# THE CONSTITUTION IN CRISIS

# THE
# CONSTITUTION
# IN CRISIS

## The High Crimes of the Bush Administration and a Blueprint for Impeachment

House Democratic Judiciary Committtee Staff

Foreword by Elizabeth Holtzman

Introduction by Representative John Conyers, Jr.

Skyhorse Publishing

www.skyhorsepublishing.com

10 9 8 7 6 5 4 3 2 1

Library of Congress Cataloging-in-Publication Data

The Constitution in crisis : the high crimes of the Bush Administration and a blueprint for impeachment / House Democratic Judiciary Staff; introduction by Representative John Conyers, Jr.
     p. cm.
  Includes bibliographical references.
  ISBN-13: 978-1-60239-009-6 (pbk. : alk. paper)
  ISBN-10: 1-60239-009-6 (pbk. : alk. paper)
  1. Bush, George W. (George Walker), 1946- —Impeachment. 2. Political crimes and offenses—United States. 3. Misconduct in office—United States. 4. Political corruption—United States. 5. Iraq War, 2003- —Causes. 6. United States—Politics and government—2001—7. United States—Foreign relations—2001—I. United States. Congress. House. Committee on the Judiciary. Democratic Staff.

E903.3.C66 2007
973.931—dc22
2006038570

Printed in Canada

973.931
C

# Table of Contents

## II. Unlawful Domestic Surveillance and the Decline of Civil Liberties Under the Administration of George W. Bush

# Foreword

By Elizabeth Holtzman

*Former Representative from New York's 16th Congressional District*

The Iraq war, now in its third year, has been a tragic, huge debacle. Both Al Gore and a former head of U.S. Army intelligence characterized it as the worst strategic military mistake in American history. Three thousand Americans have been killed and more than 22,000 have been wounded. The monetary costs could exceed $1 trillion. According to some estimates, the number of Iraqis killed may be as high as 600,000. No one can foretell what the consequences for Iraqis will be—intensified civil war, anarchy, religious dictatorship. No one knows what we, the region, and the world will reap from the whirlwind we have sown there.

The American people have finally realized the catastrophe the war has become, and with a mounting anger about it swept the Republicans out of power in the November 7, 2006 Congressional elections.

*The Constitution in Crisis* documents in vivid and brilliant detail how the war was foisted on us through a carefully orchestrated scheme of lies and deceptions, half-truths, and misstatements by a President determined for his own reasons—still unknown—to remove Saddam Hussein from power. What this book forces us to come to grips with is what we as a nation are going to do about it.

This is not a war that the American people would have supported absent these lies. And the lies cynically built both on the fear created by the attacks of 9-11 and the desire to retaliate against those attacks. President Bush and his team inflamed and manipulated these emotions in support of our invasion of Iraq.

As *The Constitution in Crisis* demonstrates, the outline of these lies is clear: 1) link Saddam to Al Qaeda and suggest to Americans that an invasion of Iraq would be justified retaliation for 9-11; 2) raise the specter of a "mushroom cloud" and make Americans fear that Saddam could attack us with nuclear weapons unless we act immediately to protect ourselves; and 3) claim that the war would be short, sweet and painless, a "cakewalk" where we would be "greeted as liberators," and where Iraqi oil revenues would pay for the costs of reconstruction.

Most Americans believed their President, whose words were echoed and amplified by Vice President Richard Cheney, Secretary of Defense Donald Rumsfeld, National

Security Adviser Condoleeza Rice, Secretary of State Colin Powell, and a host of lesser officials.

The problem *Constitution in Crisis* poses is how to hold President Bush and his team accountable. Interestingly, the book spells out a series of criminal statutes that may have been violated in the run up to the war. But there is no practical way of enforcing the statutes against the President and his team as long as the Attorney General, appointed by the very person to be investigated, remains responsible for the prosecutions.

After Watergate, a special prosecutor statute was put into place to avoid this problem. It was designed to ensure that government higher-ups, including a president, could be prosecuted for criminal misbehavior. But the excesses of Special Prosecutor Kenneth Starr in the Monica Lewinsky/Bill Clinton affair prompted Congress to let the statute expire. We need to think of resurrecting that law, but with safeguards against those excesses.

Another problem with criminal prosecution is that it is unclear whether a president may lawfully be prosecuted during his term of office. Special Watergate Prosecutor Leon Jaworski believed that President Nixon could not be prosecuted, and he did not permit the grand jury to indict him—although Nixon was named as an unindicted co-conspirator. President Bush will be out of office by the time this issue could be resolved by the courts.

The only real remedy is impeachment and removal from office. Placed in the constitution by framers who were worried about presidential abuses of power, the impeachment power was designed to protect the constitution from "subversion." There can be no greater subversion than driving our country into war through lies and deceptions, thereby undermining the ability of Congress and the American people to make a reasoned determination as to whether to go to war on a basis of the actual—not hyped or faked—facts. There is no more serious decision a country can make than whether to go to war, and our framers wisely put the power in the hands of the Congress and the American people, not just the President (except, obviously, in cases of actual or imminent attack on the US where the President must immediately mobilize forces to protect the country).

The framers wanted Congress to have a significant role in war-making. They were prompted by more than just an abstract allegiance to checks and balances or the idea that two heads are better than one. The framers knew from bitter experience with a monarchy and from their study of history that executives are more prone to start wars. They wanted a brake on that predilection, and thought Congress would act as one. As James Madison explained in a 1798 letter to Thomas Jefferson: "The Constitution supposes what the history of all governments demonstrates, that the executive is the branch of power most interested in war and most prone to it. It has accordingly . . . vested the question of war in the legislative." Although the framers did not shrink from war (after all, they had just won the Revolutionary War against King George), they knew its horrific costs, and wanted to minimize them in the future for the nation.

The advantage of impeachment is that it can remove President Bush from office, and thus put an end to the continuation of the war through a web of lies and deceptions. As *The Constitution in Crisis* notes, even after the invasion took place, the President and his team kept lying about the war, claiming, for example, that they had found the WMDs that the war was supposed to have been fought over and claiming progress even when the war was going badly. Who can forget Cheney's June 2005 statement that the insurgents were in their "last throes"? Or President Bush's pre-November 2006 assertion: "Absolutely we are winning" in Iraq—which became, post-election, "We are not winning, but we are not losing either."

Removing the President from office ends the danger that he would take us into another war the same way he took us into Iraq—with lies and deceptions. It would also stop him from continuing to violate the Foreign Intelligence Surveillance Act (which this book does not address in depth because the information have only recently surfaced) and from authorizing any further mistreatment of detainees in violation of the Geneva Conventions and the federal anti-torture statute, as well as from other violations of U.S. law.

This is the third time in the last sixty years that presidents have, through lies and deceptions, embroiled this nation in wars or substantial military actions, each of which was disastrous in its own way. In 1965, President Lyndon Johnson, a Democrat, won Congressional authorization to escalate the Vietnam War through the ruse of the Gulf of Tonkin incidents. He claimed that U.S. patrol boats had been fired upon by North Vietnam in two separate incidents and that retaliation was required. The first attack was not unprovoked and the second never took place. But Congress didn't know this, and overwhelmingly supported military action. We paid a horrific price for the Vietnam War, in blood and treasure. So did the Vietnamese people.

Only a few years later, in the spring of 1969, President Nixon, a Republican, began bombing the neutral country of Cambodia, although Congress had never authorized any military action against the country. The President also ordered that the bombing be kept absolutely secret, and directed that his generals lie about where the bombing was taking place. As with Enron, the Pentagon kept two sets of books about the bombing, one showing where the bombing actually occurred and one for Congressional and public consumption showing that the bombing took place in Vietnam. The Cambodia bombing did not prevent our defeat in the Vietnam War. Moreover, some experts, such as William Shawcross, believe that the bombing led to the rise of the Khmer Rouge, which visited unspeakable horrors on the Cambodian people.

Neither President Johnson nor President Nixon was called to account for these lies and deceptions. During the impeachment proceedings against Richard Nixon, I drafted an article of impeachment based on his deception of Congress about the Cambodia bombing. But it was not adopted. One excuse was that the War Powers Resolution, just enacted, would prevent a president from secretly starting a war secretly, so there was no need for impeachment on this ground. Another was the concern was that the American people would think the Congress was impeaching the President about the war, instead of for his lying about the bombing.

Given this history and the impunity with which two recent presidents used lies and deceptions in the exercise of their war-making powers, it was inevitable that another president, in this case George W. Bush, would follow in their footsteps.

This pattern of immunity for presidents must stop. Impeaching President Bush for lying to get us into a war will not only protect us from him, but also send an unmistakable message to future presidents: never again.

—JANUARY 2, 2007

# Introduction

By Rep. John Conyers, Jr.

Scandals such as Watergate and Iran-Contra are widely considered to be constitutional crises. They were in the sense that the executive branch was acting in violation of the law and in tension with the Majority Party in the Congress. But the system of checks and balances put in place by the Founding Fathers worked, the abuses were investigated, and actions were taken—even if presidential pardons ultimately prevented a full measure of justice.

The situation we find ourselves in today under the administration of George W. Bush is systemically different. The alleged acts of wrongdoing my staff has documented— which include making misleading statements about the decision to go to war; manipulating intelligence; facilitating and countenancing torture; using classified information to out a CIA agent; and violating federal surveillance and privacy laws—are quite serious. However, the current Majority Party* has shown little inclination to engage in basic oversight, let alone question the Administration directly. The media, though showing some signs of aggressiveness as of late, is increasingly concentrated and all too often unwilling to risk the enmity or legal challenge from the party in charge. At the same time, unlike previous threats to civil liberties posed by the Civil War (suspension of *habeas corpus* and eviction of the Jews from portions of the Southern States); World War I (anti-immigrant "Palmer Raids"); World War II (internment of Japanese Americans); and the Vietnam War (COINTELPRO), the risks to our citizens' rights today are potentially more grave, as the war on terror has no specific end point.

Although on occasion the courts are able to serve as a partial check on the unilateral overreaching of the Executive Branch—as they did in the recent *Hamdan v. Rumsfeld* decision invalidating the President's military tribunal rules—the unfortunate reality remains that we are a long way from being out of the constitutional woods under the dangerous combination of an imperial Bush presidency and a compliant GOP Congress. I say this for several reasons. The Hamdan decision itself was approved by only five Justices (three Justices dissented, and Chief Justice Roberts recused himself because he had previously ruled in favor of the Administration) and was written by 86-year-old Justice Stevens. In the event of his retirement in the next two years, the Court's balance would likely be tipped back, as he would undoubtedly be replaced by another Justice in the Scalia-Thomas-Roberts-Alito mode favoring an all-powerful "unitary" executive. In the very first hearing held on the decision, the Administration witness testified that "the president is always right" and severely chastised the Court's decision. The Republican Majority* also appears poised to use the decision to score political points rather than reassert Congressional prerogatives, as House Majority Leader Boehner disingenuously declared the case "offers a clear choice between Capitol Hill Democrats who celebrate offering special privileges to violent terrorists, and Republicans who want the President to have the necessary tools to prosecute and achieve victory in the Global War on Terror."

Thus, notwithstanding the eloquence of the *Hamdan* decision, I believe our Constitution remains in crisis. We cannot count on a single judicial decision to reclaim the rule of law or resurrect the system of checks and balances envisioned by the Founding Fathers. Rather, we need to restore a vigilant Congress, an independent judiciary, a law-abiding president, and the vigorous free press that has served our Nation so well throughout our history.

Because of the above concerns, I asked my Judiciary Committee staff to prepare the following Report. I made this request in the wake of President Bush's failure to respond to a letter submitted by 122 Members of Congress and more than 500,000 Americans in July of 2005 asking him whether the assertions set forth in the so-called "Downing Street Minutes" were accurate, and in the aftermath of the disclosure by the *New York Times* in December 2005 and *USA Today* in May 2006 that the President had approved widespread warrantless domestic surveillance of innocent Americans. I asked for this Report to be prepared because I believe it is vital that we document these allegations, learn from our mistakes, and consider laws and safeguards necessary to prevent their recurrence. I believe it is essential that we come together as a Nation to confront religious extremism and despicable regimes abroad as well as terrorist tactics at home. However, as a veteran, I recognize that we do no service to our brave armed forces by asking them to engage in military conflict under false pretenses and without adequate resources. Nor do we advance the cause of fighting terrorism if our government takes constitutionally dubious short cuts of little law enforcement value that alienate the very groups in this country whose cooperation is central to fighting this seminal battle.

Many of us remember a time when the powers of our government were horribly abused. Those of us who lived through Vietnam know the damage that can result when our government misleads its citizens about war. As one who was included on President Nixon's "enemies list," I am all too familiar with the specter of unlawful government intrusion. In the face of these lessons, I believe it is imperative that we never lose our voice of dissent, regardless of the political pressure. As Martin Luther King, Jr. told us, "there comes a time when silence is betrayal." None of us should be bullied or intimidated when the executive branch charges that those who would criticize their actions are "aiding the terrorists" and "giving ammunition to America's enemies," or when they warn that

"Americans need to watch what they say," as this Administration has done.

It is tragic that our Nation has invaded another sovereign nation because "the intelligence and facts were being fixed around the policy," and that millions of innocent Americans have been subject to government surveillance outside of proper legal process. However, it is unforgivable that Congress has been unwilling to examine these matters or take actions to prevent these circumstances from occurring again. Since the Majority Party* is unwilling to fulfill their oversight responsibilities, it is incumbent on individual Members of Congress as well as the American public to act to protect our constitutional form of government. It is with that purpose and in that spirit that I am releasing this Minority Report.

I would like to thank the "blogosphere" for its myriad and invaluable contributions to me and my staff. Absent the assistance of "blogs" and other Internet-based media, it would have been impossible to assemble all of the information, sources, and other materials necessary to the preparation of this Report. Whereas the so-called "mainstream media" has frequently been willing to look past the abuses of the Bush Administration, the blogosphere has proven to be a new and important bulwark of our Nation's first amendment freedoms.

*[ed: Since the time of this writing, the Democratic Party has retaken control of Congress.]*

# Summary

This Minority Report has been produced at the direction of Representative John Conyers, Jr., Ranking Member of the House Judiciary Committee. The Report is divided into two principal parts—Part I, released in draft form in December 2005, concerns "The Downing Street Minutes and Deception Manipulation, Torture, Retribution, and Cover-ups in the Iraq War" and Part II, released in June 2006, concerns "Unlawful Domestic Surveillance and Related Civil Liberties Abuses under the Administration of George W. Bush." (At the conclusion, we include an Addendum including additional matters which have come to light since Part I of the Report was issued in December 2005 and Part II was written in May 2006).

In preparing this Report, we reviewed tens of thousands of documents and materials, including testimony submitted at two hearings held by Rep. Conyers concerning the Downing Street Minutes and warrantless domestic surveillance; hundreds of media reports, articles, and books, including interviews with past and present Administration employees and other confidential sources; scores of government and nonprofit reports, hearings, and analyses; numerous letters and materials submitted to Rep. Conyers; staff interviews; relevant laws, cases, regulations, and administrative guidelines; and the Administration's own words and statements.

In brief, we have found that there is substantial evidence that the President, the Vice-President, and other-high ranking members of the Bush Administration misled Congress and the American people regarding the decision to go to war in Iraq; misstated and manipulated intelligence information regarding the justification for such war; countenanced torture and cruel, inhuman, and degrading treatment in Iraq; permitted inappropriate retaliation against critics of their Administration; and approved domestic surveillance that is both illegal and unconstitutional. As further detailed in the Report, there is evidence that these actions violate a number of federal laws, including:

- Making False Statements to Congress; for example, saying you have learned Iraq is attempting to buy uranium from Niger, when you have been warned by the CIA that this is not the case.

- The War Powers Resolution and Misuse of Government Funds; for example, redeploying troops and initiating bombing raids before receiving congressional authorization.

- Federal laws and international treaties prohibiting torture and cruel, inhuman, and degrading treatment; for example, ordering detainees to be ghosted and removed, and tolerating and laying the legal ground work for their torture and mistreatment.

- Federal laws concerning retaliating against witnesses and other individuals; for example, demoting Bunnatine Greenhouse, the chief contracting officer at the Army Corps of Engineers, because she exposed contracting abuses involving Halliburton.

- Federal requirements concerning leaking and other misuse of intelligence; for example, failing to enforce the executive order requiring disciplining those who leak classified information, whether intentionally or not.

- Federal regulations and ethical requirements governing conflicts of interest, for example, then Attorney General John Ashcroft's being personally briefed on FBI interviews concerning possible misconduct by Karl Rove even though Mr. Rove had previously received nearly $750,000 in fees for political work on Mr. Ashcroft's campaigns.

- Violating FISA and the Fourth Amendment; for example, intercepting thousands of communications "to or from any person within the United States" without obtaining a warrant.

- The Stored Communications Act of 1986 and the Communications Act of 1934; for example, obtaining millions of U.S. customer telephone records without obtaining a subpoena or warrant, without customer consent, and outside of any applicable "emergency exceptions."

- The National Security Act; for example, failing to keep all Members of the House and Senate Intelligence Committees "fully and currently informed" of intelligence activities, such as the warrantless surveillance programs.

With regard to the NSA's domestic surveillance programs, we have also found that members of the Bush Administration made a number of misleading statements regarding its operation and scope; the legal justifications proffered by the Bush Administration are constitutionally destabilizing; there is little evidence that the programs have been beneficial in combating terrorism and may have affirmatively placed terrorism prosecutions at risk; and the programs appear to have been designed and implemented in a manner designed to stifle legitimate concerns.

The Report rejects the frequent contention by the Bush Administration that their pre-war conduct has been reviewed and they have been exonerated. No entity has ever considered whether the Administration misled Americans about the decision to go to war. The Senate Intelligence Committee has not yet conducted a review of pre-war intelligence distortion and manipulation, while the presidentially appointed Silberman-Robb Commission Report specifically cautioned that intelligence manipulation "was not part of our inquiry."

There has also not been any independent inquiry concerning torture and other legal violations in Iraq; nor has there been an independent review of the pattern of cover-ups and political retribution by the Bush Administration against its critics, other than the very narrow and still ongoing inquiry of Special Counsel Fitzgerald into the outing of Valerie Plame. There also has been no independent review of the circumstances surrounding the Bush Administration's domestic spying scandals. The Administration summarily rejected all requests for special counsels, as well as reviews by the Department of Justice and Department of Defense Inspector Generals. When the DOJ Office of Professional Responsibility opened an investigation, the Bush Administration effectively squashed it by denying the investigators security clearances. Neither the House nor Senate Intelligence Committee have undertaken any sort of comprehensive investigation, and the Bush Administration has sought to cut off any court review of the NSA programs by repeatedly invoking the State Secrets Doctrine.

As a result of our findings, we have made a number of recommendations to help prevent the recurrence of these events in the future, including:

- Obtaining enhanced investigatory authority to access documentary information and testimony regarding the various allegations set forth in this Report
- Reaffirming that FISA and the criminal code contain the exclusive means for conducting domestic warrantless surveillance and, to the extent that more personnel are needed to process FISA requests, increasing available resources
- Requiring the President to report on the pardon of any former or current officials who could implicate the President or other Administration officials implicated by pending investigations
- Requiring the President to notify Congress upon the declassification of intelligence information
- Providing for enhanced protection for national security whistle-blowers
- Strengthening the authority of the Privacy and Civil Liberties Oversight Board.

We also make a number of additional recommendations within the jurisdiction of the House Judiciary Committee to help respond to the ongoing threat of terrorism, including:

- Increasing funding and resources for local law enforcement and first responders and insuring that anti-terrorism funds are distributed based on risk, not politics
- Implementing the 9-11 Commission Recommendations, including providing for enhanced port, infrastructure, and chemical plant security and ensuring that all loose nuclear materials are secured
- Banning corporate trade with state sponsors of terrorism and eliminating sovereign immunity protections for state sponsors of terrorism
- Enhancing laws against wartime fraud.

# I

## *The* Downing Street Minutes *and* Deception, Manipulation, Torture, Retribution, *and* Coverups *in the* Iraq War

# Chronology:
# Last Throes of Credibility

*"But I think the level of activity that we see today, from a military standpoint, I think will clearly decline. I think they're in the last throes, if you will, of the insurgency."*
—May 30, 2005, Vice President Dick Cheney's
Remarks on the Iraqi insurgency, *"Larry King Live"*[1]

The 2000 Presidential election focused on many issues relating to domestic and foreign policy.[2] However, the topic of Iraq was virtually unmentioned in the campaign. In a presidential debate with then-Vice President Al Gore, then-presidential candidate George W. Bush emphasized that he would be careful about using troops for "nation-building" purposes and that he would not launch a pre-emptive war because he believed the role of the military was to "prevent war from happening in the first place."[3] At the same time, some future members of the Bush Administration, dubbed the neoconservatives, were waiting for war with Iraq. High-ranking officials such as Dick Cheney, Richard Perle, and Paul Wolfowitz were part of this group.[4]

In the aftermath of the September 11 attacks, the Bush Administration began to hint at the coming attack on Iraq. In his January 29, 2002 State of the Union Address, the President remarked that countries like Iraq, Iran, and North Korea "constitute an axis of evil. . . . These regimes pose a grave and growing danger. . . . I will not wait on events while dangers gather."[5] On June 1, 2002, during a speech at West Point, President Bush formally enunciated his doctrine of preemption that would be used against Iraq.[6] It was also around this time that Vice President Cheney and his Chief of Staff, Scooter Libby, began making a series of unusual trips to the Central Intelligence Agency (CIA) to discuss Iraqi intelligence.[7]

At the same time, the President's public statements indicated a reluctance to use military force in Iraq. He assured the public that he had not made up his mind to go to war with Iraq and that war was a last resort.[8] However, contrary to these public statements, the Bush Administration formed the White House Iraq Group (WHIG) in August 2002 in an apparent effort to bolster public support for war with Iraq.[9]

Shortly thereafter, the Administration began making more alarming and sensational claims about the danger posed to the United States by Iraq (for example, in a September 12, 2002 address to the United Nations), and began to press forward publicly with preparations for war.[10] In the days following the President's speech to the United Nations, Iraq delivered a letter to U.N. Secretary-General Kofi Annan stating that it would allow the return of U.N. weapons inspectors "without conditions."[11] But on September 18, President Bush discredited Hussein's offer to let U.N. inspectors back into Iraq as "his latest ploy."[12]

As the Congressional vote to authorize force against Iraq approached, the President and Administration officials raised the specter of a nuclear attack by Iraq.[13] The President subsequently received from Congress on October 11, 2002, a joint resolution for the use of force in Iraq.[14] Based on the intelligence findings in the National Intelligence Estimate provided to Congress by the Administration, the resolution stated that Iraq posed a "continuing threat" to the United States by, among other things, "actively seeking a nuclear weapons capability."[15]

The President's focus then moved to the United Nations in an effort to persuade the U.N. to approve renewed weapons inspections in Iraq and sanctions for noncompliance. Once again, the President asserted his reluctance to take military action. Upon signing the resolution, the President stated: "I have not ordered the use of force. I hope the use of force will not become necessary."[16] On November 8, 2002, the United Nations Security Council adopted U.N. Resolution 1441, which stipulated that Iraq was required to readmit U.N. weapons inspectors under more stringent terms than required by previous U.N. Resolutions.[17]

On January 27, 2003, the International Atomic Energy Agency (IAEA) indicated that the Bush Administration's claim that aluminum tubes being delivered to Iraq were part of an Iraqi nuclear weapons program likely was false.[18] In the wake of this claim being discredited, President Bush introduced a new piece of evidence to the public in his State of the Union address on January 28, 2003, to demonstrate that Iraq was developing a nuclear arms program: "The British government has learned that Saddam Hussein recently sought significant quantities of uranium from Africa."[19]

On February 5, 2003, Secretary of State Colin Powell took the Bush Administration's case to the United Nations Security Council. In a presentation to the United Nations, Secretary Powell charged, among other things, that Iraq had "mobile production facilities" for biological weapons.[20] With its case to the United Nations delivered, for the first time and contrary to earlier claims that the Administration was reluctant to use force, the Administration publicly indicated its readiness and enthusiasm for going to war. The question was no longer whether force would be used, but what—if any—difficulties would accompany the use of force. Vice President Dick Cheney made an appearance on *Meet the Press* and stated that the war was not going to be long, costly, or bloody because "we will, in fact, be greeted as liberators."[21]

On March 18, 2003, the President submitted a letter to the Speaker of the House of Representatives and the President Pro Tempore of the Senate informing the Congress of his determination that diplomatic and peaceful means alone would not protect the Nation or lead to Iraqi compliance with United Nations demands.[22] On March 20, the President launched the preemptive invasion.

A little more than a month into the invasion, President Bush landed aboard the USS Abraham Lincoln and, standing beneath a massive banner reading "Mission Accomplished," he stated, "Major combat operations in Iraq have ended."[23] Immediately thereafter, it was self-evident that—despite the premature declaration of victory—numerous problems persisted with regard to the occupation. This was not the only post-war mischaracterization of the truth by the Bush Administration. Since then, they have been dogged by misstatements concerning the size and strength of the insurgency; the preparedness of Iraqi troops; the cost of the war; the existence of weapons of mass destruction (WMD); and the war's impact on terrorism, among other things.[24]

Another significant problem for the Bush Administration was its failure to find any of the WMD that it had used to justify the invasion. On July 6, 2003, Ambassador Joseph Wilson, who was sent to Niger at the behest of the CIA to investigate the uranium claim, wrote in an op-ed piece that the intelligence concerning Niger's alleged sale of uranium to Iraq was "twisted to exaggerate the Iraqi threat."[25] The following day, the White House issued a rare retraction of the uranium allegations from the President's State of the Union Address.[26] Shortly thereafter, the identity of Wilson's wife, a covert CIA agent, was revealed in the press through a Robert Novak column sourced to two officials in the Administration.[27] Later in the year, Colin Powell also conceded that the information given in his February 5, 2003 speech before the U.N. "appear[ed] not to be . . . that solid."[28] Capping these retractions were the findings of David Kay, the U.S. official responsible for the WMD search as the head of the Iraq Survey Group, who concluded that "there were not large stockpiles of newly produced weapons of mass destruction. We don't find the people, the documents, or the physical plants that you would expect to find if the production was going on."[29]

Amid these admissions that the case for war was, generously speaking, faulty, the Administration and Congressional Republicans sought to pre-empt inquiries into the White House use or manipulation of intelligence by launching more limited investigations. On February 6, 2004, President Bush created the Robb-Silberman Commission, which later found that the intelligence community was "dead wrong in almost all of its pre-war judgments about Iraq's weapons of mass destruction."[30] However, this Commission was specifically prohibited from examining the use or manipulation of intelligence by policymakers.[31]

On March 16, 2004, the Democratic staff of the U.S. House Committee on Government Reform submitted a report to Ranking Member Henry A. Waxman.[32] This report, entitled "Iraq on the Record: The Bush Administration's Public Statements on Iraq," details public statements made by senior Bush Administration officials regarding policy toward Iraq. The report indicates that "five officials made misleading statements about the threat posed by Iraq in 125 public appearances. The report and an accompanying database identify 237 specific misleading statements by the five officials."[33]

On July 7, 2004, the Senate Select Committee on Intelligence reported that it had found numerous failures in the intelligence-gathering and analysis process.[34] However, that review also was explicitly not intended to look into the Administration's use of that wrong intelligence in selling the war.[35] To date, there has never been a truly independent, comprehensive non-partisan or bipartisan review of the Administration's false claims regarding WMD or any other aspect of the war.[36]

On April 28, 2004, *60 Minutes II* made public a series of photos taken at the Abu Ghraib prison in Iraq documenting apparent torture and other cruel, inhuman, and degrading treatment by U.S. military and other personnel.[37] Since then, reports of other alleged violations of international law involving Iraqi prisoners have been reported by the media and human rights organizations.[38]

As the war continued into 2005, with U.S. casualties approaching 1,500, Iraq held elections on January 30. The Administration heralded the elections as a symbol of freedom and as an event which validated the initial invasion. By that point, however, the reason for attacking Iraq had shifted from an imminent threat of weapons of mass destruction; to combating terrorism after the September 11 attacks; to regime change; and eventually to promoting democracy and ensuring that those lives lost were not lost in vain.[39]

While evidence and accounts of Administration insiders strongly suggested a predetermination to go to war and a manipulation of intelligence to justify it, that evidence and those accounts were attacked by Administration officials as inaccurate or biased. Then, on May 1, 2005, the *Sunday London Times* published the first of a series of important documents known as the "Downing Street Minutes."[40] The Downing Street Minutes (DSM) are a collection of classified documents, written by senior British officials during the spring and summer of 2002, which recounted meetings and discussions of such officials with their American counterparts. The focus of these meetings and discussions was the U.S. plan to invade Iraq. The DSM appear to document a pre-determination to go war with Iraq on the part of U.S. officials and a manipulation of intelligence by such officials in order to justify the war.

The DSM generated significant media coverage in Great Britain in the lead up to the British elections, but initially received very little media attention in the United States. However, a concerted effort to call attention to them by Congressman John Conyers, Jr. and a number of Members of Congress, grassroots groups, and Internet activists was ultimately successful. On May 5, 2005, Congressman Conyers, the Ranking Member of the House Judiciary Committee, along with 87 other Members of Congress (eventually 121), wrote to the President demanding answers to the allegations presented in the Minutes.[41] In his letter, Representative Conyers questioned the President on whether there "was a coordinated effort with the U.S. intelligence community and/or British officials to 'fix' the intelligence and facts around the policy."[42]

On June 16, 2005, Congressman Conyers and 32 Members of Congress convened a historic hearing on the Downing Street Minutes, covered by numerous press outlets. The hearing was forced to a cramped room in the basement of the Capitol since Democrats were denied ordinary hearing room space by the Republican leadership. The Republicans tried to disrupt the hearings further by holding 12 consecutive floor votes during the hearing, an unprecedented number.[43] After the hearing, Congressman Conyers led a congressional delegation to the White House to personally deliver a letter signed by over 500,000 citizens, demanding answers from the President.[44] To date, the White House has declined to respond to these questions that were posed by these citizens and their elected representatives in Congress.

In the meantime, after some initial false starts, delays, and denials concerning possible misconduct in the Bush Administration's "outing" of Valerie Plame Wilson,[45] then-Attorney General John Ashcroft recused himself from the investigation due to conflicts of interest and, on December 30, 2003, U.S. Attorney Patrick J. Fitzgerald was appointed to conduct the investigation of the Plame leak.[46] By July 2005, it became apparent that Karl Rove, a senior aide to the President, was involved in the leak; a *Time* reporter's notes revealed that he had spoken to Karl Rove about the case.[47] Then, on July 18, 2005, President Bush conspicuously changed the standard for White House ethics from stating that he would fire anyone who leaked the information to firing someone only if he or she "committed a crime."[48] With a lack of response from the Administration or from congressional Republicans, on July 22, 2005, Congressman Henry Waxman and Senator Byron Dorgan conducted a joint Democratic hearing on the "National Security Consequences of Disclosing the Identity of a Covert Intelligence Officer."[49]

Ambassador Wilson was not the only individual facing apparent retribution from the Bush Administration for criticizing its conduct. For example, on August 27, 2005, Bunnatine Greenhouse, the Chief Contracting officer at the Army Corps of Engineers, was demoted in apparent retaliation for exposing Pentagon favoritism toward a Halliburton subsidiary in awarding no-bid contracts in Iraq.[50] As discussed later in this Report, a long line of individuals was subject to other forms of sanctions and retribution by the Administration for exposing Administration wrongdoing concerning Iraq.

On October 28, 2005, Vice Presidential Chief of Staff Scooter Libby resigned after a federal grand jury indicted him on five charges, totaling a maximum 30-year sentence, related to the leak probe.[51] Patrick Fitzgerald has yet to indict other individuals but has publicly stated that his investigation would remain open to consider other matters.[52] On November 1, 2005, after numerous attempts to open an investigation on the issue, Democrats demanded answers to the Administration's use of pre-war intelligence and led the Senate into a rare closed-door session, finally receiving a promise from the Republican majority to speed up the process.[53]

Since that time, numerous additional disclosures have come out calling into question the Bush Administration's pre-war veracity concerning WMD intelligence. On November 6, Senator Levin disclosed a classified Defense Department document showing that an Al Qaeda prisoner, Iba al Shaykh al-Libi, had been identified as a fabricator months before the Bush Administration used his claims to allege that Iraq had trained Al Qaeda members to use biological and chemical weapons.[54] On November 20, the *Los Angeles Times* revealed that German intelligence officials had informed the Administration that the Iraqi defector known as "Curveball" was not a reliable source for their mobile biological weapons charges.[55]

Today, more than half of all Americans believe the Administration "deliberately misled" the public on the reasons for going to war.[56] The invasion appears to have increased and emboldened the terrorist movement.[57] As of the date of this Report, United States casualties are in excess of 2,500. The Iraq war costs approximately $6 billion a month, and by some estimates the eventual cost could approach a trillion dollars.[58]

# Detailed Findings

# Determination to go to War
# Before Congressional Authorization

There are numerous, documented facts now in the public record that indicate that the Bush Administration had made a decision to go to war before it sought Congressional authorization or informed the American people of that decision.

Our investigation shows that while the roots of this decision existed even before George W. Bush was first elected president, it became a foregone conclusion in the aftermath of the September 11 tragedy. Due to the release of the so-called "Downing Street Minutes" materials, we are now able to confirm that there were agreements between the Bush and Blair governments in the spring and summer of 2002 to go to war in Iraq. Further evidence of that agreement to go to war exists by virtue of the Bush Administration's marketing campaign to sell the war to the American people commencing in the fall of 2002, and the efforts to use the United Nations as a pretext to go to war later in 2002 and early in 2003.

Even though the Administration had begun planning an invasion of Iraq, the President and senior Administration officials continued to issue public denials regarding this effort, including misleading statements made before Congress:

- September 8, 2002: Vice President Dick Cheney insists that "first of all, no decision's been made yet to launch a military operation."[59]

- September 16, 2002: U.S. Secretary of Defense Donald Rumsfeld states, "The President hasn't made a decision with respect to Iraq. Didn't I say that earlier? I thought I said that."[60]

- September 19, 2002: Secretary of State Colin Powell states, "Of course, the President has not decided on a military option . . . nobody wants war as a first resort . . . [n]obody is looking for a war if it can be avoided."[61]

- October 1, 2002: The President made the first in a series of statements, "Of course, I haven't made up my mind we're going to war with Iraq."[62]

- November 7, 2002: "Hopefully, we can do this peacefully . . . don't get me wrong. And if the world were to collectively come together to do so, and to put pressure on Saddam Hussein and convince him to disarm, there's a chance he may decide to do that. And war is not my first choice, don't . . . it's my last choice."[63]

- December 4, 2002: "This is our attempt to work with the world community to create peace. And the best way for peace is for Mr. Saddam Hussein to disarm. It's up to him to make his decision."[64]

- December 31, 2002: "You said we're headed to war in Iraq . . . I don't know why you say that. I hope we're not headed to war in Iraq. I'm the person who gets to decide, not you."[65]

- January 2, 2003: "First of all, you know, I'm hopeful we won't have to go war, and let's leave it at that."[66]

- March 6, 2003: "I've not made up our mind about military action."[67]

- March 8, 2003: "We are doing everything we can to avoid war in Iraq. But if Saddam Hussein does not disarm peacefully, he will be disarmed by force."[68]

- March 17, 2003: "Should Saddam Hussein choose confrontation, the American people can know that every measure has been taken to avoid war, and every measure will be taken to win it."[69]

## ■ Avenging the Father and Working with the Neo-Cons

*"From the very beginning, there was a conviction that Saddam Hussein was a bad person and that he needed to go. It was all about finding a way to do it. That was the tone of it. The president saying, 'Go find me a way to do this.'"*

—JANUARY 11, 2004, PAUL O'NEILL, "60 MINUTES"[70]

Our investigation has found, in retrospect, there were indications even before September 11, 2001 that President Bush and key members of his Administration were fixated on the military invasion of Iraq, regardless of the provocation. A key piece of the puzzle was revealed in a series of interviews between then-Governor Bush and writer and long-time family friend Mickey Herskowitz when, according to Herskowitz, Mr. Bush stated:

*"One of the keys to being seen as a great leader is to be seen as a commander-in-chief. . . . My father had all this political capital built up when he drove the Iraqis out of Kuwait and he wasted it. . . . **If I have a chance to invade . . . if I had that much capital, I'm not going to waste it.**"*[71]

According to Mr. Herskowitz, George W. Bush's beliefs on Iraq were based in part on a notion ascribed to now-Vice President Dick Cheney: "Start a small war. Pick a country where there is justification you can jump on, go ahead and invade."[72]

In addition to Mr. Bush's apparent belief that a successful military invasion could cause him to be seen as a great leader, additional possible motivations include responding to those right-wing critics who blamed his father for not entering Baghdad during the first Gulf War[73] and achieving revenge for Saddam Hussein's reported plot to assassinate his father. Discussing Saddam Hussein on September 26, 2002, Bush declared: **"After all, this is the guy that tried to kill my dad at one time."**[74]

It is also significant that key members of the Bush Administration were part of a group of so-called "neo-conservatives" or "neo-cons" who were dedicated to removing Saddam Hussein by military force. The notion of toppling Saddam Hussein and his regime dates as far back as the 1990s, when it had been a priority of a circle of neo-conservative intellectuals, led by Richard Perle, a former Assistant Secretary of Defense under President Reagan, and Paul Wolfowitz, an Undersecretary of Defense for Policy under President George H.W. Bush.[75] The neocons did not have the power to effectuate their goals during the Clinton Administration, but they remained tied to one another and to Dick Cheney through a number of right-wing think-tanks and institutes, including the Project for the New American Century.

On January 26, 1998, the Project for the New American Century issued a letter to President Bill Clinton explicitly calling for "the removal of Saddam Hussein's regime from power."[76] Foretelling of subsequent events, the letter calls for the United States to go to war alone and attack the United Nations, and instructs that the United States should not be "crippled by a misguided insistence on unanimity in the U.N. Security Council."[77] **The letter was signed by 18 individuals; ten of them, including Donald Rumsfeld and Paul Wolfowitz, became members of the current Bush Administration.** Other documentary evidence of the neocon vision for an invasion is manifested by the December 1, 1997 issue of the *Weekly Standard*, a conservative magazine, which was headlined by a bold directive: "Saddam Must Go: A How-to Guide." Two of the articles were written by current Administration officials, including Paul Wolfowitz.[78]

In September 2000, a strategy document commissioned from the Project for the New American Century by Dick Cheney argued that **"[t]he United States has for decades sought to play a more permanent role in Gulf regional security. While the unresolved conflict with Iraq provides the immediate justification, the need for a substantial American force presence in the Gulf transcends the issue of the regime of Saddam Hussein."**[79]

There is other evidence from within the highest levels of Bush's cabinet of an early fixation on invading Iraq. On *60 Minutes*, former Bush Treasury Secretary Paul O'Neill reported that as early as January 30, 2001, members of the Bush Administration were discussing plans for Saddam Hussein's removal from power: **"From the very beginning, there was a conviction that Saddam Hussein was a bad person and that he needed to go. It was all about finding a way to do it. That was the tone of it. The president saying, 'Go find me a way to do this.'"**[80]

This fixation on war with Iraq would seem to explain why, from the very beginning of the Bush Administration, key officials were consulting with outsiders on possible replacements for Saddam Hussein and contemplating possible means of exploiting Iraqi oil fields. For example, in February 2001, White House officials discussed a memo titled

"Plan for Post-Saddam Iraq," which talks about troop requirements, establishing war crimes tribunals, and divvying up Iraq's oil wealth.[81] During this time, Iraqi-born oil industry consultant Falah Aljibury was asked to interview would-be replacements for a new U.S.-installed dictator. As Mr. Aljibury stated, "It is an invasion, but it will act like a coup. The original plan was to liberate Iraq from the Saddamists and from the regime, to stabilize the country."[82] In March of 2001, a Pentagon document titled "Foreign Suitors For Iraqi Oilfield Contracts" was circulated.[83] The document outlines areas of oil exploration and includes a table listing 30 countries that have interests in Iraq's oil industry. The memorandum also includes the names of companies that have interests and the oil fields with which those interests are associated.[84]

# ■ September 11 and Its Aftermath: Beating the Drums for War

*"F\*\*\* Saddam. We're taking him out."*

> —March, 2002, President George W. Bush, poking his head into
> the office of National Security Advisor Condoleezza Rice.[25]

It was the September 11 tragedy that gave the President and members of his Administration the political opportunity to invade Iraq without provocation. It was also in the immediate aftermath of September 11 that it became clear that the President had made up his mind to invade. We know this now for several reasons—we have first-hand evidence concerning President Bush's intentions; we have direct evidence concerning the intent of other senior members of his Administration; we have information provided through high-level Administration sources; and we have documentary and other evidence concerning specific actions taken by the United States military that brought our nation on the verge of war with Iraq before Congressional authorization was sought.

Donald Rumsfeld began pushing for retaliatory attacks against Iraq almost immediately after the September 11 attacks. *CBS News* reported that at 2:40 p.m. on September 11, Secretary Rumsfeld stated: "[I want the] best info fast. Judge whether good enough hit S.H. [Saddam Hussein] at same time. Not only UBL [Osama bin Laden]."[86] Rumsfeld went on to say, "[g]o massive. Sweep it all up. Things related and not."[87] Spencer Ackerman and John Judis of *The New Republic* reported that "Deputy Defense Secretary Paul Wolfowitz floated the idea that Iraq, with more than 20 years of inclusion on the State Department's terror-sponsor list, be held immediately accountable."[88]

The first evidence regarding President Bush's inclination to invade Iraq after the September 11 attacks occurred the very next day, when he instructed National Security official Richard A. Clarke to go out of his way to find a link between Saddam Hussein and the terrorist attacks. Richard Clarke recounts the following in his book, *Against All Enemies*:

> [On September 12th] I left the Video Conferencing Center and there, wandering alone
> around the situation room, was the president. He looked like he wanted something to

do. He grabbed a few of us and closed the door to the conference room. 'Look,' he told us, 'I know you have a lot to do and all . . . but I want you, as soon as you can, to go back over everything, everything. See if Saddam did this. See if he's linked in any way.' I was once again taken aback, incredulous, and it showed. 'But, Mr. President, Al Qaeda did this.' 'I know, I know, but . . . see if Saddam was involved. Just look. I want to know any shred'. . . . 'Look into Iraq, Saddam,' the President said testily and left us. Lisa Gordon-Hagerty stared after him with her mouth hanging open.[89]

This inclination was evidenced to other senior Republicans as well. For example, Trent Lott observed in an interview on *Meet the Press* that shortly after September 11, the President made clear his intention to go after Iraq:

> Well, beginning in August that year and into the fall—in fact, beginning not too long after 9-11—as we had leadership meetings at breakfast with the president, he would go around the world and talk about what was going on, where the threats were, where the dangers were, and even in private discussions, **it was clear to me that he thought Iraq was a destabilizing force, was a danger and a growing danger, and that we were going to have to deal with that problem.**[90]

We have also received confirmation of the Bush Administration's intention to invade Iraq after the September 11 attacks from various high-level Administration sources. For example, General Wesley Clark revealed on *Meet the Press* that shortly after the September 11 attacks, the White House was asking people to link Saddam Hussein with the September 11 attacks. Clark stated:

> [T]here was a concerted effort during the fall of 2001, starting immediately after 9-11, to pin 9-11 and the terrorism problem on Saddam Hussein. . . . Well, it came from the White House . . . it came from all over. I got a call on 9-11. I was on CNN, and I got a call at my home saying, '**You got to say this is connected. This is state-sponsored terrorism. This has to be connected to Saddam Hussein.**' I said, 'But—I'm willing to say it but what's your evidence?' And I never got any evidence.[91]

On September 17, 2001, President Bush signed a 22-page document marked "TOP SECRET" that outlined the plan for going to war in Afghanistan as part of a global campaign against terrorism. As one senior Administration official commented, the direction to the Pentagon to begin planning military options for an invasion of Iraq appeared "almost as a footnote."[92]

"On September 19 and 20, an advisory group known as the Defense Policy Board met at the Pentagon—with Secretary Rumsfeld in attendance—and discussed the importance of ousting Hussein."[93] According to Administration sources:

> They met in Rumsfeld's conference room. After a C.I.A. briefing on the 9-11 attacks, Perle introduced two guest speakers. The first was Bernard Lewis, professor emeritus at Princeton, a longtime associate of Cheney's and Wolfowitz's. Lewis told the meeting that America must respond to 9-11 with a show of strength: to do otherwise would be taken in

the Islamic world as a sign of weakness—one it would be bound to exploit. At the same time, he said, America should support democratic reformers in the Middle East. "Such as," he said, turning to the second of Perle's guest speakers, "my friend here, Dr. Chalabi" . . . . At the meeting Chalabi said that, although there was as yet no evidence linking Iraq to 9-11, failed states such as Saddam's were a breeding ground for terrorists, and Iraq, he told those at the meeting, possessed W.M.D. During the later part of the second day, Wolfowitz and Rumsfeld listened carefully to the debate. "Rumsfeld was getting confirmation of his own instincts . . ." Perle says. "He seemed neither surprised nor discomfited by the idea of taking action against Iraq."[94]

The 9-11 Commission Report further notes that as early as September 20, 2001, Undersecretary of Defense for Policy Douglas Feith, suggested attacking Iraq in response to the September 11 attacks. In a draft memo, Feith "expressed disappointment at the limited options immediately available in Afghanistan and the lack of ground options. **[He] suggested instead hitting terrorists outside the Middle East in the initial offensive, perhaps deliberately selecting a non-Al Qaeda target like Iraq.**"[95] Also on September 20, it is reported that President Bush told Prime Minister Blair of the need to respond militarily with Iraq. Blair told Bush he should not get distracted from the war on terror. As noted above, Bush replied, "I agree with you, Tony. We must deal with this first. But when we have dealt with Afghanistan, we must come back to Iraq."[96]

By late November 2001, the President essentially instructed Secretary of Defense Donald Rumsfeld to develop an Iraq war plan, which Rumsfeld began to implement. In a CBS News *60 Minutes* interview about his book *Plan of Attack*, Bob Woodward describes their meeting:

> President Bush, after a National Security Council meeting, takes Don Rumsfeld aside, collars him physically, and takes him into a little cubbyhole room and closes the door and says, **"What have you got in terms of plans for Iraq? What is the status of the war plan? I want you to get on it. I want you to keep it secret."**[97]

The evidence of the President's determination to go to war continued on through 2002. On January 29, 2002, President Bush gave his State of the Union address, in which he stated that Iraq was part of an "axis of evil" along with South Korea and Iran.[98] Although Administration officials sought to temper the meaning of that reference, the President's own speech writers have subsequently made it clear that the President was intending to target Iraq. As James Mann recounts: "David Frum, then one of Bush's speech writers, later claimed that the original aim of the axis-of-evil speech was specifically to target Iraq. Mark Gerson, Bush's chief speech writer, had asked Frum first to find a justification for war against Iraq, he wrote; later Iran was added, and finally North Korea as a seemingly casual afterthought. Frum's perspective reflected both his inexperience as a speech writer and also the thinking of neoconservatives within the administration, who were eager for a regime change in Iraq."[99]

We have also learned from three sources that beginning as early as February 2002, the Bush Administration took specific concrete steps to deploy military troops and assets into Iraq. First, in February 2002, Senator Bob Graham told the Council on Foreign Relations that a military commander had said to him: "**Senator, we have stopped fighting the war on terror in Afghanistan. We are moving military and intelligence personnel and resources out of Afghanistan to get ready for a future war in Iraq.**"[100]

Second, it is clear from Bob Woodward's book *Plan of Attack* that the redeployment began in the summer of 2002, well before it was authorized by Congress:

> On July 17, Franks updated Rumsfeld on the preparatory tasks in the region. He carefully listed the cost of each and the risk to the mission if they didn't proceed along the timeline which set completion by December 1. Total cost: about $700 million . . . . Later the president praised Rumsfeld and Franks for this strategy of moving troops in and expanding the infrastructure. "It was, in my judgment," Bush said, "a very smart recommendation by Don and Tommy to put certain elements in place that could easily be removed and it could be done so in a way that was quiet so that we didn't create a lot of noise and anxiety." . . . He carefully added, "The pre-positioning of forces should not be viewed as a commitment on my part to use military." He acknowledged with a terse "Right. Yup" that the Afghanistan war and war on terrorism provided the excuse, that it was done covertly, and that it was expensive . . . **By the end of July, Bush had approved some 30 projects that would eventually cost $700 million. He discussed it with Nicholas E. Calio, the head of White House congressional relations. Congress, which is supposed to control the purse strings, had no real knowledge or involvement, had not even been notified that the Pentagon wanted to reprogram money.**[101]

In his interview on *60 Minutes*, Mr. Woodward himself points out this was a basic violation of the Constitution: "Some people are gonna look at a document called the Constitution which says that no money will be drawn from the Treasury unless appropriated by Congress."[102] The funds were diverted from appropriation laws specifically allocated for the war in Afghanistan.[103]

Third, Seymour Hersh of *The New Yorker* received similar confirmation from his Administration sources of the reallocation of intelligence assets from Afghanistan to Iraq in preparation for an invasion: "The Bush Administration took many intelligence operations that had been aimed at Al Qaeda and other terrorist groups around the world and redirected them to the Persian Gulf. Linguists and special operatives were abruptly reassigned, and several ongoing anti-terrorism intelligence programs were curtailed."[104]

Further, beginning in February 2002, senior White House officials were also confirming to the press that military ouster of Saddam Hussein was inevitable. On February 13, 2002, *Knight Ridder* reported that, according to their sources, "President Bush has decided to oust Iraqi leader Saddam Hussein from power and ordered the CIA, the Pentagon and other agencies to devise a combination of military, diplomatic and covert steps to achieve that goal, senior U.S. officials said Tuesday."[105]

White House officials were also telling Seymour Hersh that the decision to go to war had been made and that a process to support that determination had been created:

**By early March, 2002, a former White House official told me, it was understood by many in the White House that the President had decided, in his own mind, to go to war** . . . . The Bush Administration took many intelligence operations that had been aimed at Al Qaeda and other terrorist groups around the world and redirected them to the Persian Gulf. . . . Chalabi's defector reports were now flowing from the Pentagon directly to the Vice-President's office, and then on to the President, with little prior evaluation by intelligence professionals.[106]

Also in March 2002, President Bush reportedly poked his head into the office of National Security Advisor Condoleezza Rice and said "F*** **Saddam. We're taking him out.**"[107] At the time, Rice was meeting with three U.S. Senators and discussing options for dealing with Iraq through the United Nations or other peaceful means. However, a source reported, "Bush wasn't interested. He waved his hand dismissively . . . and neatly summed up his Iraq policy in that short phrase. The Senators laughed uncomfortably; Rice flashed a knowing smile."[108]

By late March 2002, Vice President Cheney was telling his fellow Republicans that a decision to invade Iraq had been made:

Dick Cheney dropped by a Senate Republican policy lunch soon after his 10-day tour of the Middle East—the one meant to drum up support for a U.S. military strike against Iraq. . . . Before he spoke, he said no one should repeat what he said, and Senators and staff members promptly put down their pens and pencils. Then he gave them some surprising news. **The question was no longer if the U.S. would attack Iraq, he said. The only question was when.**[109]

In his book, Bob Woodward describes Cheney as a "powerful, steamrolling force obsessed with Saddam and taking him out."[110]

By July of 2002, Condoleezza Rice was offering further confirmation that President Bush's mind was made up regarding a decision to invade Iraq. At this time, State Department Director of Policy Planning Richard N. Haass held a meeting with Rice and asked if they should discuss Iraq. Rice said, **"Don't bother. The president has made a decision."**[111]

We know that in early August 2002, President Bush and Prime Minister Blair spoke by telephone and cemented the decision to go to war. A White House official who read the transcript of their conversation disclosed that war was inevitable by the end of the call. On August 29, 2002, after three months of war exercises conducted by the Pentagon, President Bush reportedly approved a document entitled "Iraq goals, objectives and strategy."[112] The document cites far-reaching goals and the study refers to "some unstated objectives," including installing a pro-American government in Iraq and using it to influence events in the Middle East, especially in Syria and Iran.[113]

Not only is it clear that a decision had been made to go to war in early 2002, it has also become apparent that the U.S. was actually engaging in acts of war by May 2002. On April 28, 2002, the *New York Times* wrote: "The Bush Administration, in developing a potential approach for toppling President Saddam Hussein of Iraq, is concentrating its attention on a major air campaign and ground invasion, with initial estimates contemplating the use of 70,000 to 250,000 troops. . . . Senior officials now acknowledge that any offensive would probably be delayed until early next year, allowing time to create the right military, economic and diplomatic conditions."[114]

Bombing activity designed to increase military pressure on Iraq appears to have commenced by May 2002, and intensified in August 2002, following a meeting of the National Security Council.[115] The *Sunday London Times* reported that "[b]y the end of August [2002] the raids had become a full air offensive."[116] As former veteran CIA intelligence officer Ray McGovern testified:

> The step-up in bombing was incredible. In March-April of 2002, there were hardly any bombs dropped at all. **By the time September came along, several hundred tons of bombs had been dropped. The war had really started.**[117]

On May 27, 2002, a former U.S. Air Force combat veteran Tim Goodrich told the World Tribunal on Iraq jury in Istanbul, Turkey: "We were dropping bombs then, and I saw bombing intensify. All the documents coming out now, the Downing Street Memo and others, confirm what I had witnessed in Iraq. The war had already begun while our leaders were telling us that they were going to try all diplomatic options first. . ."[118] "Tommy Franks, the allied commander, has since admitted that this operation was designed to 'degrade' Iraqi air defenses in the same way as the air attacks that began the 1991 Gulf war."[119]

The United States and Britain initially attempted to justify these raids by claiming that "the rise in air attacks was in response to Iraqi attempts to shoot down allied aircraft."[123] However, in July 2005, in response to British MP Sir Menzies Campbell's request for data, the British Ministry of Defence released figures that would indicate that the true reason for the raids was to put pressure on the Iraqis.[121] The data shows that in "the first seven months of 2001 the allies recorded a total of 370 'provocations' by the Iraqis against allied aircraft. But in the seven months between October 2001 and May 2002 there were just 32."[122] The records show that the allies dropped twice as many bombs on Iraq in the second half of 2002 as they did in the whole of 2001.[123]

The "secret air war" was also confirmed by Iraq War Lieutenant-General Michael Moseley, who said that "in 2002 and early 2003 allied aircraft flew 21,736 sorties, dropping more than 600 bombs on 391 'carefully selected targets' before the war officially started."[124] Between March and November 2002, coalition forces attacked Iraqi installations with 253,000 pounds of bombs. In June 2002 specifically, forces bombed Iraq with 20,800 pounds of munitions; in September 2002, the tonnage amounted to 109,200 pounds of bombs.[125]

# ■ The Downing Street Minutes and Documentary Evidence of an Agreement to go to War

The Downing Street Minutes, which cover a time period from early March 2002 to July 23, 2002, provide the most definitive documentary evidence that the Bush Administration had not only made up its mind to go to war well before it sought congressional authorization, but that it had an agreement with the British government to do so. Collectively, the documents paint a picture of U.S. and British officials eager to convince the public that war in Iraq was not a foregone conclusion, even as exacting plans for war were being laid. This section of the Report includes a description of each of the critical elements of these documents as they relate to that determination to go to war by the spring and summer of 2002 and details how the Downing Street Minutes have been confirmed and corroborated as accurate. (The Downing Street Minutes also include critical documentary evidence showing Bush and Blair Administration plans concerning "marketing" the war to the public and the United Nations, as well as the manipulation of intelligence, both of which are discussed later in this Report.)

## Description and Analysis of Various Downing Street Minutes Materials

*"Bush wanted to remove Saddam, through military action, justified by the conjunction of terrorism and WMD. But the intelligence and facts were being fixed around the policy." It seemed clear that Bush had made up his mind to take military action, even if the timing was not yet decided. But the case was thin."*

—July 23, 2002, "The Downing Street Minutes"[126]

### ■ Iraq: Options Paper (March 8, 2002)

This paper, prepared by the Office of the Overseas and Defense Secretariat, is the first of four documents written by various British authorities to prepare Prime Minister Blair for his early April trip to Crawford, Texas. The document includes the seeds of the upcoming war plan by the U.S. and lays out a plan by which Iraq would reject a U.N. ultimatum, paving the way to war.

Besides summarizing various legal and political restraints, the paper warns Blair that a "legal justification for invasion would be needed. Subject to Law Officers advice, none currently exists."[127] The document also states, "[T]he U.S. has lost confidence in containment. Some in government want Saddam removed. The success of Operation Enduring Freedom [the military code name for the U.S.-led invasion of Afghanistan], distrust of U.N. sanctions and inspection regimes, and unfinished business from 1991 are all factors."[128]

In this document, we learn of a nascent plan that the rejection of United Nations weapons inspectors by Iraq would provide the needed justification for war:

A refusal to admit U.N. inspectors, or their admission and subsequent likely frustration, which resulted in an appropriate finding by the Security Council could provide the justification for military action. Saddam would try to prevent this, although he has miscalculated beofre [sic]. . .[129]

## ■ IRAQ: LEGAL BACKGROUND PAPER (EARLY MARCH 2002)

This document, the second of four papers prepared to brief Prime Minister Blair for his upcoming Crawford trip, describes various legal doctrines believed to be at play with regard to military intervention in Iraq. The most significant aspect of this document is its revelation that the British government did not agree with the Bush Administration's belief that any State can enforce United Nations resolutions. The Bush Administration ultimately relied on this view to justify preemptive war one year later.

One analysis of Security Council Resolutions suggests that, while the British hold the view that "it is for [the Security] Council to assess whether any such breach of those obligations has occurred," the **United States has "a rather different view: they maintain that the assessment of breach is for individual member States.** We are not aware of any other State which supports this view."[130] The paper also notes that "for the exercise of the right of self-defence there must be more than 'a threat.' There has to be an armed attack actual or imminent."[131]

## ■ DAVID MANNING MEMO (MARCH 14, 2002)

This memo was prepared by British national security advisor David Manning after having dinner with Condoleezza Rice. He observes that Ms. Rice is seen as an unalloyed advocate of military action against Iraq and again emphasizes how an ultimatum to Iraq on weapons inspectors could be helpful politically.

David Manning advises Prime Minister Tony Blair that President Bush had yet to find the answers to the "big" questions, such as: how to persuade international opinion that military action against Iraq is necessary and justified; what value to put on the exiled Iraqi opposition; how to coordinate a U.S./allied military campaign with internal opposition (assuming there is any); what happens on the morning after?[132]

Manning also wrote, "[T]he issue of the weapons inspectors must be handled in a way that would persuade European and wider opinion that the U.S. was conscious of the international framework, and the insistence of many countries on the need for a legal base. Renwed refused [sic] by Saddam to accept unfettered inspections would be a powerful argument."[133]

Manning also attempted to prepare Blair for his upcoming trip to Crawford: "I think there is a real risk that the Administration underestimates the difficulties. They may agree that failure isn't an option, but this really does not mean that they will avoid it." The memo went on to say: **"Condi's enthusiasm for regime change is undimmed."**[134]

## ■ THE MEYER MEMO (MARCH 18, 2002)

In this memo from Christopher Meyer, the British Ambassador in Washington, to

David Manning, we first learn that the British had agreed to join the Bush Administration in backing regime change through military action. The British also suggest giving Hussein an ultimatum that he would reject as a way of justifying war. In the memo, the Ambassador describes a lunch he recently had with Paul Wolfowitz, then U.S. Deputy Secretary of Defense:

> On Iraq I opened by sticking very closely to the script that you used with Condi Rice last week. **We backed regime change, but the plan had to be clever and failure was not an option.** It would be a tough sell for us domestically, and probably tougher elsewhere in Europe. The U.S. could go it alone if it wanted to. But if it wanted to act with partners, there had to be a strategy for building support for military action against Saddam. **I then went through the need to wrongnfoot [sic] Saddam on the inspectors and the U.N. SCRs [Security Council Resolutions]** and the critical importance of the MEPP [Middle East Peace Process] as an integral part of the anti-Saddam strategy. If all this could be accomplished skilfully, we were fairly confident that a number of countries would come on board.[135]

Meyer goes on to note that "Wolfowitz said that it was absurd to deny the link between terrorism and Saddam."[136] Meyer told Wolfowitz that "if the U.K. were to join the U.S. in any operation against Saddam, we would have to be able to take a critical mass of parliamentary and public opinion with us."[137]

Mr. Meyer had previously recalled that in the fall of 2001, Blair told Bush he should not get distracted from the war on terror. As noted above, Bush replied, "**I agree with you, Tony. We must deal with this first. But when we have dealt with Afghanistan, we must come back to Iraq.**"[138] This statement of intent by President Bush with regard to Iraq was made at a private White House dinner between the leaders on September 20, 2001.

### ■ THE RICKETTS MEMO (MARCH 22, 2002)

Peter Ricketts, the Political Director of the Foreign and Commonwealth Office, wrote this memo to the U.K. Foreign Secretary Jack Straw as the third of four documents advising the Prime Minister on his trip to Crawford. This memo is an early indication that at least the British were concerned that unmanipulated intelligence did not provide a strong case for Iraq possessing dangerous WMD that could target the United States.

In the memo, Ricketts expressed relief at the postponement of the publication of a dossier that detailed the limited state of Iraq's weapons program: "My meeting yesterday showed that there is more work to do to ensuer [sic] that the figures are accurate and consistent with those of the U.S."[139] Ricketts goes on to argue that "even the best survey of Iraq's WMD programmes will not show much advance in recent years on the nuclear, missile or CW/BW [chemical weapons/biological weapons] fronts: the programmes are extremely worrying but have not, as far as we know, been stepped up."[140]

Ricketts offered one final piece of advice: "**The truth is that what has changed is not the pace of Saddam Hussein's WMD programmes, but our tolerance of them post-11**

September . . . attempts to claim otherwise publicly will increase scepticism about our case."[141]

## ■ THE STRAW MEMO (MARCH 25, 2002)

U.K. Foreign Secretary Jack Straw wrote this final of four memos to Tony Blair before his April trip to Crawford.[142] The memo confirms once again that the Bush Administration anticipates military action to remove Saddam Hussein and again advocates the efficacy of delivering a legal ultimatum to Iraq. Straw emphasizes the need for a legal justification for military action, and the fact that "we have a long way to go" to convince the public that regime change is acceptable.[143]

According to Secretary Straw, the legal obstacles are difficult to surmount:

> **regime change per se is no justification for military action; it could form part of the method of any strategy, but not a goal.** Of course, we may want credibly to assert that regime change is an essential part of the strategy by which we have to achieve our ends— that of the elimination of Iraq's WMD capacity: but the latter has to be the goal.[144]

Echoing the advice of Peter Ricketts, Straw notes that "[O]bjectively, the threat from Iraq has not worsened as a result of 11 September."[145] **Straw cautions Blair that "[t]he rewards from your visit to Crawford will be few" and that, while the U.S. has "assumed regime change as a means of eliminating Iraq's WMD threat,"** virtually no assessment "has satisfactorily answered how that regime change is to be secured, and how there can be any certainty that the replacement regime will be better."[146] Straw also writes to Blair: "I believe that a demand for the unfettered readmission of weapons inspectors is essential, in terms of public explanation, and in terms of legal sanction for any subsequent military action."[147]

## ■ THE CABINET OFFICE PAPER (JULY 21, 2002)

The British Cabinet Office prepared a briefing paper for participants at the upcoming July 23 meeting from which the Downing Street Minutes would be generated. The paper reiterates that Prime Minister Blair had already agreed to back military action to eliminate Saddam Hussein's regime at the April summit in Crawford, Texas and again confirms U.S. determination to go to war.

The memo again highlights the need to make an ultimatum for Hussein that he would reject, and expresses concern about U.S. preparedness for occupying Iraq:

> [I]t is necessary to create the conditions in which we could legally support military action. Otherwise we face the real danger that the US will commit themselves to a course of action which we would find very difficult to support . . . U.S. plans assume, as a minimum, the use of British bases in Cyprus and Diego Garcia . . . [i]t is just possible that an ultimatum could be cast in terms which Saddam would reject (because he is unwilling to accept unfettered access) and which would not be regarded as unreasonable by the international community . . . [a] post-war occupation of Iraq could lead to a protracted

and costly nation-building exercise. As already made clear, the U.S. military plans are virtually silent on this point.[148]

The Cabinet Office Paper also provides additional evidence of the concerted strategy to use the United Nations route as a pretext for war. The Paper confirms the now accepted notion that the United Nations could be used as an excuse for going to war, and broaches the idea of using the United Nations to create a legal deadline for military action. The Paper states, "[W]e need to set a deadline, leading to an ultimatum. It would be preferable to obtain backing of a UNSCR [United Nations Security Council Resolution] for any ultimatum and early work would be necessary to explore with Kofi Annan and the Russians, in particular, the scope for achieving this."[149] Significantly, the Cabinet Office Paper goes on to conclude that the onus is on the United States to insure that the preconditions for war are met, writing, the Bush Administration would need to "creat[e] the conditions necessary to justify government military action . . ."[150]

■ **THE DOWNING STREET MINUTES (JULY 23, 2002)**

The July 23, 2002 Downing Street Minutes, the most important and well publicized of the Downing Street Minutes materials—sometimes described as the "smoking gun memo"—is a document obtained from an undisclosed source that contains the minutes taken during a meeting among the highest officials in the United Kingdom government and defense intelligence figures. The British authorities discuss the build up to the Iraq invasion of March 2003, and it is clear to those attending that President Bush intends to remove Saddam Hussein from power by force. The minutes run through military options and then consider a political strategy by which an appeal for support would be positively received by the public. They again suggest that President Bush issue an ultimatum for Saddam to allow back United Nations weapons inspectors, and that this tactic would help to make the use of force legal. Tony Blair is quoted as saying that under these conditions the British public would support regime change.[151]

Perhaps the most important passage in the July 23 Minutes is a report of a recent visit to Washington by Sir Richard Dearlove, head of MI-6 and known in official terminology as "C":

> C reported on his recent talks in Washington. **There was a perceptible shift in attitude. Military action was now seen as inevitable. Bush wanted to remove Saddam, through military action, justified by the conjunction of terrorism and WMD. But the intelligence and facts were being fixed around the policy.** The NSC had no patience with the U.N. route, and no enthusiasm for publishing material on the Iraqi regime's record. There was little discussion in Washington of the aftermath after military action.[152]

The Minutes also record British Defense Secretary Geoff Hoon as saying, "The U.S. had already begun 'spikes of activity' to put pressure on the regime."[153] In addition, Foreign Secretary Straw articulates his idea for justifying an attack in light of the fact that

Saddam was not threatening to attack his neighbors and his weapons of mass destruction program was less extensive than those of a number of other countries: "**We should work up a plan for an ultimatum to Saddam to allow back in the U.N. weapons inspectors. This would also help with the legal justification for the use of force.**"[154]

The British realized they needed "help with the legal justification for the use of force" because, as the British Attorney General pointed out, "the desire for regime change was not a legal base for military action."[155] Moreover, the Attorney General stated that of the "three possible legal bases: self-defence, humanitarian intervention, or [United Nations Security Council] authorisation," the first two "could not be the base in this case."[156] In other words, Iraq was not attacking the United States or the United Kingdom, so the leaders could not claim to be acting in self-defense; nor was Iraq's leadership in the process of committing genocide, so the United States and the United Kingdom could not claim to be invading for humanitarian reasons. This left Security Council authorization as the only conceivable legal justification for war.

At this point in the meeting Prime Minister Tony Blair weighed in. Responding to his minister's suggestion about drafting an ultimatum demanding that Saddam let United Nations inspectors back in the country, Blair acknowledged that such an ultimatum could be politically critical—but only if the Iraqi leader turned it down:

> **The Prime Minister said that it would make a big difference politically and legally if Saddam refused to allow in the U.N. inspectors.** Regime change and WMD were linked in the sense that it was the regime that was producing the WMD. . . . If the political context were right, people would support regime change. The two key issues were whether the military plan worked and whether we had the political strategy to give the military plan the space to work.[157]

As if there were any doubt about the intentions of using the United Nations to provoke war, U.K. Foreign Secretary Jack Straw observes, "[W]e should explore discreetly the ultimatum. Saddam would continue to play hard-ball with the UN."[158]

## Confirmation and Corroboration of Downing Street Minutes Materials

While the Bush Administration has sought to either ignore or diminish the Downing Street Minutes, they have ultimately proved to be important not only because they were in documentary form, but also because of their source, a critical Bush Administration ally. Unlike other disclosures by ex-Administration officials and others, which the White House has characterized as biased, these disclosures cannot be dismissed as mere sour grapes.[159]

As Cindy Sheehan stated so eloquently at the June 10, 2005 hearing on the Downing Street Minutes, convened by Representative Conyers: "I am even more convinced now that this aggression on Iraq was based on a lie of historic proportions and was blatantly unnecessary. The so-called Downing Street Memo dated 23 July 2002 only confirms what I already suspected, the leadership of his [sic] country rushed us into an illegal invasion of another sovereign country on prefabricated and cherry-picked intelligence. Iraq was no threat to the United States of America, and the devastating sanctions and bombing against the Iraqis were working."[160]

Our research indicates there is little doubt as to the accuracy of the Downing Street Minutes and related documents. Sources within the Blair and Bush Administrations have confirmed their accuracy, and we have been able to independently confirm and corroborate the major precepts of the various documents.

It is telling that when the Downing Street Minutes were first published by the *Sunday London Times*, shortly before the 2005 British election, the Blair Administration chose not to deny their authenticity. Shortly after the Minutes were released, sources within both the Bush and Blair Administrations confirmed their accuracy to the press.— former senior U.S. official told *Knight Ridder* that the Downing Street Minutes were "an absolutely accurate description of what transpired."[161] Two senior British officials, who asked not to be further identified because of the sensitivity of the material, told *Newsweek* in separate interviews that they had no reason to question the authenticity of the Downing Street Minutes.[162]

In addition, elements of the Downing Street Minutes can be independently corroborated. Consider the core, specific provisions of the July 23 Downing Street Minutes from Richard Dearlove, in which he describes his recent discussions with the Bush Administration:

- **By mid-July 2002, eight months before the war began, President Bush had decided to "remove Saddam, through military action."**

This statement that "Bush wanted to remove Saddam, through military action" has been proven true—on March 20, 2003, the U.S. military invaded Iraq and follow-up aspects of the Downing Street Minutes bear out that this decision was made well in advance of the war. In addition to the wealth of verification in Sections III(A)(1), (2), and (4) of this Report, and in particular as noted in the previous section, we know that in early August 2002, President Bush and Prime Minister Blair spoke by telephone. It was a short call, about fifteen minutes. According to a White House official who has studied the transcript of the phone call, "**The way it read was that, come what may, Saddam was going to go; they said they were going forward, they were going to take out the regime, and they were doing the right thing.** Blair did not need any convincing. There was no 'Come on Tony, we've got to get you on board.' I remember reading it then and thinking, O.K., now I know what we're going to be doing for the next year."[163] **Before the call, this official says, he had the impression that the probability of invasion was high, but still below 100 percent. Afterward, he says, "It was a done deal."**[164]

It is also worth noting that in March 2003, Tony Blair reportedly said, "[L]eft to himself, Bush would have gone to war in January. No, not January, but back in September."[165]

• **Bush had decided to "justify" the war "by the conjunction of terrorism and WMD."**

This statement is borne out by the entire "marketing campaign," which fixated on these twin justifications (see Section III(A)(4) of this Report). For example, the Bush Administration formed the White House Iraq Group (WHIG) in August 2002 to persuade the public of Saddam's supposed threat and to market the war. The Administration waited to introduce the WHIG's product to the public until September 2002, because, as White House Chief of Staff Andrew Card told the *New York Times* in an unusually candid interview, "[Y]ou don't introduce new products in August."[166]

• **Already "the intelligence and facts were being fixed around the policy."**

The statement that "the intelligence and facts were being fixed around the policy" is confirmed by the multi-layered effort by the Administration to pressure officials within the Administration to find links between Saddam and September 11 and to manipulate intelligence officials and agencies into overstating WMD threats (see Section III(B) of this Report).

• **Many at the top of the administration "had no patience" with "the U.N. route."**

This statement is consistent with the realities of the Bush Administration's intentions at the time. For example, Vice President Cheney's stated opinion was that there was no need to seek any approval from the U.N. to invade. He has stated: "A return of inspectors would provide no assurance whatsoever of his compliance with U.N. resolutions. On the contrary, there is great danger that it would provide false comfort that Saddam was somehow "back in the box."[167] Mr. Cheney, like other administration "hard-liners," was said to have feared "the U.N. route" not because it might fail but because it might succeed and thereby prevent a war that they were convinced had to be fought.[168]

• **"There was little discussion in Washington of the aftermath of military action."**

Unfortunately, this statement has been verified by events following the war (see below). Among other things, in an ironic assessment of the events to follow, Vice President Dick Cheney made an appearance on *Meet the Press* and stated that the war was not going to be long, costly, or bloody because "we will be greeted as liberators."[169] As the war unfolded, numerous gaps in planning became apparent.

• **The U.S. had already begun "spikes of activity" to put pressure on the regime.**

The statement that the U.S. had already begun "spikes of activity" to pressure Iraq has been subsequently confirmed by numerous accounts (see below). As reported in the *Sunday London Times*, in May 2002, with a conditional agreement in place with Britain for war, the U.S. and U.K. began to conduct a bombing campaign in Iraq described by British and U.S. officials as "spikes of activity" designed to put pressure on the Iraqi regime.[170] The bombing campaign was initiated a full ten months before the Bush

Administration determined that all diplomatic means had been exhausted and six months before Congressional authorization for the use of force.[171]

- **The British believed "[w]e should work up a plan for an ultimatum to Saddam to allow back in the U.N. weapons inspectors. This would also help with the legal justification or the use of force."[172]**

The initiative of the British to go back to the U.N. to force an "ultimatum" has also been proven true (see Section III(A)(5) of this Report). The U.S. and Britain asked for U.N. authorization to demand the reintroduction of weapons inspectors, which they received on November 8, 2002.

Other documents released in conjunction with the Downing Street Minutes have also been independently corroborated. For example, the Cabinet Office Paper from July 21, 2002 and the Iraq Options Paper from March 8, 2002 include the following:

- **Blair had already agreed to back military action to get rid of Saddam Hussein at a summit in Crawford, Texas in April 2002.**

This agreement has been corroborated by numerous sources, including British newspapers *The Guardian*[173] and *The Daily Telegraph*.[174]

- **U.S. plans assume, at a minimum, the use of British bases in Cyprus and Diego Garcia.**

This plan came to fruition. Akrotiri, the British air base in Cyprus, has been used extensively since the beginning of the war as a refueling and resupply base for U.S. and British aircraft and warships.[175] At the start of the war, the U.S. also used the base in Diego Garcia.[176]

- **U.K. contribution could include deployment of a Division (i.e., Gulf War-sized contribution plus naval and air forces) to making available bases.**

Britain did provide a sizable troop contribution, with over 11,000 troops currently in Iraq.[177]

- **An international coalition is necessary to provide military platform and desirable for political purposes, even though this coalition was made up of small powers, since the U.S. would probably not receive the support of the major powers for U.N. authorization.**

The U.S. ended up gathering a number of small powers to form an "international coalition," including, among others, Armenia, Bulgaria, Denmark, El Salvador, Estonia, Kazakhstan, Latvia, Mongolia, and Poland.[178]

- **"Time will be required to prepare public opinion in the U.K. that it is necessary to take military action against Saddam Hussein. There would also need to be a substantial effort to secure the support of Parliament. An information campaign will be needed which has to be closely related to an overseas information campaign designed to influence Saddam Hussein, the Islamic World and the wider international community."[179]**

The British Administration engaged in such a marketing campaign, with the Prime Minister persuading the Parliament and public of the case for war.[180]

• **"The optimal times to start action are in early spring."**

The war began on March 20, 2003, the first day of spring.

## ■ Manipulating Public Opinion

*"From a marketing point of view . . . you don't introduce new products in August."*
— AUGUST 2002, WHITE HOUSE CHIEF OF STAFF ANDREW CARD
COMMENTING ON THE FORMATION OF THE WHITE HOUSE
IRAQ GROUP (WHIG) TO MARKET THE WAR.

The Bush Administration manipulated public opinion by engaging in what Andrew Card, President Bush's Chief of Staff, described as a "marketing" plan to justify the war.[181] In retrospect, it is apparent that this marketing plan was decided and implemented well before Mr. Card's admission. The Downing Street Minutes, written in the spring and summer of 2002, provide valuable insights into the upcoming marketing of the justifications for war. Not only was the British government well aware of the planned U.S. marketing campaign, but it too was planning to engage in such an effort. Thus, the Cabinet Officer Paper notes that ministers are planning to "[a]**gree to the establishment of an ad-hoc group of officials under Cabinet Office Chairmanship to consider the development of an information campaign to be agreed with the U.S.**"[182]

In August 2002, Secretary of Defense Rumsfeld ramped up the rhetoric to a significant degree, comparing Saddam Hussein to Adolf Hitler, and deriding those asking the Bush Administration to substantiate their Weapons of Mass Destruction claims:

> Think of the prelude to World War Two. Think of all the countries that said, well, we don't have enough evidence. I mean, *Mein Kampf* had been written. Hitler had indicated what he intended to do. **Maybe he won't attack us. Maybe he won't do this or that. Well, there were millions of people dead because of the miscalculations.** The people who argued for waiting for more evidence have to ask themselves how they are going to feel at that point where another event occurs.[183]

By August 2002, the "so-called" White House Iraq Group (WHIG) was formed as a coordinating center to convince the public of the need for the Iraq war. The group met weekly in the White House Situation Room. Among its participants were Karl Rove, Karen Hughes, Mary Matalin, James R. Wilkinson, legislative liaison Nicholas E. Calio, Condoleezza Rice and her deputy, Stephen J. Hadley, and Scooter Libby.[184] According to *The Washington Post*, **"the escalation of nuclear rhetoric a year ago, including the introduction of the term 'mushroom cloud' into the debate, coincided with the formation of a White House Iraq Group."**[185] It was reportedly created to persuade the public, the Congress, and allies of the need to invade Iraq.[186]

During this time period, there is additional evidence of other Bush Administration officials seeking to manipulate public opinion to support war. For example, ABC News reported that officials both inside and outside the government said the Bush Administration would emphasize the danger of Saddam's weapons to gain the legal justification for war from the United Nations and also emphasize the danger at home to Americans, "'We were not lying,' said one official. 'But it was just a matter of emphasis.'"[187] Consider also Paul Wolfowitz's statement regarding why Iraq's supposed control over weapons of mass destruction was ultimately used to pitch the public on the war: "**[F]or bureaucratic reasons, we settled on one issue, weapons of mass destruction (as justification for invading Iraq), because it was the one reason everyone could agree on.**"[188]

Early September was a critical period in the WHIG's existence. It was on September 6 that the *New York Times* reported that Andrew Card explained the reason for delaying the roll-out of their pro-war campaign: "**From a marketing point of view. . . you don't introduce new products in August.**"[189] It is quite telling that he referred to their Iraq war initiative as a "product." Another senior Administration official made the following admission when asked why our nation really went to war: "As it was, the administration took what looked like the path of least resistance in making its public case for the war: WMD and intelligence links with Al Qaeda. If the public read too much into those links and thought Saddam had a hand in September 11, so much the better."[190]

Two days later, on September 8, the "marketing" campaign began in earnest. As described in one publication:

> The PR campaign intensified Sunday, September 8 . . . In a choreographed performance worthy of *Riverdance,* Cheney, Rumsfeld, Powell, Condoleezza Rice and Gen. Richard Myers said on separate talk shows that the aluminum tubes, suitable only for centrifuges, proved Iraq's pursuit of nuclear weapons.[191]

Frank Rich describes the flurry of activity on that day:

> All the references to nuclear threats were beginning to have their intended impact. As the *Washington Post* recounts, the administration's talk of clandestine centrifuges, nuclear blackmail and mushroom clouds had a powerful political effect, particularly on Senators who were facing fall election campaigns. "When you hear about nuclear weapons, this is the national security knock-out punch," said Senator Ron Wyden.[192]

In early October, in advance of a congressional vote to authorize military action, the WHIG released a "white paper." The paper is based on the rushed, confidential CIA intelligence assessment. As *Newsweek* reported:

> The publicly released white paper unequivocally backed up the White House's case about the dangers posed by Iraq's weapons of mass destruction (WMD) programs. It stated boldly and without caveats in the first paragraph that Baghdad "has chemical and biological weapons" and "if left unchecked, it probably will have a nuclear weapon during this decade." If Iraq obtains sufficient weapons-grade material from abroad, the white

paper further warned, Baghdad could make a nuclear weapon "within a year." To support its conclusions about an Iraqi nuclear program, it prominently cited, among other factors, Iraq's "aggressive attempts" to purchase high-strength aluminum tubes, an effort that Miller and her colleague Michael Gordon had first written about in an influential front-page story for the *New York Times* the previous September [apparently based on a leak from Scooter Libby]. . . . But . . . **the more detailed version of the NIE was hardly stronger. In fact, it revealed for the first time, in the very first paragraph, right after the sentence that** "if left unchecked, [Iraq] probably will have a nuclear weapon during this decade" **the fact that the State Department's intelligence arm, the Bureau of Intelligence and Research (INR), had an "alternative view" of the matter.**[193]

The more detailed, classified NIE also included the State and Energy Departments' dissents about the intended use of aluminum tubes. Both agencies had concluded that the tubes were not suited for use in centrifuges. Yet the publicly released white paper mentioned no disagreement on the aluminum tubes issue, removed qualifiers, and added language to distort the severity of the threat.[194]

Communications Director James Wilkinson, who played a prominent role in the writing of the white paper, emphasized the importance the group placed on nuclear threat imagery, no matter how attenuated:

By summer 2002, the **White House Iraq Group assigned Communications Director James R. Wilkinson to prepare a white paper for public release, describing the** "grave and gathering danger" **of Iraq's allegedly** "reconstituted" **nuclear weapons program.** Wilkinson gave prominent place to the claim that Iraq "sought uranium oxide, an essential ingredient in the enrichment process, from Africa." That claim, along with repeated use of the "mushroom cloud" image by top officials beginning in September, became the emotional heart of the case against Iraq. The uranium claims had never been significant to career analysts—Iraq had plenty already and lacked the means to enrich it. But the **allegations proved irresistible to the White House Iraq Group, which devised the war's communications strategy and included Libby among its members. Every layman understood the connection between uranium and the bomb, participants in the group said in interviews at the time, and it was the easiest way for the Bush Administration to raise alarms.**[195]

This characterization of the WHIG and its product, as using a no-holds barred approach to develop strategy and rhetoric designed to pursue war, is consistent with what we have learned from other sources. For example, Bush Administration officials who observed the white paper's development noted that the WHIG "wanted gripping images and stories not available in the hedged and austere language of intelligence."[196] Even Bush Administration supporter David Brooks was forced to acknowledge "**from Day One,**" the Bush White House "**decided our public relations is not going to be honest.**"[197]

The strong congressional vote on October 11 was also aided in large part by the timing—less than one month before the midterm elections. This favorable timing was not an accident. Among other things, it was anticipated as early as the July 23 Downing Street meeting that war's timing would be premised on United States elections. According to the British Defence Secretary Geoff Hoon, no decisions had been made, but "the most likely timing in U.S. minds for military action to begin was January, with the timeline beginning 30 days before the U.S. Congressional elections."[198] Although the eventual date slipped because of delays regarding U.N. approval, it is quite telling that the British thought that military engagement would commence at such a politically opportunistic time. Former United States Ambassador Raphael, who was involved in Iraq policy, acknowledged much of the timing was premised on United States elections when he said that the Administration was "not prepared" when it invaded Iraq due to "clear political pressure, election-driven and calendar-driven."[199]

Also, on September 12, 2002, President Bush gave a speech at the United Nations in which he declared that "Iraq has answered a decade of U.N. demands with a decade of defiance."[200] Simultaneously with Bush's United Nations speech, the Which House released a report, "A Decade of Deception and Defiance," seeking to set forth evidence that Iraq was violating bans on possessing chemical, biological and nuclear weapons.[201]

Other reports on the manner in which the Bush Administration was planning its campaign to convince the public and the Congress of the need for war further confirm the sense that this was more a public relations endeavor than an honest and frank sharing of information with the American public. For example, in December 2002, when the President was being briefed on WMD evidence, his basic concern appears to have been with the public relations value of the information, rather than its actual efficacy. Bob Woodward reported that when Deputy CIA Director John McLaughlin presented his best evidence of weapons of mass destruction, complete with satellite photos and flip charts, the President responded by exclaiming "**Nice try, but that isn't gonna sell Joe Public. That isn't gonna convince Joe Public. . . . This is the best we've got?**"[202]

By January, of course, there were fewer and fewer doubts that the decision to go to war had been made. As noted in Bob Woodward's "Plan of Attack," January was when the Bush White House "**was planning a big rollout of speeches and documents**" to advance the war.[203] By January 12, 2003, Secretary of State Colin Powell had become exasperated with the headlong push for war. State Department officials have said that after White House meetings, Secretary Colin Powell would return to his office on the seventh floor of the State Department, roll his eyes and say, "Jeez, what a fixation about Iraq."[204] In this regard, another Administration official added, "I do believe certain people have grown theological about this. It's almost a religion—that it will be the end of our society if we don't take action now."[205]

Finally, on January 28, 2003, President Bush gave his State of the Union Speech, in which he declared the now infamous 16 words: "The British government has learned that Saddam Hussein recently sought significant quantities of uranium from Africa."[206] Again, in retrospect, this uranium reference appears to have been part and parcel of the pre-meditated marketing plan launched earlier that summer. It has been reported that one of the speech writers conceded the phrase's marketing impact: "**For a speech writer, uranium was valuable because anyone could see its connection to an atomic bomb.**"[207]

Just as the Bush Administration engaged in a public relations style campaign to convince the nation to support the war, the record shows it also sought to manipulate public opinion to convince the American public that the upcoming occupation would be straight forward and relatively peaceful. Prior to the war, senior members of the Bush Administration repeatedly downplayed the risks and overstated the ease of the occupation. For example, rejecting Army Secretary Eric Shinseki's assessment that the mission would require large numbers of troops for a long duration, Deputy Defense Secretary Paul Wolfowitz stated: "I am reasonably certain that they will greet us as liberators, and that will help us to keep requirements down. In short, we don't know what the requirement will be, but we can say with reasonable confidence that the notion of hundreds of thousands of American troops is way off the mark."[208]

Later, Defense Secretary Rumsfeld echoed these remarks, stating that "[t]he idea that it would take several hundred thousand U.S. forces, I think, is far off the mark."[209] Vice President Dick Cheney made an appearance on *Meet the Press* and stated that the war would be quick and easy: "I really do believe that we will be greeted as liberators. I've talked with a lot of Iraqis in the last several months myself. . . . The read we get on the people of Iraq is there is no question but what they want to get rid of Saddam Hussein and they will welcome as liberators the United States when we come to do that."[210]

Also in this regard, comprehensive reports written by four ex-CIA analysts and led by former Deputy Director Richard Kerr found:

> **Policymakers worried more about making the case for the war, particularly the claim that Iraq had weapons of mass destruction, than planning for the aftermath.** . . . In an ironic twist, the policy community was receptive to technical intelligence (the weapons program), where the analysis was wrong, but apparently paid little attention to intelligence on cultural and political issues (post-Saddam Iraq), where the analysis was right.[211]

The evidence we have identified indicates that the Bush Administration deliberately chose to downplay real and credible risks regarding the occupation in order to help make the strongest case for war for the public. Thus, for example, in January 2003, when President Jacques Chirac's top advisor, Maurice Gourdault-Montagne, warned Condoleezza Rice that the war would lead to an increase in terrorism, the National Secretary Advisor ignored the warnings:

> **Gourdault-Montagne talked of the unrest that would no doubt erupt among Iraq's many ethnic groups, and he warned of increased terror.** Rice pooh-poohed his every objection. "Everything was dismissed," says a French diplomat, recalling Rice's reaction. "There is terror already in the world and the rest of the Arab world won't feel resentment. If it does, the leaders of the Arab world will support the administration. . . . **Every good reason not to go to war was irrelevant.**" It was clear, says this diplomat, "that the decision to go to war was taken."[212]

As a matter of fact, it has been reported that the National Intelligence Council specifically warned President Bush in January 2003 that "the conflict could spark factional violence and an anti-U.S. insurgency . . . [o]ne of the reports said the U.S.-led occupation could 'increase popular sympathy for terrorist objectives.'"[213]

State Department officials warned not only about the lack of planning for the occupation, but also of future human rights abuses in Iraq. On February 7, 2003, one month before the U.S. invasion, three State Department bureau chiefs prepared a secret memo for their superior and cited "serious planning gaps for post-conflict public security and humanitarian assistance."[214] The State Department officials noted that the military was reluctant "to take on 'policing' roles" in Iraq after the overthrow of Saddam Hussein.[215] The three officials also warned that "a failure to address short-term public security and humanitarian assistance concerns could result in serious human rights abuses which would undermine an otherwise successful military campaign, and our reputation internationally."[216] Again, these risks were ignored by the Bush Administration's intent on developing the strongest possible case for war.

The Downing Street Minutes also indicate that the United Kingdom had sought to warn the Bush Administration of the perils of post-war occupancy. In the spring of 2002, British Foreign Secretary Jack Straw wrote, "We have a long way to go to convince [the Bush Administration] as to . . . whether the consequence of military action really would be a compliant law abiding replacement government."[217]

There is also considerable evidence indicating that the Bush Administration went into armed conflict in Iraq without a real or viable plan for the occupation. United Kingdom Foreign Secretary Jack Straw, in writing a memo to Prime Minister Blair concerning his upcoming April 2002 trip to Crawford, Texas, expressed alarm at the Bush Administration's failure to consider these issues. He wrote:

> We have also to answer the big question—what will this action achieve? There seems to be a larger hole in this than on anything. Most of the assessments from the U.S. have assumed regime change as a means of eliminating Iraq's [weapons of mass destruction] threat. **But no one has satisfactorily answered how that regime change is to be secured, and how there can be any certainty that the replacement regime will be better.**[218]

Around the same time, British Foreign Policy Advisor David Manning wrote a memo to Prime Minister Blair in which, based on Manning's dinner with Condoleezza Rice, he continued to express concern regarding the lack of United States preparation for an Iraq occupation: "From what [Rice] said, Bush has yet to find the answers to the big questions, including what happens on the morning after?"[219] Later on in the memo, Manning again raises questions regarding the Bush Administration's preparedness for a post-occupation of Iraq noting, "I think there is a real risk that the Administration underestimates the difficulties. They may agree that failure isn't an option, but this does not mean that they will avoid it. Will the Sunni majority really respond to an uprising led by

Kurds and Shias? Will Americans really put in enough ground troops to do the job if the Kurdish/Shi'ite stratagem fails?"[220]

Perhaps most famously, in the Downing Street Minutes, when "C" (Sir Richard Dearlove) reported on his recent discussions in Washington, he discerned that the Bush Administration was not focused on post-occupation issues. Mr. Dearlove noted, "[T]here **was little discussion in Washington of the aftermath after military action.**"[221] While the British at least seemed concerned about the risks of "nation-building," their impression was that the Bush Administration was blithely ignoring these matters. Further, as detailed in the Cabinet Office Paper, "[A] post-war occupation of Iraq could lead to a protracted and costly nation-building exercise. As **already made clear, the U.S. military plans are virtually silent on this point.**"[222]

Finally, we now know that a classified State Department report, disclosed by *The Los Angeles Times*, concluded that it was unlikely that installing a new government in Iraq would encourage the spread of democracy in the region. The paper found that in the unlikely event a democracy did take root in Iraq, it would likely result in an Islamic-controlled government antipathetic to the United States.[223]

## ■ Using the United Nations as a Pretext for War

*The United States was "ready to discredit inspections in favor of disarmament."*
—OCTOBER 2002 STATEMENT BY VICE PRESIDENT CHENEY, RECOUNTED BY IRAQ SURVEY GROUP HEAD HANS BLIX AS A "PRETTY STRAIGHT WAY . . . OF SAYING THAT IF WE DID NOT SOON FIND THE WEAPONS OF MASS DESTRUCTION THAT THE U.S. WAS CONVINCED IRAQ POSSESSED . . . THE U.S. WOULD BE READY TO SAY THAT THE INSPECTORS WERE USELESS AND EMBARK ON DISARMAMENT BY OTHER MEANS."[224]

The manipulation and marketing of the Iraq war by the Bush Administration extended beyond domestic opinion to include the United Nations as well. Our review indicates that the very concept of seeking U.N. resolutions was merely to provide an ultimatum that Iraq would reject. Moreover, from the time the Bush Administration committed to obtaining United Nations approval in September 2002, it engaged in a series of actions intended to pursue military action regardless of the efficacy of the United Nations Security Council process.

From the very outset, the Bush Administration was antagonistic to any successes the United Nation inspectors might have achieved. It pursued language that would most easily have paved the way for war and then sought to discredit the very inspections process the Security Council had just approved. When the weapons inspections process appeared to be working and the votes appeared lacking to obtain a Security Council vote to authorize war, President Bush and Prime Minister Blair met on January 31, 2003, to discuss alternative scenarios of provoking war. Finally, when the plan to provoke war failed and the Security Council made clear it would not authorize military action, the Bush

Administration was forced to adopt a contorted and extreme view of international law in order to justify military intervention.

As early as August 2002, British Foreign Secretary Straw arrived in the Hamptons to "discreetly explore [an] ultimatum [given to Saddam Hussein]" with Secretary of State Powell.[225] As Bob Woodward notes in his book *Plan of Attack,* **Mr. Straw told the Secretary, "If you are really thinking about war and you want us Brits to be a player, we cannot be unless you go to the United Nations."[226]**

As we now know, this course of action was set forth in the various Downing Street Minutes materials described earlier in Section III(A)(3) of this Report. The deceptiveness of this course of events has not been lost on other observers. As Mark Danner of the *New York Review of Books* has written, these discussions were not about preserving the peace, or even allowing the inspectors to do the job, but about finding a legal justification for war:

> Though "the U.N. route" would be styled as an attempt to avoid war, its essence, as the Downing Street memo makes clear, was a strategy to make the war possible, partly by making it politically palatable . . . [T]hus, the idea of U.N. inspectors was introduced not as a means to avoid war, as President Bush repeatedly assured Americans, but as a means to make war possible. War had been decided on; the problem under discussion here was how to make, in the prime minister's words, "the political context . . . right" . . . [T]he demand that Iraq accept U.N. inspectors, especially if refused, could form the political bridge by which the allies could reach their goal: "regime change" through "military action."[227]

By September 7, 2002, Woodward detailed a personal visit by Blair to persuade President Bush to go to the United Nations: "It was critical domestically for the Prime Minister to show his own Labour Party, a pacifist party at heart, opposed to war in principle, that he had gone the U.N. route. Public opinion in the U.K. favored trying to make international institutions work before resorting to force. Going through the U.N. would be a large and much-needed plus."[228] The President told Blair that he had decided "to go to the UN" and the Prime Minister "was relieved."[229] After the session with Blair, Bush walked into a conference room and told the British officials gathered there that "your man has got *cojones.*"[230] This particular conference with Blair would be known, Bush declared, as "the *cojones* meeting."[231]

Five days later, on September 12, 2002, President Bush announced that the United States would "work with the U.N. Security Council for the necessary resolutions."[232] It is notable that the President envisaged more than one resolution. Almost immediately, however, the Bush Administration began to distance itself from any suggestion that the reintroduction of weapons inspectors would work—the purported purpose of the resolutions:

> **Four days later, on September 16, Annan stood before the microphones at the U.N. and announced he had received a letter from Iraqi authorities that said Iraq would allow inspectors access "without conditions". . . . White House staffers flew into a rage.** In their view Annan was giving Saddam the kind of wiggle room that would allow him to avert

military action. Reportedly, later that night, Powell and Rice, in a conference call, chewed out Annan for taking matters into his own hands. . . . [R]elations between the U.N. leadership and the White House deteriorated in the following days as word of American military preparations seeped out . . . **Bush's U.N. strategy was becoming clear: the goal was not to get Saddam to disarm through peaceful means, but rather to get a U.N. stamp of approval for American military action as quickly as possible.** Indeed, Bush's speech before the General Bssembly was soon seen by the delegates for what it was: a tell-'em-what-they-want-to-hear spiel even though you don't believe it.[233]

Thereafter, the Bush Administration engaged in an effort to discredit the weapons inspectors before they were even able to do their work. For example, on September 19, 2002, Donald Rumsfeld testified before the Senate that "the more inspectors that are in there, the less likely something's going to happen."[234] The same day, President Bush threatened that "if the United Nations Security Council won't deal with the problem, the United States and some of our friends will."[235] Richard Perle attacked Hans Blix by saying, "If it were up to me, on the strength of his previous record, I wouldn't have chosen Hans Blix.[236]

After this initial round of "saber-rattling," the Administration then pursued an extreme—and ultimately unsuccessful—resolution that would have allowed an automatic trigger path to military action. The initial draft of Resolution 1441, prepared by the Bush Administration, threatened the use of "all necessary means" should Iraq fail to comply with strict new inspections.[237] Hans Blix, chief inspector of the United Nations Monitoring, Verification and Inspection Commission (AUNMOVIC) remarked: "It was so remote from reality . . . [I]t was written by someone who didn't understand how (inspections) function."[238] Lacking the votes, the Bush Administration was forced to abandon the idea of an "automatic trigger," and by November 8, a revised resolution was approved. As Sir Jeremy Greenstock, the British ambassador to the UN, acknowledged: "We heard loud and clear during the negotiations about 'automaticity' and 'hidden triggers' the concerns that on a decision so crucial we should not rush into military action. . . . Let me be equally clear. . . . There is no 'automaticity' in this Resolution. If there is a further Iraqi breach of its disarmament obligations, the matter will return to the Council for discussion as required."[239]

After this failure, the Bush Administration continued to pursue its strategy of using the United Nations action to justify military action, dismissing the inspection process recently approved by the U.N. Almost immediately, United States officials made it clear that the Bush Administration would invade Iraq regardless of the outcome of the recently authorized weapons inspection process. In late November, Richard Perle, a member of the Defense Policy Board, attended a meeting on global security with members of the British Parliament. At one point he argued that the weapons inspection team might be unable to find Saddam's arsenal of banned weapons because they were so well-hidden. According to the *London Mirror*, **he then stated that the U.S. would "attack Iraq even if U.N. inspec-**

tors fail to find weapons," admitting that a "clean bill of health" from U.N. chief weapons inspector Hans Blix would not halt America's war machine.[240]

On December 7, 2002, the Iraqis issued a 12,000-page document accounting for the state of Iraq's weapons programs. The Bush Administration immediately asserted that the report constituted a "material breach,"[241] zeroing in on the charge that the Iraqi declaration failed to mention the now-discredited theory that Iraq was attempting to acquire uranium from Niger.[242] Vice President Cheney went so far as to inform Hans Blix that the purpose of the inspectors was to find WMD, and that war was coming in any event. Blix recounted that Cheney:

> stated the position that inspections, if they do not give results, cannot go on forever, and said the U.S. was "ready to discredit inspections in favor of disarmament"—pretty straight way, I thought, of saying that if we did not soon find the weapons of mass destruction that the U.S. was convinced Iraq possessed (though they did not know where), the U.S. would be ready to say that the inspectors were useless and embark on disarmament by other means.[243]

By December 2002 and January 2003, it was becoming increasingly apparent that the Bush Administration was not providing full cooperation with U.N. inspection teams. In December, UNMOVIC weapons inspection leader Hans Blix had called on the United States to share its intelligence information with inspectors. "Of course we would like to have as much information from any member state as to evidence they may have on weapons of mass destruction, and, in particular, sites," he says.[244] "Because we are inspectors, we can go to sites. They may be listening to what's going on and they may have lots of other sources of information. But we can go to the sites legitimately and legally."[245] As observed in the *New York Times*: "On one hand, administration officials are pressing him to work faster and send out more inspectors to more places to undermine Baghdad's ability to conceal any hidden programs. At the same time, Washington has been holding back its intelligence, waiting to see what Iraq will say in its declaration."[246]

On February 20, 2003, CBS News reported: "U.N. arms inspectors are privately complaining about the quality of U.S. intelligence and accusing the United States of sending them on wild goose chases . . . The inspectors have become so frustrated trying to chase down unspecific or ambiguous U.S. leads that they've begun to express that anger privately in no uncertain terms . . . U.N. sources have told CBS News that American tips have lead to one dead end after another." And whatever intelligence has been provided, reports CBS, has turned out to be "circumstantial, outdated or just plain wrong."[247]

Moreover, despite repeated assurances of cooperation, the IAEA received no information on the Niger-uranium claim until the day before Powell's United Nations presentation, even though Bush Administration officials had such information for over a year and provision of information was mandated by U. N. Resolution 1441:

> The U.S. Mission in Vienna provided the IAEA with an oral briefing while Jacques Baute

was en route to New York, leaving no printed material with the nuclear inspectors. As IAEA officials recount, an astonished Baute told his aides, "That won't do. I want the actual documentary evidence." He had to register his complaints through a United Nations Monitoring, Verification, and Inspection Commission (UNMOVIC) channel before receiving the documents the day Powell spoke. It was an incident that would characterize America's intelligence-sharing with the IAEA.[248]

By late January, the U.N. was not finding any evidence that Iraq had reinitiated its nuclear program, which in turn was leading to a furor in the Bush Administration. Thus on January 27, the U.N. issued a press release regarding Iraq's response to Resolution 1441 and stated that "it would appear that Iraq had decided in principle to provide cooperation on substance in order to complete the disarmament task through inspection."[249] Although there were some outstanding issues and questions concerning chemical and biological weapons, the press release stated that the U.N. weapons inspectors had reported that after 60 days of inspections with a total of 139 inspections at 106 locations, they had found "no evidence that Iraq had revived its nuclear weapons programme" and "no prohibited nuclear activities had been identified."[250]

According to Bob Woodward, the accounts of Iraqis cooperating with U.N. weapons inspectors by opening up buildings "infuriated" President Bush, who believed, in Woodward's words, that the "unanimous international consensus of the November [UN] resolution was beginning to fray."[251] President Bush told Rice that the "pressure isn't holding together." President Bush also commented about the antiwar protests in the United States and Europe.[252]

These issues arose in the run up to Secretary of State Colin Powell's February 5, 2003 presentation to the United Nations Security Council. To the Bush Administration's chagrin, the presentation did not produce a "smoking gun" that would cause other members of the Council to join in efforts to authorize the use of force. Indeed, it now appears clear that by this time, the Bush Administration had no intelligence of its own that could provide hard evidence to support any claim that Saddam Hussein possessed any WMD threatening the United States.

On February 14, Hans Blix appeared before the Security Council and essentially contradicted Powell's presentation: "The trucks that Powell had described as being used for chemical decontamination, Blix said, could just as easily have been used for 'routine activity.' He contradicted Powell's assertion that the Iraqis knew in advance when the inspectors would be arriving. Mohamed El Baradei of the IAEA weighed in as well, insisting that, at least on the nuclear front, there was no evidence Saddam had any viable program. Further, Blix said that Iraq was finally taking steps toward real cooperation with the inspectors, allowing them to enter Iraqi presidential palaces, among other previously proscribed sites."[253]

On February 24, 2003, the Bush Administration opted to propose the long-awaited "second resolution" authorizing war.[254] Although the resolution was ultimately withdrawn on March 17, 2003, without a vote—even though President Bush had assured all concerned that there would be a vote "no matter what the whip count is"[255]—the Bush Administration's desperate tactics to obtain passage, even to the point of wiretapping the communications of Security Council Members, belie the true purpose of the United Nations route.

For example, the Bush Administration engaged in a secret "dirty tricks" campaign against U.N. Security Council delegations as part of its struggle to win votes in favor of the requisite second resolution. A memorandum written by a top official at the U.S. National Security Agency details an aggressive surveillance operation that involved the interception of home and office telephone calls and e-mails and was particularly directed at "U.N. Security Council Members (minus U.S. and GBR, of course)."[256] The memo was directed at senior NSA officials and advises them that the agency is "mounting a surge" aimed at gleaning information not only on how delegations on the Security Council will vote on any second resolution on Iraq, but also "policies," "negotiating positions," "alliances" and "dependencies"—the "whole gamut of information that could give U.S. policymakers an edge in obtaining results favorable to U.S. goals or to head off surprises."[257]

The existence of this surveillance operation severely undercut the credibility and efforts of the Administration to win over undecided delegations. In addition, diplomats complained about the outright "hostility" of U.S. tactics to persuade them to fall in line, including threats such as receiving the "unpleasant economic consequences of standing up to the U.S."[258]

Further proof that the Bush Administration used the United Nations as a pretext for war can be seen in the fact that by March, after it was clear the votes did not exist for a second resolution, the Administration engaged in furious and frantic efforts to develop the legal cover to justify military action.[259] Thus, the Bush Administration began to argue that the invasion would be pursuant to a Security Council Resolution.[260] In a speech immediately preceding the invasion, President Bush cited three previous U.N. Security Council resolutions that purportedly conferred legal authorization for force. These were: (1) the recent Resolution 1441, which dealt with the renewed weapons inspections; (2) Resolution 678, adopted in 1990, authorizing force in the Persian Gulf war; and (3) Resolution 687, adopted shortly after the war ended, imposing economic sanctions and calling for the surrender for WMD.[261]

The Bush Administration's legal justifications for changing course and action without a second resolution also lack credibility. With respect to Resolution 1441, the clear weight of authority signaled that it did not in itself authorize force and that the Administration would need a second resolution from the Security Council. In fact, the U.K. Attorney General, Lord Goldsmith, expressed this view to Prime Minister Blair days before the invasion of Iraq.[262] With respect to a violation of Resolution 687, which would trigger the use of force contemplated in 678, the British authorities cited in the March 2002 Legal Background Paper included in the Downing Street Minutes note that the

United States was the only country in the world that was claiming that an explicit authorization from the U.N. to enforce U.N. resolutions by invading Iraq was not needed: "As the cease-fire was proclaimed by the Council in 687 (1991), it is for the Council to assess whether any such breach of those obligations has occurred . . .[T]he U.S. have a rather different view: they maintain that the assessment of breach is for individual member States. We are not aware of any other State which supports this view."[263]

Even Richard Perle, a noted war hawk, acknowledged that legal precedent did not support the unilateral action taken by the Bush and Blair Administrations. Before an audience in London, he admitted that "international law . . . would have required us to leave Saddam Hussein alone."[264]

While the Bush Administration was forced to make these farfetched legal arguments, British legal authorities found themselves in the position of having to completely reverse their initial assessments of the illegality of the war. Thus, although as recently as Spring 2002, it was clear British legal advisors understood that applicable international law did not justify military action,[265] less than one year later, British authorities were altering their legal analysis and conclusions. For example, on March 17, 2003, the British Attorney General produced a memo that provided an unequivocal justification for the use of force, which contained no caveats or reservations. His new view, which still remains contentious in Britain, was that authority to use force existed from the "combined effects" of U.N. Security Council Resolutions.[266]

This abrupt about-face led to a legal storm in the United Kingdom and a wave of resignations.[267] As Ray McGovern testified at a hearing on the Downing Street Minutes, the British documents on this point "show a panic, a veritable panic among British lawyers, and I think perhaps you can all identify with this. They were befuddled. The decision had been made for war. Their prime minister had opted on to this scheme and they were trying to figure out a way how it could be legally justified."[268]

One casualty, Elizabeth Wimshurst, Deputy Legal Advisor at the British Foreign Office, stated in he letter of resignation in protest of the war that the invasion of Iraq is a "crime of aggression."[269] She said she could not agree to military action in circumstances she described as "so detrimental to the international order and the rule of law."[270] She also noted:

> I regret that I cannot agree that it is lawful to use force against Iraq without a second Security Council resolution to revive the authorization given in SCR 678. I do not need to set out my reasoning; you are aware of it. My views accord with the advice that has been given consistently in this office before and after the adoption of U.N. Security Council resolution 1441 and with what the attorney general gave us to understand was his view prior to his letter of 7 March. (The view expressed in that letter has of course changed again into what is now the official line.)[271]

# Misstating and Manipulating the Intelligence to Justify Pre-emptive War

*"There was a great deal of pressure to find a reason to go to war with Iraq. And the pressure was not just subtle; it was blatant . . . [the official's boss] called a meeting and gave them their marching orders. And he said, "You know what? If Bush wants to go to war, it's your job to give him a reason to do so."*

—FALL/WINTER 2001, A CIA OFFICIAL WORKING ON WMD[272]

Our investigation reveals that there was a steady stream of pressure and other forms of influence placed on intelligence and other government officials by the Bush Administration to adopt assessments supporting war with Iraq. In particular, we found that members of the Bush Administration misstated, overstated, and manipulated intelligence with regard to linkages between Iraq and Al Qaeda; the acquisition of nuclear weapons by Iraq; the acquisition of aluminum tubes to be used as uranium centrifuges; and the acquisition of uranium from Niger. In this section, we will generally detail the techniques utilized by the Administration to manipulate intelligence, as well as identify several specific examples of such manipulation.

As a general matter, the record reveals that the Bush Administration engaged in several techniques to insure that the available intelligence information would be used to justify war—including the application of political pressure on intelligence officials, "stovepiping" (whereby raw and unfiltered data was forwarded directly to the White House); "cherry-picking" (by which the White House only utilized those bits of data and information, often without qualification or caveat, that supported a case for war); and selectively leaking information (including classified information) to the media.[273]

We know about these techniques from numerous and repeated disclosures by current and former intelligence and Administration officials. Perhaps most damaging are the candid assessments by life-long Republican and former Treasury Secretary Paul O'Neill and Secretary of State Powell's former Chief of Staff, Lawrence Wilkerson. Mr. O'Neill recounted, "If you operate in a certain way—by saying this is how I want to justify what I've already decided to do, and I don't care how you pull it off—you guarantee that you'll get faulty, one-sided information . . . [Y]ou don't have to issue an edict, or twist arms, or be overt."[274] Lawrence Wilkerson recently stated:

> The case that I saw for four-plus years was a case I have never seen in my studies of aberrations, bastardizations, perturbations, changes to the national security decision-making process, . . . **What I saw was a cabal between the vice president of the United States, Richard Cheney, and the Secretary of Defense, Donald Rumsfeld, on critical issues that made decisions that the bureaucracy did not know were being made** . . . [When a decision was presented to the bureaucracy], it was presented in such a disjointed, incredible way that the bureaucracy often didn't know what it was doing as it moved to carry them out.[275]

With regard to outright pressure, a former CIA analyst described the intense pressure brought to bear on CIA analysts by the Bush Administration: "The analysts at the C.I.A. were beaten down defending their assessments. And they blame George Tenet" (the CIA director) "for not protecting them. I've never seen a government like this."[276]

In a similar vein, the *Washington Post* described the pressure on intelligence officials from a barrage of high-ranking Bush Administration officials:

> Former and current intelligence officials said they felt a continual drumbeat, not only from Cheney and Libby, but also from Deputy Defense Secretary Paul D. Wolfowitz, Feith, and less so from CIA Director George J. Tenet, to find information or write reports in a way that would help the administration make the case that going into Iraq was urgent. "They were the browbeaters," said a former defense intelligence official who attended some of the meetings in which Wolfowitz and others pressed for a different approach to the assessments they were receiving. "In interagency meetings," he said, "Wolfowitz treated the analysts' work with contempt."[277]

There are numerous other instances and corroboration of this pressure. For example, on October 8, 2002, *Knight Ridder* reported that various military officials, intelligence employees, and diplomats in the Bush Administration charged "that the administration squelches dissenting views and that intelligence analysts are under intense pressure to produce reports supporting the White House's argument that Hussein poses such an immediate threat to the United States that preemptive military action is necessary."[278] It has also been reported that the Vice President's staff monitored the National Security Council staff in such a heavy-handed fashion that some N.S.C. staff "quit using e-mails for substantive conversations because they knew the Vice President's alternate national security staff was reading their e-mails now."[279] United States Diplomat John Brady Kiesling resigned his post as a diplomat because of the flaws in the intelligence process. In his resignation letter, he cited his opposition to the "distortion of intelligence, such systematic manipulation of American opinion."[280]

A CIA official working on WMD explained: "[T]here was a great deal of pressure to find a reason to go to war with Iraq." And the pressure was not just subtle; it was blatant. At one point in January 2003, the person's boss called a meeting and gave them their marching orders. "And he said, 'You know what—if Bush wants to go to war, it's your job to give him a reason to do so' . . . He said it at the weekly office meeting. And I just remember saying, 'This is something that the American public, if they ever knew, would be outraged' . . . He said it to about fifty people. And it's funny because everyone still talks about that—'Remember when [he] said that.'"[281]

With regard to stovepiping and cherry-picking, a former intelligence aid stated: "There's so much intelligence out there that it's easy to pick and choose your case . . . [i]t opens things up to cherry-picking."[282] Former CIA officer Robert Baer concluded on the CNN documentary *Dead Wrong*, that "the problem is the White House didn't go to the CIA and say 'tell me the truth,' it said 'give me ammunition.'"[283] As Spencer Ackerman and

John Judis found in their article "The First Casualty," "interviews with current and former intelligence officials and other experts reveal that the Bush Administration culled from U.S. intelligence those assessments that supported its position and omitted those that did not. The administration ignored, and even suppressed, disagreement within the intelligence agencies and pressured the CIA to reaffirm its preferred version of the Iraqi threat."[284]

Seymour Hersh similarly found that "Chalabi's defector reports were now flowing from the Pentagon directly to the Vice-President's office, and then on to the President, with little prior evaluation by intelligence professionals."[285]

Former National Security Council official, Ken Pollack, confirmed how the Bush Administration abused the intelligence process in order to justify invading Iraq, observing the Bush team had "dismantle[d] the existing filtering process that for fifty years had been preventing the policymakers from getting bad information. They created stovepipes to get the information they wanted directly to the top leadership. Their position is that the professional bureaucracy is deliberately and maliciously keeping information from them. They always had information to back up their public claims, but it was often very bad information."[286]

Similar, damaging acknowledgments of intelligence manipulations have been made by ex-CIA officials. Vincent Cannistraro, the CIA's former head of counter-intelligence admitted, "Basically, cooked information is working its way into high-level pronouncements and there's a lot of unhappiness about it in intelligence, especially among analysts at the CIA."[287] Michael Scheuer, a CIA analyst, echoed this when he stated, "[T]here was just a resignation within the agency that we were going to war against Iraq and it didn't make any difference what the analysis was or what kind of objections or countervailing forces there were to an invasion. We were going to war."[288]

In an interview on the PBS show *Frontline*, Greg Thielmann, Director of the Strategic, Proliferation and Military Affairs Office at the State Department's Intelligence Bureau, who was responsible for analyzing the Iraq's weapon threat, accused the White House of "systematic, across-the-board exaggeration" of intelligence as it made its case that Saddam Hussein posed an imminent threat to the U.S.[289] He further contended that "senior officials made statements which I can only describe as dishonest."[290] Mr. Thielmann has also stated that "**the American public was seriously misled. The Administration twisted, distorted, and simplified intelligence in a way that led Americans to seriously misunderstand the nature of the Iraq threat. I'm not sure I can think of a worse act against the people in a democracy than a president distorting critical classified information.**"[291]

It also appears that the Bush Administration engaged in an organized effort to selectively leak information to the media in order to help justify the case for war. As *Knight Ridder* reported:

A *Knight Ridder* review of the administration's arguments, its own reporting at the time and the Senate Intelligence Committee's 2004 report shows that the White House followed a pattern of using questionable intelligence, even documents that turned out to be forgeries, to support its case—**often leaking classified information to receptive journalists**—and dismissing information that undermined the case for war.[292]

This process of selective leaking appears to have had a particularly debilitating impact on the intelligence community:

> **A routine settled in: the Pentagon's defector reports, classified "secret," would be funneled to newspapers, but subsequent C.I.A. and INR analyses of the reports—invariably scathing but also classified—would remain secret.** "It became a personality issue," a Pentagon consultant said of the Bush Administration's handling of intelligence. "My fact is better than your fact. The whole thing is a failure of process. Nobody goes to primary sources." The intelligence community was in full retreat.[293]

Some of the above-described techniques can be seen in two instances—the visits by the Vice President and Scooter Libby to CIA headquarters and efforts by the Vice President and his office to influence and manipulate Secretary of State Powell's February 2003 speech before the United Nations.

It is now well known that the Vice President himself, along with his Chief of Staff, Scooter Libby, made numerous visits to CIA Headquarters in Virginia, during which they placed even greater pressure on individual analysts to develop conclusions supporting a decision to go to war. Numerous media outlets confirmed that these visits occurred, with the *Washington Post* reporting as follows:

> Vice President Cheney and his most senior aide made multiple trips to the CIA over the past year to question analysts studying Iraq's weapons programs and alleged links to Al Qaeda, creating an environment in which some analysts felt they were being pressured to make their assessments fit with the Bush Administration's policy objectives, according to senior intelligence officials. With Cheney taking the lead in the administration last August in advocating military action against Iraq by claiming it had weapons of mass destruction, **the visits by the Vice President and his chief of staff, I. Lewis "Scooter" Libby, 'sent signals . . . that a certain output was desired from here,' one senior agency official said yesterday** . . . . The exact number of trips by Cheney to the CIA could not be learned, but one agency official described them as "multiple." They were taken in addition to Cheney's regular attendance at President Bush's morning intelligence briefings and the special briefings the vice president receives when he is at an undisclosed location for security reasons.[294]

Some analysts went even further in detailing the pressure placed on them by the Vice President's visits. According to former CIA officials, the visits created a "chill factor" among those working on Iraq. There was "a kind of radical pressure" throughout 2002 and on into 2003, one former official said.[295] At a hearing convened by Representative Conyers, former CIA analyst Ray McGovern testified: "But I had never known fixing to include the Vice President abrogating the right to turn a key piece of intelligence on its head. Nor had I in all those years ever known a sitting Vice President to make multiple visits to CIA headquarters to make sure the fix was in, and this is just one example."[296]

The record also shows that the Bush Administration gave the Secretary of State significant amounts of biased and one-sided intelligence information and then pressured the Secretary to skew his presentation to the United Nations. Lawrence Wilkerson, Colin Powell's Chief of Staff at the time of the speech, has stated that when the Secretary of State first received background materials for his speech from the White House, "[Powell] came through the door that morning and he had in his hand a sheaf of papers and he said this is what I've got to present at the United Nations according to the White House and you need to look at it . . . [I]t was anything but an intelligence document. It was, as some people characterized it later, sort of a Chinese menu from which you could pick and choose."[297] Powell himself junked much of what the CIA had given him to read, reportedly calling it "bull****."[298]

This was followed by numerous meetings in which the Vice President's office sought to pressure Mr. Powell to make the case for war:

> The meetings [between the Vice President's staff and the Secretary of State's staff] stretched on for four more days and nights. Cheney's staff constantly pushed for certain intelligence on Iraq's alleged ties to terrorists to be included—information that Powell and his people angrily insisted was not reliable . . .Cheney and his staff had insisted that their intelligence was, in fact, well documented. **They told Powell not to worry. One morning a few days before the speech, Powell encountered Cheney in the hallway outside the Oval Office. 'Your poll numbers are in the 70s,' Cheney told him. 'You can afford to lose a few points.'**[299]

It also has been reported that Mr. Libby was pushing so hard to include certain intelligence information in the speech that Mr. Libby called Mr. Powell's suite at the Waldorf Bstoria hotel the night before the speech. John E. McLaughlin, then-deputy director of the CIA, has testified to Congress that "much of our time in the run-up to the speech **was spent taking out material . . . that we and the secretary's staff judged to have been unreliable.**"[300]

The eventual speech (discussed in greater length in Section III(a)(5) of this Report) "was still based on a hyped and incomplete view of U.S. intelligence on Iraq. Much of what was new in Secretary Powell's speech was raw data that had come into the CIA's possession but had not yet undergone serious analysis."[301] Mr. Powell has admitted that he saw the incident as a "blot" on his reputation.[302] On national television, Secretary Powell stated, "It was painful . . . [I]t's painful now."[303]

## ■ Links to September 11 and Al Qaeda

*"Wrong answer . . . . Do it again."*

—Fall 2001, Richard Clarke, on *60 Minutes*, describing the reaction of the Bush White House to his report finding no connection between Iraq and the September 11 attacks.[304]

Our investigation has found that members of the Bush Administration made numerous false statements alleging links between Iraq and Al Qaeda and terrorism. Not only were those statements false, but they appear to have been accompanied by deliberate efforts to pressure and manipulate intelligence. We know this from revelations in the Downing Street Minutes, statements by current and ex-Bush Administration officials, and publicly released reports and other disclosures.

Numerous members of the Bush Administration, including the President, made false statements linking Saddam Hussein to the events of September 11 and Al Qaeda. "You can't distinguish between Al Qaeda and Saddam when you talk about the war on Terror," President Bush said on September 25, 2002.[305] Secretary Rumsfeld, Secretary Powell, and National Security Advisor Rice all issued misleading statements regarding this linkage as well. For example, in September 19, 2002 testimony before the Senate Armed Services Committee, the Defense Secretary claimed, "We know that Al Qaeda is operating in Iraq today, and that little happens in Iraq without the knowledge of the Saddam Hussein regime."[306] On September 27, 2002, Secretary Rumsfeld claimed that he had "bullet-proof" evidence of ties between Saddam and Al Qaeda.[307] Powell also described a "potentially . . . sinister nexus between Iraq and the Al Qaeda terrorist network, a nexus that combines classic terrorist organizations and modern methods of murder."[308] And on September 25, 2002, Rice insisted, "There clearly are contacts between Al Qaeda and Iraq . . . There clearly is testimony that some of the contacts have been important contacts and that there's a relationship there."[309]

In particular, the Vice President made a number of false statements linking Iraq with the September 11 hijackers. Just a few months after the attacks and over a year prior to the U.S. invasion of Iraq, the Vice President appeared on *Meet the Press* on December 9, 2001 and stated: "Well, what we now have that's developed since you and I last talked, Tim [Russert], of course, was that report that's been pretty well confirmed, that [Mohammed Atta, one of the hijackers] . . . did go to Prague and he did meet with a senior official of the Iraqi intelligence service in Czechoslovakia last April, several months before the attack."[310] Even after the invasion, on October 10, 2003, the Vice President stated that Saddam Hussein "had an established relationship with Al Qaeda."[311]

In addition, both the President and Secretary of State Powell made false statements claiming that Iraq had trained Al Qaeda members to use chemical and biological weapons. In his October 7, 2002 speech in Cincinnati, shortly before the congressional vote to authorize military action, the President stated: "We've learned that Iraq has trained Al Qaeda members in bomb-making and poisons and deadly gases . . . We know that Iraq and Al Qaeda have had high-level contacts that go back a decade."[312] In his February 5, 2003 speech before the U.N., Secretary of State Powell stated: "I can trace the story of a senior terrorist operative telling how Iraq provided training in these weapons to Al Qaeda."[313] Powell also said that "[w]e are not surprised that Iraq is harboring Zarqawi and his subordinates. This understanding builds on decades-long experience with respect to ties between Iraq and Al Qaeda."[314] In 2002, *Newsweek* disclosed that information about links between Iraq and Al Qaeda came from Ibn al-Shaykh al-Libi, an aide to Osama bin Laden in U.S. custody.[315]

We now know that there statements were false. With respect to general linkages between Iraq and Al Qaeda, on June 16, 2004, the 9-11 Commission concluded that it had found no "collaborative" relationship between Iraq and Al Qaeda.[316] The 9-11 Commission further concluded that "[w]e have no credible evidence that Iraq and Al Qaeda cooperated on attacks against the United States."[317] The Senate Select Committee's Report on Pre-War Intelligence confirmed CIA assessments that "there was no evidence proving Iraqi complicity or assistance in an Al Qaeda attack" and that contacts between the two "did not add up to an established formal relationship."[318] On January 28, 2004, David Kay testified before the Senate Armed Services Committee that there is no evidence of participation by either Saddam Hussein or his principal henchmen in the WMD-sharing with Al Qaeda or any other terrorist organizations.[319] With respect to the Vice President's allegations of meetings between Mohammed Atta and Iraqi intelligence, the 9-11 Commission concluded: "We do not believe that such a meeting occurred." The Commission cited FBI photographic and telephone evidence, Czech and U.S. investigations, and reports from detainees, including the Iraqi official with whom Atta was alleged to have met.[320]

As for the allegations that Iraq had trained members of Al Qaeda to make bombs with poisons and deadly gases, and that they had high level contacts going back a decade, these statements were based on information provided by a top Al Qaeda operative, Ibn al-Shaykh al-Libi. However, Mr. al-Libi, who was captured in Pakistan at the end of 2001, recanted his claims in January 2004. In response, a month later the CIA recalled all intelligence reports based on his statements, a fact recorded in a footnote to the report issued by the 9-11 Commission.[321]

Numerous public reports and information, as well as statements by current and former Bush Administration officials, indicate that the Bush Administration must have known that these misstatements were not fully supported at the time they were made, and that members of the Bush Administration had exercised political pressure so that intelligence information would support their desired conclusions.

## General Linkages Between Iraq and Al Qaeda

With regard to general assertions linking Iraq with Al Qaeda and terrorism, we now know that intelligence experts within the Administration questioned this linkage prior to the Iraq invasion. As detailed by Richard Clarke, former National Coordinator for Counterterrorism for the National Security Council, the President requested a report on whether Iraq was behind the September 11 attacks. Clark describes: "**We got together all the F.B.I. experts, all the C.I.A. experts. We wrote the report. We sent the report out to C.I.A. and found F.B.I. and said, 'Will you sign this report?' They all cleared the report. And we sent it up to the President and it got bounced back by the National Security**

Advisor or Deputy. It got bounced and sent back saying, 'Wrong answer . . . Do it again.'"322

It was also recently disclosed that as early as September 21, 2001, the President knew there was no evidence tying Iraq and Al Qaeda. "**Ten days after the September 11, 2001, terrorist attacks on the World Trade Center and the Pentagon, President Bush was told in a highly classified briefing that the U.S. intelligence community had no evidence linking the Iraqi regime of Saddam Hussein to the attacks and that there was scant credible evidence that Iraq had any significant collaborative ties with Al Qaeda,** according to government records and current and former officials with first-hand knowledge of the matter."323 This briefing, which was confirmed by a former high-level official, was also distributed to Vice President Cheney, the President's national security advisor and deputy national security advisor, the secretaries and undersecretaries of State and Defense, and various other senior policy makers.324 The official said, "What the President was told on September 21 was consistent with everything he has been told since—that the evidence was just not there."325 It is significant that this critical briefing came before the various misstatements of Mr. Bush and other high Administration officials linking Iraq with Al Qaeda.

Moreover, a June 21, 2002 CIA report titled "Iraq and Al Qaeda: Interpreting a Murky Relationship," stated, "[O]ur knowledge of Iraqi links to Al Qaeda still contains many critical gaps" and "[s]ome analysts concur with the assessment that intelligence reporting provides 'no conclusive evidence of cooperation on specific terrorist operations.'"326

In addition, an October 2002 NIE included key judgments regarding Saddam Hussein's link to Al Qaeda. In its section on "Confidence Levels for Selected Key Judgements in This Estimate," **the NIE gave a "Low Confidence" rating to the notion of "[W]hether in desperation Saddam would share chemical or biological weapons with Al Qaeda."**327 The NIE also reported that "Baghdad for now appears to be drawing a line short of conducting terrorist attacks with conventional or CBW against the United States, fearing that exposure of Iraqi involvement would provide Washington a stronger cause for making war."

In January of 2003, the CIA issued an updated and revised version of "Iraq Support for Terrorism," initially circulated in September 2002. **The paper stated, "[T]he Intelligence Community has no credible information that Baghdad had foreknowledge of the 11 September attacks or any other Al Qaeda strike."**328 Specifically, the paper clearly forewarned in its "Scope Note" section that "[t]his paper's conclusions-especially regarding the difficult and elusive question of the exact nature of Iraq's relations with Al Qaeda-are based on currently available information that is at times contradictory and derived from sources with varying degrees of reliability."329

Michael Scheuer, a CIA analyst, described a comprehensive CIA examination of the possible linkage, which was totally disregarded by the White House. Scheuer told CNN, "Mr. Tenet, to his credit, had us go back through CIA files and **we went back for almost** ten years, reviewed nearly 20,000 documents, which came to 65,000 pages or more and could find no connection in the terms of a state-sponsored relationship with Iraq. I believe Mr. Tenet took it downtown, but it apparently didn't have any impact."[330] Another former CIA agent Bob Baer also confirmed, "But there is no evidence that a strategic partnership came out of it. I'm unaware of any evidence of Saddam pursing terrorism against the U.S."[331]

Finally, former senior State Department intelligence official Greg Thielmann has stated, "There was no significant pattern of cooperation between Iraq and the Al Qaeda terrorist operation . . . [I]ntelligence agencies agreed on the 'lack of a meaningful connection to Al Qaeda' and said so to the White House and Congress."[332]

There is also significant evidence that members of the Bush Administration not only knowingly made false statements regarding linkages between Al Qaeda and Iraq, they also pressured intelligence officials to do the same, and on at least one occasion, caused classified information to be leaked that would help support its case.

Government reports as well as numerous admissions by Bush Administration officials and CIA personnel confirm the extraordinary effort by the Administration to link Saddam Hussein with the September 11 attacks. In an important report in which a classified internal review of the CIA's pre-war intelligence was conducted, former Deputy Director of Central Intelligence Richard Kerr stated publicly that:

> There was a lot of pressure, no question . . .[T]he White House, State, Defense, were raising questions, heavily on W.M.D. and the issue of terrorism . . . some of the analysts felt there was pressure . . . some people in the agency will say, "We've been pushed too hard." Analysts will say, "You're trying to politicize it." There were people who felt there was too much pressure . . . they were being asked again and again to re-state their judgments—do another paper on this, repetitive pressures. Do it again.[333]

Kerr's conclusions were confirmed by a similar investigation conducted by the CIA Ombudsman, who told the Senate Intelligence Committee that the "hammering" by the Bush Administration on Iraq intelligence was harder than he had previously witnessed in his 32-year career with the agency.[334] A senior analyst at the Defense Intelligence Agency also testified before the Senate Intelligence Committee that he was aware of pressure being put on analysts.[335]

Another former official with the Bush National Security Counsel acknowledged, "It was a classic case of "rumint," rumor-intelligence plugged into various speeches and accepted as gospel."[336] An official with the CIA told the *New York Times* directly that the Administration was using intelligence information in any manner to link Saddam Hussein with Al Qaeda. "I remember reading the Abu Zubaydah [a top Al Qaeda leader] debriefing last year, while the administration was talking about all of these other reports [of a Saddam-Al Qaeda link], and thinking that they were only putting out what they wanted."[337]

FBI employees have also described the Bush Administration's willingness to manipulate intelligence linking Iraq and Al Qaeda. *ABC News* reported:

> At the Federal Bureau of Investigation, some investigators said they were baffled by the
> Bush Administration's insistence on a solid link between Iraq and Osama bin Laden's net-
> work. "We've been looking at this hard for more than a year and you know what, we just
> don't think it's there," a government official said. Mr. Bush asserted in his State of the
> Union address this week that Iraq was protecting and aiding Qaeda operatives, but
> American intelligence and law enforcement officials said the evidence was fragmentary and
> inconclusive . . . "It's more than just skepticism," said one official, describing the feelings
> of some analysts in the intelligence agencies. "I think there is also a sense of disappoint-
> ment with the community's leadership that they are not standing up for them at a time
> when intelligence is obviously politicized . . . Based on the terrorism experts I met during
> my period of government, I never heard anyone make the claim that there was a significant
> tie between Al Qaeda and Saddam Hussein." He added, "The Bush Administration . . .
> was misleading the public in implying there was a close connection."[338]

Another source familiar with the September 11 investigation admitted: "The FBI has
been pounded on to make this link."[339]

The attempted linkages were so attenuated that the Director of the CIA had to correct Bush Administration misstatements on numerous occasions. George Tenet testified
before the Senate Armed Services Committee that in at least three instances, he had to
correct President Bush and Vice President Cheney for making misrepresentations of intelligence in their public speeches.[340] Tenet said he also was forced to correct Vice President
Cheney for having referred to Douglas Feith's disputed memo about Iraq's connection to
Al Qaeda as "your best source of information."[341]

There is significant evidence that the Pentagon's newly created Counter Terrorism
Evaluation Group (CTEG)[342] under Douglas Feith—which is currently under investigation for wrongdoing[343]—was used to place undue pressure on both the State Department
and the CIA linking Iraq with Al Qaeda, to cherry-pick and stovepipe such information
directly to the White House, and to leak classified information regarding this linkage to
the press. A *New York Times* article concluded that "for Iraq's links to Al Qaeda, Powell's
staff was convinced that much of that material had been funneled directly to Cheney by
a tiny, separate intelligence unit set up by Defense Secretary Donald Rumsfeld. We were
so appalled at what had arrived from the White House, says one official."[344]

Mel Goodman, a CIA analyst for 24 years, also detailed the political pressure
brought to bear on career intelligence officials: "'[Vice President Cheney] was holding
forth on what he thought the situation was and why doesn't your intelligence support
what we know is out there? They assumed he was referring to [Feith's] Pentagon intelligence unit that was producing stuff that was going right downtown and had much
stronger claims about links between Saddam and Al Qaeda.'"[345]

This pressure appears to have seeped all the way down to Iraqi exiles, as they were apparently advised to tailor their information to show links to terror and WMD by Iraq:

> The Iraq National Congress (INC), an exile group based in London led by Ahmad Chalabi, had been supplying U.S. Intelligence with Iraqi defectors whose information had often proved suspect or fabricated. The problem with the INC was that its information came with an overt agenda. **As the INC's Washington advisor, Francis Brooke, admitted, he urged the exile group to do what it could to make the case for war: "I told them, as their campaign manager, 'Go get me a terrorist and some W.M.D., because that's what the Bush Administration is interested in.'"**[346]

It was also clear to British intelligence and diplomatic personnel that the Bush Administration was pushing and manipulating intelligence to link September 11 to Saddam Hussein. For example, in the March 22, 2002 Ricketts Memo, part of the Downing Street Minutes documents, Peter Ricketts, the Political Director of the Foreign and Commonwealth Office, advised the Prime Minister on his April 2002 trip to Crawford: "U.S. scrambling to establish a link between Iraq and Al-Aaida[sic] is so far frankly unconvincing" and "For Iraq, 'regime change' does not stack up. It sounds like a grudge between Bush and Saddam."[347] The Downing Street Minutes also include the following admission by the U.K. Overseas and Defense Secretariat in the March 8, 2002 Options Paper: "In the judgement of the JIC [British Joint Intelligence Committee] there is no recent evidence of Iraq complicity with international terrorism. There is therefore no justification for action against Iraq based on action in self-defence (Article 51) to combat imminent threats of terrorism as in Afghanistan."[348]

## Meeting Between Mohammed Atta and Iraqi Officials

With respect to the alleged meeting between Mohammed Atta and a senior Iraqi official in Prague, the Vice President's assertions omitted key information. The Vice President failed to acknowledge that, by late April 2002, the CIA and FBI had concluded that (1) "the meeting probably did not take place"[349]; (2) Czech government officials had developed doubts about whether this meeting occurred; and (3) American records indicated that Mr. Atta was in Virginia Beach, Virginia, at the time of the purported meeting.[350]

Administration officials also described the same type of pressure and manipulation concerning the alleged meeting between Mohammed Atta and Iraqi Intelligence. The *Washington Post* described an ongoing tug-of-war between the Vice-President's office and the CIA:

> The feud had been simmering in the run-up to the Iraq war. Cheney's office kept pushing the CIA to substantiate claims by Chalabi and other defectors that would connect Iraq to Al Qaeda and the Sept. 11, 2001 attacks. The vice president's office focused on a meeting that had allegedly taken place in Prague in April 2001 between Sept. 11 hijacker Mohamed Atta and Iraqi intelligence. **CIA analysts would literally measure ears and noses in surveillance photos of the alleged meeting to show that the report was phony, but**

Cheney's aides would tell them to go back again, and yet again. In January 2003, the CIA finally balked at being assigned over and over to confirm what it viewed as phony intelligence. In a heated conversation with Libby, CIA Deputy Director John McLaughlin is said to have insisted: "I'm not going back to the well on this. We've done our work."351

## Iraq Training Al Qaeda Members to Use Chemical and Biological Weapons

We now know that the information provided by the prisoner Ibn al-Shaykh al-Libi—that Iraqis had trained Al Qaeda members to use chemical and biological weapons—was false and that the Bush Administration knew his information was not credible. This is because of the recent declassification of a key Defense Intelligence Agency document by Senator Carl Levin:

> A high Al Qaeda official in American custody was identified as a likely fabricator months before the Bush Administration began to use his statements as the foundation for its claims that Iraq trained Al Qaeda members to use biological and chemical weapons. **The document, an intelligence report from February 2002, said it was probable that the prisoner, Ibn al-Shaykh al-Libi, "was intentionally misleading the debriefers" in making claims about Iraqi support for Al Qaeda's work with illicit weapons. . .** the D.I.A. report noted that Mr. Libi's claims lacked specific details about the Iraqis involved, the illicit weapons used and the location where the training was to have taken place. "It is possible he does not know any further details; it is more likely this individual is intentionally misleading the debriefers," the February 2002 report said. "Ibn al-Shaykh has been undergoing debriefs for several weeks and may be describing scenarios to the debriefers that he knows will retain their interest."352

There appears to be little doubt that key Administration officials knew of this important disclosure, because as an official intelligence report, labeled DITSUM No. 044-02, it would have circulated widely within the government and would have been available to the CIA, the White House, the Pentagon, and other agencies.353 **Nor could Secretary of State Powell have responsibly relied on al-Libi's information, given that a classified CIA assessment at the time stated that "the source [al-Libi] was not in a position to know if any training had taken place."**354 According to the *New York Times*, the misinformation came from a detainee "identified as a likely fabricator" months before the Bush Administration began to use his statements as the foundation for its claims that Iraq trained Al Qaeda members to use biological and chemical weapons.355

The declassified DIA document also reveals that the Presidents and Secretary of State Powell's claims of a "decade"-long relationship between Iraq and Al Qaeda were completely inappropriate, given that the DIA's declassified February 2002 report points out that "Saddam's regime is intensely secular and wary of Islamic revolutionary movements.356 Moreover, Baghdad is unlikely to provide assistance to a group it cannot control."357

FBI anti-terrorism expert, Dan Coleman, observed that "[i]t was ridiculous for interrogators to think Libi would have known anything about Iraq."[358] He went on to say: "I could have told them that. He ran a training camp. He wouldn't have had anything to do with Iraq. Administration officials were always pushing us to come up with links, but there weren't any."[359]

Another reason to question the credibility of the Bush Administration's statements relying on al-Libi's disclosure is that the Administration knew that his information flowed directly from a harsh interrogation. Current and former government officials have recently admitted that al-Libi stated that he had fabricated his statements to escape harsh treatment. The officials noted that al-Libi provided his most specific and elaborate accounts about ties between Iraq and Al Qaeda only after he was secretly handed over to Egypt by the United States in January 2002, in a process known as rendition.[360]

## ■ Resumed Efforts to Acquire Nuclear Weapons

*"We still knew enough, [and] we could watch pretty closely what was happening."*
—ACCORDING TO ONE CIA ANALYST DESCRIBING EVENTS IN 2002, U.S. INTELLIGENCE SHOWED PRECIOUS LITTLE EVIDENCE TO INDICATE A RESUMPTION OF IRAQ'S NUCLEAR PROGRAM, AS TENET'S EARLY 2002 THREAT ASSESSMENTS HAD INDICATED.[361]

Numerous members of the Bush Administration made a variety of claims to the effect that Iraq had and was attempting to acquire nuclear weapons. Most notably, Vice President Dick Cheney stated on *Meet the Press* on March 16, 2003, shortly before the war, that "we know [Saddam] has been absolutely devoted to trying to acquire nuclear weapons. And we believe he has, in fact, reconstituted nuclear weapons."[362] This was not the first time Mr. Cheney made these claims. On August 26, 2002, Mr. Cheney said, "[W]e now know that Saddam has resumed his efforts to acquire nuclear weapons."[363] Mr. Cheney went on to say that "[a]mong other sources, we've gotten this from firsthand testimony from defectors, including Saddam's own son-in-law."[364]

In addition, in his October 7, 2002, speech in Cincinnati, on the eve of congressional votes on the Iraq war resolution, the President stated, "America must not ignore the threat gathering against us. Facing clear evidence of peril, we cannot wait for the final proof—the smoking gun—that could come in the form of a mushroom cloud."[365] At a September 7, 2002 meeting at Camp David with Prime Minister Blair, President Bush declared that a new "report came out of the . . . IAEA, that they [Iraqis] were six months away from developing a weapon. I don't know what more evidence we need."[366] In his February 2003 presentation before the UN, when considering whether Iraq had reconstituted a nuclear program, Secretary Powell unequivocally stated, "there is no doubt in my mind."[367] Similar statements were made by National Security Director Rice,[368] Secretary Rumsfeld,[369] and Vice President Cheney.[370]

These statements were all false and misleading. On October 2, 2003, David Kay reported that "we have not uncovered evidence that Iraq undertook significant post-1998 steps to actually build nuclear weapons or produce fissile material."[371] In his January 28, 2004, testimony before the Senate Armed Services Committee, Dr. Kay reported that "[a]s best as has been determined . . . in 2000 they had decided that their nuclear establishment had deteriorated to such a point that it was totally useless."[372] He concluded that there was "no doubt at all" that Iraq had less of an ability to produce fissile material in 2001 than in 1991.[373] The July 7, 2004 report of the Senate Intelligence Committee concluded that "the judgment in the National Intelligence Estimate (NIE), that Iraq was reconstituting its nuclear program, was not supported by the intelligence. The Committee agreed with the State Department's Bureau of Intelligence and Research (INR) alternative view that the available intelligence "does not add up to a compelling case for reconstitution."[374]

## General Assertions

Beyond making false and misleading statements about Iraq's attempt to acquire nuclear weapons, the record shows that the Bush Administration must have known that these statements conflicted with known international and domestic intelligence at the time. As early as 2000, the intelligence community recognized that Iraq was not a nuclear threat to the United States. **For example, the IAEA reported in 1999 that there was "no indication that Iraq possesses nuclear weapons or any meaningful amounts of weapon-usable nuclear material, or that Iraq has retained any practical capability (facilities or hardware) for the production of such material."**[375] Again, in March 2003, IAEA Director-General Mohamed El Baradei reported to the U.N. Security Council that weapons inspectors had not found any evidence that Iraq was "reconstituting its nuclear program."[376]

At the same time, British Intelligence also had not identified any nuclear threat emanating from Iraq. For example, **Newsweek found that two high ranking British Officials confirmed that by 2002, Iraq's nuclear weapons program was "effectively frozen"** and there was "no recent evidence" tying Iraq to international terrorism, notwithstanding the Administration's claims to the contrary.[377]

United States intelligence information on this point was no stronger. For example, the pre-2002 CIA assessments of nuclear proliferation worldwide did not cite any specific nuclear threat from Iraq.[378] At that time, as detailed in the Senate Select Committee on Intelligence Report, **the intelligence community had come to a general consensus that "Iraq did not appear to have reconstituted its nuclear weapons program."**[379]

The State Department's Bureau of Intelligence and Research (INR) also did not support a credible case for Iraq reacquiring nuclear weapons. The Bureau found, "[T]he activities we have detected do not, however, add up to a compelling case that Iraq is currently pursuing what INR would consider to be an integrated and comprehensive approach to acquire nuclear weapons."[380] INR also stated that, "**[L]acking persuasive evidence that Baghdad has launched a coherent effort to reconstitute its nuclear weapons** program, INR is unwilling to speculate that such an effort began soon after the departure of U.N. inspectors."[381]

The December 2001 NIE clearly stated that Iraq did not have nuclear weapons and was not attempting to obtain them. In fact, the December 2001, unlike the October 2002 NIE, was conclusive on this point and contained no dissents regarding Iraq's nuclear capability.[382]

This lack of hard evidence of a nuclear threat from Iraq appears to have led the Bush Administration to pressure intelligence agencies and sources to find a nuclear link. As John Judis and Spencer Ackerman of *The New Republic* wrote:

> Within the administration, Tenet and the CIA came under an entirely different kind of pressure: Iraq hawks in the Pentagon and in the vice president's office, reinforced by members of the Pentagon's semi-official Defense Policy Board, **mounted a year-long attempt to pressure the CIA to take a harder line against Iraq . . . on the status of its nuclear program.** The intelligence community was . . . pressured to exaggerate Iraq's nuclear program. As Tenet's early 2002 threat assessments had indicated, U.S. intelligence showed precious little evidence to indicate a resumption of Iraq's nuclear program. And, while the absence of U.N. inspections had introduced greater uncertainty into intelligence collection on Iraq, according to one analyst, **"We still knew enough, [and] we could watch pretty closely what was happening."**[383]

Also, two senior policymakers stated in unauthorized interviews that the Bush Administration greatly overstated the short-term dangers of Iraq's nuclear potential. "I never cared about the 'imminent threat,'" said one of the policymakers with directly relevant responsibilities.[384] "To me, just knowing what it takes to have a nuclear weapons program, he needed a lot of equipment. You can stare at the yellowcake [uranium ore] all you want. You need to convert it to gas and enrich it. That does not constitute an imminent threat, and the people who were saying that, I think, did not fully appreciate the difficulties and effort involved in producing the nuclear material and the physics package."[385]

## Claims Regarding Hussein's Son-in-Law

According to the Vice President, Saddam Hussein's son-in-law, Hussein Kamel al-Majid, had made claims that Iraq had resumed its nuclear weapons program between the time of the Gulf War and Kamel's defection in 1995. The Administration was aware that the Vice President's claims directly conflicted with numerous sources at the time. Kamel's statements were a prime concern of UNSCOM and the IAEA. In agency debriefing notes, Professor Maurizio Zifferero of the IAEA expressed that: "It was of great importance for the IAEA to listen to the Minister's [Kamel's] explanations on the full abandonment of the nuclear weapons programme by Iraq."[386] In a September 4, 1995 report, the IAEA declared that Kamel had in fact admitted that since the Gulf War, Iraq had **not** resumed its attempts to acquire nuclear weapons:

An IAEA delegation, headed by the leader of the Action Team, went to Baghdad and held a round of talks with the Iraqi authorities, from 17 to 20 August 1995 . . . **General Hussein Kamel's statement [of August 22, 1995] was compatible with statements made in the Baghdad talks, that all nuclear weapons related activities had effectively ceased at the onset of the attack on Iraq by the coalition forces.**[387]

The *Washington Post* also had reported that known intelligence contradicted any statement made by the Vice President that Kamel was a source of intelligence on Iraq engaging in nuclear weapons activity:

But Saddam Hussein lured Kamel back to Iraq, and he was killed in February 1996, so Kamel could not have sourced what U.S. officials "now know." **And Kamel's testimony, after defecting, was the reverse of Cheney's description. In one of many debriefings by U.S., Jordanian and U.N. officials, Kamel said on Aug. 22, 1995, that Iraq's uranium enrichment programs had not resumed after halting at the start of the Gulf War in 1991.** According to notes typed for the record by U.N. arms inspector Nikita Smidovich, Kamel acknowledged efforts to design three different warheads, "but not now, before the Gulf War." **The U.S. government possessed no specific information on Iraqi efforts to acquire enriched uranium, according to six people who participated in preparing for the estimate.** It knew only that Iraq sought to buy equipment of the sort that years of intelligence reports had said "may be" intended for or "could be" used in uranium enrichment.[388]

In October 2004 the *New York Times* published similar conclusions:

In his Nashville speech, Mr. Cheney had not mentioned the aluminum tubes or any other fresh intelligence when he said, "We now know that Saddam has resumed his efforts to acquire nuclear weapons." The one specific source he did cite was Hussein Kamel al-Majid, a son-in-law of Mr. Hussein's who defected in 1995 after running Iraq's chemical, biological and nuclear weapons programs. **But Mr. Majid told American intelligence officials in 1995 that Iraq's nuclear program had been dismantled. What's more, Mr. Majid could not have had any insight into Mr. Hussein's current nuclear activities: he was assassinated in 1996 on his return to Iraq.**[389]

## *Statement that Iraq Was Six Months from Obtaining a Nuclear Weapon*

With respect to President Bush's September 7, 2002 statement regarding a new IAEA Report stating that Iraq was six months from developing a nuclear weapon, we now know that there was no new IAEA Report. As the *Washington Post* reported, "There was no new IAEA report. . . . **Bush cast as present evidence the contents of a report from 1996, updated in 1998 and 1999. In those accounts, the IAEA described the history of an Iraqi nuclear weapons program that arms inspectors had systematically destroyed.**"[390] Even the Bush Administration's after-the-fact efforts to claim that the President meant to reference United States intelligence, not the IAEA, make little sense. Prime Minister Blair was referring to an IAEA Report at the same press conference and "U.S. intelligence reports had only one scenario for an Iraqi bomb in six months to a year, premised on Iraq's immediate acquisition of enough plutonium or enriched uranium from a foreign source."[391]

## ■ Aluminum Tubes

*"[If Iraq was really trying to make centrifuges out of the aluminum tubes] we should just give them the tubes . . .[you could also] turn your new Yugo into a Cadillac, given enough time and energy and effort."* [392]

—Energy Department analyst testimony before
the Senate Intelligence Committee

The Bush Administration also misstated and unjustly overstated intelligence with regard to the charge that Iraq was acquiring aluminum tubes that could only be used as uranium centrifuges.

For example, in September 2002, Vice President Cheney stated that "it is now public that, in fact, he [Saddam] has been seeking to acquire, and we have been able to intercept and prevent him from acquiring through this particular channel, the kinds of [aluminum] tubes that are necessary to build a centrifuge . . . We do know, with absolute certainty, that [Saddam Hussein] is using his procurement system to acquire the equipment he needs in order to enrich uranium to build a nuclear weapon."[393] Also in September 2002, on an appearance on *Meet the Press*, Mr. Cheney said he knew "in fact" and "with absolute certainty" that Mr. Hussein was buying equipment to build a nuclear weapon.[394] That same day, then National Security Advisor Condoleezza Rice told CNN that: "We do know that there have been shipments going into . . . Iraq, for instance, of aluminum tubes that really are only suited to—high-quality aluminum tools that are only really suited for nuclear weapons programs, centrifuge programs."[395] In addition, Secretary of State Powell asserted to the Security Council that the tubes were manufactured to a tolerance "that far exceeds U.S. requirements for comparable rockets."[396] The uranium centrifuge claim was also made by President Bush.[397]

These statements have proved to be both false and misleading. First, on January 27, 2003, the IAEA concluded that the aluminum tubes "would be consistent with the purpose stated by Iraq and, unless modified, would not be suitable for manufacturing centrifuges."[398] The Iraq Survey Group also did not find evidence that the tubes were intended for nuclear use. In his January 28, 2004 testimony, Dr. Kay announced: "It is my judgment, based on the evidence that was collected . . . that it's more probable that those tubes were intended for use in a conventional missile program, rather than in a centrifuge program."[399] In addition, the July 7, 2004 report of the Senate Intelligence Committee concluded that "the information available to the Intelligence Community indicated that these tubes were intended to be used for an Iraqi conventional rocket program and not a nuclear program."[400]

It is now clear that the Bush Administration was aware that these claims regarding the tubes were not only controversial, but also did not stand up to the clear weight of authority from the U.S. and international intelligence communities. The claims were premised on the views of a single, isolated CIA analyst[401] and were contradicted by an overwhelming number of reviews by other credible weapons experts, including those at the Energy Department, the State Department, the Department of Defense, as well as international and outside experts and agencies.

First, there are numerous reports from the Department of Energy that contain information directly contradicting the Bush Administration's contentions.

For example, the Energy Department, the agency responsible for constructing centrifuges and operating the nation's nuclear weapons facilities, learned that on April 10, 2001, an individual identified as "Joe" at the CIA had told senior members of the Administration that the tubes "have little use other than for a uranium enrichment program."[402] The next day the Department was able to rebut the assertions by identifying a number of reasons why the tubes were not appropriate for centrifuges: "**Simply put, the analysis concluded that the tubes were the wrong size—too narrow, too heavy, too long—to be of much practical use in a centrifuge.** What was more, the analysis reasoned, if the tubes were part of a secret, high-risk venture to build a nuclear bomb, why were the Iraqis haggling over prices with suppliers all around the world? And why weren't they shopping for all the other sensitive equipment needed for centrifuges?"[403]

The next month, the Department of Energy analysts went even further, explaining that while the tubes were not suitable for uranium centrifuges, they could easily be used to construct conventional rockets.[404] Many of these concerns were published on May 9, 2001, in the Energy Department's Daily Intelligence Highlight on Intelink, a Web site for the intelligence community and the White House.[405] Among other things, the Energy Department reported, "Iraq had for years used high-strength aluminum tubes to make combustion chambers for slim rockets fired from launcher pods . . . The tubes now sought by Iraq had precisely the same dimensions—a perfect match."[406]

Additional evidence was developed by the Energy Department in the summer of 2001, after the U.S. government seized a shipment of aluminum tubes in Jordan destined for Iraq.[407] The Energy Department quickly assembled a team of its top nuclear scientists,[408] who analyzed the aluminum tubes and found them to be consistent for use with standard rockets. On Aug. 17, 2001, the team published a comprehensive analysis further elaborating concerns regarding the tubes' suitability for centrifuges:

> First, in size and material, the tubes were very different from those Iraq had used in its centrifuge prototypes before the first Gulf War. Those models used tubes that were nearly twice as wide and made of exotic materials that performed far better than aluminum. "Aluminum was a huge step backwards," Dr. Wood recalled. In fact, the team could find no centrifuge machines "deployed in a production environment" that used such narrow tubes. Their walls were three times too thick for "favorable use" in a centrifuge, the team

**wrote.** They were also anodized, meaning they had a special coating to protect them from weather. Anodized tubes, the team pointed out, are "not consistent" with a uranium centrifuge because the coating can produce bad reactions with uranium gas."[409]

By the end of 2001, Energy Department experts produced an even more definitive analysis rebutting the contention that the aluminum tubes being procured by Iraq could be used for the production of nuclear weapons. According to the WMD commission:

[A]nalysts from CIA's Weapons Intelligence, Non-Proliferation, and Arms Control Center (WINPAC) sought the assistance of the DOE National Laboratories—specifically, Oak Ridge National Laboratory—to test the tubes. The Oak Ridge laboratory concluded that, while it was technically possible to enrich uranium using tubes of the diameter the Iraqis were seeking, it would be suboptimal to do so . . . the tubes Iraq was seeking were so suboptimal for uranium enrichment that it would have taken many thousands of them to produce enough uranium for a weapon—and although Iraq was in fact seeking thousands of tubes, **DOE assessed it would have been highly unlikely for a proliferator to choose a route that would require such a large number of machines.**[410]

In other words, the analysts had found it would be so difficult, expensive, and time-consuming for Iraq to use these aluminum tubes for nuclear weapons that the likelihood could be discounted entirely. As one Energy Department analyst told Senate Intelligence Committee investigators, if Iraq really wanted to use these tubes for uranium production, "we should just give them the tubes."[411] While there may have been some infinitesimal theoretical possibility, it was so remote that an Energy Department analyst later likened it to "turn[ing] your new Yugo into a Cadillac."[412]

Other agencies within the Administration also found the claim that the aluminum tubes could be credibly used for the production of weapons grade uranium to be lacking, including the State and Defense Departments.[413] In the NIE, the State Department explained: "The very large quantities being sought, the way the tubes were tested by the Iraqis, and the atypical lack of attention to operational security in the procurement efforts are among the factors, in addition to the DOE assessment, that lead INR to conclude that **the tubes are not intended for use in Iraq's nuclear weapons program.**"[414] The NIE went on to conclude, "**INR considers it far more likely that the tubes are intended for another purpose, most likely the production of artillery rockets.**"[415]

It has also been reported that shortly before Secretary Powell's U.N. presentation on this matter, the State Department explicitly warned him not to assert the aluminum tubes claim: "[I]n a memo written two days [before his U.N. speech] Mr. Powell's intelligence experts had specifically cautioned him about those very same words. 'In fact,' they explained, 'the most comparable U.S. system is a tactical rocket—the U.S. Mark 66 air-launched 70-millimeter rocket—that uses the same, high-grade (7075-T6) aluminum, and that has specifications with similar tolerances.'"[416]

Defense Department experts also found the aluminum tubes to be consistent with use as rockets, not nuclear weapons production. When the CIA asked Pentagon engineers to review the Iraqi tubes, they found the tubes "were perfectly usable for rockets."[417]

British intelligence experts also found it farfetched that the Iraqi aluminum tubes could be used for nuclear weapons. **They believed the tubes would require "substantial re-engineering" to work in centrifuges**, according to Britain's review of its prewar intelligence. Their experts found it "paradoxical" that Iraq would order such finely crafted tubes only to radically rebuild each one for a centrifuge.[418]

The highly respected Institute for Science and International Security also issued a series of lengthy reports using non-classified data to rebut the contention that the aluminum tubes could be used for nuclear weapons production. The first of these reports was issued on September 23, 2002[419], but it received no credence or even a response by the Bush Administration.

The IAEA also scrutinized the claims that Iraq's aluminum tubes could be used to manufacture weapons-grade uranium:

> [IAEA head Jack] Baute . . . made quick work of the aluminum tubes. He assembled a team of experts—two Americans, two Britons, and a German—with 120 years of collective experience with centrifuges. After reviewing tens of thousands of Iraqi transaction records and inspecting Iraqi front companies and military production facilities with the rest of the IAEA unit, **they concluded, according to a senior IAEA official, that "all evidence points to that this is for the rockets"—the same conclusion reached by the State and Energy Departments.**[420]

As the *New York Times* reported, "Unlike 'Joe,' experts at the international agency had worked with Zippe centrifuges, and they spent hours with him explaining why they believed his analysis was flawed. They pointed out errors in his calculations. They noted design discrepancies. They also sent reports challenging the centrifuge claim to American government experts through the embassy in Vienna, a senior official said."[421] The Bush Administration sought to convince the IAEA that their analysis was flawed, but to little avail. On January 22, 2003, "'Joe' of the CIA flew to Vienna to argue his case before the international body.[422] His presentation was weak and unpersuasive. As one participant in the meeting recalled: Everybody was embarrassed when he came and made this presentation, embarrassed and disgusted. . . . We were going insane, thinking, 'Where is he coming from?'" [423]

It is also important to note that even the CIA, which nominally supported the Administration's charges regarding Iraq's use of the tubes for nuclear weapons, had a long, detailed history noting that these charges were not without controversy or caveat. Consider the following:

- A June 20, 2001 CIA paper found the tubes were "more consistent" with a centrifuge application, but "we are also considering non-nuclear applications for the tubes."[424]

- A June 30, 2001 CIA paper found that if Iraq claimed the tubes had a conventional use, "that cannot be discounted."[425]

- A November 24, 2001 CIA paper described "divergent views" about the tubes' intended use.[426]

- Toward the end of 2001, according to the WMD report, "the CIA informed senior policymakers that it believed the tubes were destined for use in Iraqi gas centrifuges," but noted "that there was disagreement within the Intelligence Community concerning the most likely use for the tubes."[427]

- An August 1, 2002 CIA memo found the tubes were "suitable" for uranium enrichment but included a text box with possible other uses.[428]

Despite the tremendous weight of evidence indicating that the aluminum tubes being procured by Iraq were not realistically usable for uranium, the Bush Administration nevertheless adopted and persisted in relying on this argument. One congressional investigator described the debate as a "holy war,"[429] while an intelligence analyst stated: **"You had senior American officials like Condoleezza Rice saying the only use of this aluminum really is uranium centrifuges. She said that on television. And that's just a lie."**[430]

It is clear from our investigation that intense political pressure played a role in this decision, as well as cherry-picking and using only intelligence that supported a decision to invade Iraq. Our investigation also shows that the Bush Administration further manipulated the intelligence regarding the aluminum tubes by selectively leaking confidential information and by selectively declassifying information that supported its pre-determined position.

We know of the intense pressure to adopt the Administration's claims that the aluminum tubes were to be used as centrifuges because of explicit admissions by Bush Administration officials. For example, intelligence analysts informed members of the Senate Intelligence Committee, **"There's so much pressure, you know, they keep telling us, go back and find the right answer."**[431] Another source learned that Energy Department personnel were pressured to silence their criticisms of the Administration's aluminum tubes theory, with one expert at the Department's Lawrence Livermore National Laboratory in California saying, "The Administration can say what it wants and we are expected to remain silent."[432] Yet another Energy Department rocket engineer complained that the proponents "had 'an agenda' and were trying 'to bias us' into agreeing that the Iraqi tubes were not fit for rockets."[433]

As David Barstow, William J. Broad, and Jeff Gerth summarized in their report in the *New York Times*, when it came to the issue of the aluminum tubes, "[S]enior administration officials repeatedly failed to fully disclose the contrary views of America's leading nuclear scientists . . . [T]hey sometimes overstated even the most dire intelligence assessments of the tubes, yet minimized or rejected the strong doubts of nuclear experts. They worried privately that the nuclear case was weak, but expressed sober certitude in public. One result was a largely one-sided presentation to the public that did not convey the depth of evidence and argument against the administration's most tangible proof of a revived nuclear weapons program in Iraq."[434]

Our investigation has also found that classified intelligence information supporting the Bush Administration's position regarding the aluminum tubes was leaked to the press. For example, on Sunday, September 8, 2002, the lead story in the *New York Times*, written by Judith Miller and Michael R. Gordon, quotes "anonymous" Administration officials as stating that "Iraq has stepped up its quest for nuclear weapons and has embarked on a worldwide hunt for materials to make an atomic bomb."[435] The article goes on to source "administration officials" for the proposition that "[i]n the last 14 months, Iraq has sought to buy thousands of specially designed aluminum tubes, which American officials believe were intended as components of centrifuges to enrich uranium" and that "[t]he diameter, thickness and other technical specifications of the aluminum tubes had persuaded American intelligence experts that they were meant for Iraq's nuclear program."[436]

Subsequent media accounts have traced the story, at least in part, to Paul Wolfowitz:

> In the summer of 2002, [Deputy Defense Secretary Paul] Wolfowitz convened a secret meeting [concerning the tubes] in his office with Francis Brooke, the I.N.C. advisor, and Khidir Hamza, a former chief of Saddam's nuclear program, who had defected to America in 1994 . . . **Wolfowitz circulated his conclusions to his administration allies.— few days later, the story of the 'nuclear' tubes was leaked to the *New York Times*, where it landed on the front page.**[437]

On the CNN documentary *Dead Wrong*, an anonymous source characterized the dissemination of this biased and slanted information to Miller and Gordon as "official leaking": "I would call it official leaking because I think these were authorized conversations between the press and members of the intelligence community that further misreported the nature of the intelligence community's disagreement on this issue."[438]

Our investigation has also learned that administration officials appear to have leaked classified information to the press well before the *New York Times* article. A July 29, 2002 article in the *Washington Times*, titled "Iraq Seeks Steel for Nukes," reported:

> Procurement agents from Iraq's covert nuclear-arms program were detected as they tried to purchase stainless-steel tubing, uniquely used in gas centrifuges and a key component in making the material for nuclear bombs, from an unknown supplier, said administration officials familiar with intelligence reports . . . U.S. **intelligence agencies believe the tubing is an essential component of Iraq's plans to enrich radioactive uranium to the point where it could be used to fashion a nuclear bomb** . . . The covert nuclear-acquisition effort was detected in mid-June, and reports about the activities were then circulated to senior Bush Administration policy officials. "This is only one sign that Iraq is reconstituting its nuclear-weapons program," one official said.[439]

The coordinated leak campaign involved the very highest levels of the Bush Administration. It began on the eve of the first anniversary of the September 11 attacks when numerous high level officials appeared on the Sunday talk shows to highlight the aluminum tube "discovery." Among other things:

- Condoleezza Rice stated: "[Iraq has obtained] high quality aluminum tubes that are only really suited for nuclear weapons programs, centrifuge programs" and "We don't want the smoking gun to be a mushroom cloud."[440]

- Vice President Dick Cheney stated: "I do know with absolutely certainty that he is using his procurement system to acquire the equipment he needs to enrich uranium to build a nuclear weapon"[441]

- Donald Rumsfeld stated: "Imagine a September 11 with weapons of mass destruction."[442]

It was the leak to the *New York Times* that enabled Bush Administration officials to even have these specific discussions on the Sunday talk shows. As *Knight Ridder* explained, "**[The leaks'] appearance in the nation's most influential paper also gave Cheney and Rice an opportunity to discuss the matter the same day on the Sunday television talk shows. They could discuss the article, but otherwise they wouldn't have been able to talk about classified intelligence in public.**"[443] Former NSC official Rand Beers observed that "[A]s [the Bush Administration] embellished what the intelligence community was prepared to say and as the press reported that information, it began to acquire its own sense of truth and reality."[444]

The September 8, 2002 leak to Miller and Gordon was not the only example of such selective leaking. The Administration went so far as to note and then dismiss the intra-Administration debate concerning the tubes in a September 13, 2002 leak to the *New York Times*. A *New York Times* article that day quoted an unnamed senior administration official dismissing the tubes debate as a "footnote, not a split."[445] Citing another unnamed administration source, the article reported that the "best technical experts and nuclear scientists at laboratories like Oak Ridge supported the CIA assessments.[446]

The leak even went so far as to misrepresent the various agencies' position on the tubes debate, as the article reported the Administration officials as claiming "it was the intelligence agencies' unanimous view that the type of tubes that Iraq has been seeking are used to make such centrifuges" and "[t]he Defense Intelligence Agency and the National Security Agency support the C.I.A. view, the officials said."[457] These claims, as we now know, were false.

The Bush Administration went even further to guarantee that its selective and one-sided leaking would go unchallenged—by muzzling anyone within the Administration who would expose any contrary views. On September 13, the day the *New York Times* article appeared, the Energy Department forwarded a directive forbidding employees from discussing the tubes matter with reporters.[448]

The Bush Administration also selectively declassified information regarding the aluminum tubes to support its case for war. This can be seen in the October 1, 2002 declassified NIE, which left out the views of those in the Administration who questioned the ability of Iraq to use the tubes as uranium centrifuges:

> On October 1, 2002, Tenet produced a declassified NIE. **But Graham and Durbin were outraged to find that it omitted the qualifications and countervailing evidence that had characterized the classified version and played up the claims that strengthened the administration's case for war.** For instance, the intelligence report cited the much-disputed aluminum tubes as evidence that Saddam "remains intent on acquiring" nuclear weapons. And it claimed, "All intelligence experts agree that Iraq is seeking nuclear weapons and that these tubes could be used in a centrifuge enrichment program"B a blatant mischaracterization. Subsequently, the NIE allowed that "some" experts might disagree but insisted that "most" did not, never mentioning that the DOE's expert analysts had determined the tubes were not suitable for a nuclear weapons program.[449]

## ■ Acquisition of Uranium from Niger

*"They got pounded on, day after day . . . and received no consistent backup from Tenet and his senior staff. Pretty soon you say F\*\*\* it. And they began to provide the intelligence that was wanted."*

— 2002 STATEMENT BY A SENIOR CIA ANALYST[450]

The Bush Administration also made numerous misstatements regarding the charge that Iraq had sought to acquire a form of uranium from Niger known as "yellow cake," which could be converted into nuclear weapons grade uranium. The record indicates that the Bush Administration made these charges without building any sort of credible foundation, and did so notwithstanding overwhelming intelligence and information to the contrary.

In his January 2003 State of the Union Address, President Bush stated, "The British government has learned that Saddam Hussein recently sought significant quantities of uranium from Africa."[451] On January 20, 2003, President Bush made a written statement to Congress that Iraq's report to the U.N. "failed to deal with issues which have arisen since 1998 including . . . attempts to acquire uranium and the means to enrich it."[452] Also, on January 26, 2003, Secretary Powell, speaking at the World Economic Forum in Davos, Switzerland, asked, "Why is Iraq still trying to procure uranium?"[453] In a January 23, 2003 Op-Ed column in the *New York Times*, Condoleezza Rice wrote that the "false declaration . . . fails to account for or explain Iraq's efforts to get uranium from abroad."[454] On January 29, 2003, Secretary of Defense Donald Rumsfeld stated at a press conference that Hussein's "regime has the design for a nuclear weapon, was working on several different methods of enriching uranium, and recently was discovered seeking significant quantities from Africa."[455]

The Secretary of Defense, in Congressional testimony, also claimed that Saddam was "aggressively pursuing nuclear weapons."[456] In a discussion about Iraq with Congressional leaders, as the President was providing Members of Congress with information to justify his request for an authorization to use force in Iraq, President Bush flatly declared that Saddam was seeking nuclear materials and could build a nuclear bomb "within a year."[457]

These statements were not true. On March 7, 2003, the head of the IAEA, Dr. Mohammed ElBaradei, informed the U.N. Security Council that the Italian Documents, "which formed the basis for the reports of recent uranium transactions between Iraq and Niger—are in fact not authentic."[458] Six months after the President's State of the Union speech, on July 7, 2003, the White House finally confirmed that the President's assertion that Iraq tried to buy uranium from Africa was based on unsubstantiated, and possibly false, information. Ari Fleischer, then-White House Press Secretary, stated, "But specifically on the yellow cake, the yellow cake for Niger, we've acknowledged that that information did turn out to be a forgery."[459] The White House also admitted that the information "should not have risen to the level of a presidential speech."[460]

A review of the record indicates that these charges were elevated and made public because of cherry-picking and pressure by the Bush Administration on intelligence officials, and also that the charges were contradicted by the overwhelming weight of intelligence information.

First, the public record demonstrates that the Bush Administration was willing to elevate, without adequate scrutiny, the allegations that Iraq was attempting to obtain uranium from Niger. It has been reported that shortly after September 11, 2001, U.S. and British governments received, at the behest of the Italian Premier, information from Italy's Military Intelligence and Security Service (SISMI) suggesting that an Iraqi ambassador had sought to acquire uranium from Niger.[461] Mr. Berlusconi was eager to help President Bush in his search for arguments for war. According to the *New York Times*, "an Italian paper," *La Repubblica*, said General Pollari, chief of SISMI, had knowingly provided the United States and Britain with forged documents.[462] "The newspaper . . . also reported that General Pollari had acted at the behest of Mr. Berlusconi, who was said to be eager to help President Bush in the search for weapons in Iraq. . . . *La Repubblica* said General Pollari had held a meeting on September 9, 2002, with a national security advisor, [Stephen Hadley]."[463]

Vice President Cheney quickly jumped on this dated and dubious intelligence assertion and pressured intelligence officials to verify the SISMI report:

> "The Vice-President saw a piece of intelligence reporting that Niger was attempting to buy uranium," Cathie Martin, the spokeswoman for Cheney, told me. Sometime after he first saw it, Cheney brought it up at his regularly scheduled daily briefing from the C.I.A., Martin said. "He asked the briefer a question. The briefer came back a day or two later and said, 'We do have a report, but there's a lack of details.'" The Vice-President was further told that it was known that Iraq had acquired uranium ore from Niger in the early nineteen-eighties but that that material had been placed in secure storage by the I.A.E.A., which was monitoring it. "End of story," Martin added. "That's all we know."

According to a former high-level C.I.A. official, however, Cheney was dissatisfied with the initial response, and asked the agency to review the matter once again. It was the beginning of what turned out to be a year-long tug-of-war between the C.I.A. and the Vice-President's office.[464]

It was during 2002 that CIA officials report severe pressure from the Bush Administration on these issues: "**Senior C.I.A. analysts dealing with Iraq were constantly being urged by the Vice-President's office to provide worst-case assessments on Iraqi weapons issues.** 'They got pounded on, day after day,' one senior Bush Administration official [stated], and received no consistent backup from Tenet and his senior staff. 'Pretty soon you say "F*** it."' And they began to provide the intelligence that was wanted."[465]

Later in 2002, when Elizabetta Burba, a reporter for an Italian magazine, turned over additional documents concerning the purported uranium sales to the U.S. Embassy,[466] the Bush Administration seized the opportunity to disseminate the charges to the highest levels of the CIA and the Pentagon. As two former CIA officials explained, "**The Embassy was alerted that the papers were coming . . . and it passed them directly to Washington without even vetting them inside the Embassy.** Once the documents were in Washington, they were forwarded by the CIA to the Pentagon."[467]

Although the charge was still largely unverified, by the time of the President's 2003 State of the Union address, the Bush Administration was facing a situation in which many of its claims—such as the aluminum tubes charge—had been discredited,[468] and the international community did not appear ready for war.[469] It was at this time, "four days before President Bush delivered his State of the Union address presenting the case for war against Iraq, the National Security Council staff put out a call for new intelligence to bolster claims that Saddam Hussein possessed nuclear, chemical and biological weapons or programs."[470] It did so because, according to Robert Walpole, the then-National Intelligence Officer for Strategic and Nuclear Programs, the NSC believed the nuclear case "was weak."[471]

Second, our investigation has confirmed that the President's and other Bush Administration officials' charges regarding uranium acquisition from Niger were made at a time when the overwhelming weight of intelligence authority was to the contrary, a fact which key Bush Administration officials were aware. We know this because of reports, filings and statements, from and on behalf of the CIA, the State Department and the IAEA.

Foremost is the fact that Ambassador Joe Wilson, who was asked by the CIA to travel to Niger in February 2002 to review the charge, found it to be false.[472] Wilson was able to confirm two critical facts eliminating any possibility that the SISMI report was accurate. First, he learned that any authentic memorandum of understanding concerning yellowcake sales would have required the signatures of each of Niger's Prime Minister, Foreign Minister, and Minister of Mines, which did not occur: "'**I saw everybody out there**' Wilson said, **and no one had signed such a document.** 'If a document purporting to be about the sale contained those signatures, it would not be authentic.'"[473] Second, Wilson ascertained that since Niger had pre-sold all of its available uranium to its Japanese and European consortium partners, it had no uranium to sell to Iraq or anyone else.[474] Upon his return, Wilson filed his report with the CIA, which in turn circulated a report on Wilson's trip—without identifying him—to the White House and other agencies.[475]

Also in February 2002, the deputy commander of U.S. Armed Forces Europe, Marine Gen. Carlton Fulford, traveled to Niger and met with the country's president. He concluded that, given the controls on Niger's uranium supply, there was little chance uranium was diverted to Iraq. His report was sent to the Chairman of the Joint Chiefs of Staff, Gen. Richard Myers. The U.S. Ambassador to Niger, Barbro Owens-Kirkpatrick was also present at the meeting and sent similar conclusions to the State Department.[476]

Other experts at the CIA were also highly skeptical of the claim.[477] Prior to the President's October 7, 2002 speech in Cincinnati, **George Tenet called Stephen Hadley, principal deputy to Condoleezza Rice, and told him that the "President should not be a fact witness on this [Niger-Uranium] issue," because his analysts had told him that the "reporting was weak."**[478] The CIA also faxed two memos to the National Security Council on October 6, 2002, one of which was also sent to National Security Advisor Condoleezza Rice, backing up Tenet's advice. One memo stated that "**the evidence is weak . . . the Africa story is overblown.**"[479] Hadley later recalled that the uranium reference, "having been taken out of Cincinnati, it should have been taken out of the State of the Union."[480] It is also notable that the Senate Intelligence Report also found that in September of 2002, a CIA analyst suggested to a staff member of the White House's NSC that the White House remove from a draft speech the claim that Iraq attempted to acquire uranium from Africa.[481] According to the CIA analyst, the NSC staff member responded by noting that removing the claim would leave the British "flapping in the wind."[482]

At the same time Tenet was sending faxes and telephoning the White House in early October 2002, his deputy was telling the Senate Select Committee on Intelligence that the American Intelligence community believed the British had stretched the case on African uranium sales to Iraq.[483]

It also has been reported that the CIA had sought to dissuade the British from asserting the NigerBIraq uranium connection.[484] A senior intelligence official interviewed by the Associated Press in June of 2003 indicated that the CIA shared with Britain the results of Joseph Wilson's trip to Niger, advising British intelligence that claims that Iraq attempted to procure uranium from Niger are unsubstantiated.[485]

State Department analysts also "considered [the Niger uranium link] suspect."[486] In fact, the Bureau of Intelligence and Research sent a memorandum to Secretary of State Colin Powell stating that claims regarding Iraqi attempts to obtain uranium from Niger are not credible.[487] By October, the National Intelligence Estimate given to Congress as it considered authorizing military action, included the **State Department's finding that "claims of Iraqi pursuit of natural uranium in Africa"** were "**highly dubious.**"[488] Moreover, on January 13, 2003, the INR Iraq nuclear analyst sent an e-mail to several intelligence community analysts outlining his reasoning why, "the uranium purchase agreement probably is a hoax" and concluded that "the uranium purchase agreement probably is a forgery."[489]

The Niger story was also rejected by the French Intelligence agency, who were explicitly sought out by the CIA:

> Alain Chouet, a senior French intelligence official] recalled that his agency was contacted by the CIA in the summer of 2001 C shortly before the attacks of Sept. 11 . . .CIA officials asked their French counterparts to check that uranium in Niger and elsewhere was secure. The former CIA official confirmed Chouet's account of this exchange. Then twice in 2002, Chouet said, the CIA contacted the French again for similar help. By mid-2002, Chouet recalled, the request was more urgent and more specific. The CIA was asking questions about a particular agreement purportedly signed by Nigerian officials to sell 500 metric tons of uranium to Iraq.[490]

After dispatching a team to Niger which did not find any sale or purchase of uranium, **the French "told the Americans, 'Bullsh\*\*. It doesn't make any sense,'** Chouet said."[491] Chouet also stated that "the question from CIA officials in the summer of 2002 seemed to follow almost word for word from the [forged] documents in question. He said that an Italian intelligence source, Rocco Martino, had tried to sell the documents to the French, but that **in a matter of days French analysts determined the documents had been forged**."[492]

The Bush Administration was able to insist on using the 16-word Niger uranium reference only after considerable back and forth with the CIA. On July 11, 2003, Tenet admitted that CIA officials who reviewed the draft of the State of the Union address and its remarks concerning the Niger-Iraqi uranium deal had "**raised several concerns about the fragmentary nature of the intelligence** with [White House] National Security Council colleagues."[493] After noting that the CIA raised these concerns, Tenet stated that "[s]ome of the language was changed."[494] Senator Levin has also noted that this was "highly deceptive" since the "only reason" to say that the British learned that Iraq was seeking uranium from Africa "was to create the impression that we believed it" although "we actually did not believe" it.[495]

By the time the President had opted to include the Iraq-Niger uranium claim in his 2003 State of the Union speech, intelligence officials were flabbergasted that the misinformation could have gone so far. Seymour Hersh describes the following discussions with intelligence officials:

> The State of the Union speech was confounding to many members of the intelligence community, who could not understand how such intelligence could have got to the President without vetting. **The former intelligence official who gave me the account of the forging of the documents told me that his colleagues were also startled by the speech. They said, "Holy sh\*\*, all of the sudden the President is talking about it in the State of the Union address!" They began to panic.**[496]

Finally, the weakness of the Bush Administration's case can be seen by its inability to provide information supporting its position to the IAEA, and in turn, the IAEA's ease in confirming the documents were fraudulent. On February 4, 2003, the Bush Administration informed the UN's IAEA that it "**cannot confirm [the uranium] reports.**"[497] On March 3, 2003, the IAEA told the American government that the documents were forgeries.[498] On March 7, 2003, the head of the IAEA, Dr. Mohammed ElBaradei, informed the United Nations Security Council that the Italian Documents, "which formed the basis for the reports of recent uranium transactions between Iraq and Niger—are in fact not authentic."[499] The Deputy Director General of the IAEA, Jacques Baute, had found that the Italian documents were so replete with errors that a 2-hour search on "Google" would suffice to discredit them[500] and was easily able to rebut these "clumsy forgeries."[501]

## ■ Chemical and Biological Weapons

*"This war's going to happen regardless of what Curveball said or didn't say, and that the Powers That Be probably aren't terribly interested in whether Curveball knows what he's talking about."*

—FEBRUARY 4, 2003, DEPUTY CHIEF OF THE CIA's
IRAQI TASK FORCE IN RESPONSE TO CIA DOCTOR[502]

The Bush Administration has also misstated and overstated intelligence information regarding (i) Iraq's possession of chemical weapons generally; (ii) a charge by an Iraqi defector that he had helped bury significant amounts of chemical and other weapons; (iii) the existence of mobile chemical weapons laboratories; and (iv) Iraq's ability to deliver such weapons using unmanned aerial vehicles (UAVs). The record shows that these misstatements were in contradiction of known countervailing intelligence information, and were the result of political pressure and manipulation.

First, in terms of misstatements regarding chemical weapons generally, in his October 7, 2002, speech in Cincinnati, President Bush stated: "In 1995, after several years of deceit by the Iraqi regime, the head of Iraq's military industries defected. It was then that the regime was forced to admit that it had produced more than 30,000 liters of anthrax and other deadly biological agents . . . This is a massive stockpile of biological weapons that has never been accounted for, and capable of killing millions."[503] In his 2003 State of the Union address, President Bush stated, "Our intelligence officials estimate that Saddam Hussein had the materials to produce as much as 500 tons of sarin, mustard, and VX nerve agent. In such quantities, these chemical agents could also kill untold thousands. He's not accounted for these materials. He has given no evidence that he has destroyed them."[504] In late September 2002, the President bluntly told leaders of Congress that "[t]he Iraqi regime possesses biological and chemical weapons."[505] In addition, Vice President Cheney, Secretary of State Powell and Secretary of State Rumsfeld made similar misstatements.[506]

Second, on September 12, 2002, as President Bush was preparing to speak before the UN, the White House rolled out a report entitled "Iraq: Denial and Deception," which prominently detailed charges by Iraqi defector Adnan Ihsan Saeed al-Haeder that he had secretly helped bury significant amounts of biological, chemical, and nuclear weapons.[507]

Third, in terms of misstatements regarding mobile weapons, on February 5, 2003, in an address before the United Nations, Secretary of State Colin Powell stated that he had learned that Iraq controlled several mobile biological weapons laboratories as a result of information derived from numerous defectors, describing one as "an eyewitness . . . who supervised one of these facilities" and was at the site when an accident killed 12 technicians.[508] Relying on supposed eyewitness accounts by an Iraqi defector known in the intelligence community as "Curveball," Powell warned that Iraq's mobile labs could brew enough weapons-grade microbes "in a single month to kill thousands upon thousands of people."[509] One week earlier, in his 2003 State of the Union speech, President Bush told the American people that as a result of information provided by three Iraqi defectors, "we know that Iraq, in the late 1990s, had several mobile biological weapons labs . . . designed to produce germ warfare agents and can be moved from place to a place to evade inspectors."[510] In February 2003, the president further stated in a radio address that "first-hand witnesses have informed us that Iraq has at least seven mobile factories" for germ warfare and that Iraq could "produce within just months hundreds of pounds of biological poisons."[511]

Fourth, in terms of misstatements regarding unmanned aerial vehicles, in his February 2003 address to the United Nations, Secretary Powell stated: "UAVs are well suited for dispensing chemical and biological weapons. There is ample evidence that Iraq has dedicated much effort to developing and testing spray devices that could be adapted for UAVs."[512] He further maintained that "every statement I make today is backed up by sources, solid sources. These are not assertions. What we're giving you are facts and conclusions based on solid intelligence."[513] Just one month earlier, President Bush stated in his October 7, 2002 speech in Cincinnati, "Iraq possesses ballistic missiles with a likely range of hundreds of miles-far enough to strike Saudi Arabia, Israel, Turkey and other nations—in a region where more the 135,000 American civilians and service members live and work."[514]

These statements have been proven to be untrue. First, with respect to a chemical weapons program, David Kay conclusively stated in congressional testimony that "[m]ultiple sources with varied access and reliability have told ISG [the Iraq Survey Group] that Iraq did not have a large, ongoing, centrally controlled CW [Chemical Weapons] program after 1991. Information found to date suggests that Iraq's large-scale capability to develop, produce, and fill new CW munitions was reduced—if not entirely destroyed—during Operations Desert Storm and Desert Fox, 13 years of U.N. sanctions and U.N. inspections."[515]

Second, with respect to the charge by the Iraqi defector at Haeder that he had buried "tons" of chemical and other weapons, the CIA confirmed this was a lie.[516]

Third, as to assertions regarding mobile biological weapons labs, on March 7, 2003, Hans Blix, the chief United Nations weapons inspector, told the Security Council that a series of searches had found "no evidence" of mobile biological production facilities in Iraq.[517] In 2004, the CIA's Iraq survey group reported they "could find nothing to corroborate Curveball's reporting."[518] The CIA issued a formal directive in May of 2004, stating that "[d]iscrepancies surfaced regarding the information provided by . . . Curveball in this stream of reporting, which indicate that he lost his claimed access in 1995. Our assessment, therefore, is that Curveball appears to be fabricating in this stream of reporting."[519]

Fourth, the Bush Administration's claims about UAV have not been substantiated. On January 28, 2004, David Kay testified on behalf of the Iraq Survey Group that Iraq's UAV program "was not a strong point," that it presented only a "theoretically possible" chance and that there was no "existing deployment capability . . . for any sort of systematic military attack."[520] With respect to the President's claims regarding Iraq's ability to effectuate long-range attacks against Americans, U.N. weapons inspectors found that the weapons in question could travel less than 200 miles—not far enough, the *Washington Post* noted, "to hit the targets Bush named."[521]

Each and every one of these four categories of misstatements were made after the Bush Administration knew they were not fully corroborated and were strongly contradicted by other sources, and, in some cases, appear to have been accompanied by political pressure.

## General Assertions Regarding Chemical and Biological Weapons

With respect to general assertions regarding chemical weapons, our investigation shows they conflicted with known reports at the time, that the Bush Administration did not reveal that one of its principal sources had provided contrary information, and that many of Secretary Powell's assertions were not fully supported.

In September 2002, the Defense Intelligence Agency (DIA) issued a report that concluded: "A substantial amount of Iraq's chemical warfare agents, precursors, munitions, and production equipment were destroyed between 1991 and 1998 as a result of Operation Desert Storm and UNSCOM (United Nations Special Commission) actions . . . [t]here is **no reliable information on whether Iraq is producing and stockpiling chemical weapons or where Iraq has—or will—establish its chemical warfare agent production facilities.**"[522]

Moreover, as noted in the discussion about the information provided by Hussein's son-in-law, by 1995 the CIA was aware that Kamel al-Majid had stated that Iraq had destroyed these weapons soon after the Gulf War and no longer possessed any WMD. In his August 22, 1995 debriefing by UNSCOM and the IAEA, Kamel stated categorically: "**I ordered destruction of all chemical weapons.** All weapons—biological, chemical, missile, nuclear—were destroyed."[523]

A declassified CIA document, apparently from a debriefing of Kamel by the United States, reads:

> HUSAYN KAMIL MADE THE FOLLOWING STATEMENTS AWARE THAT THEY WOULD REACH U.S. GOVERNMENT OFFICIALS
>
> KAMIL STRESSED THAT NO [CW] AGENT WAS HIDDEN IN IRAQ, EITHER VX OR ANY OTHER.[524]

In addition, shortly before the Iraq war, *Newsweek* published a story revealing the specifics of what Kamel had said in 1995:

> Hussein Kamel, the highest-ranking Iraqi official ever to defect from Saddam Hussein's inner circle, told CIA and British intelligence officers and U.N. inspectors in the summer of 1995 that after the Gulf War, Iraq destroyed all its chemical and biological weapons stocks and the missiles to deliver them . . . **Kamel was interrogated in separate sessions by the CIA, Britain's M.I.6 and a trio from the United Nations,** led by the inspection team's head, Rolf Ekeus. NEWSWEEK has obtained the notes of Kamel's U.N. debrief, and verified that the document is authentic. NEWSWEEK has also learned that Kamel told the same story to the CIA and M.I.6. (The CIA did not respond to a request for comment.)[525]

Finally, a comprehensive review of Secretary Powell's statements regarding chemical and biological weapons was compared to State Department and other analyses.[526] The comparison indicates that, contrary to his assertions, many of Mr. Powell's statements were not fully supportable. For example, the Secretary stated that "we know from sources that a missile brigade outside Baghdad was disbursing rocket launchers and warheads containing biological warfare agents to various locations, distributing them to various locations in western Iraq."[527] **The January 31, 2003 INR evaluation flagged this claim as "weak."**[528] A more detailed analysis of Secretary Powell's U.N. statements regarding chemical weapons is available at http://www.house.gov/judiciary_democrats/iraqrept .html. Powell later showed a slide of a satellite photograph of an Iraqi munitions bunker and stated: "The two arrows indicate the presence of sure signs that the bunkers are storing chemical munitions. . . [t]he truck you [. . .] see is a signature item. It's a decontamination vehicle in case something goes wrong.[529] **The January 31, 2003 INR evaluation also flagged this claim as "weak."**[530] Powell further stated: "UAVs outfitted with spray tanks constitute an ideal method for launching a terrorist attack using biological weapons."[531] **Like his other statements, the January 31, 2003 INR evaluation had flagged this statement as "weak."**[532]

## Assertions Regarding Buried Chemical and Other Weapons

With regard to the charges that tons of chemical, biological, and other weapons were buried underground in Iraq with the help of a defector, Aduan Ihsan Saeed al-Haideri, we now know that the Administration knew that the charges had been disproved when it released its report trumpeting the charges. As James Bamford recently wrote:

The illegal arms, according to al-Haideri, were buried in subterranean wells, hidden in private villas, even stashed beneath the Saddam Hussein Hospital, the largest medical facility in Baghdad. It was damning stuff—just the kind of evidence the Bush Administration was look for. If the charges were true, they would offer the White House a compelling reason to invade Iraq and depose Saddam. That's why the Pentagon had flown a CIA polygraph expert to Pattaya: to question al-Haideri and confirm, once and for all, that Saddam was secretly stockpiling weapons of mass destruction. **There was only one problem: It was all a lie. After a review of the sharp peaks and deep valleys on the polygraph chart, the intelligence officer concluded that al-Haideri had made up the entire story, apparently in the hopes of securing a visa.** [533]

The polygraph was completed in December 2001, ten months before the White House report was issued.[534]

## Assertions Regarding Mobile Biological Weapons

Given the massive weight of authorities raising concerns about Curveball, key officials in the Bush Administration had to have known their biological weapons charges were problematic. These doubts were brought to the Bush Administration's attention before Secretary of State Powell gave his February 2003 United Nations address, and were also raised repeatedly and persistently by German and British intelligence agencies, as well as by key officials within the CIA.

German intelligence authorities voiced many substantive concerns to the Bush Administration about relying on Curveball for mobile weapons labs charges. As the *Los Angeles Times* recently reported:

> The German intelligence officials responsible for one of the most important informants on Saddam Hussein's suspected weapons of mass destruction say that the Bush Administration and the CIA repeatedly exaggerated his claims during the run-up to the war in Iraq. Five senior officials from Germany's Federal Intelligence Service, or BND, said in interviews with *The Times* that they warned U.S. intelligence authorities that the source, an Iraqi defector code-named Curveball, never claimed to produce germ weapons and never saw anyone else do so. Curveball's German handlers for the last six years said his information was often vague, mostly secondhand and impossible to confirm. **"This [Curveball] was not substantial evidence . . . [w]e made clear we could not verify the things he said."** The German authorities . . . also said that their informant suffered from emotional and mental problems. "He is not a stable, psychologically stable guy," said a BND official who supervised the case. "He is not a completely normal person," agreed a BND analyst.[535]

As one senior German intelligence officer explained after seeing Powell's U.N. statements regarding Curveball: "'We were shocked,' the official said. '*Mein Gott!* We had always told them it was not proven . . . It was not hard intelligence.'"[536]

British intelligence officials also raised doubts.[537] The Robb-Silberman Commission found that British intelligence officials had informed the CIA that they were "**not con-vinced that Curveball is a wholly reliable source**" and that "**elements of [his] behavior strike us as typical of . . . fabricators.**"[538]

CIA officials also provided information questioning the Bush Administration's mobile biological weapons assertions before both the President's 2003 State of the Union Address and Secretary of State Powell's February U.N. address. For example, the CIA's Berlin station chief had previously forwarded a message to headquarters noting that a German official had said Curveball was "out of control" and couldn't be located.[539] The Station Chief warned about using Curveball's information on the mobile biological units in Bush's State of the Union speech because the German intelligence service considered Curveball "problematical" and said its officers had been unable to confirm his asser-tions.[540] The station chief recommended that CIA headquarters give "serious considera-tion" before using that unverified information.[541]

On February 4, 2003, the day before Secretary Powell's speech, the CIA doctor who had met with Curveball sent an urgent e-mail stating that he "was deemed a fabricator. Need I say more?"[542] The Deputy Chief of the CIA's Iraqi Task Force replied to the doc-tor, upon receiving the doctor's email: "As I said last night, let's keep in mind the fact **that this war's going to happen regardless of what Curveball said or didn't say, and that the Powers That Be probably aren't terribly interested in whether Curveball knows what he's talking about.**"[543]

Also, shortly before Mr. Powell's U.N. presentation, a CIA official questioned the sources he was using to make the mobile biological weapons labs claims. According to the Senate Intelligence Committee Report, "a [CIA] detailee [was provided] a draft of the BW [mobile biological weapons] section of Secretary Powell's United Nations speech on February 2 or 3, 2003, according to the CIA. **After reading the speech, the detailee wrote an electronic mail (e-mail) to the Deputy Chief of the Iraqi Task Force to express his concerns about the use of the four HUMINT [human intelligence] sources cited in the speech.**"[544]

Thus, for example, with respect to the first source, Curveball, the detailee wrote: "I do have a concern with the validity of the information based on CURVEBALL . . . we're having major handling issues with him and we're attempting to determine, if in fact, CURVEBALL was who he said he was. **These issues, in my opinion, warrant further inquiry, before we use the information as the backbone of one of our major finding of the existence of a continuing Iraqi BW program!**"[545] The detailee also expressed concern about the second source cited in Powell's speech—an Iraqi civil engineer in a position to know the details of the program.[546] Among other credibility issues, the detailee stated that the source "sure didn't corroborate 'curve ball's' information."[547] With respect to the fourth source—an Iraqi Major who defected and had purportedly confirmed that Iraq had mobile biological laboratories—the Defense Intelligence Agency has issued a "fabri-cation notice" on him in May of 2002.[548]

Beyond ignoring the weight of intelligence authority, the record also indicates evidence that the Bush Administration manipulated intelligence information. For example, with regard to the CIA-prepared intelligence estimate, the *Los Angeles Times* reports: "**Despite the lack of access or any new reports from Curveball, U.S. intelligence sharply upgraded its assessments of Iraq's biological weapons before the war. The shift is reflected in declassified portions of National Intelligence Estimates**, which are produced as the authoritative judgment of the 15 U.S. intelligence agencies. [Significantly], the caveats [previously expressed by intelligence officials] disappeared after the Sept. 11 attacks."[549]

A Congressional staffer who was privy to the CIA's threat assessment confirmed that the assessment merely collected arguments for going to war, without doing any substantive review or critique:

> [I]t highlighted "extensive Iraqi chem-bio programs and nuclear programs and links to terrorism" but then included a footnote that read, "This information comes from a source known to fabricate in the past." **The staffer concluded that "they didn't do analysis. What they did was they just amassed everything they could that said anything bad about Iraq and put it into a document."**[550]

### Unmanned Aerial Vehicles

Finally, the record shows that the Bush Administration made false charges regarding UAVs and Iraq's ability to direct weapons far afield, regardless of the weight of authority to the contrary. As explained in a National Intelligence Estimate, the government entity most knowledgeable about UAVs—the Air Force's National Air and Space Intelligence Center—"does not agree that Iraq is developing UAVs primarily intended to be delivery platforms for chemical and biological (CBW) agents."[551] Instead, the Air Force experts asserted that "[t]he small size of Iraq's new UAV strongly suggests a primary role of reconnaissance."[552]

Moreover, with regard to assertions by the President that biological and other weapons could be used by Iraq to target nations far abroad, including the United States, the CIA "increasingly believed that the attempted purchase of the mapping software . . . may have been inadvertent."[553] In an intelligence estimate on threats to the United States homeland published in January 2003, Air Force Defense Intelligence Agency and Army analysts agreed that the proposed purchase was "not necessarily indicative of an intent to target the U.S. homeland."[554]

# Encouraging and Countenancing Torture and Cruel, Inhuman and Degrading Treatment

Our investigation has found that the Bush Administration has not only countenanced, but also paved the way for, torture; cruel, inhuman, and degrading treatment, and other violations of international treaties. While additional violations of international treaties may well have occurred in Afghanistan and Guantanamo Bay, Cuba, our focus in this section will be on the violations that occurred in Iraq, to which this report is directed.

In April of 2004, the world was shocked when photos of torture and humiliation of Iraqi detainees in Abu Ghraib prison were leaked to the press. On May 6, President Bush stated that the "wrongdoers will be brought to justice," and "that the actions of those folks in Iraq do not represent the values of the United States of America."[555] More than a year later, our investigation has found that the abuse was not the result of a "few bad apples," as initially claimed, but that the responsibility lies within the highest levels of the Bush Administration.

# ■ Documented Instances of Torture and Other Legal Violations

*"I questioned some of the things that I saw . . . such things as leaving inmates in their cell with no clothes or in female underpants, handcuffing them to the door of their cell, and the answer I got was, 'This is how military intelligence (MI) wants it done.'"*

—January 2004, Sergeant Ivan L. Frederick II, soldier of the
372nd Military Police Company, in a letter to family describing
acts committed against Iraqi detainees at Abu Ghraib. [556]

## Torture and Murder

Investigations conducted by the military as well as international human rights organizations including Human Rights First, the International Committee of the Red Cross (ICRC), the ACLU, Amnesty International, and Human Rights Watch and media organizations have identified numerous detainee deaths, incidents of torture, and other abuses under international law in Iraq.

The "Taguba Report" was prepared by Maj. Gen. Antonio Taguba at the request of Lt. Gen. Ricardo S. Sanchez, the U.S. Commander of the Combined Joint Task Force in Iraq. The purpose was to investigate the conduct of the 800th Military Police Brigade, principally at the Abu Ghraib prison facility.[557] Over the course of a month, General Taguba headed a team that reviewed reports of prior military investigations, witness statements by military police and military intelligence personnel, potential suspects, and detainees. Moreover, the Taguba investigation conducted its own interviews and collected additional evidence.[558] In late February 2004, General Taguba issued his report, which documented numerous instances of torture and other unlawful conduct:

> Between October and December 2003, at the Abu Ghraib Confinement Facility (BCCF), **numerous incidents of sadistic, blatant, and wanton criminal abuses were inflicted on several detainees. This systemic and illegal abuse of detainees was intention-**

ally perpetrated by several members of the military police guard force . . . of the Abu Ghraib Prison (BCCF). The allegations of abuse were substantiated by detailed witness statements . . . and the discovery of extremely graphic photographic evidence.[559]

The Taguba Report has confirmed that military and intelligence personnel and DOD contractors were responsible for "numerous incidents of sadistic, blatant, and wanton criminal abuses . . . inflicted on several detainees," and that such abuses were "systemic," "illegal," and "intentionally perpetrated."[560] The Report details that intentional acts of abuse committed by military personnel include "punching, slapping and kicking detainees,"[561] rape, use of military dogs to intimidate detainees, and numerous other types of mistreatment.[562] There are detailed witness statements by numerous officers and soldiers within the 800th Brigade which substantiate these allegations.[563] Moreover, these allegations have been confirmed by photographs and videos depicting the graphic images of abuse.[564] It is important to note that Major General Taguba's investigation delved into only one brigade at one prison in Iraq.

Numerous international human rights groups have detailed even more serious abuses. Human Rights First has uncovered at least 16 detainee deaths in Iraq, including at least one at Abu Ghraib,[565] that the military itself has found to be homicides.[566] Many of those victims were found to have been tortured to death.[567] While other deaths have not been directly linked to acts of torture, evidence that detainees died while bound and blindfolded[568] increases the likelihood that these deaths were the direct result of detainee abuse. At least seven more deaths remain under investigation at the time of writing this Report, including a case where a marine broke the neck of a detainee, causing the detainee's death.[569] Moreover, Human Rights First has also found that a number of these deaths occurred after the abuses at Abu Ghraib became public.[570]

The ICRC also has made similar findings regarding the treatment of Iraqi detainees.[571] An ICRC report has concluded that acts of violence and degradation were used on a "systematic" basis and included:

• Extended time spent in stress positions

• Hanging of detainees by their arms for hours at a time

• Deprivation of sleep, food, water, clothing, and light

• Sexual assault and humiliation of male and female detainees

• Threatening and simulating electrocution and murder

• Beatings and murder.[572]

The ACLU has used Freedom of Information Act requests to collect thousands of pages of internal documents, confirming the physical and sexual abuse of detainees and citizens by military personnel in Iraq and elsewhere.[573] These internal documents reveal allegations of abuse against juveniles in Iraq, including one teenager whose jaw was broken as a result of an officer's blow to the face.[574] In another instance, military personnel electrically shocked a teenage prisoner on his feet and neck while he was in zipcuffs, and hit him with a pistol, knocking him unconscious and leaving him to bleed.[575] The internal documents also reveal that detainees were exercised to the point of extreme fatigue, which, in one instance, may have caused the death of an otherwise healthy detainee.[576]

Amnesty International has reported that acts of torture have not only occurred at detention sites but also continue to be perpetrated against Iraqis during house raids and arrests.[577] They found:

- Hooding of suspects upon arrest
- Striking of suspects with rifles
- Soldiers taking aim on suspects with rifles
- Injuring of suspects with severe blows by punching and kicking.[578]

Human Rights Watch confirmed with three officers that torture was a daily practice at the 82nd Airborne Division in Iraq.[579] Detainees singled out for interrogation or retribution were reportedly viciously abused by army personnel.[580] They were denied food and water, kept awake for days at a time, put in stress positions, or forced to do vigorous exercise until they lost consciousness. Their detention center, located only fifteen minutes from Abu Ghraib prison, became known amongst the locals for its abuse: "The Murderous Maniacs" was what they called us at our camp because they knew if they got caught by us and got detained by us before they went to Abu Ghraib then it would be hell to pay."[581]

Human Rights Watch found that others were abused for apparently no reason at all. One officer recalled a cook who came into the detention area in a bad mood, seeking to work out his "frustration:" "One day a sergeant shows up and tells a [detainee] to grab a pole. He told him to bend over and broke the guy's leg with a mini Louisville Slugger that was a metal bat. He was the f***ing cook. He shouldn't be in with no [detainee]s."[582] That officer continued, "Everyone in camp knew if you wanted to work out your frustration you show up at the PUC tent. In a way it was sport."[583]

*Newsweek* chronicled the abuse witnessed by Army Specialist Anthony Lagouranis. He said abuse was part of the job, expected of soldiers in an effort to loosen up detainees and make them talk:

> **I think our policies required abuse . . . There were freaking horrible things people were doing.** I saw [detainees] who had feet smashed with hammers. One detainee told me he had been forced by Marines to sit on an exhaust pipe, and he had a softball-sized blister to prove it. The stuff I did was mainly torture lite: sleep deprivation, isolation, stress positions, hypothermia. We used dogs.[584]

*Time* magazine recently uncovered that CIA interrogators tried to cover up the death of an Iraqi ghost detainee who died while being interrogated at Abu Ghraib prison.[585] According to documents obtained by *Time,* the death of secret detainee Manadel al-Jamadi was ruled a homicide in the Defense Department autopsy, which states that after approximately 90 minutes of interrogation in the custody of CIA officials, he died of "blunt force injuries" and "asphyxiation."[586] Further evidence of this cover-up is demonstrated by documents obtained by *Time*, including many "photographs of his battered corpse—iced to keep it from decomposing in order to hide the true circumstances of his dying . . ."[587] *Time* reported that, as a result of al-Jamadi's treatment, "Military Police at Iraq's notorious Abu Ghraib prison dubbed him the Iceman; others used the nickname Mr. Frosty."[588]

The *New York Times* has reported on substantial evidence that torture and murder were used by CIA operatives in Iraq. An elite group of CIA operatives hunting insurgents in Iraq were "accused of abusing a number of prisoners between October 2003 and April 2004 by kicking them, punching them, twisting their testicles, breaking their fingers and pointing loaded guns at them."[589] This type of abuse even led to deaths. At least three Iraqis have died while in CIA custody.[590]

## Cruel, Inhuman and Degrading Treatment

The ICRC has identified numerous incidents of cruel, inhuman, and degrading treatment (CID) in Iraq, which, while short of torture, has been found to be subject to the Geneva Conventions and the Convention Against Torture.[591]

According to the February 2004 report of the ICRC, U.S. military intelligence abuse of Iraqi detainees during interrogation was widespread, harsh, brutal, and, in some cases, "tantamount to torture."[592] The ICRC identified numerous other incidents of cruel treatment that can be confirmed by simply looking at the released photos and reports, including:

- "punching, slapping and kicking detainees[, and] jumping on their naked feet"
- "videotaping and photographing naked male and female detainees"
- "forcibly arranging detainees in various sexually explicit positions for photographing"
- "forcing detainees to remove their clothing and keeping them naked for several days at a time"
- "positioning a naked detainee on a . . . Box, with a sandbag on his head, and attaching wires to his fingers, toes, and penis to simulate electric torture"
- "placing a dog chain or strap around a naked detainee's neck and having a female Soldier pose for a picture"
- "a male MP [military police] guard having sex with a female detainee"
- "using military working dogs (without muzzles) to intimidate and frighten detainees, and in at least one case biting and severely injuring a detainee"
- taking photographs of dead Iraqi detainees."[593]

## Other Possible Violations of International Treaties

We have also identified practices designed to keep detainees hidden from the ICRC, namely detainees being moved around in Iraq in secret (known as "ghosting") and individuals being transferred out of Iraq for interrogation. Both of these practices would violate the Geneva Conventions.[594] We have learned about these practices from several sources. The *New York Times* confirmed in a report that the CIA "has secretly transport[ed] as many as a dozen detainees out of Iraq in the last six months [from April to October 2004]."[595]

Army General Paul Kern testified before the Senate Armed Services Committee in September of 2004 that the United States had held as many as 100 ghost detainees in Iraq.[596] Maj. Gen. Kern even admitted to the Committee that the ghosting was intended to keep international monitors from having contact with the prisoners: "People . . . were brought into the facilities and . . . were moved so that they could not be identified by the International Red Cross."[597] He stated that because there was no record of how many there were, he could not definitely tell the Committee how many there were, but that the CIA maintained up to three dozen ghost detainees at the now infamous Abu Ghraib facility.[598]

Moreover, it appears from statements of Col. Thomas M. Pappas, head of military intelligence operations at Abu Ghraib, that ghosting was coordinated between military and CIA commanders on the ground.[599] During his interview with investigators, Col. Pappas said that Col. Steven Boltz, then the second-ranking military intelligence officer in Iraq, approved the CIA's use of Abu Ghraib prison to store Aghost detainees."[600] Pappas also told investigators he initially "had concerns over this arrangement" and asked Col. Boltz if they were going to continue housing ghosts. "[Boltz] said yes, to facilitate [military intelligence's] request."[601]

Recent reports coming out of Iraq verify the use of a weapon called white phosphorus (WP) in combat. An Italian state broadcaster, *RAI,* recently reported that American forces used WP in Fallujah last year against insurgents.[602] According to a former American soldier who fought in Fallujah, "I heard the order to pay attention because they were going to use white phosphorus on Fallujah. In military jargon it's known as Willy Pete. . . . Phosphorus burns bodies, in fact it melts the flesh all the way down to the bone . . . I saw the burned bodies of women and children. Phosphorus explodes and forms a cloud. Anyone within a radius of 150 metres is done for."[603]

Use of WP as an incendiary weapon against civilians is banned by Protocol III of the 1980 Convention on Certain Conventional Weapons (CCW).[604] Protocol III regulates the use of weapons designed to set fire to or burn their target. The protocol proscribes targeting civilians with incendiary weapons and restricts the use of air-delivered incendiary weapons against military targets in close proximity to concentrations of noncombatants.[605] Protocol III only covers weapons created intentionally to set fire or burn, such as flamethrowers, and does not cover weapons that ignite fires or burn as a side effect. Because we have not signed Protocol III, the United States is theoretically not legally bound by the protocol's provisions. Additionally, WP is not covered by the 1993 Chemical Weapons Convention (CWC), to which the United States is a party. This is because the CWC regulates weapons whose toxicity is specific to life processes, while WP is a general incendiary weapon.

However, grave breaches are also defined within the Geneva Conventions, as "willful killing, torture or inhuman treatment, including biological experiments, willfully causing great suffering or serious injury to body or health."[606] Thus, the use of WP in combat would appear to be illegal as it would fall within this definition of grave breaches under the Conventions, to which the United States is legally bound.

# ■ Bush Administration Responsibility for Torture and Other Legal Violations

*"In recent days, there has been a good deal of discussion about who bears responsibility for the terrible activities that took place at Abu Ghraib. These events occurred on my watch. As Secretary of Defense, I am accountable for them. I take full responsibility."*

—MAY 7, 2004, SECRETARY OF DEFENSE DONALD RUMSFELD
BEFORE THE HOUSE ARMED SERVICES COMMITTEE[607]

## *Department of Justice*

### ■ FAILURE TO ADEQUATELY PROSECUTE TORTURE AND OTHER LEGAL VIOLATIONS BY CONTRACTORS AND OTHERS WITHIN ITS JURISDICTION

There appear to be numerous instances of torture that are capable of being punished within the jurisdiction of the Justice Department, which includes the authority under the Military Extraterritorial Jurisdiction Act to pursue criminal charges against military contractors, military personnel, and CIA officers.[608] **It is telling that only one such case has resulted in an official indictment, and no one has been convicted. In fact, according to Amnesty International, despite the numerous detainee deaths that occurred in Abu Ghraib as a result of torture and other legal violations, it appears that no member of the military has received a sentence of more than three years in prison.**[609]

According to a recent report by the *New York Times*, despite evidence of CIA involvement in the deaths of at least four prisoners in Iraq and Afghanistan, the Justice Department has charged only one person linked to the CIA with wrongdoing in any of the cases; that person, David A. Passaro, was a contractor, not an official CIA officer, though.[610] In a recent *New York Times* Op-Ed, Frank Rich asks, "Why have the official reports on detainee abuse at Abu Ghraib and Guantanamo spared all but a single officer in the chain of command?"[611] This failure to investigate has occurred under both former Attorney General John Ashcroft and current Attorney General Alberto Gonzales.

Human rights law expert Scott Horton surmised that not only had the Justice Department poorly executed its investigative duties, but that then-Attorney General Ashcroft had willfully disregarded his discretionary duty to prosecute.[612] He also theorized that a failure to conduct meaningful investigation would continue in the future stating:

The Attorney General, John Ashcroft, and his immediate subordinates have . . . been complicit in a scheme for the commission of war crimes and accordingly will not undertake a criminal investigation. . . The Attorney General-designate, Alberto Gonzales, is a principal author of the scheme to undertake war crimes . . . [S]enior lawyers at DOJ, acting with the knowledge and support of the Attorney General, were complicit in the scheme to introduce torture and other abusive practices into authorized regimes of treatment for detainees in GWOT. It is therefore clear that DOJ will not act on its responsibility to initiate criminal investigations or undertake prosecutions of the conspirators and implementers of this scheme.[613]

Numerous rights groups have also expressed their outrage at the failure of the Justice Department to prosecute. They have rejected the military findings that only low-level officials were complicit in the abuses at Abu Ghraib and requested that the Justice Department investigate and prosecute higher officials.[614] In an open letter to Alberto Gonzales, the ACLU wrote:

> There is an obvious public interest in investigating and prosecuting all persons committing torture or abuse or conspiring to commit those crimes against persons being held by the United States. A small number of enlisted men and women and a few low-ranking military officers should not be the only persons held responsible, if civilians and top military officers also engaged in wrongdoing.[615]

Other rights groups, including Human Rights Watch and Amnesty International, have requested that Attorney General Gonzales "appoint a special prosecutor to investigate the roles of all U.S. officials 'who participated in, ordered, or had command responsibility for war crimes or torture.'"[616] These groups have since requested that Congress conduct an independent and bipartisan investigation because there is little promise that the Justice Department will conduct any meaningful inquiries.[617] Moreover, the failure of our government to prosecute those responsible for acts of torture has led foreign nations to issue warrants for CIA operatives for their role in abductions and renditions.[618]

## ■ REMOVAL OF DETAINEES FROM IRAQ

We have clear evidence, by virtue of a March 19, 2004 memo from the Justice Department's Office of Legal Counsel, that the Justice Department paved the way for the removal of detainees identified above.[619]

The Justice Department memo undermined the Geneva Convention's prohibition against deportation and forcible removal by stating "that there is no evidence that the [Geneva Convention's prohibition against deportation and forcible removal] extended to illegal aliens from occupied territory . . . and there is no evidence that international law has ever disapproved of such removals."[620] The classified memo concludes that there is an exception to the ban against forcible transfers and deportations of protected persons, surmising that protected persons, "whether illegal aliens or not,"[621] may be "relocate[d] . . . from occupied Iraq to another country for a brief but not indefinite period, for the purposes of interrogation."[622] This memo was prepared at the request of then-White House

Counsel Alberto Gonzales, as evidenced by the appearance of Gonzales' initials handwritten on the document,[623] and presumably with the approval of then-Attorney General John Ashcroft.

There appears to be little doubt that this memo gave the CIA legal cover for removing both Iraqi citizens and foreigners found on Iraqi soil. **One intelligence official stated that "[t]he memo was a green light," and that "[t]he CIA used the memo to remove other people from Iraq."[624]**

Rights groups such as Human Rights First have closely linked the March 2004 memo with the practices of ghosting and rendition that have since become rampant in Iraq.[625] In fact, Human Rights First used evidence of Gonzales's involvement with the memo to support its opposition to Alberto Gonzales's appointment as Attorney General.[626] The group argues that "the Goldsmith memo to Gonzales sheds light on [Gonzales's] involvement in the 'ghost detainee' program of secret detentions, described by Army Maj. Gen. Antonio Taguba in his report as 'deceptive, contrary to Army doctrine and in violation of international law.'"[627]

## ■ LIMITED CONSTRUCTION OF TORTURE AND APPLICABILITY OF CID

The Department of Justice also bears significant responsibility for the acts of torture and other legal violations by virtue of the extreme and narrow legal views it has adopted. These are set forth in an August 1, 2002 memo setting forth an inappropriately narrow definition of torture and in Mr. Gonzales's January 2005 confirmation hearing testimony on the jurisdictional reach of bans on CID.

An August 1, 2002 Department of Justice memo addressed to then-White House Counsel Gonzales creates a definition of torture that is contrary to international law, domestic law, and legislative intent.[628] **The memo claims that torture consists of "extreme acts" under U.S. law, inflicting severe pain that "must be of an intensity akin to that which accompanies serious physical injury such as death or organ failure. According to the memo, severe mental pain requires suffering not just at the moment of infliction but it also requires lasting psychological harm, such as seen in mental disorders like post-traumantic [sic] stress disorder."[629]**

However, 18 U.S.C. 2340-2340A, the federal law executing the U.N. Convention Against Torture,[630] does not use the word "extreme" or otherwise suggest the conclusion that "those acts must be of an extreme nature to rise to the level of torture within the meaning of Section 2340A and the Convention."[631] Instead, the law provides:

(1) "Torture" means an act committed by a person acting under the color of law specifically intended to inflict severe physical or mental pain or suffering (other than pain or suffering incidental to lawful sanctions) upon another person within his custody or physical control;

(2) "Severe mental pain or suffering" means the prolonged mental harm caused by or resulting from—(A) the intentional infliction or threatened infliction of severe physical

pain or suffering; (B) the administration or application, or threatened administration or application, of mind-altering substances or other procedures calculated to disrupt profoundly the senses or the personality; (C) the threat of imminent death; (D) the threat that another person will imminently be subjected to death, severe physical pain or suffering, or the administration or application of mind-altering substances or other procedures calculated to disrupt profoundly the senses or personality.[632]

**There is nothing in this definition that requires the sensation of either organ failure or death or a level of mental harm rising to a disorder to invoke the law's protections.**

Mr. Gonzales has followed up this position on torture by taking the position at his confirmation hearing that the ban on Cruel, Inhuman and Degrading treatment only applies to detainees held within the United States.[633] When the Senate approved the CAT, however, it did so with the reservation that cruel, inhuman and degrading treatment was limited by our jurisprudence of the Eighth Amendment of the constitution.[634] It is therefore understood that the definition of CID treatment should be consistent with the definition of unconstitutionally "cruel" treatment under the Eighth Amendment.

However, Attorney General Gonzales has argued that the limitation was categorical and not definitional. He believes that only those individuals covered by the 8th Amendment would receive protection against cruel, inhuman or degrading treatment. If so, this means that all of those foreign nationals held overseas will be stripped of protection against CID.

Mr. Gonzales's argument has been rejected by numerous groups and scholars and has been refuted by countless groups outside of the Administration.[635] For example, the following groups have publicly objected to this new and unfounded interpretation: Human Rights First, the American Civil Liberties Union, Amnesty International, USA, Human Rights Watch and the Center for American Progress.[636] Moreover, it has been rejected by Abraham D. Sofaer, the former legal advisor to the Department of State when the Reagan Administration originally signed the Convention Against Torture in 1988, who stated in a January 2005 letter to Sen. Patrick Leahy that **"the purpose of the Senate's [reservation] was to ensure that the same standards for [CID] would apply outside of the United States, as would apply inside."**[637] Approval of recent legislative initiatives by Senator McCain and others does not alter the harm done by these extreme legal positions.

## Department of Defense

### ■ PERSONAL APPROVAL OF TORTURE AND OTHER ILLEGAL ACTIONS

In terms of Secretary Rumsfeld, first, he approved treatment in violation of the Geneva Conventions for individuals held in Guantanamo Bay, Cuba, and allowed these methods to be incorporated into the detention centers in Iraq. Second, he personally approved the ghosting and removal of Iraqi detainees.

We know about his approval of unlawful tactics because, according to a letter from William Haynes to Secretary Rumsfeld, on November 27, 2002, Mr. Rumsfeld signed the

Haynes action memo, which requested approval of counter-resistance techniques, and actually asked for harsher techniques.[638] These tactics were created for the express purpose of "enhancing [military] efforts to extract additional information" from detainees and included removal of detainee clothing, use of hoods and dogs.[639] **The most egregious of these tactics are collectively referred to as "Category III," and include the "use of scenarios designed to convince the detainee that death or severely painful consequences for him and/or his family are imminent."[640] The memo notes that such a tactic could easily be construed as a death threat, which constitutes infliction of mental pain and suffering under the Torture Convention.[641] The memo also notes that another Category III tactic—use of a "wet towel and dripping water to induce the misperception of suffocation"[642]—could also be construed as a violation of the Torture Convention since it was likely to inflict mental harm.[643]**

We also know that Mr. Rumsfeld had to have appreciated that these tactics would migrate to Iraq because, when he sent Maj. Gen. Geoffrey D. Miller to Iraq in the summer of 2003, the Iraqi prisons were known to be crowded and a hotbed for violence; further, Iraqi detainees were not providing enough "actionable intelligence."[644] General Miller's task was specifically to turn up the heat and, as one officer explained, incorporate the Guantanamo practices into the facilities there.[645] **Brig. Gen. Janis L. Karpinski, head of the prison system in Iraq, stated, "[Miller] came up there and told me he was going to 'Gitmoize' the detention operation."[646]**

Further, Larry Wilkerson, former Chief of Staff to former Secretary of State Colin Powell, charged that a cabal of senior Administration officials issued directives that led to the abuse of prisoners by United States soldiers in Iraq and Afghanistan. "It was clear to me," he said,

> that there was a visible audit trail from the vice president's office through the Secretary of Defense down to the commanders in the field that in carefully couched terms—I'll give you that—that to a soldier in the field meant two things: we're not getting enough good intelligence and you need to get that evidence—and oh, by the way, here's some ways you probably can get it.[647]

Moreover, we now know that Secretary Rumsfeld was put on notice by the International Committee of the Red Cross that these techniques he was exporting to Iraq were considered to be "**an intentional system of cruel, unusual and degrading treatment and a form of torture.**"[648] These warnings began in 2003, soon after invasion, and were made to military leadership at least as high as Deputy Defense Secretary Paul Wolfowitz.[649] Secretary Rumsfeld stated by his own admission before the House Armed Services Committee on May 7, 2004, "These events occurred on my watch. As Secretary of Defense, I am accountable for them. I take full responsibility."[650]

## ■ COMMAND RESPONSIBILITY

There is substantial evidence that not only did Secretary Rumsfeld know the conditions for abuse being set and know abuse was taking place, but also that he did very little to prevent or punish the illegal activity. Specifically, it appears that Secretary Rumsfeld was well aware of or should have known the following:

- That detainees in Iraq were being tortured, or treated in a cruel, inhuman and degrading way as the **International Committee of the Red Cross reported over 250 allegations of abuse to military officials in 2003 alone**[651] **that according to former Secretary of State Colin Powell, Secretary Rumsfeld personally kept the President "fully informed of the concerns that were being expressed" by the ICRC,**[652] and that there were no less than 14 public accounts of detainee abuse after the spring of 2002 and before the *60 Minutes II* airing of the Abu Ghraib photos.[653]

- That, as confirmed by Army Gen. Paul Kern in testimony before the Senate Armed Services Committee, detainees were kept hidden from the International Committee of the Red Cross on numerous occasions and **"the number [of ghost detainees] is in the dozens, perhaps up to 100."**[654]

Although it is clear by now that Secretary Rumsfeld either knew or should have known about the illegal practices at detention facilities in Iraq, the record shows that he refused to take serious measures either to prevent these acts from recurring or to investigate and punish those who already had mistreated detainees.

While a number of low-level individuals were punished, such a response appears to be insufficient in two important respects: the acts of torture have not been punished with the severity that is truly necessary to deter others from engaging in such conduct; and high-level officials who have encouraged or permitted the behavior in the first place have not been punished at all.

First, Human Rights First and Amnesty International estimate from publicly-available information that those who were actually punished were usually given no more than a slap on the wrist. A full 70 percent of those sanctioned by the military were given on-judicial, administrative punishments.[655] The longest sentence meted out for the death of a detainee was only three years.[656] While we can confirm that there have been no less than 410 criminal investigations as of June 2005—almost all including more than one offender and more than one victim—only 74 soldiers have been criminally charged.[657]

Further, it appears that Secretary Rumsfeld has chosen not to investigate or to punish officials high in the chain of command. There has been nearly unanimous critique of the military investigations by groups advocating the abolition of torture and cruel treatment, such as Human Rights First, which notes that "months after the Abu Ghraib photos were published—and nearly two years after the first abuse-related deaths in U.S. custody in the 'war on terror'—we are still not in a position to say that we know how to ensure that such abuses never happen again."[658] Amnesty International expresses similar critiques of the military investigations, explaining that "evidence of torture and other ill-treatment by U.S. forces in the 'war on terror' continues to mount, but no U.S. agents have been charged with war crimes or torture. Over 70 percent of official actions have resulted in non-judicial or administrative punishments."[659] Amnesty International further noted that "the response by the U.S. administration to the allegations [of torture] had been inadequate."[660]

### ■ GHOSTING AND REMOVAL OF DETAINEES

We also have an admission that George Tenet specifically approved the ghosting in Iraq of a specific individual, and that Mr. Rumsfeld admitted to approving of ghosting of detainees as a special matter. During a press conference in June 2004, Secretary Rumsfeld confirmed not only that was he asked by CIA Director George Tenet to hide a specific detainee, but also that he hid the detainee and that the detainee was lost in the system for more than eight months:

> **Q:** Mr. Secretary, I'd like to ask why last November you ordered the U.S. military to keep a suspected Ansar al-Islam prisoner in Iraq [Hiwa Abdul Rahman Rashul] secret from the Red Cross. He's now been secret for more than seven months. And there are other such shadowy prisoners in Iraq who are being kept secret from the Red Cross.
>
> **SEC. RUMSFELD:** With respect to the—I want to separate the two. Iraq, my understanding is that the investigations on that subject are going forward. With respect to the detainee you're talking about, I'm not an expert on this, but **I was requested by the Director of Central Intelligence to take custody of an Iraqi national who was believed to be a high-ranking member of Ansar al-Islam. And we did so. We were asked to not immediately register the individual. And we did that.** It would—it was—he was brought to the attention of the Department, the senior level of the Department I think late last month. And we're in the process of registering him with the ICRC at the present time. . .[661]

The CIA transferred Mr. Rashul to an undisclosed location outside Iraq to be interrogated.[662] Three months after Mr. Rashul's detention, the CIA's General Counsel determined that transferring him out of Iraq violated the Geneva Conventions.[663] Upon transferring Mr. Rashul from CIA custody to the U.S. military, Director Tenet asked that the detention be kept secret, meaning that military should "not immediately register" Mr. Rashul in any military database.[664] Secretary Rumsfeld complied, issuing a classified order that the media have reported as stating: "Notification of the presence and or status of the detainee to the International Committee of the Red Cross, or any international or national aid organization, is prohibited pending further guidance."[665] Secretary Rumsfeld's order was then transmitted down the chain of command to Lieutenant General Ricardo Sanchez, commander of U.S. forces in Iraq.

General Sanchez then issued his own order to implement Secretary Rumsfeld's order. A media report on the Sanchez order describes that it "accepts custody and detains Hiwa Abdul Rahman Rashul, a high-ranking Ansar al-Islam member;" orders that he "remain segregated and isolated from the remainder of the detainee population;" "[o]nly military personnel and debriefers will have access to the detainee. . . . Knowledge of the presence of this detainee will be strictly limited on a need-to-know basis." "Any reports from inter-rogations or debriefings will contain only the mininum [sic] amount of source informa-tion . . ."[666]

Mr. Rashul was detained at Camp Cropper, outside Baghdad Airport, where he reportedly received only one cursory interrogation when he first arrived.[667] The CIA is reported to have made little effort to follow up and, when it did inquire about him in January 2004, prison officials were unable to locate him.[668] In addition to this, several prison officials questioned superiors to determine what to do about Rashul's given his indeterminate detention, but received no official answers.[669]

After media reports began circulating in June 2004 as to the existence of an unregis-tered detainee, Mr. Rashul was finally registered. This occurred more than eight months after he was turned over to the military and almost a year after his initial capture and detention.[670]

Further, in his statement to investigators, Col. Thomas M. Pappas, the top military intelligence officer at Abu Ghraib, stated that in September 2003, the CIA requested that the military intelligence officials "continue to make cells available for their detainees and that they not have to go through the normal in processing procedures."[671] And, as Army General Paul Kern testified before the Senate Armed Services Committee in September of 2004, the U.S. had held as many as 100 ghost detainees in Iraq.[672]

In addition, Secretary Rumsfeld confirmed that the ghosting of detainees occurred on his watch on many occasions:

Q: But then why wasn't the—why wasn't the Red Cross told, and there are other such prisoners being detained without the knowledge of the Red Cross?

SEC. RUMSFELD: There are—there are instances where that occurs. And a request was made to do that, and we did.[673]

# Cover-ups and Retribution

*"It's slime and defend . . ."*
    —OCTOBER 2, 2003, REPUBLICAN AIDE ON CAPITOL HILL, DESCRIBING THE WHITE HOUSE'S
    EFFORT TO RAISE QUESTIONS ABOUT MR. WILSON'S MOTIVATIONS AND ITS SIMULTANEOUS EFFORT
    TO SHORE UP SUPPORT IN THE REPUBLICAN RANKS[674]

Inevitably, information began to seep out exposing the many falsehoods and deceptions concerning the Iraq war. The release of this information—including information detailing the Niger-Iraq uranium forgeries—led members of the Bush Administration to react with a series of leaks and other actions designed to cover up their misdeeds and obtain retribu-tion against their critics. In addition, the Bush Administration began disseminating even more falsehoods, in an apparent further effort to obscure its initial misstatements.

# ■ The Niger Forgeries and the "Sliming" of Ambassador Wilson and his Family

The most well-known example of the Bush Administration's efforts to cover up its misdeeds and exact revenge against its critics is its response to Ambassador Joseph Wilson's statements regarding the forged Niger uranium documents. Ambassador Wilson's exposures—that not only were the Niger-Iraq uranium documents forgeries, but also that the Bush Administration had been forewarned of this fact—threatened to bring down the entire house of cards of pre-war deceptions.

Beginning in the Summer of 2003, with the public disclosures concerning the Niger forgeries and the Bush Administration's apparent foreknowledge of them, members of the Administration initiated a concerted campaign to cover up their own misdeeds and taint Ambassador Wilson. The record reflects that (i) members of the Bush Administration were highly concerned about the disclosures to the point of obsession and, as a result, obtained classified information regarding Ambassador Wilson and his wife that they leaked to the press, in apparent violation of administrative requirements and non-disclosure agreements (if not criminal laws); (ii) the leak was not only in apparent retribution against the Wilsons, but also was damaging to national security; and (iii) the investigation into the leak was delayed by members of the Bush Administration, beset by conflicts of interest, and accompanied by numerous misstatements and falsehoods.[675] The leak story culminated in the federal criminal indictment, issued by Special Counsel Patrick Fitzgerald, of I. Lewis ("Scooter") Libby, Vice President Cheney's Chief of Staff (the "Libby Indictment").[676]

## Disclosure and Panic

According to the Libby Indictment, numerous media stories and inquiries into the Administration's use of faulty intelligence led to this consternation in the White House. Articles were published in the *New York Times*,[677] the *Washington Post*,[678] and the *New Republic*,[679] among others.[680]

Clearly, this media onslaught—aimed directly at one of the Bush Administration's principal rationales for the war and challenging its veracity—caused considerable turmoil in the White House. For example, after he finished a discussion on this issue with Matthew Cooper on July 11, 2003, Karl Rove expressed alarm over the damage this line of inquiry could cause the President, writing in an e-mail to Deputy Security Advisor Stephen Hadley: "When [Cooper] finished his brief heads-up he immediately launched into Niger. . . . **Isn't this damaging? Hasn't the president been hurt? I didn't take the bait, but I said if I were him I wouldn't get *Time* far out on this.**"[681]

According to White House sources, Libby became enraged over Wilson's disclosures to the point of obsession. the *Los Angeles Times* wrote, "Vice President Dick Cheney's chief of staff was so angry about the public statements of former ambassador Joseph C.

Wilson IV, a Bush Administration critic married to an undercover CIA officer, that he monitored all of Wilson's television appearances and urged the White House to mount an aggressive public campaign against him, former aides say."[682] the *Los Angeles Times* went on to say that "[T]the intensity with which Libby reacted to Wilson had many senior White House staffers puzzled, and few agreed with his counterattack plan or its rationale, former aides said."[683]

Instead of responding to these charges in an above-board and factual manner, officials in the Bush Administration chose to cover up their earlier deceptions by using their positions of authority to obtain classified information to undermine and attack Ambassador Wilson and his wife. According to the Libby Indictment and other sources, this was done in apparent violation of relevant administrative requirements, non-disclosure agreements, and potentially the criminal laws.

The Libby Indictment makes clear that Mr. Libby obtained classified information about Ambassador Wilson's trip and his wife from at least six sources within the government, including Vice President Cheney himself. This began on May 29, 2003, when Libby sought information concerning Wilson's travel from an under-Secretary of State, which he received via oral reports and fax over the course of the next two weeks.[684] (The under-Secretary is reported to be John Bolton, who is now the U.S. Ambassador to the United Nations.[685]) On June 11, 2003, Libby also sought and received similar information from a CIA officer.[686] The next day, Libby learned from Vice President Cheney that Wilson's wife worked at the CIA's Counterproliferation Division,[687] which is part of the CIA's secret Clandestine Service.[688] Libby further broached the topic of Wilson's wife on June 14, 2003 with a CIA briefer.[689] Next, on July 8, 2003, Libby asked the Vice President's counsel, David Addington, about CIA paperwork requirements for trips by spouses of CIA employees.[690] Finally, at some point before July 8, 2003, Libby obtained additional information about Wilson's wife from the Assistant to the Vice President for Public Affairs.[691]

Significantly, Libby was not the only individual in the White House soliciting or receiving information about Ambassador Wilson's wife in the wake of the disclosures about possible Bush Administration wrongdoing and misstatements. The record indicates that numerous additional officials, including Vice President Cheney,[692] Secretary of State Powell,[693] and Political Director Rove,[694] were also obtaining access to classified information concerning Wilson's wife.

Once these various high-ranking Administration officials obtained this information that they believed would help with damage control on the embarrassing Niger disclosures, it was widely shared with others in the Administration as well as the press. For example, Mr. Libby shared the classified information with his principal deputy;[695] with Karl Rove;[696] and with then-White House Press Secretary Ari Fleischer.[697] Classified information concerning Ambassador Wilson's trip and his wife's employment at the CIA was also widely shared on Air Force One on June 10, 2003,[698] and on Air Force Two on July 12, 2003.[699]

Even more significantly, although Mr. Libby and the other members of the Administration had to know the information was classified (the Libby indictment includes numerous references that make it clear that Valerie Plame's employment at the CIA is classified),[700] they nevertheless widely shared this damaging information with the press. Thus, for example, before Novak's column ran, at least four Administration officials (Mr. Libby, Mr. Rove, and two still as of yet unknown Administration officials) called at least five Washington journalists (Ms. Miller, Mr. Novak, Mr. Cooper, Mr. Pincus, and Mr. Woodward) and disclosed the identity and occupation of Wilson's wife. The Libby Indictment and related accounts describes in greater detail the White House effort to stem questions surrounding the forged Niger documents by disclosing classified information to the media:

- Washington Post Assistant Managing Editor Bob Woodward testified that yet another senior Administration official told him about CIA operative Valerie Plame and her position as early as May 2005, one month before her name was disclosed.[701]

- On or about June 23, 2003, Libby met with *New York Times* reporter Judith Miller . . . In discussing the CIA's handling of Wilson's trip to Niger, Libby informed her that Wilson's wife might work at a bureau of the CIA."[702]

- On July 8, Libby discussed with Miller Wilson's trip and criticized the CIA reporting concerning Wilson's trip. During this discussion, Libby advised Miller of his belief that Wilson's wife worked for the CIA.[703]

- On or about July 10 or 11, the indictment states that Karl Rove was one of the sources who had confirmed to Robert Novak that Ambassador Wilson's wife worked for the CIA: "On or about July 10 or July 11, 2003, Libby spoke to a senior official in the White House (Official A) who advised Libby of a conversation Official———[subsequently identified as Karl Rove] had earlier that week with columnist Robert Novak in which Wilson's wife was discussed as a CIA employee involved in Wilson's trip. Libby was advised by Official———that Novak would be writing a story about Wilson's wife."[704]

- On July 11, in the morning, Karl Rove had a short conversation with *Time* magazine reporter Matthew Cooper. Rove told Cooper that Wilson's wife worked for the CIA and had a hand in sending him to Niger.[705]

- On July 12, in the afternoon, Libby spoke by telephone to Matthew Cooper, who asked whether Libby had heard that Wilson's wife was involved in sending Wilson on the trip to Niger. Libby confirmed to Cooper, without elaboration or qualification, that he had heard this information too.[706]

- On or about July 12, 2003, in the late afternoon, Libby spoke by telephone with Judith Miller of the *New York Times* and discussed Wilson's wife and that she worked at the CIA.[707]

- On July 12, according to press reports, an administration official who has not been identified returned a call from Walter Pincus of the *Washington Post*. The official "veered off the precise matter we were discussing and told me . . . [Ambassador Wilson's trip] was a boondoggle set up by his wife," Pincus has written.[708]

Contrary to the arguments of many in the Bush Administration, these disclosures to the media do not appear to have been inadvertent or merely confirming in nature. For instance, in reference to the two senior Administration officials who provided him with Valerie Plame Wilson's status as a covert operative, **Bob Novak later admitted "I didn't dig it out, it was given to me. . . They thought it was significant, they gave me the name and I used it."**[709] Mr. Novak also stated on December 14, 2005, that he would be "amazed" if the president didn't know the source's identity and that the public should "bug the president as to whether he should reveal who the source is."[710] Also, as noted above, another administration official actually "veered" at the subject at hand to bring up Ambassador Wilson's trip and complain that it "was a boondoggle set up by Wilson's wife."[711] A senior source in the Administration also acknowledged that officials brought up Plame as part of their broader case against Wilson. **"'It was unsolicited,' the source said. 'They were pushing back. They used everything they had.'"**[712]

## Retribution and Damage

There is also significant evidence that, in addition to leaking this classified information to deflect criticism from the President and Vice-President for their false uranium and other nuclear claims, the Bush Administration was motivated by revenge and retribution. First, we have the stunning admission, by **a Republican congressional aide, that the White House strategy with respect to Ambassador Wilson's charges was to "slime and defend."**[713]

We also have the statement by the host of MSNBC's *Hardball*, Chris Matthews: "**I just got off the phone with Karl Rove who said your wife is fair game.**"[714] We also have the statement by a senior Bush Administration official that "[the leak] was meant purely and simply for revenge."[715] Asked about the motive for describing the leaks, the senior official said the leaks were "wrong and a huge miscalculation, because they were irrelevant and did nothing to diminish Wilson's credibility."[716]

There are numerous additional sources who have indicated that revenge was a motivating factor behind the series of leaks. Vince Cannistraro, a former Chief of Operations and Analysis for the CIA's Counterterrorism Center, noted the retaliatory nature of the leak: "**[Administration officials] were trying to not only undermine and trash Ambassador Wilson, but to demonstrate their contempt for CIA by bringing Valerie's name into it. Wasn't germane to their argument, but they brought it in there deliberately, vindictively in, in my judgment, a dirty trick.**"[717] Echoing this belief, former CIA Case Officer Jim Marcinkowski noted, "[T]he interest being advanced by this disclosure was certainly not national security."[718]

The *Los Angeles Times* reported that the "intensity with which Libby reacted to

Wilson had many senior White House staffers puzzled, and few agreed with his counter-attack plan, or its rationale."[719] An **ex-Administration official said "this might have been about politics on some level, but it is also personal. [Libby] feels that his honor has been questioned, and his instinct is to strike back.**"[720]

These leaks of classified information by Bush Administration officials have damaged national security.[721] At **his press conference on October 28, 2005, Fitzgerald stated that the leaks were "a serious breach of the public trust,"** and he said the disclosure of Ms. Wilson's status were a setback to the Central Intelligence Agency and its employees, at minimum as a deterrent to the recruiting of new officers.[722] Numerous ex-CIA agents also have confirmed the damaging nature of these politically motivated disclosures. For example, Arthur Brown, who retired in February as the CIA's Asian Division chief and is now a senior vice president at the consultancy firm Control Risks Group, declared that "[c]over and tradecraft are the only forms of protection one has and to have that stripped away because of political scheming is the moral equivalent to exposing forward deployed military units."[723]

Many Republicans tried to minimize the damage by challenging Mrs. Wilson's status as a covert agent.[724] For example, on July 17, House Republican Whip Roy Blunt (R-MO) read from the Republican talking points and stated, "[Y]ou know, this was a job that the ambassador's wife had that she went to every day. It was a desk job. I think many people in Washington understood that her employment was at the CIA, and she went to that office every day."[725]

However, many former CIA agents were critical of Republican efforts to dismiss Ms. Plame's job as a non-covert desk job. Larry Johnson, a former CIA analyst, and ten other former intelligence officers wrote to congressional leaders calling the disclosure of her name a "shameful event in American history."[727] Citing statements by Republican allies, they stated: "[I]ntelligence officers should not be used as political footballs. In the case of Valerie Plame, she still works for the CIA and is not in a position to publicly defend her reputation and honor."[727] At a Democratic hearing on the leak, former intelligence officers reiterated their plea that Republicans cease their attacks on Mrs. Wilson.[728]

## Delays, Conflicts, and More Lies

Once it became clear that someone in the Bush Administration had leaked classified information for political gain, rather than move quickly to identify and dismiss and, if necessary, prosecute the responsible parties—as had been initially promised—the Administration did the opposite. The record shows that members of the Bush Administration delayed and encumbered the investigation and engaged in even more lies and misstatements. In fact, from the very outset, the Bush Administration's handling of the leak has been rife with political and procedural irregularities.

The Department of Justice caused serious delays to the investigation by failing to pursue the allegations and by failing to obtain waivers from White House personnel in a timely manner. Initially, the Department failed to open an investigation into the leak. Immediately after Mr. Novak's piece was published, the CIA contacted the Justice Department four times in the span of three weeks to (1) notify it that the disclosure of Wilson's name and covert status probably violated the law and (2) request a criminal investigation.[729] On September 29, 2003, over a month after the first CIA notification, the Department finally confirmed that the FBI would investigate the leak.[730]

Unfortunately, the Department's handling of the case was subject to further delays and conflicts of interest. For example, the Department waited three days before notifying the White House of the investigation, and the then-White House Counsel Gonzalez in turn waited eleven hours before asking all White House staff to preserve any evidence. (Gonzales claimed that this day was approved by the Department of Justice).[731] Moreover, any evidence employees turned over was and continues to be screened for "relevance" by White House counsel, perhaps filtering out critical information.[732] **One reason given for these delays was that the Department was "going a bit slower on this one because it is so high-profile,"[733]** according to FBI sources.

In addition to causing delay, other aspects of the Department's handling of the investigation are of concern. For example, law enforcement officials close to the investigation have indicated that then-Attorney General Ashcroft was personally and privately briefed on FBI interviews of Karl Rove, then a senior advisor to the President and now the Deputy White House Chief of Staff.[734] **At the time of these events, Mr. Ashcroft had personal and political connections to Mr. Rove, Mr. Rove was an advisor to Mr. Ashcroft during the latter's political campaigns, earning almost $750,000 for his services.[735]**

Finally, on December 30, 2003, these conflicts led the Attorney General to recuse himself from the investigation. Then-Deputy Attorney General James Comey became the acting Attorney General for the matter and simultaneously appointed Patrick Fitzgerald, the U.S. Attorney for the Northern District of Illinois, as a special counsel to lead the investigation.[736]

However, even Mr. Fitzgerald's appointment did not stop the Administration's efforts to delay the investigation. Mr. Fitzgerald encountered numerous problems, including Administration officials' failure to execute waivers of privilege. For example, Mr. Libby's initial failure to execute a clear and unequivocal waiver of privilege to Judith Miller significantly delayed and impeded Mr. Fitzgerald's investigation.[737] Indeed, in a March 2005 filing with the court hearing the case, Mr. Fitzgerald stated he could not close the matter because of Ms. Miller's inability to testify about conversations with senior government officials.[738] Looking back at the investigation on the day the grand jury expired, Mr. Fitzgerald noted that witnesses had not been able to testify when subpoenas were issued in August 2004, lamenting that "we would have been here in October 2004 instead of October 2005."[739]

Members of the Bush Administration also have sought to cover up their own misdeeds through a series of lies and misstatements. First, the White House Press Secretary repeatedly provided false information to the American people about the leak and the investigation. At a minimum, this occurred in exchanges on September 29, 2003,[740] and on October 7, 2003,[741] which together contain at least eight falsehoods by Mr. McClellan.

With regard to Karl Rove being "involved" in the leak, Mr. McClellan asserted (i) that it was a "ridiculous suggestion"; (ii) that "it's not true"; (iii) "that he was not involved"; and (iv) "there's no truth to the suggestion that he was." With regard to whether Scooter Libby, Karl Rove, or Elliot Abrams "were the leakers," Mr. McClellan also claimed (v) it was a "ridiculous suggestion"; (vi) "it is simply not true"; (vii) "I've said it's not true"; and (viii) "there is simply no truth to that suggestion. And I have spoken with Karl about it."

In addition to Mr. McClellan's false statements, Mr. Rove also made direct misstatements to the public. Bsked on September 29, 2003 whether he had "any knowledge" of the leak or whether he leaked the name of the CIA agent, Rove answered, "No."[742]

There is also clear evidence that Vice President Cheney "misspoke" on national television when he denied any knowledge of who sent Mr. Wilson to Niger. On a September 14, 2003 appearance on *Meet the Press*, Cheney said: "I don't know Joe Wilson . . . [and have] no idea who hired him."[743] In point of fact, as the Libby Indictment reveals, "on or about June 12, 2003, Libby was advised by the Vice President of the United States that Wilson's wife worked at the Central Intelligence Agency in the Counterproliferation Division. Libby understood that the Vice President had learned this information from the CIA."[744] This clearly contradicts Cheney's statement on *Meet the Press*.

The President himself appears to have misled the American people regarding this cover-up when, among other things, he revoked his pledge to dismiss any and all leakers from his Administration. On September 30, 2003, when President Bush was asked about the matter and Rove's involvement in it, the President flatly declared: "Listen, I know of nobody—I don't know of anybody in my administration who leaked classified information. . . . If somebody did leak classified information, I'd like to know it, and we'll take the appropriate action. And this investigation is a good thing."[745]

The President was even more definitive on June 10, 2004, in the middle of his re-election campaign:

**Q.** Do you stand by your pledge to fire anyone found to have done so?

**THE PRESIDENT:** Yes.[746]

Despite these promises, on July 18, 2005, as it became increasingly clear that senior White House officials played a role in the leak, the President made it far less likely that the leakers would be subject to administrative discipline. At a press conference with the Prime Minister of India, President Bush stated, "If someone committed a crime, they will no longer work in my administration,"[747] a stunningly low threshold for ethics.[748]

# ■ Other Instances of Bush Administration Retribution Against its Critics

*"The White House press office is under new management and has become slightly more aggressive about contacting reporters."*[749]

—JULY 16, 2003, CONSERVATIVE BLOGGER MATT DRUDGE, DESCRIBING HOW THE BUSH ADMINISTRATION GAVE HIM INFORMATION IN ORDER TO OUT A REPORTER AS GAY WHO HAD INTERVIEWED UNITED STATES TROOPS FRUSTRATED WITH THE IRAQ WAR

Beyond the "sliming" of Ambassador Wilson, the Bush Administration appears to have engaged in a coordinated assault against numerous individuals and institutions that dared to challenge the Administration's assertions and conclusions about the Iraq war. These attacks were an apparent effort to both silence honest whistleblowers and shift focus away from the root of the problem—the Administration's wrongdoing.[750]

The list of persons who have suffered this fate is long, ranging from former General Shinseki, who was "sidelined for questioning the administration's projections about needed troop strength in Iraq"[751] to Jeffrey Kofman for reporting about frustrated soldiers in Iraq to a CIA analyst named "Jerry" for ascertaining the truth about "Curveball."

## Former General Eric Shinseki and Others in the Military

Former General Eric Shinseki, Chief of Staff of the United States Army, was punished and undermined for contradicting Donald Rumsfeld's pre-war assessment of troop needs in Iraq. In February 2003, **Shinseki presciently testified before the Senate Armed Services Committee that the Defense Department's troop estimate for occupying Iraq was too low and that "something on the order of several hundred thousand soldiers" would be needed.**[752] He further stated, "We're talking about post-hostilities control over a piece of geography that's fairly significant, with the kinds of ethnic tensions that could lead to other problems."[753] He continued: "It takes a significant ground force presence to maintain a safe and secure environment, to ensure that people are fed, that water is distributed, all the normal responsibilities that go along with administering a situation like this."[754]

This, however, was very different from what the Defense Department had been telling Congress and the American public, as it had put the figure for occupation troop needs closer to 100,000 troops. Deputy Defense Secretary Paul Wolfowitz called Shinseki's estimate "wildly off the mark" and said "I am reasonably certain that U.S. troops will greet us as liberators, and that will help us to keep requirements down."[755] Later, Defense Secretary Rumsfeld echoed these remarks, stating that "[t]he idea that it would take several hundred thousand U.S. forces, I think, is far off the mark."[756] It was also reported that in a semi-private meeting, the Pentagon's civilian leadership told the *Village Voice* that General Shinseki's remark was "bullshit from a Clintonite enamored of using the army for peacekeeping and not winning wars."[757]

General Shinseki refused to back down from his honest—and ultimately correct—estimate. A spokesman for the General, Col. Joe Curtin, stated, "He was asked a question and he responded with his best military judgment."[758] And, in another congressional hearing, General Shinseki stated that the number "could be as high as several hundred thousand. . . . We all hope it is something less."[759]

In the end, General Shinseki's comments, and his willingness to say them publicly, cost him his job worth and status. In revenge for his comments, Defense Department officials leaked the name of Shinseki's replacement 14 months before his retirement, rendering him a lame duck commander and "embarrassing and neutralizing the Army's top officer."[760] As one person who engaged in high-level planning for both wars said, "There was absolutely no debate in the normal sense. There are only six or eight of them who make the decisions, and they only talk to each other. And if you disagree with them in public, they'll come after you, the way they did with Shinseki."[761] Shinseki "dared to say publicly that several hundred thousand troops would be needed to occupy Iraq [and] was ridiculed by the administration and his career was brought to a close."[762] Another reporter noted that "[t]his administration has a history of undermining people who raise questions. . . . Army Chief of Staff Gen. Eric Shinseki was publicly humiliated for suggesting it would take hundreds of thousands of troops to secure a post-Saddam Iraq."[763]

A situation similar to that of General Shinseki was the retaliation against Major General John Riggs. Major General Riggs gave an interview with *The Baltimore Sun* saying the army needed at least another 10,000 soldiers because it was being stretched too thin between Iraq and Afghanistan.[764] General George W. Casey subsequently told Riggs to "stay in your lane" and not discuss the troops.[765] Riggs retired and was denied his full rank, officially for "minor infractions."[766] A retired Army Lieutenant General, Jay M. Garner, a one-time Pentagon advisor who ran reconstruction efforts in Iraq in 2003, commented that when Riggs made his comment about being overstretched in Iraq, the Administration "went bats . . . . The military part of [the defense secretary's office] has been politicized. If [officers] disagree, they are ostracized and their reputations are ruined."[767]

Another victim of the Administration's attacks was Army Spc. Thomas Wilson, a 31-year-old member of a Tennessee National Guard unit. After asking Donald Rumsfeld why vehicle armor was still scarce nearly two years after the start of the war, Mr. Wilson was trashed as an insubordinate plant of the "liberal media."[768]

## Former Secretary of Treasury Paul O'Neill and Economic Advisor Lawrence Lindsey

Former Secretary of the Treasury Paul O'Neill was punished twice by the Administration, once for opposing Bush's tax policy, for which he was forced to resign in January 2003,[769] and later for providing a first hand account of the Administration's decision-making process in the lead up to the Iraq war. In "The Price of Loyalty," written by former *Wall Street Journal* reporter Ron Suskind, O'Neill recounts how the Administration was discussing plans for going to war in Iraq in the earliest days of Bush's presidency, well before the September 11 attacks. He stated that Iraq was discussed at the first National Security Council meeting after Bush was inaugurated in January 2001. "From the very beginning, there was a conviction that Saddam Hussein was a bad person and that he needed to go," O'Neill told *60 Minutes*.[770] The only task was "finding a way to do it."[771] He also stated that he never saw any credible intelligence indicating that Saddam Hussein had weapons of mass destruction.[772]

Before the book was published, Donald Rumsfeld called Secretary O'Neill and tried to persuade his longtime friend not to go through with the project. Rumsfeld labeled it a "sour grapes" book.[773] But when Mr. O'Neill went through with the book, the Administration sought to discredit him by launching an investigation into his use of classified documents and whether he shared them with *60 Minutes* in his interviews.[774] As Paul Krugman of the *New York Times* points out, the Administration "opened an investigation into how a picture of a possibly classified document appeared during Mr. O'Neill's TV interview.[775]

The investigation did not uncover any improprieties.[776] The Treasury Department's inspector general reported that although O'Neill received the classified material after his resignation, the lapse was the fault of the department, not O'Neill.[777] It is noteworthy now sharply this contrasted with an evident lack of concern when a senior administration official, still unknown, blew the cover of a C.I.A. operative because her husband had revealed some politically inconvenient facts."[778]

The Administration also sought to minimize O'Neill's role as a high-level official and painted him to be completely out of step with reality. As one writer observed, "O'Neill's revelations have not been met by any factual rebuttal. Instead, they have been greeted with anonymous character assassination from a 'senior official': 'Nobody listened to him when he was in office. Why should anybody now?'"[779]

Press Secretary Scott McClellan said "We appreciate his service, but we are not in the business of doing book reviews. . . . It appears that the world according to Mr. O'Neill is more about trying to justify his own opinion than looking at the reality of the results we are achieving on behalf of the American people."[780] Another senior Administration official stated, "The Treasury Secretary is not in the position to have access to that kind of information, where he can make observations of that nature. . . This is a headscratcher."[781]

The Administration also went after former senior White House economic advisor Larry Lindsey. Mr. Lindsey angered the White House in September 2002 when he made a prescient prediction that a war with Iraq would cost between $100 billion and $200 billion, an estimate Administration officials at the time insisted was too high. In December 2002, the White House requested that Lindsey resign from his post.[782] Lindsey's estimate, of course, has proved to be on the far low side.[783] As Frank Rich wrote, "Lawrence Lindsey, the president's chief economic advisor, was pushed out after he accurately projected the cost of the Iraq war."[784]

## Richard Clarke

The Administration personally attacked Richard Clarke, the former counterterrorism czar, for publishing a book in which he recounted how the Bush Administration was fixated on invading Iraq. Clarke's book, *Against All Enemies: Inside the White House's War on Terror,* was published in March of 2004. Clarke, who worked for both Democratic and Republican administrations and helped shape U.S. policy on terrorism under President Reagan and the first President Bush as well as President Clinton, suggests in his book that President Bush was overly fixated on Saddam Hussein and Iraq. As a result, the President let down his guard on Al Qaeda. Clarke stated that Bush's top aides wanted to use the terrorist attacks of September 11 as an excuse to remove Saddam from power.[785] In an interview with CBS, Clarke recalled: "Rumsfeld was saying we needed to bomb Iraq. . . We all said, 'But no, no, Al Qaeda is in Afghanistan.'"[786] Rumsfeld responded: "There aren't any good targets in Afghanistan. And there are lots of good targets in Iraq."[787]

Clarke also stated that his team substantively examined whether there was a connection between Iraq and the September 11 attacks. "We got together all the FBI experts, all the C.I.A. experts. We wrote the report. We sent the report out to C.I.A. and found FBI and said, 'Will you sign this report?' They all cleared the report. And we sent it up to the president and it got bounced by the National Security Advisory or Deputy. It got bounced and sent back saying, 'Wrong answer. . . . Do it again.'"[788]

Because of these revealing accounts, the Bush Administration went into attack mode in an attempt to discredit and smear Clarke. Dan Bartlett, White House communications director, dismissed Clarke's accounts as "politically motivated," "reckless," and "baseless."[789] Scott McClellan, President Bush's spokesman, portrayed Clarke as a disgruntled former employee: "Mr. Clarke has been out there talking about what title he had . . . He wanted to be the deputy secretary of the Homeland Security Department after it was created. The fact of the matter is, just a few months after that, he left the administration. He did not get that position. Someone else was appointed."[790] National Security Advisor Condoleezza Rice alleged that: "Dick Clarke just does not know what he is talking about. He wasn't involved in most of the meetings of the Administration."[791] Vice President Cheney stated that Clarke "wasn't in the loop, frankly, on a lot of this stuff . . . It was as though he clearly missed a lot of what was going on."[792] Even Republican Majority Leader Bill Frist went after Clarke, saying "[i]n his appearance before the 9-11 commission, Mr. Clarke's theatrical apology on behalf of the nation was not his right, his privilege or his responsibility. In my view it was not an act of humility, but an act of supreme arrogance and manipulation."[793]

The Bush Administration's smear campaign against Clarke was widely discussed. As Joe Conason, a political commentator and journalist, stated, "[A]dministration officials **have been bombarding him with personal calumny and abuse. They have called him an embittered job-seeker, a publicity-seeking author, a fabricator, a Democratic partisan** and, perhaps worst of all, a friend of a friend of John Kerry."[794] Sidney Blumenthal noted, "The controversy raging around Clarke's book—and his testimony before the 9-11 commission that Bush ignored warnings about terrorism that might have prevented the attacks—revolves around his singularly unimpeachable credibility. In response, the Bush Administration has launched a full-scale offensive against him: impugning his personal motives, claiming he is a disappointed job-hunter, that he is publicity mad, a political partisan . . . as well as ignorant, irrelevant and a liar."[795] The Administration's attacks were seriously questioned by those who were aware of Clarke's qualifications. One journalist described the White House's attacks as "desperate" because "for the first time since the September 11 attacks, Bush's greatest accomplishments have been credibly recast as his greatest failures."[796]

## Cindy Sheehan

Cindy Sheehan, founder of Gold Star Families for Peace, is the mother of Casey Sheehan, a church group leader and honor roll student who enlisted in 2000 before the September 11 attacks. At the age of 24, on April 4, 2004, Casey died in a rescue mission with six other soldiers in Sadr City. This was almost a year from the date President Bush declared "mission accomplished" in Iraq and announced the end of major combat operations.

After the death of her son, Ms. Sheehan became an active leader and participant in protesting the Iraq war. On August 6, 2005, Ms. Sheehan set up camp at President Bush's ranch in Crawford, Texas, asserting that she would remain there until the President agreed to meet with her to discuss the war.[797]

Instead of meeting with Sheehan,[798] the Administration and other conservative media outlets began to attack Sheehan. Columnist Maureen Dowd noted that the "Bush team tried to discredit 'Mom' by pointing reporters to an old article in which she sounded kinder to W. If only her husband were an undercover C.I.A. operative, the Bushies could out him. But even if they send out a squad of Swift Boat Moms for Truth, there will be a countering Falluja Moms for Truth."[799]

The attacks continued as Fred Barnes of Fox News labeled Sheehan a "crackpot."[800] Conservative blogs then started talking about Sheehan's divorce. "The right-wing blogosphere quickly spread tales of her divorce, her angry Republican in-laws, her supposed political flip-flops, her incendiary sloganeering and her association with known ticket-stub-carrying attendees of 'Fahrenheit 9-11.' Rush Limbaugh went so far as to declare that Ms. Sheehan's 'story is nothing more than forged documents—there's nothing about it that's real.'"[801]

The President also joined in on the attack by criticizing Sheehan as unrepresentative of most military families he meets. He labeled anti-war protestors as dangerous isolationists and stated that they advocated policies that would embolden terrorists. "An immediate withdrawal of our troops in Iraq or the broader Middle East, as some have called for, would only embolden the terrorists and create a staging ground to launch more attacks against America and free nations," he told an audience mostly made up of Idaho National Guard members.[802]

Commenting on these typical administration smear tactics, journalist Ahmed Amr wrote the following:

> **Karl Rove has let the dogs out. A vicious campaign to maul Citizen Sheehan is in play.** Instead of answering her questions—the right wing media hacks are focusing on her motives, her mental health, her ideology and her family. These are standard and classic Rovian tactics used to smear administration critics. The predictable pundits at FOX have taken the lead by portraying Sheehan as a treasonous "crackpot" who is exploiting the death of her son to gain fame and fortune and advance the extremist political agenda of leftist "anti-American" groups. Hate radio stations across the nations are assailing Cindy's integrity and questioning her patriotism.[803]

## Jeffrey Kofman

Jeffrey Kofman, an ABC reporter, was "outed" by the Administration after giving voice to frustrated soldiers in Iraq. On July 15, 2003, one week after Donald Rumsfeld told certain troops they would be going home, Kofman covered a story in which American soldiers in Falluja described low morale in Iraq and spoke angrily of how their tour of duty had been extended yet again.[804] Kofman interviewed several troops who criticized President Bush and Donald Rumsfeld on camera, including Spc. Clinton Deitz, who said, "If Donald Rumsfeld was here, I'd ask him for his resignation."[805] The story was broadcast on ABC News *World Report*, a nightly newscast anchored by Peter Jennings.[806] It was repeated on *Good Morning America* the next day.[807]

The White House retaliated, using Matt Drudge and his Drudge Report website as the vehicle. Drudge's website contained the headline: "ABC News Reporter Who Filed Troops Complaint Story—Openly Gay Canadian."[808] When asked about the story, **Drudge pointed to the White House as his source, telling Lloyd Grove of the** *Washington Post* **that "someone from the White House communications shop" had given him the information.**[809] **Drudge was also reported as saying, "The White House press office is under new management and has become slightly more aggressive about contacting reporters."**[810]

It had become standard Administration practice to discredit the messenger rather than refute the message. As columnist Frank Rich aptly stated, "The 'outing' of Mr. Kofman (who turned out to be openly gay) almost simultaneously with the outing of Ms. Plame points to a pervasive culture of revenge in the White House and offers a clue as to who might be driving it. Joshua Green reported in detail in the *Atlantic Monthly* last year, a recurring feature of Mr. Rove's political campaigns throughout his career has been the questioning of an 'opponent's sexual orientation.'"[811]

## International Organizations: The Organization for the Prohibition of Chemical Weapons and the IAEA

Jose Bustani, a Brazilian diplomat and former director of the Organization for the Prohibition of Chemical Weapons (OPCW), which oversees the destruction of two million chemical weapons and two-thirds of the world's chemical weapon facilities, was attacked and ultimately ousted by the Bush Administration for failing to cooperate with the Administration's decision to attack Iraq. Bustani began serving as director of OPCW in 1997 and was reelected to the position of Director-General in May 2000 for the 2001-2005 term by a unanimous vote.[812]

In early 2001, Bustani sought to convince Saddam Hussein to sign the chemical weapons convention, hoping that he would eventually be able to send chemical weapons inspectors to Baghdad. It was perceived by some in the Bush Administration that sending weapons inspectors to Iraq "might have helped defuse the crisis over alleged Iraqi weapons and undermined a U.S. rationale for war."[813] Consequently, Undersecretary of State John Bolton and other Administration officials grew increasingly irritated with Bustani for his attempts to send inspectors to Iraq. According **to Bustani himself, he received a "menacing" phone call from John Bolton in June 2001.**[814] He elaborated in an interview with the French newspaper *Le Monde* in mid-2002, saying Bolton "tried to order me around," and sought to have some U.S. inspection results overlooked and certain Americans hired to OPCW positions.[815]

When Bustani refused, Bolton apparently led a campaign to have him fired and based the campaign on Bustani purported "mismanagement" of the agency. **But as one Bolton aide explicitly stated, Jose Bustani "had to go" because he was trying to send chemical weapons inspectors to Baghdad.**[816] A former Bustani aide also noted that Bolton sought Bustani's removal not because of mismanagement, for which Bolton offered no evidence, but because Bustani wanted to avoid war. As **OPCW official Bob Rigg told the Associated Press: "Why did they not want OPCW involved in Iraq? They felt they couldn't rely on OPCW to come up with the findings the U.S. wanted."**[817]

The Bush Administration went public with its campaign in March 2002, moving to terminate Bustani's tenure. On the eve of an OPCW Executive Council meeting to consider the dismissal, Bolton personally met Bustani in The Hague to seek his resignation. When Bustani refused, according to Bustani, **"Bolton said something like, 'Now we'll do it the other way,' and walked out,"** OPCW official Bob Rigg recounted.[818] In the Executive Council, the Bush Administration failed to win majority support among the 41 nations. In light of this failure, the Administration became more aggressive in its approach, sending envoys to the member-states of the OPCW to secure votes for his dismissal. **The Administration reportedly began a smear campaign against Bustani, accusing him of** "financial mismanagement," "demoralization of his staff," "bias," and "ill-reputation."[819]

The Bush Administration also called an unusual, special session of the OPCW member states in April 2002. Addressing the delegates, Bustani pleaded that the conference must decide whether genuine multilateralism "will be replaced by unilateralism in a multilateral disguise."[820] To strongarm the member nations, the U.S. delegation suggested it would withhold U.S. dues—22 percent of the budget—if Bustani stayed in office, stirring fears of an OPCW collapse.[821] With less than one-third of the member nations voting, the Bush Administration got its way and Bustani was let go. However, in a stern rebuke to the Administration, the United Nations' highest administrative tribunal in July 2003 declared that the Bush Administration's allegations were "extremely vague" and the dismissal was "unlawful." It stated that international civil servants must not be made "vulnerable to pressures and to political change."[822]

The Bush Administration also sought to undermine the IAEA and its Director-General. After Jacques Baute, the head of the IAEA's Iraq inspections unit, determined that the Niger documents were fraudulent and IAEA Director-General Mohammed ElBaradei delivered Baute's conclusions to the Security Council, Vice President Cheney publicly assaulted the credibility of the organization and ElBaradei. Vice President Cheney stated on *Meet the Press*: "I think Mr. ElBaradei frankly is wrong . . . I think, if you look at the track record of the [IAEA] and this kind of issue, especially where Iraq's concerned, they have consistently underestimated or missed what it was Saddam Hussein was doing. I don't have any reason to believe they're any more valid this time than they've been in the past.'"[823]

Beginning in late 2004, the White House made a push to oust El Baradei from the agency. The Administration's retaliation campaign included a complete halt of intelligence-sharing with the agency, recruitment of potential replacements and eavesdropping on his calls in search of ammunition to use against ElBaradei and the IAEA.[824] As the *New York Times* noted, "**Tensions [between the United States and the IAEA] were so sharp that agency officials said they suspected their phones, including Dr. ElBaradei's, were being wiretapped by American intelligence agencies.**"[825] Further:

> For most of the last year (2004), the Bush Administration had tried to block Dr. ElBaradei from assuming a third term as chief of the agency, a part of the United Nations . . . **The roots of the disagreement stretch back beore the invasion of Iraq, when Dr. ElBaradei was openly skeptical of the Bush Administration's accusations that Saddam Hussein had rebuilt a nuclear program. No weapons of mass destruction have since been found in Iraq.**[826]

Mohamed ElBaradei and the IAEA were easily vindicated by the international community and ElBaradei recently won the 2005 Nobel Peace Prize for his longstanding efforts.[827]

## Bunnatine Greenhouse

Bunnatine Greenhouse was the chief contracting officer at the Army Corps of Engineers, the agency that has managed much of the reconstruction work in Iraq. In October 2004,

Ms. Greenhouse came forward and revealed that top Pentagon officials showed improper favoritism to Halliburton when awarding military contracts to Halliburton subsidiary Kellogg Brown & Root (KBR).[828] Greenhouse stated that when the Pentagon awarded Halliburton a five-year, $7 billion contract, it pressured her to withdraw her objections, actions which she claimed were unprecedented in her experience.[829]

On June 27, 2005, Ms. Greenhouse testified before Congress, detailing that the contract award process was compromised by improper influence by political appointees, participation by Halliburton officials in meetings where bidding requirements were discussed, and a lack of competition.[830] She stated that the Halliburton contracts represented "the most blatant and improper contract abuse I have witnessed during the course of my professional career."[831] Days before the hearing, the acting general counsel of the Army Corps of Engineers paid Ms. Greenhouse a visit and reportedly let it be known that it would not be in her best interest to appear voluntarily.[832]

On August 27, 2005, the Army demoted Ms. Greenhouse, removing her from the elite Senior Executive Service and transferring her to a lesser job in the corps' civil works division.[833] As Frank Rich of the *New York Times* described the situation, "her crime was not obstructing justice but pursuing it by vehemently questioning irregularities in the awarding of some $7 billion worth of no-bid contracts in Iraq to the Halliburton subsidiary Kellogg Brown & Root."[834] The demotion was in apparent retaliation for her speaking out against the abuses, even though she previously had stellar reviews and over 20 years of experience in military procurement. "They went after her to destroy her," said Michael Kohn, her attorney, who added that the demotion was "absolutely" in retaliation for her complaints about the Halliburton contract.[835]

## The Central Intelligence Agency and Its Employees

The Bush Administration also appears to have undermined and used the CIA and its analysts as a scapegoat for its own failings. In the article *The Secret Way to War*, Mark Danner describes the Administration's approach: "[Administration] officials now explain their misjudgments in going to war by blaming them on 'intelligence failures'—that is, on the intelligence that they themselves politicized."[836]

Among other things, the White House blamed the CIA and George Tenet for the Niger reference in the State of the Union address after the CIA had sought to modify, if not delete, the reference. "Condoleezza Rice, the national-security advisor, told a television interviewer on July 13th, 'Had there been even a peep that the agency did not want that sentence in or that George Tenet did not want that sentence . . . it would have been gone.'"[837] E.J. Dionne wrote:

> After Tenet's hedged statement about the Niger affair, whatever trust remained between the White house and C.I.A. seemed to dissolve. **Then-national security advisor Condoleezza Rice blasted Tenet personally, and the White House escalated its criticisms of the C.I.A.'s intelligence failure. Tenet was gone by early 2004.**[838]

The CIA was also undermined when it resisted immediate endorsement of the Administration's theories about Iraq.[839] When the CIA did not fall in line with the Administration's assessment of a link between Iraq and Al Qaeda, "administration officials began a campaign to pressure the agency to toe the line. Perle and other members of the Defense Policy Board, who acted as quasi-independent surrogates for Wolfowitz, Cheney, and other administration advocates for war in Iraq, harshly criticized the C.I.A. in the press. The C.I.A.'s analysis of Iraq, Perle said, 'isn't worth the paper it is written on.'"[840] In addition, the Pentagon created a special intelligence operation to offer alternative intelligence analyses to the CIA.[841] Secretary Rumsfeld began "publicly discussing the creation of a new Pentagon position, an undersecretary for intelligence, who would rival the C.I.A. director and diminish the authority of the agency."[842]

**In addition, when Porter Goss replaced George Tenet as Director of the CIA, he began what one recently retired CIA official called a "political purge" of analysts in the CIA's Directorate of Intelligence.**[843] Several senior analysts who wrote dissenting papers were among those purged. One former CIA official said, "The White House carefully reviewed the political analyses of the DI so they could sort out the apostates from the true believers."[844]

We also have received information of Bush Administration retaliation against two CIA officials who sought to provide accurate information regarding the Administration's inappropriate reliance on the Iraqi defector known as "Curveball"[845] and his alleged statements regarding mobile chemical weapons laboratories. The first is "Jerry," who led a CIA unit that went to Iraq and found Curveball's claims to be blatantly false and misleading. After he did so, he was chastised and transferred. According to the *Los Angeles Times*:

> Back home . . . Jerry was "read the riot act" and accused of "making waves" by his office director, according to the presidential commission. **He and his colleague ultimately were transferred out of the weapons center.** The C.I.A. was "very, very vindictive," Kay said. Soon after, Jerry got in touch with Michael Scheuer . . . "Jerry had become kind of a nonperson," Scheuer recalled of their meeting. "There was a tremendous amount of pressure on him not to say anything. Just to sit there and shut up."[846]

A CIA spokeswoman confirmed the account but declined to comment further. Jerry still works at the CIA and could not be contacted for this report. His former supervisor, reached at home, said she could not speak to the media. "What was done to them was wrong," said a former Pentagon official who investigated the case for the presidential commission.[847]

Another victim was David Kay, head of the Iraq Survey Group, which found the Bush Administration's WMD claims to be inaccurate, including its reliance on Curveball:

> In December 2003, Kay flew back to C.I.A. headquarters. **He said he told Tenet that Curveball was a liar and he was convinced Iraq had no mobile labs or other illicit weapons. C.I.A. officials confirm their exchange. Kay said he was assigned to a window-**

less office without a working telephone. On Jan. 20, 2004, Bush lauded Kay and the Iraq Survey Group in his State of the Union Speech for finding "weapons of mass destruction-related program activities. . . . Had we failed to act, the dictator's weapons of mass destruction program would continue to this day." Kay quit three days later and went public with his concerns.[848]

Finally, others in the CIA have suffered retaliation for criticizing the Administration or calling into question the validity or wisdom of the war. For example, in spring 2001, "an informant told the CIA that Iraq had abandoned a major element of its nuclear weapons program."[849] However, according to a CIA officer, the agency did not share the information with other agencies or with senior policy makers.[850] The officer, an employee for the agency for more than 20 years, including several years in intelligence related to illicit weapons, was fired in 2004.[851] In his lawsuit, the officer states that his dismissal was punishment for his reports questioning the agency's assumptions on a series of weapons-related matters and with the agency's intelligence conclusions.[852]

# ■ Ongoing Lies, Deceptions and Manipulations

Another means by which the Bush Administration has sought to cover up and obscure its initial misstatements about the Iraq war is through additional and ongoing misinformation and manipulation concerning the status of the war,[853] including the efficacy of the occupation, the costs of the war to our nation, and the war's impact on terrorism.

The Bush Administration has even sought to alter its justification for the war after the fact, and to assert that weapons of mass destruction have been found in Iraq.

## Efficacy of the Occupation

From the very outset, the Bush Administration sought to convince the American public that the Iraq occupation would be an unmitigated success. Most famously, on May 1, 2003, President Bush landed aboard the USS Abraham Lincoln, and standing beneath a massive banner reading "**Mission Accomplished**," declared, "**In the battle of Iraq, the United States and our allies have prevailed,**" and "**major combat operations in Iraq have ended.**"[854]

In addition, the Bush Administration has consistently underestimated the size, intensity, and strength of the Iraqi insurgency, and overestimated the abilities of the Iraqis to defend themselves. Thus, for example, on June 18, 2003, when asked at a Pentagon press conference about the Iraqi resistance, Defense Secretary Rumsfeld described it as "small elements" of 10 to 20 people, not large military formations or networks of attackers, and observed that "in those regions where pockets of dead-enders are trying to reconstitute, Gen. [Tommy] Franks and his team are rooting them out. In short, the coalition is making good progress."[855] More than two years later, on June 20, 2005, Vice President Cheney stated, in a CNN interview, "**The level of activity that we see today from a mil-**

itary standpoint, I think, will clearly decline. I think they're in the last throes, if you will, of the insurgency."[856]

With regard to Iraqi troop capabilities, on March 14, 2004, Donald Rumsfeld stated: "We're making very good progress with respect to the Iraqi security forces. We're up to over 200,000 Iraqis that have been trained and equipped, and are deployed and out providing security . . . [t]he essential service work is going forward, and so, too, the governance."[857] As recently as October 4, 2005, the President emphasized progress in Iraqi troop preparation and claimed there were about "**30 Iraqi battalions in the lead.**"[858]

The reality is far different. On June 1, 2003, former Army Secretary James White said defense officials are "unwilling to come to grips" with the scale of U.S. involvement in Iraq.[859] "This is not what they were selling [before the war] . . . It's almost a question of people not wanting to 'fess up' to the notion that we will be there a long time and they might have to set up a rotation and sustain it for the long term."[860] Former military officials have acknowledged their growing frustration with a war that they feel was not properly planned by the Bush Administration. General Anthony Zinni, now retired, has said:

> There has been poor strategic thinking in this . . . [t]here has been poor operational plan-
> ning and execution on the ground. And to think that we are going to "stay the course,"
> the course is headed over Niagara Falls. **I think it's time to change course a bit, or at least
> hold somebody responsible for putting you on this course. Because it's been a failure.**[861]

A recently retired four-star general admitted that "[W]e're good at fighting armies, but we don't know how to do this. We don't have enough intelligence analysts working on this problem."[862]

As for the number of combat-ready Iraqi troops, less than a week before the President's speech stating there were 30 Iraqi battalions, **his own commanders testified that the number of Iraqi battalions capable of fighting unaided had dropped from 3 to 1**.[863] Moreover, according to the *New York Times*, a recently "declassified Pentagon assessment" explained that "half of Iraq's new police battalions are still being established and cannot conduct operations, while the other half of the police units and two-thirds of the new army battalions are only 'partially capable' of carrying out counterinsurgency missions, and only with American help. . . . Only 'a small number' of Iraqi security forces are capable of fighting the insurgency without American assistance, while about one-third of the army is capable of 'planning, executing and sustaining counterinsurgency operations' with allied support."[864]

The Bush Administration has even gone so far as to repeatedly take credit for killing or capturing al-Zarqawi's second in command when, in reality, "New York's *Daily News* would quickly report, the man in question 'may not even be one of the top 10 or 15 leaders.' By one analysis, 33 so-called 'top lieutenants' of Abu Musab al-Zarqawi who have been captured, killed or identified in the past two and a half years, with no deterrent effect on terrorist violence in Iraq, Madrid or London."[865]

The Bush Administration has also repeatedly taken to highlighting turning points in the occupation, which unfortunately has never proved true. "We have long since lost count of all the historic turning points and fast-evaporating victories hyped by this president. The toppling of Saddam's statue, 'Mission Accomplished,' the transfer of sovereignty and the purple fingers all blur into a hallucinatory loop of delusion. One such red-letter day, some may dimly recall, was the adoption of the previous, interim constitution in March 2004, also proclaimed a 'historic milestone' by Mr. Bush. Within a month after that fabulous victory, the insurgency boiled over into the war we have today, taking, among many others, the life of Casey Sheehan."[866]

At the same time, the Bush Administration has over-promised the extent and benefits of Iraqi reconstruction. For example, in 2003, the Bush Administration asked Congress to appropriate over $20 billion for Iraqi reconstruction efforts and promised the funds would be used to restore oil production to pre-war levels, increase electricity production substantially above pre-war levels, and provide drinking water to 90% of Iraqis.[867]

Again, the reality has proven starkly different. Representative Waxman has found that "[o]il production remains below pre-war levels, electricity production is unreliable and well below the goal of 6,000 megawatts of peak electricity output, and a third of Iraqis still lack access to potable water. Billions of taxpayer dollars have been spent, but there is little to show for the expenditures in Iraq."[868]

An analysis by *USA Today*, based in part on an Office of Special Inspector General for Iraq Reconstruction Report, also found rampant waste, fraud and diversion of reconstruction funds:

> Congress appropriated $18.4 billion for Iraq reconstruction in November 2003, but last year nearly $5 billion of it was diverted to help train and equip Iraq's security forces as the Insurgency grew in strength. . . . **And the security costs keep increasing. Originally estimated at 9% of total project costs, security costs have risen to between 20% and 30%, says Brig. Gen. William McCoy Jr., commander of the Army Corps of Engineers in Iraq. . . . Rebuilding it has proved tougher than first envisioned. Nearly half of all of Iraqi households still don't have access to clean water, and only 8% of the country, excluding the capital, is connected to sewage networks. . . . Besides escalating security costs, reconstruction also has been dogged by allegations of fraud and mismanagement. Nearly $100 million in Iraqi funds distributed by the Coalition Provisional Authority for reconstruction was either spent without supporting receipts or vanished.**[869]

In its headlong efforts to convince Americans of the occupation's success, the Bush Administration has taken several steps to insure that only positive stories come out of Iraq. Thus, on March 19, 2003, the Bush Administration issued a directive forbidding news coverage of "deceased military personnel returning to or departing from" air bases.[870] On the other hand, the Administration has recently opted to publicize insurgent death tolls. The *Washington Post* reported on October 24, 2005: "Eager to demonstrate success in Iraq, the U.S. military has abandoned its previous refusal to publicize enemy body counts and now cites such numbers periodically to show the impact of some counterinsurgency operations . . . a practice discredited during the Vietnam War."[871]

Also, on October 12, 2005, the Bush Administration went so far as to pre-stage and pre-script an event with ten American soldiers to tout the occupation's successes, including a soldier whose responsibility included public affairs and press.[872] According to press accounts, Allison Barber, Deputy Assistant to the Secretary of Defense for Internal Communication, could be heard asking one soldier before the start:

> [T]he president is going to ask you some questions. And he may ask all six of them, he may ask three of them, he might have such a great time talking to you, he might come up with some new questions . . . So what we want to be prepared for is to not, not stutter. **So if there's a question that the president comes up with that we haven't drilled through today, and I'm expecting the microphone to go right back to you, Captain Kennedy and you to handle.**[873]

On November 30, 2005, the *Los Angeles Times* first reported that the U.S. military was secretly paying Iraqi media outlets to run stories prepared by the Pentagon.[874] Under this program, described as "extensive, costly, and hidden,"[875] the DOD has paid the Lincoln Group some $100 million to place more than 1,000 articles in the Iraqi and Arab press. Concerning this program, a senior Pentagon official stated, "**Here we are trying to create the principles of democracy in Iraq. Every speech we give in that country is about democracy. And we're breaking all the first principles of democracy when we're doing it.**"[876] Colonel Jack N. Summe, the then-commander of the Fourth Psychological Operations Group, also admitted: "We call our stuff information and the enemy's propaganda. . . [even in the Pentagon] some public affairs professionals see us unfavorably as for propaganda. . . as lying, dirty tricksters."[877] (This was disclosed at the same time that Scott McClellan stated the U.S. is "a leader when it comes to promoting and advocating a free and independent media around the world."[878])

This Pentagon propaganda program has its roots in the Pentagon's "Office of Strategic Influence," formed in the Pentagon after the September 11 attacks, which was disbanded in February 2002 after it was planning "to provide news items, possibly even false ones, to foreign news organizations."[879] Later in 2002, **Secretary Rumsfeld told the media he gave them a "corpse" by closing the Office of Strategic Influence, but he intended to "keep doing every single thing that needs to be done."**[880]

As Mr. Rumsfeld predicted, the Pentagon has continued to engage these controversial foreign propaganda activities, outsourcing to groups such as the Lincoln Group,[881] the Rendon Group, and Ahmad Chalabi's INC Information Collection Program (which provided false information regarding Iraq's WMD Program).[882]

Beginning November 30, 2005, and continuing through the date of this report, President Bush has given a series of speeches outlining the plan to win the Iraq War. The speeches included several falsehoods and half truths. For example, Mr. Bush claimed Iraqi troops control major areas of Iraq, but this is true only if you include militias with no particular loyalty to the Iraqi government.[883] Mr. Bush also trumpeted the lead role of Iraqi battalions in fighting the insurgents, highlighting the claim that in Tal Afar "the assault was primarily led by Iraqi security forces—11 Iraqi battalions backed by 5 coalition battalions providing support." In reality, as *Time*'s Michael Ware, who was embedded with U.S. troops during the battle explained, "I was with Iraqi units right there on the front line as they were battling with Al Qaeda. They were not leading."[884] **Even the president's claim that the so-called "National Strategy for Victory in Iraq" that he released as a supposedly "declassified" version of the Administration's plan to win the war since its inception in 2003 proved false. In reality, as the *New York Times* found, the electronic version of the document was prepared by Peter Feaver, a Duke public opinion expert who has only been advising the National Security Council since June of 2005.**[885]

## Cost of the War and Occupation

The Bush Administration is also guilty of severely underestimating the costs of the war and occupation, in terms of lives expenditures, and in its impact on our armed forces. For example, in December 2002, administration officials estimated the cost of the war to be in the range of $50 to $60 billion.[886] In fact, in 2003, Deputy Defense Secretary Paul D. Wolfowitz said Iraq's oil revenues "could bring between $50 and $100 billion over the course of the next two or three years . . . [w]e're dealing with a country that can really finance its own reconstruction, and relatively soon," he told a House committee.[887]

In terms of financial costs, the reality goes well beyond the more than $277 billion already appropriated for the war.[888] When taking into account weapon replacement costs, veterans' benefits and deficit financing, one budget expert pegged the costs as $1 trillion.[889] Basic running costs of the current conflicts are $6 billion a month. Factors keeping costs high include almost exclusive reliance on expensive private contractors, costs for military personnel serving second and third deployments, extra pay for reservists and members of the National Guard, as well as more than $2 billion a year in additional foreign aid to reward cooperation in Iraq. The bill for repairing and replacing military hardware is $20 billion a year, according to figures from the Congressional Budget Office.[890] But the biggest long-term costs are disability and health payments for returning troops, which will be incurred even if hostilities were to stop tomorrow; these payments are likely to run at $7 billion a year for the next 45 years.[891]

## Ongoing Deceptions Regarding Weapons of Mass Destruction and the Decision to Go to War

The Bush Administration has also disseminated a series of confusing, if not outright deceptive, statements concerning why the nation went to war and the status of Iraq's weapons of mass destruction.

For example, on June 15, 2005, when asked about the veracity of the July 23, 2002 Downing Street Minutes, President Bush argued, "Nothing could be farther from the truth . . . Both of us didn't want to use our military. Nobody wants to commit military into combat. It's the last option."[892]

**As noted above, the President has refused to respond to a letter from Representative Conyers and 121 other Members of Congress, and more than 500,000 Americans, asking him to respond to the charges inherent in the Downing Street Minutes.**[893]

The Bush Administration also stubbornly insisted that there were weapons of mass destruction even though none were found in Iraq. On May 29, 2003, President Bush declared that "**we found the weapons of mass destruction,**"[894] **and on July 17, 2003, he repeated, "[W]e ended the threat from Saddam Hussein's weapons of mass destruction.**"[895] Similar misstatements were made by Secretary Powell, Secretary Rumsfeld and Vice President Cheney. For example, on March 30, 2003, just days after the invasion, Secretary Rumsfeld appeared on an ABC News segment and stated, "We know where [the WMDs] are.[896]

The truth, of course, is that no weapons of mass destruction have been found. The Iraq Survey Group has concluded that it was unlikely that chemical or biological stockpiles existed prior to the war. As Dr. David Kay testified: "I'm personally convinced that there were not large stockpiles of newly produced weapons of mass destruction. We don't find the people, the documents or the physical plants that you would expect to find if the production was going on."[897]

The Bush Administration also untruthfully claimed that there was no disagreement as to whether Iraq was attempting to reconstitute its nuclear weapons program or whether the President should include that claim in his 2003 State of the Union. For instance, on July 13, 2003, **Dr. Rice stated, "[H]ad there been even a peep that [the CIA] did not want that sentence in or that George Tenet did not want that sentence in, that the Director of Central Intelligence did not want it in, it would have been gone.**"[898] The CIA, however, sent two memoranda to the National Security Council, then headed by Dr. Rice, that warned the claim was specious.[899] Also, the State Department's Bureau of Intelligence and Research noted in the October 2002 National Intelligence Estimate that the claim was "highly dubious."[900]

The Bush Administration also sought to convince the American public that its rationale for war was the existence of weapons of mass destruction "programs," despite the fact that before the war the Administration was claiming the justification was links to the September 11 attacks and weapons of mass destruction. Thus, after he could no longer credibly assert that weapons of mass destruction were in Iraq, he claimed that had "we failed to act, the dictator's weapons of mass destruction programs would continue to this day."[901] Dick Cheney, in interviews with *USA Today* and the *Los Angeles Times*, perpetuated this bait and switch tactic—last year "weapons," this year "programs"—observing that "the jury's still out" on whether Iraq had WMD and that "I am a long way at this stage from concluding that somehow there was some fundamental flaw in our intelligence."[902]

The Bush Administration later sought to drop the weapons of mass destruction rationale entirely and substitute new justifications. As the *Washington Post* summarized, "As the search for weapons in Iraq continues without success, the Bush Administration has moved to emphasize a different rationale for the war against Saddam Hussein: using Iraq as the 'linchpin' to transform the Middle East and thereby reduce the terrorist threat to the United States. President Bush, who has stopped talking about Iraq's weapons, said . . . that 'the rise of a free and peaceful Iraq is critical to the stability of Middle East, and a stable Middle East is critical to the security of the American people.'"[903] Deputy Defense Secretary Wolfowitz, after a trip to Iraq, said flat out, "I'm not concerned about weapons of mass destruction . . . I'm concerned about getting Iraq on its feet. I didn't come [to Iraq] on a search for weapons of mass destruction."[904] On April 13, 2004, the President went so far as arguing that we need to stay in Iraq to insure that those who have already lost their lives there did not die in vain: "[O]ne of the things that's very important . . . is to never allow our youngsters to die in vain. And I made that pledge to their parents. Withdrawing from the battlefield of Iraq would be just that. And it's not going to happen under my watch."[905]

The Bush Administration's hurried—and incorrect—claims regarding alleged Iraqi mobile chemical weapons laboratories found in April and early May 2003 is illustrative. At that time, the CIA and DIA issued a report stating that the trailers were for making biological weapons and dismissed claims by senior Iraqi scientists that the trailers were used to make hydrogen for the weather balloons that were then used in artillery practice.[906] Although intelligence experts disputed the purpose of these trailers, senior administration officials, including Colin Powell, repeatedly asserted that the trailers were mobile biological weapons laboratories. On May 22, 2003, Secretary Powell said, "So far, we have found the biological weapons vans that I spoke about when I presented the case to the United Nations on the 5th of February, **and there is no doubt in our minds now that those vans were designed for only one purpose, and that was to make biological weapons.**"[907]

The reality is, in August 2003, the *New York Times* reported that a majority of engineers from the DIA concluded in June that the vehicles were likely used to chemically produce hydrogen for artillery weather balloons, as the Iraqis had claimed.[908] Their work had not been completed at the time of the CIA/DIA paper.

> [A] government official from a different agency said the issue of the trailers had prompted deep divisions within the Defense intelligence "agency. **The official said members of the engineering team had been angry that the agency issued the joint white paper with the CIA before their own work was completed.**[909]

The analysts of other agencies had also come to this conclusion. A former senior intelligence official reported that "only one of 15 intelligence analysts assembled from three agencies to discuss the issue in June endorsed the white paper conclusion."[910]

An official British investigation has also concluded that the trailers were not mobile germ warfare laboratories, but were actually for the production of hydrogen gas.[911] The Iraq Survey Group confirmed these accounts, according to Dr. Kay's January 28, 2004 testimony: "[T]he consensus opinion is that when you look at these two trailers, while [they] had capabilities in many areas, their actual intended use was not for the production of biological weapons."[912] Dr. Kay also explained that the trailers "were actually designed to produce hydrogen for weather balloons, or perhaps to produce rocket fuel."[913]

In their comprehensive investigation concerning chemical weapons claims in Iraq, the *Los Angeles Times* also found that many U.S. and foreign officials believed the Bush Administration's assertions regarding the two trucks were not well-founded: Bio-weapons experts in the intelligence community were sharply critical.[914] **A former senior official of the State Department's Bureau of Intelligence and Research called the unclassified report an unprecedented "rush to judgment."[915]** The DIA then ordered a classified review of the evidence. One of 15 analysts held to the initial finding that the trucks were built for germ warfare.[916] The sole believer was the CIA analyst who helped draft the original White Paper.[917] Hamish Killip, a former British army officer and biological weapons expert, flew to Baghdad in July 2003 as part of the Iraq Survey Group, the CIA-led Iraqi weapons hunt.[918] He inspected the truck trailers and was immediately skeptical:

> **"The equipment was singularly inappropriate" for biological weapons, he said. "We were in hysterics over this. You'd have better luck putting a couple of dust bins on the back of the truck and brewing it in there."[919]** The trucks were built to generate hydrogen, not germs, he said. But the CIA refused to back down. In March 2004, Killip quit, protesting that the CIA was covering up the truth. Rod Barton, an Australian intelligence officer and another bio-weapons expert, also quit over what he said was the CIA's refusal to admit error.[920]

The Bush Administration also continues to refuse to accept responsibility for false claims regarding aluminum tubes and links between Al Qaeda and Iraq. When the *New York Times* asked officials in the White House about false claims concerning the tubes, they offered two rationalizations: "First, they said they had relied on the repeated assurances of George J. Tenet, then the director of central intelligence, that the tubes were in fact for centrifuges. Second, they noted that the intelligence community, including the Energy Department, largely agreed that Mr. Hussein had revived his nuclear program."[921] The irony is that the Administration is now blaming the CIA for these falsehoods even though it was the Administration that pressured the CIA and cherry-picked information to reach these conclusions. Moreover, the claim that the Energy Department countenanced this propaganda is untenable, given that experts at the Department had thoroughly rebutted the aluminum tube claims. As one Energy Department advisor, Dr. Houston G. Wood III, stated, "I was really shocked in 2002 when I saw [the centrifuge claim] was still there . . . I thought it had been put to bed."[922]

As for the proposed meeting between Mohammed Atta and Iraqi intelligence, Vice

President Cheney refused to acknowledge his misstatements. **In June 2004, he stated that "we just don't know whether the meeting took place."**[923] Similarly, when Gloria Borger interviewed the Vice President on CNBC about his earlier claim, Mr. Cheney denied three times that he had ever said it had been **"pretty well confirmed,"**[924] even though he had used those precise words on *Meet the Press* on December 9, 2001.[925]

The President has also attempted to assert that notwithstanding the Administration's unique access to intelligence information, it was not alone in believing Iraq's weapons of mass destruction somehow justified preemptive war. This argument was proffered as early as February 17, 2004, when the President asserted: "My administration looked at the intelligence information, and we saw a danger. Members of Congress looked at the same intelligence, and they saw a danger. The United Nations Security Council looked at the intelligence, and it saw a danger."[926] And as recently as November 2005, while asserting he had been exonerated by the Robb-Silberman Commission and Senate Intelligence Committee, the President expanded the field of those who had believed Iraq had weapons of mass destruction to include both former President Clinton and foreign governments.[927]

The truth, however, is that the Administration has access to far greater information than Congress—including the President's daily brief—and Congress is totally reliant on the Administration for intelligence manipulation, much of which cannot be discussed. As for the charges about the Clinton Administration and foreign governments, the information provided to President Clinton regarding Iraq would have been several years out of date, while foreign governments not only had differing information, but this information was completely at odds with what the Bush Administration was saying. As the *New York Times* wrote,

> Mr. Clinton looked at the data and concluded that inspections and pressure were working—a view we now know was accurate. France, Russia, and Germany said war was not justified. Even Britain admitted later that there had been no evidence about Iraq, just new politics.[928]

As for the assertions of exoneration by independent reviews, the Senate Intelligence Committee has not yet conducted a review of pre-war intelligence information, while Judge Silberman wrote as follows when he issued his report: "Our executive order did not direct us to deal with the use of intelligence by policymakers, and all of us were agreed that that was not part of our inquiry."[929]

## Impact of the Iraq War on Terrorism

The Bush Administration has also attempted to convince the American public that the Iraq war has succeeded in bringing about a decline in terrorism. **On October 6, 2005, the President flatly rejected the idea that "extremism" had been "strengthened" by the ongoing U.S. war in Iraq,** taking strong issue with analysts who believe that Iraq has become a "melting pot for jihadists from around the world, a training group and an indoctrination center" for a new generation of terrorists, as the State Department's annual report on terrorism put it this year.[930]

Again, the reality is far different. As a matter of fact, there have been twice as many terrorist attacks outside Iraq in the three years after the September 11 tragedy than in the three years before.[931] Roger W. Cressey, formerly a White House counter-terrorism advisor under both President Bush and Clinton, has said, "**To say [the] Iraq [war] has not contributed to the rise of global Sunni extremism movement is delusional. We should have an honest discussion about what these unintended consequences of the Iraq war are and what do we do to counter them.**"[932] Retired Army General Lt. General William Odom has stated that the invasion of Iraq was the "greatest strategic disaster in the United States history" and that the war alienated America's Middle East allies, making it harder to prosecute a war against terrorists.[933]

# Thwarting Congress and the American Public: The Death of Accountability under the Bush Administration and the Republican-Controled Congress

Both the Bush Administration and the Republican-controlled Congress have made it difficult, if not impossible, for Democrats or the American people to obtain meaningful information or oversight concerning the various abuses and misuse of power described in this Report.

## ■ Determination to Go to War Without Congressional Authorization

*"The decline of oversight hearings on Capitol Hill reflects what many of the commentators called a loss of institutional pride in Congress. Majority Republicans see themselves first and foremost as members of the Bush team—and do not want to make trouble by asking hard questions."*
—SEPTEMBER 4, 2005, DAVID BRODER, THE *WASHINGTON POST*[934]

With regard to the charges that the Bush Administration made a decision to go to war well before seeking congressional authorization, the Administration and congressional Republicans have rejected or ignored every request to obtain information on this matter. This includes efforts to obtain information by letter, through hearings, and by way of Resolution of Inquiry.[935]

Numerous letter requests have been ignored by the Administration. For example, on May 5, 2005, Representative Conyers and 89 other Members wrote to the President asking him five questions:

1. Do you or anyone in your Administration dispute the accuracy of the leaked document?

2. Were arrangements being made, including the recruitment of allies, before you sought Congressional authorization [to] go to war? Did you or anyone in your Administration obtain Britain's commitment to invade prior to this time?

3. Was there an effort to create an ultimatum about weapons inspectors in order to help with the justification for the war as the minutes indicate?

4. At what point in time did you and Prime Minister Blair first agree it was necessary to invade Iraq?

5. Was there a coordinated effort with the U.S. intelligence community and/or British officials to "fix" the intelligence and facts around the policy as the leaked document states?[936]

To date, no response has been received.[937] In addition to the congressional letter, on June 16, 2005, more than 500,000 citizens joined in this request for information from the President, which Representative Conyers and several other Members hand-delivered to the White House. Again, there has been no response.

Also, on May 31, 2005, Representative Conyers wrote a letter to Secretary of Defense Rumsfeld requesting a response to reports that British and U.S. aircraft increased the rate of bombing Iraq in 2002 to provoke an excuse for war.[938] The Defense Department did respond to this letter, although it failed to answer the specific questions posed and thus provided no meaningful information.[939]

In addition, Democrats submitted a request for hearings to the various committees of jurisdiction to seek oversight of these serious charges. On June 30, 2005, 52 members formally requested that the House Committees on Judiciary, Armed Services, International Relations, and the Permanent Select Committee on Intelligence commence hearings on the Downing Street Minutes.[940] None of the committee chairs responded to this letter. Similarly, on June 22, 2005, Senator Kerry and other Senators urged the Senate Select Committee on Intelligence to investigate pre-war intelligence failures, noting that the "committee's efforts have taken on renewed urgency given recent revelations in the United Kingdom regarding the apparent minutes of a July 23, 2002, meeting between Prime Minister Tony Blair and his senior national security advisors."[941] In a convoluted response, Senator Pat Roberts indicated that "the opinions of a British government official as expressed in the 'Downing Street Memo' are not pertinent to the Committee's inquiry on Iraq."[942]

The Administration has also been elusive in response to Democratic attempts to obtain answers through the Freedom of Information Act. On June 30, 2005, Representative Conyers and 51 other members of Congress submitted several FOIA requests to the Administration, seeking any and all documents and materials concerning the Downing Street Minutes and the lead up to the Iraq war.[943] The Administration responded with delays and is seeking in excess of $100,000 to even process the request.[944]

Democrats have also proposed seeking information via a non-binding request for information known as a "Resolution of Inquiry." Congresswoman Barbara Lee and 26 cosponsors filed a resolution requiring the White House and State Department to "transmit all information relating to communication with officials of the United Kingdom between January 1, 2002, and October 16, 2002, relating to the policy of the United States with respect to Iraq."[945] Instead of permitting the Resolution to come to the House floor for an up or down vote, the Republicans denied a vote on the measure by sending it to the International Relations Committee, where the Resolution was defeated by a 22-21 vote.[946]

## ■ Manipulation of the Intelligence to Justify the War

The Administration has failed to address the most important questions regarding the manipulation of intelligence to justify the war in Iraq. Democrats in the House and Senate have attempted to hold the Administration accountable with letters, requests for independent investigations, requests for congressional oversight, and the introduction of Privileged Resolutions and Resolutions of Inquiry. On every occasion, however, the Administration and the Republican leadership have restricted access to information, tied the hands of investigators, and rejected oversight attempts.

Democrats first sought answers by writing letters to the Administration. Representative Waxman, for example, has sent numerous letters seeking information about officials' knowledge of false nuclear claims and any efforts to mislead the public, including two to National Security Advisor Condoleezza Rice,[947] one to Secretary of State Colin Powell,[948] and two to the President.[949] In general, the Administration's responses to these letters, or lack thereof, have been wholly inadequate.[950]

Democrats have also asked for independent reviews. For example, on February 2, 2004, House Minority Leader Pelosi, Senate Minority Leader Daschle, Senators Rockefeller and Lieberman, and Representative Waxman called for a congressionally appointed commission to examine the intelligence used to justify the Iraq war.[951] The Republican majority has ignored this request.

In addition, Democrats have sought meaningful congressional oversight, particularly once it became apparent that the Senate Intelligence Committee under Chairman Roberts did not intend to investigate whether the Bush Administration used and exaggerated the faulty intelligence.[952] In response, Democrats wrote several letters demanding the investigation take place. For example, Senator Jay Rockefeller, Ranking Member on the Intelligence Committee, said in a statement that he expected Phase II to be completed: "The Chairman agreed to this investigation and I fully expect him to fulfill his commitment."[953] And Senator Feinstein wrote a letter to Senator Roberts in July 2005, stating: "I am increasingly dismayed by the delay in completing the Committee's 'Phase II' investigation into intelligence prior to the Iraq War."[954] However, it was not until Senator Reid forced a closed session of the Senate on November 1, 2005—a tactic not employed for six years—that Senator Roberts finally agreed to complete Phase II of the investigation, although it is still unclear whether the review will be meaningful.[955]

In the House, Representative Jane Harman, Ranking Member of the Permanent

Select Committee on Intelligence, sought a formal investigation into the following aspects of pre-war intelligence: (1) the pressure felt by intelligence professionals to conform their analysis to policy judgments of the Administration; (2) the presentation of competing, differing, or dissenting views; (3) the conduct of intelligence professionals in response to statements by policymakers that purported to characterize intelligence; and (4) the development of public presentations purported to be based on intelligence.[956] During a press conference on November 10, 2005 and in a letter on that same date, Chairman Peter Hoekstra flatly rejected Harman's request to commence an investigation into the manipulation of pre-war intelligence.[957]

Democrats have also requested hearings. Congressman Henry Waxman, for example, requested hearings in the Government Reform Committee[958] and the Intelligence Committee[959] concerning issues of intelligence manipulation. Similarly, Congressman Nadler requested hearings in the Judiciary Committee to discuss whether the Administration manipulated intelligence in order to make a case for war.[960] These requests have been ignored by all three Republican Chairmen.

Democrats have also attempted to gain information by use of Privileged Resolutions and Resolutions of Inquiry. Leader Pelosi offered a Privileged Resolution in early November that called for "the Republican Leadership and Chairmen of the committees of jurisdiction to comply with their oversight responsibilities, demand[ed] they conduct a thorough investigation of abuses relating to the Iraq War, and condemn[ed] their refusal to conduct oversight of an Executive Branch controlled by the same party, which is in contradiction to the established rules of standing committees and Congressional precedent."[961] Pelosi explained that the resolution was necessary because the House was faced with, among other things, a "Republican Leadership and Committee Chairmen [who] have repeatedly denied requests by Democratic Members to complete an investigation of pre-war intelligence on Iraq and have ignored the question of whether that intelligence was manipulated for political purposes."[962] The resolution was tabled by a party line vote of 220-191.[963]

In addition, Representatives Hinchey, Waxman, and Conyers introduced a resolution on November 10, 2005, that would require the White House to provide Congress with all drafts and documents related to the crafting of the State of the Union address.[964] The resolution also sought drafts and related documents surrounding the October 2002 speech given by President Bush in which he discussed a possible mushroom cloud from an Iraqi nuclear weapon.[965] The Resolution was referred to the Committee on International Relations and was considered on December 9, 2005. The Committee deadlocked in a 24-to-24 tie vote when one Republican, Representative Leach of Iowa, voted in its favor and two other Republicans missed the vote. However, the Chairman of the Committee scheduled another vote for the following week and the Resolution was finally defeated on December 5, 2005 by a 24-19 vote.[966]

# ■ Encouraging and Countenancing Torture

In May 2004, the world was shocked when photos of torture and humiliation of Iraqi detainees in Abu Ghraib prison were leaked to the press. Since then, Democrats have been trying to obtain information through requests for hearings and documents, requests for independent reviews and commissions, and Resolutions of Inquiry. Democrats, however, have been stonewalled at every turn.

Democrats began by asking the relevant committee chairmen to conduct hearings and investigations. After it became apparent that the House "Armed Services Committee would not conduct a full and complete investigation, on June 17, 2004, Congressman Conyers and other Democratic Members of the House Judiciary Committee wrote to Chairman Sensenbrenner asking that the Committee "formally request from the Administration all executive branch memoranda, orders, and rules analyzing and implementing the Geneva Conventions, the 1994 Convention Against Torture, customary international law on torture, and federal torture statutes as they apply to detainees in Afghanistan, Iraq, and Guantanamo Bay."[967] Chairman Sensenbrenner did not reply. In addition, Representative Waxman requested that the Government Reform Committee hold hearings about allegations that private contractors participated in torture of Iraqi detainees.[968] No response was received.

After Democrats were rebuffed by the relevant committees, the Ranking Members of six committees wrote a letter to the President requesting that he provide assistance in obtaining key documents concerning torture and other alleged abuse.[969] In the letter, Democrats listed 35 items of documents that are needed to conduct a full and transparent investigation. The President never responded.

With regard to requests for independent commissions and reviews, Democrats have written to both Attorneys General Ashcroft and Gonzales on May 20, 2004 and May 12, 2005, respectively, asking for the appointment of a special counsel to investigate whether there had been violations of the War Crimes Act or the Anti-Torture Act.[970] The DOJ denied both requests with little in the way of explanation. It was not until July 11, 2005, over a year after the original letter, that the Department of Justice responded to the Ashcroft request.[971]

In addition, Democrats asked for the creation of an independent commission. On November 4, 2005, Senator Levin and others introduced an amendment to the National Defense Authorization Act that would have established a national commission on policies and practices on the treatment of detainees since September 11, 2001.[972] The amendment was defeated on the Senate floor by a vote of 43-55.[973] In the House, Representative Waxman, Democratic Leader Pelosi, and other senior Democrats twice introduced similar legislation to establish an independent commission. The first resolution, H. Res. 690,[974] was introduced in June 2004, and the second, H.R. 3003,[975] was introduced in June 2005. Neither of these pieces of legislation ever received a hearing or a vote on the House floor.

Democrats have also attempted to obtain information by introducing Resolutions of Inquiry. In June 2004, Congressman Conyers and 47 other Members of Congress introduced resolutions to gather information regarding the treatment of prisoners or detainees in Iraq, Afghanistan, or Guantanamo Bay. The resolutions were referred to the Judiciary Committee, the International Relations Committee, and the Armed Services Committee.[976] The resolutions were designed to trace the evolution of documents arguing that tortuous treatment of prisoners is not barred by American or international law, and to attempt to discover who commissioned these documents and whether the blank check given to the Administration under their rationale was ever used.[977] The Resolutions were all voted down on party line votes in all Committees.[978]

Other Democratic members have also tried to use Resolutions of Inquiry to obtain information on torture. For example, on May 12, 2004, Congressman Bell introduced H. Res.640, which requested that the Secretary of Defense provide "any picture, photograph, video, communication, or report produced in conjunction with any completed Department of Defense investigation conducted by Major General Antonio M. Taguba relating to allegations of torture or allegations of violations of the Geneva Conventions of 1949 at Abu Ghraib prison in Iraq or any completed Department of Defense investigation relating to the abuse or alleged abuse of a prisoner of war or detainee by any civilian contractor working in Iraq who is employed on behalf of the Department of Defense."[979] The Resolution was referred to the Committee on Armed Services and was voted down.[980]

Democratic efforts have been particularly important given the fact that the Bush Administration's purported investigations into the allegations of torture have been largely non-responsive. While there have been a number of investigations into the treatment of Iraqi prisoners, each one has been limited to distinct areas of the military chain of command, which has prevented any inquiry into the accountability of anyone in the Administration.[981] Nor were they tasked with investigating how ideas and direction for abuse moved amongst different units, and between entire theaters of combat. The Administration maintains these are all "isolated" events. Indeed, by setting up a dozen discrete investigations that ignore any connections between behavior, the abuse, at first blush, will of course continue to look like isolated events.[982]

## ■ Post-War Cover-Ups and Retribution and More Deceptions

The Administration has also retaliated against and publicly smeared those who have dared to speak out against the war in Iraq, including Joe Wilson and his wife, covert CIA agent Valerie Plame. When Democrats have attempted to gain insight and demand accountability, by writing letters, requesting hearings in Congress, and seeking adoption of Resolutions of Inquiry, the Administration and congressional Republicans have rejected or ignored nearly every request.

Congressional Democrats have written numerous letters to the Administration regarding the Plame leak that remain unanswered. Soon after Valerie Plame was exposed to the public as a covert CIA operative, Democrats sought President Bush's assurance that White House officials would cooperate with any investigation and would address reports that certain officials were refusing to cooperate.[983] In addition, when it became clear that Karl Rove may have been involved in the leak of Plame's name, Congressman Conyers wrote a letter to Mr. Rove asking him to resign.[984] Later, a similar letter was sent to President Bush asking him to require Mr. Rove to explain his role in the leak or resign.[985] To date, Rove has not been asked or required to explain his role, and there has been no discussion of his resignation.[986]

After Scooter Libby was indicted on October 26, 2005 for perjury and obstruction of justice for his role in the leak, Representatives Conyers, Waxman and Hinchey wrote to Vice President Cheney and requested that he "make [himself] available to appear before Congress to explain the details and reasons for [his] office's involvement—and [Cheney's] personal involvement—in the disclosure of Valerie Wilson's identity as a Central Intelligence Agency (CIA) operative."[987] To date, Vice President Cheney has failed to respond.

Congressman Conyers also asked President Bush to pledge not to pardon anyone involved in the Plame leak because of a concern that the Administration's "low ethical standards foreshadow future actions on [the Administration's] part that will allow individuals responsible for this breach of national security to evade accountability."[988] Furthermore, senior Senate Democrats, including Senators Reid, Durbin, Stabenow and Schumer, asked President Bush to pledge not to pardon anyone convicted in connection with the leak investigation.[989] The President has not responded to either of these requests.

Democrats have also written letters to the Administration in an attempt to obtain information about others who have suffered similar retaliation efforts by the Administration. For example, on August 29, 2005, Representative Waxman sent a letter to Secretary of Defense Rumsfeld requesting that the Department of Defense investigate the removal of Bunnatine Greenhouse from her position as Principal Assistant for Contracting for the Army Corps of Engineers. Representative Waxman wrote that "[t]he decision to remove Ms. Greenhouse from her position and demote her appears to be retaliation for her June 27, 2005 testimony before Congress."[990] Mr. Waxman received a response to this letter on September 27, 2005; however, the letter is unpersuasive because it asserts that there was a sufficient record to determine whether Greenhouse was properly removed because General Strock's staff put together a memo. Of course, Greenhouse's allegations specifically involved Gen. Strock and his people.[991]

In addition, in a letter dated January 14, 2004, Mr. Waxman asked Condoleezza Rice to explain "inconsistencies in how the Administration handles allegations regarding the release of sensitive information."[992] Specifically, Mr. Waxman highlighted the immediate response and retaliation against Paul O'Neill's television interview (where he voiced criticism of the Administration) and contrasted it with the Administration's delayed handling of the Plame Leak.[993] Mr. Waxman also noted the very different treatment given to Mr. O'Neill and Bob Woodward, whose book, *Bush at War,* cites notes taken during more than 50 meetings of the National Security Council and both classified and unclassified written materials. Ms. Rice never responded to this letter.

Finally, Representative Conyers wrote a letter to the President expressing concerns that the Department of Defense is "under-reporting casualties in Iraq by only reporting non-fatal casualties incurred in combat."[994] In the letter, Congressman Conyers asks the President to provide a full accounting of the American casualties in Iraq since the March 2003 invasion.[995] To date, Mr. Conyers has not received a response to the letter.

Just as Administration officials ignored and evaded Democratic efforts to reveal the truth, Congressional Republicans have similarly blocked Democratic requests for investigative hearings. On October 30, 2003, House Judiciary Committee Democrats wrote to Chairman Sensenbrenner asking him to hold hearings to investigate the Plame leak.[996] After it became apparent that Karl Rove was almost certainly involved in the leak in some capacity, Committee Democrats asked to hold hearings a second time in a letter dated July 14, 2005.[997] Democrats never received responses to these requests. Representative Waxman also pursued committee hearings, requesting investigative oversight in a letter to House Government Reform Chairman Davis on September 29, 2003.[998] Mr. Waxman tried again on October 8, 2003,[999] December 11, 2003,[1,000] and then again July 11, 2005,[1,001] in light of mounting evidence of Rove's involvement in the Plame outing. On October 28, 2005[1,002] and November 16, 2005,[1,003] Mr. Waxman made his fifth and sixth requests for the Government Reform Committee to hold hearings on the Plame leak. To date, Chairman Davis has either denied or ignored all of these requests.

In addition to oversight into the Plame leak, Democrats have also attempted to gain information about and hold the Administration accountable for activities occurring in Iraq. First, in May 2004, Representative Waxman and other Members of Congress asked Chairman Davis to investigate allegations that civilian contractors participated in the abuse of detainees at Abu Ghraib.[1,004] Chairman Davis did not respond to this letter. Second, Mr. Waxman tried to enlist Chairman Davis in seeking documents from the Pentagon about reports that the U.S. military is secretly paying Iraqi newspapers to run stories presenting a positive image of the United States in Iraq.[1,005] Again, Chairman Davis has not responded to this request to date.

Democrats also pursued Resolutions of Inquiry. On July 29, 2005, Congressman Holt, along with other Members of Congress, attempted to request the Administration to provide information about the identity of the source of the Plame leak.[1,006] The Resolutions were referred to four Committees, including the Judiciary Committee, the International Relations Committee, the Armed Services Committee, and the Intelligence Committee.

The Republicans voted all of the Resolutions down, arguing that there was an ongo-

# Chronology: Democracy Without Checks and Balances

*"I don't email, however. And there's a reason. I don't want you reading my personal stuff. There has got to be a certain sense of privacy. You know, you're entitled to how I make decisions. And you're entitled to ask questions, which I answer. I don't think you're entitled to be able to read my mail between my daughters and me."*

—April 14, 2005, President George W. Bush, responding to questions at
an American Society of Newspaper Editors conference in Washington.[1,009]

In the days and weeks after the horrific attacks of September 11, members of both political parties recognized the need to insure that law enforcement had the tools and resources to respond to terrorist threats, while at the same time respecting our Nation's core constitutional principles. With that goal in mind, Judiciary Committee Chairman F. James Sensenbrenner and Ranking Member John Conyers introduced legislation that would both enhance law enforcement while providing for necessary safeguards to protect civil liberties.[1,010] Their legislation passed the usually contentious Judiciary Committee by a unanimous vote of 36-0 on October 3, 2001.[1,011]

Unfortunately—and ominously—the Bush Administration reneged on the bipartisan compromise and chose to go its own route by substituting a 342-page Administration draft. The Administration's substitute was inserted in the middle of the night and brought to the House floor a few hours later on October 12 with no amendments permitted. Final legislation passed the House on October 23, in the midst of an anthrax scare while most Members and staff were locked out of their offices and in no position to read, let alone understand, the legislation.[1,012]

Among the more controversial sections of the PATRIOT Act added or expanded by the Bush Administration were provisions concerning: (i) "sneak and peak" warrants lowering the standard for the FBI to enter an individual's home and take property without notification; [1,013] (ii) business records permitting the FBI to obtain any record, including medical, and library and bookstore reading information, with recipients "gagged" from informing others they received the request; [1,014] (iii) National Security Letters (NSLs), permitting the FBI to mandate that businesses (including Internet and telecommunications companies) turn over specific financial, telephone, Internet and other consumer records with no judicial oversight or approval, with recipients again "gagged" from informing others they received the request;[1,015] and (iv) material support, permitting immigrants to be deported for donating funds to groups they did not know had terrorist ties and by criminalizing vaguely defined aspects of "material support" for terrorism.[1,016] (Eventually, the National Security Letter provision was held to violate the First and Fourth Amendments by two separate courts,[1,017] while the material support provisions were held to violate both the First Amendment right to freedom of speech and advocacy and the Fifth Amendment right to due process.[1,018])

# II

## Unlawful Domestic Surveillance

## *and the* Decline *of* Civil Liberties

## Under *the* Administration

## *of* George W. Bush

ing criminal investigation into the matter and the resolutions competed with that investigation.[1,007] This argument would seem to be disingenuous, given that there are numerous precedents for congressional committees investigating concurrently with the Justice Department and with other matters under criminal review by the Executive Branch[1,008], most notably many concurrent investigations by the Republican Congress involving the Clinton Administration.

The enactment of the PATRIOT Act was followed by a series of unilateral actions taken by the Bush Administration that raised significant civil liberties and constitutional issues. For example, in the fall of 2001, the Administration elected to close many depoaration proceedings to the public, a practice the Sixth Circuit held violated the First Amendment, by "seeking to uproot people's lives, outside the public eye, and behind a closed door. Democracies die behind closed doors."[1,019] Also, in late 2001, the Justice Department indefinitely detained more than 1,200 individuals in the U.S., the vast majority of Arab or Muslim descent.[1,020] In addition, during this period we learned of additional instances of the Bush Administration choosing to conduct law enforcement activities based on race and ethnicity with regard to immigration registration, "voluntary" interrogations of Middle Eastern men, and other federal police activities.[1,021] On November 13, 2001, the Administration announced the creation of secret military tribunals, again without any authorization or even input from Congress. The initial order was not limited to persons detained abroad or engaged in terrorism, but could apply to millions of immigrants who were in our nation lawfully. [1,022]

On May 30, 2002, then Attorney General Ashcroft unilaterally announced that the Department had made major revisions to the guidelines that governed how it conducted investigations, removing a number of safeguards that had been included in the guidelines adopted by Attorney General Edward H. Levi in the wake of the Watergate and COINTELPRO surveillance scandals.[1,023] Concerning the new guidelines, conservative columnist William Safire wrote that the Administration "gutted guidelines put in place a generation ago to prevent the abuse of police power by the federal government."[1,024] This in turn, contributed to a series of instances in which the Bush Administration began investigating innocent Americans for engaging in constitutionally protected activities, such as protesting the war and protecting the environment.[1,025] By late fall of 2002, reports began to circulate concerning the misuse and abuse of the material witness laws, with the principal targets again being individuals of Arab and Muslim descent.[1,026]

In February 2003, the Administration began circulating its so-called "PATRIOT II" legislation. This bill would have, among other things, authorized secret arrests, permitted the construction of detailed government databases based on information concerning innocent Americans, allowed the secret revocation of citizenship, and expanded the government's ability to search homes and tap phones without a warrant.[1,027]

Throughout this period and his entire presidency, George W. Bush has unilaterally claimed the authority to disregard hundreds of laws duly passed by Congress. The *Boston Globe* reported that as of April 2006, President Bush has "claimed the authority to disobey more than 750 laws enacted since he took office, asserting that he has the power to set aside any statute passed by Congress when it conflicts with his interpretation of the Constitution."[1,028] Among the laws Mr. Bush asserts he can ignore are torture bans, provisions requiring reports to Congress regarding the implementation of the PATRIOT Act, laws against using illegally obtained evidence, whistle-blower protections, and affirmative action requirements.[1,029] Reacting to this unprecedented use of signing statements to ignore laws passed by Congress, Phillip Cooper, a legal expert on executive power, stated, "There is no question that this administration has been involved in a very carefully thought-out, systematic process of expanding presidential power at the expense of other branches of government."[1,030]

There is no better illustration of the full-blown constitutional crisis inherent in these unilateral actions taken by the Bush Administration than the series of circumstances concerning both the warrantless wiretapping of Americans by the Bush Administration and their creation of a database comprised of the calls of millions of innocent citizens (the focus of this Part of the Report). The National Security Agency (NSA)'s warrantless wiretapping activities were initially disclosed on December 16, 2005, by the *New York Times*.[1,031] This disclosure raised an obvious conflict with both the Foreign Intelligence Surveillance Act (FISA), which applies to the "interception of international wire communications *to or from any person (whether or not a U.S. person) within the United States* without the consent of at least one party"[1,032] and the Fourth Amendment.[1,034] Government sources have stated that pursuant to this program "the NSA eavesdrops without warrants on up to 500 people in the United States at any given time." the *Washington Post* has reported that "[t]wo knowledgeable sources placed that number in the thousands, one of them, more specific, said about 5,000."[1,035]

Attorney General Gonzales has asserted that pursuant to the program, the NSA intercepts the contents of communications where there is a "reasonable basis to believe" that a party to the communication is "a member of Al Qaeda, affiliated with Al Qaeda, or a member of an organization affiliated with Al Qaeda or working in support of Al Qaeda."[1,036] General Hayden, the Principal Deputy Director for National Intelligence, has stated that the judgment of whether to target a communication is made by operational personnel at the NSA using the information available to them at the time,[1,037] and that judgment is made by two people, signed off only by a shift supervisor.[1,038]

In early 2004, Jack Goldsmith, the head of the DOJ Office of Legal Counsel, raised concerns with James Comey, the Deputy Attorney General, about the legality of the program.[1,039] Mr. Comey was acting as Attorney General while John Ashcroft was in the hospital. Mr. Comey reportedly agreed with Mr. Goldsmith that the program raised serious legal and constitutional concerns and refused to reauthorize it. As a result, Andrew Card, then White House chief of staff, and Albert Gonzales, then-White House Counsel, visited Mr. Ashcroft in the hospital in a further unsuccessful effort to persuade him to reverse his deputy. [1,040] These refusals reportedly led to the temporary shut down of the program and eventually the creation of a secret audit of the program examining several cases to determine how the NSA was running the program and to review the parameters for determining reasonable belief. Thereafter, DOJ and NSA are reported to have developed a checklist to follow in determining whether "reasonable belief" existed.[1,041]

The Administration and the Department of Justice also encountered resistance from the FISA court. Judge Colleen Kollar-Kotelly complained that information obtained under the program was being improperly used as the basis for FISA wiretap warrant requests.[1,042] Judge Royce Lamberth, the U.S. District Court judge who preceded Kollar-Kotelly as the head of the FISA court, also raised doubts regarding the program. According to government sources, "[b]oth judges expressed concern to senior officials that the president's program, if ever made public and challenged in court, ran a significant risk of being declared unconstitutional . . . . Yet the judges believed they did not have the authority to rule on the president's power to order the eavesdropping . . . and focused instead on protecting the integrity of the FISA process."[1,043] As a result, in early 2002 the FISA court and DOJ reportedly reached a compromise, by which in any case involving warrantless surveillance where the government subsequently sought an official FISA warrant was to be "tagged" as such, and that a FISA warrant would only be sought based on independently gathered information presented to the presiding judge.[1,044] However, by 2004, James Baker, DOJ's liaison to the FISA court, was forced to acknowledge to the court that NSA was not providing DOJ with the information needed to implement the tagging system, and as a result, Judge Kollar-Kotelly complained to Attorney General Ashcroft, which also reportedly helped lead to the program's suspension.[1,045] Eventually, the Department agreed that a high-level official would certify that the information provided to the FISA court was accurate, or face possible perjury charges.[1,046] Once the program was disclosed to the public, another judge on the court, James Robertson, became so concerned about the program's legality that he resigned his position in protest.[1,047]

After initially attempting to downplay the significance of disclosure of the domestic spying program, the Bush Administration realized it had a major controversy on its hands and crafted a full-scale legal and public relations offensive. The Department of Justice was called upon to issue an ever-expanding set of after-the-fact legal rationales—on December 22, 2005, they wrote a four-page letter to the House and Senate Intelligence Committees;[1,048] on January 19, 2006 they issued a 42-page "White Paper;"[1,049] and on January 27, 2006, the Department issued a 27-point "Myth vs. Fact" memorandum.[1,050]

The domestic spying program has engendered widespread opposition, including from a number of Republicans, conservatives, and non-partisan groups. Those who have raised questions or challenged the legal and constitutional underpinnings of the NSA program include: Senate Judiciary Chairman Arlen Specter (R-PA), Senators Chuck Hagel (R-NE), Olympia Snowe (R-ME), Richard Lugar (R-IN), Susan Collins (R-ME), John Sununu (R-NH), Larry Craig (R-ID), Lindsey Graham (R-SC), and John McCain (R-AZ); former GOP Congressman Bob Barr; conservative activists Grover Norquist, David Keene, and Paul Weyrich; former Republican officials such as Judge and former Reagan FBI Director William Sessions, former Reagan Associate Deputy Attorney General Bruce Fein and former Nixon White House Counsel John Dean; conservative legal scholars such as CATO's Robert Levy and University of Chicago Professor Richard Epstein, noted conservative columnists William Safire, George Will, and Steve Chapman; the American

Bar Association, the Congressional Research Service, and numerous current and former members of the Bush Administration. Among other things, Senator Specter stated that the Administration's legal interpretation "just defies logic and plain English,"[1,051] and David S. Kris, the former Associate Deputy Attorney General at the Department of Justice for national security, issued a 23-page legal analysis finding that the Administration's arguments were "weak" and unlikely to be supported by the courts.[1,052]

It has also been reported that senior members of the Bush Administration specifically sought and obtained information from the NSA concerning the identity of American citizens who were swept up in the warrantless surveillance program. *Newsweek* reported the "NSA received—and fulfilled—between 3,000 and 3,500 requests from other agencies to supply the names of U.S. citizens and officials . . . that initially were deleted from raw intercept reports . . . . About one third of such disclosures were made to officials at the policymaking level."[1,053] One case involved John Bolton, the then Under Secretary of State for Arms Control, who stated at his April, 2005 confirmation hearing for U.N. Ambassador that in the last four years he had obtained from the NSA the names of American citizens on numerous occasions, in apparent violation of NSA rules requiring the blacking out of such names when intelligence reports are distributed.[1,054]

On May 11, 2006, another aspect of the domestic spying scandal erupted. *USA Today* reported that according to individuals with first-hand knowledge, "[t]he NSA has been secretly collecting the phone call records of tens of millions of Americans."[1,055] The newspaper reported that "[t]he NSA program reaches into homes and businesses across the nation by amassing information about the calls of ordinary Americans—most of whom aren't suspected of any crime."[1,056] According to individuals familiar with the program, "[i]t's the largest database ever assembled in the world," and the NSA's goal is "to create a call of every call ever made" in the U.S.[1,057] The NSA database program was reportedly developed in the fall of 2001, with the cooperation of three telecommunications companies—AT&T, Verizon, and BellSouth—under the direction of then-NSA Director General Michael Hayden.[1,058] Under the program the various telephone numbers as well as the time and destination of the calls, known as "call detail records," are turned over to the NSA. While the program apparently does not include specific names or addresses,[1,059] there is little doubt the government can ascertain this information through access to commercial databases and other sources.[1,060]

The basic contours of the NSA domestic database program have been confirmed—either directly or indirectly—by a number of sources beyond those relied on by *USA Today* in its May 11 article. First and foremost is the fact that Qwest has provided a specific statement that it rejected the NSA's request in the fall of 2001.[1,061] Second, although neither the President nor his staff would officially confirm or deny the domestic database story, the *New York Times* reported on May 12 that "[o]ne senior government official who was granted anonymity to speak publicly about the classified program confirmed that the N.S.A. had access to records to most telephone calls in the U.S."[1,062] Similarly, *Time* reported that a White House official confirmed the existence of the program when he told them the program was "just digits . . . just a bunch of numbers."[1,063] Government sources have also confirmed the existence of the NSA database program to Seymour Hersch of the *New Yorker*.[1,064] Two Republican Senators on the Intelligence Committee have indirectly confirmed the existence of the program: Senator Trent Lott (R-MS) informed Bloomberg News that he had been briefed on the database program,[1,065] while Senator Kit Bond (R-MO) told PBS that "I'm a member of the subcommittee on the Intelligence Committee that's been thoroughly briefed on this [the NSA database] program."[1,066] The allegations were taken so seriously by the Bush Administration that it even threatened prosecution of the press for the disclosure.[1,067]

About one week after the *USA Today* story broke, both BellSouth and Verizon sought to distance themselves from the NSA program in somewhat qualified terms.[1,068] However, as the *New York Times* noted, "The statement by Verizon left open the possibility that MCI, the long-distance carrier it bought in January, did turn over such records— or that the unit, once absorbed into Verizon, had continued to do so."[1,069] With respect to the BellSouth denial, the *Washington Post* noted "BellSouth did not address whether it might have provided such records outside of a contract or to an agency other than the NSA."[1,070] Skepticism regarding these denials was further fueled by a report in *Business Week* that some companies are willing to serve as intermediaries between telephone companies and the government[1,071] and the disclosure of a May 5 presidential memorandum permitting the NSA to authorize corporations to conceal activities concerning national security without violating the securities laws.[1,072]

A number of prominent conservatives and Republicans have also expressed reservations about the NSA data-base program. Former GOP Speaker Newt Gingrich declared, "I'm not going to defend the indefensible."[1,073] Senator Charles Grassley (R-IA) asked "Why are the telephone companies not protecting their customers' privacy?"[1,074] and House Majority Leader John Boehner stated, ". . . I'm not sure why it would be necessary to keep and have that kind of information."[1,075]

Beyond this series of disturbing events in the U.S., a number of reports also surfaced describing abuses of liberties and rights abroad. In addition to the many reports of abuses reported at Guantanamo Bay,[1,076] the Supreme Court has found the Administration's treatment of detainees to be violation of due process;[1,077] while other courts have questioned the Bush Administration's actions in detaining Jose Padilla in military custody for several years, without trial, lawyer, charges, or access to the outside world.[1,078] There is also significant evidence that the Administration has engaged in "extraordinary rendition," the process by which detainees are sent to nations which engage in torture,[1,079] and it has been reported that the Administration has set up a network of secret CIA prisons in Eastern Europe and other locations where individuals may be detained free of congressional or human rights oversight.[1,080] There is little evidence these actions have produced actionable intelligence.[1,081]

## Detailed Findings

# Domestic Surveillance: Spying On Innocent Americans without Court Approval and Outside of the Law

*"If the lickspittle lawyer [defending the program] thinks all this is legal, 'he's smoking Dutch Cleanser.'"*

—February 7, 2006, Senate Judiciary Chairman Arlen Specter,
during an interview with the *Washington Post*[1,082]

As a result of our review, we have been able to make a number of preliminary findings and determinations based on the facts we are aware of. First, we have found that the warrantless wiretapping program is clearly unlawful, that the massive domestic database created by the NSA also appears to violate several statutes, and that the limited Congressional briefings surrounding these programs contravened the National Security Act. Just as dangerously, the legal justifications used by the Administration to justify the warrantless wiretap program could establish a legal precedent which provides for no meaningful limitation on executive branch authority. Third, in attempting to justify the programs, President Bush and other members of the Bush Administration appear to have made a number of misleading statements. Also, we have found that while there is little evidence that the programs have been beneficial in the war against terror, there is a considerable risk they will affirmatively harm terrorism prosecutions. Finally, the NSA programs appear to have been implemented in a manner designed to stifle legitimate concerns within the Administration.

## ■ The warrantless wiretap program violates FISA and the Fourth Amendment; the NSA database program appears to violate the Stored Communications Act and the Communications Act of 1934; and the programs have been briefed in violation of the National Security Act.

The Bush Administration has laid out a number of arguments to defend the warrantless wiretapping program disclosed by the *New York Times* in December: first they claim that the program does not violate FISA because the September 11 Use of Force Resolution authorized the surveillance program; second, they argue that the program falls within the President's inherent authority as Commander-in-Chief; and third, they claim that the Fourth Amendment warrant requirement does not apply to the programs. The Bush

Administration has not directly sought to specifically defend the NSA database program, but that program appears to be unlawful as well. They also offer a number of non-legal justifications for the programs namely that the FISA procedures are too cumbersome; the NSA programs could have prevented the 9-11 attacks; and that both President Carter and Clinton have engaged in warrantless surveillance. Our review—and the review of the overwhelming majority of outside and independent experts—has found that these arguments are neither credible nor legally sustainable.

## September 11 Use of Force Resolution

The Bush Administration has put forth four separate legal justifications for the proposition that the so-called Authorization for the Use of Military Force (AUMF)[1,083] authorizes warrantless wiretapping within the United States. First, the Administration highlights a provision in the AUMF preamble that reads, "[the attacks of September 11th] render it both necessary and appropriate that the United States exercise its right to self-defense and to protect United States citizens both at home and abroad."[1,084] Second, the Administration relies on a 2004 Supreme Court decision, *Hamdi v. Rumsfeld*,[1,085] in which in upholding the Non-Detention Act the Court noted that the AUMF "clearly and unmistakably authorize[s]" the "fundamental incident[s] of waging war."[1,086] Third, the Administration points to a provision of FISA which "makes it unlawful to conduct electronic surveillance, 'except as authorized by statute'"[1,087] and argues that the AUMF provides such explicit statutory authority.[1,088] Fourth, the Administration argues that the canon of constitutional avoidance requires resolving conflicts between FISA's proscriptions and executive branch authority in favor of the President.[1,089]

Our review indicates that the overwhelming weight of legal authority contravenes each and every one of these assertions. First, with regard to the claims that the AUMF resolution directly authorized warrantless wiretapping or other surveillance in the U.S., Tom Daschle, the Senate Majority Leader at the time the AUMF was enacted, has stated the Senate rejected a last minute request from the White House that the AUMF authorize "all necessary and appropriate force in the United States and against those nations, organizations or persons [the President] determines planned, authorized, committed or aided" the attacks of September 11.[1,090] **Senator Daschle explains that "this last-minute change would have given the president broad authority to exercise expansive powers not just overseas—where we all understood he wanted authority to act—but right here in the United States, potentially against American citizens."**[1,091]

Republican Senator Sam Brownback (R-KS) has concurred with Senator Daschle, stating, "I do not agree with the legal basis on which [the Administration] are basing their surveillance—that when the Congress gave the authorization to go to war that gives sufficient legal basis for the surveillance."[1,092] Senate Judiciary Chairman Arlen Specter (R-PA) has stated that "I do not think that any fair, realistic reading of the September 14 resolution gives you the power to conduct electronic surveillance,"[1,093] while Senator

Lindsey Graham (R-SC) declared, "I will be the first to say when I voted for it, I never envisioned that I was giving to this President or any other President the ability to go around FISA carte blanche."[1,094] Senator John McCain (R-AZ) has stated, "I think it's probably clear we didn't know we were voting for [domestic warrantless surveillance]."[1,095] Significantly, in a 44-page memorandum, the nonpartisan Congressional Research Service has concluded that based on their review of the law, "it appears unlikely that a court would hold that Congress has expressly or impliedly authorized the NSA electronic surveillance operations here under discussion."[1,096]

Moreover, it is difficult for the Administration to credibly claim that the AUMF authorizes warrantless wiretapping when they have also acknowledged that Congress was not supportive of such a proposal.[1,097] **On December 19, 2005, Attorney General Gonzales stated that "[w]e have had discussions with Congress in the past [after the September 11 attacks]—certain members of Congress—as to whether or not FISA could be amended to allow us to adequately deal with this kind of threat, and we were advised that would be difficult, if not impossible."**[1,098] As conservative columnist George Will has written, "Administration supporters incoherently argue that the AUMF authorized NSA surveillance—and that if the Administration had asked, Congress would have refused to authorize it."[1,099] The Administration's tepid response in this area—they have admitted they never even bothered to inquire about the possibility of amending FISA with Members on the Judiciary Committee which has jurisdiction over FISA[1,100]— may in part be due to the fact that this argument was apparently developed well after the fact.[1,101] It is also informative that efforts to further modify FISA were either dropped because they were too controversial (such as the PATRIOT II proposal)[1,102] or shot down by the Administration itself (such as a proposal by Senator DeWine to require only reasonable suspicion for FISA warrants).[1,103]

Second, the Administration's contention that the *Hamdi* decision supports the proposition that the AUMF authorizes the President to engage in warrantless wiretapping is contradicted by the fact that the majority of the Court found that Mr. Hamdi has a right to due process and that the U.S. was not permitted to detain him for an indefinite period of time, writing, "indefinite detention for the purpose of interrogation [of enemy combatants]. . . is not authorized."[1,104] In addition, the *Hamdi* decision itself is limited to operations abroad and to enemy combatants of the United States.[1,105] By contrast, the domestic wiretapping program applies in the U.S. to U.S. persons who have not been shown to have done anything harmful to the U.S. As constitutional expert Professor Laurence Tribe notes, it is therefore difficult to argue that *Hamdi* supports the idea of warrantless surveillance of Americans, when they "are not even *alleged* to be enemies, much less *enemy combatants*."[1,106]

Third, in its White Paper, the Administration goes to great pains to claim that FISA contemplated exceptions to it, and that those who dispute their interpretations are somehow arguing that one Congress can bind a future Congress.[1,107] Clearly, one Congress cannot bind a future Congress; however, that is not in dispute. The problem for the Bush Administration is that when Congress enacted FISA in 1978, it went to great lengths to state that FISA was the exclusive authority concerning electronic surveillance, that the only exceptions to that law were some "technical activities," such as so-called "trap and trace" monitoring, and that it was intended that any future exemptions should be clear and specific, not vague and general as is the case with the Administration's AUMF assertion. As the House Committee explained in legislative history, FISA "carries forward the criminal provisions of chapter 119 [of Title 18, U.S.C.] and makes it a criminal offense for officers or employees of the United States to intentionally engage in electronic surveillance under color of law except as specifically authorized in chapter 119 of title III [of the Omnibus Crime Control and Safe Streets Act of 1968] and this title [concerning pen register activities]."[1,108] In reviewing this legislative history, the Congressional Research Service observed, "the legislative history appears to reflect an intention that the phrase 'authorized by statute' was a reference to chapter 119 of Title 18 of the U.S. Code (Title III) and to FISA itself, rather than having a broader meaning, in which case a clear indication of Congress's intent to amend or repeal it might be necessary before a court would interpret a later statute as superceding it."[1,109]

Thus, while FISA certainly is subject to amendment, it is clear that the AUMF does not come close to meeting the standards of precision contemplated by Congress.[1,110] In the present case, not only did the AUMF not explicitly amend FISA as Congress intended, it is not even clear the AUMF constitutes a "statute" within the meaning of FISA. As Professor Turley explained in the House Democratic Hearing, "the Force Resolution is not a statute for the purpose of Section 1809 [of FISA]."[1,111]

The Department's fourth assertion—that the canon of constitutional avoidance should lead to an implicit statutory repeal of FISA—is also not legally sustainable. The case law holds such repeals by implication can be established only by "overwhelming evidence"—which is clearly not the case with regard to the NSA domestic wiretapping program. A 2001 Supreme Court decision held that "the only permissible justification for a repeal by implication is when the earlier and later statutes are irreconcilable,"[1,112] while another 2001 Supreme Court case found that "the canon of constitutional avoidance has no applications in the absence of statutory ambiguity."[1,113] The interpretational rule which does apply in the present case is the doctrine that specific statutes prevail over general statutes when there is a possible conflict.[1,114] Accordingly, as Judge Sessions and other legal scholars explained, "[c]onstruing FISA and the AUMF according to their plain meanings raises no serious constitutional questions regarding the President's duties under Article II . . . [c]onstruing the AUMF to permit unchecked warrantless wiretapping without probable cause, however, would raise serious questions under the Fourth Amendment."[1,115]

## Inherent Authority as Commander-In-Chief

As an alternative to its statutory authority argument, the Administration also claims it has authority to conduct domestic warrantless wiretapping by virtue of the President's "inherent" constitutional authority as Commander-in-Chief.[1,116] The Bush Administration has developed three rationales to support this claim. First, the Administration asserts the Founding Fathers intended that the executive branch be "cloathed with all the powers requisite" to protect the Nation[1,117] and compares the current executive surveillance program to the intelligence methods of President George Washington, who intercepted mail between Britain and Americans in the revolutionary war; President Woodrow Wilson, who in WWI intercepted cable communication between the U.S. and Europe; and President Franklin Roosevelt, who intercepted mail after the bombing of Pearl Harbor.[1,118] Second, the Administration relies on Justice Jackson's concurrence in *Youngstown Sheet & Tube Co. v. Sawyer*[1,119] to argue that the President's wartime authority to act is at its "zenith" with respect to warrantless surveillance."[1,120] Third, the Administration repeatedly cites a passage in the *In re Sealed Case* that "[w]e take for granted that the President does have [inherent wiretap authority] and, assuming that it is so, FISA could not encroach on the President's constitutional power,"[1,121] which case in turn refers to three earlier circuit court decisions.[1,122]

The Administration's contention that the intent of the Founding Fathers supports its inherent authority argument belies any viable understanding of the founding of the United States. It was Benjamin Franklin who declared, "[t]hey that can give up essential liberty to purchase a little temporary safety, deserve neither liberty not safety,"[1,123] and it was James Madison who warned that wartime is "the true nurse of executive aggrandizement."[1,124] A close review of Federalist 23 reveals that it argues for a strong federal government, not a strong executive.[1,125] **Moreover, in Federalist 47, Madison further warned about the dangers of excess of power in the executive, writing, "[t]here can be no liberty where the legislative and executive powers are united in the same person," or "if the power of judging be not separated from the legislative and executive powers."**[1,126] If the Administration truly appreciated history, they would recognize that the Founding Fathers provided for a Fourth Amendment with a strong warrant requirement in reaction to the colonists' well-founded fears regarding the British "general warrant" of the 1700s, under which the British authority "could break into any shop or place suspected of containing evidence of potential enemies of the state."[1,127]

The argument that warrantless surveillance has been going on since as early as General George Washington does not appear to be legally or constitutionally credible. Not only did some of the "precedents" cited by the Administration occur before the Constitution, Bill of Rights, or Fourth Amendment were in place, but the cited actions by President Woodrow Wilson and Franklin Roosevelt occurred before the Supreme Court held in 1967 that the Fourth Amendment applies to electronic surveillance,[1,128] before FISA was enacted in 1978, and before Congress repealed a provision of law deferring to the President with respect to foreign intelligence information.[1,129]

The Administration's argument that the *Youngstown Steel* decision supports the claim of inherent authority is also legally tenuous. The holding of *Youngstown Steel* rejected the idea that President Truman had inherent presidential authority to seize steel mills during the Korean military conflict, with the Supreme Court finding that such important questions as the authority to seize private property "is a job for the Nation's lawmakers, not for its military authorities."[1,130] Properly understood, the *Youngstown Steel* case severely undermines, rather than supports the Administration's position. In his critical concurring opinion, Justice Jackson explained that "the presidential powers are not fixed, but fluctuate, depending upon their disjunction or conjunction with those of Congress,"[1,131] and that when the President defies "the expressed or implied will of Congress," his authority is "at its lowest ebb" and "Presidential power [is] most vulnerable to attack and in the least favorable of possible constitutional postures."[1,132]

In the present case, there appears to be little doubt that the warrantless wiretapping program disclosed by the *New York Times* is operating against the express as well as the implied will of Congress, and that the President is therefore at his "lowest ebb" in terms of constitutional authority. The legislative history of FISA makes it abundantly clear that Congress intended to and indeed did "express its will" and "occupy the field" with respect to the area of surveillance impacting Americans.[1,133] Thus, when Congress approved FISA in 1978, it refused to provide an exception to enable the President to conduct warrantless surveillance involving Americans[1,134] and, as noted above, explicitly repealed the provision which the executive branch had previously relied upon in claiming inherent presidential authority for warrantless surveillance.[1,135]

The legislative history from the House, Senate, and Conference Report all supports this understanding. **The House Report provides, "[e]ven if the President has the inherent authority in the absence of legislation to authorize warrantless electronic surveillance for foreign intelligence purposes, Congress has the power to regulate the conduct of such surveillance by legislating a reasonable procedure, which then becomes the exclusive means by which such surveillance may be conducted."**[1,136] The Senate Judiciary Committee was also clear on this point, finding FISA "constitutes the exclusive means by which electronic surveillance . . . may be conducted."[1,137]

The Conference report—the final and most definitive explanation of Congress's legislative intent—firmly reiterates that **Congress intended to occupy the field regarding domestic warrantless surveillance: "The intent of the conferees is to apply the standard set forth in Justice Jackson's concurring opinion in the Steel Seizure case: 'When a President takes measures incompatible with the express or implied will of Congress, his power is at the lowest ebb, for then he can rely only upon his own constitutional power minus any constitutional power of Congress over the matter.'"**[1,138]

Although the Bush Administration attempts to assert that contemporaneous statements of the Carter Administration indicate their support for warrantless surveillance,[1,139] the legislative history is also quite clear that at the time of its passage, the executive branch understood and accepted that the FISA law would occupy the field. Testifying before the

House Intelligence Committee in 1978, Attorney General Griffin Bell stated, "I would particularly call your attention to the improvements in this bill over a similar measure introduced in the last Congress. First, *the current bill recognizes no inherent power of the President to conduct electronic surveillance.* Whereas the bill introduced last year contained an explicit reservation of Presidential power for electronic surveillance within the United States, this bill specifically states that the procedures in the bill are the exclusive means by which electronic surveillance, as defined in the bill, and the interception of domestic wire and oral communications may be conducted."[1,140]

The Bush Administration's reliance on language in *In re Sealed Case* and the three court of appeals decisions noted therein is not persuasive for several reasons. The actual statement in the *In re Sealed Case* is *dicta*—the issue before the FISA court was whether the new "significant purpose" test for FISA warrants enacted pursuant to the PATRIOT Act complied with the Fourth Amendment, not whether warrantless domestic surveillance was constitutional.[1,141] Also, all three court of appeals decisions cited by the Administration were decided prior to the enactment of the 1978 FISA law and are easily distinguishable.[1,142] After reviewing these cases, the non-partisan Congressional Research Service concluded, "[i]n the wake of FISA's passage, the Court of Review's reliance [in the *In re Sealed Case*] on these pre-FISA cases or cases dealing with pre-FISA surveillance as a basis for its assumption of the continued vitality of the President's inherent authority to authorize the warrantless electronic surveillance for the purpose of gathering foreign intelligence information might be viewed as somewhat undercutting the persuasive force of the Court of Review's statement."[1,143]

## Fourth Amendment

Even if the Administration is able to establish that warrantless domestic wiretapping was statutorily or otherwise legally authorized—which does not appear to be the case—in order to be lawful, it must also be shown to comply with the Fourth Amendment's warrant requirement (which has been definitively held to apply to electronic surveillance[1,144]). For its part, the Bush Administration argues that the NSA program should be considered reasonable, both under a general "balancing of interests" test under the Fourth Amendment[1,145] and pursuant to a "special needs" exception to the Fourth Amendment set forth in various court decisions.[1,146]

The Administration's contention that the domestic wiretapping program complies with the Fourth Amendment fails for several reasons. First, the cases cited by the Justice Department can be easily distinguished, and are either pre-FISA or include mitigating factors that are not present in the Bush Administration's warrantless surveillance program.[1,147] As the letter signed by former FBI Director Sessions Professor Van Alstyne and other scholars and officials explained:

> The NSA spying program has none of the safeguards found critical to upholding "special needs" searches in other contexts. It consists not of a minimally intrusive brief stop on a highway or urine test, but of the wiretapping of private telephone and email com-

munications. It is not standardized, but subject to discretionary targeting under a standard and process that remain secret. Those whose privacy is intruded upon have no notice or choice to opt out of the surveillance. And it is neither limited to the environment of a school nor analogous to a brief stop for a few seconds at a highway checkpoint. Finally, and most importantly, the fact that FISA has been used successfully for almost thirty years demonstrates that a warrant and probably cause regime is not impracticable for foreign intelligence surveillance.[1,148]

Second, the essential test set forth by the Bush Administration for conducting warrantless wiretapping—an NSA determination that there is a "reasonable basis to believe" that a party to the communication is a member of Al Qaeda, affiliated with Al Qaeda, or a member of an organization affiliated with Al Qaeda or working in support of Al Qaeda"—is inconsistent with the Fourth Amendment's probable cause requirement. Although the Attorney General has attempted to argue that "it's the same standard,"[1,149] George Washington Law School Professor Jeffrey Rosen has observed, "[I]t's not the same standard: Probable cause is clearly more demanding."[1,150] Another legal expert, President Bush's Chief of the FBI's national security law unit Michael J. Woods, explained that this lower legal threshold may be the reason the Administration decided to opt out of FISA to begin with.[1,151]

Third, and in any event, it does not appear that the surveillance being performed under the NSA program can meet even the Administration's lower self-imposed "reasonable basis" standard, which would need to be applied by a court and not the Administration. According to government sources, and as noted at greater length below, the NSA program had little discernible impact on the government's ability to prevent terrorist plots by Al Qaeda.[1,152] It has been reported by official sources that fewer than ten U.S. persons per year have aroused sufficient suspicion during warrantless surveillance to warrant seeking a full fledged FISA warrant.[1,153] Accordingly, both national security lawyers working for and outside the Bush Administration have stated that this low "washout" rate make it doubtful the program could be deemed "reasonable" and pass muster under the Fourth Amendment.[1,154]

A government lawyer who has closely examined the NSA wiretapping program has stated that the minimum conceivable definition of "reasonable basis" would require that evidence derived from the eavesdropping would be "right for one out of every two guys at least."[1,155] This individual stated that the people who developed the program "knew they could never meet that standard—that's why they didn't go through" the FISA court.[1,156] Michael J. Woods has reiterated that even the Administration's own "reasonable basis" standard would necessitate, as a constitutional matter, evidence "that would lead a prudent, appropriately experienced person" to believe the American was a terrorist agent, and if the program returned "a large number of false positives, I would have to conclude that the factor is not a sufficiently reliable indicator and thus would carry less (or no) weight."[1,157]

## NSA Domestic Database Program

Our review indicates that creating a massive NSA database program first disclosed by *USA Today* has also resulted in apparent legal violations. These include ongoing civil violations of the Stored Communications Act and the Communications Act, and potentially criminal violations as well.[1,158] The Stored Communications Act of 1986[1,159] (SCA) prohibits the knowing disclosure of customer telephone records to the government unless pursuant to subpoena, warrant,[1,160] or a National Security Letter (or other Administrative subpoena);[1,161] with the customer's "lawful consent;"[1,162] when there is a business necessity;[1,163] or when there is an emergency involving danger of death or serious physical injury.[1,164] None of these exceptions apply to the circumstances described in the *USA Today* story.

Qwest has already stated that with regard to the subpoena or warrant, "no such authority had been granted." As the program is being run through the NSA, not the FBI, no NSLs would have been issued to obtain the data.[1,165] There is also no colorable argument of business necessity; if anything, releasing the records was deleterious to the phone companies' business. With regard to customer consent,[1,166] this would not seem applicable under the present circumstances because the provision is analogous to the consent exception of the closely related Federal Wiretap Act,[1,167] requiring that "the user actually agreed to the action, either explicitly or implicitly based on the user's decision to proceed in light of actual notice, and there is no indication such opt-in notice was provided."[1,168] As for the "emergency" exception, there is no indication either the post-2006 ("the provider, in good faith, believes that an emergency involving danger or death, or serious physical injury to any person"), or pre-2006 (the provider "reasonably believed that there was an immediate danger of death or physical injury") statutory language was in any way intended by Congress to exempt wholesale requests by the NSA for entire databases on an ongoing basis. Moreover, given that the NSA database program has been operating continuously for nearly five years—through a range of color-coded threats—it would seem to be an impossible task to claim for the government to claim that at all times and in all regions there was an "immediate danger" to life.[1,169]

Section 222 of the Communications Act[1,170] prohibits the disclosure of telephone customer information to any third party except as required by law,[1,171] with the approval of the customer,[1,172] or for other specific business exigencies.[1,173] Again, none of these exceptions apply in the present situation. There has been no court approved warrant or subpoena issued and none of the identified business exigencies apply. With respect to the customer consent argument, this would again require affirmative opt-in by millions of customers as required by the analogous Federal Wiretap Act, as well as the applicable regulations.[1,174]

The NSA would have separately violated the criminal law if it obtained the customer information on a "real-time" basis, through so-called "trap and trace" or "pen register" mechanisms. This is a concern given that a former intelligence official has stated, "[t]his is not about getting a cardboard box of monthly phone bills in alphabetical order. The N.S.A. is getting real time and actionable intelligence."[1,175] The Pen Register and Trap and Trace Statute (18 U.S.C. Sec. 3121) prohibits the installation of any pen register or trap and trace device without first obtaining a court order under FISA or under the general criminal wiretap law.[1,176] Again, in the present circumstances there is no indication that a request for a warrant was made by the Justice Department under either FISA or the criminal wiretap laws. As a result, both the Center for Democracy and Technology (CDT) and the Center for National Security Studies have concluded that the Administration's actions were likely unlawful. CDT wrote, "[i]f the program involved real-time interception, it probably violated both the Foreign Intelligence Surveillance Act and the statute on interception of call detail information in criminal cases."[1,177] Kate Martin, the Director of the Center wrote,"[i]f the NSA used a pen register or trap and trace device in real time, it was required to obtain an order from the FISA court, either under the specific pen register provisions . . . or under the provisions for electronic surveillance generally."[1,178]

Finally, although the Supreme Court held in 1979 in *Smith v. Maryland* [1,179] by a 5-4 vote that the use of a pen register recording numbers from a specific phone is not considered a "search" for Fourth Amendment purposes, there are some indications that the decision may not have continued viability given changes in technology over the years.  As Professor Tribe wrote of the 1979 decision, "[un]convincing then, those words ring hollow today, now that information technology has made feasible the NSA program whose cover was blown [in May]. That program profiles virtually every American's phone conversations, giving government instant access to detailed knowledge of the numbers, and thus indirectly the identities, of whomever we phone, when and for how long, and what other calls the person phoned has made or received. As Justice Stewart recognized in 1979, a list of numbers called "easily could reveal. . . the most intimate details of a person's life."[1,180] If Professor Tribe is correct, the NSA database program would also constitute a violation of the Fourth Amendment as well as the above referenced statutory prohibitions.

## Additional Non-Legal Justifications

The Bush Administration has also propounded a number of non-legal justifications for the NSA surveillance programs.  First, they have argued that it is impractical and cumbersome for the Administration to comply with FISA, which they assert needs to be "modernized."[1,181] Second, Vice President Cheney, General Hayden, and others have asserted that had warrantless domestic spying programs been in place in the early part of 2001, they would have been able to prevent the September 11 attacks—by intercepting the communications involving two of the 9-11 hijackers (Nawaf Alhazmi and Khalid Almidhar)[1,182] or their co-conspirator Zacarias Moussaoui.[1,183] Third, members of the Bush Administration,[1,184] the Republican National Committee[1,185] and their allies have asserted that Presidents Jimmy Carter and Bill Clinton authorized comparable forms of surveillance programs during their administrations through Executive Orders and Project Echelon.

The Bush Administration's contention that FISA is too "cumbersome and burdensome"[1,186] and has not been "modernized" is belied by the fact that FISA clearly permits the Attorney General to conduct emergency surveillance so long as they obtain court approval within three days.[1,187] The Bush Administration has never adequately explained why this three-day retroactivity requirement was not appropriate for their needs, other than to say that processing FISA applications requires significant manpower and resources.[1,188] However, we are not aware of any request by the Administration to obtain the necessary personnel or resources to allow them to comply with the law.

FISA itself has been updated on numerous occasions to respond to concerns regarding its "agility." Soon after the September 11 attacks, Congress amended FISA to extend its emergency exemption from 24 to 72 hours.[1,189] The PATRIOT Act included some twenty-five separate updates to FISA[1,190] including: (i) expanding the scope of FISA pen register authority;[1,191] (ii) lowering the standard for FISA pen-traps;[1,192] (iii) lowering the legal standard for FISA surveillance;[1,193] (iv) extending the duration of FISA warrants;[1,194] (v) expanding the scope of business records that can be sought with a FISA order;[1,195] (vi) allowing for "John Doe" roving wiretaps;[1,196] (vii) requiring the intelligence community to set FISA requirements and assist with dissemination of FISA Information;[1,197] (viii) immunizing those complying with FISA orders;[1,198] (ix) lowering the standard for National Security Letters;[1,199] and (x) expanding NSL approval authorities.[1,200] Subsequent to the passage of the PATRIOT Act, Congress has again at the Administration's request broadened FISA to allow surveillance of "Lone Wolf" terrorists.[1,201]

Moreover, the *Washington Post* has reported that **"[s]everal FISA judges said they . . . remain puzzled by Bush's assertion that the court was not 'agile' or 'nimble' enough to help catch terrorists. The court had routinely approved emergency wiretaps 72 hours after they had begun, as FISA allows, and the court's actions in the days after the Sept. 11 attacks suggested that its judges were hardly unsympathetic to the needs of their nation at war."**[1,202] Indeed, the ease of use of both the standard warrant and the emergency provisions is illustrated by the fact that between 1979 and 2004 the FISA court approved 18,748 warrants and rejected only five applications,[1,203] while between 2001 and April 1, 2003, DOJ had successfully employed the emergency FISA provisions 170 times—nearly four times as often as it has been used by all previous administrations combined.[1,204]

**In addition, the FISA court has specifically acceded to adopting new procedures to streamline the FISA warrant process.** On September 12, 2001, one day after the attacks, when FBI Director Robert Mueller and other Justice officials asked then-FISA presiding judge Lamberth to allow for expedited FISA procedures, he immediately agreed. According to an informed government official: "The requirement for detailed paperwork was greatly eased, allowing the NSA to begin eavesdropping the next day on anyone suspected of a link to Al Qaeda, every person who had ever been a member or supporter of militant Islamic groups, and everyone ever linked to a terrorist watch list in the United States or abroad."[1,205] **Even former Secretary of State Colin Powell acknowledged that it would not have been "that hard" for the Bush Administration to obtain warrants to comply with FISA requirements.**[1,206]

The Administration's claims that the NSA programs could have prevented the September 11 attacks also do not appear to comport with the facts. With respect to Nawaf Alhazmi and Khalid Almihdhar, the September 11th Commission found the government had already compiled significant information on these individuals prior to the attacks, writing, "[o]n May 15, [2001], [a CIA official] reexamined many of the old cables from early 2000, including the information that Mihdhar had a U.S. visa, and that Hazmi had come to Los Angeles on January 15, 2000. The CIA official who reviewed the cables took no action regarding them."[1,207] Under FISA, the Administration could have used the information to seek permission to monitor the suspects' phone calls and e-mails without risking any disclosure of the classified information. It is also not at all clear that warrantless surveillance would have been useful in averting the 9-11 attacks, since the Administration was unable to locate where the two suspects were living in the United States and according to the FBI "had missed numerous opportunities to track them down in the 20 months before the attacks."[1,208] **Senator Bob Kerry, who was a member of the 9-11 Commission, specifically criticized General Hayden for suggesting that the NSA warrantless wiretapping program could have prevented the September 11 attack stating: "[t]hat's patently false and an indication that he's willing to politicize intelligence and use false information to help the President."**[1,209]

As for the Administration's claims regarding Zacarias Moussaoui, a 2003 Senate Judiciary Committee Report found that the evidence gathered against him would have met the standard for acquiring a FISA warrant, and that FBI personnel "failed miserably" in its attempts to secure approval for a warrant.[1,210] More recently, FBI Agent Harry Samit, who had interrogated Mr. Moussaoui before the September 11 attacks, testified he had warned his superiors more than 70 times, and as recently as September 10, 2001, that he believed that Moussaoui was a terrorist involved in a plot to hijack an airplane, but the warnings were ignored by the FBI's Bin Laden unit.[1,211] It also has been reported that the FBI ignored warnings from Phoenix FBI Agent Kenneth Williams that he had uncovered a scheme by Al Qaeda to send terrorists to the U.S. to obtain flight training.[1,212]

Third, it is not factually correct to assert that either Presidents Carter or Clinton authorized surveillance comparable to President Bush's NSA programs. In attempting to divert attention from President Bush's conduct, the Republican National Committee asserted that both Presidents Carter and Clinton had authorized comparable forms of "search [or] surveillance without court orders."[1,213] However, the RNC misstated the impact of a Clinton Executive Order; EO 12949 merely clarified the existing FISA authority for warrantless surveillance in emergency situations.[1,214] The RNC left out the requirement, included in the same sentence of the Executive Order, that any warrantless search not involve "the premises, information, material or property of a United States person."[1,215] The Carter Executive Order 12139 also only permitted warrantless surveillance on "foreigners who are not protected by the Constitution."[1,216]

With regard to the argument that under President Clinton Project Echelon was comparable to the Bush Administration's domestic database program, that program was premised on court-approved warrants. Thus, then-CIA Director George Tenet in his April 12, 2002 testimony before the Senate Intelligence Committee stated that Project Echelon utilized the warrant process: "We do not target [the phone calls of U.S. residents] for collection in the United States unless a FISA warrant has been obtained from the FISA Court by the Justice Department."[1,217]

## Intelligence Briefings In Violation of the National Security Act

Members of the Bush Administration have repeatedly pointed to the value and significance of their briefing certain members of House and Senate Leadership and the Chairs and Ranking Members of the House and Senate Intelligence Committees regarding the domestic spying programs.[1,218] The NSA briefings concerning both the warrantless wiretap and domestic database programs were conducted by the Administration as so-called "Gang of Eight" briefings—which included the Speaker and Minority Leader of the House, the Majority and Minority Leaders of the Senate, and the Chairmen and Ranking Members of the Congressional Intelligence Committees.[1,219]

Briefings of this nature would appear to be in violation of the National Security Act of 1947,[1,220] which governs the manner in which Members of Congress are to be briefed on intelligence activities.[1,221] The law requires the President to keep all Members of the House and Senate Intelligence Committees "fully and currently informed" of intelligence activities. Only in the case of a highly classified covert action (when the U.S. engages in operations to influence political, economic, or military conditions of another country) does a statute expressly permit the President to limit briefings to a select group of Members.[1,222] Covert actions, pursuant to the statute, do not include "activities the primary purpose of which is to acquire intelligence."[1,223] The Act makes clear that the requirement to keep the committees informed may not be evaded on the grounds that "providing the information to the congressional intelligence committees would constitute the unauthorized disclosure of classified information."[1,224] (Eventually, on May 12, 2006, the White House relented and permitted full briefings of the House and Senate Intelligence Committees, but this appeared to simply be an effort to ease Gerald Hayden's confirmation hearings before the Senate Intelligence Committee scheduled for the next day.)[1225]

In the report, "Statutory Procedures Under Which Congress Is To Be Informed of

U.S. Intelligence Activities, Including Covert Actions," the Congressional Research Service concludes that "[b]ased upon publicly reported descriptions of the program, the NSA surveillance program would appear to fall more closely under the definition of an intelligence collection program, rather than qualify as a covert action program as defined by statute."[1,226] Under this characterization, **according to Congressional Research Service, "limiting congressional notification of the NSA program to the Gang of Eight . . . would appear to be inconsistent with the law."**[1,227]

It is also disingenuous for members of the Bush Administration to assert that the briefings themselves somehow gave the warrantless or domestic database programs enhanced legitimacy or legality,[1,228] as those Members who were briefed were constrained from taking actions to preempt the program. Suzanne Spaulding, former legal counsel for both Republican and Democratic leaders on the House and Senate Intelligence Committees explained the inherent limitations of the "Gang of Eight" briefings: "They are provided only to the leadership of the House and Senate and of the intelligence committees, with no staff present. The eight are prohibited from saying anything about the briefing to anyone, including other intelligence panel members. The leaders for whom I worked never discussed the content of these briefings with me. It is virtually impossible for individual members of Congress, particularly members of the minority party, to take any effective action if they have concerns about what they have heard in one of these briefings. It is not realistic to expect them, working alone, to sort through complex legal issues, conduct the kind of factual investigation required for true oversight and develop an appropriate legislative response."[1,229] Intelligence Committee Ranking Democrat Jane Harmann agreed, writing, "Gang of Eight briefings do not provide for effective oversight. Members of the Gang of Eight cannot take notes, seek the advice of counsel, or even discuss the issues raised with their committee colleagues."[1,230]

## ■ The legal justifications used to justify the NSA programs threaten to establish a constitutionally destabilizing precedent.

*"To borrow from Justice Robert Jackson's dissent in* Korematsu v. United States *(1944), the chilling danger created by President Bush's claim of wartime omnipotence to justify the NSA's eavesdropping is that the precedent will lie around like a loaded weapon ready for the hand of the incumbent or any successor who would reduce Congress to an ink blot."*

—JANUARY 26, 2006, FORMER REAGAN ASSOCIATE DEPUTY
ATTORNEY GENERAL BRUCE FEIN, TESTIFYING AT HOUSE
DEMOCRATIC HEARINGS ON THE NSA WIRETAP SCANDAL[1,231]

One of the most problematic aspects of the domestic wiretapping program is the after-the-fact legal rationales developed by the Justice Department to justify the program to the public. By articulating far-fetched and extravagant legal justifications, the Bush

Administration has compounded the initial problem by asserting a legal precedent without any meaningful limitation on executive authority, which sends a signal that the president considers himself to be above the law.

As *Barron's Magazine* Associate Editor Thomas G. Donlan wrote, the existence of the NSA wiretapping program "was worrisome on its face, but in justifying their actions, officials have made a bad situation much worse: Administration lawyers and the president himself have tortured the Constitution and extracted a suspension of the separation of powers."[1,232] Similarly, Jonathan Schell noted that "if [the president] can suspend FISA at this whim and in secret, then what law can he not suspend? What need is there, for example, to pass or not pass the Patriot Act if any or all of its provisions can be secretly exceeded by the President? If abuses of power are kept secret, there is still the possibility that, when exposed, they will be stopped. But if they are exposed, and still permitted to continue, then every remedy has failed, and the abuse is permanently ratified. In this case what will be ratified is a presidency that has risen above the law."[1,233] In a similar vein, **during the Senate Judiciary Committee hearings, Republican Senator Lindsey Graham told the Attorney General, "[r]eally, Mr. Attorney General, you could use the inherent authority argument of a Commander-in-Chief at a time of war to almost wipe out anything Congress wanted to do."**[1,234]

The Administration's response to this concern has been somewhat inconsistent and contradictory. When asked about the limits of executive power during an interview on January 31, 2006 on CBS News, the President responded that he believed his power had limits even in wartime: "I don't think a president can order torture, for example. I don't think a president can order the assassination of a leader of another country with which we're not at war . . . There are clear red lines."[1,235] However, the President has not articulated where these "clear red lines" are derived from, if not the types of statutory and constitutional limitations that were ignored in connection with the warrantless surveillance program itself. Moreover, Attorney General Gonzales has contradicted the president's statements about what those limitations may be. When Senator Graham asked if it was lawful for the Congress to tell the executive that he cannot physically abuse a prisoner of war, he stated, "I am not prepared to say that, Senator. I think that is—I think you can make an argument that is part of the rule the Government . . . ."[1,236] In addition, the President's assertions of limitations are undermined by his own signing statement that he was not bound by the recently enacted congressional limitations on torture.[1,237]

Many observers have seen through the Administration's arguments and found real danger in the breadth and brazenness of their legal contentions. *New York Times* columnist Bob Herbert has explained that by operating independently of the courts, the Bush Administration is jeopardizing the principal of "separation of powers, which is the absolutely crucial cornerstone of our form of government—our bulwark against tyranny. An elaborate system of checks and balances (you need a warrant from a court to wiretap, for example) prevents the concentration of too much power in any one branch, or any one person. Get rid of the checks and balances and you've gotten rid of the United States as we know it."[1,238] Others recognized that by legally justifying warrantless surveillance, the Administration was using the very same arguments it had wrongfully used to justify torture and other unchecked abuses of executive power. The *Washington Post* warned, "[t]his [legal] interpretation [of domestic spying], with its expansive view of the commander in chief's powers, would call into question Congress's ability to prevent the administration from engaging in torture or cruel and inhuman treatment or to establish rules for detainees and military tribunals . . . ."[1,239]

Web commentator Glen Greenwald has observed that the same dangerous and limitless legal argument appeared in the now infamous "Bybee Memo" justifying torture in contravention of applicable international treaties and legal structures. Just as in the case of domestic spying, the Bybee Memo contended, "it must be admitted, as a necessary consequence, that there can be *no limitation* of that authority, which is to provide for the defense and safety of the community, *in any matter essential to its efficacy* . . . . The Constitution's sweeping grant vests in the President an *unenumerated* Executive power . . . The Commander in Chief Power and the President's obligation to protect the Nation *imply the ancillary powers necessary to their successful exercise.*"[1,240] *U.S. News & World Report* recently reported that soon after the September 11, 2001 terror attacks, lawyers in the White House and the Justice Department argued that the same legal authority that allowed warrantless electronic surveillance inside the U.S. could also be used to justify physical searches of terror suspects homes and businesses without court approval.[1,241]

Fears that the legally expansive rationales behind the warrantless wiretapping program would be used to justify other unilateral actions which may impinge on our citizens' civil liberties have been validated during the limited hearings held by the Senate and House Judiciary Committees. At the Senate Judiciary hearing on February 6, 2006, Attorney General Gonzales refused to respond to Senator Schumer's question as to whether the Administration had entered the homes of any American citizens without warrants.[1,242] Moreover, subsequent to the hearing, the Attorney General wrote an ominous letter creating the impression that there were indeed additional top secret programs using such authority outside of the domestic spying program. The *Washington Post* wrote, "Attorney General Alberto R. Gonzales appeared to suggest yesterday that the Bush Administration's warrantless domestic surveillance operations may extend beyond the outlines that the president acknowledged in mid-December."[1,243]

Other examples of the dangerous nature of the legal precedent set by the warrantless surveillance program can be illustrated by the response to questions submitted by Members of the House Judiciary Committee. Among other things, the Department of Justice made clear that even if Congress passed legislation restricting the domestic warrantless wiretapping program and the President signed it and agreed to it, the president was subsequently free to ignore these restrictions under the inherent authority argument.[1,244] **Of particular concern, at the House Judiciary hearings, the Attorney General essentially** admitted that under the inherent authority argument, the Administration would also have the legal authority to intercept purely domestic communications between American citizens without a court approved warrant. In response to a question from Rep. Adam Schiff (D-CA), Mr. Gonzales stated, "I'm not going to rule it out."[1,245]

# ■ President Bush and other high ranking members of the Bush Administration appear to have made a number of misleading statements concerning the NSA programs.

*"Now, by the way, any time you hear the United States government talking about wiretap, it requires—a wiretap requires a court order. Nothing has changed, by the way. When we're talking about chasing down terrorists, we're talking about getting a court order before we do so . . . constitutional guarantees are in place when it comes to doing what is necessary to protect our homeland, because we value the Constitution."*

—APRIL 20, 2004, PRESIDENT GEORGE W. BUSH, BUFFALO, NY,
IN A SPEECH DISCUSSING THE ENACTMENT OF THE USA PATRIOT ACT[1,246]

As part of the efforts to justify the NSA surveillance programs, it appears that President Bush and members of his Administration made a number of inaccurate statements. These include statements to the effect that domestic wiretapping was being done according to court approved warrants, indicating that no purely domestic communications were intercepted, that the government was not monitoring U.S. calls on a widespread basis, and mischaracterizing the extent and nature of concerns raised by Members during the course of classified briefings.

## Statements that the government was only intercepting communications involving American citizens pursuant to court approved warrants

Separate and apart from the question of the legality of the warrantless wiretapping program, it appears that Members of the Bush Administration misled Members of Congress and the American people when discussing this issue before the December, 2005 *New York Times* disclosure of the program. The public record reveals that on numerous occasions prior to this disclosure, President Bush and others in his Administration indicated that wiretapping of Americans would only occur pursuant to a court order:

- On September 10, 2002, then-Associate Attorney General David Kris testified before the Senate Judiciary Committee that "both before and after the PATRIOT Act, FISA can be used only against foreign powers and their agents, and only when there is at least a significant foreign intelligence purpose for the surveillance. Let me repeat for emphasis, we cannot monitor anyone today whom we could not have monitored at this time last year."[1,247]

- On April 19, 2004, President Bush stated, "law enforcement uses so-called roving wiretaps to investigate organized crime. You see, what that meant is if you got a wiretap by court order—and, by the way, everything you hear about requires court order, requires there to be permission from a FISA court, for example."[1,248]

- On April 20, 2004, President Bush stated: "Now, by the way, any time you hear the United States government talking about wiretap, it requires—a wiretap requires a court order. Nothing has changed, by the way. When we're talking about chasing down terrorists, we're talking about getting a court order before we do so . . . constitutional guarantees are in place when it comes to doing what is necessary to protect our homeland, because we value the Constitution."[1,249]

- On July 14, 2004, the President stated, "[f]irst of all, any action that takes place by law enforcement requires a court order. In other words, the government can't move on wiretaps or roving wiretaps without getting a court order."[1250]

- On January 6, 2005, in response to Senator Feingold asking "Does the President, in your opinion, have the authority, acting as Commander in Chief, to authorize warrantless searches of American's homes and wiretaps of their conversations in violation of the criminal and foreign intelligence surveillance statutes of this country?" Mr. Gonzalez responded, "It's not the policy or the agenda of this President to authorize actions that would be in contravention of our criminal statutes."[1251] When Senator Feingold followed up by asking if Mr. Gonzales would "commit to notify Congress if the President makes this type of decision and not wait two years until a memo is leaked about it," he replied, "I will commit to advise the Congress as soon as I reasonably can, yes, sir."[1252]

- On June 9, 2005, President Bush stated, "Law enforcement officers need a federal judge's permission to wiretap a foreign terrorists phone, a federal judge's permission to track his calls, or a federal judge's permission to search his property."[1253] Similarly, on July 20, 2005, President Bush stated: "Law enforcement officers need a federal judge's permission to wiretap a foreign terrorist's phone, or to track his calls, or to search his property."[1254]

These statements do not comport with the Administration's responsibility to be careful and forthright in their statements to the Congress or the American people. The principal defense offered by President Bush is that "I was talking about roving wiretaps, I believe, involving the PATRIOT Act. This is different from the NSA program."[1252] This defense is incomplete at best, and misleading at worst.

First, the blanket defense does not apply to the many misleading statements made by members of the Bush Administration. Thus, on September 10, 2002, when Associate Attorney Kris stated, "We cannot monitor anyone today whom we could not have monitored at this time last year," this would seem false by any construction. The context of the statement indicates that with or without the PATRIOT Act, checks and balances—

in the form of court-approved surveillance—are in place. It is also clearly misleading, when in January 2005, Attorney General Gonzales, who was integrally involved in the creation of the domestic spying program, told Senator Feingold that warrantless surveillance was not occurring, and pledged to let him know if such a program was initiated (which he never did). The Attorney General's response was in no way limited to PATRIOT Act authorities.

With regard to the President's statements, while they were made in speeches during which the PATRIOT Act was discussed, it is not at all clear that the President was intending to limit his remarks—which did not include specific qualifications—to the PATRIOT Act. Read in context, it would seem the more reasonable interpretation of the statements is as part of an overall effort to convince the public that the Justice Department was not over reaching in their investigations. This construction is supported by the fact that most investigations involve a variety of authorities, some under the PATRIOT Act, and some under other authorities. For example, the so-called "roving wiretaps" referred to by the president in his defense exist under both the PATRIOT Act and general criminal law.[1,256]

## Statements that no purely domestic communications were intercepted under the warrantless wiretapping program

On numerous occasions, members of the Bush Administration have asserted that the NSA warrantless wiretapping program does not include purely domestic communications. For example, on January 25, 2006, President Bush stated the NSA program was limited to international calls, stating, "[i]n other words, one end of the communication must be outside the United States."[1,257] On December 19, 2005, Attorney General Gonzales indicated that "[t]he President has authorized a program to engage in electronic surveillance of a particular kind, and this would be the intercepts of contents of communications where one of the—one party to the communication is outside the United States."[1,258] On January 19, 2006, Vice President Cheney stated that the surveillance program consists of "international communications, one end of which [the NSA] have reason to believe is related to Al Qaeda or to terrorist networks affiliated with Al Qaeda."[1,259] Furthermore, on January 23, 2006, General Hayden said that "[o]ne end of any call targeted under this program is always outside the United States."[1,260]

These statements do not appear to be accurate. Government sources and other media reports indicate that purely domestic communications have been intercepted in connection with the warrantless wiretapping program, and that this occurs by virtue of the program accidently capturing domestic-to-domestic cell phone and other communications and by intentionally capturing communications by Americans as part of an expanding chain of intercepts which may have began abroad.

First, government officials have specifically indicated that the eavesdropping program "has captured what are purely domestic communications."[1,261] According to Robert

Morris, a former senior scientist at the NSA, it is "difficult, even for the NSA, to determine whether someone is inside or outside the United States when making a cell phone call or sending an email message."[1,262] As a result, telecommunications experts believed that the "people [the NSA] may think are outside the United States are actually on American soil."[1,263] Government officials, confirming that there are accidental intercepts of purely domestic calls, revealed that there have been instances of "someone using an international cell phone [being] thought to be outside the United States when in fact both people in the conversation were in the country."[1,264]

That there is little question that purely domestic communications have been at least inadvertently captured can be seen by the fact that at Judiciary Committee hearings, the Justice Department indicated that such communications are destroyed when they are identified.[1,265] It is also telling that the Administration has not responded to charges that the program may have specifically targeted American citizens. For example, NBC implied in an interview with James Risen that CNN's chief international correspondent, Christiane Amanpour, was targeted by the NSA domestic surveillance program.[1,266] In the interview, Andrea Mitchell asked Mr. Risen, "You don't have any information, for instance, that a very prominent journalist, Christiane Amanpour, might have been eavesdropped upon?" The transcript from the interview was posted on the MSNBC.com website, but NBC later redacted the portion of the transcript concerning the line of questioning on the wiretapping of Amanpour.[1,267] Mr. Conyers and 27 other Members asked President Bush to respond to this charge, in a letter dated January 5, 2006;[1,268] however, we have never received a response to this letter.[1,269]

Second, there is evidence the NSA warrantless wiretapping program includes purely domestic communications by individuals located in the U.S. who have been linked to foreign parties. Officials familiar with the warrantless surveillance program indicated that initially the NSA program was intended to exploit computers, cell phones, and personal directories of Al Qaeda operatives that had been seized by the CIA overseas.[1,270] However, in addition to eavesdropping on data retrieved from the seized items, according to the government officials, the "NSA began monitoring others linked to them, creating an expanding chain."[1,271] Although most of the numbers and addresses were overseas, according to officials, "hundreds [of the telephone numbers and email addresses] were in the United States."[1,272] According to the *New York Times*, "In addition to eavesdropping on those numbers and reading e-mail messages to and from the Qaeda figures, the N.S.A. began monitoring others linked to them, creating an expanding chain. While most of the numbers and addresses were overseas, hundreds were in the United States, the officials said."[1,273]

The *Washington Times* confirmed the nature of this ever-expanding chain pulling in domestic-to-domestic communications based on their discussions with law enforcement officials:

The [law enforcement] sources provided guidelines to how the administration has employed the surveillance program. They said the National Security Agency in cooperation with the FBI was allowed to monitor the telephone calls and e-mails of any American believed to be in contact with a person abroad suspected of being linked to Al Qaeda or other terrorist groups. *At that point, the sources said, all of the communications of that American would be monitored, including calls made to others in the United States. The regulations under the administration's surveillance program do not require any court order.*[1,274]

Current and former government officials as well as private sector sources have confirmed the basic outlines on the program, and its impact on purely American communications. On February 5, 2006, the *Washington Post* wrote:

> The program has touched many . . . Americans . . . . Surveillance takes place in several stages, officials said, the earliest by machine. Computer-controlled systems collect and sift basic information about hundreds of thousands of faxes, e-mails and telephone calls into and out of the United States before selecting the ones for scrutiny by human eyes and ears. Successive stages of filtering grow more intrusive as artificial intelligence systems rank voice and data traffic in order of likeliest interest to human analysts. But intelligence officers, who test the computer judgements by listening initially to brief fragments of conversation "wash out" most of the leads within days or weeks."[1,275]

In the May 29 issue of the *New Yorker*, Seymour Hersh confirmed that the Bush Administration was using this technique known as "chaining" to eavesdrop on domestic calls without a warrant:

> The N.S.A. also programmed computers to map the connections between telephone numbers in the United States and suspected numbers abroad, focusing on a geographic area, rather than on a specific person—for example, a region of Pakistan. Such calls often triggered a process known as "chaining" in which subsequent calls to and from the American number were monitored and linked . . . . The N.S.A. began, in some cases, to eavesdrop on callers (often using computers to listen for key words) . . . . A government consultant told me that tens of thousands of American had their calls monitored in one way or another. "In the old days, you needed probable cause to listen in. But you could not listen in to generate probable cause."[1,276]

## Statements that the government is not monitoring telephone calls and other communications within the U.S.

The President and other members of the Bush Administration have also made a number of statements to the effect that the Administration was not monitoring calls or other domestic communications. For example, on December 27, 2005, White House spokesman Trent Duffy stated that the NSA program was "a limited program. This is not about monitoring phone calls designed to arrange Little League practice or what to bring to a potluck dinner."[1,277] On May 8, 2006, when Intelligence Director John Negroponte declared the Bush Administration was "absolutely not" monitoring domestic calls without warrants and added, "I wouldn't call it domestic spying."[1,278] On the day of the *USA Today* disclosure of the domestic database scandal, President Bush said, "[t]he privacy of ordinary Americans is fiercely protected in all our activities. We're not mining or trolling through the personal lives of millions of innocent Americans."[1,279]

In light of the *USA Today* disclosure, it was incomplete at best, and misleading at worst, for Mr. Duffy and Mr. Negroponte to state that U.S. calls were not being monitored, given that, as the article makes clear, "[t]he NSA has been secretly collecting the phone call records of tens of millions of Americans" and the "NSA program reaches into homes and businesses across the nation by amassing information about the calls of ordinary Americans—most of whom aren't suspected of any crime."[1,280]

President Bush's statement that his Administration is not "mining or trolling through the personal lives of millions of Americans" also appears difficult to defend in light of the *USA Today* story. Even beyond the article's disclosure of the existence of the NSA database program, there is ample evidence the Bush Administration monitors the domestic communications of innocent Americans and maintain data bases of numerous aspects of our personal lives. Consider the following revelations which were disclosed independently of the May 11 *USA Today* article:

• In October 2002, then-Senate Intelligence Chairman Bob Graham stated that "briefers told him in Cheney's office . . . that Bush had authorized the [NSA] to tap into [domestic telephone] junctions . . . . and allowed the NSA to intercept conversations . . . that went through a transit facility inside the United States.'"[1,281]

• In October 2002, NSA Director General Michael Hayden testified, "I have met personally with prominent corporate executive officers. (One senior executive confided that the data management needs we outlined to him were larger than any he had previously seen). [ . . . ] And last week we cemented a deal with another corporate giant to jointly develop a system to mine data . . . ."[1,282]

• In November 2002, the *New York Times* reported that the Pentagon was developing a tracking system called Total Information Awareness (TIA), which would have been capable of searching countless public and private databases and combining the information to find patterns and associations, peering into the lives of 300 million Americans.[1,283] Although Congress eliminated funding for the controversial project in September 2003,[1,284] TIA has been replaced by a number of programs, including: (i) the NSA's "Advanced Research and Development Activity" (ARDA)(the National Journal reported that research under TIA was moved to ARDA);[1,285] (ii) the Pentagon's "Threat and Local Observation Notice" (TALON) Program[1,286] (a memo obtained by Newsweek shows that the deputy Defense secretary admitted that TALON reports likely contain information on innocent U.S. citizens and groups);[1,287] (iii) the Department of Homeland Security's "Analysis, Dissemination, Visualization, Insight, and Semantic Enhancement" (ADVISE) Program (designed to assemble a database by linking information from blogs, e-mail and government records);[1,288] and (iv) the Pentagon's Counter Intelligence Field Activity (CIFA) (which was found to have "failed to follow policies regarding the collection and retention of information about U.S. persons").[1,289] In May 2004, the GAO issued a report confirming that the Bush Administration was engaged in "199 data mining efforts. . . [of which] 122 used personal information."[1,290] According to the GAO, the data mining included personal information from private and government sources.[1,291]

- On December 23, 2005, the *New York Times* reported that according to government officials, "the NSA has gained the cooperation of American telecommunications companies to obtain backdoor access to streams of domestic and international communications"[1,292] and the leading telecommunication companies "have been storing information on calling patterns and giving it to the federal government . . . ."[1,293] The *Times* further reported that according to a telecommunications industry source, "efforts to obtain call details go back to early 2001, predating the 9-11 attacks" and the "the NSA approached U.S. carriers and asked for their cooperation in a 'data-mining operation,' which might eventually cull 'millions' of individual calls and e-mails."[1,294]

- On January 20, 2006, Congressman Conyers sent letters to twenty companies— including telephone companies, cable companies, and Internet service providers—concerning their involvement in data mining and surveillance of American citizens.[1,295] While several companies said that they would not support government surveillance except pursuant to a compulsory order,[1,296] the responses of AT&T and Verizon appear to have been drafted to leave open the possibility that they had provided access and information without a court order or subpoena.[1,297]

- On January 31, 2006, the Electronic Frontier Foundation filed a lawsuit alleging that AT&T gave the NSA access to massive databases of telephone and email messages. The lawsuit was supported by affidavits filed by Mark Klein, who stated that in 2003, the NSA set up a "secret room" at AT&T's San Francisco and other West Coast offices capable of sweeping in telephone and Internet communications.[1,298]

## Statements that Members of Congress briefed by the Bush Administration had not questioned the legality or appropriateness of the NSA Programs

Members of the Bush Administration have claimed that during the various Congressional briefings, members of Congress did not raise any objections regarding the programs.[1,299] For example, White House Counselor Dan Bartlett declared that lawmakers who have been briefed on the NSA wiretapping program "believed we are doing the right thing," and that Democrats "briefed on these programs would be screaming from the mountaintops" if they thought the program was illegal.[1,300] With respect to the NSA domestic database program, White House Deputy Press Secretary Dana Perino stated that "all appropriate Members of Congress had been briefed."[1,301] We have found, however, that numerous Members who were briefed about the spying programs did express concerns regarding both the scope of the briefing and the substance of the programs.

For example, **in 2003, the Ranking Democrat on the Senate Intelligence Committee, Senator Rockefeller (D-WV) handwrote a letter to Vice President Cheney expressing serious reservations about NSA warrantless wiretapping operations, noting "[c]learly, the activities we discussed raise profound oversight issues"**[1,302] **and that "[w]ithout more information and the ability to draw on any independent legal or technical expertise, I simply cannot satisfy lingering concerns raised by the briefing we received."**[1,303] Nancy Pelosi (D-CA) stated that when she was the Ranking Member of the House Intelligence Committee, she forwarded a letter to the National Security Agency in October 2001 indicating that because of President Bush's "overly broad interpretation" of the terms "'classified or sensitive law enforcement information,' it has not been possible to get answers to my questions,"[1,304] and that "[u]ntil I understand better the legal analysis regarding the sufficiency of the authority which underlies your decision on the appropriate way to proceed on this matter, I will continue to be concerned."[1,305] Bob Graham, the former Chairman of the Senate Intelligence Committee, also expressed concerns with these briefings, noting that "his recollection from an initial briefing in late 2001 or early 2002 was that there had been no specific discussion that the program would involve eavesdropping on American citizens."[1,306]

Former Senator Democratic Leader Tom Daschle has stated that the White House "omitted key details about the surveillance programs related to the war on terrorism during classified briefings with lawmakers."[1,307] He added, "[t]he presentation was quite different from what is now being reported in the press. I would argue that there were omissions of consequence."[1,308] Current Majority Leader Reid (D-NV) also indicated that he received only "a single, very short briefing" and "key details about the program apparently were not provided to [him]."[1,309] Also, with regard to the briefings on the NSA's domestic data base program, House Minority Leader Pelosi stated she "hadn't been told all of the information included in the *USA Today* story. And all but a handful of lawmakers learned of the program for the first time in the news account."[1,310]

### There is little indication the domestic spying programs have been beneficial in the war against terror, while there is a significant risk the programs may be affirmatively harming terrorism prosecutions and tying up law enforcement resources.

*"[The leads provided by the NSA wiretapping program] were 'viewed as unproductive, prompting agents to joke that a new bunch of tips meant more calls to Pizza Hut'."*
—January 17, 2006, Statement of FBI Field Supervisor to the *New York Times*[1,311]

We have found little, if any evidence, that the domestic spying programs have led to significant leads in the war against terror, and there is a very real risk that the existence of the programs may jeopardize terrorism prosecutions.

In December 2005, law enforcement officials told the media that the warrantless wiretapping program had not led to the detention of any Al Qaeda agents in the U.S. Law enforcement sources informed the *Washington Times* that, "more than four years of surveillance by the National Security Agency has failed to capture any high-level Al Qaeda operative in the United States. They said Al Qaeda insurgents have long stopped using the phones and even computers to relay messages. Instead, they employ couriers. 'They have been way ahead of us in communications security,' a law enforcement source said. 'At most, we have caught some riff-raff. But the heavies remain free and we believe some of them are in the United States.'"[1,312] According to the *New York Times*, "[t]he law enforcement and counterterrorism officials said the program had uncovered no active Qaeda networks inside the United States planning attacks. 'There were no imminent plots—not inside the United States,' the former F.B.I. official said."[1,313] On February 2, 2006, FBI Director Mueller testified that the warrantless surveillance program had not identified a single Al Qaeda representative in the United States since the September 11 attacks.[1,314] The *Washington Post* also confirmed in February that "[i]ntelligence officers who eavesdropped on thousands of Americans in overseas calls under authority from President Bush have dismissed nearly all of them as potential suspects after hearing nothing pertinent to a terrorist threat, according to accounts from current and former government officials and private-sector sources with knowledge of the technologies in use."[1,315] A former senior prosecutor stated that "[t]he information was so thin, and the connections were so remote, that they never led to anything, and I never heard any follow-up."[1,316]

FBI officials have indicated skepticism regarding the importance of the streams of NSA intelligence and complained that they were overloaded with tips gathered from the NSA electronic surveillance. One official source acknowledged, "[i]t affected the FBI in the sense that they had to devote so many resources to tracking every single one of these leads, and, in my experience, they were all dry leads," and that the program "led to dead ends or innocent Americans."[1,317] In response to complaints by the FBI, the NSA "began ranking its tips on a three-point scale, with three being the highest priority and one the lowest."[1,318] Even after the NSA began using this ranking system, according to an official that supervised FBI field agents, the leads continued to be "viewed as unproductive, prompting agents to joke that a new bunch of tips meant more calls to Pizza Hut."[1,319]

Because of legal and constitutional concerns with the domestic wiretap program, there is a risk that it will undermine pending and completed terrorism prosecutions. As First Amendment attorney Martin Garbus predicted, every defendant in a terrorism case will use the existence of the program to challenge evidence being used against them.[1,320] Terror prosecutions in Florida, Ohio, Oregon, and Virginia have already been challenged by defense attorneys arguing that illegal wiretaps were used to obtain valid warrants, undercutting the legality of all the evidence used against their clients.[1,321] The attorneys have also filed pleadings asserting that they should have had access to the materials under normal discovery rules so they are able to provide a full defense for their clients.[1,322] At the Senate Judiciary hearings in February, FISA judges testified that "the program could imperil criminal prosecutions that grew out of the wiretaps."[1,323]

Numerous additional terrorism cases involving FISA warrants may also have been threatened, even though, as noted above, the FISA court laid down strict requirements to insure that the information obtained pursuant to warrantless surveillance does not taint subsequent warrants or criminal prosecutions.[1,324] According to two sources, at least twice in the last four years, James A. Baker, the counsel for intelligence policy in the Justice Department's Office of Intelligence Policy and Review, was forced to disclose to the FISA court that such information may have been wrongfully used to obtain FISA warrants.[1,325]

There is also little evidence the NSA's domestic data base program has aided in the apprehension of terrorists. For example, on May 22, 2006, *Newsweek* reported that "administration officials [it] interviewed . . . questioned whether the fruits of the NSA [database] program—which they doubted, though not publicly at the risk of losing their jobs—have been worth the cost to privacy."[1,326] One Pentagon consultant admitted, "[t]he vast majority of what we did with the [NSA] intelligence was ill-focused and not productive. It's intelligence in real time, but you have to know where you're looking and what you're after."[1,327] When Senate Majority Leader Bill Frist (R-TN) was interviewed by Wolf Blitzer on May 14, 2006, Mr. Frist, while defending the program's lawfulness, refused to identify or even knowledge any specific successes against terrorism, even though he was asked three separate times whether "there has been one success story that you can point to."[1,328]

# ■ The NSA programs appear to have been implemented in a manner designed to stifle objections and dissent within the Administration.

*"Miffed that [Deputy Attorney General James] Comey, a straitlaced, by-the-book former U.S. attorney from New York, was not a 'team player' on this and other issues, President George W. Bush dubbed him with a derisive nickname, 'Cuomo,' after the man who vacillated over running for president in the 1980's."*

—FEB. 6, 2006, STATEMENT OF GOVERNMENT SOURCE TO *NEWSWEEK*[1,329]

Defenders of the Administration have contended that even if the warrantless surveillance programs are unlawful, the Administration engaged in the programs in good faith.[1,330] However, it is difficult to confirm such a claim when the Administration refuses to turn over the secret legal opinions and related material involved in the NSA program's initial approval[1,331] and will not even disclose the names of those individuals involved in the initial authorization of the programs.[1,332]

At the same time, the public record appears to show that the warrantless wiretapping programs were created in a manner specifically designed to facilitate its approval. Thus, officials within the Bush Administration told *Time* that when the warrantless wiretapping program was created, "the 'lawyers group,' an organization of fewer than half a dozen government attorneys the National Security Council convenes to review top-secret intelligence programs, was bypassed. Instead, the legal vetting was given to Alberto Gonzales, then the White House counsel."[1,333] Similarly, *Newsweek* reported, "[t]he eavesdropping program was very closely held, with cryptic briefings for only a few congressional leaders . . . [then-counsel to the Vice President David] Addington and his allies made sure the possible dissenters were cut out of the loop."[1,334] Among others, the Vice President himself "played a direct role in the controversial surveillance program."[1,335] Incredibly, then-Deputy Attorney General Larry Thompson, who had been involved in nearly all of the Administration's classified counterterrorism activities, was not involved or otherwise given access to the program.[1,336]

We have also identified a pattern by which senior members of the Bush Administration appear to have sought retaliation against those individuals who have expressed concerns regarding the warrantless wiretapping program. The most notable example of this retribution comes in the form of the Justice Department's "leak" investigation into the whistleblowing activity that led to the disclosure of the NSA program.[1,337] This was specifically referred to by President Bush, who claimed it was "a shameful act for someone to disclose this very important program in a time of war. The fact that we're discussing the program is helping the enemy."[1,338] In an apparent effort to make sure there was no doubt that the "aggressive and fast-moving"[1,339] legal reaction by the Bush Administration was noted, the Department of Justice took the highly unusual step of publicly announcing that it had commenced an investigation on December 30, 2005.[1,340]

Of course, when asked what possible fallout could come from disclosing the rather unexceptional fact that terrorists might be subject to surveillance, the only argument the Administration could muster was that it somehow "reminded" the terrorists to be careful.[1,341] As George Will noted, "surely America's enemies have assumed that our technologically sophisticated nation has been trying, in ways known and unknown, to eavesdrop on them."[1,342] Frank Rich also pointed out that "[a]lmost two weeks before the *New York Times* published its scoop about our government's extralegal wiretapping, the cable network Showtime blew the whole top-secret shebang. In its mini-series *Sleeper Cell*, about Islamic fundamentalist terrorists in Los Angeles, the cell's ringleader berates an underling for chatting about an impending operation during a phone conversation with an uncle in Egypt. 'We can only pray that the N.S.A. is not listening,' the leader yells at the miscreant, who is then stoned for blabbing."[1,343]

The few attorneys at Justice willing to voice legal concerns regarding the wiretapping program also faced severe criticism and threats from high-ranking officials within the Administration, according to current and former DOJ officials.[1,344] This led Deputy Attorney General James Comey to state in his farewell speech at DOJ, "the people committed to getting it right—and to doing the right thing . . . know who they are. Some of them did pay a price for their commitment to right."[1,345] These individuals included former Assistant Attorney General in charge of the Office of Legal Counsel Jack Goldsmith and Patrick Philbin, a national security aide to the Deputy Attorney General, both of whom raised questions regarding the NSA program.[1,346] According to sources, although Philbin "had been the in-house favorite to become deputy solicitor general . . . his chances of securing any administration job [were] derailed when [David] Addington, who had come to see him as a turncoat on national-security issues, moved to block him from promotion, with Cheney's blessing."[1,347] *Newsweek* **further reported that within the Justice Department, those who raised questions regarding the program "did so at their peril; [they were] ostracized . . . denied promotions, while others left . . . .** Some went so far as to line up private lawyers in 2004, anticipating that the president's eavesdropping program would draw scrutiny from Congress, if not prosecutors."[1,348]

When Mr. Comey himself registered concerns with the NSA wiretapping program, which led to a secret audit of the program, the displeasure went all the way up to the President. The *New York Post* reported that as a result of this disloyalty, President Bush began referring to Mr. Comey as "Cuomo," after former New York Democratic Governor Mario Cuomo, who was considered not to be a "team player."[1,349] *Newsweek* also confirmed that "[m]iffed that Comey, a straitlaced, by-the-book former U.S. attorney from New York, was not a 'team player' on this and other issues, President George W. Bush dubbed him with a derisive nickname, '"Cuomo,' after the man who vacillated over running for president in the 1980's."[1,350]

With respect to the domestic database program, there is also evidence that it was set up in a manner designed to eliminate dissent and avoid scrutiny by attorneys at the Justice Department. Intelligence historian Matthew Aid explained, "it does seem clear that the Justice Department was excluded from all of this, or at least the parts of the Justice Department that would normally have some oversight over this . . . . They kept the number of people within the Justice Department who had knowledge of the program to a small number of people. I think they feared that if they passed it down to other departments that might have some purview over the program, they might have encountered a stream of objections."[1,351]

There are also reports the Bush Administration applied inappropriate pressure to Qwest in an effort to force it to participate in the NSA database program. *USA Today* reported that according to its sources, after Qwest refused to voluntarily participate, "**the agency suggested that Qwest's foot-dragging might affect its ability to get future classified work with the government.** Like other big telecommunications companies, Qwest already had classified contracts and hoped to get more."[1,352]

# Continued Stonewalling of Congress and the American People

*"When the President does it, that means it's not illegal."*

—MAY 20, 1977, PRESIDENT RICHARD NIXON EXPLAINING HIS INTERPRETATION
OF EXECUTIVE PRIVILEGE IN AN INTERVIEW WITH DAVID FROST[1,353]

As we learned when reviewing the deceptions and manipulations associated with the Downing Street Minutes and the War in Iraq, the Bush Administration has shut down any semblance of independent review or meaningful oversight associated with the domestic spying scandal. As Senate Judiciary Chairman Specter observed, "[t]hey want to do just as they please, for as long as they can get away with it. I think what is going on now without congressional intervention or judicial intervention is just plain wrong."[1,354]

First, the Administration spurned attempts to have an independent special counsel review the legality of the NSA programs, even though such a review would clearly meet the criteria set forth in the regulations.[1,355] When Rep. Zoe Lofgren (D-CA) and 17 other Members requested a special counsel regarding the warrantless wiretapping program, the White House Press Secretary, stated that there was not any basis for appointing a special counsel and that Members "ought to spend their time on what was the source of the unauthorized disclosure of this vital and critical program."[1,356] After *USA Today* revealed the existence of a massive NSA database program, Rep. Lofgren and 53 other Members of Congress extended the request to include all of the domestic surveillance programs.[1,357] There has been no response to this letter. Rep. Conyers asked the Attorney General about the Department's record of having failed to appoint a single special counsel during the entire Bush Administration. Mr. Gonzales appeared to not even appreciate that he had the authority to appoint a special counsel pursuant to DOJ regulations.[1,358]

Democrats have also been rebuffed in their efforts to obtain an independent review outside of the special counsel regulations, with both the Department of Justice Inspector General[1,359] and the Department of Defense Inspector General[1,360] claiming they did not have jurisdiction to consider the matters. Although in February 2006, the DOJ Office of Professional Responsibility (OPR) did initially agree to investigate whether Department attorneys had violated any ethical rules in approving the warrantless wiretap program,[1,361] by May, the Bush Administration had squashed this investigation as well by denying OPR attorneys security clearances needed to review DOJ's role in the program.[1,362] Requests by the House Democratic Leadership to conduct hearings and create an independent panel to examine the programs have also been ignored by the Republican Leadership,[1,363] as have been efforts by Sen. Byrd in the Senate and Rep. Conyers in the House to have a blue ribbon commission review the programs.[1,364]

Second, the Senate and House Judiciary Committees were unsuccessful in obtaining meaningful information from the Bush Administration regarding the domestic spying scandal. At the Senate hearings, in a break with regular order, the Attorney General was not even sworn in.[1,365] At the hearings, Members became so exasperated by Mr. Gonzales's failure to respond to their questions that Ranking Member Leahy was forced to state, "[o]f course, I'm sorry, Mr. Attorney General, I forgot; you can't answer questions that might be relevant to this."[1,366] After initially raising no objection to the Committee's request that former Attorney General Ashcroft or former Deputy Attorney General Comey testify—both of whom had first-hand knowledge regarding the legal foundations for the warrantless wiretapping program—the Department of Justice subsequently blocked them from testifying.[1,367] The Bush Administration also killed an effort by Senate Judiciary Chairman Arlen Specter to ask telephone executives to testify regarding the NSA's domestic database program.[1,368]

The Department also failed to respond to the vast majority of the written questions submitted by both Democrats and Republicans on the House Judiciary Committee in advance of general oversight hearings.[1,369] This failure caused Chairman Sensenbrenner to accuse the Department of "stonewalling": "I think that saying that how the review was done and who did the review is classified is stonewalling. And if we're properly to determine whether or not the program was legal and funded—because that's Congress's responsibility—we need to have answers, and we're not getting them."[1,370]

The GOP-controlled Senate and House Intelligence Committees also have failed to fulfill their oversight responsibilities. The Senate Intelligence Committee initially appeared to be considering a meaningful investigation of the NSA wiretapping program; however, after intense White House lobbying, the Committee voted against such an investigation on a party-line basis.[1,371] After **the Committee vote, Ranking Democrat John Rockefeller (D-WI) declared, "[t]he committee is, to put it bluntly, basically under the control of the White House."**[1,372] The *New York Times* wrote, "[t]he [NSA] program violates the law. Congress knows it. The public knows it. Even President Bush knows it. (He just says the law doesn't apply to him.) In response, the Capitol Hill rebels are boldly refusing to investigate the program—or any other warrantless spying that is going on . . . . And meanwhile, they've created new subcommittees to help the president go on defying the law."[1,373]

In addition, Senate Republicans introduced two bills, one by Senator DeWine and another by Senator Specter, which would effectively ratify the practice of warrantless surveillance of innocent Americans. The DeWine legislation would "entirely remove intelligence gathering related to terrorism from the [FISA] law;"[1,374] while the Specter legislation would "grant legal cover, retroactively, to the one spying program Mr. Bush has acknowledged. It also covers any other illegal wiretapping we don't know about—including, it appears, entire programs that could cover hundreds, thousands, or millions of unknowing people."[1,375] Rather than investigate the domestic spying program, the Chairman of the Senate Intelligence Committee has proposed new legislation to broaden the coverage of leaks, cracking down on the very whistleblowers who have helped disclose the illegal NSA program.[1,376]

The Republican Leadership has also blocked legislative efforts to obtain further information about the NSA spying programs. Representatives Lee,[1,377] Conyers,[1,378] Slaughter,[1,379] and Wexler[1,380] have all introduced separate Resolutions of Inquiry to direct the Administration to provide documents concerning the authorization of the warrantless wiretapping program.[1,381] The rejection of these resolutions by the Majority has prevented Congress from obtaining copies of the original legal opinions issued concerning the domestic surveillance programs.[1,382] At the same time, on May 22, the GOP-dominated FCC also rejected a request by Rep. Markey (D-MA) that they investigate the legality of the NSA database program.[1,383]

The Bush Administration has compounded the oversight difficulties through misstating facts and their proclivity toward secrecy. For example, while the Bush Administration argues it has convicted hundreds upon hundreds of individuals in terrorism cases, a careful review reveals that the vast majority of these cases bear no relation to terrorism. Thus, in June 2005, the *Washington Post* reported that only 39 people—not the 200 implied by President Bush—have been convicted of terrorism-related crimes since the September 11 attacks.[1,384] Another independent review of cases brought in 2003 by the *Miami Herald* found that the Justice Department claimed to have charged 56 people as "terrorists"; however, 41 of these cases were found to have had nothing to do with terrorism.[1,385] The *Daily Iowan* also reported that numerous individuals whom the Administration claimed had been convicted of terrorism were found to have actually been implicated in far more minor offenses.[1,386] A GAO Report found that in 2002, "at least 132 of the 288 convictions. . . were misclassified as terrorism-related."[1,387]

By making numerous changes to narrow FOIA, expanding the classification rules, and repeatedly asserting the state secrets doctrine, the Bush Administration has also unilaterally acted to make it far more difficult for Congress, the media, and the American people to have access to government documents concerning these abuses. (The notable exception to these sweeping increases in secrecy is in cases where members of the Bush Administration have chosen to selectively declassify documents for political purposes.[1,388])

First, the Bush Administration significantly narrowed the scope of the FOIA by providing that agencies are entitled to the government's full legal support for withholding information from the public. The GAO found that this led federal agencies to significantly inhibit the release of previously public information.[1,390] Second, the Administration dramatically expanded the use of the "state secret doctrine" to block access to government documents.[1,391] Among other things, the doctrine was used by the Administration to block Sibel Edmonds, an FBI translator, from seeking redress as an intelligence whistleblower;[1,392] to limit information concerning the case of Maher Arar, a Canadian citizen sent to Syria where he was tortured;[1,393] and to seek dismissal of suits challenging the NSA's wiretapping program brought against AT&T,[1,394] two suits challenging the legality of the NSA's warrantless wiretap program brought by the ACLU and the Center for Constitutional Rights,[1,395] twenty lawsuits brought against telephone companies alledging that they had improperly provided customer call data to the NSA[1,396], and a lawsuit alleging that the CIA had wrongfully imprisoned a German citizen.[1,397] Third, President Bush has eliminated the presumption of disclosure when the federal government makes classification decisions,[1,398] resulting in a significant increase in the number of documents classified each year.[1,399]

President Bush has also used presidential signing statements in an effort to negate laws providing for congressional oversight. This includes statements that he can ignore statutes requiring reports on the use of national security wiretaps against American citizens; disclosure of memorandums setting forth new interpretations of domestic spying laws; reports on civil liberties, security clearance and border security; reports on possible vulnerabilities in chemical plants and baggage screening at airports; and notification regarding diversions of funds for secret "black sites."[1,400] Concerning this practice, NYU Law Professor David Golove has warned, a "President who ignores the court, backed by a Congress that is unwilling to challenge him, can make the Constitution simply disappear."[1,401]

# Addendum

Since Part I of this Report concerning Iraq and the Downing Street Minutes was issued in December 2005, and Part II of the Report concerning unlawful government surveillance was written in May 2006, a number of additional events have transpired. The following is a brief summary of those matters, divided by section corresponding to the Report:

## The Downing Street Minutes and Deception, Manipulation, Torture, Retribution and Coverups in the Iraq War

## Determination to go to War Before Congressional Authorization

- On February 3, the *London Guardian* detailed the minutes of a White House meeting between President Bush and Prime Minister Blair in which President Bush indicated on January 31, 2003 that he would invade Iraq regardless of whether U.N. inspectors found evidence of WMD. At the January meeting, President Bush reportedly stated, "the diplomatic strategy had to be arranged around the military planning." A memo described by prominent British lawyer Phillipe Sands in his book *Lawless World* revealed that at the meeting, President Bush stated that he was so concerned by the failure to find WMD that he proposed that the U.S. "fly . . . U2 reconnaissance aircraft planes with fighter cover over Iraq, painted in U.N. colours," and added: "[i]f Saddam fired on them he would be in breach [of U.N. resolutions]." (Neither the Blair nor the Bush Administrations have challenged the accuracy of this new document).

## Misstating and Manipulating the Intelligence to Justify Pre-emptive War

- On January 18, the *New York Times* reported that a high-level intelligence assessment by the Bush Administration concluded in March 2002 that the sale of uranium from Niger to Iraq was "unlikely" because of a host of economic, diplomatic, and logistical obstacles. The State Department assessment concluded that the sale would have required Niger to send "25 hard-to-conceal 10-ton tractor-trailers" filled with uranium across 1,000 miles and at least one international border.

- On February 2, Murray Waas of the *National Journal* reported that a highly classified CIA memo issued on June 17, 2003 determined that "[w]e no longer believe there is sufficient" credible information to "conclude that Iraq pursued uranium from abroad," and that "[s]ince learning that the Iraqi-Niger uranium deal was based on false documents earlier this spring, we no longer believe that there is sufficient other reporting to conclude that Iraq purchased uranium from abroad." Vice President Cheney and his then-Chief of Staff Scooter Libby were personally informed of these findings. (The Administration did not withdraw or correct their misstatement until July 7, 2003, six months after the President's State of the Union address.

- On February 10, in an article in the journal "Foreign Affairs," veteran CIA agent, Paul Pillar, who oversaw intelligence assessments about the Middle East from 2000 to 2005, accused the Bush Administration of "cherry-picking" intelligence on Iraq to justify a decision it had already reached to go to war. Mr. Pillar wrote that "[i]ntelligence was misused publicly to justify decisions that had already been made," chiefly to topple Mr. Hussein in order to "shake up the sclerotic power structures of the Middle East." He also wrote that as a result of political pressure, analysts began to "sugarcoat" their conclusions regarding the threat posed by Iraqi weapons and about ties between Mr. Hussein and Al Qaeda.

- On March 2, Murray Waas reported that two highly classified intelligence reports delivered directly to President Bush before the war undermined important assertions the Administration had made concerning WMD. In October, 2002, President Bush personally received a one-page summary of a National Intelligence Estimate that concluded that both the Energy and State Departments believed the aluminum tubes being procured by Iraq were "intended for conventional weapons." In early January 2003, President Bush received another one-page summary of an NIE that concluded that Saddam Hussein was unlikely to attack the U.S. except if "ongoing military operations risked the imminent demise of his regime."

- On April 9, the *Washington Post* revealed that in January 2003, the National Intelligence Council, the senior coordinating body for the fifteen agencies that then constituted the U.S. intelligence community, informed the Administration that the Niger uranium claim was unequivocally false. Four U.S. officials with firsthand knowledge said in interviews that the January 2003 memo, which has not been reported before, arrived at the White House as Bush and his highest-ranking advisors made the uranium story a centerpiece of their case for the rapidly approaching war against Iraq.

- On April 13, the *Washington Post* reported that a secret fact-finding mission including nine U.S. and U.K authorities unanimously issued a 122-page report on May 27, 2003 concluding that the two small trailers captured by the U.S. that month "had nothing to do with biological weapons." One expert stated, "there was no connection to anything biological," while another described the trailers as "the biggest sand toilets in the world." The *Post* article was based on its interviews with six government officials who either participated in the review or had direct knowledge of the Report. (Notwithstanding the 122-page report, on May 29, 2003, President Bush declared that because of the trailers, "we have found the weapons of mass destruction.")

- On April 23, *Sixty Minutes* interviewed retired CIA Officer Tyler Drumheller, who headed up the CIA's covert operations in Europe before the war. He confirmed that prior to the War, the vast majority of individuals who worked in the intelligence community recognized that the Niger uranium story was false. He stated on the show, "Most people came to the opinion that there was something questionable about [the Italian intelligence service report]. . . [t]hat was our reaction from the very beginning. The report didn't hold together." Drumheller explained that the White House lost interest in information provided by Naji Sabri, Iraq's former Foreign Minister, after Sabri had reported that "[Iraq] had no active weapons of mass destruction program." As Drumheller stated on Sixty Minutes, "It just sticks in my craw every time I hear them say it's an intelligence failure . . . This was a policy failure . . .[t]he policy was set . . .[t]he war in Iraq was coming. And they were looking for intelligence to fit into that policy, to justify the policy." On June 25, the *Washington Post* further reported when Drumheller saw a claim in a draft U.N speech for Mr. Powell that Iraq had mobile chemical weapons labs, supported by statements from the Iraqi defector known as "Curveball," he "took his pen and crossed out the whole paragraph" and that when he received a late evening phone call from CIA Director Tenet the night before Powell's speech Drumheller told him, "[h]ey, boss, you're not going to use that stuff in the speech . . . ? There are real problems with that." However, when Mr. Drumheller later "turn[ed] on the television . . . there it [the reference to mobile chemical weapons labs] was again."

- On June 27, the Senate Democratic Policy Committee held informal hearings on pre-war intelligence. Lawrence Wilkerson, former Chief of Staff to Secretary of State Colin Powell, testified that "the Vice President was using portions of the intelligence documents in ways that the documents themselves did not seem to report . . . . [and that] [o]thers in the Administration were participating in the distortion." At the hearing, Wayne White, the former Deputy Director of the State Department's Office of Analysis for the Near East and South Bsia, testified that the most senior Administration officials involved "did intervene in the process of intelligence analysis . . . ."

# Cover-ups and Retribution:
# The Niger Forgeries and the "Sliming"
# of Ambassador Wilson and his Family

- On April 6, Special Counsel Fitzgerald filed documents with the federal court indicating that President Bush had authorized the Vice President's former Chief of Staff, Scooter Libby to leak classified information to the press in an effort to undermine Ambassador Wilson. Fitzgerald wrote that Libby "testified that he was specifically authorized to disclose the key judgments of the classified NIE to [former *New York Times* reporter Judith] Miller, and that "[defendant further testified that he at first advised the Vice President that he could not have this conversation with reporter Miller because of the classified nature of the NIE  Defendant testified that the Vice President later advised him that the President had authorized defendant to disclose the relevant portions of the NIE." The following day, White House Press Secretary Scott McClellan responded to the leak by stating, "There is a difference between providing declassified information to the public when it's in the public interest and leaking classified information that involved sensitive national intelligence regarding our security."

- In the April 6 filing, Mr. Fitzgerald further described a "concerted action" by "multiple people in the White House" using classified information to "discredit, punish or seek revenge against" Ambassador Wilson. He also found that the Vice President and his staff perceived Wilson as a threat to "the credibility of the Vice President (and the President) on a matter of signal importance: the rationale for the war in Iraq." On May 12, Mr. Fitzgerald released a copy of a note hand-written by the Vice President on Wilson's op-ed specifically deriding the former Ambassador and his wife. The Vice President wrote: "Have they done this sort of thing before? Send an Amb[assador] to answer a question? Do we ordinarily send people out pro bono to work for us? Or did his wife send him on a junket?" Murray Waas of *The National Journal* subsequently reported that according to persons familiar with the President's interview with Patrick Fitzgerald "President Bush told the special prosecutor in the CIA leak case that he directed Vice President Cheney to personally lead an effort to counter allegations made by former Ambassador Joseph C. Wilson IV that his administration had misrepresented intelligence information to make the case to go to war with Iraq" and that "he had directed Cheney, as part of a broader effort, to disclose highly classified intelligence information that would . . . discredit Wilson."

- On April 9, 2006, the *Washington Post* reported that what the Special Counsel did not mention was that "the evidence Cheney and Libby selected to share with reporters had been disproved months before." At Cheney's instruction, Libby was to tell Miller some of the key judgments of the NIE "and that the NIE stated that Iraq was vigorously trying to procure uranium." However, as the *Post* explained: "In fact, the alleged effort to buy uranium was not among the estimate's key judgments, which were identified by a headline and bold type and set out in bullet form in the first five pages of the 96-page document."

- On May 25, the *National Journal* reported that on September 29, 2003, three days after it had become known that the CIA had asked the DOJ to investigate the outing of Valerie Plame, "Robert Novak telephoned White House senior advisor Karl Rove to assure Rove that he would protect him from being harmed in the investigation, according to people with firsthand knowledge of the federal grand jury testimony of both men." On the same day, it was disclosed in a court filing by Mr Fitzgerald that the Vice President was personally angered and upset by Ambassador Wilson's column.

- On June 8, Murray Waas reported that Attorney General Ashcroft had been personally briefed on the Valerie Plame investigation for a full two months in later 2003 prior to his recusal on December 30, 2003. These briefings occurred after Mr. Ashcroft had been informed that Scooter Libby and Karl Rove were "trying to mislead the FBI to conceal their roles in the leak, according to government records and interviews." According to legal ethics expert Professor Stephen Gillers, the Attorney General should have recused himself "once he learned the people professionally trained to draw these inferences believed there was substantial reason that Rove and Libby were involved in the leak."

- On July 11, Robert Novak finally acknowledged that Karl Rove had been one of the sources for his column outing Valerie Plame as a CIA operative.

# Cover-ups and Retribution: Other Instances of Bush Administration Retribution Against Its Critics

- On February 16, Samuel J. Provance, an Army intelligence officer, testified that he was demoted and stripped of his clearance after speaking out in 2004 about the abuse of detainees at the Abu Ghraib prison. Provance stated, "[w]hen I made clear to my superiors that I was troubled about what had happened [at Abu Ghraib] I was shown that the honor of my unit and the Army depended on either withholding the truth or outright lies." He added that his military career had been "derailed" and his duties in Germany consist of "picking up trash and guard duty."

- On February 7, 2006, Warren P. Strobel of Knight Ridder reported that a State Department reorganization led by then Undersecretary of State John Bolton targeted key career weapons experts. A dozen State Department employees wrote that "the process has been gravely flawed from the outset, and smacks plainly of a political vendetta against career Foreign Service and Civil Service (personnel) by political employees."

# Thwarting Congress and the American Public: The Death of Accountability Under the Bush Administration and the Republican-Controlled Congress

- After Representative Conyers and 51 other Members of Congress sent the initial Freedom of Information Act request regarding the Downing Street Minutes on June 30, 2005 to the State Department and the Defense Department, and after two follow-up letters to the State Department (dated September 19, 2005 and April 19, 2006) and two follow-up letters to the Defense Department (dated July 28, 2005 and April 19, 2006), the State Department finally furnished some documents in a letter dated April 21, 2006. The 28 documents from the State Department include only written and publicly given statements by then-Secretary Powell, questions taken by a State Department spokesman, and press releases—all of the documents were simply taken from the State Department's website. As of this date Rep. Conyers has not received a response from the Defense Department regarding his narrowed request for documents and request for a public interest fee waiver.

## Unlawful Domestic Surveillance and the Decline of Civil Liberties Under the Administration of George W. Bush

- On June 21, *Salon* reported that in addition to maintaining a secret room in San Francisco, AT&T and the government also utilized a "secret, highly secured room" in its St. Louis network operations center. Former AT&T employees were told that "employees working inside the room were 'monitoring network traffic' and that the room was being used by a 'government agency.'" As for the likely government agency involved, NSA expert Matthew Aid stated, "It's safe that it's NSA," while former NSA officer Russ Tice explained, "[y]ou're talking about a backbone for computer communications, and that's NSA."

- On June 26, Jane Mayer of the *New Yorker* wrote a lengthy article detailing the extent Cheney advisor David Addington had excluded key decision makers—including then Secretary of State Powell and National Security Advisor Rice—from being able to raise questions concerning the domestic wiretapping program and other controversial Administration initiatives. Among other direct quotes included in the article were Powell's statement when he belatedly learned about the NSA wiretap program that "[i]t's Addington. He doesn't care about the Constitution;" former Reagan DOJ official Bruce Fein's statement that "the idea of reducing Congress to a political cipher was already in play. It was Cheney and Addington's political agenda;" ex-Pentagon lawyer Richard Shiffrin indication after a White House meeting that he was "left with the impression that Addington 'doesn't believe there should be co-equal branches,'" while another participant added, "if you favored international law, you were in danger of being called 'soft on terrorism' by Addington."

- On June 30, *USA Today* updated its story concerning the NSA's domestic database program based on discussions with numerous members of the House and Senate Intelligence Committees. The paper reported that 19 lawmakers confirmed the existence of the massive telephone database program; 5 members confirmed that AT&T participated in the program; and 3 members confirmed that while Verizon was not involved, its new subsidiary, long-distance company MCI, did participate. *USA Today* also reported that five Members informed them it BellSouth did not directly participate in the program, but Senator Saxby Chambliss indicated BellSouth customers could be tracked through long distance calls routed through AT&T. Another lawmaker acknowledged that "[t]he database is not complete. We don't know if it works yet."

- On June 30, the Supreme Court issued its landmark ruling in *Hamdan v. Rumsfeld.* As a matter of law, the decision held that President Bush's order creating rules for military tribunals was inconsistent with both federal law (in the form of the Uniform Code of Military Justice) and international treaty obligations (in the form of Article 3 of the Geneva Conventions). The majority opinion by Justice Stevens reasoned, "the Executive is bound to comply with the Rule of Law," while Justice Breyer and Kennedy wrote in concurring opinions that "Congress has not issued the executive a blank check," and "the Constitution is best preserved by reliance on standards tested over time and insulated from the pressure of the moment." On July 11, the Pentagon issued a memorandum acknowledging that all detainees held by the U.S. were entitled to human rights protections pursuant to the Geneva Conventions. However, on the same day, in hearings before the Senate Judiciary Committee, Justice Department witness Steven Bradbury testified that "the president is always right" and derided the *Hamdan* decision, referring to it as "suprising and disappointing."

- More importantly, the decision undercuts the Administration's legal rationalization supporting many of their other secret programs, including the NSA's domestic warrantless wiretap program. Harvard Law Professor Tribe stated that the Administration's legal argument for the NSA program "is blown out of the water and is obliterated." Even the principal legal architect of many of the Administration's program, former DOJ official John Yoo, admitted the *Hamdan* decision "could affect detention conditions, interrogation methods, the use of force," and other Administration programs.

- With regard to the Administration's argument that the AUMF authorized increased presidential authority regarding tribunals, the Court wrote, "[T]here is nothing in the text or the legislative history of the AUMF even hinting that Congress intended to expand or alter" the Military Code of Justice statute. This holding should apply with equal force against the Administration's AUMF argument in the context of its warrantless wiretapping program. Justice Kennedy also rejected the Administration's contention that the President could act with greater authority than the applicable statute specified during time of war, writing, "[i]f the President has exceeded [the limits set by statute], this becomes a case of conflict between the Presidential and congressional action—a case within Justice Jackson's third category [in the *Steel Seizure* case where presidential authority is at its lowest ebb], not the second or first." The Court also rebuffed any contention that the President has "inherent authority" to act in a war time setting in contravention of law, writing in a key footnote that "[w]hether or not the President has independent power, absent congressional authorization, to convene military commissions, he may not disregard limitations that Congress has, in proper exercise of its own war powers, placed on his powers."

- On July 9, it was revealed that the Chairman of the House Intelligence Committee, Peter Hoekstra (R-MI), had written a letter to President Bush, charging the Administration with possible violations of the National Security Act for failing to properly brief the Committee concerning covert programs, stating, "the U.S. Congress simply should not have to play Twenty Questions to get the information that it deserves under our Constitution." In his letter, Mr. Hoekstra indicated that there were additional secret programs that he had recently been apprised of a result of information provided by whistleblowers and which had not yet been made public.

# Analysis

## Determination to go to War Before Congressional Authorization

## Misleading Congress and the American Public Concerning the Decision to Go to War: Determination to Go to War Before Congressional Authorization

Our investigation has found that President Bush and members of his Administration made numerous public statements to the effect that a decision had not been made to invade Iraq, when in fact the record indicates that such a decision had been made.

Among other things, we have found: Immediately after the September 11 attacks, President Bush and members of his Administration displayed an immediate inclination to blame Iraq—the President asked Richard Clarke to determine if Hussein is "linked in any way;" White House officials instructed Wesley Clark to state that the attack was "connected to Saddam Hussein;" and Undersecretary of Defense Douglas Feith proposed that the U.S. select "a non Al Qaeda target like Iraq." The Downing Street Minutes provide unrebutted documentary evidence that in the spring and summer of 2002 it was understood by the Blair government that the Bush Administration had irrevocably decided to invade Iraq. These documents reveal that President Bush had told Prime Minster Blair "when we have dealt with Afghanistan, we must come back to Iraq" (Fall, 2001); "Condi's enthusiasm for regime change is undimmed" (March 14, 2002); the U.S. has "assumed regime change as a means of eliminating Iraq's WMD threat" (March 25, 2002) and; and "Bush wanted to remove Saddam through military action, justified by the conjunction of terrorism and WMD" and "the intelligence and facts were being fixed around the policy" (July 23, 2002).

Among other things, we have also found: The "marketing" campaign for the war which included the creation of the so-called "White House Iraq Group;" the "rollout of speeches and documents;" the release of a white paper inaccurately describing a "grave and gathering danger" of Iraq's allegedly "reconstituted" nuclear weapons program; and the deliberate downplaying of the risks of occupation. The plan by which the Bush and Blair Administration sought to use the U.N. to "wrongfoot Saddam on the inspectors and the U.N. SCRs [Security Council Resolutions]" in the winter of 2002 and spring of 2003, constitutes further evidence that the decision to invade Iraq had been made. This is reflected by the fact that Defense Policy Board Member, Richard Perle admitted the U.S. "would attack Iraq even if U.N. inspectors fail to find weapons;" Vice President Cheney reportedly acknowledged to Hans Blix that the U.S. was "ready to discredit inspectors in favor of disarmament;" and President Bush was "infuriated" by reports of Iraq's cooperating with U.N. inspectors. In addition, it has also been disclosed that at a January 31, 2003 meeting with Prime Minister Blair, President Bush was so concerned by the failure to locate WMD that he proposed the U.S. "fly . . . UC reconnaissance aircraft planes with fighter cover over Iraq, painted in U.N. colours" and that "[i]f Saddam fired on them he would be in breach [of U.N. resolutions]."

# Unauthorized War Actions and Provocations

Our investigation has found that there is evidence the Bush Administration redeployed military assets in the immediate vicinity of Iraq and conducted bombing raids on Iraq in 2002 in possible violation of the War Powers Resolution, Pub. L. No. 93-148, and laws prohibiting the Misuse of Government Funds, 31 U.S.C. §1301.

Among other things, we have found: A military commander told Senator Bob Graham in February 2002 that "[w]e are moving military and intelligence personnel and resources out of Afghanistan to get ready for a future war in Iraq;" and "[b]y the end of July [2002], Bush had approved some 30 projects that would eventually cost $700 million." The bombing campaign engaged in by the U.S. and Great Britain in 2002 and early 2003 involved more than 21,000 sorties and hundreds of thousands of pounds of bombs, has been described as "a full air offensive;" and a former U.S. combat veteran stated that based on what he had witnessed, "[t]he war had already begun."

## Misstating and Manipulating the Intelligence to Justify Preemptive War

# Links to September 11 and Al Qaeda

Our investigation has found that President Bush and members of his Administration made numerous false statements regarding linkages between Iraq and the September 11 attacks, and also may have sought to manipulate intelligence to support these statements. This includes misstatements concerning general linkages between Iraq and Al Qaeda; an alleged meeting between Mohammed Atta and Iraqi Intelligence officials; and allegations that Iraq was training Al Qaeda members to use chemical and biological weapons.

With regard to general linkages between Iraq and Al Qaeda, members of the Bush Administration ignored at least five separate reports from within their own Administration, including

- a report shortly after September 11 prepared by Counterterrorism Coordinator Richard Clarke finding no connection with Iraq that was "bounced back," with his superiors saying "[w]rong answer. . . . Do it again."

- a September 21, 2001 classified intelligence briefing that "the U.S. intelligence community had no evidence linking the Iraqi regime of Saddam Hussein to the attacks and that there was scant credible evidence that Iraq had any significant collaborative ties with Al Qaeda."

- a June 21, 2002 CIA report which found "no conclusive evidence of cooperation on specific terrorist operations."

- the October 2002 NIE, which gave a "Low Confidence" rating to the notion of "[w]hether in desperation Saddam would share chemical or biological weapons with Al Qa'ida."

- a January, 2003 CIA report that the "Intelligence Community has no credible information that Baghdad had foreknowledge of the 11 September attacks or any other Al Qaeda strike." Given this record, it is particularly hard to justify Administration statements such as Secretary Rumsfeld's September 22, 2002 claim that he had "bulletproof" evidence of ties between Saddam and Al Qaeda.

The evidence that members of the Bush Administration sought to manipulate and pressure intelligence officials on this linkage includes Deputy Director of the CIA Richard Kerr's report that people at the CIA have stated they have been "pushed too hard" on this point and felt "too much pressure;" a CIA ombudsman who reported unprecedented "hammering" on this issue; an FBI official who stated that the "Bush Administration. . . was misleading the public in implying there was a close connection [between Iraq and Al Qaeda];" and former CIA Agent Paul Pillar's statement that "[i]ntelligence was misused publicly to justify decisions that had been already made."

We also have found evidence that Vice President Cheney's December 9, 2001 statement that the meeting between Mohammed Atta and an Iraqi intelligence official in Prague had been "pretty well confirmed" was either knowingly or recklessly false. This includes the fact that Czech government officials had expressed doubts the meeting had occurred; both the CIA and FBI had concluded that "the meeting probably did not take place;" and

Administration records indicated that Mr. Atta was in Virginia Beach, Virginia at the time of the meeting. There is also evidence that the Vice President's office put undue pressure on the CIA to substantiate this meeting, with the Deputy Director of the CIA insisting to Mr. Libby, "I'm not going back to the well on this. We've done our work."

Statements by President Bush on October 7, 2002 that "Iraq has trained Al Qaeda members in bomb-making and poisons and deadly gases;" and Secretary Powell on February 5, 2003, "trac[ing] the story of a senior terrorist operative telling how Iraq provided training in these weapons to Al-Quaeda;" with both saying this relationship goes back for "decades" were also false. Among other things, we have found that a declassified Defense Intelligence Agency report from February 2002 indicated that the source of this information, Ibn al-Shaykh al-Libi, "was intentionally misleading the debriefers in making these claims;" that it was unlikely any relationship between Iraq and Al Qaeda went back decades since "Saddam's regime is intensely secular and wary of Islamic revolutionary movements;" a classified CIA report found that Mr. al-Libi was "not in a position to know if any training had taken place;" and Administration officials knew or should have known he fabricated his statements to avoid torture.

# Resumed Efforts to Acquire Nuclear Weapons

Our investigation has found that President Bush and members of his Administration made false statements regarding Iraq's effort to acquire nuclear weapons, including general claims regarding such acquisition; assertions based on claims by Saddam Hussein's son-in-law; and a statement by Mr. Bush that Iraq was within six months of obtaining a nuclear weapon.

The Bush Administration appears to have ignored numerous intelligence reports indicating that there was no credible evidence of an ongoing nuclear program in Iraq, including:

- a 1999 IAEA report that there was "no indication that Iraq possesses nuclear weapons. . . or any practical capability. . . for the production of such material."
- British intelligence officials confirmation that Iraq's nuclear weapon's program was "effectively frozen."
- the pre-2002 CIA NIE indicating that Iraq did not have and was not trying to reacquire nuclear weapons; and the State Department INR's finding that it lacked "persuasive evidence that Baghdad has launched a coherent effort to reconstitute its nuclear weapons program." Given this record, it is difficult to defend statements such as Mr. Cheney's March 16, 2003 declaration that "we believe [Saddam] has, in fact, reconstituted nuclear weapons."

There is also evidence that the Vice President's statement on August 26, 2002 that the Administration had learned about Hussein's efforts to reacquire nuclear weapons from

"Saddam's own son-in-law," Hussein Kamel al-Majid, was knowingly or recklessly false. This is first because Kamel was killed in February, 1996, so he "could not have sourced what U.S. officials 'now know;'" and second because Kamel's testimony to the IAEA was, according to the *Washington Post*, "the reverse of Cheney's description" which was debriefed to U.S. officials.

President Bush's statement on September 7, 2002 that the IAEA had issued a new report that Iraq was "six months away from developing a [nuclear] weapon" also appears to be false and misleading, as the *Washington Post* found "there was no new IAEA report . . . . Bush cast as present evidence the contents of a report from 1996, updated in 1998 and 1999. In those accounts, the IAEA described the history of an Iraqi nuclear weapons program that arms inspectors had systematically destroyed."

# Aluminum Tubes

**Our investigation has found that President Bush and members of his Administration made numerous false statements that Iraq was seeking to acquire aluminum tubes in order to build a uranium centrifuge and leaked classified information to the press in order to further buttress their arguments for war.**

Members of the Bush Administration appear to have ignored reports and information provided by at least five agencies and foreign intelligence sources, including:

- several reports by the Department of Energy which found that the tubes were "too narrow, too heavy, too long—to be of much practical use in a centrifuge"

- the State Department's INR [Bureau of Intelligence and Research], which "considers it far more likely that the tubes are intended for another purpose"

- the Defense Department which found the tubes "were perfectly usable for rockets"

- British Intelligence that found the tubes would require "substantial re-engineering" to serve as centrifuges

- The International Atomic Energy Agency which found "all evidence points to that this is for the rockets"

- a one-page summary of National Intelligence Estimate personally delivered to President Bush in October, 2002, concluding that both the Energy and State Departments believed the aluminum tubes were "intended for conventional weapons."

Statements by the Vice President and Ms. Rice that they knew about Iraq's proposed use of the tubes for centrifuges with "absolute certainty" and that the tubes were "only really suited for nuclear weapons programs" are particularly questionable, since the dispute within the Administration has been described as a "holy war" and Administration sources have stated that Ms. Rice "was aware of the differences of opinion" and that her statements were "just a lie."

The evidence also shows that a September 8 lead article in the *New York Times* and a July 29, 2002 article in the *Washington Times* included classified information leaked by Administration officials. Among other things, the *New York Times* article quoted "anonymous" Administration officials as stating that "Iraq has stepped up its quest for nuclear weapons and has embarked on a worldwide hunt for materials to make an atomic bomb;" and the *Washington Times* article stated, "U.S. intelligence agencies believe the tubing is an essential component of Iraq's plans to enrich radioactive uranium to the point where it could be used to fashion a nuclear bomb." Special Prosecutor Fitzgerald has also filed documents detailing that President Bush authorized the leaking of classified information to the press in order to undermine Ambassador Wilson.

# Acquisition of Uranium from Niger

We have found that President Bush and members of his Administration made numerous false statements that Iraq had sought to acquire enriched uranium from Niger. In particular, President Bush's statements and certifications before and to Congress may constitute Making a False Statement to Congress in violation of 18 U.S.C. §1001.

There is evidence that members of the Bush Administration, including the Vice President, have elevated intelligence information which supports this claim without adequate scrutiny, and may have applied undue pressure to intelligence officials to reach these conclusions. Among other things, a former high-level CIA official has stated that when CIA personnel were unable to verify these claims, Cheney became dissatisfied and it "was the beginning of what turned out to be a year-long tug-of-war between the C.I.A and the Vice-President's office;" another senior official reported that CIA analysts got "pounded on, day after day" on these issues; two former CIA officials explained that information on the charge was "passed directly to Washington without vetting them in the [U.S.] Embassy" in Rome; and former CIA agent Tyler Drumheller told *60 Minutes* "[t]he war in Iraq was coming. And they [the Administration] were looking for intelligence to fit into that policy."

The Bush Administration ignored numerous, contrary intelligence findings before making these false statements, including:

- Ambassador Wilson's finding that "no one had signed such a document."
- the CIA's warning to to Ms. Rice directly that "the evidence is weak."
- the State Department's finding that the charges were "highly dubious."
- statements by French Intelligence authorities that the story "doesn't make any sense."
- the conclusion of the National Intelligence Council, delivered to the White House in January, 2003, that the Niger uranium claim was unequivocally false.

The President's own statement in his State of the Union address that "the British government has learned that Saddam Hussein recently sought significant quantities of uranium from Africa" is particularly difficult to defend, given that, among other things, the CIA had told the President's staff before his October 7, 2002 speech that the "President should not be a fact witness on this [Niger-Uranium] issue;" the CIA Araised several concerns about the fragmentary nature of the intelligence" before the State of the Union; and after the speech his Administration informed the U.N. it "cannot confirm [the uranium] reports" (which the IAEA quickly found to be "not authentic").

# Chemical and Biological Weapons

Our investigation has found that President Bush and members of his Administration have made numerous false statements regarding Iraq's chemical and biological weapons capability. These include false statements regarding Iraq's possession of chemical weapons generally; a charge by an Iraqi defector that he had helped bury significant amounts of chemical and other weapons; the existence of mobile chemical weapons laboratories; and Iraq's ability to deliver such weapons using unmanned aerial vehicles.

We have found evidence that members of the Bush Administration made misleading statements regarding Iraq's chemical weapons capability generally, even though they were aware of contrary intelligence provide by the DIA, the CIA, and the State Department. Among other things, the September 2002 DIA report found "[t]here is no reliable information on whether Iraq is producing or stockpiling chemical weapons, or where Iraq has or will establish its chemical warfare agent production facilities;" as early as 1995 the CIA had been informed that "after the Gulf War, Iraq destroyed all its chemical and biological weapons stock;" and the State Department's INR flagged many of Secretary Powell's statements regarding chemical weapons as being "weak." There is also evidence that the Administration's September 2002 statement that an Iraqi defector, Adnan Ihsan Saeed al-Haideri, had secretly helped bury tons of biological and chemical weapons was also knowingly and recklessly made, as the CIA determined by December 2001 that "the intelligence officer concluded that al-Haideri had made up the entire story, apparently in the hopes of securing a visa."

Further, there is evidence of the misleading nature of the Bush Administration's misstatements regarding mobile chemical weapons laboratories by virtue of the fact that they ignored numerous contrary information provided by the German and British Intelligence, as well as CIA officials. Among other things, German Intelligence informed the Administration "[t]his [Curveball] was not substantial evidence . . . [w]e made clear we could not verify the things he said;" British Intelligence officials informed the CIA they are "not convinced that Curveball is a wholly reliable source;" and shortly before Mr. Powell's speech, the CIA doctor who had met with Curveball noted that he "was deemed a fabricator," only to be told by his superior that "this war's going to happen regardless of what Curveball said or didn't say." Given the depth and credibility of these concerns, it is particularly difficult to defend the President's statement in his January 28, 2003 State of the Union address that as a result of information provided by defectors "we know that Iraq, in the late 1990s, had several mobile biological weapons labs . . . designed to produce germ warfare agents and can be moved from place to a place to evade inspectors."

Finally in this regard, there is also evidence that then-Secretary of State Powell and President Bush also made knowingly or recklessly false claims regarding Iraq's unmanned aerial vehicles. Contrary to their assertions, the Air Force was found to "not agree that Iraq is developing UAVs primarily intended to be delivery platforms for chemical and biological (CBW) agents;" while the CIA "believed that the attempted purchase of the mapping software . . . may have been inadvertent."

# Encouraging and Countenancing Torture and Cruel, Inhuman, and Degrading Treatment

Our investigation has found that there is evidence that individuals within the Bush Administration have violated a number of domestic laws and international treaty obligations concerning the mistreatment of detainees, including the Anti-Torture Statute, 18 U.S.C. §2339; the War Crimes Act; 18 U.S.C. §2441; the Geneva and Hague Conventions; the Convention Against Torture, Cruel, Inhuman, and Degrading Treatment; and the legal principle of command responsibility.

# Department of Justice

We have identified evidence that then-Attorney General Ashcroft and then-White House Counsel Gonzales may bear responsibility for unlawful removal of detainees from Iraq in contravention of the War Crimes Act. Among other things, Mr. Ashcroft and Gonzales appear to have requested and approved a March 19, 2004 legal memorandum which, according to intelligence officials "was a green light" for the CIA to improperly remove detainees from Iraq.

Then-Attorney General Ashcroft also appears to be responsible for approving a legal memorandum defining torture as acts consisting of "extreme acts" inflicting "severe pain," such as that accompanying "death or organ failure," which such standard is inconsistent with the Anti-Torture Stature, 18 U.S.C. §2339. Finally, there is further evidence that Attorney General Gonzales bears responsibility for adopting a legal position that the ban on cruel, inhuman, and degrading treatment (CID) does not apply to detainees held outside of the United States, in contravention of the Convention Against Torture, Cruel, Inhuman and Degrading Treatment. Among other things, the former Legal Advisor to the U.S. Department of State has concluded that the ban on CID Awould apply outside the U.S."

# Department of Defense and CIA

There is evidence that Secretary Rumsfeld bears responsibility for certain torture and other illegal conduct in violation of the Anti-Torture Statute. Among other things, Secretary Rumsfeld approved a November 27, 2002 memorandum which includes the use of scenarios designed to convince the detainee that death or severely painful consequences for him and/or his family are imminent."

There is also evidence that Secretary Rumsfeld is responsibile under the command responsibility doctrine. Among other things, Secretary Rumsfeld has been appraised of numerous incidents of torture and CID as well as "ghosting" of detainees, yet has initiated no major action to hold those who committed the acts responsible or effectuated policy changes designed to prevent such misconduct from reoccurring.

There is also evidence that both Secretary Rumsfeld and then-CIA Director Tenet have personally been aware of and approved the "ghosting" of at least one, and potentially further detainees, in potential violation of the Geneva and Hague Conventions. Specifically, with regard to the detaineee Hiwa Abdul Rahman Rashul, Secretary Rumsfeld admitted that Mr. Tenet asked him "not to immediately register the individual" (who was not registered for several additional months).

## Cover-ups and Retaliation

# The Niger Forgeries and the "Sliming" of Ambassador Wilson and His Family

Our investigation has found there is evidence (i) the President has abrogated his obligation under Executive Order 12958 to take corrective action concerning acknowledged leaks of classified information within his Administration; (ii) these leaks appear to have been committed to, among other things, exact retribution against Ambassador Wilson for disclosing that the Bush Administration should have known that the Niger documents were forgeries; and (iii) then-Attorney General Ashcroft participated in a pending criminal investigation involving Karl Rove at a time when he had a personal and political relationship with Mr. Rove in violation of applicable conflict of interest requirements, namely 28 C.F.R. §452, §2-2.170 of the U.S. Attorneys Manual, and Sec. 1.7(b)(4) of the D.C. Rules of Professional Conduct. In addition, we have found that there have been a number

**of misstatements and delays by Members of the Bush Administration since the criminal investigation into the leak was commenced.**

There is evidence as documented in the Libby Indictment and related media accounts that at least four administration officials (including Mr. Libby and Mr. Rove) called at least five Washington journalists (Ms. Miller, Mr. Novak, Mr. Cooper, Mr. Pincus, and Mr. Woodward) and disclosed the identity and occupation of Wilson's wife as a CIA operative. These disclosures do not appear to have been inadvertent, rather they were, according to relevant reporters "given to me," "unsolicited," and obtained when the Administration official "veered" off topic. While it is uncertain whether these leaks violated specific criminal laws, there appears to be little doubt that leaks by Mr. Rove and Mr. Libby violated the requirements of their non-disclosure obligations, including Executive Order 12958 concerning the protection of national security secrets. This Order applies not only to negligent disclosure of classified information but also to persons simply "confirming" information to the media. Under the Executive Order, the President—about whom Robert Novak now claims he would "be amazed" if he did not know the leaker's identity—has an affirmative obligation to take "appropriate and prompt corrective action." (As *Newsweek* explained: "[a]ny reasonable reading of the events covered in the indictment would consider Rove's behavior "reckless [under the EO].")

There is significant evidence that the motivation for disclosure of Ms. Plame's name was to obtain retribution against Ambassador Wilson. Among other things, our investigation has shown that the White House strategy concerning Mr. Wilson was to "slime and defend;" Karl Rove reportedly admitted that Mr. Wilson's wife "is fair game;" a former Administration official acknowledged they "were trying to not only undermine and trash Ambassador Wilson, but to demonstrate their contempt for CIA by bringing Valerie's name into it;" and Special Prosecutor Fitzgerald described a "concerted action" by "multiple people in the White House" using classified information to "discredit, punish, or seek revenge" against Ambassador Wilson, and released a hand-written note by the Vice President specifically questioning the Ambassador's actions.

There is also evidence that then-Attorney General Ashcroft violated applicable conflict of interest requirements, namely 28 C.F.R. §452, Sec. 2-2.170 of the U.S. Attorneys Manual, and Sec. 1.7(b)(4) of the D.C. Rules of Professional Conduct. Even though Mr. Rove had previously advised Mr. Ashcroft as a political candidate (earning almost $750,000 for his services) and was considered by many to be responsible for Mr. Ashcroft being named as Attorney General, the Attorney General was personally and privately briefed on FBI interviews with Karl Rove. It has also been reported that then-Attorney General Ashcroft had been personally briefed on the Plame investigation a full two months after he was informed that Scooter Libby and Karl Rove were "trying to mislead the FBI to conceal their roles in the leak, according to government records and interviews." This conflict raises serious questions regarding the one-month delay between the time the CIA contacted the Department of Justice regarding possible criminal misconduct and the time the Department initiated a criminal investigation, the Department's subsequent delay in notifying the White House Counsel, and the White House Counsel's delay in asking White House staff to preserve relevant evidence. This may also explain why an FBI official admitted that the Department was "going a bit slower on this one because it is so high-profile."

We have also found evidence that there have been a number of additional misstatements by members of the Bush Administration concerning the leak, as well as numerous delays that they have caused. Among other things, then-White House Press Secretary Scott McClellan is responsible for at least eight misstatements concerning the involvement of Mr. Rove, Mr. Libby, and other Administration officials in the leak, and Karl Rove also appears to have falsely denied whether he leaked the name or had "any knowledge" of the leak. There is also evidence Vice President Cheney misspoke on national television in September 2003, when he denied knowledge of who sent Mr. Wilson to Niger, when the Libby Indictment reveals the Vice President had been briefed on that very matter "on or about June 12, 2003."

# Other Instances of Bush Administration Retribution Against its Critics

We have also found evidence that members of the Bush Administration have engaged in a pattern of seeking to exact retribution against a series of individuals, both inside and outside of the Administration, who have exposed wrongdoing or otherwise criticized their misconduct with regard to the Iraq War.

There is evidence that the Army's actions in demoting Bunnatine Greenhouse as the Chief Contracting Officer of the Army Corps of Engineers was in retribution for her testimony before Congress that undue favoritism was shown toward Halliburton in awarding contracts in Iraq. Among other things, it has been charged that "they went after her to destroy her;" and reported that "[h]er crime was not obstructing justice but pursuing it by vehemently questioning irregularities in the awarding of some $7 billion worth of no bid contracts in Iraq to the Halliburton subsidiary Kellogg Brown & Root."

There is also evidence that members of the Bush Administration improperly harmed General Erik Shinseki by leaking the name of his replacement 14 months before his retirement, rendering him a lame duck and, according to media accounts, "embarrassing and neutralizing the Army's top officer." This appears to have been done in retaliation for his testimony before the Senate Armed Services Committee that the Defense Department's troop estimate was too low and "something on the order of several hundred thousand soldiers" would be needed. Among other things, an official acknowledged, "if you disagree with them in public, they'll come after you, the way they did with Shinseki;" while others have stated "Shinseki was publicly humiliated for suggesting it would take hundreds of thousands of troops to secure a post-Saddam Iraq."

There is further evidence that members of the Bush Administration sought to exact political retribution against a number of other individuals who exposed their misconduct regarding Iraq. Among other things, when ABC reporter Jeffrey Kofman reported on frustrated troops in Iraq, Matt Drudge reported that Mr. Kofman was gay, admitting "someone from the White House communications shop" had given him the information; when a CIA employee named "Jerry" found that Curveball was providing false information, he was transferred and "read the riot act;" and Samuel J. Provance, an Army intelligence officer, was demoted and stripped of his clearance after he "made clear to [his] superiors that [he] was troubled about what had happened [at Abu Ghraib]."

# Ongoing Lies, Deceptions, and Manipulation

Our investigation has found that the pattern of misstatements by individuals in the Bush Administration has continued well after the invasion of Iraq.

Among other things, President Bush and Vice President Cheney have made misstatements, such as the President declaring on May 1, 2003 that "major combat operations in Iraq have ended" and the Vice President stating in June, 2005, that "they're in the last throes, if you will, of the insurgency." On October 4, 2005, President Bush stated that there were "30 Iraqi battalions in the lead," when his own generals found that the number of combat ready Iraqi battalions had declined from three to one. In May 2003, President Bush stated "we found the weapons of mass destruction; and Secretary Powell asserted "we have found the biological weapons vans;" however, the *Washington Post* subsequently reported that on May 27, 2003, a U.S./U.K. fact finding mission issued a unanimous 122-page report concluding that the vans "had nothing to do with biological weapons."

# Domestic Spying

The warrantless wiretap program disclosed by the *New York Times* directly violates the Foreign Intelligence Surveillance Act, 50 U.S.C. §1801; and the warrant requirement of the Fourth Amendment, and, just as dangerously, threatens to create a precedent that may be used to violate numerous additional laws. The NSA's domestic database program disclosed by *USA Today* also appears to violate the Stored Communications Act and the Communications Act of 1934. In addition, the Administration appears to have briefed Members of the Intelligence Committees regarding these programs in violation of the National Security Act, 50 U.S.C. §401, and we have found little evidence that they provided useful intelligence or law enforcement information.

# Legal Violations

With regard to the warrantless wiretapping program, there is little doubt that the AUMF was not intended by Congress to statutorily authorize domestic surveillance as the Administration contends. The Senate Majority Leader Tom Daschle has directly contradicted the Administration's argument, writing that the Senate rejected a "last-minute change [from the White House that] would have given the president broad authority to exercise expansive powers not just overseas—where we all understood he wanted authority to act—but right here in the United States, potentially against American citizens." The Attorney General himself acknowledged that Congressional leaders told him it would be "difficult, if not impossible" to obtain Congressional approval for warrantless domestic surveillance. The Bush Administration's argument that the *Hamdi* case (involving the detention of enemy combatants) supports their expansive view of the AUMF is also not credible. Among other experts, noted constitutional scholar Professor Laurence Tribe explains, it is difficult to argue that *Hamdi* supports the idea of warrantless surveillance of Americans, when they "are not even *alleged* to be enemies, much less *enemy combatants*." Likewise, the Administration's argument that the AUMF would constitute a statutory exception as envisioned by FISA is contradicted by the legislative history as well as the review by the non-partisan Congressional Research Service. Perhaps most significantly, in the recent *Hamdan* decision, the Supreme Court held that with regard to the analogous situation of military tribunals, there was "nothing in the text of the legislative history of the AUMF even hinting that Congress intended to expand or alter" the Administration's legal authority.

The Administration's assertion that it nevertheless has inherent constitutional authority to engage in domestic spying pursuant to the *Youngstown Steel Seizure* case is directly contradicted by the House-Senate Conference Report regarding FISA, which stated it is "[t]he intent of the conferees is to apply the standard set forth in Justice Jackson's concurring opinion in the *Steel Seizure* case: 'When a President takes measures incompatible with the express or implied will of Congress, his power is at the lowest ebb, for then he can rely only upon his own constitutional power minus any constitutional power of Congress over the matter.'" With regard to the Bush Administration's contention that a passage in the *In re Sealed Case* supports their inherent authority to conduct domestic warrantless surveillance, these cases are inoperative, as they are all pre-FISA. The Congressional Research Service has concluded, "[i]n the wake of FISA's passage, the Court of Review's reliance [in the *In re Sealed Case*] on these pre-FISA cases. . . as a basis for its assumption of the continued vitality of the President's inherent authority. . . might be viewed as somewhat undercutting the persuasive force of the Court of Review's statement." Again, of particular importance in the *Hamdan* decision, the Court shot down the Administration's "inherent authority" argument, writing, "[w]hether or not the President had independent power, absent congressional authorization, to convene military commissions, he may not disregard limitations that Congress has, in proper exercise of its own war powers, placed on his powers."

With regard to the Fourth Amendment, the Department of Justice's assertion that warrantless domestic spying should be considered "reasonable" pursuant to the "special needs" exception to the Amendment's warrant requirement is undermined by the overwhelming weight of case law. This is summarized in the letter signed by Reagan FBI Director William Sessions and other legal experts ("the NSA spying program has *none* of the safeguards found critical to upholding 'special needs' searches in other contexts"). It is also difficult for the Administration to assert that warrantless surveillance is "reasonable" within the meaning of the Fourth Amendment when national security lawyers working for the Bush Administration have admitted that the low "washout" rate associated with the domestic spying program make it doubtful the program could be deemed sufficiently reasonable to pass muster under the Fourth Amendment.

The NSA's domestic database program would appear to violate both the Stored Communications Act, which prohibits the knowing disclosure of customer telephone records to the government, and the Communications Act, which prohibits the disclosure of telephone records to third parties. If the information was obtained on a "real-time basis," as some government sources have indicated, it would also constitute a criminal violation of the Pen Register and Trap and Trace Statute.

With regard to the National Security Act, that law clearly specifies that the President is required to keep all Members of the House and Senate Intelligence Committees "fully and currently informed" of all intelligence activities except in the case of a highly classified covert action. Based on their review, the non-partisan Congressional Research Service concluded, "the NSA surveillance program would appear to fall more closely under the definition of an intelligence collection program, rather than qualify as a covert action program as defined by statute."

Of additional concern is the fact that the legal justifications developed by the Bush Administration to support the NSA programs threaten to endanger even greater rights and liberties. For example, during the course of House Judiciary Committee hearings, Attorney General Gonzales acknowledged that based on these legal considerations, he was "not going to rule out" the intentional surveillance of purely domestic communications without a court approved warrant. As Republican Senator Lindsey Graham warned, "you could use the inherent authority argument of a Commander-in-Chief at a time of war to almost wipe out anything Congress wanted to do."

At the same time that the domestic spying programs have intruded on the civil liberties of millions of Americans, there is little evidence they have provided any appreciable intelligence or law enforcement benefit, and may have jeopardized numerous terrorism prosecutions. Government officials "have dismissed nearly all of [the NSA call leads] as potential suspects afer hearing nothing pertinent to a terrorist threat," stating that "[t]he information was so thin, and the connections were so remote, that they never led to anything," with FBI agents "jok[ing] that a new bunch of tips meant more calls to the Pizza Hut." FISA judges have testified that "the [warrantless wiretapping] program could imperil criminal prosecutions that grew out of the wiretaps." With regard to the domestic database program, an administration official "questioned whether the fruits of the NSA [database] program . . . have been worth the cost to privacy, while a Pentagon consultant admitted, "[t]he vast majority of what we did with the [NSA] intelligence was ill-focused and not productive."

# Evidence of Misleading Statements and Possible Bad Faith

President Bush and other high-ranking members of the Bush Administration appear to have made a number of misleading statements concerning the NSA programs to Congress and the public. These include statements that (i) the government was only intercepting communications involving Americans pursuant to court approved surveillance; (ii) no purely domestic communications were intercepted under the warrantless wiretapping program; (iii) the government is not monitoring telephone calls and other communications within the U.S.; (iv) Members of Congress briefed by the Bush Administration had not questioned the legality or propriety of the NSA programs; and (v) if the surveillance programs had been in place prior to September 11, the government could have prevented the Al Qaeda attacks. We have also found evidence the NSA programs were developed in a manner designed to stifle legitimate opposition within the Administration.

With respect to the issue of whether the government engaged in domestic warrantless wiretapping, President Bush and members of his Administration made a number of misleading statements. Among other things, prior to the disclosure by the *New York Times*, then Associate Attorney General David Kris testified that "both before and after the PATRIOT Act, FISA can be used only against foreign powers and their agents;" President Bush himself declared that "any time you hear the United States government talking about wiretap, it requires. . . a court order;" and Attorney General Gonzales testified, "It's not the policy or the agenda of this President to authorize actions that would be in contravention of our criminal statutes."

The Bush Administration's claims that no domestic communications were intercepted under the warrantless wiretapping program also appear to be misleading. Government officials have acknowledged that the eavesdropping program "has captured what are purely domestic communications." The *Washington Times* reported that government sources stated, "the National Security Agency in cooperation with the FBI was allowed to monitor the telephone calls and e-mails of any American believed to be in contact with a person abroad suspected of being linked to Al Qaeda or other terrorist groups."

Similarly, the Administration's claims that the government was not monitoring calls or, in President Bush's words, "trolling through the personal lives of millions of innocent Americans" within the U.S. is belied by the *USA Today* revelations, as well as previous revelations by the *New York Times* (telecommunications companies "have been storing information on calling patterns and giving it to the federal government"); former AT&T employee Mark Klein (the NSA set up a "secret room" in AT&T's offices capable of sweeping in telephone and Internet communications); and numerous reports of government programs set up to replace the discredited "Total Information Awareness" Program.

It also appears misleading for members of the Bush Administration, such as White House Counselor Dan Bartlett, to state that lawmakers who have been briefed on the NSA programs "believed they were doing the right thing." In reality, numerous Members of Congress raised legal concerns. Among other Members, the Ranking Democrat on the Senate Intelligence Committee, Senator Rockefeller handwrote a letter to Vice President Cheney, stating, "[c]learly, the activities we discussed raise profound oversight issues," and House Minority Leader Pelosi stated, "she hadn't been told all of the information included in the *USA Today* story."

It also appears inappropriate for the Administration to assert that the NSA warrantless surveillance programs could have prevented the September 11 attacks, given that the 9-11 Commission concluded the government had compiled significant information regarding the responsible individuals and "took no action regarding them," and the FBI "had missed numerous opportunities to track down [the individuals] in the 20 months before the attacks."

The information we have been able to access concerning the creation of the domestic spying program indicates that there is evidence of possible bad faith in its development and implementation on the part of the Bush Administration. For example, officials within the Bush Administration have admitted that when the domestic warrantless wiretapping program was created, "the 'lawyers group,' an organization of fewer than half a dozen government attorneys the National Security Council convenes to review top-secret intelligence programs, was bypassed." *Newsweek* reported that then-counsel to the Vice President David Addington and his allies "made sure the possible dissenters [to the NSA wiretap program] were cut out of the loop," and within the Justice Department those who raised questions regarding the program "did so at their peril; [they were] ostracized. . . denied promotions, while others left" DOJ entirely. It has also been reported that the domestic database program was set up outside of the Justice Department because "they feared that if they passed it down to other departments that might have some purview over the program they might have encountered a stream of objections."

# Thwarting and Stonewalling Congress and the American People

Members of the House and Senate have been essentially stymied by both the Bush Administration and the Republican Congress from obtaining information concerning the matters described in this Report. As David Broder wrote, "Majority Republicans see themselves first and foremost as members of the Bush team—and do not want to make trouble by asking hard questions."

With regard to the allegations of abuse concerning the Downing Street Minutes and Iraq, the President has refused to respond to a letter from 122 Members of Congress, along with more than 500,000 Americans, asking him to explain whether the assertions set forth in the Downing Street Minutes were accurate; House Republican Chairmen of all relevant committees have refused to respond to a letter signed by 52 Members calling for hearings concerning the Downing Street Minutes; and the Administration has essentially ignored questions submitted by Democratic Members concerning false statements regarding nuclear claims and other misstatements concerning the Iraq war.

In addition, the Senate and House Intelligence Committees have refused to conduct any meaningful investigation concerning intelligence manipulation; House Republican Chairmen have refused numerous requests by Members to conduct meaningful hearings on torture and other abuses in Iraq; and the Administration has ignored a request for information concerning such abuses submitted by the Ranking Members of six committees. The President and Vice President have also ignored letters submitted by Members asking them to explain or act on the leaking of Valerie Plame's name to the press in apparent retaliation against her husband, and Republican Chairmen have refused requests to hold hearings on the leaks. Republicans in the House have also rejected myriad attempts by Members to ask the Administration to provide information regarding all of these matters pursuant to Resolutions of Inquiry.

Members of the House and Senate have also, by and large, been blocked by the Bush Administration from obtaining information concerning the domestic spying scandals. First, the Bush Administration rejected without explanation Democratic requests for a special counsel to review the allegations of possible criminal misconduct concerning warrantless domestic surveillance. Second, the Administration stymied any meaningful attempt at congressional oversight, with Senate Judiciary Chairman Specter complaining, "[t]hey want to do just as they please, for as long as they can get away with it." Moreover, House Republican leaders rejected repeated Democratic proposals to create an independent panel or commission to review the NSA program, while Republican Committee Chairman rejected Democratic efforts to pursue Resolutions of Inquiry directing the Bush Administration to respond to congressional inquiries. When the Senate Intelligence Committee fell in line behind the Administration in rejecting an investigation, the

Ranking Democrat John Rockefeller declared, "[t]he committee is, to put it bluntly, basically under the control of the White House." The Administration has pursued various changes to FOIA and classification laws, and repeatedly invoked the state secrets doctrine in an effort to help insulate their conduct from outside or court scrutiny.

# Recommendations

Based upon our investigation of the misconduct of the Bush Administration, we recommend that Congress should consider a number of actions that could deter such abuses in the future, including:

- *Exercising its oversight responsibility to obtain information from the Administration*— A number of bills have been introduced that would provide authority to investigate the various allegations identified in this Report. These include: (i) H. Res. 635, introduced by Rep. Conyers, establishing a Select Committee to investigate the various charges identified in Part I of this Report (The Committee would be equally comprised of Democrats and Republicans, selected by the Speaker and the Minority Leader and make appropriate recommendations if agreed to on a bipartisan basis); (ii) Sen. Robert Byrd (D-WV) and Rep. Conyers introduced S. 2362 and H.R. 5223, to establish a blue ribbon commission to investigate the various allegations identified in Part II of this Report; and (iii) H.R. 3003, introduced by Rep. Waxman and nineteen other Ranking Members, as well as the House Democratic Leader and House Democratic Whip, would establish a bipartisan blue ribbon commission to investigate the alleged torture and other abuses at Guantanamo and Abu Ghraib. None of these bills have received any hearings or other consideration by the Republican Majority.

- *Reaffirming that the Foreign Intelligence Surveillance Act and the criminal code contain the exclusive means for conducting domestic surveillance*—Under the guise of exercising oversight of the warrantless surveillance, Republican Members of Congress have introduced legislation that merely attempts to grant the program constitutional and legal validation. To the extent legislation is needed to improve intelligence gathering capabilities, the preferable approach is to reaffirm that FISA and the criminal code contain the exclusive means for conducting domestic surveillance, to the extent necessary, and increasing resources for warrantless FISA wiretaps that may be authorized under current law. Two bills have been introduced this Congress to further this goal: (i) H.R. 4570, introduced by Reps. Jane Harman (D-CA) and Conyers, and (ii) H.R. 4976, introduced by Reps. Adam Schiff (D-CA) and Jeff Flake (R-AZ).

- *Requiring the President to report on the pardon of any individual who could implicate the President or other officials implicated by pending investigations*—Congress should consider legislation, such as H.R. 5961, requiring that the President notify Congress of the pardon of any individual who is or was an Administration official. The notification should include the nature of the pardon and the effects it might have on any pending investigations. Such legislation is needed to allow for full disclosure should the President pardon individuals as a means of preventing an investigation from running its course and, perhaps, uncovering information critical of the Administration. This is a particular concern because the President refused to respond to a July 25, 2005 letter from Rep. Conyers seeking his assurance that he would not pardon any former or current officials involved in the leak of CIA officer Valerie Plame Wilson's name.

- *Requiring the President to notify Congress upon the declassification of classified information*— The Administration appears to have selectively leaked numerous items of classified information to buttress their case for war, and that President himself secretly authorized the declassification of information without notice to the media in an effort to respond to Ambassador Wilson's op-ed concerning the Administration's uranium claims. The public would have better access to information were the White House to issue public notices upon declassification. Sen. Dianne Feinstein (D-CA) has introduced S. 2660 to require such notice.

- *Enhancing protections for national security whistleblowers*—Federal employees should be encouraged to try to correct and report wrongdoing at federal agencies. Among other things, Congress should consider limiting exemptions from the whistleblower protection laws and permitting whistleblowers to report problems directly to Congress and the President instead of having to go through an agency's chain of command. Sens. Daniel Akaka (D-HI) and Frank Lautenberg (D-NJ) have proposed whistleblower reforms in S. 494 and S. 2285. Congress also should consider legislation providing for a procedure to enable whistleblowers to enforce their rights against reprisal by protecting them from Executive Branch assertions of state secrets privileges, as provided for in H.R. 5112, introduced by Reps. Tom Davis (R-VA) and Henry Waxman (D-CA).

- *Strengthening the authority of the Privacy and Civil Liberties Oversight Board*—Upon the recommendation of the 9-11 Commission, Congress created a board to review the privacy and civil liberties implications of White House policies. Unfortunately, the Board was established within the Executive Office of the President instead of as an independent agency. Under H.R. 1310, introduced by Rep. Carolyn Maloney (D-NY), the Board would be independent of the President and possess subpoena powers.

Congress also should take additional measures to address the threat of terrorism, including:

- *Increasing funding for COPS and other first responders and base anti-terror funding on risk not politics*—Despite the success of the Community Oriented Policing Program in reducing crime across the country and the fact that local police will be the first on the scene at any terrorist or other catastrophic event, the Bush Administration continues to seek cuts in the program's funding. Congress should make it a national priority to fully fund COPS and provide firefighters, emergency workers, and police with the training, personnel, and technology they need. In addition, anti-terrorism funding for state and local governments should be based on need and terror risk, not politics. Such proposals have passed the House but were not considered in the Senate in the form of section 128 of H.R. 3199, the House-passed extension of the PATRIOT Act; H.R. 1544, which was introduced by then-Homeland Security Committee Chairman Christopher Cox (R-CA); and H.R. 1419, introduced by then-Rep. Robert Menendez (D-NJ).

• *Implementing the 9-11 Commission recommendations, including enhancing port, infrastructure, and chemical plant security*—Only a small percentage of incoming cargo is screened for potential terrorist threats, such as dirty bombs. While the House passed H.R. 4954 to increase security, that bill failed to require screening of all cargo, to increase the number of radiation portal monitors, and to require a review of contracts for port operations where a terrorist-sponsored entity might be involved. We also must secure our airports, mass transit systems, chemical and nuclear plants, and food and water supplies. Finally, this would include ensuring that would-be terrorists do not have access to loose nuclear materials.

• *Banning corporate trade with state sponsors of terror and eliminating sovereign immunity protections for state sponsors of terror*—Current law prohibits U.S. companies from engaging in trade with terrorist nations, but they are able to circumvent the restriction by setting up foreign subsidiaries. The law should be extended to apply to foreign subsidiaries. In the 108th Congress, Sen. Frank Lautenberg (D-NJ) offered amendment S.A. 3151 to a Senate bill, S. 2400, to accomplish this goal. Also, many victims of terror and their families, have sued foreign states for damages arising out of terrorism. Unfortunately, the State and Justice Departments have opposed such lawsuits on the grounds that sovereign immunity protects foreign states from U.S. law. Rep. Jim Saxton (R-NJ) has introduced legislation, H.R. 865, to permit private lawsuits against foreign states for terrorism.

• *Enhancing Laws Against Wartime Fraud*—Legislation should be enacted to extend the statutes of limitations for criminal fraud perpetrated by corporations against the United States during wartime. In the 108th Congress, Rep. Rahm Emanuel (D-IL) introduced H.R. 3673 to penalize wartime profiteering, whether during a declared war or military conflict.

# Conclusion

Our examination of both major matters described in this Report, "The Downing Street Minutes and Deceptions, Manipulation, Torture, Retribution and Coverups in the Iraq War," and "Unlawful Domestic Surveillance and the Decline of Civil Liberties Under the Administration of George W. Bush," has revealed a number of persistent and disturbing pattern of conduct involving the Bush Administration. This includes:

- The apparent willingness of members of the Bush Administration to see their actions as not being subject the law
- A number of false and misleading statements made by members of the Bush Administration which helped to cover up or delay disclosure of their conduct
- Using the power of the executive branch to threaten and undermine political opponents of the Bush Administration
- Using the tragic events of September 11 as a means of justifying unrelated objectives of the Administration
- Acting to limit possible oversight and accountability for the Administration's actions.

Thus, over the last six years, the Bush Administration appears to have ignored a number of laws and legal requirements, such as executive orders concerning the protection of national security secrets; supervising an investigation of the Valerie Plame leak in a manner inconsistent with conflict of interest requirements; mistreatment of detainees in possible violation of international and domestic laws and treaties concerning torture and cruel, inhuman and degrading treatment; warrantless domestic wiretaps and customer telephone databases in contravention of the Foreign Intelligence Surveillance Act, the Stored Communications Act and the Communications Act; and failure to notify Members of the Intelligence Committees of intelligence activities in violation of the National Security Act.

At the same time, all too frequently, members of the Bush Administration appear to have placed political expediency above veracity. Whether it was then-White House Press Secretary stating that "I spoke with [Karl Rove and Scooter Libby], so that I could come back to you and say that they were not involved" in the leak of Valerie Plame's name, or President Bush declaring that "any time you hear the United States government talking about a wiretap it requires . . . a court order," there have been numerous instances where political convenience appears to have taken precedence over the principle of communicating fully, frankly, and honestly with the American people and their representatives.

Our Report has also found a number of instances where public criticism of the Bush Administration and their policies has placed the careers of government officials and even their families' careers in jeopardy. Thus, Bunnantine Greenhouse was demoted from the Army Corps of Engineers after she testified the Administration was improperly favoring Haliburton in awarding contracts in Iraq; Valerie Plame was outed as a covert CIA agent after her husband wrote that the Iraq uranium claims were false; and attorneys at the Department of Justice who questioned the NSA's warrantless wiretapping program "did so at their own peril," according to government sources.

In terms of taking political advantage of the September 11 tragedy, we learned that as early as January 30, 2001, former Bush Secretary of Treasury Paul O'Neill stated that "[f]rom the beginning . . . . It was all about finding a way" to get rid of Saddam, with the President saying "go find me a way to do this;" while immediately after the September 11 attacks, the White House told Wesley Clark, "[y]ou got to say this is connected. . . . This has to be connected to Saddam Hussein." Both Vice President Cheney and General Hayden sought to justify the Administration's domestic spying program by claiming it would have prevented the September 11 attacks, even though this was contrary to the findings of the 9-11 Commission, causing Commission Member Bob Kerry to assert that the Administration claim was "patently false and an indication that [Hayden] is willing to politicize intelligence and use false intelligence to help the President."

The single overriding characteristic running through all of the allegations of misconduct identified in our Report has been the unwillingness of the Bush Administration to allow its actions to be subject to any form of meaningful outside review. Not only were 122 Members of Congress unable to obtain any response to their questions posed regarding the Downing Street Minutes, but neither the House nor the Senate has ever engaged in any serious review of the facts surrounding the NSA domestic spying programs. The institutional damage resulting from such constitutional neglect will likely be felt for many years, if not generations.

The lesson of this Report is that if we allow intelligence, military, and law enforcement to do their work free of political interference, if we give them requisite resources and modern technologies, if we allow them to "connect the dots" in a straight-forward and non-partisan manner, we can protect our citizens. We all want to fight terrorism, but we need to fight it the right way, consistent with our Constitution, and in a manner that serves as a model for the rest of the world.

# Endnotes

1. *Larry King Live*: "Interview with Dick Cheney and Lynne Cheney" (CNN television broadcast, May 30, 2005) (emphasis added), *available at* http://transcripts.cnn.com/TRANSCRIPTS/0505 /30/lkl.01.html.

2. Texas Governor George W. Bush's campaign focused on issues of "compassionate conservatism," his stated view that conservative policies could be brought to bear to address social ills. Another focus of his campaign was the perceived ethical transgressions of the Clinton Administration, and the Starr Investigation in particular. Governor Bush promised to restore "honor and dignity to the White House." "Capital Gang: Lieberman Takes the Heat; Bush, McCain Meet in Arizona; Are the Democrats Getting Tough on Hollywood?" (CNN television broadcast, Aug. 13, 2000) *available at* http://transcripts.cnn.com/TRANSCRIPTS/0008 /13/cg.00.html.

3. See Commission on Presidential Debates, Unofficial Debate Transcript, Oct. 3, 2000, *available at* http://www.debates.org/pages/trans2000a.html. Vice President Cheney also stated in an interview, in the midst the 2000 presidential campaign, that the U.S. should not act as though "we were an imperialist power, willy-nilly moving into capitals in that part of the world, taking down governments." *Meet the Press*: "Interview with Vice President Dick Cheney" (NBC television broadcast, Aug. 27, 2000).

4. Bryan Burrough, Evgenia Peretz, David Rose, & David Wise, "The Path to War," *Vanity Fair*, May 1, 2004, at 228, 232.

5. President George W. Bush, State of the Union Address (Jan. 29, 2002), *available at* http://www.whitehouse .gov/news/releases/2002/01/20020129-11.html.

6. President George W. Bush, Graduation Speech at West Point (June 1, 2002), *available at* http://www.white house.gov/news/releases/2002/06/20020601-3.html. He further noted that "[t]he war on terror will not be won on the defensive. We must take the battle to the enemy. . . . And this nation will act." Ibid.

7. On "multiple" occasions, Cheney and Libby questioned analysts studying alleged Iraq's weapons programs and links to Al Qaeda.. Walter Pincus, "Some Iraq Analysts Felt Pressure From Cheney," *The Washington Post*, June 5, 2003, at A1

8. For example, on August 22, 2002, the President stated that he was willing to "look at all options." Adam Nagourney & Thom Shanker, "A 'Patient' Bush Says He'll Weigh All Iraq Options", the *New York Times*, Aug. 22, 2002, at A1. Later that year, he stated, "Of course, I haven't made up my mind we're going to war with Iraq." President George W. Bush, Remarks on Terrorism Insurance (Oct. 1, 2002), *available at* http://www.whitehouse.gov/news/releases/2002/10/20021001-1.html.

9. Frank Rich, "It's Bush-Cheney, Not Rove-Libby", the *New York Times*, Oct. 16, 2005, at 12.

10. The President stated that Iraq was a "grave and gathering danger." President George W. Bush, Remarks at the U.N. General Bssembly (Sept. 12, 2002), *available at* http://www.whitehouse.gov/news/releases /2002/09/20020912-1.html. He also said that the U.S. would "not allow any terrorist or tyrant to threaten civilization with weapons of mass murder." President George W. Bush, Remarks to the Nation on the Anniversary of Terrorist Attacks (Sept. 11, 2002), *available at* http://www.whitehouse.gov/news /releases/2002/09/20020911-3.html.

11. Letter from Dr. Naji Sabri, Iraq Minister of Foreign Affairs, to Kofi Annan, U.N. Secretary-General (Sept. 16, 2002), *available at* http://www.sfgate.com/cgi-bin/article.cgi?f=/news/archive/2002/09/16/interna tional1954EDT0706.DTL.

12. President George W. Bush, President Discusses Iraq, Domestic Agenda with Congressional Leaders (Sept. 18, 2002), *available at* http://www.whitehouse.gov/news/releases/2002/09/20020918-1.html. The next day, the President stated how important it was that Congress pass a resolution authorizing the use of force in Iraq. President George W. Bush, President Bush to Send Iraq Resolution to Congress Today (Sept. 19, 2002), *available at* http://www.whitehouse.gov/news/releases/2002/09/20020919-1.html.

13. On October 7, 2002, President Bush warned that the final proof of Iraq's weapons of mass destruction (WMD) could come in the form of a "mushroom cloud" and subsequently requested Congressional authorization for war. President George W. Bush, Remarks on Iraq (Oct. 7, 2002), *available at* http://www.white house.gov/news/releases/2002/10/20021007-8.html.

14. H.J. Res. 114, 107th Cong. 2d Sess. (2002) (enacted as Authorization for Use of Military Force Bgainst Iraq Resolution of 2002, Pub. L. No. 107-243, 116 Stat. 1498 (2002)). Several Members of Congress, including Ranking Member Conyers, filed suit in Federal court arguing the resolution was Constitutionally deficient. Among other things, the suit alleged that the text of the resolution did not explicitly invoke the War Powers Act and unconstitutionally delegated the Congressional power to declare war to the Executive Branch. The suit was ultimately unsuccessful [Doe v. Bush, 323 F.3d 133 (1st Cir. 2003).] While substantial questions remain about whether this resolution appropriately authorized the use of force in Iraq, it has come to be known as a joint resolution "for the use of force" and will be referred to as such in this report.

15. See *Ibid*.

16. President George W. Bush, Remarks at the Signing of the Iraq Resolution (Oct.16, 2002), *available at* http://www.whitehouse.gov/news/releases/2002/10/20021016-1.html

17. S.C. Res 1441, U.N. SCOR, 4644th mtg., S/2002/1198 (2002), *available at* http://www.un.int/usa /sresiraq.htm. The resolution made clear that only the United Nations Security Council had the right to take punitive action against Iraq in the event of noncompliance. *Ibid*.

18. Mohamed ElBaradei, Report to the U.N. Security Council (Jan. 27, 2003), *available at* http://www .un.org/News/dh/iraq/elbaradei27jan03.htm. According to the IAEA, the tubes were not suitable for manufacturing centrifuges as the Administration had claimed. *Ibid*.

19. President George W. Bush, State of the Union Address (Jan. 28, 2003), *available at* www.whitehouse .gov/news/releases/2003/01/20030128-19.html.

20. Secretary Colin Powell, Remarks to the U.N. Security Council (Feb. 5, 2003), *available at* http://www .whitehouse.gov/news/releases/2003/02/20030205-1.html. During his speech, he assured the world that, "every statement I make today is backed up by sources, solid sources. These are not assertions. What we're giving you are facts and conclusions based on solid intelligence." *Ibid*.

21. *Meet the Press*: "Interview with Vice President Cheney" (NBC television broadcast, Mar. 16, 2003), *available at* http://msnbc.msn.com/id/3080244/s.

22. The letter stated that "Reliance by the United States on further diplomatic and other peaceful means alone will neither (A) adequately protect the national security of the United States against the continuing threat posed by Iraq nor (B) likely lead to enforcement of all relevant United Nations Security Council resolutions regarding Iraq." Letter from President George W. Bush to Congress (Mar. 18, 2003), *available at* http://www.whitehouse.gov/news/releases/2003/03/20030319-1.html.

23. President George W. Bush, Remarks from the U.S.S. Abraham Lincoln (May 1, 2003), *available at* http://www.whitehouse.gov/news/releases/2003/05/iraq/20030501-15.html.

24. Massive unchecked looting, including that of radioactive material, may have taken place days after the fall of Baghdad. See Barton Gellman, "U.S. has Not Inspected Iraq Nuclear Facility", *The Washington Post*, Apr. 25, 2003, at A14. The Administration's disbanding of the Iraqi army effectively created 400,000 or so available recruits for the insurgency. See Ellen Knickmeyer, "Under U.S. Design, Iraq's New Army Looks a Good Deal Like the Old One", *The Washington Post*, Nov. 21, 2005, at A1. In addition, months after the invasion, up to 51,000 American military and civilian personnel had not been provided with proper body armor and thus had to ask friends and relatives in the United States to buy and mail off-the-shelf models. Peter

Brownfield, "U.S. Troops in Iraq have limited Body Armor", *FoxNews.com*, Oct. 24, 2003, *available at* http://www.foxnews.com/story/0,2933,101061,00.html.

25. Joseph C. Wilson IV, Op-Ed, "What I Didn't Find in Africa," the *New York Times*, July 6, 2003, §4, at 9.

26. White House Press Secretary Ari Fleischer, Press Gaggle (July 7, 2003), *available at* http://www.white-house.gov/news/releases/2003/07/20030707-5.html#9.

27. Robert D. Novak, "Mission to Niger," *The Washington Post*, July 14, 2003, at A21. Around July 7, just a week prior to the Novak column, a State Department memorandum containing information about CIA officer Valerie Plame in a paragraph marked "(S)" for secret was circulated within the administration, a clear indication that any Bush Administration official who read it should have been aware the information was classified. See Walter Pincus & Jim VandeHei, "Plame's Identity Marked as Secret", *The Washington Post*, July 21, 2005, at A1.

28. "Powell: Some Iraq Testimony Not Solid", *CNN.com*, Apr. 3, 2004, *available at* http://www.cnn.com/2004/US/04/03/powell.iraq.

29. James Risen, "Ex-Inspector Says CIA Missed Disarming in Iraqi Arms Program", the *New York Times*, Jan. 26, 2004, at A1. Kay's conclusion was confirmed by the CIA chief weapons inspector, Charles A. Duelfer, in his report released later in the year. Special Advisor to the DCI on Iraq's WMD, Comprehensive Report (Sept. 20, 2004), *available at* http://www.cia.gov/cia/reports/iraq_wmd_2004/transmittal.html.

30. The Comm'n on the Intelligence of the U.S. Regarding Weapons of Mass Destruction, Report to the President of the U.S. (2005) (transmittal letter).

31. The Situation Room: Debate Continues Over Iraq Withdrawal; Holiday Crunch Hits Home; Hillary vs. Condoleezza in 2008? (CNN television broadcast Nov. 23, 2005) *available at* http://transcripts.cnn.com/TRANSCRIPTS/0511/23/sitroom.01.html.

32. Minority Staff of H. Comm. on Gov't Reform, 108th Cong., Report on Iraq on the Record (Comm. Print 2004).

33. *Ibid.* at i.

34. S. Rep. No. 108-301(2004).

35. *Ibid.* (additional views of Vice Chairman John D. Rockefeller, IV, Sen. Carl Levin * Sen. Dick Durbin).

36. The Administration also attempted to minimize its mistakes or misdeeds. At a black-tie dinner for journalists on March 24, 2004, President Bush narrated a slide show attempting to make light of the failure to find WMD. One picture showed the President looking under a piece of furniture in the Oval Office, at which he remarked: "Those weapons of mass destruction have got to be here somewhere." "Bush's Iraq WMD Joke Backfires", *BBC News*, Mar. 26, 2004, *available at* http://news.bbc.co.uk/2/hi/americas/3570845.stm.

37. *60 Minutes II* (CBS television broadcast, Apr. 28, 2004).

38. See, e.g., *Human Rights Watch*, "Getting Away with Torture: Command Responsibility for the U.S. Abuse of Detainees" (Apr. 2005).

39. Farah Stockman, "Bush Calls Vote 'Resounding Success' for Democracy", *The Boston Globe*, Jan. 31, 2005, at A1.

40. Michael Smith, "Blair Planned Iraq War From Start", *The Sunday Times*, May 1, 2005, *available at* http://www.timesonline.co.uk/article/0,,2087-1592724,00.html.

41. Letter from 87 Members of Congress to the President (May 5, 2005), *available at* http://www.house.gov/judiciary_democrats/letters/bushsecretmemoltr5505.pdf.

42. *Ibid.*

43. Congressman Charles Rangel summed up the hearing best: "Quite frankly, evidence that appears to be building up points to whether or not the president has deliberately misled Congress to make the most important decision a president has to make, going to war." Democratic Hearing on the Downing Street Minutes, Before the H. Comm. on the Judiciary, 109th Cong. (2005).

44. Letter to President George W. Bush (June 16, 2005), *available at* http://www.johnconyers.com /index.asp?Type'sUPERFORMS&SEC={8771D3DA-2F3D-49F7-895C-DF473CAEFA2C}. On July 23, 2005, nationwide hearings were held concerning the Downing Street Minutes in Boston, Detroit, Los Angeles, New York, and Seattle, as well as in individual homes around the country.

45. Letter from Stanley M. Moskowitz, Director of Congressional Affairs, CIA, to the Honorable John Conyers, Jr., Ranking Member, Committee on the Judiciary (Jan. 30, 2004).

46. Letter from James B. Comey, Acting Attorney General, to Patrick J. Fitzgerald, U.S. Attorney (Dec. 30, 2003), *available at* http://www.usdoj.gov/usao/iln/osc/documents/ag_letter_december_30_2003.pdf.

47. Matthew Cooper, "What I Told the Grand Jury", *Time*, July 25, 2005, *available at* http://www.time .com/time/archive/preview/0,10987,1083899,00.html. On July 14, 2005, Congressman Conyers wrote a letter to President Bush, signed by 91 members of Congress, urging the President to demand either that Karl Rove explain his role in the leak or that Karl Rove resign. Letter from 91 Members of Congress to President George W. Bush (July 14, 2005), *available at* http://www.house.gov/judiciary_democrats /letters/presroveltr71405.pdf.

48. President George W. Bush, Remarks in the East Room (July 18, 2005), *available at* http://www.whitehouse.gov/news/releases/2005/07/20050718-1.html.

49. National Security Implications of Disclosing the Identity of a Covert Intelligence Officer: Hearing Before the S. Democratic Policy Comm. & Democratic Members of the H. Gov't Reform Comm., 109th Cong., 1st Sess. (2005).

50. Erik Eckholm, "Army Contract Official Critical of Halliburton Pact is Demoted", the *New York Times*, Aug. 29, 2005, at A9.

51. David Johnston & Richard W. Stevenson, "Cheney Aide Charged with Lying in Leak Case", the *New York Times*, Oct. 29, 2005, at A1. See also United States v. Libby (D.D.C. Oct. 26, 2005) (grand jury indictment), *available at* www.usdoj.gov/usaoil/n/osc/libby_indictment_28102005.pdf. There was one count of obstruction of justice, two counts of perjury and two counts of making false statements. *Ibid.*

52. Special Counsel Patrick J. Fitzgerald, Press Conference (Oct. 28, 2005).

53. Carl Hulse & David D. Kirkpatrick, "Partisan Quarrel Causes Senators to Bar the Doors in an Unusual Closed Session", the *New York Times*, Nov. 2, 2005, at A22.

54. Press Release, Senator Carl Levin, Levin Says Newly Declassified Information Indicates Bush Administration's Use of Pre-War Intelligence Was Misleading (Nov. 6, 2005), *available at* http://levin.senate.gov/newsroom/release.cfm?id=248339.

55. Bob Drogin & John Goetz, "How U.S. Fell Under the Spell of 'Curveball'", *Los Angeles Times*, Nov. 20, 2005, at A1.

56. Richard Morin & Dan Balz, "Survey Finds Most Support Staying in Iraq; Public Skeptical About Gains Bgainst Insurgents," *The Washington Post*, June 28, 2005, at A1.

57. Warren P. Strobel, "Iraq Emerges as a Terrorist Training Ground", *Knight Ridder*, July 5, 2005, *available at* http://seattletimes.nwsource.com/html/nationworld/2002357529_iraqterror05.html. *According* to classified studies by the CIA and the State Department, "Iraq has replaced Afghanistan as the prime training ground for foreign terrorists who could travel elsewhere across the globe and wreak havoc." *Ibid.*

58. Linda Bilmes, Op-Ed, "The Trillion-Dollar War", the *New York Times*, Aug. 20, 2005, at A13 ("Factors keeping costs high include inducements for recruits and for military personnel serving second and third deployments, . . . as well as more than \$2 billion a year in additional foreign aid to Jordan, Pakistan, Turkey and others to reward their cooperation in Iraq and Afghanistan. . . . The biggest long-term costs are disability and health payments for returning troops, which will be incurred even if hostilities were to stop tomorrow. . . . These payments are likely to run at \$7 billion a year for the next 45 years.").

59. *Meet the Press*: "Interview with the Vice President" (NBC television broadcast), Sept. 8, 2002.

60. Secretary Donald Rumsfeld, Press Briefing (Sept. 16, 2002).

61. U.S. Policy Toward Iraq: Hearing before the U.S. House Comm. on International Relations, 107th Cong., 2d Sess. (Sept. 19, 2002) (statement of Secretary Powell) (emphasis added).

62. President George W. Bush, Remarks After Meeting with Members of Congress (Oct. 1, 2002), *available at* http://www.whitehouse.gov/news/releases/2002/10/20021001-1.html (emphasis added).

63. President George W. Bush, Remarks at Presidential Hall (Nov. 7, 2002), *available at* http://www.white house.gov/news/releases/2002/11/20021107-2.html (emphasis added).

64. President George W. Bush, President Bush Signs Child Internet Safety Legislation (Dec. 4, 2002), *available at* http://www.whitehouse.gov/news/releases/2002/12/20021204-1.html.

65. President George W. Bush, Remarks on Iraq and North Korea (Dec. 31, 2002), *available at* http://www.whitehouse.gov/news/releases/2002/12/20021231-1.html.

66. President George W. Bush, Remarks at Prairie Chapel Ranch, (Jan.2, 2003), *available at* http://www.whitehouse.gov/news/releases/2003/01/20030102.html.

67. President George W. Bush, Address to the Nation (Mar. 6, 2003), *available at* http://www.whitehouse.gov/news/releases/2003/03/20030306-8.html.

68. President George W. Bush, President's Radio Address (Mar. 8, 2003), *available at* http://www.whitehouse.gov/news/releases/2003/03/20030308-1.html.

69. President George W. Bush, Address to the Nation (Mar. 17, 2003), *available at* http://www.whitehouse.gov/news/releases/2003/03/20030317-7.html

70. 60 Minutes (CBS television broadcast, Jan. 11, 2004) (emphasis added), *available at* http://www.cbsnews.com/stories/2004/01/09/60minutes/main592330.shtml.

71. Russ Baker, "Bush Wanted to Invade Iraq if Elected in 2000", GNN.tv, Oct. 27, 2004 (emphasis added), *available at* http://www.gnn.tv/articles/article.php?id=761

72. *Ibid.*

73. See Bryan Bender, "Indictments Put Focus on Neoconservatives", *The Boston Globe*, Oct. 29, 2005, at A12.

74. The President, Remarks by the President at John Cornyn for Senate Reception (Sept. 26, 2002) (emphasis added), *available at* http://www.whitehouse.gov/news/releases/2002/09/20020926-17.html. Former President H.W. Bush visited Kuwait between April 14 and April 16, 1993, to commemorate the victory over Iraq in the Persian Gulf War. During Bush's visit, Kuwaiti authorities arrested 17 people, allegedly linked to Saddam Hussein, who were involved in a plot to kill him. "Suspect Admits Targeting Bush for Bomb, Kuwaiti Says", Chicago Tribune, Apr. 28, 1993, at 7.

75. See Bryan Burrough, Evgenia Peretz, David Rose, & David Wise, "The Path to War", *Vanity Fair*, May 1, 2004, at 228.

76. Letter from Elliott Abrams, Richard L. Armitage, William J. Bennett, Jeffrey Bergner, John Bolton, Paula Dobriansky, Francis Fukuyama, Robert Kagan, Zalmay Khalilzad, William Kristol, Richard Perle, Peter W. Rodman, Donald Rumsfeld, William Schneider, Jr., Vin Weber, Paul Wolfowitz, R. James Woolsey & Robert B. Zoellick to President William J. Clinton (Jan. 26, 1998), *available at* http://www.newamerican century.org/iraqclintonletter.htm

77. *Ibid.*

78. Zalmay Khalilzad & Paul Wolfowitz, "Overthrow Him", Weekly Standard, Dec. 1, 1997, at 14; see also Glenn Kessler, "U.S. Decision on Iraq Has Puzzling Past: Opponents of War Wonder When, How Policy was Set", January 12, 2003, *The Washington Post*, at A1.

79. Project for a New American Century, Rebuilding America's Defenses: Strategy, Forces and Resources for a New Century 14 (Sept. 2000) (emphasis added), *available at* http://newamericancentury.org/Rebuilding AmericasDefenses.pdf.

80. *60 Minutes* (CBS television broadcast, Jan. 11, 2004) (emphasis added), *available at* http://www.cbsnews.com/stories/2004/01/09/60minutes/main592330.shtml

81. *Ibid.* (statement of Ron Suskind).

82. *BBC News*: "the Secret U.S. Plan for Iraq's Oil" (BBC television broadcast, Mar. 21, 2005), *available at* http://www.gregpalast.com/detail.cfm?artid=419&row=1

83. The Pentagon, Foreign Suitors for Iraqi Oil Field Contracts (Mar. 5, 2001), *available at* http://www.judicialwatch.org/IraqOilFrgnSuitors.pdf.

84. *Ibid.*

85. George Packer, The Bssassins' Gate 45 (Farrar, Straus, and Giroux, 2005).

86. "Plans for Iraq Attack Began on 9-11", *CBSnews.com*, Sept. 4, 2002, *available at* http://www.cbsnews.com/stories/2002/09/04/september11/main520830.shtml.

87. *Ibid.*

88. John B. Judis & Spencer Ackerman, "The First Casualty", *The New Republic*, June 30, 2003, at 14.

89. Richard A. Clarke, "Against All Enemies: Inside America's War on Terror" at 32 (Free Press, 2004) (emphasis added) (Clarke recounting conversation with the President).

90. *Meet the Press*: "Interview with Senator Trent Lott" (NBC television broadcast, Aug. 21, 2005) (emphasis added), *available at* http://www.msnbc.msn.com/id/8926876/.

91. *Meet the Press*: "Interview with General Wesley Clark" (NBC television broadcast, June 15, 2003) (emphasis added), *available at* http://securingamerica.com/ccn/node/1147.

92. Glenn Kessler, "U.S. Decision on Iraq Has Puzzling Past: Opponents of War Wonder When, How Policy was Set", Jan. 12, 2003, *The Washington Post*, at A1.

93. *Ibid.* The board's meetings amount to a form of "organized brainstorming" with the Defense Secretary, his key lieutenants, and a group of well-informed outsiders, all of whom are cleared to have access to classified intelligence.

94. Bryan Burrough, Evgenia Peretz, David Rose & David Wise, "The Path to War", *Vanity Fair*, May 2004, at 236 (emphasis added).

95. National Commission on Terrorist Attacks upon the United States, The 9-11 Commission Report 559-560 n.75 (2004), *available at* http://www.9-11commission.gov/report/911Report.pdf (emphasis added).

96. David Rose, "Bush and Blair Made Secret Pact for Iraq War", *The Observer*, Apr. 4, 2004, at 1.

97. *60 Minutes*: "Interview with Bob Woodward" (CBS television broadcast, Apr. 18, 2004) (emphasis added).

98. President George W. Bush, State of the Union Address (Jan. 29, 2002), *available at* http://www.whitehouse.gov/news/releases/2002/01/20020129-11.html

99. James Mann, "Rise of the Vulcans: The History of Bush's War Cabinet 318" (Penguin Group, 2004) (internal citations omitted).

100. Senator Bob Graham, Remarks to the Council on Foreign Relations (Mar. 26, 2004) (emphasis added), *available at* http://www.cfr.org/publication/6905/senator_bob_graham_remarks_to_the_council_on_foreign_relations.html?breadcrumb=default.

101. Bob Woodward, Plan of Attack 136-37 (Simon & Schuster, 2004) (emphasis added).

102. *60 Minutes*: "Interview with Bob Woodward" (CBS television broadcast, Apr. 18, 2004), available at http://www.cbsnews.com/stories/2004/04/15/60minutes/main612067.shtml..

103. 2002 Supplemental Appropriations Act for Further Recovery From and Response to Terrorist Attacks on the United States, Pub. L. No. 107-206, 116 Stat. 820 (2002) (does not mention Iraq); Department of Defense and Emergency Supplemental Appropriations for Recovery from and Response to Terrorist Attacks on the United States Act of 2002, Pub. L. No. 107-117, 115 Stat. 2230 (2002) (does not mention Iraq)

104. Seymour Hersh, "Annals of National Security: Stovepipe", *The New Yorker*, Oct. 27, 2003, at 77.

105. Warren P. Strobel & John Walcott, "Bush Has Decided to Overthrow Hussein", *Knight Ridder*, Feb.13, 2002, *available at* http://www.realcities.com/mld/krwashington/news/special_packages/11809605.htm?template=contentModules/printstory.jsp.

106. Seymour Hersh, "Annals of National Security: Stovepipe", *The New Yorker*, Oct. 27, 2003, at 77 (emphasis added)

107. George Packer, The Bssassins' Gate 45 (Farrar, Straus, and Giroux, 2005) (emphasis added).

108. Michael Elliott & James Carney, "First Stop, Iraq", *Time*, Mar. 31, 2003, at 172.

109. Daniel Eisenberg, "We're Taking Him Out", *Time*, May 13, 2002, at 36 (emphasis added).

110. *60 Minutes*: Interview with Bob Woodward (CBS television broadcast, Apr. 18, 2004), *available at* http://www.cbsnews.com/stories/2004/04/15/60minutes/main612067.shtml.

111. Glenn Kessler, "U.S. Decision on Iraq Has Puzzling Past", *The Washington Post*, Jan. 12, 2003, at A1.

112. Rowan Scarborough, "U.S. Rushed Post-Saddam Planning", *The Washington Times*, Sept. 3, 2003, *available at* http://www.washingtontimes.com/national/20030903-120317-9393r.htm.

113. Adel Safty, "Forcible Occupation of Iraq Is a Man-made Disaster," *Gulf News*, January 3, 2005, *available at* http://search.gulfnews.com/articles/05/01/03/146204.html

114. Thom Shanker & David E. Sanger, "U.S. Envisions Blueprint on Iraq Including Big Invasion Next Year", the *New York Times*, Apr. 28, 2002, at A1.

115. Michael Smith, "British Bombing Raids Were Illegal, Says Foreign Office", *The Sunday Times*, June 19, 2005, at 7.

116. Michael Smith, "RAF Bombing Raids Tried to Goad Saddam into War", *The Sunday Times*, May 29, 2005. The decision to increase military activity in order to add pressure on Iraq appears to have been discussed as early as December 2001, when General Tommy Franks said to Secretary Rumsfeld that he was thinking of "spurts of activity followed by periods of inactivity. We want the Iraqis to become accustomed to military expansion, and then apparent contraction." General Tommy Franks, American Soldier 342 (2004) (emphasis in original).

117. Democratic Hearing on the Downing Street Minutes, Before the H. Comm. on the Judiciary, 109th Cong. (2005) (testimony of Ray McGovern) (emphasis added)

118. Larisa Alexandrova & John Byrne, "The Unofficial War: U.S., Britain Led Massive Secret Bombing Campaign Before Iraq War Was Declared", RawStory.com, June 27, 2005, *available at* http://rawstory.com/news/2005/The_unofficial_war_U.S._and_Britain_led_massive_air_campaign_before_Iraq_war_be_0627.html.

119. Michael Smith, "RAF Bombing Raids Tried to Goad Saddam Into War", *The Sunday Times*, May 29, 2005, at 2.

120. Robert Winnett, "Key No 10 Aides were Split over War", *The Sunday Times*, July 31, 2005, *available at* http://www.timesonline.co.uk/article/0,,2087-1715005_1,00.html.

121. *Ibid.*

122. *Ibid.*

123. Michael Smith, "RAF Bombing Raids Tried to Goad Saddam Into War", *The Sunday Times*, May 29, 2005, at 2.

124. Michael Smith, "General Admits to Secret Air War", *The Sunday Times*, June 26, 2005, at 2.

125. John Byrne, "U.S. Changed Iraq Policy to Begin Airstrikes Months Before War", Rawstory.com, *available at* http://rawstory.com/news/2005/U.S._changed_Iraq_policy_to_begin_airstrikes_months_before_0630.html

126. Memorandum from Matthew Rycroft to David Manning, U.K. Foreign Policy Advisor (July 23, 2002), at 1 (emphasis added), *available at* http://www.timesonline.co.uk/article/0,,2087-1593607,00.html [hereinafter Downing Street Minutes].

127. Memorandum from the Office of the Overseas and Defense Secretariat to Personal Secret U.K. Eyes Only (Mar. 8, 2002), at 1, *available at* http://downingstreetmemo.com/docs/iraqoptions.pdf [hereinafter Options Paper].

128. *Ibid.* at 4 (emphasis added).

129. *Ibid.* at 10 (emphasis added).

130. Memorandum from the Foreign and Commonwealth Office to the Prime Minister (Mar. 2002), *available at* http://www.timesonline.co.uk/article/0,,2087-1654697,00.html [hereinafter Legal Background Paper].

131. *Ibid.*

132. Memorandum from David Manning, U.K. Foreign Policy Advisor, to the Prime Minister (Mar. 14, 2002), *available at* http://downingstreetmemo.com/docs/manning.pdf [hereinafter David Manning Memo].

133. *Ibid.*

134. *Ibid.* (emphasis added).

135. Memorandum from Christopher Meyer, U.K. Ambassador to U.S., to David Manning, U.K. Foreign Policy Advisor (Mar. 18, 2002) (emphasis added), *available at* http://www.afterdowningstreet.org/?q=node/837 [hereinafter Meyer Memo

136. *Ibid.*

137. *Ibid.*

138. David Rose, "Bush and Blair Made Secret Pact for Iraq War", *The Observer*, Apr. 4, 2004, at 1 (emphasis added).

139. Memorandum from Peter Ricketts, Political Director of the U.K. Foreign and Commonwealth Office, to Jack Straw, U.K. Foreign Secretary (Mar. 22, 2002), *available at* http://downingstreetmemo.com/docs/ricketts.pdf [hereinafter Ricketts Memo]

140. *Ibid.*

141. *Ibid.* (emphasis added)..

142. Memorandum from Jack Straw, U.K. Foreign Secretary, to the Prime Minister (Mar. 25, 2002), *available at* http://downingstreetmemo.com/docs/straw.pdf [hereinafter Straw Memo].

143. *Ibid.*

144. *Ibid.* (emphasis added)

145. *Ibid.*

146. *Ibid.* (emphasis added).

147. *Ibid.* at 3.

148. Memorandum from Cabinet Office (July 21, 2002) (emphasis added), *available at* http://www.timesonline.co.uk/article/0,,2089-1648758_1,00.html [hereinafter Cabinet Office Paper].

149. *Ibid.* ¶ 12 (emphasis added).

150. *Ibid.*

151. Downing Street Minutes at 1.

152. *Ibid.* (emphasis added).

153. Downing Street Minutes at 2.

154. *Ibid.* (emphasis added).

155. *Ibid.*

156. *Ibid.*

157. *Ibid.* (emphasis added).

158. *Ibid.*; see also Cabinet Office Paper.

159. See Carmen Yarrusso, "Downing Street Memos explained in Plain English", *AfterDowningStreet.org*, June 24, 2005 (explaining that Bush Administration characterizations of the leaked Downing Street Minutes as insignificant is incorrect since the documents clearly indicate the "beliefs of people working closely with Bush's top war planners, with access to privileged U.S. information"), *available at* http://www.afterdowning street.org/?q=node/506

160. Democratic Hearing on the Downing Street Minutes, Before the H. Comm. on the Judiciary, 109th Cong. (2005) (testimony of Cindy Sheehan).

161. Warren P. Strobel & John Walcott, "Downing Street Memo Indicates Bush Made Intelligence Fit Iraq Policy", *Knight Ridder*, May 5, 2005, *available at* http://www.realcities.com/mld/krwashington/11574296.htm.

162. Michael Isikoff & Mark Hosenball, "From Downing Street to Capitol Hill", *Newsweek.com*, June 17, 2005, *available at* http://www.msnbc.msn.com/id/8234762/site/newsweek/.

163. Bryan Burrough, Evgenia Peretz, David Rose & David Wise, "The Path to War", *Vanity Fair*, May 2004, at 284.

164. *Ibid.* (emphasis added).

165. Robin Cook, Internet Diary: The Road to War, December 19, 2001, *Why-War.com*, Oct. 5, 2003, *available at* http://www.why-war.com/news/2003/10/05/theroadt.html

166. Elisabeth Bumiller, "Bush Aides Set Strategy to Sell Policy on Iraq", the *New York Times*, Sept. 7, 2002, at A1.

167. Mark Danner, "The Secret Way to War", the *New York Review of Books*, June 9, 2005, *available at* http://www.nybooks.com/articles/18034

168. *Ibid.*

169. *Meet the Press*: "Interview with Vice President Dick Cheney" (NBC television broadcast, Mar. 16, 2003), replayed on Meet the Press: Interview with Vice President Dick Cheney (NBC television broadcast, Sept. 14, 2003), *available at* http://msnbc.msn.com/id/3080244/s.

170. In his autobiography, retired U.S. General Tommy Franks, who led the 2003 invasion of Iraq, wrote that he was telling Defense Secretary Rumsfeld in December 2001: "spurts of activity followed by periods of inactivity. We want the Iraqis to become accustomed to military expansion, and then apparent contraction." General Tommy Franks, American Soldier 342 (2004) (emphasis in original).

171. A total of 21,736 sorties were flown over southern Iraq between June 2002 and the beginning of the war. According to a document found by Larisa Alexandrova of *RawStory.com*, Lieutenant-General T Michael Moseley said that the "spikes of activity" were part of a covert air war. According to Moseley, the attacks, "laid the foundation" for the war. John Byrne, U.S. Changed Iraq Policy to Begin Air Strikes Months before War, *Rawstory.com*, *available at* http://rawstory.com/news/2005/U.S._changed_Iraq_policy_to _begin_airstrikes_months_before_0630.html.

172. Downing Street Minutes, at 2.

173. Richard Norton-Taylor & Patrick Wintour, "Papers Reveal Commitment to War", *The Guardian*, May 2, 2005, *available at* http://politics.guardian.co.uk/election/story/0,15803,1474755,00.html

174. Michael Smith, "Failure is not an option, but it doesn't mean they will avoid it", *Sunday Telegraph*, Sept. 18, 2004, at 4, *available at* http://www.telegraph.co.uk/news/main.jhtml?xml=/news/2004/09 /18/nwar118.xml.

175. "War Protesters Keep Pressure On", CBSNews.com, Mar. 30, 2003, *available at* http://www.cbsnews .com/stories/2003/03/31/iraq/main547001.shtml

176. Andrew Brookes, International Institute for Strategic Studies, Combat Air Force Bssets in Place Around Iraq As at 21 March 2003, *available at* http://www.iiss.org/iraqCrisis-more.php?itemID=6.

177. Iraq Coalition Troops: Non US-Forces In Iraq, *available at* globalsecurity.org/military/ops /iraq_orbat _coalition.htm

178. The White House, Operation Iraqi Freedom: Statement of Support from Coalition (Mar. 26, 2003), *available at* http://www.whitehouse.gov/news/releases/2003/03/20030326-7.html

179. Memorandum from Cabinet Office ¶ 20 (July 21, 2002), *available at* http://www.timesonline.co.uk/article/0,,2089-1648758_1,00.html

180. See i.e Prime Minister Blair, Speech to Parliament (Mar. 18, 2003), *available at* http://politics.guardian .co.uk/iraq/story/0,12956,916790,00.html

181. Elisabeth Bumiller, "Bush Aides Set Strategy to Sell Policy on Iraq", the *New York Times*, Sept. 7, 2002, at A1.

182. As Robert Parry explained, "From the start of its drive to invade Iraq, the administration treated the war like a public relations game, with the goal of manufacturing consent or at least silencing any meaningful opposition." Robert Parry, "Why U.S. Intelligence Failed", *Consortiumnews.com*, Oct. 22, 2003, *available at* http://www.consortiumnews.com/2003/102203.html.

183. The Cabinet Office Paper includes several additional expectations concerning the Blair government's design to sell the public on the need for preemptive military action. Among other things, the paper explains that a condition for military action includes "the preparation of domestic opinion" and goes on to emphasize that "[t]ime will be required to prepare public opinion in the U.K. that it is necessary to take military action against Saddam Hussein . . . [a]n information campaign will be needed . . . [t]his will need to give full coverage to the threat posed by Saddam Hussein, including his WMD." Ricketts Memo, at 1. The Ricketts Memo goes on to emphasize the difficult public relations problem expected by the Iraq war, observing that "we are still left with a problem of bringing public opinion to accept the imminence of a threat from Iraq. This is something the Prime Minister and President need to have a frank discussion about." *Ibid.* Later on, the Ricketts Memo emphasizes how "much better" it will be to use weapons of mass destruction as the rationale for war: "For Iraq, 'regime change' does not stack up. It sounds like a grudge between Bush and Saddam. Much better, as you have suggested, to make the objective ending the threat to the international community from Iraqi [weapons of mass destruction] before Saddam uses if or gives it to terrorists. This is at once easier to justify in terms of international law but also more demanding." *Ibid.*

Other portions of the Downing Street Minutes further anticipate the British government's need to emphasize public relations and marketing with regard to the justification for the upcoming war:

British Ambassador Christopher Meyer wrote that when he met with Paul Wolfowitz, "[i]f the U.K. were to join with the U.S. in any operation against Saddam, we would have to be able to take a critical mass of parliamentary and public opinion with us. Memorandum from Christopher Meyer, U.K. Ambassador to U.S., to David Manning, U.K. Foreign Policy Advisor (Mar. 18, 2002) (emphasis added), *available at* http://www.afterdowningstreet.org/?q=node/837.

The British Office of the Overseas and Defense Secretariat in the Iraq Options Paper stated that attacking Iraq required "sensitising the public: a media campaign to warn of the dangers that Saddam poses and to prepare public opinion both in the U.K. and abroad." Memorandum from the Office of the Overseas and Defense Secretariat to Personal Secret U.K. Eyes Only (Mar. 8, 2002), at 10 (emphasis added), *available at* http://downingstreetmemo.com/docs/iraqoptions.pdf.

U.K. Foreign Secretary Jack Straw acknowledged that while regime change was the goal, it needed to be cloaked by reference to weapons of mass destruction: "regime change per se is no justification for military action; it could form part of the method of any strategy, but not a goal. Of course, we may want credibly to assert that regime change is an essential part of the strategy by which we have to achieve our ends—that of the elimination of Iraq's WMD capacity: but the latter has to be the goal . ." Memorandum from Jack Straw, U.K. Foreign Secretary, to the Prime Minister (Mar. 25, 2002) (emphasis added), *available at* http://downingstreetmemo.com/docs/straw.pdf.

184. Bret Baer, "Rumsfeld: Iraq Can't Wait", *FoxNews.com*, Aug. 20, 2002 (interview with Secretary Rumsfeld) (emphasis added)..

185. Barton Gellman & Walter Pincus, "Depiction of Threat Outgrew Supporting Evidence", *The Washington Post*, Aug. 10, 2003, at A1.

186. *Ibid.* (emphasis added)..

187. Elisabeth Bumiller, "Traces of Terror: The Strategy", the *New York Times*, Sept. 7, 2002, at A1.

188. ABC News Transcript, April 25, 2003, Page 301.

189. Sam Tanenhaus, "Bush's Brain Trust", *Vanity Fair*, July 2003, at 114 (emphasis added)

190. Elisabeth Bumiller, "Traces of Terror: The Strategy", the *New York Times*, Sept. 7, 2002, at A1 (emphasis added).

191. Walter Russell Mead, "The Revolutionary", *Esquire*, Nov. 1, 2004.

192. Elizabeth De La Vega, "The White house Criminal Conspiracy", *The Nation*, November 14, 2005.

193. David Barstow, William J. Broad, & Jeff Gerth, "How White House Embraced Suspect Iraq Arms Intelligence", the *New York Times*, Oct. 3, 2004, at A1.

194. *Ibid.*

195. Barton Gellman, "A Leak, Then Then a Cascade; Did a Bush loyalist overstep the bounds in protecting the administration's case for war in Iraq and obstruct an investigation?" *The Washington Post*, Oct. 30, 2005, at A1 (emphasis added).

196. Barton Gellman and Walter Pincus, "Depiction of Threat Outgrew Supporting Evidence", *The Washington Post*, Aug. 10, 2003.

197. Barton Gellman and Walter Pincus, "Depiction of Threat Outgrew Supporting Evidence", *The Washington Post*, Aug. 10, 2003

198. *The Chris Matthews Show* (MSNBC television broadcast, Sept. 11, 2005) (emphasis added).

199. Memorandum from Matthew Rycroft to David Manning, U.K. Foreign Policy Advisor (July 23, 2002), at 1, *available at* http://www.timesonline.co.uk/article/0,,2087-1593607,00.html.

200. President's Remarks at the United Nations General Bssembly (Sept. 12, 2002), *available at* http://www.whitehouse.gov/news/releases/2002/09/20020912-1.html

201. Jonathan S. Landay, "CIA leak illustrates selective use of intelligence on Iraq",

*Knight Ridder*, Oct. 26, 2005.

202. *60 Minutes*: Interview with Bob Woodward (CBS television broadcast, Apr. 18, 2004) (emphasis added).

203. Bob Woodward, Plan of Attack 286 (Simon & Schuster, 2004) (emphasis added).

204. Glen Kessler, "U.S. Decision On Iraq Has Puzzling Past; Opponents of War Wonder When, How Policy Was Set", *The Washington Post*, Jan. 12, 2003, at A1

205. *Ibid.*

206. President George W. Bush, State of the Union (Jan. 28, 2003) *available at* http://www.whitehouse.gov/news/releases/2003/01/20030128-19.html.

207. Barton Gellman and Walter Pincus, "Depiction of Threat Outgrew Supporting Evidence", *The Washington Post*, Aug. 10, 2003.

208. Department of Defense Budget Priorities FY 2004: hearing Before the House Comm. on Budget, 108th Cong. 9 (2003) (statement of the Hon. Paul D. Wolfowitz, Deputy Secretary of Defense).

209. Secretary of Defense Donald Rumsfeld, Media Availability with Afghan President Karzai (Feb. 27, 2003) *available at* http://www.defenselink.mil/transcripts/2003/t02272003_t0227ap.html

210. *Meet the Press*: Interview with Vice President Dick Cheney (NBC television broadcast, Mar. 16, 2003), *available at* http://msnbc.msn.com/id/3080244/s.

211. John Diamond, "CIA Review Faults Prewar Plans", *USA Today*, Oct. 12, 2005, at A1 (emphasis added).

212. Bryan Burrough, Evgenia Peretz, David Rose & David Wise, "The Path to War", *Vanity Fair*, May 20, 2004, at 228 (emphasis added).

213. *Ibid.*

214. Bradley Graham, "Prewar Memo Warned of Gaps in Iraq Plans", *The Washington Post*, Aug. 18, 2005, at A13

215. *Ibid.*

216. *Ibid.*

217. Memorandum from Jack Straw, U.K. Foreign Secretary, to the Prime Minister (Mar. 25, 2002), *available at* http://downingstreetmemo.com/docs/straw.pdf

218. *Ibid.* at 4 (emphasis added).

219. Memorandum Memorandum from David Manning, U.K. Foreign Policy Advisor, to the Prime Minister

(Mar. 14, 2002), *available at* http://downingstreetmemo.com/docs/manning.pdf

220. *Ibid.*

221. *Ibid.* (emphasis added).

222. Memorandum from Cabinet Office (July 21, 2002) (emphasis added), *available at* http://www.timeson-line.co.uk/article/0,,2089-1648758_1,00.html

223. David Corn, The Lies of George W. Bush 240 note (Random House, 2004).

224. Hans Blix, Disarming Iraq 86 (Pantheon, 2004) (quoting the Vice President).

225. Bob Woodward, Plan of Attack 162 (Simon & Schuster, 2004).

226. *Ibid.* (emphasis added).

227. Mark Danner, "The Secret Way to War", 52 the *New York Review of Books* 10, June 9, 2005 (emphasis added).

228. Bob Woodward, Plan of Attack 177-78 (Simon & Schuster, 2004)

229. *Ibid.*

230. *Ibid.* Bush told Woodward, "And of course these Brits don't know what cojones are." *Ibid.*

231. *Ibid.*

232. President George W. Bush, Remarks at the United Nations General Bssembly (Sept. 12, 2002), *available at* http://www.whitehouse.gov/news/releases/2002/09/20020912-1.html.

233. Bryan Burrough, Evgenia Peretz, David Rose, & David Wise, "The Path to War", *Vanity Fair*, May 1, 2004, at 285 (emphasis added).

234. Testimony Regarding Iraq: Hearing Before the S. Comm. on Armed Services, 107th. Cong., 2d Sess. (2002) (statement of Secretary of Defense Donald H. Rumsfeld), *available at* http://www.dod.gov /speeches/2002/s20020919-secdef2.html.

235. President George W. Bush, Remarks from the Oval Office (Sept. 19, 2002), *available at* http://www.white house.gov/news/releases/2002/09/20020919-1.html

236. Ewen MacAskill & Edward Pilkington, "Threat of War", *The Guardian*, Nov. 13, 2002, at 13 (quoting Richard Perle).

237. S.C. Res 1441, U.N. SCOR, 4644th mtg., S/2002/1198 (2002), *available at* http://www.un.int/usa /sresiraq.htm.

238. Bryan Burrough, Evgenia Peretz, David Rose, & David Wise, "The Path to War", *Vanity Fair*, May 1, 2004, at 286.

239. Mark Danner, "The Secret Way to War", 52 *The New York Review of Books* 10, June 9, 2005, at 72.

240. Paul Gilfeather, "Bush Aide: Inspections or Not, We'll Attack Iraq", *Mirror*, Nov. 20, 2002, *available at* http://www.mirror.co.uk/news/allnews/page.cfm?objectid=12377231&method=full&siteid=50143 (Emphasis added). Peter Kilfoyle, a former defense minister and Labour backbencher, tells The Mirror: "America is duping the world into believing it supports these inspections. President Bush intends to go to war even if inspectors find nothing. This make a mockery of the whole process and exposes America's real determination to bomb Iraq." Ibid

241. "Bush: 'A Disappointing Day' for Peacez', *CNN.com*, Dec. 20, 2002, *available at* http://archives.cnn .com/2002/US/12/20/sproject.irq.un/.

242. *Ibid.*

243. Hans Hans Blix, Disarming Iraq 86 (Pantheon, 2004) (emphasis added).

244. *Ibid.*

245. *Ibid.*

246. Julia Preston, "Threats And Responses: The Inspections; Weapon Inspector Bsks U.S. To Share Secret Iraq Data", the *New York Times*, Dec. 7, 2002, at 1.

247. "Inspectors Call U.S. Tips 'Garbage,'" *CBSNews.com*, Feb. 20, 2003, *available at* http://www.cbsnews.com /stories/2003/01/18/iraq/main537096.shtml.

248. John B. Judis & Spencer Ackerman, "The First Casualty", *The New Republic*, June 30, 2003 at 24 (emphasis added).

249. Press Release, United Nations Security Council, Security Council Briefed by Chief U.N. Weapons Experts on First 60 Days of Inspections in Iraq (January 27, 2003), *available* ¿

250. *Ibid.*

251. Bob Woodward, Plan of Attack 253 (Simon & Schuster, 2004).

252. *Ibid.*

253. Bryan Burrough, Evgenia Peretz, David Rose, & David Wise, The Path to War, *Vanity Fair*, May 1, 2004, at 290.

254. The Resolution stated that Iraq "has failed to take the final opportunity afforded it in Resolution 1441." U.S., U.K., Spain Draft Resolution, U.S. Dep't of State, Feb. 24, 2003, *available at* http://www.state .gov/p/io/rls/othr/17937.htm. Again, high level British intelligence documents reveal that the Bush Administration was only viewing the United Nations process as a pretext to war, not an actual mechanism for finding and eliminating WMD. The U.S. edition of Philippe Sands' book "Lawless World" refers to a conversation between President Bush and Prime Minister Blair on January 30, 2003, about whether to seek a second United Nations resolution. President Bush was reported to have agreed with Mr. Blair that "it made sense to try for a second resolution, which he would love to have." But President Bush was also said to be "worried about Saddam playing tricks" and that Hans Blix, the top United Nations weapons inspector, would report "that Saddam was beginning to cooperate." Philippe Sands, Lawless World 185-7 (Viking, 2004).

255. The following interchange occurred with the press:

Q: As you said, the Security Council faces a vote next week on a resolution implicitly authorizing an attack on Iraq. Will you call for a vote on that resolution, even if you aren't sure you have the vote?

THE PRESIDENT: Well, first, I don't think—it basically says that he's in defiance of 1441. That's what the resolution says. And it's hard to believe anybody is saying he isn't in defiance of 1441, because 1441 said he must disarm. And, yes, we'll call for a vote.

Q: No matter what?

THE PRESIDENT: No matter what the whip count is, we're calling for the vote. We want to see people stand up and say what their opinion is about Saddam Hussein and the utility of the United Nations Security Council. And so, you bet.

President George W. Bush, Press Conference (Mar. 6, 2003), *available at* http://www.whitehouse.gov /news/releases/2003/03/20030306-8.html.

256. Martin Bright, Ed Vulliamy & Peter Beaumont, "Revealed: U.S. Dirty Tricks To Win Vote on Iraq War", *The Observer*, Mar. 2, 2003, at 1..

257. *Ibid.*

258. *Ibid.*

259. A similar scramble took place in the U.K. Consider the following reported admission from Michael Boyce, the former British Chief of Defense Staff, on why he demanded an unequivocal assurance from British lawyers that the war was legal: "I wanted to make sure that we had this anchor which has been signed by the government law officer . . . [i]t may not stop us from being charged, but, by God, it would make sure other people were brought into the frame as well." Martin Bright, Ed Vulliamy & Peter Beaumont, "Revealed: U.S. Dirty Tricks to Win Vote on Iraq War", *The Observer*, Mar. 2, 2003 at 1. When questioned by The Observer whether he meant the Prime Minister and the Attorney General, Boyce replied: "Too bloody right." *Ibid.*

260. As described by Professor Philippe Sands, "[b]y early March the only argument left, the only plausible jus-

tification, would be to run the argument that the Security Council had somehow already authorized the use of force." Philippe Sands, Lawless World 178 (Penguin Group, 2005)

261. President George W. Bush, Address to the Nation (Mar. 17, 2003) *available at* http://www.whitehouse.gov /news/releases/2003/03/20030317-7.html. Of course, as noted above, it is clear that the opposite is true. For example, as the Cabinet Office Paper observes, "U.S. views of international law vary from that of the U.K. and the international community. Regime change per se is not a proper basis for military action under international law." Cabinet Office Paper at 2. In addition, as the British legal advisors concluded in their March 8, 2002 Legal Background Memo, "[f]or the exercise of the right of self-defense there must be more than 'a threat.' There has to be an armed attack actual or imminent. The development of posses-sion of nuclear weapons does not in itself amount to an armed attack; what would be needed would be clear evidence of an imminent attack." Legal Background Memo

262. Memorandum from Lord Goldsmith, U.K. Attorney General, to the Prime Minister (Mar. 7, 2003), *available at* http://www.number-10.gov.uk/files/pdf/Iraq%20Resolution%201441.pdf.

263. Memorandum from the Foreign and Commonwealth Office to the Prime Minister (Mar. 2002), *available at* http://www.timesonline.co.uk/article/0,,2087-1654697,00.html.

264. Oliver Burkeman & Julian Borger, "War Critics Bstonished as U.S. Hawk Admits Invasion was Illegal", *Guardian*, Nov. 20, 2003, at 4

265. The March 8, 2002 Iraq Options Paper clearly articulates this: "[O]f itself, REGIME CHANGE has no basis in international law" and "[a] legal justification for invasion would be needed. Subject to Law Officers advice, none currently exists." See Options Paper at 8. In addition, at the Blair war cabinet meet-ing of July 23, 2002, the then-U.K. Attorney General, Lord Goldsmith, directly informed Blair of the ille-gality of an invasion: "The Attorney-General said that the desire for regime change was not a legal base for military action. There were three possible legal bases: self-defense, humanitarian intervention, or UNSCR authorization. The first and second could not be the base in this case." See Downing Street Minutes at 2. (Of course, as we now know, United Nations Security Council authority, while eventually sought, was never achieved).

266. The Attorney-General's Written Answer of 17 March 2003 Setting Out His View of the Legal Basis for the Use of Force Bgainst Iraq (Mar. 17, 2003), *available at* http://www.fco.gov.uk/Files/kfile/AG%20 Written%20Answer%20of%2017%20March%202003,0.pdf.

267. On March 18, 2003, the Leader of the House of Commons and former Foreign Secretary Robin Cook resigned from the British Cabinet. Mr. Cook made clear his views on the adequacy of the intelligence and rejected the claim that Saddam had WMD. Matthew Tempest, Cook Doubts Saddam Threat, The Guardian Unlimited, June 17, 2003, *available at* http://politics.guardian.co.uk/iraq/story /0,12956,979260,00.html.

268. Democratic Hearing on the Downing Street Minutes, Before the H. Comm. on the Judiciary, 109th Cong. (2005) (testimony of Ray McGovern).

269. Letter from Elizabeth Wilmshurst, Deputy Legal Advisor to the Foreign Office, to Michael Wood, Legal Advisor, (Mar. 20, 2003), *available at* http://news.bbc.co.uk/2/hi/uk_news/politics/4377605.stm.

270. *Ibid.*

271. *Ibid.* (emphasis added). This last sentence was redacted from the resignation letter made public in March of 2005. The unredacted version, containing this sentence, surfaced shortly thereafter, causing further difficulties for the British Attorney General and Blair government, who would now be accused of engaging in censorship

272. James Bamford, A Pretext for War 333 (Doubleday, 2004).

273. Col. Lawrence Wilkerson, Chief of Staff to Former Secretary of State Colin Powell, Remarks before the New America Foundation (Oct. 19, 2005), *available at* http://www.newamerica.net/Download _Docs/pdfs/Doc_File_2644_1.pdf

274. Ron Suskind, "Without A Doubt", *N.Y. Times Magazine*, Oct. 17, 2004, at 44.

275. Glenn Kessler, "CIA Leak Linked to Dispute over Iraq Policy", *The Washington Post*, Oct. 25, 2005, at A3 (emphasis added).

276. M. Hersh, "Annals of National Security: The Stovepipe", *The New Yorker*, Oct. 27, 2003, at 75. Mel Goodman, a 24-year veteran of the CIA, who lectures at the State Department's Foreign Service Institute, has recounted what his students from the intelligence agencies told him about the political pressure they faced regarding Iraq:

> I get into the issue of politicization . . . [t]hey [the students] don't say much during the question period, but afterwards people come up to me, D.I.A. and C.I.A. analysts who have had this pressure. I've gotten stories from D.I.A. people being called into a supervisor's office and told they might lose their job if they didn't revise a paper. "This is not what the administration is looking for. You've got to find W.M.D.'s, which are out there."

Bryan Burrough, Evgenia Peretz, David Rose & David Wise, "The Path to War", *Vanity Fair*, May 2004, at 242 (emphasis added).

277. Walter Pincus & Dana Priest, "Some Iraq Analysts Felt Pressure From Cheney Visits", *The Washington Post*, June 5, 2003, at A1 (emphasis added).

278. Warren P. Strobel, Jonathan S. Landay & John Walcott, "Some in Bush Administration Have Misgivings about Iraq Policy", *Knight Ridder*, Oct. 8, 2002.

279. Maureen Dowd, "Fashioning Deadly Fiascos", the *New York Times*, Nov. 5, 2005, at A17 (quoting Col. Lawrence Wilkerson).

280. The Diplomat's Goodbye, *The Washington Post*, Mar. 9, 2003, at B3.

281. Spencer Ackerman & John B. Judis, "The First Casualty", *The New Republic*, June 30, 2003, at 14.

282. Seymour M. Hersh, "Annals of National Security: The Stovepipe", *The New Yorker*, Oct. 27, 2003, at 80.

283. *CNN Presents*: "Dead Wrong" (CNN television broadcast, Aug. 21, 2005) (quoting unidentified male).

284. Spencer Ackerman & John B. Judis, "The First Casualty", *The New Republic*, June 30, 2003, at 14.

285. Seymour M. Hersh, "Annals of National Security: The Stovepipe", *The New Yorker*, Oct.27, 2003, at 80.

286. *Ibid.* at 75 (quoting Kenneth Pollack). Pollack later wrote himself that: Throughout the spring and fall of 2002 and well into 2003 I received numerous complaints from friends and colleagues in the intelligence community, and from people in the policy community, about [how the Bush Administration handled the intelligence]. . . . Many Administration officials reacted strongly, negatively, and aggressively when presented with information or analysis that contradicted what they already believed about Iraq. . . . Intelligence officers who presented analyses that were at odds with the pre-existing views of senior Administration officials were subject to barrages of questions and requests for additional information. They were asked to justify their work sentence by sentence. . . . The Administration gave greatest credence to accounts that presented the most lurid picture of Iraqi activities. In many cases intelligence analysts were distrustful of those sources, or knew unequivocally that they were wrong. But when they said so, they were not heeded; instead, they were beset with further questions about their own sources.

Kenneth M. Pollack, Spies, *Lies, and Weapons: What Went Wrong, The Atlantic Monthly*, Jan. 1, 2004 (emphasis added).

287. Julian Borger, "Threat of War: U.S. Intelligence Questions Bush Claims on Iraq", *The Guardian*, Oct. 9, 2002, at 12.

288. *CNN* Presents: Dead Wrong (CNN television broadcast, Aug. 21, 2005) (statement of Michael Scheuer).

289. *Frontline*: Truth, War & Consequences (PBS television broadcast, Aug. 12, 2003).

290. *Ibid.*

291. Bryan Burrough, Evgenia Peretz, David Rose & David Wise, "The Path to War", *Vanity Fair*, May 2004, at 204 (quoting Greg Thielmann) (emphasis added).

292. Jonathan S. Landay, "CIA Leak Illustrates Selective Use of Intelligence on Iraq", *Knight Ridder*, Oct. 25, 2005 (emphasis added).

293. Seymour M. Hersh, "Annals of National Security: The Stovepipe", *The New Yorker*, Oct. 27, 2003, at 81 (emphasis added).

294. Walter Pincus & Dana Priest, "Some Iraq Analysts Felt Pressure from Cheney Visits", *The Washington Post*, June 5, 2003, at A1 (emphasis added).

295. Michael Smith, "Exclusive: Downing Street Reporter Dissects Pre-War Iraq Intelligence", *The Raw Story*, Aug. 24, 2005, available at http://rawstory.com/news/2005/Downing_Street_reporter_dissects_Iraq _intelligence_in_leadup_0824.html.

296. Democratic Hearing on the Downing Street Minutes, Before the H. Comm. on the Judiciary, 109th Cong. (2005) (statement of Ray McGovern).

297. CNN Presents: Dead Wrong (CNN television broadcast, Aug. 21, 2005).

298. See Bruce B. Auster, Mark Mazzetti & Edward Pound, "Truth and Consequences", *U.S. News & World Report*, June 9, 2003, at 14.

299. Bryan Burrough, Evgenia Peretz, David Rose, & David Wise, "The Path to War", *Vanity Fair*, May 1, 2004, at 230 (emphasis added).

300. Hearing on Findings of the 9-11 Commission Before the Senate Armed Services Committee, 108th Cong. (2004) (testimony of John E. McLaughlin, Acting Director of Central Intelligence).

301. John B. Judis & Spencer Ackerman, "The First Casualty" *The New Republic*, June 30, 2003, at 23-4.

302. Colin Powell on Iraq, Race, and Hurricane Relief, ABC News, Sept. 8, 2005, available at http://abcnews.go.com/2020/Politics/story?id=1105979&page=1

303. *Ibid.*

304. 60 Minutes: Interview with Richard Clarke (CBS television broadcast, Mar. 21, 2004) (emphasis added), available at http://www.cbsnews.com/stories/2004/03/19/60minutes/main607356.shtml.

305. President George W. Bush, Remarks in Meeting with President Alvaro Uribe of Colombia (Sept. 25, 2002), available at http://www.whitehouse.gov/news/releases/2002/09/20020925-1.html

306. Hearing on U.S. Policy on Iraq: Before the U.S. Senate Comm. on Armed Services, 107th Cong., 2d Sess. (statement of Secretary Rumsfeld).

307. Eric Schmitt, "Rumsfeld Says U.S. Has 'Bulletproof' Evidence of Iraq's Links to Al Qaeda", *The New York Times*, Sept. 28, 2002, at A9.

308. John John B. Judis and Spencer Ackerman, "The First Casualty", *The New Republic*, June 30, 2003, at 24.

309. "Rice: Iraq trained Al Qaeda in chemical weapons", CNN.com, Sept. 26, 2002, available at http://archives .cnn.com/2002/US/09/25/us.iraq.alqaeda/.

310. Meet the Press: Interview with Vice President Dick Cheney (NBC television broadcast, Dec. 9, 2001).

311. Fox News: Interview with Vice President Dick Cheney (Fox News television broadcast, June 28, 2004), available at http://www.foxnews.com/story/0,2933,123794,00.html).

312. President George W. Bush, Remarks on Iraq (Oct. 7, 2002), available at http://www.whitehouse.gov /news/releases/2002/10/20021007-8.html..

313. Secretary of State Colin Powell, Remarks to the U.N. Security Council (Feb. 5, 2003), available at http://www.whitehouse.gov/news/releases/2003/02/20030205-1.html.

314. *Ibid.*

315. Michael Isikoff & Daniel Klaidman, "Al Qaeda's Man in Iraq", *Newsweek*, Oct. 7, 2002, at 42.

316. National Commission on Terrorist Attacks Upon the United States, The 9-11 Commission Report 66 (2004). In a hearing of the panel, a senior FBI official and a senior CIA analyst concurred with the finding. See Walter Pincus & Dana Milbank, "Al Qaeda-Hussein Link is Dismissed", *The Washington Post*, June 17, 2004 at A1.

317. National Commission on Terrorist Attacks Upon the United States, The 9-11 Commission Report (2004).

318. S. Rep. No. 108-301, at 347 (2004).

319. Testimony on Efforts to Determine the Status of Iraqi Weapons of Mass Destruction and Related Programs: Hearing Before the S. Comm. on Armed Services, 108th Cong., 2d Sess. (2004) (statement of David Kay).

320. National Commission on Terrorist Attacks Upon the United States, The 9-11 Commission Report 228-29 (2004).

321. Douglas Jehl, "Report Warned Bush Team About Intelligence Suspicions", *The New York Times*, Nov. 6, 2005 at 14.

322. 60 Minutes: Interview with Richard Clarke (CBS television broadcast, Mar. 21, 2004), available at http://www.cbsnews.com/stories/2004/03/19/60minutes/main607356.shtml (describing the reaction of the Bush White House to his report finding no connection between Iraq and the September 11 attacks)(emphasis added).

323. Murray Waas, "Key Bush Intelligence Briefing Kept from Hill Panel", *The National Journal*, Nov. 22, 2005, *available at* http://nationaljournal.com/about/njweekly/stories/2005/1122nj1.htm (emphasis added).

324. *Ibid.*

325. *Ibid.*

326. S. Rep. No. 108-301, at 306 (2004)(emphasis added).

327. National Intelligence Council, Iraq's Continuing Program for Weapons of Mass Destruction: Key Judgements (from October 2002 National Intelligence Estimate) (declassified July 18, 2003)(emphasis added). See also S. Rep. No. 108-301, at 331 (2004). In an October 7, 2002 letter to Senator Bob Graham, CIA Director George Tenet again asserted strong qualifiers regarding a relationship between Iraq and Al Qaeda: "Our understanding of the relationship between Iraq and al-Qai'da is evolving and is based on sources of varying reliability." Letter from CIA Director George Tenet to the Honorable Bob Graham, Chairman, Select Committee on Intelligence (Oct. 7, 2002).

328. S. Rep. No. 108-301, at 332 (2004)(emphasis added).

329. *Ibid.*

330. CNN Presents: Dead Wrong (CNN television broadcast, Aug. 21, 2005) (emphasis added).

331. Oliver Burkeman & Julian Borger, "War Critics Bstonished as U.S. Hawk Admits Invasion was Illegal", *Guardian*, Nov. 20, 2003, at 4 (emphasis added).

In her book, *Blowing My Cover*, Lindsay Moran detailed the following discussions she had with C.I.A. analysts regarding CIA knowledge of possible relationships between Iraq and Al Qaeda:

"[A] CIA analyst, whose opinion I'd solicited about the connection between Al-Qa'ida and Iraq, looked at me almost shamefacedly, shrugged, and said, "They both have the letter q?" And a colleague who worked in the office covering Iraqi counterproliferation reported to me that her mealy-mouthed pen pusher of a boss had gathered together his minions and announced, "Let's face it. The president wants us to go to war, and our job is to give him a reason to do it." Lindsay moran, *Blowing My Cover: My Life as a CIA Spy* 55 (Putnam Adult Books, 2004) (emphasis added).

332. "Bush Overstated Iraq Links to Al Qaeda, Former Intelligence Officials Say", *USA Today*, July 13, 2003, available at http://www.usatoday.com/news/washington/2003-07-13-bush-alqaeda_x.htm.

333. Bryan Burrough, Evgenia Peretz, David Rose & David Wise, "The Path to War", *Vanity Fair*, May 2004, at 228 (emphasis added).

334. S. Rep. No. 108-301, at 449 (2004).

335. The unnamed individual testified: "Generally it was understood how receptive [the Office of the Secretary of Defense] civilians were to our assessments and what kind of assessments they would not be receptive to . . ." S. Rep. No. 108-301, at 280 (2004). A senior official at the Defense Department stated that on September 11, Paul Wolfowitz told senior officials at the Pentagon that he believed Iraq might have been responsible. "I was scratching my head because everyone else thought of Al Qaeda," the former senior defense official stated. Walter Pincus and Dana Priest, Some Iraq Analysts Felt Pressure From Cheney Visits, Wash. Post, June 5, 2003. Days after September 11, Colin Powell warned the Administration not to make up a link. Bob Woodward, in his book *Bush at War*, conveyed Powell's perspective:

Don't go with the Iraq option right away, or we'll lose the coalition we've been signing up. "They'll view it as bait-and-switch—it's not what they signed up to do." If we weren't going after Iraq before September 11, why would we be going after them now when the current outrage is not directed at Iraq, Powell asked. Nobody could look at Iraq and say it was responsible for September 11. It was important not to lose focus. "Keep the Iraq options open if you get the linkages," he said. "Maybe Syria, Iran'—the chief state sponsors of terrorism in the 1980s—"but doubt you'll get the linkages."

Bob Woodward, *Bush at War*, at 87-88 (Simon & Schuster, 2002)(emphasis added).

336. Spencer Ackerman & John B. Judis, "The First Casualty", *The New Republic*, June 30, 2003, at 16 (emphasis added).

337. James Risen, "Threats and Responses: C.I.A.; Captives Deny Qaeda Worked With Baghdad", *The New York Times*, June 10, 2003, at A1.

338. ABC News Transcript, April 25, 2003, Page 304 (emphasis added).

339. Julian Borger, ", *The Guardian*, Oct. 9, 2002, at 12.

340. Current and Future Worldwide Threats to U.S. National Security: Hearing Before the Senate Committee on Armed Services, 108th Cong. (2004) (statement of George Tenet, Director, Central Intelligence Agency).

341. *Ibid.*

342. The CTEG was created under Paul Wolfowitz and Under Secretary of Defense for Policy, Douglas Feith, and ultimately answerable to Donald Rumsfeld. CNN's documentary Dead Wrong noted, "at the Pentagon, Secretary of Defense Donald Rumsfeld set up a special office to provide him with alternative intelligence analysis, focusing on a possible link between Saddam and Al Qaeda." CNN Presents: Dead Wrong (CNN television broadcast, Aug. 21, 2005). In this regard, Former CIA and State Department Official Larry Johnson responded that "they even briefed their findings to the [intelligence] community and the community would come back and say, wait a second, you don't know what you're talking about. That's garbage. That's misleading, that misrepresents." . *Ibid.*. Referring to the work of the special unit, Lt. Colonel Karen Kwiatkowski, a former Air Force officer who served in the Pentagon's Near East and South Bsia unit, has stated, "it wasn't intelligence,—it was propaganda . . . [t]hey'd take a little bit of intelligence, cherry-pick it, make it sound much more exciting, usually by taking it out of context, often by juxtaposition of two pieces of information that don't belong together." Robert Dreyfuss & Jason Vest, The Lie Factory, Mother Jones, January/February 2004, available at http://www.motherjones.com/news/feature/2004/01/12_405.html.

343. On November 14, 2005, the Pentagon's Inspector General announced an investigation into whether Mr. Feith and others associated with his group engaged in "unauthorized, unlawful, or inappropriate intelligence activities." Murray Waas, "Key Bush Intelligence Kept From Hill Panel", *The National Journal*, Nov. 22, 2005, *available at* http://nationaljournal.com/about/njweekly/stories/2005/1122nj1.htm. Mr. Feith also put together a series of classified findings indicating that Iraq intelligence agents had worked with Al Qaeda for over a decade in a memorandum to the Senate Intelligence Committee. This memorandum was leaked to the conservative Weekly Standard and formed the basis of its November 24, 2003 article entitled "Case Closed" by Stephen F. Hayes. Stephen F. Hayes, "Case Closed", *The Weekly Standard*, Nov. 24, 2003. Although the contents were highly classified, they were leaked to The Weekly Standard, a journal closely associated with the neoconservatives. "If you don't understand how intelligence works," a Pentagon official told The New York Times, "you could look at this memo and say, 'Aha, there was an operational connection between Saddam and Al Qaeda.'" Douglas Jehl, "More Proof of Iraq-Qaeda Link, or Not?", *The New York Times*, Nov. 20, 2003, at A18.

344. Bryan Burrough, Evgenia Peretz, David Rose & David Wise, "The Path to War", *Vanity Fair*, May 2004, at 230.

345. *Ibid.* at 242. Former DIA Chief of Mideast Operations, Pat Lang, described how the CTEG bypassed standard intelligence channels to provide unfiltered information to the White House: "That unit had meetings with senior White House officials without the CIA or the Senate being aware of them. That is

not legal. There has to be oversight." Richard Sale, "DIA Targets DOD Unit", *The Washington Times*, July 29, 2004. According to Lang, "the two men [of the CTEG] had gone to the White House several times to brief officials without notifying CIA analysts because the agency analysts differed in their conclusions." According to Congressional staffers, the men allegedly briefed Stephen Hadley, the deputy national security advisor, and Lewis "Scooter" Libby, chief of staff for Vice President Richard Cheney. *Ibid.*

346. Bryan Burrough, Evgenia Peretz, David Rose & David Wise, "The Path to War", *Vanity Fair*, May 2004, at 230.

347. Memorandum from Peter Ricketts, Political Director of the U.K. Foreign and Commonwealth Office, to Jack Straw, U.K. Foreign Secretary (Mar. 22, 2002), available at http://downingstreetmemo.com /docs/ricketts.pdf at 1-2. To British officials, it was equally clear that Bush Administration charges were to the contrary, there was no credible link between Iraq and the September 11 attacks or Al Qaeda. In the March 25, 2002 Straw Memo, United Kingdom Foreign Secretary Jack Straw noted that "If 11 September had not happened, it is doubtful that the U.S. would now be considering military action against Iraq . . .[o]bjectively, the threat from Iraq has not worsened as a result of 11 September." Memorandum from Jack Straw, U.K. Foreign Secretary, to the Prime Minister (Mar. 25, 2002), available at http://downingstreet-memo.com/docs/straw.pdf at 2.

348. Memorandum from the Office of the Overseas and Defense Secretariat to Personal Secret U.K. Eyes Only (Mar. 8, 2002), at 1, available at http://downingstreetmemo.com/docs/iraqoptions.pdf at 8.

349. Michael Isikoff, "Phantom Link to Iraq", *Newsweek*, Apr. 28, 2002.

350. James Risen, "Iraqi Agent Denies He Met 9-11 Hijacker in Prague Before Attacks in the U.S.", *The New York Times*, December 13, 2003, at A10. "Credit card and phone records appear to demonstrate that Atta was in Virginia Beach, Va., at the time of the alleged meeting, according to law enforcement and intelligence officials. Al-Ani, the Iraqi intelligence official with whom Atta was said to have met in Prague, was later taken into custody by U.S. authorities. He not only denied the report of the meeting with Atta, but said that he was not in Prague at the time of the supposed meeting, according to published reports." Murray Waas, "Key Bush Intelligence Kept From Hill Panel", *The National Journal*, Nov. 22, 2005, *available at* http://nationaljournal.com/about/njweekly/stories/2005/1122nj1.htm

351. David Ignatius, "The Real Crime, White House vs. CIA Was the Wrong Battle", *The Washington Post*, October 30, 2005 at B7 (emphasis added).

352. Douglas Jehl, "Report Warned Bush Team About Intelligence Suspicions", *The New York Times*, Nov. 6, 2005, at 14 (emphasis added).

353. *Ibid.*

354. *Ibid.* (emphasis added).

355. *Ibid.*

356. Walter Pincus, "Newly Released Data Undercut Prewar Claims, Source Tying Baghdad, Al Qaeda Doubted", *The Washington Post*, Nov. 6, 2005 at A22.

357. *Ibid.*

358. Jane Mayer, "Annals of Justice, Outsourcing Torture", *The New Yorker*, Feb. 14, 2005 at 116.

359. *Ibid.*

360. Douglas Jehl, "Qaeda-Iraq Link U.S. Cited is Tied to Coercion Claim", *The New York Times*, Dec. 9, 2005, at 1.

361. John B. Judis & Spencer Ackerman, "The First Casualty", *The New Republic*, June 30, 2003, at 17.

362. Meet the Press: Interview with Vice President Dick Cheney (NBC television broadcast, March 16, 2003).

363. Vice President Dick Cheney, Remarks by the Vice President to the Veterans of Foreign Wars 103rd National Convention (Aug. 26, 2002), available at http://www.whitehouse.gov/news/releases /2002/08/20020826.html. Similarly Colin Powell testified before the House International Relations Committee that, "[w]ith respect to the nuclear program, there is no doubt that the Iraqis are pursuing it."

The President's International Affairs Budget Request for FY2003: Hearing Before the H. Comm. on International Relations, 107th. Cong., 2d Sess. (2002) (Testimony of Colin Powell).

364. Vice President Dick Cheney, Remarks by the Vice President to the Veterans of Foreign Wars 103rd National Convention (Aug. 26, 2002), available at http://www.whitehouse.gov/news/releases /2002/08/20020826.html.

365. President George W. Bush, Remarks on Iraq (Oct. 7, 2002), available at http://www.whitehouse.gov /news/releases/2002/10/20021007-8.html.

366. President George W. Bush, Remarks by the President and Prime Minister Tony Blair (Sept. 7, 2002), available athttp://www.whitehouse.gov/news/releases/2002/09/20020907-2.html

367. Secretary of State Colin Powell, Remarks to United Nations Security Council, (February 5, 2003) available at http://www.state.gov/secretary/rm/2003/17300.htm

368. Secretary Rice stated on September 8, 2002: "There will always be some uncertainty about how quickly [Saddam] can acquire nuclear weapons. But we don't want the smoking gun to be a mushroom cloud." CNN's Late Editon with Wolf Blitzer (CNN television broadcast, Sept. 8, 2002).

369. Secretary Rumsfeld stated on September 8, 2002: "Imagine a September eleventh with weapons of mass destruction. It's not three thousand—it's tens of thousands of innocent men, women, and children." CBS, Face the Nation (CBS television broadcast, Sept. 8, 2002).

370. Vice President Dick Cheney stated in August 2002 that Mr. Hussein could acquire nuclear weapons "fairly soon" and that Saddam, "armed with an arsenal of these weapons of terror," could "directly threaten America's friends throughout the region and subject the United States or any other nation to nuclear blackmail." Vice President Dick Cheney, Remarks by the Vice President to the Veterans of Foreign Wars 103rd National Convention (Aug. 26, 2002) available at http://www.whitehouse.gov/news/releases /2002/08/20020826.html.

371. Statement by David Kay on the Interim Progress Report on the Activities of the Iraq Survey Group (ISG) before the House Permanent Select Committee on Intelligence, the House Committee on Appropriations, Subcommittee on Defense, and the Senate Select Committee on Intelligence (Oct. 2, 2003).

372. Testimony on Efforts to Determine the Status of Iraqi Weapons of Mass Destruction and Related Programs: Hearing Before the S. Comm. on Armed Services, 108th Cong., 2d Sess. (2004) (Testimony of David Kay).

373. *Ibid.*

374. S. Rep. No. 108-301, at 129 (2004).

375. Letter from Dr. Mohamed ElBaradei, Director General of the International Atomic Energy Agency, to Kofi A. Annan, U.N. Secretary General (Apr. 7, 1999) (emphasis added), available at http://www.iaea.org /OurWork/SV/Invo/reports/s_1999_393.pdf.

376. IAEA Director General Dr. Mohamed ElBaradei, The Status of Nuclear Inspections in Iraq: An Update, March 7, 2003, available at http://www.iaea.org/NewsCenter/Statements/2003/ebsp2003n006.shtml. Notably, Vice President Cheney made his "reconstituted" claim a little more than a week later.

377. Micheal Isikoff & Mark Hosenball, "From Downing Street to Capital Hill", *Newsweek*, June 17, 2005 (emphasis added), *available at* http://www.msnbc.msn.com/id/8234762/site/newsweek/.

378. Central Intelligence Agency, Unclassified Report to Congress on the Acquisition of Technology Relating to Weapons of Mass Destruction and Advanced Conventional Munitions, 1 January Through 30 June 2001 (2001), available at http://www.nti.org/e_research/official_docs/cia/11-63001CIA.pdf. The review said only, "We believe that Iraq has probably continued at least low-level theoretical R&D associated with its nuclear program. A sufficient source of fissile material remains Iraq's most significant obstacle to being able to produce a nuclear weapon." *Ibid.*

379. S. Rep. No. 108-301, at 85 (emphasis added).

380. National Intelligence Council, Iraq's Continuing Program for Weapons of Mass Destruction: Key Judgments (from October 2002 NIE) (declassified July 18, 2003).

381. *Ibid.* (emphasis added).

382. Elizabeth De La Vega, "The White House Criminal Conspiracy", *The Nation*, Nov. 14, 2005, at 14.

383. John B. Judis & Spencer Ackerman, "The First Casualty", *The New Republic*, June 30, 2003, at 17 (emphasis added)

384. Barton Gellman and Walter Pincus, "Depiction of Threat Outgrew Supporting Evidence", *The Washington Post*, Aug. 10, 2003 at A1.

385 *Ibid.*

386. The meeting was attended by Prof. M Zifferero (IAEA), N. Smidovich, and a person from King of Jordan court who served as an interpreter. Meeting of the Executive Chairman of the Special Commission and General Hussein Kamal (Aug. 22, 1995), available at http://www.globalsecurity.org/wmd/library/news /iraq/un/unscom-iaea_kamal-brief.html.

387. International Atomic Energy Agency, The Implementation of United Nations Security Council Resolutions 687, 707 and 715 (1991) Relating to Iraq (1995), available at http://www.iaea.org/About /Policy/GC/GC39/Resolutions/gc3910a1.html (emphasis added).

388. Barton Gellman and Walter Pincus, "Depiction of Threat Outgrew Supporting Evidence", *The Washington Post*, Aug. 10, 2003, at A1 (emphasis added).

389. David Barstow, William J. Broad, & Jeff Gerth, "How the White House Embraced Disputed Iraqi Arms Intelligence", *The New York Times*, Oct. 3, 2004, at A1 (emphasis added).

390. Barton Gellman and Walter Pincus, "Depiction of Threat Outgrew Supporting Evidence", *The Washington Post*, Aug. 10, 2003, at A1 (emphasis added).

391. *Ibid.*

392. S. Rep. No. 108-301, at 85, 112.

393. Meet the Press: Interview with Vice President Dick Cheney (NBC television broadcast, Sept. 8, 2002).

394. *Ibid.*

395. CNN Late Edition: Interview With Condoleezza Rice (Sept. 8, 2002).

396. Secretary of State Colin Powell, Remarks to the U.N. Security Council (Feb. 5, 2003), available at http://www.whitehouse.gov/news/releases/2003/02/20030205-1.html.

397. In his January 2003 State of the Union Address, the President stated that Saddam Hussein was trying to buy tubes "suitable for nuclear weapons production." See President George W. Bush, State of the Union (Jan. 28, 2003), available at http://www.whitehouse.gov/news/releases/2003/01/20030128-19.html.

398. Dr. Mohamed ElBaradei, Remarks to the U.N. Security Council on the Status of Nuclear Inspections in Iraq (Jan. 23, 2003), available at http://www.iaea.org/NewsCenter/Statements/2003/ebsp2003n003 .shtml.

399. Testimony on Efforts to Determine the Status of Iraqi Weapons of Mass Destruction and Related Programs: Hearing Before the S. Comm. on Armed Services, 108th Cong., 2d Sess. (2004) (Testimony of David Kay).

400. S. Rep. No. 108-301, at 131 (2004).

401. The analyst was named "Joe." As the *New York Times* reported, "Suddenly, Joe's work was ending up in classified intelligence reports being read in the White House. Indeed, his analysis was the primary basis for one of the agency's first reports on the tubes, which went to senior members of the Bush Administration on April 10, 2001. The tubes, the report asserted, 'have little use other than for a uranium enrichment program.' This alarming assessment was immediately challenged by the Energy Department, which builds centrifuges and runs the government's nuclear weapons complex." David Barstow, William J. Broad, & Jeff Gerth, "How the White House Embraced Disputed Iraqi Arms Intelligence", the *New York Times,* Oct. 3, 2004, at A1.

402. S. Rep. No. 108-301, at 88 (2004).

403. David Barstow, William J. Broad, & Jeff Gerth, "How the White House Embraced Disputed Iraqi Arms Intelligence", the *New York Times*, Oct. 3, 2004, at A1.

404. S. Rep. No. 108-301, at 89 (2004).

405. *Ibid.*

406. David Barstow, William J. Broad, & Jeff Gerth, "How the White House Embraced Disputed Iraqi Arms Intelligence", the *New York Times*, Oct. 3, 2004, at A1. "Back in 1996, inspectors from the International Atomic Energy Agency had even examined some of these tubes, also made of 7075-T6 aluminum, at a military complex, the Nasser metal fabrication plant in Baghdad, where the Iraqis acknowledged making rockets. According to the international agency, the rocket tubes, some 66,000 of them, were 900 millimeters in length, with a diameter of 81 millimeters and walls 3.3 millimeters thick." *Ibid.*

407. S. Rep. No. 108-301, at 91-92 (2004).

408. At the Energy Department, those examining the tubes included scientists who had spent decades designing and working on centrifuges and intelligence officers steeped in the tricky business of tracking the nuclear ambitions of America's enemies. They included Dr. Jon A. Kreykes, head of Oak Ridge's national security advanced technology group; Dr. Duane F. Starr, an expert on nuclear proliferation threats; and Dr. Edward Von Halle, a retired Oak Ridge nuclear expert. Dr. Houston G. Wood III, a professor of engineering at the University of Virginia, who had helped design the 40-foot American centrifuge, advised the team and consulted with Dr. Zippe. On questions about nuclear centrifuges, this was unambiguously the A-Team of the intelligence community, many experts say. David Barstow, William J. Broad, & Jeff Gerth, "How the White House Embraced Disputed Iraqi Arms Intelligence", the *New York Times*, Oct. 3, 2004, at A1

409. *Ibid.*

410. The Comm'n on the Intelligence of the U.S. Regarding Weapons of Mass Destruction, Report to the President of the U.S. (2005) (emphasis added).

411. S. Rep. No. 108-301, at 85.

412. *Ibid.* at 112.

413. National Intelligence Council, Iraq's Continuing Program for Weapons of Mass Destruction: Key Judgements (from October 2002 NIE) (declassified July 18, 2003) (emphasis added).

414. *Ibid.*

415. *Ibid.* Greg Thielman, the Director of Strategic, Proliferation and Military affairs in the State Department's Bureau of Intelligence and Research stated the following on the CNN documentary Dead Wrong:

DAVID ENSOR [CNN Correspondent]: The three feet by three inch tubes are the only piece of physical evidence that might suggest a bomb building program.

THIELMANN: We were really agnostic at the beginning of it but we listened to the experts and more and more evidence came in that told us, no, this can't be true.

CNN Presents: Dead Wrong (CNN television broadcast, Aug. 21, 2005) (emphasis added).

416. David Barstow, William J. Broad, & Jeff Gerth, "How the White House Embraced Disputed Iraqi Arms Intelligence", the *New York Times*, Oct. 3, 2004, at A1.

417. S. Rep. No. 108-301, at 85.

418. David Barstow, William J. Broad, & Jeff Gerth, "How the White House Embraced Suspect Arms Intelligence", the *New York Times*, Oct. 3, 2004, at A1 (emphasis added).

419. Institute for Science and International Security, Aluminum Tubing Is an Indicator of an Iraqi Gas Centrifuge Program: But Is the Tubing Specifically for Centrifuges (2002), available at http://www.isis-online.org/publications/iraq/aluminumtubes.html.

420. Spencer Ackerman & John B. Judis, "The First Casualty", *The New Republic*, June 30, 2003, at 17.

421. David Barstow, William J. Broad, & Jeff Gerth, "How the White House Embraced Suspect Arms Intelligence", the *New York Times*, Oct. 3, 2004, at A1.

422. Barton Gellman & Walter Pincus, "Depiction of Threat Outgrew Supporting Evidence", *The Washington Post*, Aug. 10, 2003, at A1.

423. David Barstow, William J. Broad, & Jeff Gerth, "How the White House Embraced Suspect Arms Intelligence", the *New York Times*, Oct. 3, 2004, at A1.

424. The Comm'n on the Intelligence of the U.S. Regarding Weapons of Mass Destruction, Report to the President of the U.S. (2005).

425. *Ibid.*

426. *Ibid.*

427. *Ibid.*

428. *Ibid.*

429. *Ibid.*

430. Spencer Ackerman & John B. Judis, "The First Casualty", *The New Republic*, June 30, 2003, at 14 (emphasis added). In addition, a Senior Administration official has acknowledged, "[Condoleezza Rice] was aware of the differences of opinion." David Barstow, William J. Broad, & Jeff Gerth, "How the White House Embraced Suspect Arms Intelligence", the *New York Times*, Oct. 3, 2004 , at A1.

431. Spencer Ackerman & John B. Judis, "The First Casualty," *The New Republic,* June 30, 2003, at 17.

432. Oliver Burkeman & Julian Borger, "War Critics Bstonished as U.S. Hawk Admits Invasion was Illegal", *The Guardian*, Nov. 20, 2003, at 4.

433. David Barstow, William J. Broad, & Jeff Gerth, "How the White House Embraced Suspect Arms Intelligence", the *New York Times*, Oct. 3, 2004, at A1.

434. *Ibid.*

435. Michael R. Gordon & Judith Miller, "U.S. Says Hussein Intensifies Quest for A-Bomb Parts", the *New York Times*, Sept. 8, 2002, at 1.6.

436. *Ibid.*

437. Bryan Burrough, Evgenia Peretz, David Rose & David Wise, "The Path to War", *Vanity Fair*, May 2004, at 281.

438. CNN Presents: Dead Wrong (CNN television broadcast, Aug. 21, 2005). Other intelligence officials complained about the selective leaking of information associated with the aluminum tubes debate. David Albright of the Institute for Science and International Security noted, "I became dismayed when a knowledgeable government scientist told me that the administration could say anything it wanted about the tubes while government scientists who disagreed were expected to remain quiet." Spencer Ackerman & John B. Judis, "The First Casualty", *The New Republic*, June 30, 2003 at 14.

439. Bill Gertz, "Iraq Seeks Steel for Nukes", *The Washington Times*, July 29, 2002, at A1.

440. CNN Late Edition: Interview with Condoleezza Rice (CNN television broadcast, Sept. 8, 2002).

441. Meet the Press: Interview with Vice President Dick Cheney (NBC television broadcast, Sept. 8, 2002).

442. Face the Nation: Interview with Donald Rumsfeld (CBS television broadcast, Sept. 8, 2002).

443. *The Miami Herald*, "CIA leak illustrates selective use of intelligence on Iraq (The Aluminum Tubes)", by Jonathan S. Landay, Knight Ridder Newspapers.

444. CNN Presents: Dead Wrong (CNN television broadcast, Aug. 21, 2005).

445. Judith Miller and Michael R. Gordon, "White House Lists Iraq Steps to Build Banned Weapons", the *New York Times*, Sept. 13, 2002, at A13.

446. *Ibid.*

447. *Ibid.*

448. See David Barstow, William J. Broad, & Jeff Gerth, "How the White House Embraced Suspect Arms Intelligence", the *New York Times*, Oct. 3, 2004, at A1.

449. Ray McGovern, Sham Dunk: Cooking Intelligence for the President, available at http://www.afterdowningstreet.org/downloads/mcgovern.pdf (emphasis added).

450. Seymour Hersh, "Annals of National Security: Stovepipe", *The New Yorker*, Oct. 27, 2003, at 77.

451. President George W. Bush, State of the Union Address (Jan. 29, 2002), available at http://www.whitehouse.gov/news/releases/2002/01/20020129-11.html.

452. H. Rep. No. 108-23 (2003).

453. Barton Gellman, "A Leak, Then a Deluge", *The Washington Post*, Oct. 30, 2005, at A1.

454. Condoleezza Rice,Op-Ed, "Why We Know Iraq is Lying", the *New York Times*, Jan. 23, 2003, at A25.

455. Francis T. Mandanici, "Bush's Uranium Lies: The Case for a Special Prosecutor That Could Lead to Impeachment", June 29, 2005, available at http://democracyrising.us/content/view/269/164/.

456. Hearing on U.S. Policy on Iraq: Before the S. Comm. on Armed Services, 107th Cong., 2d Sess. (statement of Secretary Donald Rumsfeld).

457. President George W. Bush, President Discusses Iraq with Congressional Leaders (Sept. 26, 2002), available at http://www.whitehouse.gov/news/releases/2002/09/20020926-7.html.

458. IAEA Director General Dr. Mohamed ElBaradei, Statement to the United Nations Security Council (Mar. 7, 2003), available at http://www.iaea.org/NewsCenter/Statements/2003/ebsp2003n006.shtml.

459. Press Secretary Ari Fleischer, White House Press Briefing (July 7, 2003), available at http://www.whitehouse.gov/news/releases/2003/07/20030707-5.html.

460. Press Secretary Ari Fleischer, White House Press Briefing (July 14, 2003), available at http://www.whitehouse.gov/news/releases/2003/07/20030707-5.html.

461. Seymour Hersh, "Annals of National Security: Stovepipe", *The New Yorker*, Oct. 27, 2003, at 77. "SISMI" delivered to the CIA a report describing a visit by Wissam al-Zahawie, the then Iraqi Ambassador to the Vatican, to Niger in February 1999. The report apparently suggested that the purpose of his visit was to provide nuclear uranium and that the Niger President had allegedly given his stamp of approval for the agreement. At the original time of the visit, both the American Ambassador and British Intelligence filed standard reports certifying the visits, but did not raise any concerns. *Ibid.*

46. Elaine Sciolino & Elisabetta Povoledo, "Italy's Top Spy Names Freelance Agent as Source of Forged Niger-Iraq Uranium Documents", the *New York Times*, Nov. 4, 2005, at A24.

463. *Ibid.*

464. Seymour Hersh, "Annals of National Security: Stovepipe", *The New Yorker*, Oct. 27, 2003, at 77 (emphasis added).

465. *Ibid.*

466. S. Rep. No. 108-301, at 57 (2004). Elisabetta Burba, a reporter for Panorama, an Italian magazine, was offered photocopies of 22 pages of additional documents describing purported sales of uranium from Niger to Iraq for approximately $10,000. Her editor asked her to turn the documents over to the American Embassy, which she did. *Ibid.*

467. Seymour Hersh, "Annals of National Security: Stovepipe", *The New Yorker*, Oct. 27, 2003, at 77.

468. See Section III.B.3.

469. For example, at this time, the United Nations was not finding any evidence that Iraq had reinitiated its nuclear program. On January 27, the U.N. issued a press release regarding Iraq's response to Resolution 1441 and stated that "it would appear that Iraq had decided in principle to provide cooperation on substance in order to complete the disarmament task through inspection." Press Release, United Nations Security Council, Security Council Briefed by Chief U.N. Weapons Experts on First 60 Days of Inspections in Iraq (January 27, 2003), available :

470. Walter Pincus, "PreWar Findings Worried Analysts", *The Washington Post*, May 22, 2005, at A1.

471. S. Rep. No. 108-301, at 56 (2004).

472. *Ibid.* at 44-45 (2004). On February 19, 2002, one in a series of meetings was held at CIA headquarters pursuant to the Vice President's request. Attendees included WMD intelligence analysts from the CIA and

the State Department as well as former Ambassador Joseph Wilson. *Ibid.* at 40. At the beginning of the meeting, Ambassador Wilson's wife, Valerie Plame Wilson, introduced her husband and left after three minutes. *Ibid.* The purpose was to evaluate whether Ambassador Wilson should be sent to Niger to determine the veracity of the claim that Iraq sought yellowcake from that country. Ambassador Wilson is considered an expert on Africa, has served as U.S. Ambassador to Gabon, was stationed in Niger, was familiar with the uranium trade, and had served in the administrations of President George H.W. Bush and President Bill Clinton. In addition, Ambassador Wilson had previously traveled to Niger on the CIA's behalf. *Ibid.* at 39. The next day, the CIA asked the Ambassador to undertake the Niger mission, and he subsequently departed on February 21, 2002. *Ibid.* at 41.

473. Seymour Hersh, "Annals of National Security: Stovepipe", *The New Yorker*, Oct. 27, 2003, at 77.

474. Bryan Burrough, Evgenia Peretz, David Rose, & David Wise, "The Path to War", *Vanity Fair*, May 1, 2004, at 228.

475. Seymour Hersh, "Annals of National Security: Stovepipe", *The New Yorker*, Oct. 27, 2003, at 77.

476. "16 Words", *The New Republic*, July 28, 2003, at 8.

477. A former senior CIA official acknowledged there was no supporting evidence or a substantiation of the claim: "I can fully believe that SISMI would put out a piece of intelligence like that . . . but why anybody would put credibility in it is beyond me." Seymour Hersh, "Annals of National Security: Stovepipe", *The New Yorker*, Oct. 27, 2003, at 77.

478. S. Rep. No. 108-301, at 56 (2004). (emphasis added)

479. *Ibid.* at 56-7. (emphasis added).

480. Joseph Cirincione, Niger Uranium: Still a False Claim, Proliferation Brief, Vol. 7, No. 12, Carnegie Endowment Publications (Aug. 28, 2004), available at http://www.carnegieendowment.org/publications /index.cfm?fa=view&id=1595&proj=znpp.

481. S. Rep. No. 108-301, at 51 (2004).

482. *Ibid.*

483. Democratic Hearing on the Downing Street Minutes, Before the H. Comm. on the Judiciary, 109th Cong. (2005) (testimony of Ambassador Joseph Wilson).

484. John J. Lumpkin, "CIA Had Doubted Claims, Later Found to be Based on Forged Documents, that Iraq Tried to Import Uranium", *AP*, June 12, 2003; Kamal Ahmed, "Blair Ignored CIA Weapons Warnings", *The Observer*, July 13, 2003; Mitch Frank, "Tale of the Cake", *Time*, July 21, 2003, at 24. *The Guardian* in London the following month cites a series of letters to the British Foreign Affairs Committee which show that the U.S. had asked Britain not to use the Africa-uranium claim, but did not provide details about Wilson's mission to Niger.

485. *Ibid.*

486. S. Rep. No. 108-301, at 36 (2004).

487. See *Ibid.* at 239-56.

488. *Ibid.* at 53.

489. *Ibid.* at 62.

490. Tom Hamburger, Peter Wallsten and Bob Drogin, "French Told CIA of Bogus Intelligence", *Los Angeles Times*, Dec. 11, 2005, at A1.

491. *Ibid.*

492. *Ibid.*

493. Statement by George J. Tenet, Director of Central Intelligence, July 11, 2003, available at http://www.cia .gov/cia/public_affairs/press_release/2003/pr07112003.html. However, even the Administration's own explanation does not make complete sense. One observer has explained the stated reason for the switch from "we" to the British was the desire to identify in the speech a source for the uranium claim that was

not classified, and the British White Paper source was not classified while the American source was classified. However, the original draft that the White House sent apparently did not name any source for America's knowledge but merely said "we." There was no need to further identify any sources. Concerning other claims against Hussein, President Bush in his speech actually used the phrase "intelligence sources" without providing any specifics on the sources. Francis T. Mandanici, Bush's Uranium Lies: The Case for a Special Prosecutor That Could Lead to Impeachment, June 29, 2005, available at http://democracyrising.us/content/view/269/164/.

494. Francis T. Mandanici, Bush's Uranium Lies: The Case for a Special Prosecutor That Could Lead to Impeachment, June 29, 2005, available at http://democracyrising.us/content/view/269/164/.

495. *Ibid.*

496. Seymour M. Hersh, "Annals of National Security: The Stovepipe", *The New Yorker*, Oct. 27, 2003 (emphasis added). The pressure to confirm the Iraq-Niger uranium link was felt within the CIA as high up as Director George Tenet. It appears that many within the CIA believed Tenet only grudgingly supported including a reference to the Niger threat in the January 30, 2002 report to Congress because of his concern that he would be fired if he did not support the Administration. Based on his discussion with CIA analysts, Seymour Hersh has explained:

The CIA assessment reflected both deep divisions within the agency and the position of its director, George Tenet, which was far from secure. (The agency had been sharply criticized, after all, for failing to provide any effective warning of the September 11th attacks.) In the view of many CIA analysts and operatives, the director was too eager to endear himself to the Administration hawks and improve his standing with the President and the Vice-President.

497. On that date the American government gave the IAEA copies of documents that supposedly supported the claim that Iraq attempted to acquire the uranium. Francis T. Mandanici, Bush's Uranium Lies: The Case for a Special Prosecutor That Could Lead to Impeachment, June 29, 2005, available at http://democracyrising.us/content/view/269/164/.

498. S. Rep. No. 108-301, at 69 (2004).

499. Mohamed El Baradei, Remarks to the U.N. Security Council on the Status of Nuclear Inspections in Iraq (Mar. 7, 2003), available at http://www.iaea.org/NewsCenter/Statements/2003/ebsp2003n006.shtml.

500. John B. Judis & Spencer Ackerman, "The First Casualty", *The New Republic*, June 30, 2003, at 14.

501. *Ibid.* John Pike, director of the Washington military watchdog Globalsecurity.org. says the Administration's line on the Niger documents raises questions. "The thing that was so embarrassing about the episode was not simply that the documents were forgeries, but that they were clumsy forgeries, as was so quickly determined by the IAEA . . . It is one thing to be taken in, but to be so easily taken in, suggested either bewildering incompetence or intentional deception, or possibly both." Larisa Alexandrova, "Senate Intelligence Chairman Quietly 'Fixed' Intelligence, and Diverted Blame from White House Over Iraq", *RawStory.com*, August 11, 2005, http://rawstory.com/news/2005/HowSenate_Intelligence_chairman_fixed_intelligence_and_diverted_blame_fromWhite_House__0811.html

502. S. Rep. No. 108-301, at 426 (2004).

503. President George W. Bush, Remarks on Iraq (Oct. 7, 2002), available at http://www.whitehouse.gov/news/releases/2002/10/20021007-8.html.

504. President George W. Bush, State of the Union Address (Jan. 29, 2003), available at http://www.whitehouse.gov/news/releases/2003/01/20030128-19.html .

505. President George W. Bush, President Bush Discusses Iraq with Congressional Leaders (Sept. 26, 2002), available at http://www.whitehouse.gov/news/releases/2002/09/20020926-7.html.

506. Minority Staff of H. Comm. on Gov't Reform, 108th Cong., Report on Iraq on the Record, at 16 (Comm. Print 2004).

507. James Bamford, "The Man Who Sold the War", *Rolling Stone* (Nov.17, 2005), at 52-62.

508. Secretary of State Colin Powell, Address to the United Nations Security Council (Feb. 5, 2003), available at http://www.whitehouse.gov/news/releases/2003/02/20030205-1.html.

509. *Ibid.*

510. President George W. Bush, State of the Union Address (Jan. 29, 2002), available at http://www.whitehouse.gov/news/releases/2002/01/20020129-11.html.

511. President George W. Bush, President's Radio Address (Feb. 8, 2003) available at http://www.whitehouse.gov/news/releases/2003/02/20030208.html.

512. Secretary of State Colin Powell, Address to the United Nations Security Council (Feb. 5, 2003), available at http://www.whitehouse.gov/news/releases/2003/02/20030205-1.html.

The pre-war unclassified white paper prepared by the CIA and presented to the public as the case for war stated that, according to "most analysts," Iraq was developing an unmanned aerial vehicle or missile that was "probably intended to deliver biological warfare agents" and could even threaten the "U.S. homeland." Central Intelligence Agency White Paper: Iraq's Continuing Programs for Weapons of Mass Destruction (Oct. 1, 2002), available at http://www.gwu.edu/~nsarchiv/NSAEBB/NSAEBB129/nie.pdf.

513. Secretary of State Colin Powell, Address to the United Nations Security Council (Feb. 5, 2003), available at http://www.whitehouse.gov/news/releases/2003/02/20030205-1.html.

514. President George W. Bush, Remarks on Iraq (Oct. 7, 2002), available at http://www.whitehouse.gov/news/releases/2002/10/20021007-8.html.

515. Statement by David Kay on the Interim Progress Report on the Activities of the Iraq Survey Group (ISG) before the House Permanent Select Committee on Intelligence, the House Committee on Appropriations, Subcommittee on Defense, and the Senate Select Committee on Intelligence (Oct. 2, 2003).

516. James Bamford, "The Man Who Sold the War", *Rolling Stone* (Nov. 17, 2005), at 52-62.

517. Dr. Hans Blix, Oral introduction of the 12th quarterly report of UNMOVIC to the U.N. Security Council (March 7, 2003), available at http://www.un.org/Depts/unmovic/SC7asdelivered.htm.

518. Bob Drogin and John Goetz, "How U.S. Fell Under the Spell of 'Curveball'", *Los Angeles Times*, Nov. 20, 2005, at A1.

519. *Ibid.*

520. Testimony on Efforts to Determine the Status of Iraqi Weapons of Mass Destruction and Related Programs: Hearing Before the S. Comm. on Armed Services, 108th Cong., 2d Sess. (2004) (Testimony of David Kay).

521. Walter Pincus and Dana Milbank, "Bush Clings to Dubious Allegations About Iraq", *The Washington Post*, Mar. 18, 2003, at A13.

522. Minority Staff of H. Comm. on Gov't Reform, 108th Cong., Report on Iraq on the Record 15 (Comm. Print 2004) (emphasis added).

523. UNSCOM/IAEA, Note for the File 13 (1995), available at http://www.un.org/Depts/unmovic/new/documents/hk.pdf. In an interview with CNN, Kamel was asked "Can you state, here and now, does Iraq have any weapons of mass destruction left?" Kamel replied: "No. Iraq does not possess any weapons of mass destruction." "Saddam Hussein's son-in-law says torture common in Iraq", CNN.com, Sept. 21, 1995, available at http://www.cnn.com/WORLD/9509/iraq_defector/ (emphasis added).

524. Central Intelligence Agency, Comments On Iraqi Weapons Of Mass Destruction (1995).

525. John Berry, "The Defector's Secrets", *Newsweek*, March 3, 2003, at 6. While the CIA did not comment on the Newsweek story initially, it eventually did so in a follow-up story by Reuters. Then-CIA spokesman Bill Harlow denied the Newsweek story was accurate, directly contradicting all publicly available information:

The CIA on Monday denied a Newsweek magazine report that Saddam Hussein's son-in-law told the U.S. intelligence agency in 1995 that Iraq after the Gulf War destroyed all its chemical and biological weapons and missiles to deliver them.

It is incorrect, bogus, wrong, untrue," CIA spokesman Bill Harlow said of the Newsweek report's allegations that Hussein Kamel told the CIA that Iraqi President Saddam Hussein had destroyed all of his weapons of mass destruction.

"U.S., Britain Deny Newsweek Defector Report", *Reuters*, Feb.24, 2003.

526. S. Rep. No. 108-301, at 424 (2004).

527. Secretary of State Colin Powell, Remarks to the U.N. Security Council (Feb. 5, 2003), available at http://www.whitehouse.gov/news/releases/2003/02/20030205-1.html.

528. S. Rep. No. 108-301, at 424 (2004)(emphasis added) ("WEAK. Missiles with biological warheads reportedly dispersed. This would be somewhat true in terms of short-range missiles with conventional warheads, but is questionable in terms of longer-range missiles or biological warheads.").

529. Secretary of State Colin Powell, Remarks to the U.N. Security Council (Feb. 5, 2003), available at http://www.whitehouse.gov/news/releases/2003/02/20030205-1.html.

530. S. Rep. No. 108-301, at 424 (2004) (emphasis added).

531. Secretary of State Colin Powell, Remarks to the U.N. Security Council (Feb. 5, 2003), available at http://www.whitehouse.gov/news/releases/2003/02/20030205-1.html.

532. S. Rep. No. 108-301, at 426 (2004).

533. James Bamford, "The Man Who Sold The War", *Rolling Stone*, Nov. 17, 2005, at 52-62 (emphasis added).

534. *Ibid.*

535. Bob Drogin and John Goetz, "How U.S. Fell Under the Spell of 'Curveball'", *Los Angeles Times*, Nov. 20, 2005, at A1 (emphasis added).

536. *Ibid.*

537. *Ibid.*

538. *Ibid.* (emphasis added).

539. *Ibid.*

540. The Commission on the Intelligence Capabilities of the United States Regarding Weapons of Mass Destruction, Report to the President of the United States 102 (2005).

541. *Ibid.*

542. S. Rep. No. 108-301, at 248 (2004).

543. *Ibid.* at 249. (Emphasis added.)

544. *Ibid.* at 247. (Emphasis added.)

545. *Ibid.* at 248. (Emphasis added.)

546. *Ibid.*

547. *Ibid.*

548. The *Los Angeles Times* recently reported "of the three sources the CIA said had corroborated Curveball's story, two had ties to Chalabi. All three turned out to be frauds, the most important, a former major in the Iraqi intelligence services, was deemed a liar by the CIA and DIA. In May 2002, a fabricator warning was posted in U.S. intelligence databases." Bob Drogin and John Goetz, "How U.S. Fell Under the Spell of 'Curveball'", *Los Angeles Times*, Nov. 20, 2005, at A1.

549. *Ibid.* (emphasis added.)

550. Spencer Ackerman & John B. Judis, "The First Casualty", *The New Republic*, June 30, 2003, at 14.

551. Key Judgments from the National Intelligence Estimate on Iraq's Continuing Programs for Weapons of Mass Destruction (2002).

552. *Ibid.*

553. S. Rep. No. 108-301, at 139 (2004).

554. *Ibid.* at 230.

555. President George W. Bush, Remarks with His Majesty King Abdullah II of the Hashemite Kingdom of

Jordan (May 6, 2004) available at http://www.whitehouse.gov/news/releases/2004/05/20040506-9.html.

556. Seymour Hersh, "Torture at Abu Ghraib", *The New Yorker*, May 10, 2004, at 42 (emphasis added).

557. ARTICLE 15-6 INVESTIGATION OF THE 800th MILITARY POLICE BRIGADE, available at <http://news.findlaw.com/hdocs/docs/iraq/tagubarpt.html>. [hereinafter "Taguba Report"] (conducted by Maj. Gen. Antonio M. Taguba, Deputy Commanding General Support, Coalition Forces Land Component Command).

558. Maj. Gen. Antonio M. Taguba, Deputy Commanding General Support, Coalition Forces Land Component Command, Article 15-6 Investigation Of The 800th Military Police Brigade (2004), available at http://www.npr.org/iraq/2004/prison_abuse_report.pdf [hereinafter "Taguba Report"]. The report was not meant for public release, but—even though portions of it were classified—it was leaked and became widely available by May 2004 on the Internet. In addition, English translations of statements by several of the abused detainees were also leaked to the public. See, e.g., Translation of Sworn Statement Provided by ___, Detainee # ___ (Jan. 21, 2004), at <http://www.washingtonpost.com/wp-srv/world/iraq/abughraib/swornstatements042104.html> (the name of the detainee was withheld for privacy reasons) (describing, among other things, an act of sodomy by military police using a nightstick). *Ibid.*

559. Taguba Report at 16 (emphasis added).

560. *Ibid.*

561. *Ibid.*

562. *Ibid.* at 16-17.

563. *Ibid.* at 18-19.

564. *Ibid.* at 16.

565. Human Rights First, One Year After Abu Ghraib: Torture Photos: U.S. Government Response Grossly Inadequate, available at http://www.humanrightsfirst.org/us_law/etn/statements/abu-yr-042605.htm #_ednref1.

566. Press Release, Human Rights First, Twenty-Seven Detainee Homicides in U.S. Custody, (Oct. 19, 2005), available at http://www.humanrightsfirst.org/media/2005_alerts/etn_1019_dic.htm.

567. *Ibid.*

568. *Ibid.*

569. *Ibid.*

570. *Ibid.*

571. Report Of The International Committee Of The Red Cross (ICRC) On The Treatment By The Coalition Forces Of Prisoners Of War And Other Protected Persons By The Geneva Conventions In Iraq During Arrest, Internment And Interrogation (Feb. 2004), available at http://www.stopwar.org.uk/Resources /icrc.pdf [hereinafter ICRC Report].

572. *Ibid.*

573. ACLU, Government Documents on Torture, available at http://www.aclu.org/torturefoia/ (last modified Oct. 24, 2005)

574. *Ibid.* http://www.aclu.org/torturefoia/released/032505/1181_1280.pdf.

575. *Ibid.*

576. *Ibid.*

577. Amnesty International, One Year After Abu Ghraib, Torture Continues, Apr. 28, 2005, available at http://web.amnesty.org/pages/irq-280405-feature-eng.

578. Amnesty International Report, United States of America: Human Dignity Denied Torture and Accountability in the 'War on Terror,' available at http://web.amnesty.org/library/Index /ENGAMR511 452004.

579. Human Rights Watch, Leadership Failure: Firsthand Accounts of Torture of Iraqi Detainees by the U.S.

Army's 82nd Airborne Division, Vol. 17, No. 3(G) (Sept. 2005), available at http://hrw.org/reports/2005/us0905/us0905.pdf.

580. *Ibid.*

581. *Ibid.* at 9.

582. *Ibid.* at 11-12.

583. *Ibid.* at 1.

584. Michael Hirsh, "The Truth About Torture", *Newsweek*, Nov. 7, 2005 (emphasis added).

585. Adam Zagorin, "Haunted by 'The Iceman'", *Time*, Nov. 21, 2005, at 38.

586. *Ibid.*

587. *Ibid.*

588. *Ibid.*

589. Scott Scott Shane, "The Reach of War: Detainees", the *New York Times*, Oct. 29, 2004 at A10.

590. John Hendren, "The Conflict in Iraq; CIA May Have Held 100 'Ghost' Prisoners", *Los Angeles Times*, Sept. 10, 2004 at A1.

591. ICRC Report (documenting the practice of keeping prisoners "completely naked in totally empty concrete cells and in total darkness, allegedly for several days at a time"). *Ibid.* at 12.

592. *Ibid.* at 3; see also Scott Wilson, "Ex-Detainee Tells of Anguishing Treatment at Iraq Prison", The Washington Post, May 5, 2004, at A18 ("the men were made to masturbate against a wall, crawl on top of one another to form a pyramid and ride each other 'as if we were riding a donkey.'"); "Iraqi Inmate: 'Treated like Dogs,'" *BBC News Online*, May 6, 2004, available at http://news.bbc.co.uk/1/hi/world/americas/3689371.stm ("They cut our clothes off with blades."). Ibid

593. Taguba Report at 17.

594. Geneva Convention Relative to the Treatment of Prisoners of War, Aug. 12, 1949, 6 U.S.T. 3316, 75 U.N.T.S. 135, [hereinafter "GC III"]; Geneva Convention Relative to the Protection of Civilian Persons in Time of War, Aug. 12, 1949, 6 U.S.T. 3516, 75 U.N.T.S. 287, [hereinafter "GC IV"], (entered into force Oct. 21, 1950). The U.S. and Iraq are both parties to the Conventions.

595. Dana Priest, "Memo Lets CIA Take Detainees Out of Iraq; Practice Is Called Serious Breach of Geneva Conventions", *The Washington Post*, October 24, 2004 at A01 (citing an unnamed DOJ official who provided the classified memorandum during an interview); see also Douglas Jehl, "U.S. Action Bars Rights of Some Captured In Iraq", the *New York Times*, October 26, 2004 at A1.

596. Testimony on the Investigation of the 205th Military Intelligence Brigade at Abu Ghraib Prison, Iraq Before the S. Armed Services Committee, 108th Cong. (2004) (statement of Army Commanding Gen. Paul Kern).

597. *Ibid.*

598. *Ibid.*

599. Josh White, "Army Documents Shed Light on CIA 'Ghosting,'" *The Washington Post*, Mar. 24, 2005, at A15.

600. *Ibid.*

601. *Ibid.*; see also R. Jeffrey Smith, "Abu Ghraib Officer Gets Reprimand; Non-Court-Martial Punishment for Dereliction of Duty Includes Fine", *The Washington Post*, May. 12, 2005, at A16.

602. Peter Popham, U.S. Forces "'Used Chemical Weapons' During Bssault on City of Fallujah", *The Independent*, Nov. 8, 2005.

603. *Ibid.*

604. Protocol III of the 1980 Convention on Certain Conventional Weapons (CCW) available at http://www.globalsecurity.org/military/library/policy/int/convention_conventional-wpns_prot-iii.htm. The operative provisions of the CCW are contained in five protocols, four of which are currently in force.

605. *Ibid.*

606. GC III, art. 130.

607. Testimony on treatment of Iraqi Prisoners: Hearing before the H. Comm. on Armed Services, 108th Cong. 2d Sess. (2004) (statement of Secretary of Defense Rumsfeld) (emphasis added).

608. 18 U.S.C. §§ 3161-3167 (2002).

609. Amnesty International, "Abu Ghraib: One Year Later, Who's Accountable?" at http://www.amnestyusa.org /stoptorture/agfactsheet.html.

610. Douglas Jehl and Tim Golden, "C.I.A. is Likely to Avoid Charges in Most Prisoner Deaths", the *New York Times*, Oct. 23, 2005, at 6.

611. Frank Rich, "One Step Closer to the Big Enchilada", the *New York Times*, Oct. 30, 2005, at 12.

612. Scott Horton, Betr: Strafanzeige gegen den US-Verteidigungsminister Donald Rumsfeld, u.a. Expert Report of Scott Horton, Jan. 28, 2005, at 2, available at http://www.ccr-ny.org/v2/legal/september_11th /docs/ScottHortonGermany013105.pdf.

613. *Ibid.* at 3 (emphasis added).

614. Josh White, "Rights Groups Reject Prison Abuse Findings", *The Washington Post*, Apr. 24, 2005 at A20.

615. Letter from Anthony Romero, Executive Director, ACLU, to Alberto Gonzales, Attorney General, United States Department of Justice (Mar. 30, 2005), available at http://www.aclu.org//safefree/general/17554leg 20050330.html (emphasis added).

616. Josh White, "Rights Groups Reject Prison Abuse Findings", *The Washington Post*, Apr. 24, 2005 at A20.

617. *Ibid.*

618. Italy Orders Further CIA Warrants, BBC News, available at http://news.bbc.co.uk/2/hi/europe /4297966.stm (reporting a total of 22 warrants issued for those found involved in the abduction of Osama Mustafa Hassan on Italian soil and his rendition to Egypt for interrogation).

619. Memorandum from Jack Goldsmith, Assistant Attorney General, Office of Legal Counsel to William H. Taft IV, General Counsel, Department of State (March 19, 2004), available at http://www.humanrights-first.com/us_law/etn/gonzales/memos_dir/memo_20040319_Golds_Gonz.pdf.

620. See *Ibid.* at 5; see also GCIV, art. 49.

621. Memorandum from Jack Goldsmith, Assistant Attorney General, Office of Legal Counsel to William H. Taft IV, General Counsel, Department of State at 15. (March 19, 2004), available at http://www.human-rightsfirst.com/us_law/etn/gonzales/memos_dir/memo_20040319_Golds_Gonz.pdf (emphasis added

622. *Ibid.* at 15.

623. *Ibid.*

624. Dana Priest, "Memo Lets CIA Take Detainees Out of Iraq", *The Washington Post*, Oct. 24, 2004 at A1 (emphasis added).

625. Human Rights First, Human Rights First Opposes Alberto Gonzales To Be Attorney General, Jan 24. 2005, available at http://www.humanrightsfirst.org/us_law/etn/gonzales/statements/hrf_opp_gonz_full _012405.asp.

626. *Ibid.*

627. *Ibid.*

628. Memorandum from Jay Bybee, Assistant Attorney General to Alberto Gonzales, Counsel to the President (Aug. 1, 2002), available at http://news.findlaw.com/hdocs/docs/doj/bybee80102ltr.html. See also, Evan Thomas and Michael Hirsh, "The Debate Over Torture", *Newsweek*, Nov. 21, 2005 at 30.

629. Memorandum from Jay Bybee, at 2 (emphasis added).

630. United Nations Convention Bgainst Torture and Other Cruel, Inhuman or Degrading Treatment or Punishment, G.A. Res. 39/46, Annex, 39 U.N. GAOR Supp. No. 51, U.N. Doc. A/39/51 (1984).

631. Memorandum from Jay Bybee, at 1.

632. 18 U.S.C. § 2340A (2002).

633. David Luban, "The False Premise of the Interrogation Debate", *The Washington Post*, Nov. 27, 2005 at B1.

634. S. Doc. No. 101-30, at 36(1990), Convention Bgainst Torture and Other Cruel, Inhuman or Degrading Treatment or Punishment, Aug. 30, 1990.

635. See David Luban, "The False Premise of the Interrogation Debate", *The Washington Post*, Nov. 27, 2005 at B1.

636. See Josh White, "Rights Groups Reject Prison Abuse Findings", *The Washington Post*, Apr. 24, 2005 at A20.

637. Letter from Abraham D. Sofaer, Hoover Institution on War Revolution and Peace to the Hon. Patrick J. Leahy, Ranking Member, Senate Judiciary Committee (Jan. 21, 2005) (on file with author) (emphasis added).

638. Memorandum from William J. Haynes, II, General Counsel, to Donald Rumsfeld, Secretary of Defense (Nov. 27, 2002), available at http://www.dod.gov/news/Jun2004/d20040622doc5.pdf

639. Memorandum from Michael B. Dunlavey, Major General, to Commander U.S. South Command (Oct. 11, 2002) at 1, 4, available at http://news.findlaw.com/hdocs/docs/dod/dunlavey101102mem.pdf.

640. *Ibid.* at 4 (emphasis added).

641. *Ibid.* at 5 (emphasis added).

642. *Ibid.* at 4 (emphasis added).

643. *Ibid.* at 5 (emphasis added). In fact, the ultimate list contained many tactics barred by then-current army doctrine. As one former military prosecutor himself said, many of these are "patent violations of the laws of war" and still others could become so if applied in a strict enough manner. Jordan J. Paust, Executive Plans And Authorization to Violation International Law Concerning Treatment and Interrogation of Detainees, 43 Colum. J. of Transnat'l L.811, 845 (2005).

> Human Rights Watch terms these tactics as an "unprecedented expansion of army doctrine" and that, "depending on how they are used, these methods also likely violate the Geneva Conventions' prohibition on torture or inhuman treatment of prisoners" and "would thus constitute a war crime." Human Rights Watch, Getting Away With Torture: Command Responsibility for the U.S. Abuse of Detainees, Apr. 2005 at 33.

644. Taguba Report at 7. The report was not meant for public release, but—even though portions of it were classified—it was leaked and became widely available by May 2004 on the Internet. In addition, English translations of statements by several of the abused detainees were also leaked to the public. See, e.g., Translation of Sworn Statement Provided by ___, Detainee # ___ (Jan. 21, 2004), at <http://www.washingtonpost.com/wp-srv/world/iraq/abughraib/swornstatements042104.html> (the name of the detainee was withheld fro privacy reasons) (describing, among other things, an act of sodomy by military police using a nightstick).

645. John Barry, Michael Hirsh and Michael Isikoff, "The Roots of Torture", *Newsweek*, May 24, 2004, at 26. See, Secretary of Defense Donald H. Rumsfeld, Memorandum for the Commander, U.S. Southern Command, on Counter-Resistance Techniques in the War on Terrorism, Tab A, at 1-2 (Apr. 16, 2003), at <http://www.washingtonpost.com/wp-srv/nation/documents/041603rumsfeld.pdf>; see also Dana Priest & Bradley Graham, "Guantanamo List Details Approved Interrogation Methods", *The Washington Post*, June 10, 2004, at A13; Neil A. Lewis & Eric Schmitt, "Lawyers Decided Bans on Torture Didn't Bind Bush", the *New York Times*, June 8, 2004, at A1.

On April 16, 2003, Secretary Rumsfeld approved twenty-four interrogation techniques (out of thirty-five examined by the working group) for use at Guantanamo Bay, including "significantly increasing the fear level in a detainee" and "attacking or insulting the ego of a detainee, not beyond the limits that would apply to a POW." *Ibid.*

646. Scott Wilson and Sewell Chan, "As Insurgency Grew, So Did Prison Abuse; Needing Intelligence, U.S. Pressed Detainees", *The Washington Post*, May 10, 2004 at A1 (emphasis added).

647. Interview by Steve Inskeep with Larry Wilkerson, Morning Edition, National Public Radio (Nov. 3, 2005).

648. Jordan J. Paust, Executive Plans And Authorization to Violation International Law Concerning Treatment and Interrogation of Detainees, 43 Colum. J. of Transnat'l L.811, 850 (2005) (emphasis added).

649. *Ibid.* at 846-848. Others told directly of the abuse include Secretary of State Colin Powell, and National Security Advisor Condoleezza Rice.

650. Testimony on treatment of Iraqi Prisoners: Hearing before the H. Comm. on Armed Services, 108th Cong. 2d Sess. (2004) (Statement of Secretary of Defense Rumsfeld).

651. Human Rights Watch, Getting Away With Torture: Command Responsibility for the U.S. Abuse of Detainees, 2005 at 44-45 (emphasis added); See Jordan J. Paust, Executive Plans And Authorization to Violation International Law Concerning Treatment and Interrogation of Detainees, 43 Colum. J. of Transnat'l L.811, 846-48 (2005).

652. Mark Mathews, "Powell Says Bush Was Informed of Red Cross Concerns", *Baltimore Sun*, May 12, 2004 (emphasis added).

653. Human Rights Watch, Getting Away With Torture: Command Responsibility for the U.S. Abuse of Detainees, Apr. 2005 at 45-8, which accounts for numerous press accounts and complaints from various human rights organizations, beginning immediately after the invasion of Iraq.

654. *Ibid.* (emphasis added).

655. Amnesty International, One year after Abu Ghraib, torture continues (last modified Apr.28, 2005), available at <http://web.amnesty.org/pages/irq-280405-feature-eng>.

656. Amnesty International, Abu Ghraib: One Year Later, Who's Accountable?, available at www.amnestyusa.org/stopturture/agfactsheet.html.

657. Human Rights First, Torture: Quick Facts, available at www.humanrightsfirst.org.

658. Josh White, "Rights Groups Reject Prison Abuse Findings", *The Washington Post*, Apr. 24, 2005 at A20.

659. Amnesty International, One year after Abu Ghraib, torture continues (last modified Apr.28, 2005), available at http://web.amnesty.org/pages/irq-280405-feature-en.

660. *Ibid.*

661. Secretary of Defense Donald Rumsfeld, Press Briefing (June 17, 2004) (emphasis added), available at www.denfenselink.mil/transcripts.

662. Eric Schmitt and Thom Shanker, "The Reach of War", the *New York Times*, June 17, 2004, at A1; Dana Priest and Bradley Graham, "U.S. Struggled Over How Far to Push Tactics", *The Washignton Post*, June 24, 2004 at A1. Rashul may have also been interrogated in Iraq at Camp Cropper before he was transported outside Iraq.

663. Dana Priest and Bradley Graham, "U.S. Struggled Over How Far to Push Tactics", *The Washington Post*, June 24, 2004 at A1.

664. Secretary of Defense Donald Rumsfeld, Press Briefing (June 17, 2004), available at

665. See Mark Fass, "Rumsfeld ID's Secret Detainee", *Daily News* (New York), June 20, 2004, at 34.

666. Jordan J. Paust, Executive Plans And Authorization to Violation International Law Concerning Treatment and Interrogation of Detainees, 43 Colum. J. of Transnat'l L.811, 850 (2005).

667. Eric Schmitt and Thom Shanker, "The Reach of War", the *New York Times*, June 17, 2004, at A1; see also Mark Fass, "Rumsfeld ID's Secret Detainee", *Daily News* (New York), June 20, 2004, at 34.

668. *Ibid.*; see also Dana Priest & Josh White, "Detainee Reportedly Was Lost in System: CIA Criticized for Hiding Some Prisoners", *The Washington Post*, June 17, 2004, at A19.

669. *Ibid.*

670. John Hendren, "The Conflict in Iraq: CIA May Have Held 100 'Ghost' Prisoners", *Los Angeles Times*, Sept. 10, 2004, at A1.

671. Josh White, "Army, CIA Agreed on 'Ghost' Prisoners", *The Washington Post*, Mar. 11, 2005, at A16.

672. Testimony on the Independent Panel to Review Department of Defense Detention Operations: Hearing before the S. Comm. on Armed Services, 108th Cong. 2d Sess. (2004) (Statement of Army Gen. Paul Kern).

673. *Ibid.* (emphasis added).

674. Richard W. Stevenson & Eric Lichtblau, "White House Looks to Manage Fallout Over C.I.A. Leak Inquiry", the *New York Times*, Oct. 2, 2003, at A24.

675. Articulating the magnitude of the matter, Senate Minority Leader, Harry Reid, stated: "This case is bigger than the leak of highly classified information. It is about how the Bush White House manufactured and manipulated intelligence in order to bolster its case for the war in Iraq, and to discredit anyone who dared to challenge the president." Press Release, Senator Harry Reid (D-NV), Reid Statement on Indictment (Oct. 28, 2005), available at http://reIbid.senate.gov/record2.cfm?id=247954.

676. United States v. Libby (D.D.C. Oct. 28, 2005) (hereinafter "Libby Indictment"). Noting the historical significance of Libby's indictment, the *New York Times* explained: "The chain of events that led to this indictment is not entirely unlike the one that prompted the Nixon White House to try to discredit Daniel Ellsberg, the former Pentagon analyst who provided reporters with the secret government history detailing the growth of American involvement in Vietnam that came to be known as the Pentagon Papers. In that case, as in this, a White House sought to cast doubt on a critic of its foreign policy, only to enmesh itself in far deeper political and legal trouble by trying to hush up its efforts." Todd S. Purdum, "Shift in Focus for Prosecutor", the *New York Times*, Oct. 29, 2005, at A1.

677. On May 6, 2003, the *New York Times* published a Nicholas Kristof Op-Ed challenging the veracity of the sixteen words in the President's State of the Union alleging an Iraq-Niger uranium connection. Nicolas D. Kristof, "Missing in Action: Truth", the *New York Times*, May 6, 2003, at A1; see also Libby Indictment 3. ("The column reported that, following a request from the Vice President's office for an investigation of allegations that Iraq sought to buy uranium from Niger, an unnamed former ambassador was sent on a trip to Niger in 2002 to investigate the allegations. According to the column the ambassador reported back to the CIA and State Department in early 2002 that the allegations were unequivocally wrong and based on forged documents.").

678. On June 12, 2003, the *Washington Post* published an article by Walter Pincus not only challenging the accuracy of the sixteen words, but also indicating that the CIA knew that the Niger story was false. Walter Pincus, "CIA Says It Cabled Key Data To White House", *The Washington Post*, June 12, 2003, at A16; see also Libby Indictment 10 ("[The Pincus article] described Wilson as a retired ambassador but not by name, and reported that the CIA had sent him to Niger after an aide to the Vice President raised questions about purported Iraqi efforts to acquire uranium. Pincus's article questioned the accuracy of the 'sixteen words,' and stated that the retired ambassador had reported to the CIA that the uranium purchase story was false.").

679. An article in the July 28, 2003 New Republic questioned the sixteen words as well as the overall misuse of pre-war intelligence. Editorial, "16 Words", *New Republic*, July 28, 2003, at 8; see also Libby Indictment 12 ("The article included a quotation attributed to the unnamed ambassador alleging that administration officials 'knew the Niger story was a flat-out lie.' The article also was critical of how the administration, including the Office of the Vice President, portrayed intelligence concerning Iraqi capabilities with regard to weapons of mass destruction, and accused the administration of suppressing dissent from the intelligence agencies on this topic.").

680. The run of damaging news for the Bush Administration continued on July 6, 2003, when Ambassador Wilson himself wrote his first-hand accounts as an Op-Ed in the *New York Times*. the *Washington Post* published an article based on an interview with Mr. Wilson, and Mr. Wilson appeared on Meet the Press. See

Libby Indictment 15 ("In his Op-Ed article and interviews in print and on television, Wilson asserted, among other things, that he had taken a trip to Niger at the request of the CIA in February 2002 to investigate allegations that Iraq had sought or obtained uranium yellowcake from Niger, and that he doubted Iraq had obtained uranium from Niger recently, for a number of reasons. Wilson stated that he believed, based on his understanding of government procedures, that the Office of the Vice President was advised of the results of his trip."). The press deluge continued into the next week, as media inquiries were coming in from Matthew Cooper of Time, among others. *Ibid.* 22-24..

681. David Johnston & Richard W. Stevenson, "Prosecutor Narrows Focus in Leak Case", the *New York Times*, Nov. 4, 2005, at A25 (emphasis added).

682. Peter Wallsten & Tom Hamburger, "Bush Critic Became Target of Libby, Former Aides Say", *Los Angeles Times*, Oct. 21, 2005, at A1.

683. *Ibid.*

684. Libby Indictment 4-6:

On or about May 29, 2003, in the White House, Libby asked an Under Secretary of State ('Under Secretary') for information concerning the unnamed ambassador's travel to Niger to investigate claims about Iraqi efforts to acquire uranium yellowcake. The Under Secretary thereafter directed the State Department's Bureau of Intelligence and Research to prepare a report concerning the ambassador and his trip. The Under Secretary provided Libby with interim oral reports in late May and early June 2003, and advised Libby that Wilson was the former ambassador who took the trip.

On or about June 9, 2003, a number of classified documents from the CIA were faxed to the Office of the Vice President to the personal attention of Libby and another person in the Office of the Vice President. The faxed documents, which were marked as classified, discussed, among other things, Wilson and his trip to Niger, but did not mention Wilson by name. After receiving these documents, Libby and one or more other persons in the Office of the Vice President handwrote the names "Wilson" and "Joe Wilson" on the documents.

On or about June 11 and 12, 2003, the Under Secretary of State orally advised Libby in the White House that, in sum and substance, Wilson's wife worked at the CIA and that State Department personnel were saying that Wilson's wife was involved in the planning of his trip.

685. See Larisa Alexandrovna & Jason Leopold, "Bolton's Chief of Staff Gave Information on Outed Agent to Libby, Lawyers Involved in Leak Case Say", *RawStory* (Nov. 2, 2005), available at http://rawstory.com/news/2005/Lawyers_involved_in_leak_case_say_1102.html ("[Attorneys involved in the investigation] said that two former Libby aides, John Hannah and David Wurmser, told the special prosecutor that Libby had actually first contacted Bolton to dig up the information.").

686. Libby Indictment 7 ("On or about June 11, 2003, Libby spoke with a senior officer of the CIA to ask about the origin and circumstances of Wilson's trip, and was advised by the CIA officer that Wilson's wife worked at the CIA and was believed to be responsible for sending Wilson on the trip.").

687. *Ibid.* 9 ("On or about June 12, 2003, Libby was advised by the Vice President of the United States that Wilson's wife worked at the Central Intelligence Agency in the Counterproliferation Division. Libby understood that the Vice President had learned this information from the CIA.").

688. See See David Corn, "After the Libby Indictment", *The Nation*, Nov. 2, 2005.

689. Libby Indictment 11 ("On or about June 14, 2003, Libby met with a CIA briefer. During their conversation he expressed displeasure that CIA officials were making comments to reporters critical of the Vice President's office, and discussed with the briefer, among other things, 'Joe Wilson' and his wife 'Valerie Wilson,' in the context of Wilson's trip to Niger.").

690. *Ibid.* 18 ("Also on or about July 8, 2003, Libby met with the Counsel to the Vice President in an anteroom outside the Vice President's Office. During their brief conversation, Libby asked the Counsel to the Vice President, in sum and substance, what paperwork there would be at the CIA if an employee's spouse undertook an overseas trip.").

691. *Ibid.* 19 ("Not earlier than June 2003, but on or before July 8, 2003, the Assistant to the Vice President for Public Affairs learned from another government official that Wilson's wife worked at the CIA, and advised Libby of this information.").

692. The Libby Indictment establishes that the Vice President advised Libby that Mrs. Wilson worked at the CIA's Counterproliferation Division on June 12, 2003, and that Mr. Cheney obtained this information from the CIA. Libby Indictment 9 ("On or about June 12, 2003, Libby was advised by the Vice President of the United States that Wilson's wife worked at the Central Intelligence Agency in the Counterproliferation Division. Libby understood that the Vice President had learned this information from the CIA."). The CIA source is believed to have been Director George Tenet. See Tom Hamburger & Peter Wallsten, "Cheney Said to Have Told Aide of Plame", *Los Angeles Times*, Oct. 25, 2003, at A13.

693. It has been widely reported that on June 12, 2003, the State Department sent Powell a classified memorandum written a month earlier identifying Wilson's wife as a CIA employee and saying it was believed she recommended Wilson for the Niger mission. Powell was traveling with Bush to Africa, and sources said the memorandum was widely circulated among officials with appropriate clearances aboard Air Force One. See Barton Gellman, "A Leak, Then a Deluge", *The Washington Post*, Oct. 30, 2005, at A1.

694. It is now clear that Karl Rove learned about Wilson's wife being employed at the CIA either from Mr. Libby or other sources within the Administration. Libby Indictment 21 ("On or about July 10 or July 11, 2003, Libby spoke to a senior official in the White House ('Official A') who advised Libby of a conversation Official B had earlier that week with columnist Robert Novak in which Wilson's wife was discussed as a CIA employee involved in Wilson's trip. Libby was advised by Official B that Novak would be writing a story about Wilson's wife."). This is because it has been confirmed that the "Official A" referred to in the indictment document is Karl Rove. See Pete Yost, "Mysterious 'Official A' is Karl Rove", *Editor & Publisher*, Oct. 28, 2005, available at http://www.editorandpublisher.com/eandp/news/article_display .jsp?vnu_content_id=1001392393 ("Friday's indictment says 'Official A' is a 'senior official in the White House who advised Libby on July 10 or 11 of 2003' about a chat with Novak about his upcoming column in which Plame would be identified as a CIA employee. Late Friday, three people close to the investigation, each asking to remain unidentified because of grand jury secrecy, identified Rove as Official A.").

695. Libby Indictment 13 ("Shortly after publication of the article in The New Republic, Libby spoke by telephone with his then Principal Deputy and discussed the article.").

696. Pete Yost, "Mysterious 'Official A' is Karl Rove", *Editor & Publisher*, Oct. 28, 2005, available at http://www.editorandpublisher.com/eandp/news/article_display.jsp?vnu_content_id=1001392393 ("Friday's indictment says 'Official A' is a 'senior official in the White House who advised Libby on July 10 or 11 of 2003' about a chat with Novak about his upcoming column in which Plame would be identified as a CIA employee. Late Friday, three people close to the investigation, each asking to remain unidentified because of grand jury secrecy, identified Rove as Official A.").

697. Libby Indictment 16 ("On or about July 7, 2003, Libby had lunch with the then White House Press Secretary and advised the Press Secretary that Wilson's wife worked at the CIA and noted that such information was not widely known.").

698. Richard Keil & William Roberts, "Prosecutors Probe Centers on Rove, Memo, Phone Calls", *Bloomberg News*, July 18, 2005; Tom Hamburger & Sonni Efron, "Memo May Hold Key to CIA Leak", *Los Angeles Times*, July 17, 2005, at A22.

699. Libby Indictment 22 ("On or about July 12, 2003, Libby flew with the Vice President and others to and from Norfolk, Virginia, on Air Force Two. On his return trip, Libby discussed with other officials aboard the plane what Libby should say in response to certain pending media inquiries, including questions from Time reporter Matthew Cooper.").

700. On or about June 9, 2003, a number of classified documents from the CIA were faxed to the Office of the Vice President to the personal attention of Libby and another person in the Office. The faxed documents were marked as classified. *Ibid.* 5. Libby's principal Deputy asked Libby whether information about Mr. Wilson's trip could be shared with the press to rebut the allegations that the Vice President had sent Mr.

Wilson to Niger. Mr. Libby responded that there would be complications at the CIA in disclosing that information publicly, and that he could not discuss the matter on a non-secure telephone line. *Ibid.* 13. On or about July 7, 2003, Libby had lunch with the then-White House Press Secretary and advised the Press Secretary that Wilson's wife worked at the CIA and noted that such information was not widely known. *Ibid.* 16. On or about the morning of July 8, 2003, Libby met with New York Times reporter Judith Miller. When the conversation turned to the subject of Joseph Wilson, Libby asked that the information he provided on the topic of Wilson be attributed to a "former Hill staffer" rather than to a "senior administration official," as had been the understanding with respect to other information that Libby provided to Miller during this meeting. *Ibid.* 17.

701. Jim VandeHei & Carol D. Leonning, "Woodward Was Told of Plame More Than Two Years Ago", *The Washington Post*, Nov. 16, 2005, at A1.

702. Libby Indictment 14

703. *Ibid.* 17.

704. *Ibid.* 21; see also Pete Yost, "Mysterious 'Official A' is Karl Rove", *Editor & Publisher*, Oct. 28, 2005, available                                                                                                                                                          at http://www.editorandpublisher.com/eandp/news/article_display.jsp?vnu_content_id=1001392393.

705. Michael Isikoff, "Matt Cooper's Source", *Newsweek*, July 18, 2005, *available at* http://msnbc.msn.com/id/8525978/site/newsweek/page/2/.

706. Libby Indictment 8.

707. *Ibid.* 24.

708. Walter Pincus, "Anonymous Sources: Their Use in a Time of Prosecutorial Interest", Neiman Reports 27 (Summer 2005).

709. Timothy M. Phelps & Knut Royce, "Columnist Blows CIA Agent's Cover", *Newsday*, July 22, 2003 (emphasis added).

710. Carol D. Leonnig, "Columnist Says Bush Knows Who Leaked Name", *The Washington Post*, Dec. 15, 2005, at A07.

711. Walter Pincus, "Anonymous Sources: Their Use in a Time of Prosecutorial Interest", Neiman Reports 27 (Summer 2005). As Newsweek recently explained: "Any reasonable reading of the events covered in the indictment would consider Rove's behavior "reckless [under the EO]." Evan Thomas & Michael Isikoff, "Secrets and Leaks", *Newsweek*, Oct. 13, 2003, at 26 (emphasis added). The fact that he discussed Plame's identity with reporters more than once constitutes a pattern. In the past, other officials have lost their security clearances for similar disclosures—even without a pattern. Former CIA director John Deutch and former National Security Advisor Sandy Berger (who got in trouble after leaving office) both lost their clearances when they took classified information home without proper authorization. More recently, officials of the Coast Guard were sanctioned when they warned relatives of a possible terrorist threat against the New York City subways before public disclosure of the threat. *Ibid.*

712. Walter Pincus & Mike Allen, "Probe Focuses on Month Before Leak to Reporters", *The Washington Post*, Oct. 12, 2003, at A1 (emphasis added).

713. Richard W. Stevenson & Eric Lichtblau, "White House Looks to Manage Fallout Over CIA Leak Inquiry", the *New York Times*, at Oct. 2, 2003.

714. Evan Thomas and Michael Isikoff, "Secrets and Leaks", *Newsweek*, Oct. 13, 2003, at 26.

715. Mike Allen & Dana Priest, "Bush Administration is Focus of Inquiry, CIA Agent's Identity Was Leaked to Media", *The Washington Post*, Sept. 28, 2003, at A1.

716. *Ibid.* The Administration's bad animus toward Ambassador Wilson appeared to infect its reliable ally, Robert Novak, who, when asked by a bystander on the street, said "Wilson's an asshole. The CIA sent him. His wife, Valerie [Plame], works for the CIA. She's a weapons of mass destruction specialist. She sent him." Joseph Wilson, The Politics of Truth: Inside the Lies that Led to War and Betrayed My Wife's CIA Identity, at 24 (2004).

717. National Security Implications of Disclosing the Identity of an Intelligence Operative, Before the Senate Democratic Policy Committee, 108th Cong. (2003) (statement of Vince Cannistraro) (emphasis added).

718. National Security Implications of Disclosing the Identity of an Intelligence Operative, Before the Senate Democratic Policy Committee, 108th Cong. (2003) (statement of James Marcinkowski).

719. Peter Wallsten & Tom Hamburger, "Bush Critic Became Target of Libby, Former Aides Say", *Los Angeles Times*, Oct. 21, 2005, *available at* http://www.latimes.com/news/nationworld/nation/la-na-libby21oct21,0,6448189,full.story?coll=la-home-headlines.

720. Murray Waas, "Cheney Libby Blocked Papers To Senate Intelligence Panel", *National Journal*, Oct. 27, 2005 (emphasis added), *available at* http://nationaljournal.com/about/njweekly/stories/2005/1027 nj1.htm.

721. In the Libby Indictment, Special Counsel Fitzgerald notes that the outing of Ms. Plame could damage national security in a number of respects: "Disclosure of the fact that . . . individuals [such as Valerie Plame] were employed by the CIA had the potential to damage the national security in ways that ranged from preventing the future use of those individuals in a covert capacity, to compromising intelligence-gathering methods and operations, and endangering the safety of CIA employees and those who dealt with them." Libby Indictment 1d.

722. Special Counsel Patrick Fitzgerald, Press Conference (Oct. 28, 2005) (emphasis added).

723. Dafna Linzer, "CIA Checks its Exposure in Plame Case", *The Washington Post*, Oct. 29, 2005.

724. On January 12, Victoria Toensing and Bruce W. Sanford published an Op-Ed:

Since Plame had been living in Washington for some time when the July 2003 column was published, and was working at a desk job in Langley (a no-no for a person with a need for cover), there is a serious legal question as to whether she qualifies as "covert."

Victoria Toensing & Bruce W. Sanford, Op-Ed, "The Plame Game: Was this a Crime?", *The Washington Post*, Jan. 12, 2005, at A21. Victoria Toensing was quoted in a news story as saying, "[Wilson] had a desk job in Langley. . . . When you want someone in deep cover, they don't go back and forth to Langley." Richard W. Stevenson, "At White House, A Day of Silence on Role of Rove", the *New York Times*, July 12, 2005, at A1. She also appeared on radio and television news and restated these talking points. See All Things Considered (NPR radio broadcast July 11, 2005). Conservative talk show host Michael Medved echoed Toensing's remarks: "Mrs. Plame, Mrs. Wilson, had a desk job at Langley. She went back and forth every single day. It was well known in Washington parlance." Larry King Live (CNN television broadcast July 12, 2005).

On July 15, Republican officials renewed their questions about Wilson's cover. Senator Pat Roberts (R-KS), the Republican Chairman of the U.S. Senate's Select Committee on Intelligence, was shown on the Fox News Channel questioning Wilson's cover. Mr. Roberts argued that "[t]he mere fact that one works for the CIA is not in and of itself classified." Fox Special Report with Brit Hume (Fox News Channel television broadcast July 15, 2005) (video footage of Senate Chairman). Similarly, Republican consultant Tara Setmayer told CNN that "Karl Rove did not break any laws. . . . [Wilson] was at a desk job. No laws have been broken, and Democrats need to get an agenda." American Morning (CNN television broadcast July 15, 2005).

725. Face the Nation (CBS television broadcast July 17, 2005). In addition, former Republican presidential nominee and former Senate Majority Leader Bob Dole wrote an Op-Ed in the *New York Times*:

[O]ne of the requirements [for a violation of the Intelligence Identities Protection Act] is that the federal government must be taking "affirmative measures" to conceal the agent's intelligence relationship with the United States. Yet we now know that Ms. Wilson had a desk job at CIA headquarters and could be seen traveling to and from work. The journalist Robert D. Novak, whose July 14, 2003 column mentioned Ms. Wilson, using her maiden name, and set off the investigation, has written that CIA officials confirmed to him over the telephone that she was an employee before he wrote his column.

Bob Dole, Op-Ed, "The Underprivileged Press", the *New York Times*, Aug. 16, 2005, at A15.

726. Letter from Larry Johnson, former Analyst, CIA, et al., to the Honorable J. Dennis Hastert, Speaker, U.S. House, et al. (July 18, 2005).

727. *Ibid.*

728. National Security Implications of Disclosing the Identity of an Intelligence Operative: Hearing Before the U.S. Senate Democratic Policy Committee, 109th Cong., 1st Sess. (July 22, 2005). Larry Johnson testified that:

What we've seen, particularly over the last two or three weeks, is one of the most malicious, disingenuous smear campaigns, not only of Ambassador Wilson, who can publicly defend himself, but of Valerie Plame his wife, who is still an officer at the Central Intelligence Agency and is unable to speak out publicly, is unable to defend herself and to correct the record.

*Ibid.* (statement of Larry Johnson). Another former CIA officer, Jim Marcinkowski, further stated;

By ridiculing, for example, the degree of cover or the use of post office boxes, you lessen the confidence that foreign nationals place in our covert capabilities, especially when they're involved in a community of intelligence collection, they know how these things work. They know how they're used.

*Ibid.* (statement of Jim Marcinkowski).

729. Letter from Stanley M. Moskowitz, Director of Congressional Affairs, CIA, to the Honorable John Conyers, Jr., Ranking Member, House Judiciary Committee (Jan. 30, 2004).

730. Letter from William Moschella, Assistant Attorney General, Department of Justice, to the Honorable John Conyers, Jr., Ranking Member, House Judiciary Committee (Jan. 20, 2004).

731. "Investigating Leaks", the *New York Times*, Oct. 2, 2003, at A30 (editorial).

732. Richard Stevenson & Eric Lichtblau, "Leaker May Remain Elusive, Bush Suggests", the *New York Times*, Oct. 8, 2003, at A28.

733. Richard Stevenson & Eric Lichtblau, "Attorney General is Closely Linked to Inquiry Figures", the *New York Times*, Oct. 2, 2003, at A1 (emphasis added).

734. Murray Waas, "What Now, Karl? Rove and Ashcroft Face New Allegations in the Valerie Plame Affair," *Village Voice*, Aug. 13, 2005. On October 21, 2003, the Assistant Attorney General for the Criminal Division, Christopher Wray, testified before the Senate Judiciary Committee that he was keeping the Attorney General up-to-date on the investigation. This included identifying the names of individuals being interviewed by the Department and enough detail "for [the Attorney General] to understand meaningfully what is going on in the investigation." Criminal Terrorism Investigations and Prosecutions: Hearing before the Senate Judiciary Committee, 108th Cong. (2003) (statement of Assistant Attorney General Christopher Wray).

735. Michael Duffy, "Leaking With a Vengeance", *Time*, Oct. 13, 2003, at 28 (released Oct. 5, 2003).

736. See U.S. Dep't of Justice, Deputy Attorney General Comey Holds Justice Department News Conference (Dec. 30, 2003) (statement of the Deputy Attorney General). The manner in which the Department appointed Fitrzgerald, however, led Fitzgerald to believe he was not granted the authority to issue a report at the conclusion of his investigation. See Letter from the Honorable Patrick Fitzgerald, Special Counsel, U.S. Dep't of Justice, to the Honorable John Conyers, Jr., et al. (Oct. 28, 2005). If the Department instead had used its express regulatory authority to appoint Mr. Fitzgerald as special prosecutor, such a report would have been required. 28 C.F.R. § 600.8-.9.

737. As the *Washington Post* reported, "[e]ven some White House aides privately wonder whether Libby was seeking to protect Cheney from political embarrassment. One of them noted with resignation, 'Obviously, the indictment speaks for itself.'" Carol D. Leonnig and Jim VandeHei, "Libby May Have Tried to Mask Cheney's Role", *The Washington Post*, Nov. 13, 2005, at A6.

738. See In re: Special Counsel Investigation, 374 F. Supp. 2d 238 (D.D.C. 2005). In response to similar concerns expressed by Mr. Fitzgerald about Time reporter Matthew Cooper, Karl Rove, the Deputy White

House Chief of Staff, granted a personal waiver to Mr. Cooper. In an effort to spur Mr. Libby's cooperation and the investigation's progress, four Democratic Members of Congress wrote to Mr. Libby seeking his personal waiver for Ms. Miller. See Letter from the Honorable John Conyers, Jr., et al., to I. Lewis Libby, Chief of Staff, Office of the Vice President (Aug. 8, 2005) ( "Your failure to grant such a waiver to Ms. Miller has apparently lead her to refuse to testify about her conversation(s) with you and, in turn, led to her recent incarceration for civil contempt for days"). While Mr. Libby claimed to have provided Ms. Miller with a personal waiver, Ms. Miller denied that had occurred. See Letter from the Honorable I. Lewis Libby, Chief of Staff, Office of the Vice President, to Judith Miller, New York Times (Sept. 15, 2005); Judith Miller, "Judith Miller's Farewell", the New York Times, Nov. 10, 2005 (letter to the editor) ("After 85 days, more than twice as long as any other American journalist has ever spent in jail for this cause, I agreed to testify before the special prosecutor Patrick J. Fitzgerald's grand jury about my conversations with my source, I. Lewis Libby Jr. I did so only after my two conditions were met: first, that Mr. Libby voluntarily relieve me in writing and by phone of my promise to protect our conversations; and second, that the special prosecutor limit his questions only to those germane to the Valerie Plame Wilson case. Contrary to inaccurate reports, these two agreements could not have been reached before I went to jail."). Furthermore, on September 12, 2005, Mr. Fitzgerald stated quite clearly that he would welcome such a communication reaffirming Mr. Libby's waiver as it might assist the investigation and lead to Ms. Miller's release, lending credence to Ms. Miller's account that there was no personal waiver. See Letter from the Honorable Patrick Fitzgerald, Special Counsel, U.S. Dep't of Justice, to Joseph A. Tate, Dechert LLP (Sept. 12, 2005).

739. Special Counsel Patrick Fitzgerald, Press Conference (Oct. 28, 2005). Indeed, it has not gone unnoticed that this delay—from October 2004 to October 2005—permitted the indictments and disclosure of the Bush Administration's cover-up to be delayed until after President Bush was reelected. As E. J. Dionne wrote in The Washington Post:

Has anyone noticed that the coverup worked? . . . Note the significance of the two dates: October 2004, before President Bush was reelected, and October 2005, after the president was reelected. Those dates make clear why Libby threw sand in the eyes of prosecutors, in the special counsel's apt metaphor, and helped drag out the investigation . . . As long as he was claiming that journalists were responsible for spreading around the name and past CIA employment of Wilson's wife, Valerie Plame, Libby knew that at least some news organizations would resist having reporters testify. The journalistic "shield" was converted into a shield for the Bush Administration's coverup.

E. J. Dionne, Jr., "What the 'Shield' Covered Up", The Washington Post, Nov. 1, 2005, at A25.

740. In a press briefing on September 29, 2003, White House Press Secretary Scott McClellan had the following exchange with reporters:

Q. You said this morning, quote, 'The president knows that Karl Rove wasn't involved.' How does he know that?

McCLELLAN: Well, I've made it very clear that it was a ridiculous suggestion in the first place . . . I've said that it's not true . . . And I have spoken with Karl Rove.

Q: It doesn't take much for the president to ask a senor official working for him to just lay the question out for a few people and end this controversy today.

McCLELLAN: Do you have specific information to bring to our attention? . . . Are we supposed to chase down every anonymous report in the newspaper? We'd spend all our time doing that.

Q: When you talked to Mr. Rove, did you discuss, 'Did you ever have this information?'

McCLELLAN: I've made it very clear, he was not involved, that there's no truth to the suggestion that he was.

McCLELLAN: Dana, I mean, think about what you're asking. If you have specific information to bring to our attention –

Q: No, but you say that—

McCLELLAN:—that suggests White House involvement. There are anonymous reports all the time in the media. The President has set high standards, the highest of standards for people in his administration. He's made it very clear to people in his administration that he expects them to adhere to the highest standards of conduct. If anyone in this administration was involved in it, they would no longer be in this administration.

White House Press Secretary Scott McClellan, Press Briefing (Sept. 29, 2003), available at http:// ww. wwhitehouse.gov/news/releases/2003/09/20030929-7.html.

741. White House Press Secretary Scott McClellan, Press Briefing (Oct. 7, 2003), available at http://www.whitehouse.gov/news/releases/2003/10/20031007-4.html#2:

Q. You have said that you personally went to Scooter Libby (Vice President Dick Cheney's chief of staff), Karl Rove and Elliott Abrams (National Security Council official) to ask them if they were the leakers. Is that was happened? Why did you do that? And can you describe the conversations you had with them? What was the question you asked?

McCLELLAN: Unfortunately, in Washington, DC, at a time like this there are a lot of rumors and innuendo. There are unsubstantiated accusations that are made. And that's exactly what happened in the case of these three individuals. They are good individuals. They are important members of our White House team. And that's why I spoke with them, so that I could come back to you and say that they were not involved. I had no doubt with that in the beginning, but I like to check my information to make sure it's accurate before I report back to you, and that's exactly what I did.

742. ABC News, "The Note" (Sept. 29, 2003), available at http://www.abcnews.go.com/sections/politics /TheNote/TheNote_Sep29.html

743. Meet the Press: Interview with Vice President Dick Cheney (NBC television broadcast, Sept. 14, 2003); see also Richard W. Stevenson & Anne E. Kornblut, "Leak Counsel is Said to Press on Rove's Role", the *New York Times*, Oct. 26, 2005.

744. Libby Indictment 9. This, of course also calls into question Mr. McClellan's denial of this misinformation at an October 30, 2005 White House briefing. Bsked whether the Vice President always told the truth to the American people, Scott McClellan, the White House press secretary apparently answered, "Yes." Richard W. Stevenson & Anne E. Kornblut, "Leak Counsel is Said to Press on Rove's Role", the *New York Times*, Oct. 26, 2005.

745. President George W. Bush, Press Conference (Oct. 28, 2003), available at http://www.whitehouse.gov /news/releases/2003/10/20031028-2.html.

746. President George W. Bush, Press Conference of the President After G8 Summit, (June 10, 2004) available at http://www.whitehouse.gov/news/releases/2004/06/20040610-36.html.

747. President George W. Bush, President, Prime Minister of India Discuss Freedom and Democracy (July 18, 2005), available at http://www.whitehouse.gov/news/releases/2005/7/20050718-1.html.

748. This stands in sharp contrast to when the President offered strong ethical pledges during his first campaign for president, when he said "Americans are tired of investigations and scandal, and the best way to get rid of them is to elect a new president who will bring a new administration, who will restore honor and dignity to the White House." CNN Today (CNN television broadcast Sept. 14, 2000) (video clip of then-Governor George W. Bush).

749. Antonia Zerbisias, "TV Man Is (Shock) Gay, And (Horror) Canadian", *Toronto Star*, July 19, 2003, at A15.

750. As columnist Frank Rich so aptly stated, "When the Bush mob attacks critics like Ms. Sheehan, its highest priority is to change the subject. If we talk about Richard Clarke's character, then we stop talking about the administration's pre-9-11 inattentiveness to terrorism. If Thomas Wilson is trashed as an insubordinate plant of the 'liberal media,' we forget the Pentagon's abysmal failure to give our troops adequate armor (a failure that persists today, eight months after he spoke up). If we focus on Joseph Wilson's wife, we lose the big picture of how the administration twisted intelligence to gin up the threat of Saddam's nonexist-

ent W.M.D.'s." Frank Rich, Op-Ed, "The Swift Boating of Cindy Sheehan", the *New York Times*, Aug. 21, 2005, § 4 at 11; see also Editorial, "Banished Whistle-Blowers", the *New York Times*, Sept. 1, 2005, at A22 ("The Bush Administration is making no secret of its determination to punish whistle-blowers and other federal workers who object to the doctoring of facts that clash with policy and spin.").

751. Editorial, "Banished Whistle-Blowers", the *New York Times*, Sept. 1, 2005, at A22.

752. Department of Defense Budget Priorities FY 2004: Hearing Before the H. Comm. on Budget, 108th Cong. 9 (2003) (statement of the Hon. Paul D. Wolfowitz, Deputy Secretary of Defense)(emphasis added).

753. *Ibid.*

754. *Ibid.*

755. Eric Schmitt, "Pentagon Contradicts on Iraq Occupation Force's Size", the *New York Times*, Feb. 27, 2003, at A1.

756. *Ibid.*

757. Matthew Engel, "Scorned General's Tactics Proved Right", *The Guardian*, Mar. 29, 2003, at 10.

758. Eric Schmitt, "Pentagon Contradicts on Iraq Occupation Force's Size", the *New York Times*, Feb. 27, 2003, at A1.

759. U.S. Army Posture and Acquisition Programs: Hearing Before the Defense Subcomm. of the House Appropriations Comm. 108th Cong. (2003) (statement of Gen. Eric K. Shinseki).

760. Warren P. Strobel and John Walcott, "Post-War Planning Non-Existent", *Knight-Ridder*, Oct. 17, 2004, *available at* http://www.realcities.com/mld/krwashington/9927782.htm. See also Glenn Kessler and Ceci Connolly, "Plenty of Flaws Among the Facts; Candidates Made Questionable Claims", *The Washington Post*, Oct. 9, 2004, at A20.

761. James Fallows, "Bush's Lost Year", *Atlantic Monthly*, Oct. 1, 2004, at 68.

762. Bob Herbert, Op-Ed, "No End in Sight", the *New York Times*, Apr. 2, 2004, at A19.

763. Basu Rekha, "Retaliation Bgainst War Critics", *Des Moines Register*, July 13, 2005, at 11A.

764. See Tom Bowman, "Unceremonious End to Army Career: Outspoken General Fights Demotion", *Baltimore Sun*, May 29, 2005, at 1A.

765. *Ibid.*

766. *Ibid.*

767. *Ibid.*

768. Frank Rich, Op-Ed, "The Swift Boating of Cindy Sheehan", the *New York Times*, Aug. 21, 2005, § 4 at 11.

769. See 60 Minutes (CBS television broadcast, Jan. 11, 2004), available at http://www.cbsnews.com/stories/2004/01/09/60minutes/main592330.shtml ("[N]ine days after that meeting in which O'Neill made it clear he could not publicly support another tax cut, the vice president called and asked him to resign").

770. *Ibid*

771. *Ibid.*

772. *Ibid.*

773. Thom Shanker, "Rumsfeld Says He Contacted Ex-Official on Bush Book", the *New York Times*, Jan. 14, 2004, at A13.

774. Investigation Regarding Release of Documents to Paul H. O'Neill—Former Treasury Secretary, U.S. Department of Treasury, Office of the Inspector General, Mar. 17, 2004.

775. Paul Krugman, Op-Ed, "The Awful Truth", the *New York Times*, Jan. 13, 2004, at A25.

776. Investigation Regarding Release of Documents to Paul H. O'Neill—Former Treasury Secretary, U.S. Department of Treasury, Office of the Inspector General, Mar. 17, 2004.

777. *Ibid.*

778. Paul Krugman, Op-Ed, "The Awful Truth", the *New York Times*, Jan. 13, 2004, at A25.

779. Sidney Blumenthal, "He Cannot Tell a Lie", *Salon*, Jan. 15, 2004, available at http://archive.salon.com /opinion/blumenthal/2004/01/15/o_neill/index_np.html?x.

780. "O'Neill: Bush Planned Iraq Invasion Before 9-11", *CNN.com*, Jan. 10, 2004, available at http://www.cnn.com/2004/ALLPOLITICS/01/10/oneill.bush/.

781. *Ibid.*

782. Edmund L. Andrews, "Upheaval in the Treasury: Bush, In Shake-Up of Cabinet, Ousts Treasury Leader", the *New York Times*, Dec. 7, 2002, at A1.

783. The Congressional Research Service, after looking at actual money spent and appropriated for Fiscal Year 2006, estimates the cost of the Iraq war at $ 251 Billion. Amy Belasco, "The Cost of Iraq, Afghanistan and Enhanced Base Security Since 9-11", *Congressional Research Service*, Oct. 7, 2005.

784. Frank Rich, Op-Ed, "Bring Back Warren Harding", the *New York Times*, Sep. 25, 2005.

785. Corbett B. Daly, "Ex-Bush Aide: Iraq War Planning Began After 9-11", *CNN.com*, May 20, 2004, available at http://www.cnn.com/2004/US/03/20/clarke.cbs/.

786. 60 Minutes (CBS television broadcast, Mar. 21, 2004), available at http://www.cbsnews.com/stories/2004/03/19/60minutes/main607356.shtml.

787. *Ibid.*

788. *Ibid.*

789. Judith Miller, "Former Terrorism Official Faults White House on 9-11", the *New York Times*, Mar. 22, 2004, at A18.

790. Press Secretary Scott McClellan, White House Press Briefing (Mar. 22, 2004), available at http://www.whitehouse.gov/news/releases/2004/03/20040322-4.html.

791. Good Morning America (ABC television broadcast, Mar. 22, 2004).

792. The Rush Limbaugh Show: Interview with Vice President Dick Cheney (Mar. 22, 2004), available at http://www.rushlimbaugh.com/home/daily/site__032204/content/stack_a.guest.html.

793. 150 Cong. Rec. S3209 (daily ed. Mar. 26, 2004) (statement of Sen. Frist).

794. Joe Conason, "Richard Clarke Terrorizes the White House", *Salon*, Mar. 24, 2004 (emphasis added), available at http://archive.salon.com/news/feature/2004/03/24/clarke/print.html.

795. Sidney Blumenthal, "Bush's War—Bgainst Richard Clarke", *Salon*.com, Mar. 25, 2004, available at http://archive.salon.com/opinion/blumenthal/2004/03/25/clarke/print.html.

796. Ryan Lizza, "Logic Jam", *The New Republic Online*, Mar. 24, 2004, available at http://www.tnr.com /doc.mhtml?i=express&s=lizza032304.

797. In addition, on August 10, 2005, Congressman Conyers and 41 other members of Congress signed a letter to President Bush asking him to meet with Ms. Sheehan. See Letter from Congressman John Conyers, Jr., Ranking Member, House Committee on the Judiciary, et al., to President George W. Bush (Aug. 10, 2005), available at http://www.house.gov/judiciary_democrats/letters/presssheehanltr81005.pdf.

798. Bush's decision not to meet with Sheehan is a perfect example of what Maureen Dowd describes as Bush's life in "meta-insulation. His rigidly controlled environment allows no chance encounters with anyone who disagrees. He never has to defend himself to anyone, and that is cognitively injurious." Maureen Dowd, Op-Ed, "Why No Tea and Sympathy?", the *New York Times*, Aug. 10, 2005, at A21.

799. *Ibid.*

800. Frank Rich, Op-Ed, "The Swift Boating of Cindy Sheehan", the *New York Times*, Aug. 21, 2005, § 4 at 11.

801. *Ibid.*

802. Elisabeth Bumiller, "For 3rd Day in a Row, Bush Says Withdrawal Now From Iraq Would Embolden Terrorists", the *New York Times*, Aug. 25, 2005, at A10.

803. Ahmed Amr, "Counteroffensive: Bush Launches 'Operation Cindy Sheehan'", *Palestine Chronicle*, Aug. 28, 2005 (emphasis added), available at www.globalresearch.ca/index.php?context=viewArticle&code =AMR20050828&articleId=875.

804. Frank Rich, Op-Ed, "Eight Days in July", the *New York Times*, July 24, 2005, § 4 at 13.

805. Antonia Zerbisias, "TV Man Is (Shock) Gay, And (Horror) Canadian", *Toronto Star*, July 19, 2003, at A15.

806. *Ibid.*

807. *Ibid.*

808. See Lloyd Grove, "The Reliable Source", *The Washington Post*, July 18, 2003, at C3; see also Editorial, Matt Drudge, a Gay Who Backs the Gay Bashers, Part II, Buzzflash.com, July 15, 2004, available at www.buzzflash.com/editorial/04/07/edi04051.html.

809. Lloyd Grove, "The Reliable Source", *The Washington Post*, July 18, 2003, at C3 (emphasis added).

810. Antonia Zerbisias, "TV Man Is (Shock) Gay, And (Horror) Canadian", *Toronto Star*, July 19, 2003, at A15 (emphasis added).

811. See Frank Rich, Op-Ed, "Eight Days in July", *The New York Times*, July 24, 2005, § 4 at 13.

812. See George Monbiot, "Chemical Coup D'Etat: The U.S. Wants to Depose the Diplomat Who Could Take Away Its Pretext for War With Iraq", *The Guardian*, Apr. 16, 2002, available at http://www.guardian .co.uk/Archive/Article/0,4273,4394862,00.html.

813. Charles J. Hanley, "Bolton Said to Orchestrate Unlawful Firing", Associated *Press*, June 5, 2005, available at http://www.commondreams.org/headlines05/0605-05.htm.

814. See "AP Probe on Bolton Finds Disturbing Links to Iraq War", Associated *Press*, June 4, 2005, available at http://www.mediainfo.com/eandp/news/article_display.jsp?vnu_content_id=1000946569.

815. *Ibid.*

816. *Ibid.*

817. Charles J. Hanley, "Bolton Said to Orchestrate Unlawful Firing", Associated *Press*, June 5, 2005 (emphasis added).

818. "AP Probe on Bolton Finds Disturbing Links to Iraq War", Associated *Press*, June 4, 2005 (emphasis added), available at http://www.mediainfo.com/eandp/news/article_display.jsp?vnu_content_id= 1000946569.

819. George Monbiot, "Chemical Coup D'Etat: The U.S. Wants to Depose the Diplomat Who Could Take Away Its Pretext for War With Iraq", *The Guardian*, Apr. 16, 2002 (emphasis added), available at http://www.guardian.co.uk/Archive/Article/0,4273,4394862,00.html.

820. "AP Probe on Bolton Finds Disturbing Links to Iraq War", Associated *Press*, June 4, 2005, available at http://www.mediainfo.com/eandp/news/article_display.jsp?vnu_content_id=1000946569.

821. *Ibid.*

822. *Ibid.*

823. Meet the Press: Interview with Vice President Dick Cheney (NBC television broadcast, March 16, 2003), available at http://msnbc.msn.com/id/3080244/.

824. Dafna Linzer, "Nuclear Arms Inspectors Get Peace Prize", *The Washington Post*, Oct. 8, 2005, at A1.

825. Craig S. Smith, "Atomic Agency and Chief Win the Peace Prize", the *New York Times*, Oct. 8, 2005, at A1 (emphasis added).

826. *Ibid.* (emphasis added).

827. *Ibid.*

828. Erik Eckholm, "A Top U.S. Contracting Official for the Army Calls for an Inquiry in the Halliburton Case", the *New York Times*, Oct. 25, 2004, at A13.

829. *Ibid.*

830. An Oversight Hearing on Waste, Fraud, and Abuse in U.S. Government Contracting in Iraq Before the Senate Democratic Policy Comm., 109th Cong. (2005) (statement of Bunnatine Greenhouse), available at http://democrats.senate.gov/dpc/hearings/hearing22/transcript.pdf.

831. *Ibid.*

832. *Ibid.*

833. Erik Eckholm, "Army Contract Official Critical of Halliburton Pact Is Demoted", the *New York Times*, Aug. 29, 2005, at A9.

834. Frank Rich, Op-Ed, "Bring Back Warren Harding", the *New York Times*, Sept. 25, 2005, § 4, at 11.

835. Christian Miller, "Democrats Demand Probe of Demotion", *Los Angeles Times*, Aug. 30, 2005, at A8.

836. Mark Danner, "The Secret Way to War", 2 N.Y. Rev. of Books 10, June 9, 2005.

837. Seymour M. Hersh, "The Stovepipe", *The New Yorker*, Oct. 27, 2003, at 77.

838. E.J. Dionne Jr., Op-Ed, "What the 'Shield' Covered Up", *The Washington Post*, Nov. 1, 2005, at A25 (emphasis added).

839. The Administration's efforts to pressure the CIA to manipulate the intelligence is discussed in more detail in Section III(B): Misstating and Manipulating the Intelligence to Justify Pre-emptive War.

840. *Ibid.*

841. *Ibid.*

842. *Ibid.*

843. See Seymour M. Hersh, "The Coming Wars", *The New Yorker*, January 24, 2005, at 40.

844. *Ibid.*

845. The Administration's efforts to retaliate against CIA officials seeking to set the record straight on the Iraqi defector known as "Curveball" is discussed in greater detail in Section III(B)(5): Misstating and Manipulating the Intelligence to Justify Pre-emptive War: Chemical and Biological Weapons (emphasis added).

846. Bob Drogin and John Goetz, "How U.S. Fell Under the Spell of 'Curveball'", *Los Angeles Times*, Nov. 20, 2005, at A1 (emphasis added).

847. *Ibid.*

848. *Ibid.* (emphasis added).

849. James Risen, "Spy's Notes on Iraqi Aims Were Shelved, Suit Says", the *New York Times*, Aug. 1, 2005, at A8.

850. *Ibid.*

851. See *Ibid.*

852. See *Ibid.*

853. Robert Parry, Why U.S. Intelligence Failed, Consortiumnews.com, Oct. 22, 2003, available at http://www.consortiumnews.com/2003/102203.html. According to Robert Parry:

As the Iraqi death toll mounts and the price tag for the U.S. occupation grows, a similar process of intelligence manipulation is now being applied to the so-called 'reconstruction' phase. Bush and his surrogates are picking and choosing the evidence that is designed to sell the public on the notion that 'Operation Iraqi Freedom' is still going great. The administration's misleading rhetoric has switched from exaggerating the danger posed by Saddam Hussein to exaggerating the gains attributable to the invasion. New half-truths and lies are quickly replacing the old ones, lest Americans begin to wonder how they had been misled by the previous bogus rationales.

854. President George W. Bush, Remarks from the USS Abraham Lincoln (May 1, 2003), available at http://www.whitehouse.gov/news/releases/2003/05/iraq/20030501-15.html.

855. Secretary Donald H. Rumsfeld, Department of Defense News Transcript (June 18, 2003), available at http://www.dod.mil/transcripts/2003/tr20030618-secdef0282.html.

856. "Iraq insurgency in 'last throes' Cheney says", CNN.com, June 20, 2005, available at http://www.cnn.com/2005/US/05/30/cheney.iraq/.

857. Face the Nation: Interview with Secretary Donald H. Rumsfeld (CBS television broadcast, Mar. 14, 2004).

858. President George W. Bush, Press Conference (Oct. 4, 2005), available at http://www.whitehouse.gov/news/releases/2005/10/20051004-1.html.

859. Dave Moniz, "Ex-Army Boss: Pentagon Won't Admit Reality in Iraq", *USA Today*, June 2, 2003, at 1A.

860. *Ibid.*

861. See e.g., 60 Minutes: Interview with General Anthony Zinni (CBS television broadcast, May 21, 2004), available at http://www.cbsnews.com/stories/2004/05/21/60minutes/main618896.shtm.

862. Joe Klein, "Saddam's Revenge: The Secret History of U.S. Mistakes, Misjudgments and Intelligence Failures that Let the Dictator and His Allies Launch an Insurgency Now Ripping Iraq Apart", *Time*, Sept. 26, 2005, at 44.

863. See Testimony on the United States Military Strategy and Operations in Iraq and the Central Command Area: Hearing Before the S. Comm. on Armed Services, 109th. Cong. (2005) (Testimony of John P. Abizaid, U.S. Army, Commander, U.S. Central Command).

864. Eric Schmitt, "Iraqis Not Ready to Fight Rebels on Their Own, U.S. Says", the *New York Times*, July 20, 2005, at A1.

865. Frank Rich, Op-Ed, "The Faith-Based President Defrocked", the *New York Times*, Oct. 9, 2005, §4, at 13.

866. Frank Rich, Op-Ed, "The Vietnamization of Bush's Vacation", the *New York Times*, Aug. 28, 2005.

867. See Minority Staff of H. Comm. on Gov't Reform, 109th Cong., The Bush Administration Record: The Reconstruction of Iraq (2005), available at http://www.democrats.reform.house.gov/Documents/20051018102134-35570.pdf.

868. *Ibid.*

869. Rick Jervis, "Iraq Rebuilding Slows as U.S. Money for Projects Dries Up", *USA Today*, Oct. 10, 2005, at 1A (emphasis added).

870. Dana Milbank, "Curtains Ordered for Media Coverage of Returning Coffins", *The Washington Post*, Oct. 21, 2003, at A23.

871. Bradley Graham, "Enemy Body Counts Revived: U.S. Is Citing Tolls to Show Success in Iraq", *The Washington Post*, Oct 24, 2005, at A1.

872. According to the Village Voice, "The soldier on the left side of the front row was actually a flack herself, though she didn't reveal it during the regime's 24-minute infomercial. Her name is Corine Lombardo....David Axe, who's made several forays into Iraq for the Voice ... knows Corine Lombardo from having spent time in Tikrit. He tells me: 'Her job when I was with the 42nd Infantry Division included taking reporters to lunch. She lives in a fortified compound in Tikrit and rarely leaves. Many public-affairs types in Iraq never leave their bases, and they're speaking for those who do the fighting and dying.'" "Bush Launches New Flack Attack", *Village Voice*, Oct. 13, 2005, available at http://www.villagevoice.com/blogs/bushbeat/archive/001948.php.

873. CNN Live at Daybreak (CNN television broadcast, Oct. 14, 2005), available at http://transcripts.cnn.com/TRANSCRIPTS/0510/14/lad.04.html (emphasis added).

874. Mark Mazzetti & Borzou Daragahi, "U.S. Military Covertly Pays to Run Stories in Iraqi Press", *Los Angeles Times*, Nov. 30, 2005, at 1.

875. Jeff Gerth, "Military's Information War Is Vast and Often Secretive", the *New York Times*, Dec. 11, 2005, at 1.

876. Mark Mazzetti & Borzou Daragahi, "U.S. Military Covertly Pays to Run Stories in Iraqi Press", *Los Angeles Times*, Nov. 30, 2005, at 1.

877. Jeff Gerth, "Military's Information War Is Vast and Often Secretive", the *New York Times*, Dec. 11, 2005, at 1.

878. Maureen Dowd, Op-Ed, "W's Head in the Sand", the *New York Times*, Dec. 3, 2005, at A29.

879. Jeff Gerth, "Military's Information War Is Vast and Often Secretive", the *New York Times*, Dec. 11, 2005, at 1.

880. *Ibid.*

881. The Lincoln Group has signed a $16 million propaganda contract with the Pentagon and disseminated false stories such as the claim that Adnan Ihsan Saeed al-Haideri had helped buy tons of biological, nuclear and chemical weapons described in Section III.B.5 above. James Bamford, "The Man Who Sold the War", *Rolling Stone*. Nov.17, 2005, at 52-62.

882. "The Information Collection Program succeeded in heavily influencing coverage in the Western press in the run-up to the war. A report issued by the Defense Intelligence Agency last fall concluded that almost all the information given to the government through the ICP and its roster of defectors before the war was useless.... [Although] the group's agreement with the State Department strictly barred the INC from "attempting to influence the policies of the United States government or Congress, or propagandizing the American people.... There is little doubt that influencing public opinion through the American and European media was always central to the INC's mission (of the 108 stories on Qanbar's list, fifty appeared in U.S. news outlets.)" Douglas McCollam, "How Chalabi Played the Press", *Columbia Journalism Review*, July/August 2004, available at www.cjr.org/issues/2004/4/mccollam-list.asp.

883. Editorial, "Plan: We Win", the *New York Times*, Dec. 1, 2005, at A32.

884. Maureen Dowd, Op-Ed, "W's Head in the Sand", the *New York Times*, Dec. 3, 2005, at A29.

885. Scott Shane, "Bush's Speech On Iraq Echoes Analyst's Voice", the *New York Times*, Dec. 4, 2005, at 1 (emphasis added).

886. Elizabeth Bumiller, "Threats and Responses: The Cost; White House Cuts Estimate of Cost of War With Iraq", the *New York Times*, Dec. 31, 2002, at A1.

887. Hearing Before the House Armed Services Committee, 108th Cong. (2004).

888. See H.R. J. Res. 73, 109th Cong., 1st Sess. (2005).

889. Carl Kaysen, et. al, "War With Iraq: Costs, Consequences and Alternatives" (2002), *available at* http://www.amacad.org/publications/monographs/War_with_Iraq.pdf.

890. Linda Bilmes, "The Trillion-Dollar War", the *New York Times*, Aug. 20, 2005, at A13.

891. *Ibid.*

892. John Daniszewski, "New Memos Detail Early Plans for Invading Iraq", *Los Angeles Times*, June 15, 2005, at A1.

893. See Letter to President George W. Bush (June 16, 2005), *available at* http://www.johnconyers.com/index.asp?Type'sUPERFORMS&SEC={8771D3DA-2F3D-49F7-895C-DF473CAEFA2C}. As of December 19, 2005, there has been no response from the Bush Administration.

894. President George W. Bush, Interview by TVP, Poland (May 29, 2003), *available at* http://www.white-house.gov/g8/interview5.html (emphasis added).

895. President George W. Bush, Remarks at a Press Conference with British Prime Minster Tony Blair (July 17, 2003), *available at* http://www.whitehouse.gov/news/releases/2003/07/20030717-9.html (emphasis added).

896. ABC News This Week (ABC television broadcast, Mar. 30, 2003).

897. James Risen, "Ex-Inspector Says C.I.A. Missed Disarray in Iraqi Arms Program", the *New York Times*, Jan. 26, 2004, at A1.

898. Face the Nation (CBS television broadcast, July 13, 2003) (emphasis added).

899. Press Briefing on Iraq Weapons of Mass Destruction and the State of the Union Speech, (July 22, 2003) *available at* http://www.whitehouse.gov/news/releases/2003/07/20030722-12.html.

900. National Intelligence Council, Iraq's Continuing Program for Weapons of Mass Destruction: Key Judgements (from October 2002 NIE) (declassified July 18, 2003).

901. President George W. Bush, State of the Union Address (Jan. 20, 2004), *available at* http://www.whitehouse.gov/news/releases/2004/01/20040120-7.html.

902. Judy Keen, "Cheney Says its Too Soon to Tell on Iraqi Arms", *USA Today*, Jan. 19, 2004, at 7A; see also Maura Reynolds, "Cheney Calls Ex-Friend O'Neill a 'Big Disappointment'", *Los Angeles Times*, Jan. 19, 2004, at A22.

903. Dana Milbank & Mike Allen, "U.S. Shifts Rhetoric On Its Goals in Iraq", *The Washington Post*, Aug. 1, 2003, at A14.

904. "Wolfowitz: WMD secondary issue in Iraq", *USA Today*, July 22, 2003, *available at* http://www.usatoday.com/news/world/iraq/2003-07-22-wolfowitz-iraq_x.htm.

905. President George W. Bush, Press Conference (Apr. 13, 2004), *available at* http://www.whitehouse.gov/news/releases/2004/04/20040413-20.html.

906. Iraqi Mobile Biological Warfare Agent Production Plants, CIA/DIA Report, May 28, 2003, *available at* http://www.cia.gov/cia/reports/iraqi_mobile_plants/paper_w.pdf.

907. Secretary Colin Powell, Interview with French Television (May 22, 2003), *available at* http://www.state.gov/secretary/former/powell/remarks/2003/20908.htm.

908. Douglas Jehl, Iraqi Trailers Said to Make Hydrogen, "Not Biological Arms", the *New York Times*, August 9, 2003, at A1.

909. *Ibid.*

910. Douglas Jehl & David E. Sanger, "Powell's Case, a Year Later: Gaps in Picture of Iraq Arms", the *New York Times*, Feb. 1, 2004, at 1.

911. Joseph Cirincione, Jessica Tuchman Mathews, and George Perkovich, with Alexis Orton, "WMD in Iraq: Evidence and Implications", *Carnegie Endowment Report*, January 2004, at 36, *available at* http://www.carnegieendowment.org/publications/index.cfm?fa=view&id=1435&prog=zgp&proj=znpp.

912. Statement by David Kay on the Interim Progress Report on the Activities of the Iraq Survey Group (ISG) before the House Permanent Select Committee on Intelligence, the House Committee on Appropriations, Subcommittee on Defense, and the Senate Select Committee on Intelligence (Oct. 2, 2003).

913. *Ibid.*

914. Bob Drogin and John Goetz, How U.S. Fell Under the Spell of 'Curveball', *Los Angeles Times*, Nov. 20, 2005, at 13.

915. *Ibid.* (emphasis added).

916. *Ibid.*

917. *Ibid.*

918. *Ibid.*

919. *Ibid.* (emphasis added).

920. *Ibid.*

921. David Barstow, William J. Broad, & Jeff Gerth, "How the White House Embraced Disputed Iraqi Arms Intelligence", the *New York Times*, Oct. 3, 2004, at A1.

922. *Ibid.*

923. Judd Legum, Faiz Shakir, Nico Pitney, Amanda Terkel, Payson Schwin, and Christy Harvey, The Progress Report, American Progress Action Fund, Nov. 17, 2005.

924. Frank Rich, "One Step Closer to the Big Enchilada", the *New York Times*, Oct. 30, 2005, at 12.

925. *Meet the Press*: Interview with Vice President Dick Cheney (NBC television broadcast, Dec. 9, 2001).

926. President George W. Bush, Remarks to Military Personnel at Fort Polk, Louisiana (Feb. 17, 2004), *available at* http://www.whitehouse.gov/news/releases/2004/02/20040217-5.html.

927. He said that "those people who have looked at that issue, some committees on the Hill in Congress, and also the Silberman-Robb Commission, have concluded that it did not happen."

928. Editorial, "Decoding Mr. Bush's Denials", the *New York Times*, Oct. 15, 2005, at 26.

929. Dana Milbank and Walter Pincus, "Asterisks Dot White House's Iraq Argument", *The Washington Post*, Nov. 12, 2005, at A1.

930. Peter Baker & Susan B. Glasser, Bush Says 10 Plots by Al Qaeda Were Foiled, *The Washington Post*, Oct. 7, 2005, at A1.

931. Frank Rich, Falluja Floods the Superdome, the *New York Times*, Sept. 4, 2005, §4, at 10.

932. Peter Baker & Susan B. Glasser, "Bush Says 10 Plots by Al Qaeda Were Foiled", *The Washington Post*, Oct. 7, 2005, at A1.

933. *Ibid.*

934. David Broder, "Our Back-Seat Congress", *The Washington Post*, Sept. 4, 2005, at B07 (emphasis added).

935. H. R. R. XIII § 7, 109th Cong. (2005) (Resolutions of Inquiry) (describing procedure used to request documents from the Executive Branch. Under House rules, a Resolution of Inquiry is to be voted on by all Members of Congress unless negative action is taken in the relevant committee within 14 legislative days).

936. Letter from the Honorable John Conyers, Jr., Ranking Member, House Judiciary Committee, et al., to the Honorable George W. Bush, President (May 5, 2005), *available at* http://www.house.gov/judiciary _democrats/letters/bushsecretmemoltr5505.pdf. Throughout the month, 39 members added their names to the letter, bringing the total of members seeking answers to 122, including Leader Pelosi.

937. On May 17, 2005, Scott McClellan told reporters that the White House saw "no need" to respond to the letter from Congress regarding the Downing Street Minutes. See Kelley Beaucar Vlahos, Downing Street Memo mostly ignored in US, FoxNews.com., June 1, 2005, *available at* http://www.foxnews.com /story/0,2933,158228,00.html. Again on June 16, 2005, during a press briefing, McClellan was asked if the President had responded to the letter that Representative Conyers and 88 other members of Congress had sent. (The correct number is 89). The following dialogue ensued:

Q:Has the President or anyone else responded?

MR. McCLELLAN: Not that I'm aware of.

Q Why not?

MR. McCLELLAN: Why not? Because I think that this is an individual who voted against the war in the first place and is simply trying to rehash old debates that have already been addressed. And our focus is not on the past. It's on the future and working to make sure we succeed in Iraq.

These matters have been addressed, Elaine. I think you know that very well. The press—

Q Scott, 88 members of Congress signed that letter.

MR. McCLELLAN: The press—the press have covered it, as well.

Q What do you say about them?

Q But, Scott, don't they deserve the courtesy of a response back?

MR. McCLELLAN: Again, this has been addressed. Go ahead.

Q Scott, on John Conyers, John Conyers is walking here with that letter again, as you have acknowledged from Elaine's comment. But 88 leaders on Capitol Hill signed that letter. Now, I understand what you're saying about him, but what about the other 88 who signed this letter, wanting information, answers to these five questions?

MR. McCLELLAN: How did they vote on the war—the decision to go to war in Iraq?

Q Well, you have two—well, if that's the case, you have two Republicans who are looking for a timetable. How do you justify that?

MR. McCLELLAN: I already talked about that.

Q I understand, but let's talk about this.

MR. McCLELLAN: Like I said—

Q Well, just because—I understand—but wait a minute, that's not—if leaders from Congress—if you're talking about unifying and asking for everyone to come together, why not answer, whether they wanted the war or not, answer a letter where John Conyers wrote to the President and then 88 congressional leaders signed? Why not answer that?

MR. McCLELLAN: For the reasons I stated earlier. This is simply rehashing old debates that have already been discussed.

See White House Press Secretary Scott McClellan, Press Briefing (June 16, 2005) (transcript *available at* http://www.whitehouse.gov/news/releases/2005/06/20050616-5.html.

938. Letter from the Honorable John Conyers, Jr., Ranking Member, Committee on the Judiciary, to the Honorable Donald H. Rumsfeld, Secretary of Defense (May 31, 2005), *available at* http://www.house.gov/judiciary_democrats/letters/rumsfeldairstrikesltr53105.pdf.

939. Letter from Peter W. Rodman to the Honorable John Conyers, Jr., Ranking Member, Committee on the Judiciary (July 28, 2005), *available at* http://www.house.gov/judiciary_democrats/responses/rumsfeldairstrikesresp72805.pdf.

940. Letter from the Honorable John Conyers, Jr., Ranking Member, Committee on the Judiciary, et al., to the Honorable James Sensenbrenner, Jr., Chairman, Committee on the Judiciary; the Honorable Duncan Hunter, Chairman, Committee on Armed Forces; the Honorable Henry J. Hyde, Chairman, Committee on International Relations; and the Honorable Peter Hoekstra, Chairman, Permanent Select Committee on Intelligence (June 30, 2005), *available at* http://www.house.gov/judiciary_democrats/letters/chair-downingltr63005.pdf.

941. Letter from the Honorable John F. Kerry, et al., to the Honorable Pat Roberts, Chairman, Select Committee on Intelligence, and the Honorable John D. Rockefeller, IV, Vice Chairman, Select Committee on Intelligence (June 22, 2005), *available at* http://www.kerry.senate.gov/v3/headlines/pdf/SSCI_Letter_Downing_Street.pdf.

942. Letter from the Honorable Pat Roberts, Chairman, Select Committee on Intelligence, to the Honorable John F. Kerry (July 20, 2005).

943. Letter from the Honorable John Conyers, Jr., Ranking Member, House Judiciary Committee, et al., to Mr. Brett Gerry, Associate Counsel, Office of Counsel to the President; Ms. Margaret P. Grafeld, Information and Privacy Coordinator, U.S. Department of State; and Mr. C.Y. Talbott, Chief, Office of Freedom of Information and Security Review, U.S. Department of Defense (June 30, 2005), *available at* http://www.house.gov/judiciary_democrats/letters/downingfoialtr63005.pdf.

944. Neither the State Department nor the White House responded to the original FOIA request within the prescribed period of time. Thus, on August 11, 2005, Representative Conyers sent a follow-up letter requesting the information. See Letter from the Honorable John Conyers, Jr., Ranking Member, House Judiciary Committee, to Mr. Brett Gerry, Associate Counsel, Office of Counsel to the President, and Ms. Margaret P. Grafeld, Information and Privacy Coordinator, U.S. Department of State (Aug. 11, 2005), *available at* http://www.house.gov/judiciary_democrats/letters/downingfoiafollowupltr81105.pdf.

The State Department then called the House Judiciary Committee Democratic staff asking for a clarification letter. That letter was sent on September 19, 2005, see Letter from the Honorable John Conyers, Jr.,

Ranking Member, House Judiciary Committee, to Ms. Charlene Wright Thomas, Chief, Requestor/Liaison Division, U.S. Department of State (Sept. 19, 2005), *available at* http://www.house.gov/judiciary_democrats/letters/dosfollowupfoialtr91905.pdf, and the State Department responded on September 27, 2005, stating that the request was being processed. See Letter from Lorraine B. Temple, Requester Communications Branch, U.S. Department of State, to the Honorable John Conyers, Jr., Ranking Member, House Judiciary Committee (September 27, 2005), *available at* http://www.house.gov/judiciary_democrats/responses/dosfollowupfoiaresp92705.pdf. Since then, staff members have called periodically to check on the status of the request but have been told on each occasion that the Department is still working on it. To date, the White House has neither responded to nor acknowledged these requests.

The Department of Defense responded by phone call to the House Judiciary Committee Democratic staff, asking for a clarification letter. The Department stated that the request was very lengthy and complex and that it would behoove the signatories to narrow the request so that the Department could more easily comply. Per the Department's statements, Congressman Conyers sent a clarification letter—with specific changes suggested by the Department—on July 28, 2005. See Letter from the Honorable John Conyers, Jr., Ranking Member, House Judiciary Committee, to Mr. Jim Hogan, Office of Freedom of Information and Security Review, U.S. Department of Defense (July 28, 2005), *available at* http://www.house.gov /judiciary_democrats/letters/downingfoiafollowupltr72805.pdf.

After waiting several months for a response, Congressman Conyers finally received a letter on November 30, 2005, stating that the "revised request is still highly complex and will take a considerable time to process," despite the fact that specific changes were made to avoid this result. See Letter from Will Kramer, Chief, Office of Freedom of Information, Department of Defense, to the Honorable John Conyers, Jr. The Department also denied the request for a fee waiver because the request "offered no information on how you plan to disseminate the information to the general public." Ibid. In addition, the Department indicated that the request will be significantly delayed because the Department will not even begin to process the request until receiving a statement of willingness to pay applicable fees, which the Department estimates to be around $110,000, not including reproduction charges. This decision is appealable, but such an appeal would come at the expense of having to wait months, if not years, before receiving information of vital public import.

945. H.R. Res. 375, 109th Cong. (2005). Congressman Maurice Hinchey introduced a similar resolution requesting "all documents in the possession of the President and Secretary of Defense relating to communications with officials of the United Kingdom related to the policy of the United States with respect to Iraq." H.R. Res. 408, 109th Cong. (2005). The International Relations Committee reported the resolution adversely to the House by a record vote of 23 yeas to 22 nays. H.R. Rep. No. 109-224 (2005).

946. H.R. Rep. No. 109-223 (2005).

947. Letter from the Honorable Henry A. Waxman, Ranking Member, Committee on Government Reform, to Dr. Condoleezza Rice, Assistant to the President for NSA (June 10, 2003); Letter from the Honorable Henry A. Waxman, Ranking Member, Committee on Government Reform, to Dr. Condoleezza Rice, Assistant to the President for NSA (July 29, 2003).

948. Letter from the Honorable Henry A. Waxman, Ranking Member, Committee on Government Reform, to Secretary of State Colin L. Powell (July 21, 2003).

949. Letter from the Honorable Henry A. Waxman, Ranking Member, Committee on Government Reform, to President George W. Bush (March 17, 2003); Letter from the Honorable Henry A. Waxman, Ranking Member, Committee on Government Reform, to President George W. Bush (June 2, 2003).

950. Even though Secretary of State Powell responded, National Security Advisor Rice ignored the two requests. President Bush's response to Representative Waxman's March 17, 2003 was an ambiguous one-page letter from the State Department and the President did not respond to Mr. Waxman's letter of June 2, 2003.

951. Letter from the Honorable Nancy Pelosi, et al., to President George W. Bush (Feb. 2, 2004), *available at* http://www.house.gov/pelosi/press/releases/Feb04/IraqReview020204.html. An independent review was essential because the Commission established by President Bush in February 2004, the Silberman-Robb

Commission on Intelligence Capabilities of the United States Regarding Weapons of Mass Destruction, was limited to investigating how intelligence was developed and did not authorize inquiry into how policymakers used the intelligence. In fact, the Commission was barred from interviewing President Bush and Vice President Cheney.

952. These assessments were relegated to a "Phase II" of the investigation, which Chairman Roberts more or less abandoned, stating that "we have now heard it all regarding prewar intelligence. I think that it would be a monumental waste of time to replow this ground any further." Remarks by the Honorable Pat Roberts on the WMD Commission Report (Mar. 31, 2005), *available at* http://roberts.senate.gov/03-31-2005.htm.

953. Shaun Waterman, Robert calls for constant change in intel, UPI, March 10, 2003, *available at* http://www.washtimes.com/upi-breaking/20050310-060505-9514r.htm.

954. Letter from the Honorable Dianne Feinstein to the Honorable Pat Roberts, Chairman, Senate Intelligence Committee (July 29, 2005), *available at* http://feinstein.senate.gov/05releases/r-intel-robrts.htm.

955. See 151 Cong. Rec. 142, S12099 (daily ed. Nov. 1, 2005). Senator Reid also issued a fact sheet to reporters showing that at every turn, "Republicans have blocked efforts to investigate how intelligence was used in the run-up to the war in Iraq." Democrats detail times their efforts to examine intel were blocked, The Raw Story, Nov. 1, 2005, *available at* http://rawstory.com/news/2005/Democrats_detail_times _their_effort_to_1101.html. The fact sheet details a timeline from March 2003 through September 2005 of letters and requests for information and hearings. The vast majority of these requests were either ignored or glossed-over by the Administration and Republicans in Congress. *Ibid.*

956. Memorandum from the Honorable Jane Harman, Ranking Member, Permanent Select Committee on Intelligence, to the Honorable Peter Hoekstra, Chairman, Permanent Select Committee on Intelligence (Nov. 4, 2005), *available at* http://www.house.gov/harman/press/releases/2005/051110_pre-war.html.

957. Letter from the Honorable Peter Hoekstra, Chairman, Permanent Select Committee on Intelligence, to the Honorable Jane Harman, Ranking Member, Permanent Select Committee on Intelligence (Nov. 10, 2005).

958. Letter from the Honorable Henry Waxman, Ranking Member, House Government Reform Committee, to the Honorable Tom Davis, Chairman, House Government Reform Committee (Oct. 4, 2005), *available at* http://www.democrats.reform.house.gov/story.asp?ID=710&Issue=Iraq+Intelligence+and+Nuclear +Evidence

959. Letter from the Honorable Henry Waxman, Ranking Member, Committee on Government Reform, to the Honorable Porter J. Goss, Chairman, Permanent Select Committee on Intelligence, and the Honorable Jane Harman, Ranking Member, Permanent Select Committee on Intelligence (July 15, 2003), *available at* http://www.democrats.reform.house.gov/story.asp?ID=327&Issue=Iraq+Intelligence+and +Nuclear+Evidence. The request was for hearings on President Bush's use of the false information about Iraq's nuclear capacity in the State of the Union address.

960. Letter from the Honorable Jerrold Nadler to the Honorable F. James Sensenbrenner, Jr., Chairman, Committee on the Judiciary (Oct. 31, 2005), *available at* http://www.house.gov/apps/list/press /ny08_nadler/JudHearingIraqWar103105.html.

961. 151 Cong. Rec. H9566-H9568 (daily ed. November 3, 2005) (Privileged Resolutions on Iraq).

962. *Ibid.*

963. *Ibid.*

964. H. Res. 549, 109th Cong. (2005).

965. Representative Kucinich also introduced H. Res. 505, which sought documents and records relating to White House Iraq Group, which was organized by Andrew Card and consists of Karl Rove, Karen Hughes, Mary Matalin, Nicholas E. Calio, James R. Wilkinson, Condoleezza Rice, Stephen Hadley and I. Lewis Libby. The resolution was defeated on a party line vote. H. Res. 505, 109th Cong. (2005).

966. Markup of H.Res. 549, before the H. Comm. on Int'l Relations, 109th Cong. (2005).

967. Letter from the Honorable John Conyers, Jr., Ranking Member, House Judiciary Committee, et al., to the

Honorable F. James Sensenbrenner, Chairman, House Judiciary Committee (June 17, 2004).

968. Letter from the Honorable Henry A. Waxman, Ranking Member, Committee on Government Reform, to the Honorable Tom Davis, Chairman, Committee on Government Reform (May 4, 2004).

969. Letter from the Honorable Henry A. Waxman, Ranking Member, Committee on Government Reform, the Honorable John Conyers, Jr., Ranking Member, Committee on the Judiciary, the Honorable David R. Obey, Ranking Member, Committee on Appropriations, the Honorable Ike Skelton, Ranking Member, Committee on Armed Services, the Honorable Tom Lantos, Ranking Member, Committee on International Relations, and the Honorable Jane Harman, Ranking Member, Permanent Select Committee on Intelligence, to The President (June 3, 2004), *available at* http://www.house.gov/judiciary_democrats/bushiraqiprisondocrequestltr6304.pdf.

970. Letter from the Honorable John Conyers, Jr., Ranking Member, House Judiciary Committee, et al., to the Honorable John D. Ashcroft, Attorney General of the United States, U.S. Department of Justice (May 20, 2004), available at http://www.house.gov/judiciary_democrats/agiraqspeccounselltr52004.pdf; Letter from the Honorable John Conyers, Jr., Ranking Member, House Judiciary Committee, to the Honorable Alberto R. Gonzales, Attorney General of the United States, U.S. Department of Justice (May 12, 2005), *available at* http://www.house.gov/judiciary_democrats/letters/agspecialcounseltortureltr51205.pdf.

971. Letter from William E. Moschella, Assistant Attorney General, Department of Justice, to the Honorable John Conyers, Jr., Ranking Member, House Judiciary Committee (July 11, 2005), *available at* http://www.house.gov/judiciary_democrats/responses/agiraqspeccounselresp71105.pdf; Letter from William E. Moschella, Assistant Attorney General, Department of Justice, to the Honorable John Conyers, Jr., Ranking Member, House Judiciary Committee (Oct. 14, 2005), *available at* http://www.house.gov/judiciary-democrats/responses/agspecialcounseltortureresp101405.pdf. In all, Democrats have written more than a dozen letters to Bush Administration officials requesting public accountability for the inexcusable offenses at Abu Ghraib. Very few of these letters have ever engendered a response from the Executive Branch; what responses have been received are of exceptionally limited substance.

972. S. 1042 (109th Congress, 1st Sess.), S. Amdt. 2430 offered by Sen. Carl Levin.

973. 151 Cong. Rec. S12479-S12516 (daily ed Nov. 8, 2005).

974. H. Res. 690, 108th Cong. (2004).

975. H.R. 3003, 109th Cong. (2005).

976. H. Res 689, 108th Cong. (2004); H. Res 699, 108th Cong. (2004); H. Res 700, 108th Cong. (2004).

977. H.R. Rep. No. 108-658 at 47 (2004).

978. Republicans argued that the Administration has substantially complied with the requests contained in the three resolutions; many of the documents requested are sensitive as they relate to military operations in a time when the country is at war; and there are competing investigations. *Ibid.* at 11. These arguments, however, are spurious. First, because none of the ongoing investigations have inquired into the Justice Department's role in sanctioning such behavior, the Resolutions of Inquiry would not interfere or duplicate any ongoing investigations. Moreover, as noted in the Democratic dissenting views, the documents the administration released "are so far afield of the legal consensus in the American and International legal community, an investigation into their creation and to what extent they evolved and were utilized is necessary." *Ibid.* at 50. In addition, the administration did not release all relevant documents and, in fact, released a selection of documents that leave large gaps not only in time, but in substance. Finally, the resolutions would have requested a much larger field of documents that had already been released.

979. H. Res 640, 108th Cong. (2004).

980. The Committee reported the resolution adversely because it concluded that the Department of Defense has provided the requested materials to the committee, and that, with respect to information regarding investigations into alleged contractor abuses of detainees, the Department had not completed any specific investigations. H.R. Rep. No. 108-547 at 5 (2004). Again, these arguments are disingenuous. In the Democratic dissenting views, the members note that the Taguba report Aleaves unaddressed important questions of per-

sonal accountability and systemic deficiencies that the committee can and should explore. *Ibid.* at 10.

981. Numerous reports have been filed, including the Taguba Report, which investigated allegations of abuse committed by the 800th Military Police Brigade at Abu Ghraib prison. In the report, Maj. Gen. Antonio M. Taguba found systematic abuse in order to loosen up detainees before interrogation. See Article 15-6 Investigation of the 800th Military Police Brigade, *available at* www.findlaw.com. There was also the report of the Independent Panel to Review Department of Defense Detention Operations, prepared by former Secretary of Defense James Schlesinger. Independent Panel to Review Department of Defense Detention Operations, Aug. 2004, at 3, *available at* www.defenselink.mil. Although this report found Athe abuses were not just the failure of some individuals to follow known standards, and they are more than the failure of a few leaders to enforce proper discipline,it concluded that the failures in leadership had already been sufficiently dealt with, that senior level administrators in the Administration did not know about the abuse and were therefore not culpable, and that they just need to find a better way to communicate so- called Abad news. *Ibid.* at 92

The Army Inspector General's report reviewed doctrine, training and procedure in the Central Command area and did not review policy actions or inactions taken by the Administration. See Department of the Army, Inspector General, Detainee Operations Inspection, July 21, 2004, at 3, *available at* www.defenselink.mil. The Navy Inspector Generals report, prepared by Vice Adm. Albert T. Church, reviewed interrogation policies and practices in Iraq and elsewhere. It found the abuse in Abu Ghraib to be isolated and that those who abused detainees did so of their own accord and not out of any approval B explicit or implicit B from leadership. It afforded the least critical review to date. See Executive Summary, Report of Vice Admiral Albert T. Church, III, Navy Inspector General at 10-11. Finally, the AR 15-6 Investigation of the Abu Ghraib Prison and 205th Military Intelligence Brigade report, prepared by Generals Jones and Fay, investigated the intelligence brigade at Abu Ghraib prison, and interviewed 170 people, ranking as high as Maj. General Geoffrey Miller, head of the Guantanamo facilities. It described the abuse as the result of confusion about or misinterpretations of interrogation policy by individual soldiers. It confirmed repeated use of sexual exploitation, beatings, unmuzzled dogs and other abuse. See Article 15-6 Investigation of the 800th Military Police Brigade, *available at* www.findlaw.com.

In addition, there have been eight other reports, investigating other locations such as Guantanamo and Afghanistan. Collectively, these Iraq-related reports did not investigate the role of senior level officers nor civilian commanders within the Pentagon. Army doctrine forbids an officer from investigating the action of anyone higher in rank than himself.

982. There has also been substantial evidence that these investigations were not conducted in a regular or sincere way. For example, one officer of the 82nd has come forward and stated that he spent 17 months trying to report incidents of abuse and clarify what standard of treatment was acceptable. Leadership Failure: Firsthand Accounts of Torture of Iraqi Detainees by the U.S. Army's 82nd Airborne Division, Human Rights Watch, September 2005, Volume 17, No. 3(G), available at www.hrw.org. However, his complaints were not investigated until he informed the military that he was speaking to a U.S. Senator. *See* Eric Schmitt, "Officer Criticizes Detainee Abuse Inquiry", the *New York Times*, Sept. 28, 2005.

983. Letter from the Honorable John Conyers, Jr., Ranking Member, Committee on the Judiciary, and the Honorable Henry A. Waxman, Ranking Member, Committee on Government Reform, to President George W. Bush (Feb. 10, 2004). In addition, on July 14, 2005, Congressman Waxman wrote to White House Chief of Staff Andrew Card asking whether the White House complied with an order requiring an internal investigation and the implementation of remedial measures. Letter from Honorable Henry A. Waxman, Ranking Member, Committee on Government Reform, to White House Chief of Staff Andrew Card (July 14, 2005), *available at* http://www.democrats.reform.house.gov/Documents/2005 0714122956-30175.pdf.

984. Letter from the Honorable John Conyers, Jr., Ranking Member, House Judiciary Committee, to the Honorable Karl Rove, Senior Advisor to the President (Oct. 7, 2003), *available at* http://www.house .gov/judiciary_democrats/roveresignltr10703.pdf.

985. Letter from the Honorable John Conyers, Jr., Ranking Member, House Judiciary Committee, et al., to President George W. Bush (July 14, 2005). Senator Schumer sent a similar letter seeking information about Rove's involvement in the leak, the President's understanding of that involvement, and an explanation of why the President had not taken action against Rove–either firing him or revoking his security clearance–once his involvement had been learned. See Letter from the Honorable Charles E. Schumer to President George W. Bush (Oct. 19, 2005). We are unaware of any response to this letter.

986. Senate Democrats also sought to revoke Rove's security clearance after passing an amendment to strip the security clearance of anyone who knowingly revealed classified information. S. 1042, 109th Cong.'1072 (2005)(enacted) (Amendment No. 2478 of Sen. Frank Lautenberg, reprinted in 151 Cong. Rec. S.12,575 (2005)). In a letter dated November 14, 2005, Senator Lautenberg, along with Senators Durbin, Reed, Harkin and Dayton, sought confirmation from Mark Frownfelter, the official in charge of security clearances for White House officials, that he is investigating and reevaluating the security clearances of Karl Rove and other administration officials referenced in the Libby indictment. Letter from Senators Frank Lautenberg, Richard Durbin, Jack Reed, Tom Harkin and Mark Dayton to Mark Frownfelter, Associate Director, Security Division, Executive Office of the President (November 14, 2005).

987. Letter from the Honorable Maurice Hinchey, et al., to Vice President Richard B. Cheney (Nov. 3, 2005). As noted in The Nation, this letter, which followed Senator Reid's success in forcing the Senate into a closed session to discuss intelligence issues related to Iraq, "offers the latest signal that Congressional Democrats are determined to hold key players in the administration, particularly Cheney, to account." Congressmen Want Cheney to Testify, www.thenation.com/blogs/thebeat?bid+1&pid=33242 (Nov. 3, 2005, 5:27pm).

989. Letter from the Honorable John Conyers, Jr., Ranking Member, House Judiciary Committee, to President George W. Bush (July 25, 2005), *available at* http://www.house.gov/judiciary_democrats/letters/prespardonltr72505.pdf.

989. Letter Letter from Senator Harry Reid, Democratic Leader, U.S. Senate, to the Honorable George W. Bush (Nov. 8, 2005).

990. Letter from the Honorable Henry Waxman, Ranking Member, Committee on Government Reform, to Secretary of Defense Donald Rumsfeld (August 29, 2005) *available at* http://www.democrats.reform.house.gov/Documents/20050829160953-04500.pdf.

991. Letter from the Honorable Francis Harvey, Acting Secretary of the Army, to Honorable Henry A. Waxman, Ranking Member, Committee on Government Reform (September 27, 2005).

992. Letter from the Honorable Henry A. Waxman, Ranking Member, House Committee on Government Reform, to Condeleeza Rice, Secretary of State (January 14, 2004), *available at* http://www.democrats.reform.house.gov/Documents/20040607092010-21572.pdf.

993. *Ibid.*

994. Letter from the Honorable John Conyers, Jr., Ranking Member, Committee on the Judiciary, to President George W. Bush (December 7, 2005).

995. *Ibid.*

996. Letter from the Honorable John Conyers, Jr., Ranking Member, House Judiciary Committee, et al., to the Honorable F. James Sensenbrenner, Jr., Chairman, House Judiciary Committee (October 30, 2003), *available at* http://www.house.gov/judiciary_democrats/cialeakltr103003.pdf.

997. Letter from the Honorable John Conyers, Jr., Ranking Member, House Judiciary Committee, et al., to the Honorable F. James Sensenbrenner, Jr., Chairman, Committee on the Judiciary (July 14, 2005), *available at* http://www.house.gov/judiciary_democrats/letters/rovehrgrequestltr71405.pdf.

998. Letter from the Honorable Henry Waxman, Ranking Member, House Committee on Government Reform, to the Honorable Tom Davis, Chairman, House Committee on Government Reform (September 29, 2003), *available at* http://www.democrats.reform.house.gov/Documents/20040607092402-66614.pdf.

999. Letter from the Honorable Henry Waxman, Ranking Member, House Committee on Government Reform, to the Honorable Tom Davis, Chairman, House Committee on Government Reform (October 8, 2003).

1,000. Letter from the Honorable Henry Waxman, Ranking Member, House Committee on Government Reform, to the Honorable Tom Davis, Chairman, House Committee on Government Reform (December 11, 2003), *available at* http://www.democrats.reform.house.gov/Documents/20040607092 233-06397.pdf.

1,001. Letter from the Honorable Henry Waxman, Ranking Member, House Committee on Government Reform, to the Honorable Tom Davis, Chairman, House Committee on Government Reform (July 11, 2005), *available at* http://www.democrats.reform.house.gov/Documents/20050711131514-97754.pdf.

1,002. Letter from the Honorable Henry Waxman, Ranking Member, House Committee on Government Reform, to the Honorable Tom Davis, Chairman, House Committee on Government Reform (October 28, 2005), *available at* http://www.democrats.reform.house.gov/Documents/20051028172902-79173.pdf.

1,003. Letter from the Honorable Henry Waxman, Ranking Member, House Committee on Government Reform, to the Honorable Tom Davis, Chairman, House Committee on Government Reform (November 16, 2005), *available at* http://www.democrats.reform.house.gov/Documents/20051116181 144-65736.pdf.

1,004. Letter from the Honorable Henry Waxman, Ranking Member, House Committee on Government Reform, to the Honorable Tom Davis, Chairman, House Committee on Government Reform (May 11, 2004), *available at* http://www.democrats.reform.house.gov/Documents/20040607093652-55156.pdf.

1,005. Letter to from the Honorable Henry Waxman, Ranking Member, House Committee on Government Reform, to the Honorable Tom Davis, Chairman, House Committee on Government Reform (November 30, 2005), *available at* http://www.democrats.reform.house.gov/Documents/20051130143 916-94287.pdf.

1,006. H.R. 420, 109th Cong. (2005); H. Res. 417, 109th Cong. (2005); H. Res. 418, 109th Cong. (2005) and H. Res. 419, 109th Cong. (2005).

1,007. H.R. Rep. No. 109-230 at 7 (2005).

1,008. *Ibid.* at 28 (2005) (Dissenting Views). For example, in 1997, the Committee held hearings on campaign improprieties in the 1996 presidential election. See Oversight of the Department of Justice: Hearing Before the House Comm. on the Judiciary, 105th Cong., 1st Sess. (1997). In 1995, the Subcommittee on Crime heard several days of testimony as part of a congressional investigation into federal actions at Waco, with soldiers, officers, ATF, FBI and Treasury Department officials testifying. See Activities of Federal Law Enforcement Agencies toward the Branch Davidians: Hearings Before the Subcomm. on Crime of the H. Comm. on the Judiciary, 104th Cong., 1st Sess. (July 28, 31 & Aug. 1, 1995). In 1990-92, the Committee investigated whether the Justice Department helped run INSLAW, a small computer company into insolvency. See The INSLAW Affair, H. Rep. No. 102-857 (1992). In the 1970's, congressional committees held extensive hearings on Watergate as the Justice Department investigation was on-going. See Impeachment of Richard M. Nixon, President of the United States, H. Rep. No. 93-1305; Debate on Articles of Impeachment: Hearings Before the H. Comm. on the Judiciary, 93rd Cong., 2d Sess. (July 24-27, 29-30, 1974); Impeachment Inquiry: Hearings Before the H. Comm. on the Judiciary, 93rd Cong., 2d Sess. (Jan. 31-July 23, 1974).

1,009. President Addresses American Society of Newspaper Editors Convention (Apr. 14, 2005), *available at* http://www.whitehouse.gov/news/releases/2005/04/20050414-4.html.

1,010. H.R. 2975, 107th Cong., 2d Sess. (2001).

1,011. H.R. Rep. No. 236, 107th Cong., 2d Sess. (2001).

1,012. Uniting and Strengthening America by Providing Appropriate Tools Required to Intercept and Obstruct Terrorism Act (PATRIOT Act), Pub. L. No. 107-56, 115 Stat. 272 (2001). As enacted, the PATRIOT Act included more than 150 separate sections, with the vast majority not limited to terrorism cases, and with 16 surveillance sections to sunset on December 31, 2005, extended to March 10, 2006. When the 16 expiring provisions of the Act were reauthorized in 2006, at the Administration's insistence, a number of civil liberties safeguards were eliminated, such as protecting libraries from receiving National Security Letters. USA PATRIOT Improvement and Reauthorization Act, Pub. L. No. 109-177 (2006).

1,013. Patriot Act, §213. Warrants authorizing these secret searches no longer require, as they did in some circuit courts, that notice be given within seven days after the secret search. Instead, an undefined "reasonable time" is the new standard.

1,014. Patriot Act, §215. Before the PATRIOT Act, these requests were required to be directed to "agents of a foreign power," under the Act they can now be used against anyone, based only on a minimum standard of relevance.

1,015. Patriot Act, §505. Before the PATRIOT Act, these requests were required to be directed to "agents of a foreign power," under the Act they can now be used against anyone, based only on a minimum standard of "relevance."

1,016. Patriot Act, §§ 411, 805. Section 411 was written to apply retroactively, so it covers donations made before the law was passed. Section 805 expanded the offense of providing material support for terrorist activities and organizations. In general, "material support" is defined as financial resources, expert advice or assistance, assets, housing, personnel, training, or communications equipment. 18 U.S.C. § 2339A. This statute's definition of 'material support or resources' also is used to prohibit the provision of material support or resources to foreign terrorist organizations under section 2339B of title 18. Section 805 added the terms "expert advice and assistance" to this list.

1,017. A New York federal court found the Act's gag restrictions violated the First Amendment (the non-disclosure requirement was seen as a prior restraint on speech) and Fourth Amendment (finding a reasonable person would not realize they had a right to contest the letter). Doe v. Ashcroft, 334 F. Supp. 2d 471, 503 (S.D.N.Y. 2004). In its decision, the court noted that "democracy abhors undue secrecy;" and that "an unlimited government warrant to conceal, effectively a form of secrecy per se, has no place in our open society." The U.S. District Court for the District of Connecticut also found section 505's nondisclosure requirement to be a prior restraint on speech and a content-based speech restriction in violation of the First Amendment. Doe v. Gonzales, 126 S. Ct. 1 (2005). In this case, the plaintiff was the recipient of a national security letter and sued the government for a violation of the First, Fourth, and Fifth Amendments. The District Court granted the plaintiff's motion for a preliminary injunction on the grounds that the NSL gag order violated the First Amendment. The court also issued a stay of the injunction so the government could appeal. Ultimately, the Second Circuit and the Supreme Court refused the plaintiff's request to lift the stay, saying the plaintiff could disclose the receipt of an NSL.

1,018. The Ninth Circuit found that the PATRIOT Act attributes "the intent to commit unlawful acts punishable by life imprisonment to persons who acted with innocent intent" and that "the terms 'personnel' and 'training' are void for vagueness under the First and Fifth Amendments because they bring within their ambit constitutionally protected speech and advocacy." Humanitarian Law Project v. United States DOJ, 352 F.3d 382, 397, 403 (9th Cir. 2003). In 2004, Congress amended the law to specify that "training" was limited to "instruction or teaching designed to impart a specific skill, as opposed to general knowledge," that "expert advice or assistance" was meant to encompass "scientific, technical, or other specialized knowledge;" and to add "services" to the list of prohibited activities. Intelligence Reform and Terrorism Prevention Act of 2004, Pub. L. No. 108-458, § 6603, 118 Stat. 3638, 3763. The District Court reviewed the new language in 2005 and found that these terms continued to be unconstitutionally vague, finding, for example, that statute leaves "the term 'training' impermissibly vague because it easily encompasses protected speech and advocacy, such as teaching international law for peacemaking resolutions or how to petition the United Nations to seek redress for human rights violations." Humanitarian Law Project v. Ashcroft, 380 F. Supp. 2d 1134, 1150 (C.D. Cal. 2005).

1,019. Detroit Free Press v. Ashcroft, 303 F.3d 681, 683 (6th Cir. 2002). In a separate case, the Third Circuit upheld the Department's ability to hold a secret hearing. North Jersey Media Group v. Ashcroft, 308

F.3d 198 (3d. Cir. 2002), cert. denied, 2003 U.S. LEXIS 4082 (2003). As a result of the Third and Sixth Circuit holdings, there was a split in the federal appellate courts as to whether deportation hearings could be held in secret. The media companies that lost in the Third Circuit sought certiorari in the Supreme Court. In its brief opposing a grant of certiorari, the Solicitor General stated that these procedures were under review and could be revised, such that further closed deportation hearings might not occur again. Brief for the Respondents in Opposition at 13, North Jersey Media Group (No. 02-1289). The Supreme Court ultimately denied certiorari on May 27, 2003, likely because of the Justice Department's brief.

1,020. A June 2003 report by the DOJ Inspector General reported "significant problems in the way the detainees were handled," that officers "slammed detainees against the wall, twisted their arms and hands in painful ways, stepped on their leg restraint chains, and punished them by keeping them restrained for long periods of time," all of which was captured on videotape. Despite being seen on videotape, these officers denied any involvement upon the Inspector General inquiry. The Inspector General also found that government employees had engaged in a "pattern of physical and verbal abuse," and found that detainees were held in lock downs 23 hours per day with lights constantly on in their cells. Some detainees were found to have been thrown against the wall naked and subjected to such verbal taunts as "you're going to die here" and "you will feel pain." Office of Inspector General, U.S. Dep't of Justice, Supplemental Report on September 11 Detainees' Allegations of Abuse at the Metropolitan Detention Center in Brooklyn, New York (2003).

1,021. The California State Senate Office of Research found that the National Security Entry-Exit Registration System (NSEERs) program did not identify any terrorists. California State Senate Office of Research, The Patriot Act, Other Post 9-11 Enforcement Powers and The Impact on California's Muslim Communities 23 (2004).: "No suspected connection to terrorism formed the criteria for sanctions ... the government...used national origin as a proxy for evidence of dangerousness" Id. at 21 (2004). With regard to the Department's "voluntary interrogation program," the GAO found the program to be of no intelligence value, and that the information gathered from the interviews sits in federal databases without any specific plans for use, finding: "[n]one of the law enforcement officials with whom [the GAO] spoke could provide examples of investigative leads that resulted from the project." U.S. Gen. Accounting Office, Homeland Security: Justice Department's Project to Interview Aliens After September 11, 2001 16 (2003). The GAO further found that even though the Department's guidelines specified that the interviewees were to be sources of information, not suspects, they were routinely asked incriminating questions. Finally, the GAO found that according to some law enforcement officials, the interviews negatively affected relations with the Arab community, observing, "Federal law enforcement officials at ... districts we visited expressed the view that the interview project had a negative effect on relations between the Arab community and law enforcement personnel." Concerning the Department's investigation and detention of Brandon Mayfield, a Muslim-American attorney wrongfully detained by the FBI in connection with the Madrid, Spain bombings in March 2004, a January 2006 report issued by the Department of Justice Inspector General found that not only were the FBI fingerprint examiners reckless in their duties, but "that Mayfield's [legal] representation of a convicted terrorist and other facts developed during the field investigation, including his Muslim religion, also likely contributed to the examiners' failure to sufficiently reconsider the identification after legitimate questions were raised." Office of the Inspector General, U.S. Dep't of Justice, A Review of the FBI's Handling of the Brandon Mayfield Case 12 (Jan. 2006) (hereinafter OIG Mayfield Report).

1,022. The White House, press release, President Issues Military Order (Nov. 13, 2001), available at http://www.whitehouse.gov/news/releases/2001/11/20011113-27.html. In 2004, the Supreme Court overruled part of the military commission orders and held that military detainees have the right to challenge their detentions in federal courts. Rasul v. Bush, 542 U.S. 466 (2004). Ultimately, the Bush Administration established Combatant Status Review Tribunals for detainee challenges, ignoring the requirement that challenges be permitted in civilian courts. Eventually, at the Administration's urging,

Congress passed legislation limiting detainee access to the courts. National Defense Authorization Act for Fiscal Year 2006, Pub. L. No. 109-163 (2006).

1,023. Neil A. Lewis, "Traces of Terror: The Inquiry; Ashcroft Permits F.B.I. to Monitor Internet and Public Activities", the *New York Times*, May 31, 2002, at A20. The new guidelines authorize the collection and use of information from databases either public, commercial or non-profit, otherwise known as "data mining." Agents are also authorized to "attend any place or event" or "conduct research including online research, accessing online sites and forums." The guidelines declare that files kept as a result of new investigations are not subject to the protections of the Privacy Act.

1,024. William Safire, "J. Edgar Mueller", the *New York Times*, June 3, 2002, at A15.

1,025. In March 2006, the *Washington Post* reported, "[a]n FBI report from November 2002 indicates that an agent photographed members from the Thomas Merton Center as they handed out leaflets opposing the impending war in Iraq. The report called the group a 'left-wing organization advocating, among many political causes, pacificism.' The same memo notes that one of the leaflet distributors 'appeared to be of Middle Eastern descent' but that no other participants appeared to be from the Middle East." Dan Eggen, "FBI Took Photos of Antiwar Activists in 2002", *The Washington Post*, Mar. 15, 2006 at A5. Freedom of Information Act (FOIA) requests have also confirmed that in June 2002, environmental activists who protested a lumber association meeting were investigated because they taught "nonviolent methods of forest defense ... security culture, street theater and banner making." Nicholas Riccardi, "FBI Keeps Watch on Activists", *Los Angeles Times*, March 27, 2006 at A1. FOIA requests have also shown that the FBI has opened a preliminary terrorism investigation into People for the Ethical Treatment of Animals (PETA). The papers offer no proof of PETA's involvement in illegal activity, but more than 100 pages of heavily censored FBI files show the agency used secret informants and tracked the group's events for years, including an animal rights conference in Washington in July 2000, a community meeting at an Indiana college in spring 2003 and a planned August 2004 protest of a celebrity fur endorser. Other FBI documents indicate that agents in Indianapolis planned to conduct surveillance as part of a "Vegan Community Project," and refer to the Catholic Workers group's "semi-communistic ideology." Spencer S. Hsu, "FBI Papers Show Terror Inquires into PETA; Other Groups Tracked", *The Washington Post*, Dec. 20, 2005, at A11. On December 14, 2005, NBC news obtained a secret 400-page Defense Department document including a DOD database that includes nearly four dozen anti-war meetings or protests, including some that have taken place far from any military installation, post or recruitment center. Lisa Myers, Douglas Pasternak, & Rich Gardella, "Is the Pentagon Spying on Americans", msnbc.com, Dec. 14, 2005, *available at* http://www.msnbc.msn.com/id/10454316.

1,026. A November 2002 the *Washington Post* article identified 44 material witnesses and found that almost half of them never testified before a grand jury. Steven Fainaru & Margot Williams, "Material Witness Law has Many in Limbo; Nearly Half Held in War on Terror Haven't Testified", *The Washington Post*, Nov. 24, 2002, at A1. In June 2005, Human Rights Watch and the American Civil Liberties Union released a detailed report identifying 70 individuals detained pursuant to the material witness law, with "[a]ll but one [being] Muslim by birth or conversion [and] [a]ll but two were of Middle Eastern, African, or South Bsian descent or African-American." Human Rights Watch & American Civil Liberties Union, Witness to Abuse: Human Rights Abuses Under the Material Witness Law Since September 11 at 16 (2005) The Report also found that of these 70 cases, 42 suspects never faced any charges, and only seven faced any terrorism-related charges, and that more than one-third of the suspects were jailed for two months or longer, often in solitary confinement.

1,027. John Conyers, "Two Unpatriotic Acts: Don't Let Troops Come Home to a Nation That Destroys Civil Liberties", *Legal Times*, April 14, 2003. As a result of the public outcry, the Administration opted not to introduce the legislation.

1,028. Charlie Savage, "Bush Challenges Hundreds of Law: President Cites Powers of his Office", *Boston Globe*, April 30, 2006, at A1.

1,029. Charlie Savage, "Bush Challenges Hundreds of Law: President Cites Powers of his Office", *Boston Globe*, April 30, 2006, at A1.

1,030. Charlie Savage, "Bush Challenges Hundreds of Law: President Cites Powers of his Office", *Boston Globe*, April 30, 2006, at A1.

1,031. James Risen & Eric Lichtblau, "Bush Lets U.S. Spy on Callers Without Courts", the *New York Times*, Dec. 16, 2005, at A1. The next day, the President publicly stated he "authorized the National Security Agency . . . to intercept the international communications of people with known links to Al Qaeda and related terrorist organizations." President George W. Bush, President's Radio Address (Dec. 17, 2005), available at http://www.whitehouse.gov/news/releases/2005/12/print/20051217.html. The Attorney General acknowledged that the NSA surveillance is the "kind" that ordinarily "requires a court order before engaging in" it. Attorney General Alberto Gonzales and Principal Deputy Director for National Intelligence General Michael Hayden, Press Briefing (Dec. 19, 2005), *available at* www.whitehouse.gov/news/releases/2005/12/20051219-1.html. President Bush has stated "that the program was reviewed for reauthorization every 45 days by the President, the Attorney General, the CIA director, the President's legal counsel, and the Office of Legal Counsel in the Justice Department." President George W. Bush, President's Radio Address (Dec. 17, 2005), *available at* http://www.whitehouse.gove/news/releases/2005/12/print/20051217.html. He also stated that the program's review is based on "a fresh intelligence assessment of terrorist threats to the continuity of [the United States] government and the threat of catastrophic damage to our homeland." According to General Hayden, the NSA program is also reviewed by the NSA's general counsel, the NSA Inspector General, and the Department of Justice for compliance with the President's authorization. General Michael Hayden, Remarks at the National Press Club (Jan. 23, 2006), *available at* http://www.cq.com. President Bush further acknowledged that he had reauthorized the program more than 30 times since September 11th and has asserted his intent to continue to do so. President George W. Bush, President's Radio Address (Dec. 17, 2005).

1,032. Foreign Intelligence Surveillance Act of 1978, Pub. L. 95-511, Title I, 92 Stat. 1796 (Oct. 25, 1978) codified as amended.

1,033. The Fourth Amendment provides "[t]he right of the people to be secure in their persons, houses, papers, and effects, against unreasonable searches and seizures, shall not be violated, and no Warrants shall issue, but upon probable cause, supported by Oath or affirmation, and particularly describing the place to be searched, and the persons or things to be seized." U.S. Const. amend. IV. It remains unclear when the domestic spying program was initiated. According to President Bush in his December 17, 2005 radio address, the program began "in the weeks following the terrorist attacks on [the United States]." President George W. Bush, President's Radio Address (Dec. 17, 2005). At the Senate Judiciary Hearings, the Attorney General stated the program began "subsequent to the authorization of the use of military force and prior to the PATRIOT Act." Wartime Executive Power and the NSA's Surveillance Authority (Part I): Hearing before the Senate Judiciary Committee (Senate NSA Hearing), 109th Cong., 109-110 (2006) (testimony of Attorney General Alberto Gonzales). However, current and former government officials have indicated that before President Bush officially authorized the program, the NSA was conducting warrantless eavesdropping on all telephone calls and email messages between the United States and Afghanistan. James Risen & Eric Lichtblau, "Eavesdropping Effort Began Soon After Sept. 11 Attacks", the *New York Times*, Dec. 18, 2005, at A44.

1,034. James Risen & Eric Lichtblau, "Bush Lets U.S. Spy on Callers Without Courts", the *New York Times*, Dec. 16, 2005, at A1. James Risen's sources recounted in the *New York Times*, "roughly 500 people in the United States" were eavesdropped on "every day over the past three to four years." MSNBC.com: Interview by Andrea Mitchell with James Risen, (Jan. 3, 2006), *available at* http://www.msnbc.msn.com/it/10697484/page/4/print/1/displaymode/1098/. Some reports indicated that the total number of people monitored domestically has reached into the thousands, while others have indicated that significantly more people have been spied upon. Eric Lichtblau & James Risen, "Spy

Agency Mined Vast Data Trove, Officials Report", the *New York Times*, Dec. 23, 2005, at A1.

1,035. James Risen & Eric Lichtblau, "Spy Agency Mined Vast Data Trove, Officials Report", the *New York Times*, Dec. 23, 2005, at A1. According to a former technology manager at one of the major telecommunications companies, the "data is mined with the cooperation of the government and [then] shared with [the government]." It is unclear is what, if anything, the Bush Administration is doing with the massive amounts of unused data generated by the domestic spying program. According to a national security lawyer who represents a participant in the program, staff is becoming increasingly "uncomfortable with the mountain of data they have now begun to accumulate," including so-called "non-threatening U.S. e-mails and conversations that the NSA intercepts."

1,036. Attorney General Alberto Gonzales and Principal Deputy Director for National Intelligence General Michael Hayden, Press Briefing (Gonzales and Hayden Press Briefing) (Dec. 19, 2005), available at www.whitehouse.gov/news/releases/2005/12/20051219-1.html. Various members of the Administration, including the President, have omitted the Attorney General's caveats at various times, asserting, for example, that the only communications being intercepted were "communications, back and forth, from within the United States to overseas with members of Al Qaeda."

1,037. General Michael Hayden, Principal Deputy Director for National Intelligence, Press Briefing (Hayden Press Briefing) (Dec. 19, 2005), *available at* http://www.whitehouse.gov/news/releases/2005 /12/print/20051219-1.html.

1,038. Hayden Press Briefing (Dec. 19, 2005). Because the judgement is made "without the burden of obtaining warrants," General Hayden conceded that the NSA Program has used a "quicker trigger" and "a subtly softer trigger" when it decides to target someone than is required to be made under FISA. "Charlie Savage, Wiretaps Said to Sift All Overseas Contacts Vast U.S. Effort Seen on Eavesdropping", *The Boston Globe*, Dec. 23, 2005, at A1.

1,039. Daniel Klaidman, Stuart Taylor Jr., & Evan Thomas, "Palace Revolt", *Newsweek*, Feb 6, 2006, at 34.

1,040. Evan Thomas and Daniel Klaidman, "Full Speed Ahead", *Newsweek*, Jan. 9, 2006, at 22.

1,041. Evan Thomas and Daniel Klaidman, "Full Speed Ahead", *Newsweek*, Jan. 9, 2006, at 22.

1,042. James Risen and Eric Lichtblau, "Bush Secretly Lifted Some Limits on Spying in U.S. After 9-11, Officials Say", the *New York Times*, Dec. 15, 2005 ("One official familiar with the episode said the judge insisted to Justice Department lawyers at one point that any material gathered under the special N.S.A. program not be used in seeking wiretap warrants from her court").

1,043. Carol D. Leonnig, "Secret Court's Judges Were Warned About NSA Spy Data", *The Washington Post*, Feb. 9, 2006, at A1.

1,044. *Ibid.*

1,045. *Ibid.*

1,046. *Ibid.*

1,047. Carol D. Leonnig, "Surveillance Court is Seeking Answers", *The Washington Post*, Jan. 5, 2006 at A2.

1,048. Letter from William E. Moschella, Assistant Attorney General, U.S. DOJ, to the Honorable Pat Roberts, Chairman Senate Select Committee on Intelligence, the Honorable John D. Rockefeller, IV, Vice Chairman, Senate Select Committee on Intelligence, *et. al.*(Dec. 22, 2005).

1,049. U.S. Department of Justice, Legal Authorities Supporting the Activities of the National Security Agency Described by the President (White Paper) (Jan. 19, 2006), *available at* http://www.usdoj.gov/opa /whitepaperonnsalegalauthorities.pdf.

1,050. U.S. Department of Justice memorandum, Myth v Fact (Jan 27, 2006), *available at* http://releases .usnewswire.com/printing.asp?id=59973. On February 9, 2006, President Bush held a special press conference to declare how effective their anti-terrorism efforts have been, claiming that they used the program to disrupt a plot to fly hijacked planes into Los Angeles's Library Tower (now known as the U.S. Bank Tower). Peter Baker and Dan Eggan, "Bush Details 2002 Plot to Attack L.A. Tower", *The*

*Washington Post*, Feb. 10, 2006, at A4. However, one intelligence official said the NSA program had "no connection" to the west coast plot, while others have attributed the President's decision to reveal more detailed information regarding the plot to politics, asserting that "there is deep disagreement within the intelligence community over the seriousness of the Library Tower scheme and whether it was ever much more than talk."

1,051. Wartime Executive Power and the NSA's Surveillance Authority: Hearing before the Senate Judiciary Committee, 109th Cong. (2006) (statement of Senator Arlen Specter). Numerous government officials who are familiar with the warrantless surveillance program consider it to be "unlawful and possibly unconstitutional, amounting to an improper search." James Risen & Eric Lichtblau, "Bush Lets U.S. Spy on Callers Without Courts", the *New York Times*, Dec. 16, 2005, at A1. Other officials were quoted as stating that "an investigation should be launched into the way the Bush Administration has turned the intelligence community's most powerful tools against the American people, while officials at the NSA indicated they wanted nothing to do with the program and were fearful that it was an illegal operation. James Bamford, "Where Spying Starts and Stops: Tracking an Embattled CIA and a President at War", the *New York Times*, Jan. 9, 2006, at E6; James Risen & Eric Lichtblau, "Bush Lets U.S. Spy on Callers Without Courts", the *New York Times*, Dec. 16, 2005, at A1.

1,052. Dan Eggen & Walter Pincus, "Ex-Justice Lawyer Rips Case for Spying", *The Washington Post*, Mar. 9, 2006, at A03. In addition, Thomas H. Kean, Chairman of the 9-11 Commission "counted himself among those who doubted the legality of the program. He said in an interview that the Administration did not inform his commission about the program and that he wished it had." Eric Lichtblau & Scott Shane, "Basis for Spying in the U.S. is Doubted", the *New York Times*, Jan. 7, 2006, at A1. One government official involved in the operation of the NSA program said that he privately complained to a Congressional official about his doubts about the program's legality, but nothing came of his inquiry. James Risen & Eric Lichtblau, "Bush Lets U.S. Spy on Callers Without Courts", the *New York Times*, Dec. 16, 2005, at A1. Another former senior intelligence official at the NSA explicitly stated "there was apprehension, uncertainty in the minds of many about whether or not the President did have that constitutional or statutory authority." Richard Lacayo, "The Spying Controversy: Has Bush Gone Too Far?", *Time*, Jan. 9, 2006, at 25.

1,053. Mark Hosenball, "Spying: Giving Out U.S. Names", *Newsweek*, May 2, 2006.

1,054. Newsweek reported, "the Senate intelligence committee's chairman, Pat Roberts, and its top Democrat, Jay Rockefeller, got a closed-door briefing on Bolton's NSA dealings from the deputy intel czar, Gen. Michael Hayden. . . Rockefeller complained that Bolton sought out a State Department official whose name was supplied by the NSA 'to congratulate him'—for unspecified reasons—which . . . was 'not in keeping' with Bolton's request for the uncensored NSA report." Mark Hosenball, "Bolton: Secrets Spilled?" *Newsweek*, June 6, 2005. As a New York Times editorial stated "[i]f the National Security Agency provides officials with the identities of Americans on its tapes, what is the use of making secret those names in the first place? . . . [w]e now know that this hasn't been the case—the agency has been listening to Americans' phone calls, just not reporting any names. And Bolton's experience makes clear that keeping those names confidential was a formality that high-ranking officials could overcome by picking up the phone." "Big Brother and the Bureaucrats", the *New York Times*, Aug. 11, 2005, at A21.

1,055. Leslie Cauley, "NSA Has Massive Database of Americans' Phone Calls", *USA Today*, May 11, 2006 at A1.

1,056. Leslie Cauley, "NSA Has Massive Database of Americans' Phone Calls", *USA Today*, May 11, 2006 at A1. This is a significant departure from previous practice under which, according to The Washington Post, "government agencies traditionally have been required to obtain a warrant before monitoring Americans conversations or call logs." Barton Gellman and Arshad Mohmmed, "Data on Phone Calls Monitored: Extent of Administration's Domestic Surveillance Decried in Both Parties", *The Washington Post*, May 12, 2006 at A1.

1,057. Leslie Cauley, "NSA Has Massive Database of Americans' Phone Calls", *USA Today*, May 11, 2006 at

A1. Four days later, ABC News reported that a senior law enforcement official had told them that the Bush Administration was tracking "phone calls and contacts by reporters for ABC News along with the *New York Times* and The Washington Post." It is unclear whether or not this tracking was occurring pursuant to or in the same manner as the NSA's domestic database, although one commentator speculated that the surveillance was occurring pursuant to National Security Letters. Brian Ross and Richard Esposito, "Federal Source to ABC News: We Know Who You're Calling", *ABC News: The Blotter*, May 15, 2006, *available at* http://blogs.abcnews.com/theblotter/2006/05/federal_source_.html.

1,058. Leslie Cauley, "NSA Has Massive Database of Americans' Phone Calls", *USA Today*, May 11, 2006 at A1. The three implicated telephone companies provide phone service to approximately 224 million customers, representing some 80% of the land line phones and more than 50% of wireless phones. Barton Gellman and Arshad Mohmmed, "Data on Phone Calls Monitored: Extent of Administration's Domestic Surveillance Decried in Both Parties," *Washington Post*, May 12, 2006 at A1.

1,059. Leslie Cauley, "NSA Has Massive Database of Americans' Phone Calls", *USA Today*, May 11, 2006 at A1.

1,060. Barton Gellman and Arshad Mohmmed, "Data on Phone Calls Monitored: Extent of Administration's Domestic Surveillance Decried in Both Parties", *The Washington Post*, May 12, 2006 at A1.

1,061. John Markoff, "Questions Raised for Phone Giants in Spy Data Furor", the *New York Times*, May 13, 2006 at A1. The Qwest statement provided: "Mr. Nacchio [the then CEO] made inquiry as to whether a warrant or other legal process had been secured in support of that request. When he learned that no such authority had been granted, and that there was a disinclination on the part of the authorities to use any legal process," he determined the requests were unlawful and refused to comply."

1,062. Eric Lichtblau and Scott Shane, "Bush is Pressed Over New Report on Surveillance", the *New York Times*, May 12, 2006 at A1.

1,063. Karen Tumulty, "Inside Bush's Secret Spy Net: Your phone records have been enlisted in the war on terrorism. Should that make you worry more or less?", *Time Magazine*, May 14. 2006 at 32.

1,064. Seymour M. Hersh, "The Talk of the Town: National Security Department, Listening In", *The New Yorker*, May 29, 2006, at 24. Hersh wrote that his sources had told him that not only was the NSA monitoring domestic calls, but was doing so on a "real time" basis. A security consultant working with a "major telecommunications carrier" told Hersh: "What the companies are doing is worse than turning over records. They're providing total access to the data. [A former intelligence official added], [t]his is not about getting a cardboard box of monthly phone bills in alphabetical order. The N.S.A. is getting real time and actionable intelligence."

1,065. Robert Schmidt and Nicholas Johnston, "NSA Collected Phone Records in the U.S., Lott Says", *Bloomberg News*, May 11, 2006, *available at* http://www.bloomberg.com/apps/news?pid =10000103&sid=aXoEofLLKuUY&refer=us.

1,066. NewsHour with Jim Lehrer: NSA Wire Tapping Program Revealed (PBS television broadcast, May 11, 2006) *available at* http://www.pbs.org/newshour/bb/law/jan-june06/nsa_05-11.html.

1,067. In a May 21 appearance on ABC's "This Week," Attorney General Gonzales indicated that the Justice Department would go so far as to actually prosecute those newspapers which disclosed the illegal NSA programs. When asked if journalists could be prosecuted for such actions, he stated, "[t]here are some statutes on the book which, if you read the language carefully, would seem to indicate that it is a possibility" and "[w]e have an obligation to enforce those laws." Ed O'Keefe, "Alberto Gonzales: Build the Wall", *ABC News*, May 21, 2006.

1,068. Letter from Randal S. Milch, Senior Vice President and General Counsel at Verizon Business to Congressman John Conyers (Feb. 17, 2006). Letter from Marc Gary, Executive Vice President and General Counsel at Bell South to Congressman John Conyers (April 4, 2006).

1,069. Ken Belson and Matt Richtel, "Verizon Denies Turning Over Local Phone Data", the *New York Times*, May 17, 2006.

1,070. Arshad Mohammed, "BellSouth Wants Story Retractions", *The Washington Post*, May 19, 2006 at A7.

1,071. Peter Svensson, "Verizon: The NSA didn't ask us for records", *Business Week*, May 16, 2006.

1,072. Greg Sargent, "New Presidential Memorandum Permits Intelligence Director to Authorize Telcos to Lie without Violating Security Laws", *Think Progress*, May 17, 2006, available at http://thinkprogress.org /2006/05/17/new-executive-order/.

1,073. Cameron: "Democrats complaining about the NSA programs" without knowing all the details "is precisely why Republicans say Democrats just aren't serious about security," Media Matters, May 15, 2006, *available at* http://mediamatters.org/items/200605150001.

1,074. Leslie Cauley, "NSA Has Massive Database of Americans' Phone Calls", *USA Today*, May 11, 2006 at A1.

1,075. Despite bipartisan outcry over NSA phone call database, CNN's Henry said, "Democrats obviously are already pouncing on this" Media Matters, May 11, 2006, *available at* http://mediamatters.org /items/200605110009.

1,076. In May 2003, Amnesty International stated in its annual report that the Bush Administration's treatment of foreign nationals and Guantanamo Bay was a "human rights scandal" and that their actions in that regard, "far from making the world a safer place, has made it more dangerous by curtailing human rights, undermining the rule of international law and shielding governments from scrutiny." Amnesty International, Report 2003: Counter-terrorism and Human Rights, *available at* http://web.amnesty.org /report2003/index-eng. These abuse would appear to stem, at least in part, from a series of controversial legal opinions issued by the Department of Justice which provided that 1) the Geneva Conventions and other international laws banning torture did not apply to our detainees, 2) if they did, they could be construed so narrowly that events such as those at Abu Ghraib are not legally "torture," and 3) even if those acts could be defined as "torture," the Administration and its military are not liable under the President's Commander-in-chief authority and other defenses.

1,077. In its June 2004 decision in Hamdi v. Rumsfeld, the Supreme Court held that the more than 600 detainees at Guantanamo were entitled to due process by contesting their status in a court of law. Justice O'Connor rebuked the Administration's handling of the detainees, stating, "a state of war is not a blank check for the President when it comes to the rights of the Nation's citizens. The Supreme Court also found that the Bush Administration's position "serves only to condense power into a single branch of government." Hamdi v. Rumsfeld, 542 U.S. 507, 536 (2004).

1,078. Mr. Padilla was arrested at O'Hare International Airport in May 2002 and President Bush later declared Padilla an enemy combatant. For three years, the Administration claimed he posed such a grave threat that it had the right to detain him without trial as an enemy combatant. His case made its way up to the Supreme Court in Rumsfeld v. Padilla, but the Court dismissed the case on procedural grounds. Rather than risk a substantive review of its policy by the Supreme Court, the Administration indicted Mr. Padilla on comparatively minor criminal charges. When the Administration asked the 4th Circuit Court for permission to transfer Padilla from military custody to jail, the once-cooperative court flatly refused, expressing amazement that the Administration suddenly would decide Mr. Padilla could be treated like a common purse snatcher—a reversal that, they said, comes "at substantial cost to the government's credibility." See Jerry Markon, "Justices Order Padilla Terror Case Moved to Civilian Court", *The Washington Post*, Jan. 5, 2006, at A1.

1,079. Perhaps the most notorious case of extraordinary rendition by the Bush Administration involved Maher Arar who was detained by the INS during a layover at JFK airport in New York in September, 2002. After authorities were unable to obtain any intelligence from Mr. Arar or establish a connection between him and Al Qaeda, Deputy Attorney General Larry Thompson ordered him deported to Syria–despite his professed Canadian citizenship and his request return to Canada. Arar was jailed and tortured in Syria for ten months before his release in October 2003. The Administration has not been able to connect Mr. Arar to terrorism or to Al Qaeda. See Jane Mayer, "Outsourcing Torture; The secret history of America's "extraordinary rendition" program", *The New Yorker*, Feb. 14 2005. On December 16, 2003, Congressman Conyers wrote the Justice Department and Department of Homeland Security Inspectors

General, requesting that Mr. Arar's rendition be investigated. The Inspector General of DHS accepted, and despite a lack of cooperation from Administration staff, has been inquiring how Mr. Arar was sent to be tortured for over two years now. See Letter from Clark Kent Ervin, Inspector General, to the Honorable John Conyers, Jr., regarding the investigation of Maher Arar's rendition, July 14, 2004.

1,080. On November 2, 2005, the *Washington Post* reported that the CIA has been conducting interrogations of Al Qaeda captives in secret prisons in Eastern Europe. The system of prisons has been in existence for over four years, yet even the most "basic information about the system [has been kept] secret from the public, foreign officials and nearly all members of Congress charged with overseeing the CIA's covert actions." Dana Priest, "CIA Holds Terror Suspects in Secret Prisons", *The Washington Post*, Nov. 2, 2005, at A1.

1,081. An FBI agent corroborated that no actionable intelligence is being gathered through abuse at Guantanamo Bay and is in fact jeopardizing prosecutions: "These tactics have produced no intelligence of a threat neutralization nature to date and . . . have destroyed any chance of prosecuting this detainee." Dan Eggen & R. Jeffrey Smith, "FBI Agents Allege Abuse at Guantanamo Bay", *The Washington Post*, Dec. 21, 2004, at A1. Recent reviews of tribunal transcripts find that detainees are now revoking previous confessions that were apparently made under coercive torture tactics. Tim Golden, "Voices Baffled, Brash and Irate in Guantanamo", the *New York Times*, Mar. 6, 2006, at A1.

1,082. Charles Babington, "Activists on the Right, GOP Lawmakers Divided on Spying; Privacy Concerns, Terror Fight at Odds", *The Washington Post*, Feb. 7, 2006 at A04. See Maureen Dowd, "Smoking Dutch Cleanser", the *New York Times*, Feb. 11, 2006 at A6.

1,083. The operative provision of the AUMF provides "the President is authorized to use all necessary and appropriate force against those nations, organizations, or persons he determines planned, authorized, committed, or aided the terrorist attacks of September 11, 2001, or harbored such organizations or persons, in order to prevent any future acts of international terrorism against the United States by such nations, organizations or persons." 115 Stat. 224(2)(a) (2001).

1,084. White Paper at 12. In emphasizing the "at home" language, the Administration explains, "[t]o take action against those linked to the September 11th attacks involves taking action against individuals within the United States."

1,085. 542 U.S. 507 (2004).

1,086. White Paper at 2.

1,087. Letter from the Honorable William E. Moschella, Assistant Attorney General, to the Honorable Pat Roberts, Chairman, Senate Select Committee on Intelligence, the Honorable John D. Rockefeller, IV, Vice Chairman, Senate Select Committee on Intelligence, et al. (Dec. 22, 2005).

1,088. *Ibid.*

1,089. White Paper at 28.

1,090. Tom Daschle, "Power We Didn't Grant", *The Washington Post*, Dec. 23, 2005 at A21.

1,091. Tom Daschle, "Power We Didn't Grant", *The Washington Post*, Dec. 23, 2005 at A21.

1,092. Scott Rothschild, "Senator: Bush's Spying Raises Serious Concerns", *Lawrence Journal-World*, Dec. 24, 2005, *available at* http://www2.ljworld.com/news/2005/dec/24/senator_bushs_spying_raises_concerns/?city_local.

1,093. Senate NSA Hearing (Sen. Arlen Specter, Chairman, Senate Judiciary Committee).

1,094. Senate NSA Hearing (Sen. Lindsey Graham, Senate Judiciary Committee).

1,095. Susan Page, "Bush's Defense of Domestic Spying Meets Skepticism", *USA Today*, Dec. 21, 2005 at 6A.

1,096. CRS Memo at 44.

1,097. Indeed, it would be odd if the AUMF was to be interpreted as giving the Administration greater legal authority than an actual declaration of war, as under FISA, war time warrantless surveillance is limited to 15 days. 50 U.S.C. § 1811 (1978).

1,098. Gonzales and Hayden Press Briefing (Dec. 19, 2005).

1,099. George F. Will, "No Checks, Many Imbalances", *The Washington Post*, Feb. 16, 2006, at A27. On this point, Harvard Law School Professor Laurence Tribe stated, "to argue that one couldn't have gotten congressional authorization ... after arguing that ... one did get congressional authorization takes some nerve." Letter from Laurence H. Tribe, Carl M. Loeb University Professor, Harvard University Law School, to the Honorable John Conyers, Jr. (Tribe Letter) (Jan. 6, 2006).

1,100. When asked at the Senate Judiciary Committee whether the Administration raised the idea of amending FISA with any Members of the Committee, Attorney General Gonzales responded, "I have no personal knowledge that anyone on this Committee was told." Senate NSA Hearing (testimony of Attorney General Alberto Gonzales).

1,101. At his confirmation hearing, General Hayden acknowledged that he "did not recall any substantive discussion about the Congressional authorization in September 2001 to use all necessary force against Al Qaeda." Erich Lichtblau, "Nominee Says N.S.A. Stayed Within Law on Wiretaps", the *New York Times*, May 19, 2006, A20.

1,102. In 2003, the Administration proposed a draft "PATRIOT II" bill, which would have among other things, changed current law authorizing wartime warrantless surveillance for up to 15 days without court approval, to "allow the wartime exception to be invoked after Congress authorizes the use of military force, or after the United States has suffered an attack creating a national emergency." The Bush Administration dropped the proposal amidst a storm of criticism. See Sandy Bergo, "Draft Legislation Undercuts Bush Domestic Spying Rationale", The Center for Public Integrity Report, Jan. 31, 2006. Dan Eggen, "2003 Draft Legislation covered Eavesdropping", *The Washington Post*, Jan. 28, 2006 at A2.

1,103. In June 2002, Senator Dewine, offered legislation that would have permitted "reasonable suspicion" rather than "probable cause" to serve as the standard for obtaining surveillance warrants for non-U.S. citizens believed to be connected to terrorism (S. 2659, 107th Cong. (2002); however, the Bush Administration objected, asserting the proposal raised "both significant legal and practical issues." Hearing on Proposals to Amend the Foreign Intelligence Surveillance Act of 1978, Before the S. Select Comm. on Intelligence, 107th Cong. (2002) (testimony of James A. Baker).

1,104. 542 U.S. 507, 521 (2004). "With respect to Hamdi, the Bush Administration also cited a 2004 Harvard Law Review article which they claim supported their interpretation of the case: "'the clear inference is that the AUMF authorizes what the laws of war permit.' Curtis A. Bradley & Jack L. Goldsmith, Congressional Authorization and the War on Terrorism, 118 Harv. L. Rev. 2048, 2092 (2005) (emphasis added)." White Paper at 13. However, the co-author of the piece, Curtis A. Bradley, has stated that the quotes "were taken out of the context of a larger discussion." and "I don't know of anything in the laws of war that contemplates this sort of surveillance." Eric Lichtblau and Adam Liptak, "Bush and His Senior Aids Press On in Legal Defense for Wiretapping Program", *The Washington Post*, Jan. 28, 2006, at A1. Another distinction between Hamdi and FISA is that FISA, unlike the statute interpreted by the Court in Hamdi, explicitly states that it "shall be the exclusive means" for electronic surveillance.

1,105. 542 U.S. 507, 516 (2004).

1,106. Tribe Letter (emphasis in original). The Bush Administration's contention on this point is also undercut by a legal memorandum prepared by 14 legal experts and former government officials, including President Reagan's FBI Director, William S. Sessions and prominent conservative legal scholar, William Van Alstyne which concludes, "[i]t is one thing, however, to say that foreign battlefield capture of enemy combatants is an incident of waging war that Congress intended to authorize. It is another matter entirely to treat unchecked, warrantless domestic spying as included in that authorization, especially where an existing statute specifies that other laws are the 'exclusive means' by which electronic surveillance may be conducted." Letter from Beth Nolan, Curtis Bradley, David Cole, Geoffrey Stone, Harold Hongju Koh, Kathleen M. Sullivan, Laurence H. Tribe, Martin Lederman, Philip B. Heymann, Richard Epstein, Ronald Dworkin, Walter Dellinger, William S. Sessions, and William Van Alstyne to Members of Congress (Legal Scholar Letter) (Jan. 9, 2005). The Congressional Research Service has contradicted the Bush Administration's legal justifications for the domestic spying program, concluding, among other things, "[t]here is reason, however, to limit Hamdi to actual military operations on the battlefield as that concept is traditionally understood." CRS Memo at 34.

1,107. White Paper at 22.

1,108. H. Conf. Rep. 95-1720, at 33.

1,109. CRS Memo at 40.

1,110. In the White Paper, the Bush Administration was somewhat dismissive of clear congressional intent, noting "some Members of Congress believed that any such authorization would come in the form of a particularized amendment to FISA itself." White Paper at 26. The Administration failed to note that "some Members" came in the form of the Committee Report filed by the House Intelligence Committee, which was most responsible for writing the legislation.

1,111. Democratic Briefing on the "Constitution in Crisis: Domestic Surveillance and Executive Power," Before the H. Comm. on the Judiciary, 109th Cong. (2006) (statement of Prof. Jonathan Turley). The Congressional Research Service also concluded, "[a]lthough section 109(a) of FISA does not explicitly limit the language "as authorized by statute" to refer only to Title III and to FISA, the legislative history suggests that such a result was intended." CRS Memo at 43.

1,112. J.E.M. Ag. Supply v. Pioneer Hi-Bred, 534 U.S. 124, 141-142 (2001) (quoting Morton v. Mancari, 417 U.S. 535, 550 (1974)).

1,113. U.S. v. Oakland Cannabis Buyers Corp., 532 U.S. 483, 494 (2001).

1,114. Morales v. TWA, 504 U.S. 374, 384-85 (1992).

1,115. Legal Scholar Letter (Jan. 9, 2005).

1,116. U.S. Attorney General Alberto Gonzales, Prepared Remarks for Attorney General Alberto R. Gonzales at the Georgetown University Law Center, (Jan. 24, 2006), *available at* http://www/usdoj.gov/ag/speeches/2006/ag_speech_0601241.html.

1,117. The Federalist No. 23 (Alexander Hamilton); White Paper at 7.

1,118. Attorney General Alberto Gonzales remarks (Jan 24, 2006), *available at* http://www.usdoj.gov/ag/speeches/2006/ag_speech_0601241.html. It is instructive to note that the Administration did not point to the warrantless wiretapping engaged in by the Nixon Administration or their efforts to rely on inherent executive authority, however the Supreme Court did reject President Nixon's assertion of such authority to enjoin the publication of the Pentagon Papers. See New York Times v. Sullivan, 376 U.S. 254 (1964).

1,119. 343 U.S. 579 (1952). See White Paper at 7.

1,120. 343 U.S. 579 (1952). See White Paper at 7.

1,121. 310 F.3d 717, 742. See White Paper at 8.

1,122. United States v. Truong Dinh Hung, 629 F.2d 908 (4th Cir. 1980); United States v. Butenko, 494 F.2d 593 (3rd Cir. 1974), cert. denied sub nom. Ivanov v. United States, 419 U.S. 881 (1974); and United States v. Brown, 484 F.2d 418, 426 (5th Cir. 1973). See White Paper at 8.

1,123. Benjamin Franklin, Pennsylvania Bssembly: Reply to the Governor (Nov. 11, 1755), reprinted in The Papers of Benjamin Franklin 242 (Leonard W. Labaree, ed., Yale Univ. Press) (1963).

1,124. James Madison, Letters of Helvidius, no. 1 (Aug. 24—Sept. 14, 1793).

1,125. Federalist 23 states, "[t]he necessity of the Constitution, at least equally energetic with the one proposed, to the preservation of the Union, is the point at the examination of which we are now arrived ... . Its distribution and organization will more properly claim our attention under the succeeding head." The Federalist No. 23 (Alexander Hamilton).

1,126. The Federalist No. 47 (James Madison).

1,127. Wartime Executive Power and the NSA's Surveillance Authority (Part II): Hearing before the S. Comm. on the Judiciary, 109th Cong. (2006) (testimony of Harold Hongju Koh, Dean, Yale Law School).

1,128. 389 U.S. 347 (1967).

1,129. 50 U.S.C. §§ 1801 et. seq.

1,130. Democratic Briefing on the "Constitution in Crisis: Domestic Surveillance and Executive Power," Before the H. Comm. on the Judiciary, 109th Cong. (2006) (statement of Prof. Jonathan Turley).

1,131. 343 U.S. 579, 635 (1952).

1,132. 343 U.S 579, 637-640 (1952); see also Legal Scholar Letter (Jan. 9, 2005). As Justice Frankfurter articulated, "[i]t is one thing to draw an intention of Congress from general language and to say that Congress would have explicitly written what is inferred, where Congress has not addressed itself to a specific situation. It is quite impossible, however, when Congress did specifically address itself to a problem, as Congress did to that of seizure, to find secreted in the interstices of legislation the very grant of power which Congress consciously withheld. To find authority so explicitly withheld is . . . to disrespect the whole legislative process and the constitutional division of authority between President and Congress." 343 U.S. 579, 609.

1,133. As Professor Tribe observed, "an unchecked presidential program of secretly recording the conversations of perhaps thousands of innocent private citizens in the United States in hopes of gathering intelligence potentially useful for the ongoing war on a global terrorist network not only falls outside that category but misses it by a mile." Tribe Letter.

1,134. Congress refused to enact language proposed by the Ford administration that: "[n]othing contained in this chapter shall limit the constitutional power of the President to order electronic surveillance for the reasons stated in section 2511(3) of title 18, United States Code." 94th Cong. 2d Sess, § 2528 (Mar. 23, 1976), reprinted in Hearings on S. 743, S. 1998, S. 3197 Before the Subcomm. On Criminal Laws and Procedures of the Senate Judiciary Comm., 94th Cong., 2d Sess. 134 (1976) (stating in the first page of the report that S. 3197 was identical to the measure transmitted to the Senate by the President on March 23, 1976).

1,135. The repealed provision provides: "Nothing contained in this chapter or in section 605 of the Communications Act of 1934 shall limit the constitutional power of the President to take such measures as he deems necessary to protect the Nation against actual or potential attack or other hostile acts of a foreign power, to obtain foreign intelligence information deemed essential to the security of the United States, or to protect national security information against foreign intelligence activities. Nor shall anything contained in this chapter be deemed to limit the constitutional power of the President to take such measures as he deems necessary to protect the United States against the overthrow of the Government by force or other unlawful means, or against any other clear and present danger to the structure or existence of the Government. The contents of any wire or oral communication intercepted by authority of the president in the exercise of the foregoing powers may be received in evidence in any trial hearing, or other proceeding only where such interception was reasonable, and shall not be otherwise used or disclosed except as is necessary to implement that power." Pub.L.No. 90-351, 82 Stat. 212 (codified as amended at 18 U.S.C. §§ 2510-2520 (1968)) (provision repealed).

1,136. H.R. Rep. No. 95-1283, pt. 1, at 24 (1978).

1,137. S. Rep. No. 95-604, pt. I, at 6 (1978) (emphasis added). To eliminate any doubt concerning the legislative intent, the Senate Report concludes that FISA was "designed . . . to curb the practice by which the Executive Branch may conduct warrantless electronic surveillance on its own unilateral determination that national security justifies it." Ibid. at 8. When it comes to electronic surveillance covered by FISA, "the Congress has declared that this statute, not any claimed presidential power, controls." Id. at 64.

1,138. Joint Explanatory Statement of the Committee of the Conference, House Conference Rep. No. 95-1720, 35 (Oct. 5, 1978) (emphasis added). The Report further stated, "[t]he Senate Bill provided that the procedures in this bill and in Chapter 119 of Title 18, United States Code, shall be the exclusive means by which electronic surveillance, as defined in this bill, and the interception of domestic wire and oral communications may be conducted. The House amendments provided that the procedures in this bill and in Chapter 119 of Title 18, U.S.C. shall be the exclusive statutory means by which electronic surveillance as defined in this bill and the interception of domestic wire and oral communications may be conducted. The Conference substitute adopts the Senate provision which omits the word "statutory" . . . . The conferees agree that the establishment by this act of exclusive means by which the President may conduct electronic surveillance does not foreclose a different decision by the Supreme Court."

1,139. The White Paper notes while FISA was being debated during the Carter Administration, Attorney General Griffin Bell testified that "the current bill recognizes no inherent power of the President to conduct electronic surveillance, and I want to interpolate here to say that this does not take away the power [of] the President under the Constitution." White Paper at 8.

1,140. Foreign Intelligence Electronic Surveillance Act of 1978: Hearings on H.R. 5764, Congressional Hearing on H.R. 9745, H.R. 7308, and H.R. 5632, Before the Subcomm. on Legislation of the H. Comm. on Intelligence, 95th Cong. (1978) (statement of Attorney General Griffin Bell) (emphasis added). During the House Hearings, John M. Harmon, the Assistant Attorney General, Office of Legal Counsel, admitted that "it seems unreasonable to conclude that Congress, in the exercise of its powers in this area, may not vest in the courts the authority intelligence surveillance." Also, when President Carter signed FISA into law, he specifically acknowledged that the law requires "a prior judicial warrant for all electronic surveillance for foreign intelligence or counterintelligence purposes in the United States in which communications of U.S. persons might be intercepted." Jimmy Carter, Statement on Signing S.1566 into Law (Oct. 25, 1978), available at http://www.cnss.org/Carter.pdf (emphasis in original).

1,141. In re Sealed Case, 310 F.3d at 746.

1,142. In Truong, the court found that pre-FISA, judicial review of warrants of foreign surveillance was not appropriate because of the desire to avoid undue delay, the need for secrecy, the competence of the judiciary, and sensitivity to separation of powers. 629 F.2d at 914. All of these concerns have been addressed and incorporated in the FISA law—emergency surveillance is permitted; the proceedings are secret; special judges have been chosen; and Congress has enacted procedures which balance the separation of powers. In Butenko, 494 F.2d 593 (3rd Cir. 1974), cert. denied sub nom. Ivanov v. United States, 419 U.S. 881 (1974), while the court held that warrantless electronic surveillance of foreign nationals was lawful, it stated that it would be unlawful if the interception were to be conducted on a domestic group for law enforcement purposes. 494 F.2d at 606. In Brown, 484 F.2d 418, 426 (1973), the Court also recognized the legality of a challenged warrantless wiretap for the purpose of gathering foreign intelligence, but in so doing partially relied upon since repealed statutory language indicating congressional intent to defer to the President on these matters. Title III of the Omnibus Crime Control and Safe Streets Act of 1968, 18 U.S.C.A. § 2511(3) (1968) (provision repealed).

1,143. CRS Memo at 32. The fourth pre-FISA circuit court decision to address this decision, Zweibon v. Mitchell, firmly rejected the idea of warrantless surveillance. 516 F.2d 594 (D.C. Cir. 1975) (en banc).

1,144. The two seminal Supreme Court precedents in this area make it clear that widespread domestic surveillance necessitates a judicially approved warrant. In Katz v. U.S., 389 U.S. 347 (1967), the only instance in which the Supreme Court considered the issue of national security wiretaps, the Court held that the Fourth Amendment requires adherence to judicial processes, and searches conducted outside the judicial process, are per se unreasonable under the Fourth Amendment, subject only to a few specifically established and well-delineated exceptions. In United States v. United States District Court (the Keith case), 407 U.S. 297 (1972), the Court specifically held that, in the case of intelligence gathering involving domestic security surveillance, prior judicial approval was required to satisfy the Fourth Amendment. Ibid. at 313-14, 317, 319-20. The Court stated: "These Fourth Amendment freedoms cannot properly be guaranteed if domestic security surveillances may be conducted solely within the discretion of the Executive Branch." Ibid. at 317-18.

1,145. White Paper at 37.

1,146. See In re Sealed Case, 310 F.3d 717 (Foreign Intel. Surv. Ct. of Rev. 2002); Vernonia School District 47J v. Acton, 515 U.S. 646 (1995), and Michigan Dep't of State Police v. Sitz, 496 U.S. 444 (1990).

1,147. In re Sealed Case merely represents the principle that before FISA was enacted, the President had inherent authority to engage in certain foreign intelligence surveillance, since that time, of course, Congress has enacted in the form of FISA an entire statutory framework governing surveillance activities. See 310 F.3d 717 (Foreign Intel. Surv. Ct. of Rev. 2002). In Vernonia, the Court upheld school drug testing programs because students have diminished expectations of privacy in school, the programs were limited to students engaging in extracurricular programs, and the drug testings were standardized and tested only for the presence of drugs—no factor like this is present with respect to the NSA program. See 515 U.S. 646 (1995). Similarly, in Sitz, the Court upheld highway drunk driving checkpoints because they were standardized, the stops were brief and minimally intrusive, and a warrant and probable cause requirement were found to defeat the purpose of keeping drunk drivers off the road—again, none of this can be said about the NSA program. See 496 U.S. 444 (1990).

1,148. Tribe Letter. Professor Tribe has written, the wiretapping scheme that the Administration employs is "so indiscriminate and sweeping" in its intrusion into American citizens' private communications that no balancing test can save it from violating those rights protected by the Fourth Amendment to be secure against unreasonable searches and seizures. Professor Tribe argues that this is especially so when the scheme is administered by one branch of government without adequate checks on that power. This applies even when such activity may be a constitutional power entrusted to the President by Article II or delegated to the President by Congress in exercising its powers by Article I.

1,149. Senate NSA Hearing (testimony of Attorney General Alberto Gonzales).

1,150. Jeffrey Rosen, "Alberto Gonzales's Spin", *The New Republic Online*, Feb. 27, 2006, *available at* http://www.tnr.com/doc.mhtml?i=20060227&s=rosen022706.

1,151. Woods has stated that the lower reasonable basis standard "in my mind, is a much more likely reason why they maintained this [surveillance program]." Richard B. Schmitt and David G. Savage, "Legal Test Was Seen as Hurdle to Spying; Some Say the Court's Tougher Standard of 'Probable Cause' Led to the Surveillance Order", *Los Angeles Times*, Dec. 20, 2005, at A1.

1,152. Barton Gellman, Dafna Linzer, & Carol D. Leonnig, "Surveillance Net Yields Few Suspects", *The Washington Post*, Feb. 5, 2006, at A1

1,153. *Ibid.*

1,154. *Ibid.*

1,155. *Ibid.*

1,156. *Ibid.*

1,157. *Ibid.*

1,158. As the non-partisan Congressional Research Service wrote, the actions by the telecommunications companies may well "expose the telephone companies to ... civil remedies or criminal sanctions." Elizabeth B. Bazan, Gina Marie Stevens, and Brian T. Yeh, Legislative Attorneys, American Law Division, Government Access to Phone Calling Activity and Related Records: Legal Authorities, Congressional Research Service Memorandum (May 17,2006) at 1.

1,159. 18 U.S.C. § 2702 et seq. (2006). A cause of action lies for violation of this law and damages of up to $1000 per violation can be assessed against the guilty party as well as attorney's fees and punitive damages in certain circumstances.

1,160. 18 U.S.C. § 2702(c)(1) (2006).

1,161. 18 U.S.C. §§ 2702(c)(1) & 2709 (2006).

1,162. 18 U.S.C. § 2702(c)(2) (2006).

1,163. 18 U.S.C. § 2702(c)(3) (2006).

1,164. 18 U.S.C. § 2702(c)(4) (2006). There is also a general exception to privacy requirements for telecommunications providers responding to law enforcement requests set forth in 18 U.S.C. § 2511, however that is limited to actual "content" rather than identifying data, and is also limited to requests by the Attorney General or designated law enforcement officer, which does not appear to be the case here.

1,165. See 18 U.S.C. § 2709 (2006); John Markoff, "In Spy Data Furor, Ex-Qwest Chief Balked-Lawmakers Vow Closer Inquiry on Program", the *New York Times*, May 13, 2006 at 13.

1,166. Barton Gellman and Arshad Mohammed, "Data on Phone Calls Monitored, Extent of Administrations's Domestic Surveillance Decried in Both Parties", *The Washington Post*, May 12, 2006, *available at* http://www.washingtonpost.com/wpdyn/content/article/2006/5/11/AR200 (The government lawyer stated "It is within their terms of service because you have consented to that...and if they do it voluntarily, the U.S. government can accept it.").

1,167. 18 U.S.C. §. 2510-22 (2006).

1,168. Processor Orin Kerr , a former federal prosecutor and an expert on the Fourth Amendment, agrees that any consent granted within the small print in companies' Terms of Service will not suffice to provide the consent necessary for the consent exception. Anita Ramasastry, The Recent Revelations about the NSA's Access to our Phone Records: the Laws that were Probably Broken and the Likely Consequences, May 15, 2006, *available at* http://writ.news.findlaw.com/ramasastry.

1,169. Beginning in 2006, the Attorney General is required to submit to the Committee of the Judiciary in both the House and the Senate a report containing the "number of accounts from which the Department of Justice has received voluntary disclosures under the emergency exception," and a summary for the basis of those disclosures in some instances. 18 U.S.C. § 2702 (2006).

1,170.47 U.S.C. § 222 et seq. (2006). Anyone who violates this act is subject to fines of up to $10, 000 or up to one year imprisonment or both.(§501-503)

1,171. 47 U.S.C. § 222(c)(1) (2006).

1,172. 47 U.S.C. § 222(c)(1) (2006).

1,173. 47 U.S.C. § 222(c)(1) (2006) (Specifically, the telecommunications companies may disclose this information in order to provide the telecommunications service from which the information is derived or when such disclosure is otherwise necessary to provide service or services necessary to provide this service, including, for example, the publishing of directories).

1,174. 47 U.S.C. § 222 (2006). The Federal Communications Commission issued its Customer Proprietary Network Information Regulations to implement this law. The rules require that the companies obtain express consent from their customers before disclosing the information to third parties or affiliates that do not provide communications-related services. However, carriers may disclose this information to affiliates only after obtaining a customer's "opt-out" consent. "Opt out" consent requires that the telephone company send the customer a notice saying it will consider the customer to have given approval to use the customer's information for marketing unless the customer tells it not to do so(usually within 30 days). 47 C.F.R. § 64.2005-2008 (2006).

1,175. Seymour M. Hersh, "The Talk of the Town: National Security Department, Listening In", *The New Yorker*, May 29, 2006 at 24.

1,176. 18 U.S.C. § 3123 (2006).

1,177. Letter from the Center for Democracy and Technology: Preliminary Analysis of NSA Datamining Program, (May 11, 2006). *available at* http://www.cdt.org.

1,178. Kate Martin, "NSA Again Violates the Law "(May 11,2006) *available at* http://www.acsblog.org/bill-of-rights-2835-guest-blogger-nsa-again-violates-the-law.html.

1,179. 442 U.S. 735 (1979).

1,180. Laurence H. Tribe, "Bush Stomps on Fourth Amendment", *The Boston Globe*, May 16, 2006.

1,181. Michael V. Hayden, "What American Intelligence and Especially the NSA Have Been Doing to Defend the Nation," National Press Club, Washington, D.C. (Jan 23, 2006)("I don't think that anyone can make the claim that the FISA statute is optimized to deal with our prevent a 9-11 or to deal with a lethal enemy who likely already had combatants inside the United States.").

1,182. Michael Hayden has stated, "[H]ad this program been in effect prior to 9-11, it is my professional judgment that we would have detected some of the 9-11 Al Qaeda operatives in the United States and we would have identified them as such." White House Steps Up Defense Of Domestic Easdropping, Cnn.com, Jan. 23, 2006, available at http://www.cnn.com/2006/POLITICS/01/23/nsa.strategy/. On January 4, 2006, Vice President Cheney when speaking at the Heritage Foundation claimed "[i]f we'd been able to do this before 9-11, we might have been able to pick up on two of the hijackers who flew a jet into the Pentagon. They were in the United States, communicating with Al Qaeda associates overseas. But we didn't know they were plotting until it was too late:"Vice President Richard Cheney, Remarks on Iraq and the War on Terror, The Heritage Foundation, Washington, D.C. (Jan. 4, 2006). On May 11, FOX News head Washington correspondent, Jim Angle asserted, "[f]or instance, if this had been in place before 9-11, and the U.S. had thephone number used by Al Qaeda planner Khalid Shaikh Mohammed, it could have searched the database to locate whyich numbers he was calling in the U.S., which might have led to the hijackers before they boarded their planes." Media Matters, Myths and Falsehoods on the NSA domestic call tracking program, May 12, 2006, *available at* http://mediamatters.org/items/200605120018.

1,183. Bush Administration allies such as William Kristol have also pointed to the case of Zacarias Moussaoui to support the proposition that FISA impeded the Administration from stopping the 2001 terrorist attacks and stated that the probable-cause requirements under FISA are too high to obtain a warrant. See William Kristol and Gary Schmitt, "Vital Presidential Power", *The Washington Post*, Dec. 20, 2005, at A31.

1,184. Scott McClellan, Remarks at Press Briefing (Jan. 17, 2006), *available at* http://www.whitehouse.gov/news/releases/2006/01/20060117-3.html ("It was the Clinton administration that used warrantless physical searches. An example is what they did in the case of Aldrich Ames."); Fox News: Interview by Sean Hannity with Alberto Gonzales, Attorney General (Fox News Television Broadcast Jan. 17, 2006), available at http://www.foxnews.com/story/0,2933,181882,00.html ( The Attorney General stated, " I will say to the American people, however, that, under the Clinton administration, the department — I mean, the administration was engaged in physical searches without a warrant. Aldrich Ames is an example, where his house was searched without a warrant.").

1,185. Barton Gellman, "RNC Points to Spy Orders By Carter, Clinton", *The Washington Post*, Dec. 22, 2005, at A12. The RNC quoted fragments of Clinton's Executive Order 12949, authorizing the attorney general to "approve physical searches, without a court order, to acquire foreign intelligence information," and Carter's Executive Order 12139, authorizing the attorney general to "approve electronic surveillance to acquire foreign intelligence information without a court order."

1,186. Senate NSA Hearing (testimony of Attorney General Alberto Gonzales).

1,187. Foreign Intelligence Surveillance Act of 1978, 50 U.S.C. § 1805(f) (providing the Attorney General with the power to authorize electronic surveillance "when the Attorney General reasonably determines that an emergency situation exists with respect to the employment of electronic surveillance to obtain foreign intelligence information before an order authorizing such surveillance can with due diligence be obtained, and the factual basis for issuance of an order under [FISA's subchapter on electronic surveillance] to approve such surveillance exists"). Beyond the three day requirement, FISA also permits the government to wiretap a foreign government for up to an entire year without warrants if the Attorney General can certify that the information will only be used for foreign intelligence purposes. 50 U.S.C. § 1802.

1,188. As the *New York Times* wrote, "[i]n other words, there is not a shred of proof that the illegal program produced information that could not have been obtained legally, had the administration wanted to bother to stay within the law." "Kabuki Congress", the *New York Times*, Mar. 6, 2006. At House Judiciary Briefings, Department of Justice representatives essentially admitted that their principal objection to using this program was that it would necessitate additional resources and manpower, even though in the most recent fiscal year, the Department had a budget of more than $22 billion and more than 112,000 employees. See U.S. Dept. of Justice, FY2005 Performance and Accountability Report, *available at* http://www.usdoj.gov/ag/annualreports/pr2005/TableofContents.htm.

1,189. FISA previously allowed the government to begin surveillance without a warrant, in an emergency, so long as a warrant request was presented to the FISA Court within 24 hours. The Intelligence Authorization Act of 2002 extended that 24-hour exception to 72 hours. 22 U.S.C. 7301.

1,190. See Summary of Post 9-11Changes to FISA and Related Laws, Prepared by the Democratic Staffs of the House Intelligence and Judiciary Committees (Jan. 20, 2006).

1,191. The Patriot Act expanded pen register and trap and trace authority under FISA to include addressing and routing information from e-mail and Internet traffic, in addition to the previously authorized interception of incoming and outgoing telephone numbers.

1,192. Prior to the Patriot Act, the government could obtain an order for a FISA pen register and trap and trace ("pen-traps") only upon certifying that there was reason to believe that the line to be monitored is being used or about to be used by a suspected spy or terrorist. Under the Patriot Act, a FISA pen-trap order may be obtained "for any investigation to gather foreign intelligence information" where the government certifies that the information sought is "relevant" to an ongoing investigation. This lower standard of relevance also applies to e-mail and Internet traffic.

1,193. Prior to the passage of the Patriot Act, the government could conduct surveillance under FISA only where gathering foreign intelligence information was the purpose for the surveillance. The Patriot Act changed FISA to allow collection when gathering foreign intelligence information is a significant purpose of the surveillance.

1,194. The Patriot Act significantly extended the duration for FISA warrants for certain categories of surveillance and physical searches.

1,195. Before September 11, only common carriers, hotels, storage facilities, or car rental agencies were subjected to FISA's business record authority. Section 215 of the PATRIOT Act eliminated restrictions on the categories of records that could be sought and permitting FISA subpoenas to be issued for "any tangible things," including the records of libraries, booksellers, financial institutions, internet service providers and others.

1,196. To address the problem of unknown suspected terrorists switching phones or computers, FISA was amended by the Patriot Act to allow for a generic warrant authorizing covering communications by an unidentified target, regardless of the specific communications device used.

1,197. The Patriot Act amended the law to require the Director of Central Intelligence (now Director of National Intelligence) to establish FISA requirements and priorities, and provide assistance to the Attorney General to ensure proper dissemination of FISA-derived information.

1,198. The Patriot Act amended FISA to shield from causes of action, in any court, companies and individuals who provide assistance pursuant to FISA court orders.

1,199. Previously, government officials could issue NSLs for financial, credit, telephone, and other business records only upon certifying there were "specific articulable facts giving reason to believe" that the subject of an investigation was a "foreign power or the agent of a foreign power." The Patriot Act lowered the standard. Now, the government is required only to assert that the records or things are "sought for" a foreign intelligence investigation or to protect against international terrorism or clandestine intelligence activities.

1,200. The Patriot Act also deleted the requirement for high-level FBI headquarters approval for NSLs. Now, Special Agents-in-Charge of FBI field offices can approve the issuance of NSLs.

1,201. In the Intelligence Reform and Terrorism Prevention Act of 2004, Congress for the first time allowed FISA surveillance of any non-U.S. person who engages in or prepares for international terrorism. Previously, FISA surveillance was available only where the government could show a nexus to a foreign power or international terrorist group. See S. 2845, 108th Cong. (2004).

1,202. Carol D. Leonnig, "Secret Court's Judges Were Warned About NSA Spy Data", *The Washington Post*, Feb 9, 2006, at A1.

1,203. Carol D. Leonnig, "Secret Court's Judges Were Warned About NSA Spy Data", *The Washington Post*, Feb 9, 2006, at A1.

1,204. Dan Eggen & Robert O'Harrow Jr., "U.S. Steps Up Secret Surveillance; FBI, Justice Dept. Increase Use of Wiretaps, Records Searches", *The Washington Post*, Mar. 24, 2003, at A1.

1,205. Carol D. Leonnig, "Secret Court's Judges Were Warned About NSA Spy Data", *The Washington Post*, Feb 9, 2006, at A1.

1,206. Steven R. Weisman, "Powell Speaks Out on Domestic Spy Program", the *New York Times*, Dec. 26, 2005, at A1.

1,207. National Commission on Terrorist Attacks Upon the United States, The 9-11 Commission Report at 267 (2004).

1,208. Jim VandeHei and Dan Eggan, "Cheney Cites Justifications for Domestic Eavesdropping", *The Washington Post*, Jan. 5, 2006, at A2. See also The 9-11 Commission Report, Final Report of the National Commission on Terrorist Attacks Upon the United States 37 (W.W. Norton & Co. 2004).

1,209. Seymour M. Hersh, "National Security Dept. Listening In", *The New Yorker*, May 29, 2006, at 24.

1,210. "In our view, the FBI applied too cramped an interpretation of probable cause and 'agent of a foreign power' in making the determination of whether Moussaoui was an agent of a foreign power. FBI Headquarters personnel in charge of reviewing this application focused too much on establishing a nexus between Moussaoui and a 'recognized' group, which is not legally required. Without going into the actual evidence in the Moussaoui case, there appears to have been sufficient evidence in the possession of the FBI which satisfied the FISA requirements for Moussaoui application." Senator Charles Grassley, Senator Patrick Leahy, and Senator Arlen Specter, FISA Implementation Failures: Interim Report on FBI Oversight in the 107th Congress, Before the Senate Judiciary Committee, Feb. 2003, at 26.

1,211. Jerry Markon & Timothy Dwyer, "FBI Was Warned About Moussaoui", *The Washington Post*, Mar. 21, 2006, at A1.

1,212. Maureen Dowd, "Fly Into a Building? Who Could Imagine?" the *New York Times*, Mar. 22, 2006, at 25. There also would not appear to have been any legal impediment to prevent the Bush Administration from, on September 10, 2001, conducting surveillance without pre-approval when the government intercepted Al Qaeda calls outside the United States, which revealed that an attack was highly imminent, as well as intercepts such as "the match begins tomorrow" and "tomorrow is zero hour" the Administration could have proceeded with an emergency wiretap. See, e.g., David Ensor, Kate Snow, and Kelly Wallace, "Justice May Probe Leaked Pre-9-11 Intercepts", *CNN*, June 21, 2002; James Bamford, "The Agency That Could Be Big Brother", *The Nation*, Dec. 25, 2005, at 1.

1,213. Republican National Comm., Research Briefing: Dems Play Politics Again with National Security (Dec. 21, 2005), *available at* http://www.gop.com/media/PDFs/122105NationalSecurity.pdf.

1,214. Exec. Order 12949 (Feb. 9, 1995).

1,215. Exec. Order 12949 (Feb. 9, 1995).

1,216. Barton Gellman, "RNC Points to Spy Orders By Carter, Clinton", *The Washington Post*, Dec. 22, 2005, at A12. Since the initial accusations that President Carter and Clinton engaged in warrantless surveillance, Attorney General Gonzales has subsequently acknowledged that not only was this not the case, but that no president since the enactment of FISA in 1978 other than President George W. Bush had engaged in domestic warrantless surveillance. Senate NSA Hearing (testimony of Attorney General Alberto Gonzales).

1,217. "Myths and Falsehoods on the NSA Domestic Call-Tracking Program", *Media Matters*, May 15, 2006.

1,218. Press Release, White House Press Secretary Scott McClellan, Setting the Record Straight: Democrats Continue to Attack Terrorist Surveillance Program (Jan. 22, 2006) *available at* http://www.whitehouse.gov/news/releases/2006/01/20060122.html.

1,219. Ironically, it was Senator Shelby, a Republican and former Chairman of the Senate Select Committee on Intelligence, who reportedly leaked classified information to the press in 2002. See Allan Lengel and Dana Priest, "Investigators Concluded Shelby Leaked Message", *The Washington Post*, Aug. 5, 2004, at A17.

1,220. 50 USC § 401.

1,221. 50 USC § 413(a)(1).

1,222. 50 USC § 413b(e).

1,223. 50 USC § 413b(e)(1).

1,224. 50 USC § 413(e).

1,225. David Morgan, "Bush agrees to full NSA oversight by Congress", *Reuters*, May 16, 2006, *available at* http://go.reuters.com/newsArticle.jhtml?type=topNews&storyID=12227749&src=rss/topNews.

1,226. Alfred Cumming, "Specialist in Intelligence and National Security, Foreign Affairs, Defense and Trade Division, Statutory Procedures Under Which Congress Is To Be Informed of U.S. Intelligence Activities, Including Covert Actions", Congressional Research Service Memorandum (Jan. 18, 2006) at 7.

1,227. Alfred Cumming, Specialist in Intelligence and National Security, Foreign Affairs, Defense and Trade Division, Statutory Procedures Under Which Congress Is To Be Informed of U.S. Intelligence Activities, Including Covert Actions, Congressional Research Service Memorandum (Jan. 18, 2006) at 8. Representative Harman, the House Intelligence Committee's Ranking Member, cited the National Security Act of 1947 in a letter dated January 4, 2006, asserting that Bush violated the law: "I have reviewed the law and now believe that the practice of briefing only certain Members of the intelligence committees violates the specific requirements of the National Security Act." She states that "failure to provide briefings to the full congressional intelligence committees is a continuing violation of the National Security Act." Harman goes on to write that "[a]s a general matter, Gang of Eight briefings do not provide for effective oversight. Members of the Gang of Eight cannot take notes, seek the advice of their counsel, or even discuss the issues raised with their committee colleagues. It is precisely for this reason that the law requires briefings for the full committee." Letter from the Honorable Jane Harman, Ranking Member on the House Permanent Select Committee on Intelligence to President George W. Bush (Jan. 4, 2006).

1,228. See Scott Shane, "Key Dem Rips Spy Program Briefings", the *New York Times*, Jan. 5, 2006, at A4. President Discusses Global War on Terror at Kansas State University (Jan. 23, 2006) *available at* http://www.whitehouse.gov/news/releases/2006/01/20060123-4.html ("We briefed members of the United States Congress, one of whom was Senator Pat Roberts, about this program. You know, it's amazing, when people say to me, well, he was just breaking the law—if I wanted to break the law, why was I briefing Congress?"); Vice President's Remarks on Iraq and the War on Terror at the Manhattan Institute for Policy Research (Jan. 19, 2006), *available at* http://www.whitehouse.gov/news /releases/2006/01/20060119-5.html ("It is important to note that leaders of Congress have been briefed more than a dozen times on the President's authorization, and on the activities conducted under it. I've personally presided over most of those briefings."); Prepared Remarks for Attorney General Alberto R. Gonzales at the Georgetown University Law Center, The Department of Justice, Jan. 24, 2006, *available at* http://www.usdoj.gov/ag/speeches/2006/ag_speech_0601241.html ("The leadership of Congress, including the leaders of the Intelligence Committees of both Houses of Congress, have been briefed about this program more than a dozen times since 2001.").

1,229. Suzanne E. Spaulding, "Power Play; Did Bush Roll Past the Legal Stop Signs", *The Washington Post*, Dec. 25, 2005, at B01.

1,230. Letter from The Honorable Jane Harman, Ranking Member on the House Permanent Select Committee on Intelligence, to The Honorable George W. Bush, United States President (Jan. 4, 2006).

1,231. Democratic Congressional Briefing on Constitution in Crisis: Domestic Surveillance and Executive Power Before the Democratic Judiciary Comm., 109th Cong. (2006) (prepared statement submitted by Bruce Fein).

1,232. Thomas G. Donlan, Editorial Commentary, "Unwarranted Executive Power", *Barron's*, Dec. 26, 2005, *available at* http://online.barrons.com/public/main.

1,233. Jonathan Schell, "Letters From Ground Zero: The Hidden State Steps Forward", *The Nation*, Jan. 9, 2006, at 8.

1,234. Senate NSA Hearing (testimony of Attorney General Alberto Gonzales).

1,235. Eric Lichtblau and Adam Liptak, "Bush and His Senior Aides Press On in Legal Defense for Wiretapping Program", the *New York Times*, Jan. 28, 2006, at A13.

1,236. Senate NSA Hearing (testimony of Attorney General Alberto Gonzales).

1,237. "Statement of President George W. Bush on signing H.R. 2863, Department of Defense, Emergency Supplemental Appropriations to Address Hurricanes in the Gulf of Mexico, and Pandemic Influenza Act, 2006 (Dec. 30, 2005), *available at* http://www.whitehouse.gov/news/releases/2005/12/20051230-8.html.

1,238. Bob Herbert, Op-Ed, "The Nixon Syndrome", the *New York Times*, Jan. 9, 2006, at A21.

1,239. "The President's End Run", Editorial, *The Washington Post*, Jan. 23, 2006, at A14.

1,240. Memorandum from Jay S. Bybee, Assistant Attorney General, to Alberto R. Gonzalez, Counsel to the President, Re. Standards of Conduct for Interrogation under 18 U.S.C. §§ 2340-2340A (Aug. 1 2002) *available at* http://www.gwu.edu/~nsarchiv/NSAEBB/NSAEBB127/02.08.01.pdf.

1,241. Chirtra Ragavan, "The Letter of the Law", *U.S. News and World Report*, Mar. 27, 2006 at 27. The article noted that according to two current and former government officials, the Bush Administration lawyers presented the arguments to senior FBI officials who expressed strong reservations about their proposal.

1,242. When Senator Schumer asked, "Has the Government searched someone's home, and American citizen, or office, without a warrant since 9-11, let's say?," the Attorney General responded, "Sir to my knowledge, that has not happened under the terrorist surveillance program, and I am not going to go beyond that." When Senator Kennedy asked, "[S]ince September 11th, has the President authorized any other surveillance program within the United States under his authority as Commander-in-Chief or under the authorization for use of military force in Afghanistan," the Attorney General responded, "Senator, I can't answer that question in terms of other operations." Senate NSA Hearing (testimony of Attorney General Alberto Gonzalez).

1,243. In his letter to the Senate Judiciary Committee, Gonzales wrote, "I did not and could not address ... any other classified intelligence activities.... At least one constitutional scholar who testified before the committee yesterday said in an interview that Gonzales appeared to be hinting that the operation disclosed by the *New York Times* in mid-December is not the full extent of eavesdropping on U.S. residents conducted without court warrants." Charles Babington & Dan Eggen, "Gonzalez Seeks to Clarify Testimony on Spying; Extent of Eavesdropping May Go Beyond NSA Work", The Washington Post, Mar. 1, 2006, at A08.

1,244. *Ibid.*

1,245. Oversight Hearing on U.S. Department of Justice: Hearing Before the House Judiciary Committee 109th Cong. 24 (2006) (testimony by Attorney General Gonzales). The Attorney General further stated that in considering the legal question, he would look to the same legal justifications used in the domestic spying program—"You would look at precedent. What have previous commander in chiefs done?" and he referred to President Wilson's authorizing cables to and from Europe "based upon the Constitution and his inherent role as commander in chief."

1,246. President George W. Bush, Speech given in Buffalo, NY (Apr. 20, 2004), *available at* http://www.areavoices.com/commonsense/?blog=1189.

1,247. The USA Patrito Act In Practice: Shedding Light on the FISA Process: Hearing on the Foreign Intelligence Surveillance Act Before the Senate Judiciary Committee, 107th Cong. (2002) (statement of Associate Attorney General David Kris). Mr. Kris' written testimony was cleared by both DOJ and the White House.

1,248. President George W. Bush, President Bush Calls for Renewing the USA Patriot Act (Apr. 19, 2004), *available at* http://www.whitehouse.gov/news/releases/2004/04/20040419-4.html.

1,249. President Bush: Information Sharing, Patriot Act Vital to Homeland Security (Apr. 20, 2004), *available at* http://www.whitehouse.gov/news/releases/2004/04/print/20040420-2.html.

1,250. President George W. Bush, Remarks at Ask President Bush Event (Jul. 14, 2004), *available at* http://www.whitehouse.gov/news/releases/2004/07/20040714-11.html.

1,251. Confirmation Hearings on the Nomination of Alberto R. Gonzales to be Attorney General of the United States, Before the Senate Judiciary Committee, 109th Cong. (Jan. 6, 2005).

1,252. Confirmation Hearing on the Nomination of Alberto R. Gonzales to be Attorney General of the United States, S. Hrg. 109-4 (statement of Alberto Gonzales). On April 26, 2005, James A. Baker, the Justice Department's Counsel for Intelligence Policy, testified under oath at a Crime Subcommittee hearing. When Rep. Bobby Scott asked him, "Suppose a U.S. citizen has information, and would be—you find out that they are going to be talking about your target, and you can find out where they are going to be, . . . Can you wiretap—as part of the investigation of the target, can you wiretap somebody else to get information about your target?" Baker responded, "No. Only if I could show that person was an agent of a foreign power. I would have to separately show . . . things I have to show under FISA: that the target is an agent of a foreign power, and I have to establish that by probable cause, and the second thing, that the target is going to use the facilities or places of which surveillance is going to be directed. Implementation of the USA PATRIOT Act: Sections of the Act that Address the Foreign Intelligence Surveillance Act (FISA): Hearing Before the Subcomm. on Crime, Terrorism, and Homeland Security of the House Comm. on the Judiciary, 109th Congress, 27 (2005).

1,253. President George W. Bush, Remarks at Ohio State Highway Patrol Academy (Jun. 9, 2005), *available at* http://www.whitehouse.gov/news/releases/2005/06/20050609-2.html

1,254. President Bush Encourages Renewal of Patriot Act Provisions (Jul. 20, 2005), *available at* http://www.whitehouse.gov/news/releases/2005/07/20050720-4.html

1,255. President George W. Bush, President Visits Troops at Brooke Army Medical Center (Jan. 1, 2006), *available at* http://www.whitehouse.gov/news/releases/2006/01/20060101.html.

1,256. Compare USA PATRIOT Act Pub. L. No. 107-56, 115 Stat 282, § 206 (codified in 28 U.S.C.) with 28 U.S.C. § 2510-2522.

1,257. President George Bush, President Visits National Security Agency (Jan. 25, 2006), *available at* http://www.whitehouse.gov/news/releases/2006/01/20060125-1.html.

1,258. Attorney General Alberto Gonzales, Press Briefing (Dec. 19, 2005), *available at* http://www.whitehouse.gov/news/releases/2005/12/print/20051219-1.html.

1,259. Vice President Dick Cheney, Vice President's remarks on Iraq and the War on Terror at the Manhattan Institute for Policy Research (Jan. 19, 2006), *available at* http://www.whitehouse.gov/news/releases/2006/01/20060119-5.html.

1,260. General Michael V. Hayden, Remarks at National Press Club (Jan. 23, 2006), *available at* http://www.freerepublic.com/focus/f-news/1564046/posts.

1,261. *Ibid.*

1,262. *Ibid.*

1,263. *Ibid.*

1,264. *Ibid.*

1,265. Senate NSA Hearing (testimony of Attorney General Alberto Gonzales).

1,266. Blogometer: When It Rains, It Amanpours, The Hotline, Jan. 5, 2006, *available at* http://nationaljournal.com/cgi-bin/ifetch4?ENG+HOTLINE-_-HOTLINE_WORLD_EXTRA-_-HOUSE_RACE_HOTLINE-_-POLL_TRACK-_-AD_SPOTLIGHT+7-hotindex+1173899-REVERSE+0+1+158+F+1+4+1+amanpours; David Ensor, "NSA: Amanpour, other CNN reporters not targeted for surveillance", CNN.com, Jan.5, 2006, *available at* http://www.cnn.com/2006/POLITICS/01/06/nsa.amanpour/index.html.

1,267. David Ensor, "NSA: Amanpour, other CNN reporters not targeted for surveillance", CNN.com, Jan.6, 2005, *available at* http://www.cnn.com/2006/POLITICS/01/06/nsa.amanpour/index.html.

1,268. Letter from the Hon. John Conyers, Jr., Ranking Members of the House Judiciary Committee, and 27 Members of Congress, to President George W. Bush (Jan. 5, 2006).

1,269. In response to the uproar over the reported wiretapping of Amanpour, a senior intelligence official assured CNN that he would look into the matter and explained that occasionally "NSA surveillance overseas 'inadvertently' acquires recordings or copies of communications involving Americans—or what the government calls 'U.S. persons,' which includes most U.S. residents and employees of American companies . . . however, such materials [by law] are required to be erased or destroyed immediately." David Ensor, "NSA: Amanpour, other CNN reporters not targeted for surveillance", CNN.com, Jan.6, 2006, *available at* http://www.cnn.com/2006/POLITICS/01/06/nsa.amanpour/index.html.

1,270. James Risen & Eric Lichtblau, "Bush Lets U.S. Spy on Callers Without Courts" the *New York Times*, Dec. 16, 2005, at A1.

1,271. *Ibid.*

1,272. *Ibid.*

1,273. *Ibid.*

1,274. Jack O'Neill, "Connecting the Dots", *The Washington Times*, Dec. 26, 2006, at A16 (emphasis added).

1,275. Barton Gellman, Dafna Linzer & Carol D. Leonnig, "Surveillance Net Yields Few Suspects", *The Washington Post*, Feb. 5, 2006, at A1.

1,276. Seymour M. Hersh, "National Security Dept. Listening In", *The New Yorker*, May 9, 2006, at 24.

1,277. Dan Eggen, "Negroponte Had Denied Domestic Call Monitoring", *The Washington Post*, May 15, 2006, at A3.

1,278. Dan Eggen, "Negroponte Had Denied Domestic Call Monitoring", *The Washington Post*, May 15, 2006, at A3.

1,279. Barton Gellman & Arshad Mohammed, "Data on Phone Calls Monitored", *The Washington Post*, May 12, 2006, at A1.

1,280. Leslie Cauley, "NSA Has Massive Database of Americans' Phone Calls", *USA Today*, May 11, 2006 at A1.

1,281. Barton Gellman, Dafna Linzer & Carol D. Leonnig, "Surveillance Net Yields Few Suspects", *The Washington Post*, Feb. 5, 2006, at A1.

1,282. Statement of Lieutenant General Michael V. Hayden, USAF Director, National Security Agency Chief, Statement Before the Joint Inquiry of the Senate Select Committee on Intelligence and the House Permanent Select Committee on Intelligence, October 17, 2002.

1,283. The database would be populated by transaction data contained in current databases such as financial records, medical records, communication records, travel records and intelligence data. Eric Lichtblau, "F.B.I. Watched Activist Groups, New Files Show", the *New York Times*, Dec. 20, 2005 at A1.

1,284. In 2003, it was disclosed that the Bush Administration was developing a futures market to allow investors to bet on the probability of coups, assassinations, terrorist strikes, and other events in the Middle East. Bradley Graham and Vernon Loeb, "Pentagon Drops Bids For Futures Market; Investors Could Bet on Terrorism, Coups", *The Washington Post*, July 30, 2003, at A17. The Administration was quickly forced to abandon the ideas. Pub. L. No. 108-87 § 8131, 117 Stat. 1054, 1102 (2003).

1,285. Shane Harris, "TIA Lives On", *National Journal*, Feb. 25, 2006, at 66. The National Journal reported that when asked whether the government could have used the tools apart from TIA, The former No. 2 official in Poindexter's office, Robert Popp replied, "I can't speak to that." Bsked to comment on TIA projects that moved to ARDA, Don Weber, an NSA spokesman said, "As I'm sure you understand, we can neither confirm nor deny actual or alleged projects or operational capabilities; therefore, we have no information to provide."

1,286. Initiated by former Deputy Secretary Paul Wolfowitz in 2003, TALON has been used to collect information on a wide range of groups unrelated to terrorism, including peace activists such as the Quaker Meeting House in Lake Worth, Florida. In the program's first year, the agency reportedly received more than 5,000 TALON reports. Lisa Myers, Douglas Pasternak, & Rich Gardella, "Is the Pentagon spying on Americans?", MSNBC.com, Dec. 14, 2005, *available at* http://www.msnbc.msn.com/id/10454316.

1,287. The number of reports with names of U.S. persons could be in the thousands, according to a senior Pentagon official who asked not to be named because of the sensitivity of the subject. Michael Isikoff, "The Other Big Brother", *Newsweek*, Jan. 30, 2006, at 32.

1,288. Mark Clayton, "U.S. plans massive data sweep", *Christian Science Monitor*, Feb. 9, 2006 at A1.

1,289. Walter Pincus, "Lawmakers Want More Data on Contracting Out Intelligence", *The Washington Post*, May 7, 2006 at A7.

1,290. United States General Accounting Office, Data Mining: Federal Efforts Cover a Wide Range of Uses, May 2004 at 1. ("Of 54 efforts to mine data from the private sector (such as credit reports or credit card transactions), 36 involve personal information. Of 77 efforts to mine data from other federal agencies, 46 involve personal information (including student loan application data, bank account numbers, credit card information and taxpayer identification numbers))." The GAO also found that "[m]ining government and private databases containing personal information creates a range of privacy concerns. Through data mining, agencies can. . . obtain information on individuals or groups by exploiting large databases containing personal information aggregated from public and private records.") *Ibid.*

1,291. United States General Accounting Office, Data Mining: Federal Efforts Cover a Wide Range of Uses, May 2004 at 1.

1,292. James Risen & Eric Lichtblau, "Spy Agency Mined Vast Data Trove, Officials Report", the *New York Times*, Dec. 23, 2005, at A1.

1,293. James Risen & Eric Lichtblau, "Spy Agency Mined Vast Data Trove, Officials Report", the *New York Times*, Dec. 23, 2005, at A1.

1,294. James Risen & Eric Lichtblau, "Spy Agency Mined Vast Data Trove, Officials Report", the *New York Times*, Dec. 23, 2005, at A1.

1,295. Of the twenty letters sent, Rep Conyers received written responses from eleven of the companies—T-Mobile, Cox, Microsoft, Charter, Comcast, Time Warner, Verizon, AT&T, BellSouth, Google and CenturyTel. Earthlink met with Rep. Conyers staff and provided an official statement from its chief privacy officer. He received no response from eight of the companies—Sprint, Citizens Communications, Qwest, Adelphia, Cablevision, Yahoo!, Cingular, and United Online. Letter from Congressman John Conyers to Presidents and CEO's of 20 Telecommunications Companies concerning President Bush's Secret Spying Program (Jan. 20, 2006).

1,296. For example, Comcast stated that it has not allowed access to customer communications and has not provided customer records in the absence of valid legal process, articulating it's "policy and practice to require valid, appropriate legal process such as a subpoena, court order, or search warrant, in response to all requests for customer information," while Time Warner said that its companies "provide narrowly tailored responses to such requests, and require the government to furnish process appropriate to the nature of the data sought (such as court order or subpoena)." Other companies indicated they have not been approached to provide such assistance For example, Earthlink publicly stated that "[w]e've never even been asked to give information without the benefit of a subpoena or a court order behind it. And our policy is to require a subpoena or court order, basically to require a court of law behind the inquiry."

1,297. For example, AT&T wrote, "[w]ithout commenting in any way on press reports, let me assure you that AT&T abides by all applicable laws, regulations and statutes in its operations and, in particular, with requests for assistance from governmental authorities." Verizon responded that the issue is a matter of national security and that it "accordingly cannot either confirm or deny cooperation in any such program."

1,298. Ryan Singel, "Whistle-Blower Outs NSA Spy Room", *Wired News*, April 7, 2006, *available at* http://www.wired.com/news/technology/1,70619-0.html.

1,299. Press Release, White House Press Secretary Scott McClellan, Setting the Record Straight: Democrats Continue to Attack Terrorist Surveillance Program (Jan. 22, 2006) *available at* http://www.white house.gov/news/releases/2006/01/20060122.html. McClellan said that "[i]t defies common sense for Democrats to now claim the administration is acting outside its authority while their own party leaders have been briefed more than a dozen times."

1,300. Dan Eggen and Walter Pincus, "Varied Rationales Muddle Issue of NSA Eavesdropping", *The Washington Post*, January 27, 2006 at A5.

1,301. Leslie Cauley, "NSA has massive database of Americans' phone calls", *USA Today*, May 11, 2006, at A1.

1,302. See Charles Babington and Dafna Linzer, "Senator Sounded Alarm in '03", *The Washington Post*, Dec. 20, 2005, at A10.

1,303. Charles Babington and Dafna Linzer, "Senator Sounded Alarm in '03", *The Washington Post*, Dec. 20, 2005, at A10.

1,304. Letter from the Honorable Nancy Pelosi, Ranking Democrat, House Intelligence Committee, to Lieutenant General Michael V. Hayden, USAF Director National Security Agency, (Oct. 11, 2001).

1,305. Letter from the Honorable Nancy Pelosi, Ranking Democrat, House Intelligence Committee, to Lieutenant General Michael V. Hayden, USAF Director National Security Agency, (Oct. 11, 2001). Leader Pelosi also authored an op-ed in the *Washington Post* soon after the story of the program broke, stating "[b]ut when the administration notifies Congress in this manner, it is not seeking approval. There is a clear expectation that the information will be shared with no one, including other members of the intelligence committees. As a result, only a few members of Congress were aware of the president's surveillance program, and they were constrained from discussing it more widely." Nancy Pelosi, "The Gap in Intelligence Oversight", *The Washington Post*, Jan. 15, 2006, at B07.

1,306. Douglas Jehl, "Spy Briefings Failed to Meet legal Test, Lawmakers Say", the *New York Times*, Dec. 21, 2005, at A36.

1,307. Diana Marrero, "Daschle says White House Omitted Key Details About NSA Spying Program", *Gannett News Service*, Dec. 20, 2005.

1,308. Evan Thomas & Daniel Klaidman, "Full Speed Ahead", *Newsweek*, Jan. 9, 2006, at 22.

1,309. Greg Miller and Maura Reynolds, "U.S. Spying Plan Lacked Congress' Scrutiny, Leading Democrat Says", *Los Angeles Times*, Dec. 20, 2005, at A32.

1,310. Susan Page, "NSA Secret Database Report Triggers Fierce Debate in Washington", *USA Today*, May 11, 2006, available at http://www.usatoday.com.

1,311. Lowell Bergman, Scott Shane, Don Van Natta, Jr. & Eric Lichtblau, "Spy Agency Data After Sept. 11 Led F.B.I. to Dead Ends", the *New York Times*, Jan. 17, 2006, at A1.

1,312. "Wiretaps Fail to Make Dent in Terror War; Al Qaeda Used Messengers", *Insight Magazine*, Dec. 26, 2005—Jan. 1, 2006, *available at* http://www.insightmag.com/media/mediaManager/wiretaps_0.htm.

1,313. Eric Lichtblau & James Risen, "Spy Agency Mined Vast Data Trove, Officials Report", the *New York Times*, Dec. 24, 2005, at A1.

1,314. James Gordon Meek, "Taps Found Clues, Not Al Qaeda, FBI Chief Says", *NY Daily News*, Feb. 3, 2006, at 17. When asked whether the program had led to any leads during his Senate Judiciary testimony, Attorney General Gonzales refused to say. Senate NSA Hearing (testimony of Attorney General Alberto Gonzales).

1,315. Barton Gellman, Dafna Linzer & Carol D. Leonnig, "Surveillance Net Yields Few Suspects", *The Washington Post*, Feb. 5, 2006, at A1.

1,316. Lowell Bergman, Eric Lichtblau, Scott Shane, and Don Van Natta Jr., "Spy Agency Data After Sept. 11 Led F.B.I. to Dead Ends", the *New York Times*, January 17, 2006 at A1.

1,317. *Ibid.*

1,318. *Ibid.*

1,319. Lowell Bergman, Scott Shane, Don Van Natta, Jr. & Eric Lichtblau, "Spy Agency Data After Sept. 11 Led F.B.I. to Dead Ends", the *New York Times*, Jan. 17, 2006, at A1. FBI Director Robert Mueller, testified that "most leads [received by the FBI], whether it be from the NSA or overseas from the CIA, ultimately turn out not to be valid or worthwhile." Hearing on the Worldwide Threats to the United States Before the Senate Select Intelligence Committee, 109th Cong. (2006) (Testimony of Robert Mueller, FBI Director).

1,320. Martin Garbus, "Impeachment is Now Real", *The Huffington Post*, Dec. 28, 2005 at http://www.huffingtonpost.com/martin-garbus/impeachment-is-now-real_b_12972.html.

1,321. Eric Lichtblau & James Risen, "Defense Lawyers in Terror Cases Plan Challenges Over Spy Efforts", the *New York Times*, Dec. 28, 2005, at A1. On January 9, 2006, a defense attorney petitioned the Fourth Circuit on behalf of Ali Al-Timimi, who was previously convicted on terrorism charges. Jerry Markon, "Terror Defendant Seeks Hearing To Find Whether He Was Spied On", *The Washington Post*, Jan. 10, 2006, at B1.

1,322. Eric Lichtblau & James Risen, "Defense Lawyers in Terror Cases Plan Challenges Over Spy Efforts", the *New York Times*, Dec. 28, 2005, at A1.

1,323. Senate NSA Hearing.

1,324. Eric Lichtblau & James Risen, "Defense Lawyers in Terror Cases Plan Challenges Over Spy Efforts", the *New York Times*, Dec. 28, 2005, at A1.

1,325. Carol D. Leonnig, "Secret Court's Judges Were Warned About NSA Spy Data", *The Washington Post*, Feb. 9, 2006, at A1.

1,326. Mark Hosenball & Evan Thomas, "Hold The Phone", *Newsweek*, May 22, 2006 at 22.

1,327. Seymour M. Hersh, "Listening In", *The New Yorker*, May 29, 2006 at 24.

1,328. Wolf Blitzer, CNN Late Edition, "Interview with Bill Frist", (May 14, 2006), *available at* http://transcripts.cnn.com/TRANSCRIPTS/0605/14/le.01.html.

1,329. Daniel Klaidman, Stuart Taylor Jr., & Evan Thomas, "Palace Revolt", *Newsweek*, Feb. 6, 2006, at 34.

1,330. Republican Senator Lindsey Graham argued that Bush did not deserve punishment for authorizing warrantless wiretapping because, unlike President Richard Nixon during the Watergate scandal, Bush had acted in good faith: "This is apples and oranges. . . . Anybody who believes that Richard Nixon was relying on some inherent-authority argument is recreating history." David D. Kirkpatrick, "Call to Censure Bush Is Answered by a Mostly Empty Echo", the *New York Times*, April 1, 2006, at A11.

1,331. Eric Lichtblau, "Panel Rebuffed on Documents on U.S. Spying", the *New York Times*, Feb. 2, 2006, at A1. On January 5, 2006, Rep. Conyers and 27 other Members of Congress sent a letter to President Bush requesting, among other things, "[a]ny and all legal opinions and memorandum concerning the lawfulness of the [NSA] program." Letter from The Honorable John Conyers Jr., Ranking Member on the House Judiciary Committee, and 27 other Members of Congress to The Honorable George W. Bush, United States President (Jan. 5, 2006). To date, the Administration has failed to respond to this letter.

1,332. During the Department of Justice oversight hearing in the House Judiciary Committee, Chairman Sensenbrenner asked Attorney General Gonzales "who was included in the review prior to the [NSA] program being authorized," Gonzales responded, "who is read into the program is a classified matter so I can't—— I can't get into specific discussions about specifically who was involved in reviewing the legal authorities for the President of the United States in authorizing this program." Oversight Hearing on U.S. Department of Justice: Hearing Before the H. Comm. on the Judiciary, 109th Cong. (2006).

1,333. Richard Lacayo, "The Spying Controversy: Has Bush Gone Too Far?", *Time*, Jan. 9, 2006, at 25.

1,334. Daniel Klaidman, Stuart Taylor Jr., & Evan Thomas, "Palace Revolt", *Newsweek*, Feb. 6, 2006, at 34.

1,335. Bob Drogin, "Lawmakers Urge Review of U.S. Spy Program", *Los Angeles Times*, Dec. 19, 2005, at A11 ("I sat in my office" with Lt. Gen. Michael V. Hayden, who was then head of the National Security Agency and is now deputy director of national intelligence, to brief Graham at the time, Cheney said.").

1,336. Eric Lichtblau and James Risen, "Justice Deputy Resisted Parts of Spy Program", the *New York Times*, January 1, 2006, at A1.

1,337. The Justice Department opened a criminal investigation at the end of December 2005, within two weeks of initial disclosure of the program. Dan Eggen, "Justice Dept. Investigating Leak of NSA Wiretapping", *The Washington Post*, Dec. 31, 2005, at A1.

1,338. President George W. Bush, Press Conference, (Dec. 19, 2005), *available at* http://www.whitehouse.gov /news/releases/2005/12/20051219-2.html.

1,339. David Johnston, "Inquiry Into Wiretapping Article Widens", the *New York Times*, Feb. 12, 2006, at 26.

1,340. David Johnston, "Inquiry Into Wiretapping Article Widens", the *New York Times*, Feb. 12, 2006, at 26.

1,341. At the Senate Judiciary Hearings, the Attorney General stated, "[y]ou would assume that the enemy is presuming that we are engaged in some kind of surveillance. But if they're not constantly reminded about it all the time in newspapers and in stories, they sometimes forget." Senate NSA Hearing (testimony of Attorney General Alberto Gonzales).

1,342. Dan Eggen, "Justice Dept. Role in Eavesdropping Decision Under Review", *The Washington Post*, Feb. 16, 2006, A04.

1,343. Frank Rich, "The Wiretappers Who Couldn't Shoot Straight", the *New York Times*, Jan. 8, 2006, A15. The Bush Administration has even raised the specter of using the Justice Department to prosecute the press directly for publishing information critical of the Administration provided to them by whistleblowers. Walter Pincus, "Press Can Be Prosecuted for Having Secret Files, U.S. Says", *The Washington Post*, Feb. 22, 2006, at A03. ("The Bush Administration said that journalists can be prosecuted under current espionage laws for receiving and publishing classified information.... .")

1,344. Daniel Klaidman, Stuart Taylor Jr., & Evan Thomas, "Palace Revolt", *Newsweek*, Feb 6, 2006, at 34.

1,345. *Ibid.*

1,346. *Ibid.*

1,347. *Ibid.*

1,348. Daniel Klaidman, Stuart Taylor Jr., & Evan Thomas, "Palace Revolt", *Newsweek*, Feb 6, 2006, at 34; Evan Thomas & Daniel Klaidman, "Full Speed Ahead", *Newsweek*, Jan. 9, 2006, at 22.

1,349. Dan Mangan, "Bush Dissed Justice Big As Cuomo", *The New York Post*, Jan. 2, 2006, at 6.

1,350. Daniel Klaidman, Stuart Taylor Jr., & Evan Thomas, "Palace Revolt", *Newsweek*, Feb 6, 2006, at 34.

1,351. Kim Zetter, "The NSA is on the line–all of them: An intelligence expert predicts we'll soon learn that cellphone and Internet companies also cooperated with the NSA to eavesdrop on us", *Salon.com*, May 15, 2006.

1,352. Leslie Cauley, "NSA Has Massive Database of Americans' Phone Calls", *USA Today*, May 11, 2006 at A1.

1,353. Transcript of David Frost- Richard Nixon interview, the *New York Times*, May 20, 1977, at A16.

1,354. Katherine Shrader, "Vocal critic of spying program to shepherd bills through Senate", Associated *Press*, March 23, 2006. the *Washington Post* observed, this "is the way this executive branch treats its supposedly equal partner: as an annoying impediment to the real work of government. It provides information to Congress grudgingly, if at all. It handles letters from lawmakers like junk mail, routinely tossing them aside without responding." Ruth Markus, "Contempt for Congress", *The Washington Post*, Jan. 25, 2006, at A19.

1,355. The Department's rules require the appointment of an outside special counsel when (1) criminal investigation of a matter is warranted; (2) the investigation of that matter presents a conflict of interest for the Department; and (3) the appointment of a Special Counsel is in the public interest. 28 C.F.R. part

600. Under the FISA statute, surveillance of U.S. persons without a warrant would be a crime punishable by imprisonment. Given Attorney General Gonzales' potential authorization of surveillance under this program and his highly public defense of it, Justice Department officials under his supervisory control clearly would have a conflict of interest in investigating this program.

1,356. White House Press Secretary Scott McClellan, Press Briefing (Feb. 27, 2006), *available at* http://www .whitehouse.gov/news/releases/2006/02/20060227-1.html. McClellan said that he does not "think there's any basis for a special counsel, and. . . Attorney General has spoken about that." *Ibid.* In addition, the ACLU requested that Attorney General Gonzales appoint an outside special counsel to investigate and prosecute any criminal acts committed by any member of the Executive Branch in the NSA warrantless electronic surveillance program. Letter from Anthony Romero, Executive Director, ACLU, *et. al.,* to Alberto Gonzales, Attorney General, Department of Justice (Dec. 21, 2005), available at http://www.aclu.org/safefree/general/23184leg20051221.html. After over three months, the Department of Justice responded with a one-paragraph letter that sidestepped the ACLU request and indicated that the Department would merely "act consistently with special counsel regulations." Letter from Steven G. Bradbury, Acting Assistant Attorney General, Department of Justice, to Anthony Romero, Executive Director, ACLU, *et. al.* (March 8, 2005).

1,357. Letter from Congresswoman Lofgren to President Bush (May 11, 2006).

1,358. Oversight Hearing on U.S. Department of Justice: Hearing Before the H. Comm. on the Judiciary, 109th Cong. (2006). When asked why there has not been a special counsel appointed in over five years, Attorney General Gonzales appeared unfamiliar with the term as he asked, "are you talking about— are you thinking in terms of more like an independent counsel?" *Ibid.*

1,359. Letter from Glenn A. Fine, Inspector General, Department of Justice, to Congresswoman Zoe Lofgren et. al. (Jan. 4, 2006).

1,360. Letter from Thomas F. Gimble, Acting Inspector General, Department of Defense, to Congresswoman Zoe Lofgren et. al. (Jan. 10, 2006).

1,361. Dan Eggen, "Justice Dept. Role in Eavesdropping Decision Under Review", The Washington Post, Feb. 16, 2006, at A4.

1,362. Associated Press, "Security Issue Kills Domestic Spying Inquiry: NSA Won't Grant Justice Department Lawyers Required Security Clearance" (May 10,2006) *available at* http://www.msnbc.msn.com/id /12727867/. It was subsequently revealed by senior government officials that the "only classified information that OPR investigators were seeking about the NSA's eavesdropping program was what had already been given to Ashcroft, Gonzales and other department attorneys in their original approval and advice on the program." Shane Harris and Murray Waas, "Justice Department Probe Foiled", *National Journal*, May 25, 2006, *available at* http://news.nationaljournal.com/articles/0525nj2.htm.

1,363. Letter from Democratic Leader Nancy Pelosi, et. al., to Speaker of the House Dennis Hastert (Dec. 17, 2005), *available at* http://www.house.gov/pelosi/press/releases/Dec05/investigate.html ("we believe . . .the justifiable concern of the American people over the allegations in the Times article, require the House of Representatives to take steps immediately to conduct hearings on the scope of Presidential power in the area of electronic surveillance. These hearings would benefit substantially if an independent panel of Constitutional scholars and experts on the laws affecting intelligence activities was to examine existing statutes, regulations, practices and precedents. We urge that you and the Democratic Leader establish such a panel jointly.").

1,364. Surveillance Activities Commission Act of 2006, S. 2362, 109th Cong. (2006); Surveillance Activities Commission Act of 2006, H.R. 5223, 109th Cong. (2006).

1,365. Wartime Executive Power and the NSA's Surveillance Authority: Hearing Before the Senate Comm. on the Judiciary, 109th Cong. (2006).

1,366. Wartime Executive Power and the NSA's Surveillance Authority: Hearing Before the Senate Comm. on the Judiciary, 109th Cong. (2006) (Ranking Member Patrick Leahy).

1,367. Letter from Assistant Attorney General William E. Moschella to Honorable Arlen Specter (Feb.15, 2006).

1368. "Specter warns of "confrontation" over NSA hearings", CNN.com, June 8, 2006, *available at* http://www.cnn.com/2006/POLITICS/06/07/nsa/

1,369. Letter from William E. Moschella, Assistant Attorney General, to the Hon. F. James Sensenbrenner, Chairman, Committee on the Judiciary (March 24, 2006). The Department provided vague and unresponsive answers to all but two of the 45 questions submitted by Judiciary Committee Democrats and most of the questions posed by Judiciary Committee Chairman Sensenbrenner.

1,370. Dan Eggen, "Warrantless Wiretaps Possible in the U.S.", *The Washington Post*, April 7, 2006, at A3. During the House Judiciary Committee oversight hearing of the Department of Justice, Chairman Sensenbrenner queried the Attorney General in reference to the NSA spying program asking, "how can we discharge our oversight responsibilities if every time we ask a pointed question we are told that the answer is classified? "Oversight Hearing on U.S. Department of Justice: Hearing Before the H. Comm. on the Judiciary, 109th Cong. (2006). Furthermore, in response to the Administration's continued effort to keep Congress in the dark on the NSA program, Mr. Sensenbrenner indicated that he is "really concerned that the Judiciary Committee has been kind of put in the trash heap."

1,371. They instead opted to set up a subcommittee to continue to simply "oversee" the program.

1,372. David Kirkpatrick & Scott Shane, "G.O.P. Senators Say Accord is Set on Wiretapping", the *New York Times*, March 8, 2006, at A1.

1,373. Editorial, "About that Rebellion", the *New York Times*, March 11, 2006, at A14.

1,374. Editorial, "Kabuki Congress", the *New York Times*, March 6, 2006, at A20. Regarding the DeWine legislation, the Philadelphia Daily News wrote, "[t]o us, this is mopping up after spilled milk, while the guy who spilled it, the president, gets off with a smirk." Editorial, "The Fix is in for Bush", *Philadelphia Daily News*, March 23, 2006, at 17.

1,375. Editorial, "Kabuki Congress", the *New York Times*, March 6, 2006, at A20.

1,376 .Intelligence Authorization Act for Fiscal Year 2006, S. 1803, 109th Cong. (2005); Walter Pincus, "Senator May Seek Tougher Law on Leaks", *The Washington Post*, Feb. 17, 2006, at A4. The House Intelligence Committee has been even less aggressive in its oversight. Instead of a serious review, they appear to be planning a continuation of the same oversight process that led to the problems in the first place. As the *New York Times* wrote, "the chairman of the House Intelligence Committee, Peter Hoekstra, is turning [their investigation] into a pro forma review that would end with Congress rewriting the foreign-intelligence law the way Mr. Bush wants." Editorial, "Kabuki Congress", the *New York Times*, March 6, 2006, at A20.

1,377. H. Res. 641, 109th Cong. (2005).

1,378. H. Res. 643, 109th Cong. (2005).

1,379. H. Res. 644, 109th Cong. (2005).

1,380. H. Res. 645, 109th Cong. (2005).

1,381. H.R. Rep. No. 109-385 (2006,

1,382. This was the case even though, for example, the Conyers resolution was specifically crafted to permit redaction of any classified information included in the legal opinion. H. Res. 643, 109th Cong. (2005). The request made in the Conyers Resolution was "subject to necessary redactions or requirements for handling classified documents."

1,383. Letter from the Federal Communications Commission to Honorable Markey, (May 22, 2006).

1,384. Dan Eggen & Julie Tate, "U.S. Campaign Produces Few Convictions on Terrorism Charges; Statistics Often Count Lesser Crimes", *The Washington Post*, June 12, 2005, at A1. the *Washington Post* found that 80 of the people charged in these "terrorism probes" had no demonstrated connection to terrorism or terrorist groups; most people were convicted of minor crimes such as making false statements. For example, 60 of 62 "terror prosecutions" in New Jersey in 2002 were against Middle Eastern men who paid others to take school-related English proficiency tests for them.

1,385. Mark Fazlollah, "Dozens of Cases Misclassified as Terror", *Miami Herald*, July 17, 2003, at 16A. Some of the cases included: (i) "28 Hispanics charged with working illegally at the airport in Austin, most of them using phony Social Security numbers;" (ii) "A Middle Eastern man indicted in Detroit for allegedly passing bad checks who had the same name as a Hezbollah leader;"and (iii) "A Middle Eastern college student charged in Trenton, N.J., with paying a stand-in to take his college English-proficiency test."

1,386. Editorial, "Justice Dept.'s Absurdity on Terrorism", *Daily Iowan*, July 20, 2004. They found, for example, "five Mexicans faced terrorism charges after stealing baby formula to sell to a man of Arab descent" who later resold the baby formula for himself, and in Waterloo, Iowa, five Pakistanis were labeled terrorists after they tried to have sham marriages so they could stay in the area to work.

1,387. U.S. Gen. Accounting Office, Justice Department: Better Management Oversight and Internal Controls Needed to Ensure Accuracy of Terror-Related Statistics 2 (2003).

1,388. The Administration selectively made public various classified documents in an apparent effort to discredit political rivals and deflect criticism on its handling of the war on terrorism. For example, then Attorney General John Ashcroft accused former Clinton Deputy Attorney General Jamie Gorelick, of building up the "wall" that prevented the flow of information between law enforcement and intelligence in terrorism investigations when he publicly released 29 pages of internal documents, including a memorandum authored by Gorelick in 1995 about intelligence sharing. Eric Lichtblau, "White House Criticizes Justice Dept. Over Papers", the *New York Times*, Apr. 30, 2004, at A24. In 2003, after Congress had voted to restrict the library and bookstore provisions of Section 215 of the PATRIOT Act, Mr. Ashcroft set out on a nationwide speaking tour to rally support for the PATRIOT Act and "agreed to declassify data on demands for library records to counter 'misinformation' and because department has been unable to tilt debate in its favor." President Bush employed a similar tactic when he selectively declassified parts of a March 2002 National Intelligence Estimate so as to discredit former Ambassador Joe Wilson, who found no evidence that Saddam Hussein was procuring uranium from Niger. "Bush Acknowledges Declassifying Intelligence", CNN.com, April 11, 2006, *available at* http://www.cnn .com/2006/POLITICS/04/10/whitehouse.leak/index.html.

1,389. Memorandum from John Ashcroft, Attorney General, to Heads of all Federal Departments and Agencies (Oct 12. 2005).

1,390. Gen. Accounting Office, Freedom of Information Act: Agency Views on Changes Resulting from New Administration Policy 20 (2003).

1,391. The state secrets doctrine was first used in 1953 to protect information about a plane crash, and dismiss a suit by the crash victims' families. United States. v. Reynolds, 345 U.S. 1 (1953). The doctrine has been used sixty times by various courts to dismiss legal actions at the government's assertion that the suit would endanger national security. William Fisher, "'State Secrets' Privilege Not so Rare", *InterPress Service*, Aug. 16, 2005, *available at* http://ipsnews.net/news.asp?idnews=29902. Its use has become more prevalent under the Bush Administration. "A growing body of declassified documents suggests that in the past, at least, the privilege has been used to protect presidential power, not national secrets, according to Thomas Blanton, director of the National Security Archive at the George Washington University, which works to expand public access to government documents." Andrew Zajac, "Bush Wielding Secrecy Privilege to End Suits", *Chicago Tribune*, Mar. 3, 2005, at C1.

1,392. William Fisher, "'State Secrets' Privilege Not so Rare", *InterPress Service*, Aug. 16, 2005, *available at* http://ipsnews.net/news.asp?idnews=29902.

1,393. For Maher Arar's court filings, see http://www.ccr-ny.org/v2/legal/september_11th/sept11Article .asp?ObjID=zPvu7s2XVJ&Content=377. The United States District Court for the Eastern District of New York has still not ruled on whether Mr. Arar's case will be dismissed.

1,394. First Statement of Interest of the United States, Hepting v. AT&T Corp. (N.D.C.A. 2006).

1,395. David Caruso, "Dismissal of Lawsuits Over NSA Eavesdropping Sought", *The Washington Post*, May 27,2006 at A13.

1,396. Andrew Harris, "U.S. to Bsk Courts to Toss Phone Suits," *The Washington Post*, June 8, 2006, D03.

1,397. Dana Priest, "Secrecy Privilege Invoked in Fighting Ex-Detainee's Lawsuit", *The Washington Post*, May 13, 2006 at A03.

1,398. In 1995, President Clinton created a presumption of disclosure policy, stating that "[i]f there is significant doubt about the need to classify information, it shall not be classified." However, President Bush subsequently reversed the presumption of disclosure.

1,399. In 2004, the federal government classified 15.6 million new documents, an 80 percent increase from 2001. At the same time, the federal government declassified only 28.4 million pages last year, the lowest number of pages since 199, a 72 percent drop in the number of declassified pages since 2001. Hearings Before the Subcomm. on National Security, Emerging Threats, and International Relations of the House Comm. on Government Reform, 109th Cong. (2005) (statement of Timothy H. Edgar, Legislative Counsel, American Civil Liberties Union). J. William Leonard, director of the Information Security Oversight Office, the arm of the National Archives and Records Administration responsible for the security classification program, warned "[p]eople also need to see that national security can be adversely impacted if information is improperly hoarded." Similarly, the 9-11 Commission report recognized that excessive classification almost certainly represents the greatest barrier to effective information sharing, explaining "[n ]o one has to pay the long-term costs of over-classifying information, though these costs . . . are substantial." National Commission on Terrorist Attacks Upon the United States, The 9-11 Commission Report 399-428 (2004).

1,400. Charlie Savage, "Bush Challenges Hundreds of Laws: President Cites Powers of His Office," *Boston Globe*, April 30, 2006 at A1.

1,401. Charlie Savage, "Bush Challenges Hundreds of Laws: President Cites Powers of His Office", *Boston Globe*, April 30, 2006 at A1. Boston University Professor Jack Beerman explained, the "president is daring Congress to act against his positions, and they're not taking action because they don't want to appear to be too critical of the president, given that their own fortunes are tied to his because they are all Republicans."

# Legal Standards *and* Authorities

The following is a description of various laws, regulations and other legal requirements potentially applicable to the various matters identified in the Report.

1. Deception of Congress and the American Public
   a. Committing a Fraud Bgainst the United States (18U.S.C. § 371)
   b. Making False Statements to Congress (18 U.S.C. § 1001)
   c. War Powers Resolution (Public Law 93-148)
   d. Misuse of Government Funds (31 U.S.C. § 1301)

2. Improper Detention, Torture, and Other Inhumane Treatment
   a. Anti-Torture Statute (18 U.S.C. §§ 2340-40A)
   b. The War Crimes Act (18 U.S.C. § 2441)
   c. The Geneva Conventions and Hague Convention: International Laws Governing the Treatment of Detainees
   d. United Nations Convention Bgainst Torture, and Cruel, Inhuman and Degrading Treatment: International Laws Governing the Treatment of Detainees
   e. Command Responsibility
   f. Material Witness (18 U.S.C. § 3144)

3. Retaliating against Witnesses and Other Individuals
   a. Obstructing Congress (18 U.S.C. § 1505)
   b. Whistleblower Protection (5 U.S.C. § 2302)
   c. The Lloyd-LaFollette Act (5 U.S.C. § 7211)
   d. Retaliating against Witnesses (18 U.S.C. § 1513)

4. Leaking and other Misuse of Intelligence and other Government Information
   a. Revealing Classified Information in Contravention of Federal Regulations (Executive Order 12958/ Classified Information Nondisclosure Agreement)
   b. Statutory Prohibitions on Leaking Information

5. Laws and Guidelines Prohibiting Conflicts of Interest

6. Laws Governing Electronic Surveillance
   a. Foreign Intelligence Surveillance Act (50 U.S.C. § 1801 et seq.)
   b. National Security Act of 1947 (50°U.S.C. chapter 15)
   c. Communications Act of 1934 (47 U.S.C. § 222)
   d. Stored Communications Act of 1986 (18 U.S.C. § 2702)
   e. Pen Registers or Trap and Trace Devices (18 U.S.C. § 3121)

### 1. Deception of Congress and the American Public
#### a. Committing a Fraud Bgainst the United States (18 U.S.C. § 371)

This statute makes it a crime, punishable by a fine and up to five years in prison, to conspire "to defraud the United States, or any agency thereof in any manner or for any purpose, and one or more of such persons do any act to effect the object of the conspiracy." "Defrauding the government" has been defined quite broadly and does not need an underlying criminal offense and alone subjects the offender to prosecution. United States v. Harmas, 974 F.2d 1262, 1266 (11th Cir. 1992).

For nearly 80 years this statute has been used to prosecute government officials and citizens alike who commit a fraud in the most liberal use of the term. The law is clear: the government need not be defrauded of money or property to trigger this statute. It is enough that the government was prevented from being able to exercise its lawful duties and authorities. As the Supreme Court stated, the law applies to those who:

interfere with or obstruct one of its lawful governmental functions by deceit, craft or trickery, or at least by means that are dishonest. It is not necessary that the Government shall be subjected to property or pecuniary loss by the fraud, but only that its legitimate official action and purpose shall be defeated by misrepresentation, chicanery or the overreaching of those charged with carrying out the governmental intention. United States v. Harmas, 974 F.2d 1262, 1266 (11th Cir. 1992).

Another more recent case repeats that principle of law. The Second Circuit held that "this statute does not restrict its application to documents that are required to be given to Congress, does not require proof that any statements made to effect the object of the conspiracy were made directly to Congress, and does not require that the conspiracy was successful." United States v. Ballistrea, 101 F.3d 827, 831-832 (2nd Cir. 1996), *cited by* Francis T. Mandanici, *Bush's Uranium Lies: The Case for a Special Prosecutor That Could Lead to Impeachment* (June 29, 2005), *available at* http://democracyrising.us/content/view/269/164. One treatise has defined fraud as "a generic term which embraces all the multifarious means which human ingenuity can devise and are resorted to by one individual to gain an advantage over another by false suggestions or by suppression of the truth." Corpus Juris Secundum § 2. Francis T. Mandanici, "Bush's Uranium Lies: The Case for a Special Prosecutor That Could Lead to Impeachment," (June 29, 2005).

Lawrence E. Walsh, Independent Counsel in charge of the Iran-Contra investigation pointed out that the deception of Congress statute applies even when the official is involved in official government policy. In his final report, he concluded, "Fraud is criminal even when those who engage in the fraud are Government officials pursuing presidential policy." Lawrence E. Walsh, Final Report of the Independent Counsel for Iran/Contra Matters, Volume I: Investigations and Prosecutions, Aug. 4, 1993.

Under these precedents, anyone—including the President and his Administration—is prohibited from intentionally misleading the Congress or any other part of the government in pursuit of his or her policy. While this statute is similar to obstructing or lying to Congress (described below), it is broader. It covers acts that may not technically be lying or communications that are not formally before Congress. Indeed, it need only be "overreaching," in the words of the Supreme Court, (*Hammerschmidt*, 265 U.S. at 188.) an exaggeration, if the intent is to influence the government.

This statute was used in the prosecution of numerous Administration and military officials in the Iran-Contra scandal. *Ibid.* It was also used by the Justice Department to prosecute members of the Nixon Administration who used the CIA to interfere with the FBI investigation of the Watergate break-in. United States. v. Haldeman, 559 F.2d 31 (D.C. Cir. 1976) (upholding conviction of violation of 18 U.S.C.A. § 371). One commentator has explained further how the statute was applied in the Watergate context:

In criminal law, a conspiracy is an agreement "between two or more persons" to follow a course of conduct that, if completed, would constitute a crime. The agreement doesn't have to be express; most conspiracies are proved through evidence of concerted action. But government officials are expected to act in concert. So proof that they were conspiring requires a comparison of their public conduct and statements with their conduct and statements behind the scenes. A pattern of double-dealing proves a criminal conspiracy. The concept of interfering with a lawful government function is best explained by reference to two well-known cases where courts found that executive branch officials had defrauded the United States by abusing their power for personal or political reasons. One is the Watergate case, where a federal district court held that Nixon's Chief of Staff,

H.R. Haldeman, and his crew had interfered with the lawful government functions of the CIA and the FBI by causing the CIA to intervene in the FBI's Investigation into the burglary of Democratic Party headquarters. The other is United States v. North, where the court found that Reagan Administration National Security Advisor John Poindexter, Poindexter's aide Oliver North and others had interfered with Congress's lawful power to oversee foreign affairs by lying about secret arms deals during Congressional hearings into the Iran/contra scandal. Elizabeth De La Vega, *The White House Criminal Conspiracy*, The Nation (Nov. 14, 2005)

### b. Making False Statements to Congress (18 U.S.C. § 1001)

Federal law proscribes the submission of false statements or evidence to Congress or congressional committees. It is a criminal offense to knowingly and willfully:

(1) falsif[y], conceal, or cover up by any trick, scheme, or device a material fact; (2) make any materially false, fictitious, or fraudulent statement or representation; or (3) make or use any false writing or document knowing the same to contain any materially false, fictitious, or fraudulent statement or entry. 18 U.S.C. § 1001(a). The penalty includes a fine, imprisonment for not more than five years, or both. *Id.*

With respect to the proceedings before Congress, this prohibition applies to administrative matters and to "any investigation or review, conducted pursuant to the authority of any committee, subcommittee, commission or office of the Congress, consistent with applicable rules of the House or Senate." *Ibid.* § 1001(c). The statute's parameters were extended to Congress only in 1996. False Statements Accountability Act of 1996, Pub. L. No. 104-292, § 2, 110 Stat. 3459 (1996); *see also* United States v. Oakar, 111 F.3d 146, 151 (1997).

There is no limitation on the definition of what constitutes an "investigation or review" by Congress. As such, the term could encompass any hearing, markup, deposition, interrogatory, informal request for information, or speech before Congress or one of its committees or subcommittees. For example, Article II of the Constitution directs the President "from time to time [to] give to the Congress Information of the State of the Union, and recommend to their Consideration such Measures as he shall judge necessary and expedient." U.S. Const. art. II, § 3. To further this requirement, a House concurrent resolution is agreed to by both chambers directing both Houses of Congress to assemble in the Hall of the House on the date and time for the address. *See* H.R. Con. Res. 20, 109th Cong., 1st Sess. (2005). As a result, even the President's State of the Union address could be considered an "investigation or review" conducted pursuant to Congress's authority.

In addition, legal treatises have further explained the meaning of the term "fraudulent misrepresentation." The term "fraudulent misrepresentation" includes "half truths calculated to deceive; and a half truth may be more misleading than an outright lie. A representation literally true is actionable if used to create an impression substantially false, as where it is accompanied by conduct calculated to deceive or where it does not state matters which materially qualify that statement." Corpus Juris Secundum § 24. Francis T. Mandanici, "Bush's Uranium Lies: The Case for a Special Prosecutor That Could Lead to Impeachment," (June 29, 2005).

### c. War Powers Resolution (Public Law 93-148)

It is unconstitutional and illegal for the President to engage the U.S. Armed Forces without timely congressional authorization. As a constitutional matter, the War Powers Clause, contained in article I, section 8, of the Constitution, gives Congress the sole authority to declare war.

As a statutory matter, in 1973 Congress passed the War Powers Resolution (WPR), which governs what powers the President is provided in order to send armed forces into hostilities absent a congressional declaration of war. War Powers Resolution, Pub. L. No. 93-148 (1973). The WPR requires the President to consult with Congress "in every possible instance" before sending troops into hostilities and to submit reports to Congress whenever forces are introduced. *Ibid.* Under the WPR, within sixty days after an initial report to Congress is submitted or should have been submitted, the President must terminate any use of armed forces unless Congress (1) declares war or authorizes the use of force, (2) extends the sixty-day period, or (3) cannot meet due to an attack on the United States. The D.C. Circuit Court of Appeals has interpreted this to mean that if the President engages U.S. armed forces, he has sixty days in which to obtain congressional authorization for the use of force or to cease such military activity. *See* Campbell v. Clinton, 203 F.3d 19, 20 (D.C. Cir. 2000).

### d. Misuse of Government Funds (31 U.S.C. § 1301)

Federal law makes it illegal to use government funds appropriated to the government for any purpose other than those specifically permitted by the appropriations. It specifically states that "appropriations shall be applied only to the objects for which the appropriations were made except as otherwise provided by law." 31 U.S.C. § 1301. The illegal use of funds would cause an automatic diminution in funds available to the guilty agency. *Id*

To determine whether a government activity is legal, it is important to understand whether the agency or office that engaged in the activity was permitted to expend funds for that specific purpose. *See* U.S. General Accounting Office, Principles of Federal Appropriations Law 4-9 (3d ed. 2004). As a general rule, of course, none of the functions of government offices include the dissemination of false information, the dissemination of information for political ends, or retribution against political opponents. For example, the Constitution provides that the President shall be commander-in-chief of the Armed Forces, have the authority to grant pardons, have the power to sign treaties, and nominate civil officers and ambassadors and judges. U.S. Const. art. II, § 2. Congress has provided funds to the President to hire staff and carry out his responsibilities; none of these appropriated funds is conditioned upon the President misleading the public or manipulating government agencies. *See* Pub. L. No. 108-7, Division J, title III (appropriations for fiscal year 2003 enacted in early 2003). The Constitution directs that the vice president will vote as a tie-breaker in instances in which the Senate has a tie vote. U.S. Const. art I, § 3. In addition, the vice president becomes the President when the President either is removed or otherwise unable to perform his duties. *Ibid.* amend. XXV.

Thus, the use of government funds for anything other than these enumerated purposes would violate the law. Using appropriated funds to criticize other officials or private citizens or to disseminate information for political purposes would be illegal.

### 2.Improper Detention, Torture, and Other Inhumane Treatment

Pursuant to federal law and numerous international treaties and conventions, the United States has the authority to prohibit and punish acts of torture and other inhumane treatment. The Justice Department has the authority to prosecute military contractors and other officials applying torture techniques in numerous ways: First, under the Military Extraterritorial Jurisdiction Act, which provides for the prosecution of anyone accompanying the military overseas, including military contractors. 18 U.S.C. §§ 3261-67 (2005). It was extended in 2004 to include contractors of other agencies, such as the CIA. Pub. L. No. 108-375, Div. A, Title X, § 1088, 118 Stat. 2066 (2004). Moreover, the Justice Department does have the authority to charge members of the military for their criminal acts over seas if either a) they are no long in the military, or b) committed the acts with non-military accomplices. Specifically, it allows the Justice Department to prosecute those acts over seas that would be felonies, crimes punishable by at least 6 months in prison, if committed on American soil. 18 U.S.C. §§ 3261-67 (2005).

### a. Anti-Torture Statute (18 U.S.C. §§ 2340-40A)

Federal law prohibits torture, which is defined as: "an act committed by a person acting under the color of law specifically intended to inflict severe physical or mental pain or suffering . . . upon another person within his custody or physical control." 18 U.S.C. § 2340(1). This statute's application does not rely on the location of the abuse, the nationality of the victim, nor the combat or civilian status of the person in custody; all U.S. citizens are subject to the jurisdiction of this statute if they abuse those lawfully in their custody. Amnesty International, Denounce Torture (Nov. 2001), *available at* www.amnestyusa.org/stoptorture/law.html; Human Rights First, U.S. Law For Prosecuting Torture and Other Serious Abuses Committed by Civilians Abroad, *available at* www.humanrightsfirst.org/us_law/detainees/us_toture_laws.htm. This statute can also be used to prosecute foreign nationals who are apprehended on U.S. soil.

In practice, "torture" has been defined broadly by our own government. The military's own manual lists techniques such as the abuse of stress positions and sleep deprivation as torture and prohibits their use. Human Rights Watch, Getting Away With Torture: Command Responsibility for the U.S. Abuse of Detainees, Apr. 2005 at 34 (citing Army *Field Manual 34-52*). Further, our State Department has categorized other nations as human rights violators for practicing these precise techniques, including food, sleep and sensory deprivation, isolation and stress positions. Country Reports, U.S. Department of State, *available at* http://www.state .gov/g/drl/hr/c1470.htm.

It is also important to note that we have prosecuted others for war crimes for the same behavior. After World War II, the United States prosecuted hundreds of Japanese military members for abuse such as stress positions, sleep and sensory deprivation, forced nudity, solitary confinement and failure to notify the Red Cross of detainees. Jess Bravin, *Will Old Rulings Play a Role in Terror Case?*, WSJ, Apr. 7, 2005 at B1.

Those who order torture, or in other ways conspire to commit torture, can be held criminally liable under this statute—the statute doesn't require a person to actually commit torture with his own hands. Amnesty International, Denounce Torture (Nov. 2001), *available at* www.amnestyusa.org/stoptorture/law.html. In addition to the traditional conspiracy and aiding and abetting charges, military personnel and officials can be held liable under the command responsibility doctrine. *See* Human Rights Watch, Getting Away With Torture: Command Responsibility for the U.S. Abuse of Detainees (Apr. 2005), *available at* http://www.hrw.org /reports/2005/us0405/.

Conspiring to violate this prohibition is explicitly recognized in the statute and is punishable up to life in prison if death results, and for twenty years in prison otherwise. 18 U.S.C. § 2340A(c).

Notably, the Administration itself has recognized that its officials could be prosecuted for their role in condoning torture under this statute in particular. In fact, the Bush Administration has taken great pains to craft a legal defense to a charge under this statute noting that someday officials in the Bush Administration may be prosecuted for their role in the abuse of detainees.

### b. The War Crimes Act (18 U.S.C. § 2441)

The War Crimes Act of 1996 criminalizes actions that would be either "grave breaches"
of the Geneva Conventions Geneva Convention Relative to the Treatment of Prisoners of War, Aug. 12, 1949, 6 U.S.T. 3316, 75 U.N.T.S. 135, [hereinafter "GC III"]; Geneva Convention Relative to the Protection of Civilian Persons in Time of War, Aug. 12, 1949, 6 U.S.T. 3516, 75 U.N.T.S. 287, [hereinafter "GC IV"], (*entered into force* Oct. 21, 1950). The U.S. and Iraq are both parties to the Conventions.
or violations of Common Article 3 of the Geneva Conventions. 18 U.S.C. § 2441 As President Bush has admitted himself, Iraqi detainees held in Iraq are covered by the Geneva Conventions. However, he maintains that non-Iraqis captured in Iraq are not. *See* Terry Frieden, *Justice Dept: Geneva Conventions Limited in Iraq*, CNN.com, Oct. 26, 2004, *available at* http://www.cnn.com/2004/LAW/10/26/noniraqi.prisoners/.

Grave breaches are defined within the Conventions as "wilful killing, torture or inhuman treatment, including biological experiments, willfully causing great suffering or serious injury to body or health;" (GC III, art. 130; GC IV art. 147) and "wilfully depriving a protected person of the rights of fair and regular trial prescribed in the present Convention." GC IV, art. 147. *See also* GC III, art. 130 which requires that Prisoners of War also receive fair trials. urther, it is a grave breach to remove a detained from the country where he is located, except when his removal is necessary for his own safety. Protocol Additional to the Geneva Conventions of 12 August 1949, and relating to the Protection of Victims of International Armed Conflicts (Protocol 1), June 8, 1977, art. 85, 1125 U.N.T.S. 3 [hereinafter Additional Protocol I] ("4. In addition to the grave breaches defined in the preceding paragraphs and in the Conventions, the following shall be regarded as grave breaches of this Protocol, when committed willfully and in violation of the Conventions or the Protocol:

(a) the transfer by the occupying Power of parts of its own civilian population into the territory it occupies, or the deportation or transfer of all or parts of the population of the occupied territory within or outside this territory, in violation of Article 49 of the Fourth Convention").

Common Article 3 prohibits "[v]iolence to life and person, in particular murder of all kinds, mutilation, cruel treatment and torture;...outrages upon personal dignity, in particular humiliating and degrading treatment." GC III, art. 3; GC IV, art. 3.

The Administration has admitted it is subject to prosecution under this statute. The Attorney General in fact cited his concern with prosecution under the War Crimes Act as a justification for declaring Afghan detainees devoid of protection under the Geneva Conventions. Memorandum from White House Counsel Alberto R. Gonzales to President George W. Bush (Jan 25, 2002), *available at* http://www.humanrightsfirst.com /us_law/etn/gonzales/memos_dir/memo_20020125_Gonz_Bush.pdf.

Because this provision can only be used to prosecute abuse of those protected by the Conventions, withholding those protections would allow the government to use techniques barred by international law without fear of prosecution in American courts.

It is important to note that despite the focus in the media concerning what exactly constitutes "torture," "torture" isn't necessary to a conviction under this statute. It is just as much a war crime to:
- treat a detainee "inhumanly"
- cause "great suffering" or "serious injury"
- denying detainees the right to a fair trial
- practice "cruel treatment"
- commit "outrages upon personal dignity, in particular humiliating and degrading treatment" GC III, art. 130; GC IV, art. 147; Additional Protocol 1, arts. 11, 85. *See* International Committee of the Red Cross, *How 'Grave Breaches' are Defined in the Geneva Conventions and Additional Protocols,* June 6, 2004, *available at* www.icrc.org.

### c. The Geneva Conventions and Hague Convention: International Laws Governing the Treatment of Detainees

The United States, along with 191 other countries, is a party to the Geneva Conventions. The United States ratified the Conventions on February 8, 2005. The Geneva Conventions provide basic human rights to everyone in Iraq. Whether a combatant covered by the third Geneva Convention as a prisoner of war, or as a protected person (civilian) under the fourth Geneva Convention, detainees must be treated humanely. GC III, art. 13; GC IV, art. 27. Detainees are protected against "violence to life and person, in particular murder of all kinds, mutilation, cruel treatment and torture;...outrages upon personal dignity, in particular, humiliating and degrading treatment..." (GC III, art. 3; GC IV, art. 3.) and "wilfully depriving a protected person of the rights of fair and regular trial prescribed in the present Convention." GC IV, art. 147. *See also* GC III, art. 130, which requires that prisoners of war also receive fair trials. Additional protocols accepted by the United States clarify that no matter a person's status, they are to be protected against the above mentioned abuses. Additional Protocol I, art. 75.

Violation of the above provisions are considered "grave breaches" and obligate our government to investigate and punish those responsible. The Conventions make clear that it is up to participating countries to enforce its provisions, as it is the only way that those protections will be observed. Jennifer Elsea, U.S. Treatment of Prisoners in Iraq: Selected Legal Issues, Cong. Research Serv. 9-10 (May 24, 2004)

Member nations are required to provide the framework for such enforcement and then to use that framework once violations occur.

The Geneva Conventions afford many other protections that the U.S. is obligated to enforce, even if not through criminal prosecution. Those include:

Holding civilians only as long as they are a demonstrable security risk, and then reviewing their detention at least every six months in an independent tribunal; GC IV, art. 41- 42.

Allowing the International Committee of the Red Cross access to detainees/internees; GC IV, art. 143.

Preventing the use of weapons that cause the "superfluous injury or unnecessary suffering" of combatants. GC Protocol I, art. 35(2). Similarly, civilians "shall enjoy general protection against dangers arising from military operations." GC Protocol I, art. 51.

Similarly, the Hague Conventions regulate the laws of war. An Annex to the Hague Conventions, entitled Respecting the Laws and Customs of War on Land, prohibits the use of weapons or other devices that cause unnecessary suffering. Convention on the Laws and Customs of War on Land (Hague IV Annex); October 18, 1907 (it is forbidden "to employ arms, projectiles, or material calculated to cause unnecessary suffering.).

### d. United Nations Convention Bgainst Torture, and Cruel, Inhuman and Degrading Treatment: International Laws Governing the Treatment of Detainees

The United States is also a party to the UN's Convention Bgainst Torture and Cruel, Inhuman and Degrading Treatment, which prohibits the use of torture, defined as "any act by which severe pain or suffering, whether physical or mental, is intentionally inflicted on a person." Convention against Torture and Other

Cruel, Inhuman or Degrading Treatment or Punishment, Dec. 10, 1984, art.1, 1465 U.N.T.S. 85 (entered into force June 26, 1987) [hereinafter "CAT"]. The United States ratified the CAT on October 21, 1994.

Most notably, it also bans the use of cruel, inhuman and degrading treatment of those in U.S. custody, regardless of the nationality of the detainee or his combatant status. Although those terms are not defined, they have been limited in scope to those practices that are banned by the Fifth, Eighth and Fourteenth Amendments, which the Senate generally noted reflect the international case law interpreting at least the terms cruel and inhuman. When the Senate ratified this treaty it clarified "That the United States considers itself bound by the obligation under article 16 to prevent `cruel, inhuman or degrading treatment or punishment', only insofar as the term `cruel, inhuman or degrading treatment or punishment' means the cruel, unusual and inhumane treatment or punishment prohibited by the Fifth, Eighth, and/or Fourteenth Amendments to the Constitution of the United States." Convention Bgainst Torture and Other Cruel, Inhuman or Degrading Treatment or Punishment, Aug. 30, 1990, S. Doc. No. 101-30, at 25-26. U.S. courts have stated that, "Generally, cruel, inhuman, or degrading treatment includes acts which inflict mental or physical suffering, anguish, humiliation, fear and debasement, which do not rise to the level of 'torture.'" Mehinovic v. Vuckovic, 198 F. Supp. 2d 1322, 1348 (N.D. Ga. 2002); Tachiona v. Mugabe, 234 F. Supp. 2d 401 (S.D.N.Y. 2002); Jama v. INS, 22 F. Supp. 2d 353 (D. N.J. 1998)

As Amnesty International explains, there is no distinct line between torture and CID, although the latter has been defined broadly to make sure nothing abhorrent can slip through a "loophole" in the definition. Amnesty International, Torture and the Law (November 2001) *at* www.amnestyusa.org/stoptorture/law.html. Behavior of this nature is prohibited by the Geneva Conventions and the Convention Bgainst Torture.

However, Human Rights First has noted that other nations that have been subjected to terrorism for decades have refrained from using CID techniques. Human Rights First, U.S. Laws Prohibits Torture and other Cruel, Inhuman or Degrading Treatment or Punishment, *at* www.humanrightsfirst.org.

Israel and the United Kingdom, for example, have been fighting terrorism for years, yet their courts have upheld bans on CID treatment. *Ibid.* Noted legal expert and Professor Mary Ellen O'Connell reviewed the history of CID techniques and noted that "military and U.S. law enforcement officers know how to interrogate without using coercive or cruel techniques—as do the military and police of our peer nations. They have done so successfully for decades." Mary Ellen O'Connell, *Affirming the Ban on Coercive Interrogation*, 66 Ohio St. L. J. ___ (2005) (forthcoming article on file with the House Judiciary Committee Democratic staff).

Our own courts interpreting these phrases will look at a totality of the circumstances to see if treatment rises to the level of a CID violation. Jama v. INS, 22 F. Supp. 2d 353 (D. N.J. 1998). For example, a federal court found cruel and inhuman treatment in a New Jersey prison used to hold illegal immigrants. Jama v. INS, 22 F. Supp. 2d 353 (D. N.J. 1998).

The court found the following treatment violated the ban on CID: sleep deprivation; forced nakedness; ethnic and sexual taunts; sexual touch less than and including sexual assault; deprivation of clothing; deprivation of fresh food; shackling of detainees to their beds; months of solitary confinement; and the trading of sexual favors from female detainees in exchange for the ability to contact their lawyers. *Ibid.* at 358-59.

This is consistent with international tribunals and other courts that have interpreted the ban on CID treatment. They have found that acts, which may not be illegal alone, when applied in concert can rise to the level of CID, including hooding, sleep deprivation, loud music, and long durations in stress positions. *Ibid.*

Again, the onus is on the member countries to enact whatever framework is necessary to deter and punish not only those who commit these acts, but those who are "complicit" in their execution. CAT, art. 4 ("Each State Party shall ensure that all acts of torture are offences under its criminal law. The same shall apply to an attempt to commit torture and to an act by any person which constitutes complicity or participation in torture."). This includes instituting "prompt and impartial investigation, wherever there is reasonable ground to believe that an act of torture has been committed." *Ibid.* at art. 12.

Columnist Bob Herbert further noted:

The Universal Declaration of Human Rights, adopted in 1948, states simply that "No one shall be subject to torture or cruel, inhuman or degrading treatment or punishment." The International Covenant on Civil and Political Rights, to which the U.S. is a signatory, states the same. The binding Convention Bgainst Torture, negotiated by the Reagan administration and ratified by the Senate, prohibits cruel, inhuman and degrading treatment. . . . But since last year's [defense] bill, a strange legal determination was made that the prohibition in the Convention Bgainst Torture against cruel, inhuman, or degrading treatment does not legally apply to foreigners held outside the U.S. They can, apparently, be treated inhumanely. This is the [Bush] administration's position, even though Judge Abe Sofaer, who negotiated the Convention Bgainst Torture for President Reagan, said in a recent letter that the Reagan administration never intended the prohibition against cruel, inhuman or degrading treatment to apply only on U.S. soil. Bob Herbert, *Who Isn't Bgainst Torture?*, N.Y. Times, Oct. 10, 2005, at A19.

### e. Command Responsibility

The United States has long recognized the legal principle of command responsibility—that military officials can be held criminally responsible for acts of their subordinates if they knew—or should have known—of the transgressions and failed to stop them or even punish them after the fact. See Human Rights Watch, Getting Away With Torture: Command Responsibility for the U.S. Abuse of Detainees, Apr. 2005.

In re Yamashita, 327 U.S. 1 (1946), the preeminent case on command responsibility, held that a commander could be held criminally responsibility for the actions of his subordinates. General Tomoyuki Yamashita, the military governor of the Philippines and commander of Japanese forces, argued that he could not be prosecuted for the war crimes committed by his soldiers during World War II. *Ibid.* However, the Supreme Court stated that the laws of war would be eviscerated if commanders could turn a blind eye to the criminal acts of their subordinates:

Its purpose to protect civilian populations and prisoners of war from brutality would largely be defeated if the commander of an invading army could with impunity neglect to take reasonable measures for their protection. Hence the law of war presupposes that its violation is to be avoided through the control of the operations of war by commanders who are to some extent responsible for their subordinates. *Ibid.* at 15.

Deciding that Yamashita would stand trial before military commissions for the atrocities committed by his soldiers, the court held that a commander has "an affirmative duty to take such measures as were within his power and appropriate in the circumstances to protect prisoners of war and the civilian population." *Ibid.* at 16. Yamashita was eventually found guilty of war crimes for failing to control his troops and executed. Human Rights Watch, Getting Away With Torture: Command Responsibility for the U.S. Abuse of Detainees, Apr. 2005, Annex—B Note on Command Responsibility.

U.S. and international law has since developed a three prong test to impose command responsibility for military commanders and civilian officials with constructive control over military forces: (1) a superior-subordinate relationship must exist, (2) the superior must have knowledge or reason to know that a crime was about to be committed or had been committed, and (3) the superior failed to prevent the crime or punish it after the fact. *Ibid.* This doctrine is reflected in the current Army Field Manual, (U.S. Army Field Manual 27-10, The Law of Land Warfare (July 18, 1956), § 501.) guidelines for U.S. instituted military tribunals, (Department of Defense, Military Commission Instruction No. 2, Crimes and Elements for Trials by Military commission, Apr. 30, 2003, *available at* www.defenselink.mil.) individual recovery under the Alien Tort Claim Act (Kadic v. Karadzic, 70 F.3d 232 (2nd Cir. 1995); Xuncax v. Gramajo, 886 F.Supp. 162 (D.Mass.1995) and the Torture Victim Protection Act, (Ford v. Garcia, 289 F3d 1283, (11th Cir. 2002) (defining the three elements of command responsibility in an action under the Torture Victim Protection Act); Xuncax v. Gramajo, 886 F.Supp. 162 (D.Mass.1995) and international law. Study on Customary International Law, International Committee of the Red Cross, July 21, 2005, *available at* www.icrc.org. As the Ninth Circuit stated, "The principle of 'command responsibility' that holds a superior responsible for the actions of subordinates appears to be well accepted in U.S. and international law in connection with acts committed in wartime." Hilao v. Estate of Ferdinand Marcos, 103 F.3d 767 (9th Cir. 1996).

First, there must be a superior-subordinate relationship. Courts will find such a relationship where it is explicit, such as in the military command structure, but also where actual or effective control exists. Ford, 289 F.3d at 1290-91. It therefore can be extended to civilian and political superiors. Major Michael L. Smidt, *Yamashita Medina and Beyond: Command Responsibility in Contemporary Military Operations*, 164 Mil. L. Rev. 155 (2000); Human Rights Watch, Getting Away With Torture: Command Responsibility for the U.S. Abuse of Detainees, Apr. 2005, Annex—B Note on Command Responsibility.

Second, the superior must know, or have reason to know, that a crime was about to be committed, or had been committed. One military commentator has explained that the "should have known" standard "is primarily linked to time. Where reports are received over time or where large numbers of crimes are committed by large numbers of subordinates, creating a basis of constructive notice, it is reasonable to say that the commander should have known." *Ibid.* at 199.

Finally, the superior must have either failed to prevent the violation he foresaw or failed punish it after it occurred. It is customary international law and now standard in U.S. courts that a superior has a duty to take all measures that are "necessary and reasonable" to prevent a crime by his subordinates. Ford, 289 F.3d at 1292-93. In other words, "[I]f the commander gains actual knowledge and does nothing, then he may become a principal in the eyes of the law in that by his inaction he manifests an aiding and encouraging support to his troops, thereby indicating that he joins in their activity and wishes the end product to come about." Major Michael L. Smidt, *Yamashita Medina and Beyond: Command Responsibility in Contemporary Military Operations*, 164 Mil. L. Rev. 155, 198 (2000) (*citing* Kenneth A. Howard, *Command Responsibility for War Crimes*, 21 J. Pub. L. 7, 16 (1972). Some international courts have held that superiors "are even responsible for failure to prevent if they fail to take into account factors such as the age, training or similar elements that point to obvious conclusions regarding the likelihood that such crimes would be committed" (Ilias Bantekas, *The Contemporary Law of Superior Responsibility*, 93 Am. J. Int'l. L. 573, 590 (1999).)

This third prong may also be met when a superior to fails to investigate and punish a crime once it has occurred. Ford, 289 F.3d at 1292-93.

### f. Material Witness (18 U.S.C. § 3144)

Federal law governs how individuals with information about a crime may be detained. Section 3144 of title 18, United States Code, provides that if the government was not certain that a subpoena would compel a witness to appear in court, then the court could issue a warrant for the person's detention as a material witness. 18 U.S.C. § 3144. The individual would have to be provided with access to counsel during detention. The person may not be held at all, however, if their testimony could be secured by a deposition. *Ibid.* Finally, the individual must be released when justice would no longer be served by the detention. *Ibid.*

### 3. Retaliating against Witnesses and Other Individuals
### a. Obstructing Congress (18 U.S.C. § 1505)

It is a federal criminal offense to impede any due exercise of congressional authority. More specifically, section 1505 of title 18 makes it illegal to:

corruptly, or by threats or force, or by any threatening letter or communication influences, obstructs, or impedes or endeavors to influence, obstruct, or impede . . . the due and proper exercise of the power of inquiry under which any inquiry or investigation is being had by either House, or any committee of either House or any joint committee of the Congress. 18 U.S.C. § 1505. The penalty for violations of this prohibition includes a fine, imprisonment for not more than five years, or both. *Ibid.*

In general, the statute prohibits persons from "corruptly" influencing or impeding the exercise of congressional power. This has been construed to apply to situations when the defendant causes another to violate his or her legal duty to Congress, such as by coercing or threatening a witness before Congress to testify falsely or inaccurately. United States v. Poindexter, 951 F.2d 369, 385 (D.C. Cir. 1991). It is not required that the defendant have gained anything from his or her conduct in order for that conduct to be corrupt within the meaning of the statute. *See ibid.* at 386.

Finally, it is important to recognize that a congressional inquiry does need not be formally authorized for the section 1505 prohibition to apply. Instead the courts have found:

the question of whether a given congressional investigation is a 'due and property exercise of the power of inquiry' for purposes of § 1505 cannot be answered by a myopic focus on formality. Rather, it is properly answered by a careful examination of all the surrounding circumstances. If it is apparent that the investigation is a legitimate exercise of investigative authority by a congressional committee within the committee's purview, it should be protected by § 1505. . . . To give § 1505 the protective force it was intended, corrupt endeavors to influence congressional investigations must be proscribed even when they occur prior to formal committee authorization. United States v. Mitchell, 877 F.2d 294, 300 (4th Cir. 1989).

Thus, any exercise of a committee or Congress' power, formal or informal, is protected from corruptive influence or obstruction. It would be unlawful, therefore, for any person in an official or unofficial capacity to coerce another individual to provide false statements or testimony to Congress or to force such individual to respond inaccurately to any congressional inquiry. Such inquiry could be initiated pursuant to formal Committee action or merely as part of an informal investigation.

### b. Whistleblower Protection (5 U.S.C. § 2302)

In 1989, Congress passed the Whistleblower Protection Act to ensure that those who came forward to expose lawlessness and waste in the federal government would not be discouraged by fear of reprisal. 5 U.S.C. § 2302.

5 U.S.C.A. § 2302 delineates different "prohibited personnel practices" and applies to almost every government agency employee. Excepted positions include those within the FBI, the CIA, the Defense Intelligence Agency, the National Security Agency and military employees of the Department of Defense. *Ibid.* at (a)(2)(B)-(C); Homeland and National Security Whistleblower Protections: The Unfinished Agenda, Project on Government Oversight, Apr. 28, 2005 at 5, 8 [hereinafter POGO Report]. Other non-covered agencies include the Government Accountability Office, Defense Mapping Agency, Airport Baggage Screeners and government contractors.

One of those prohibited practices is adverse employment actions for whistleblowing activities. For positions besides those listed above, the government is barred from taking, or failing to take, a personnel action in retaliation for the employee's:

Disclosure of information. . . which the employee or applicant reasonably believes evidences—

(i) a violation of any law, rule or regulation, or

(ii) mismanagement, a gross waste of funds, an abuse of authority, or a substantial and specific danger to pubic health or safety. 5 U.S.C.§ 2303(a). However, the employee's disclosure must be lawful itself for the employee to receive the statutory protection.

The head of the applicable agencies are responsible for ensuring these prohibited practices do not take place. *Ibid.* at (c). However, if they do, the employee may seek redress from the Office of Special Counsel, the Merit Systems Protection Board, and the federal court system. POGO Report, at 8.

c. The Lloyd-LaFollette Act (5 U.S.C. § 7211)

Also known as the "anti-gag rule," this statute passed in response to the Taft and Theodore Roosevelt Administrations' attempt to silence their employees. It ensures that agency employees can provide Congress with the information necessary to do its job. Memorandum from Jack Maskell, Cong. Research Serv., to the Honorable Charles Rangel at 4 (Apr. 26, 2004) [hereinafter Maskell Memo], *available at* http://www.pogo.org/m/gp/wbr2005/AppendixD.pdf. It states that:

The Right of employees, individually or collectively, to petition Congress or a Member of Congress, or to furnish information to either House of Congress or to a committee or Member thereof, may not be interfered with or denied. 5 U.S.C. § 7211.

Far broader than the Whistleblower Protection Act, this statute applies to everyone in the government's employ, even those in the intelligence field that are not protected under that statute. Moreover, it does not limit the sort of information that is protected. It reflects what the Supreme Court has found to be the fundamental right and necessity of Congress receiving information: "a legislative body cannot legislate wisely or effectively in the absence of information regarding conditions which the legislation is intended to affect or change." Maskell memo *supra* at 3. In fact, this right is so paramount that the Court has presumptively construed every statute in the U.S. banning information disclosure to not apply to Congress unless it very specifically states so. *Ibid.*

To give teeth to the Lloyd-LaFollette Act, Congress has repeatedly passed a spending restriction in the annual Treasury Appropriations bill to prevent paying the salary of anyone who interferes with an employee's effort to provide information to the Congress. The requirement is clear: federal money shall not be spent to help suppress the first amendment rights of federal employees:

No part of any appropriation contained in this or any other Act shall be available for the payment of the salary of any officer or employee of the Federal Government, who—

(1) prohibits or prevents, or attempts or threatens to prohibit or prevent, any other officer or employee of the Federal Government from having any direct oral or written communication or contact with any Member, committee, or subcommittee of the Congress in connection with any matter pertaining to the employment of such other officer or employee or pertaining to the department or agency of such other officer or employee in any way, irrespective of whether such communication or contact is at the initiative of such other officer or employee or in response to the request or inquiry of such Member, committee, or subcommittee; or

(2) removes, suspends from duty without pay, demotes, reduces in rank, seniority, status, pay, or performance of efficiency rating, denies promotion to, relocates, reassigns, transfers, disciplines, or discriminates in regard to any employment right, entitlement, or benefit, or any term or condition of employment of, any other officer or employee of the Federal Government, or attempts or threatens to commit any of the foregoing actions with respect to such other officer or employee, by reason of any communication or contact of such other officer or employee with any Member, committee, or subcommittee of the Congress as described in paragraph (1).

*See e.g.* H.R. 3058, 109th Cong. § 918 (2005) (as engrossed by the House); S. 1446, 109th Cong. (2005); *see also*, for example, Consolidated Appropriations Act, 2005, Pub. L. No. 108-447, § 618 of Division H, 118 Stat. 2809 (2004); Consolidated Appropriations Act, 2004, Pub. L. No. 108-99, § 618 of Division F, 117 Stat. 1176 (2003); Consolidated Appropriations Resolution, 2003, Pub. L. No. 108-7, §§ 617, 620, 117 Stat. 11 (2003); Treasury and General Government Appropriations Act of 2002, Pub. L. No. 107-67, §§ 617, 620, 115 Stat. 514 (2001).

### d. Retaliating against Witnesses (18 U.S.C. § 1513)

The government may not retaliate against individuals who provide truthful information to law enforcement officials. Section 1513(e) of title 18 prohibits anyone from "knowingly, with the intent to retaliate, takes any action harmful to any person, including interference with the lawful employment or livelihood of any person, for providing to a law enforcement officer any truthful information relating to the commission or possible commission of any Federal offense . . . ." 18 U.S.C. § 1513(e).

The term "law enforcement officer" is defined as "an officer or employee of the Federal Government . . . or serving the Federal Government as an advisor or consultant (A) authorized under law to engage in or supervise the prevention, detection, investigation, or prosecution of an offense; or (B) serving as a probation or pretrial services officer under this title." 18 U.S.C. § 1515(a)(4). The penalty for witness retaliation consists of a fine, imprisonment for not more than 10 years, or both. 18 U.S.C. § 1513(e).

Because of the definition of "law enforcement officer," this statute would apply to retaliating against any federal employee with investigative authority. For instance, a "law enforcement officer" would include any Justice Department employee (including attorneys, FBI agents, DEA agents, and ATFE agents) as well as inspectors general. This is because each inspector general must "provide policy direction for and to conduct, supervise, and coordinate audits and investigations relating to the programs and operations of [the relevant office]." 5 U.S.C. app. 3, § 4 (emphasis added). Any person who informed such officials of violations of federal law would be protected from any form of retaliation, such as firing, demotion, or rescission of security clearance or other tools necessary for job performance.

A violation of section 1513 is a predicate offense under RICO. 18 U.S.C. § 1961. It thus is unlawful to acquire and invest income or to acquire any interest in any enterprise through a pattern of section 1513 violations. *Ibid.* § 1962. Penalties for violating RICO include a fine, imprisonment for not more than twenty years, or both, as well as forfeiture of any proceeds from the illegal activity. *Ibid.* § 1963.

Finally, it is a separate criminal offense to conspire to commit the crime of witness retaliation. *Ibid.* § 1513. The penalty for conspiring to commit such an offense is the same as for the crime that was the object of the conspiracy.

### 4. Leaking and other Misuse of Intelligence and other Government Information

Numerous federal laws and regulations make it a crime to disclose national security or intelligence information without proper authorization.

**a. Revealing Classified Information in Contravention of Federal Regulations (Executive Order 12958/ Classified Information Nondisclosure Agreement**

First, there are administrative sanctions for misuse of classified information. Presidential Executive Order 12958 prescribes a uniform system for classifying, declassifying, and protecting information related to the national defense. Exec. Order No. 12948, 32 C.F.R. § 2001.10 *et seq.* (2005). It requires each agency head to implement controls over the distribution of classified information. *Ibid.* Section 5.5 provides that, if the Director of the Information Security Oversight Office finds a violation of the Order has taken place, the Director must report to the appropriate agency head so correction action may occur. *Ibid.* Further, sanctions for such violations include: "reprimand, suspension without pay, removal, termination of classification authority, loss or denial of access to classified information, or other sanctions in accordance with applicable law and agency regulation." *Ibid.*

The Order further requires that the supervisors of those who divulge classified information take remedial action against such officials. Such action can include the removal of security clearance and other measures to prevent further disclosure.

In effect, any supervisor of an individual with access to classified information must sanction such individual if he or she illegally discloses the information. For instance, the President would be responsible for ensuring that White House officials and staff having access to classified information complied with the Executive Order and would have to punish any such individual who violated the Order.

Also, prior to obtaining access to classified information, government officials must sign a Classified Information Nondisclosure Agreement, known as a Standard Form 312 or SF-312. The Agreement states that breaches (i.e., disclosure of classified information) could result in the termination of security clearances and removal from employment. The Agreement, signed by White House officials such as Mr. Rove, states: "I will never divulge classified information to anyone" who is not authorized to receive it. Information Security Oversight Office, Classified Information Nondisclosure Agreement (Standard Form 312): Briefing Booklet 73 (emphasis added). *See also* The Honorable Henry A. Waxman, Ranking Member, U.S. House Comm. on Gov't Reform, Fact Sheet: Karl Rove's Nondisclosure Agreement 1-2 (July 15, 2005).

It also is important to note that even confirming the accuracy of classified information in a public source is a violation of the agreement. Information Security Oversight Office, Classified Information Nondisclosure Agreement (Standard Form 312): Briefing Booklet 73 (emphasis added). *See also* The Honorable Henry A. Waxman, Ranking Member, U.S. House Comm. on Gov't Reform, Fact Sheet: Karl Rove's Nondisclosure Agreement 1-2 (July 15, 2005).

The agreement specifically states:

However, before disseminating the [classified] information elsewhere or confirming the accuracy of what appears in the public source, the signer of the SF 312 must confirm through an authorized official that the information has, in fact, been declassified. If it has not, further dissemination of the information or confirmation of its accuracy is also an authorized disclosure. Information Security Oversight Office, Classified Information Nondisclosure Agreement (Standard Form 312): Briefing Booklet 73.

In short, if a White House official signs the agreement yet proceeds to disclose or confirm classified information, the President would be required to terminate that individual's security clearance and remove him or her from their position.

**b. Statutory Prohibitions on Leaking Information**

Numerous federal statutes make it a criminal offense to convey anything of value that belongs to the United States. Section 641 of title 18 imposes criminal penalties on anyone who "embezzles, steals, purloins, or knowingly converts to his use or the use of another, or without authority, sells, conveys, or disposes of any record, voucher, money, or thing of value of the United States or of any department or agency thereof." 18 U.S.C. § 641. The penalty for a violation of this statute is a fine, imprisonment for not more than ten years, or both; however, if the value of the property is less than $1,000, then the prison term cannot exceed one year. *Ibid.*

This statute has been interpreted broadly, giving latitude to what constitutes a "thing of value." The Fourth Circuit Court of Appeals has held that the classification of information is, in and of itself, relevant to determining whether that information is a "thing of value" to the United States. United States v. Zettl, 889 F.2d 51, 54 (4th Cir. 1989). Similarly, the Sixth Circuit ruled that the term pertains to both tangible and intangible property. United States v. Jeter, 775 F.2d 670 (6th Cir. 1985). The Bush Justice Department has already determined that government information is a "thing of value." *See* John Dean, *It Doesn't Look Good for Karl Rove*, CNN.com, July15, 2005, *available at* http://www.cnn.com/2005/LAW/07/15/dean.rove/. Jonathan Randel, a former Drug Enforcement Administration employee, leaked to the British media the fact that the name Lord Michael Ashcroft of Great Britain appeared in the DEA's money laundering files. Press Release, U.S. Attorneys' Office, Northern District of Georgia, Former DEA Worker Sentenced to Prison for Selling Information (Jan. 9, 2003), *available at* http://www.usdoj.gov/usao/gan/press/01-09-03_2.html. In 2002, the Justice Department obtained an indictment against Mr. Randel for violating section 641. Mr. Randel ultimately pled guilty and was sentenced to one year in prison and three years of probation. *Id.* While he was sentencing Mr. Randel, U.S. District Judge Richard Story stated, "Anything that would affect the security of officers and of the operations of the agency would be of tremendous concern, I think, to any law-abiding citizen in this country." John Dean, *supra.*

Because "thing of value" is a broad term, the prohibition in turn is broad. Information such as U.S. intelligence data or analyses could be considered "of value" and thus prohibited from disclosure, even such information is not classified. Even analyses of foreign military and defense capabilities would be protected as "of value" to the United States.

The *mens rea*, or intent, requirement under the statute also is interpreted broadly. The government need only establish that the defendant transmitted information without authority. *Jeter*, 775 F.2d at 681. It is irrelevant whether the defendant knew the information was "of value" to the United States. *See Ibid.*

Second, it is illegal for any person to willfully disclose information related to the national defense. Subsection 793(d) of title 18 applies to persons having lawful possession of vital information. Criminal liability assigns to anyone:

who has lawful possession of, access to, control over, or being entrusted with any document, writing, code book, signal book, sketch, photograph, photographic negative, blueprint, plan, map, model, instrument, appliance, or note relating to the national defense, or information relating to the national defense which information the possessor has reason to believe could be used to the injury of the United States or to the advantage of any foreign nation, [and] willfully communicates, delivers, transmits or causes to be communicated, delivered, or transmitted or attempts to communicate, deliver, or transmit or cause to be communicated, delivered or transmitted the same to any person not entitled to receive it, or willfully retains the same and fails to deliver it on demand to the officer or employee of the United States entitled to receive it." 18 U.S.C. § 793(d).

The penalty for violating this prohibition includes a fine, imprisonment for not more than ten years, or both. *Id.* § 793. The penalty for conspiring to commit such an offense, and engaging in any act in furtherance of such, is the same as for the underlying offense. *Id.* § 793(g).

This means that it is unlawful to divulge any information related to U.S. military bases, defense installations, war plans, intelligence capabilities, or intelligence information. As stated above this prohibition applies to officials and employees who have lawful access to the information in question.

Courts have construed this prohibition broadly. For instance, prohibited disclosures are not limited to foreign agents; it is illegal to disclose defense information to the media, as well. United States v. Morison, 844 F.2d 1057 (4th Cir. 1988). Further, it is not necessary for the information in question to be classified for it to be protected from disclosure. United States v. Harris, 40 C.M.R. 308 (1969).

Third, it is a highly serious offense to transmit any defense information to a foreign agent or foreign government, regardless of whether the foreign entity is friendly or an enemy. *See* United States v. Rosenberg, 195 F.2d 583 (2d Cir.1952). Subsection 794(a) of title 18 prohibits the transmission or delivery of any document or information related to national defense to any foreign government or foreign agent. 18 U.S.C. § 794(a). The penalty includes death (in cases involving death of an American agent or military systems) or imprisonment for any term of years. *Id.* The penalty for conspiring to commit such an offense, and engaging in any act in furtherance of such, is the same as for the underlying offense. *Id.* § 794(c).

Such conduct is illegal if the transmission is direct or indirect. *Ibid.* § 794(a). The disclosure must occur with the intent or reason to believe that it would be used to injure the United States or to the advantage of a foreign nation. *Ibid.*

In other words, government officials and private citizens are prohibited from leaking to foreign governments any information related to our national defense. This prohibition applies to information about U.S. intelligence capabilities, military plans, defense strategy, or knowledge of foreign military assets. Any person who released such information later obtained by a foreign government, whether through speeches or press releases or leaks to the news media, would be acting unlawfully.

Finally, it also can be a specific federal crime to disclose the name of a covert U.S. agent. Subsection 421(a) of title 50 makes it unlawful for someone, having or having had access to classified information that identifies a covert agent, to intentionally disclose such information to an unauthorized recipient knowing the disclosure identifies the agent and knowing that the government is taking affirmative measures to conceal the agent's relationship to the United States. 50 U.S.C. § 421(a). The penalty includes a fine, imprisonment for not more than ten years, or both. *Ibid.* Similarly, subsection 421(b) of title 50 makes it unlawful for someone who, as a result of having access to classified information, learns the identity of a covert agent and intentionally discloses any information disclosing that identity to any person not authorized to receive it. The defendant must know that the information disclosed identifies the agent and that the government is taking steps to conceal the identity. *Ibid.* § 421(b). The penalty includes a fine, imprisonment for not more than five years, or both. *Ibid.* As such, it is a crime to intentionally disclose the identity of a covert agent to someone who is not allowed to have the information. Our review indicates that no prosecutions have been brought under this section 421 of title 50.

## 5. Laws and Guidelines Prohibiting Conflicts of Interest

Existing law and rules of professional conduct govern when Department attorneys must recuse themselves from particular investigations. Federal law requires the Attorney General to promulgate rules mandating the disqualification of any officer or employee of the Justice Department "from participation in a particular investigation or prosecution if such participation may result in a personal, financial, or political conflict of interest, or the appearance thereof." 28 U.S.C. § 528 (emphasis added). Pursuant to this requirement, the Department has promulgated regulations stating that:

No employee shall participate in a criminal investigation or prosecution if he has a personal or political relationship with: (1) any person . . . substantially involved in the conduct that is the subject of the investigation or prosecution; or (2) any person . . . which he knows or has a specific and substantial interest that would be affected by the outcome of the investigation or prosecution. 28 C.F.R. § 45.2.

To reiterate the importance of preventing conflicts of interest, the Justice Department has further explicated the guidelines in its U.S. Attorneys' Manual. The Attorneys' Manual provides that:

When United States Attorneys, or their offices, become aware of an issue that could require a recusal in a criminal or civil matter or case as a result of a personal interest or professional relationship with parties involved in the matter, they must contact General Counsel's Office (GCO), EOUSA. The requirement of recusal does not arise in every instance, but only where a conflict of interest exists or there is an appearance of a conflict of interest or loss of impartiality. U.S. Dep't of Justice, U.S. Attorneys' Manual § 3-2.170.

Furthermore, rules of professional conduct bar lawyers from matters in which they have conflicts of interest. Because Department attorneys must follow the ethical rules of the bar in which they practice, 28 U.S.C. § 530B, officials at Main Justice are obligated to comply with the District of Columbia Bar's Rules of Professional Conduct. These Rules state that, without consent, a lawyer shall not represent a client if "the lawyer's professional judgment on behalf of the client will be or reasonably may be adversely affected by the lawyer's responsibilities to or interests in a third party or the lawyer's own financial, business, property, or personal interests." District of Columbia Bar, Rules of Professional Conduct 1.7(b)(4). The American Bar Bssociation mimics this guideline in Rule 1.7 of its own Model Rules of Professional Conduct. *See* American Bar Bssociation, Model Rules of Professional Conduct 1.7(a)(2).

## 6. Laws Governing Electronic Surveillance

The general rule regarding electronic surveillance is that it is illegal for any person to "engage in electronic surveillance under color of law except as authorized by statute." 50 U.S.C. § 1809.

There are two statutes that govern electronic surveillance: (1) Title III of the Omnibus Crime Control and

Safe Streets Act of 1968 (the "Wiretap Act"), 18 U.S.C. §§ 2510-2521.which governs wiretapping in criminal cases; and (2) the Foreign Intelligence Surveillance Act of 1978 ("FISA"), 50 U.S.C. § 1801 *et seq.*

which governs electronic surveillance of foreign powers or agents of foreign powers in national security investigations. These two statutes are the "exclusive means by which electronic surveillance ... and the interception of wire and oral communication may be conducted." 18 U.S.C. § 2511.

a.  Foreign Intelligence Surveillance Act (50 U.S.C. § 1801 et seq)

In discussing Presidential authority to conduct warrantless electronic surveillance to gather foreign intelligence, the Foreign Intelligence Surveillance Act (FISA) is the applicable statute. In fact, FISA applies to the "interception of international wire communications to or from any person (whether or not a U.S. person) within the United States without the consent of at least one party" (Foreign Intelligence Surveillance Act of 1978, Pub. L. 95-511, Title I, 92 Stat. 1796 (Oct. 25, 1978) codified as amended. Under FISA, the government must seek an order from the FISA court (sometimes referred to as a FISA "warrant") before conducting electronic surveillance for foreign intelligence information. The application for the order must state that there is probable cause to believe that the target of the surveillance is a foreign power or an agent of a foreign power. 50 U.S.C. § 1805. For example, if a U.S. citizen, who is suspected of terrorist activity, is talking on his telephone from his home in Virginia. The government must obtain a FISA warrant prior to monitoring his calls.

Exceptions to this warrant requirement exist when there is an emergency and during wartime. If the Attorney General certifies that there is an emergency need to conduct electronic surveillance, he may authorize the surveillance, but must apply for a FISA warrant as soon as practicable, and not more than 72 hours later. *Ibid.* § 1805(f). For example, if a U.S. citizen, who is suspected of terrorist activity, begins talking on his telephone, the government can begin monitoring his conversations without a warrant but must apply for the warrant within 72 hours.

Wartime also creates an exception to FISA's warrant requirement. FISA expressly governs wiretapping procedures "during time of war" and provides that "the President, through the Attorney General, may authorize electronic surveillance without a court order under this title to acquire foreign intelligence information for a period not to exceed fifteen days following a declaration of war by the Congress." *Ibid.* § 1811.

If the electronic surveillance is directed solely at communications between or among foreign powers and there is "no substantial likelihood" that the surveillance will acquire the contents of any communication to which a U.S. person is a part, then the President may authorize surveillance without a FISA warrant for up to one year. *Ibid.* § 1802. A U.S. person is defined under FISA as a citizen, a lawful permanent resident, a U.S. corporation, or an unincorporated association a substantial number of members of which are U.S. citizens.

FISA's most notable provisions in this particular context are provisions that make criminal any electronic surveillance not authorized by statute *(Ibid.* § 1809.) and provisions that expressly establish FISA and specified provisions of the federal criminal code as the "exclusive means by which electronic surveillance . . . may be conducted." 18 U.S.C. § 2511(2)(f).

b. National Security Act of 1947 (50 U.S.C. chapter 15)

The National Security Act of 1947, and amendments thereto, governs the nation's counterintelligence apparatus. 50 U.S.C. chapter 15. Briefings are limited to the Gang of Eight only when intelligence activities involve "covert action" or activities of the United States Government to influence political, economic, or military conditions abroad, where it is intended that the role of the United States Government will not be apparent." 50 U.S.C. § 413b(e). Covert actions, pursuant to the statute, do not include "activities the primary purpose of which is to acquire intelligence." *Ibid.* § 413b(e)(1).

Unless a "covert action" is involved, the National Security Act requires that "the President shall ensure that the congress intelligence committees are kept fully and currently informed of the intelligence activities of the United States." *Ibid.* § 413(a)(1). The Act makes clear that the requirement to keep the committees informed may not be evaded on the grounds that "providing the information to the congressional intelligence committees would constitute the unauthorized disclosure of classified information." *Ibid.* § 413(e).

. **Communications Act of 1934 (47 U.S.C. § 222)**

Section 222 of the Communications Act generally states that every telecommunications carrier has a duty to protect the confidentiality of the proprietary information of their customers. 47 U.S.C. § 222(a). Proprietary information is: (a) information that relates to the quantity, technical configuration, type, destination, location, an amount of use of a telecommunications service subscribed to by any customer of a telecommunications carrier, and that is made available by the customer solely by virtue of the carrier-customer relationship; and (b) information contained in the bills pertaining to telephone exchange service or telephone service received by a customer of a carrier. *Id.* § 222(h)(1)(A-B).A carrier may only use, disclose, or permit access to individually-identifiable customer information in its provision of the telecommunications service or services necessary to the provision of such service. *Ibid.* § 222(c)(1). The law provides that the carrier may disclose such information if it is required by law, if it has customer approval, or if it falls under one of the exceptions outlined in the chapter. *Ibid.* § 222.

The Communications Act provides several exceptions to the prohibition on disclosure of communications content. Specifically, the law provides that a carrier may disclose the content of communications in order to (1) provide or initiate services and collect or bill for services rendered; (2) to protect the rights or property of the carrier, or to protect users of those services from fraudulent, abusive, or unlawful use of, or subscription to, such services; (3) to provide telemarketing, referral, or administrative services to the customer; or (4) to provide call location information in the case of an emergency. *Ibid.* § 222(d).

Carriers in violation of the requirements provided in the Communications Act are subject to a variety of penalties under the Act. Specifically, the law provides for criminal penalties for any knowing and willful violation of any provision of the Act. 47 U.S.C. § 501. The resulting criminal penalty provided by the Act is a fine of up to $10,000, imprisonment for up to one year, or both; and in the case of a person previously convicted of violating the Act, a fine up to $10,000, imprisonment up to two years, or both. *Ibid.* In addition, the law also punishes the willful and knowing violations of Federal Communication Commission regulations that result from a violation of the Act. *Ibid.* § 502. This section provides that any person who willfully and knowingly violates any rule, regulation, restriction, or condition made or imposed by the Commission is, in addition to other penalties provided by law, subject to a maximum fine of $500 for each day on which a violation occurs. *Ibid.*

### d. Stored Communications Act of 1986 (18 U.S.C. § 2702)

Under the Stored Communications Act of 1986, it is a federal criminal offense for a provider of electronic communications services or of remote computing services to disclose the contents of a communication that are in electronic storage. 18 U.S.C. § 2702(a). The penalty for violating this prohibition is a fine and up to ten years imprisonment for serious and repeat offenders. *Ibid.* § 2701. In addition, persons harmed by knowing or intentional violations of the law may bring civil actions in court for damages, attorney's fees, and equitable relief. *Ibid.* § 2707.

Exceptions to the prohibition on disclosure of communications content exist, such as for transmissions that are incident to the provision of communications service and pursuant to specific criminal statutes. *Ibid.* § 2702(b). There is also an exception wherein a provider may divulge a communication to a governmental entity if, in good faith, the provider believes that an emergency involving danger of death or serious physical injury to any person requires disclosure. *Ibid.* Furthermore, in analyzing another statute that permits voluntary disclosure of customer records, a court has held that there must be a good faith nexus between the alleged suspicious activity and the disclosure of the protected information for there to be statutory protection for the disclosure. Lopez v. First Union Nat'l Bank, 129 F.3d 1186 (11th Cir. 1997). Defendant evoked the safe harbor provision of the Annunzio-Wylie Anti-Money Laundering Act of 1992 (31 U.S.C. § 5318 (g)(3)).

There also are exceptions that allow for disclosure of customer records. 18 U.S.C. § 2702(c). These include: the consent of the subscriber, necessarily incident to the provision of service, to a government entity if the provider believes an emergency involving danger of death or serious injury requires disclosure. *Ibid.* Additional provisions of the Stored Communications Act require that the Attorney General submit to the Committee on the Judiciary in both the House and the Senate a report containing the number of accounts from which the Department of Justice has received voluntary disclosures under the emergency exception, and a summary for the basis of those disclosures in some instances on an annual basis. 18 U.S.C. § 2702(d).

**e. Pen Registers or Trap and Trace Devices (18 U.S.C. § 3121)**

Pen registers are surveillance devices that capture in real-time the phone numbers dialed on outgoing telephone calls; (18 U.S.C. § 3127(3)) trap and trace devices capture the numbers identifying incoming calls. 18 U.S.C. § 3127(4). These devices are not designed to reveal the content of communications, or even identify the parties to a communication or whether a call was connected at all. The law on pen registers and trap and trace devices expressly prohibits their installation and use without first obtaining a court order either under the criminal wiretap law (18 U.S.C. § 3123.) or under FISA. 18 U.S.C. § 3121. This prohibition does not apply to use by an electronic or wire service provider relating to the operation, maintenance and testing of a service or protection of the rights or property of the service provider, or to use where the consent of the user of the service has been obtained. *Ibid.* Furthermore, a government agency authorized to install and use a pen register or trap and trace device under the provisions of this statute, must use technology reasonably available to it that restricts the recording or decoding of electronic impulses utilized in the processing and transmitting of wire or electronic communications in a manner that does not include the contents of that communication. 18 U.S.C. § 3123.

# Major Reports

The following is a listing of signficiant government reports used in connection with the preparation of this Report.

## A. Executive Branch

1. Comprehensive Report of the Special Advisor to the Director of Central Intelligence on Iraq's Weapons of Mass Destruction ("Duelfer Report") (September 30, 2004), available at www.cia.gov/cia/reports/iraq_wmd _2004/.

   Report prepared by Charles Duelfer, head of the Iraq Survey Group, which found that Iraq's illicit weapons capability had been destroyed and research stopped many years before the United States led the invasion of Iraq in March 2003.

2. U.S. Department of Justice, Legal Authorities Supporting the Activities of the National Security Agency Described by the President (White Paper) (Jan. 19, 2006), available at http://www.usdoj.gov/opa/white paperonnsalegalauthorities.pdf.

   This White Paper describes the President's legal justification for the domestic spying program arguing that the President has inherent war powers under the Constitution to order warrantless eavesdropping on U.S. citizens and that the President's inherent authority seemingly supersedes FISA in a time of war.

3. The Commission on the Intelligence Capabilities of the United States Regarding Weapons of Mass Destruction ("Robb-Silberman Report") (March 31, 2005), available at http://www.wmd.gov/report/

   This Report found that the "Intelligence Community was dead wrong in almost all of its pre-war judgments about Iraq's weapons of mass destruction. This was a major intelligence failure."

4. Office of the Inspector General, U.S. Department of Justice, THE SEPTEMBER 11 DETAINEES: A REVIEW OF THE TREATMENT OF ALIENS HELD ON IMMIGRATION CHARGES IN CONNECTION WITH THE INVESTIGATION OF THE SEPTEMBER 11 ATTACKS (April 2003), available at http://www.fas.org/irp/agency/doj/oig/detainees.pdf.

   The report found "significant problems in the way the September 11 detainees were treated. . . .the evidence indicates a pattern of physical and verbal abuse by some correctional officers . . . [and] certain conditions of confinement were unduly harsh . . ."

5. Office of Inspector General, U.S. Department of Justice, SUPPLEMENTAL REPORT ON SEPTEMBER 11 DETAINEES' ALLEGATIONS OF ABUSE AT THE METROPOLITAN DETENTION CENTER IN BROOKLYN, NEW YORK (December 2003), available at http://www.usdoj.gov/oig/special /0312/final.pdf.

   The Inspector General report "found evidence that some officers slammed detainees against the wall, twisted their arms and hands in painful ways, stepped on their leg restraint chains, and punished them by keeping them restrained for long periods of time."

6. Office of the Inspector General, U.S. Department of Justice, A REVIEW OF THE FBI'S HANDLING OF THE BRANDON MAYFIELD CASE (UNCLASSIFIED AND REDACTED) (March 2006) available at http://www.usdoj.gov/oig/special/s0601/PDF_list.htm.

The Report found that the FBI fingerprint examiners were reckless in their duties and "that Mayfield's [legal] representation of a convicted terrorist and other facts developed during the field investigation, including his Muslim religion, also likely contributed to the examiners' failure to sufficiently reconsider the identification after legitimate questions were raised."

# B. Legislative Reports

1. U.S. Senate Select Committee on Intelligence, Report on the U.S. Intelligence Community's Prewar Intelligence Bssessments on Iraq (July 2004), available at http://intelligence.senate.gov/iraqreport2.pdf

# C. Government Accountability Office

1. JUSTICE DEPARTMENT: BETTER MANAGEMENT OVERSIGHT AND INTERNAL CONTROLS NEEDED TO ENSURE ACCURACY OF TERROR-RELATED STATISTICS (January 2003) available at http://www.gao.gov/new.items/d03266.pdf.

The GAO found that "DOJ does not have sufficient management oversight and internal controls in place, as required by federal internal control standards, to ensure the accuracy and reliability of its terrorism-related conviction statistics." For example, the DOJ misclassified close to 46% of terrorism related convictions which hindered "Congress's ability to accurately assess terrorism-related performance outcomes of the U.S. criminal justice system."

2. HOMELAND SECURITY: JUSTICE DEPARTMENT'S PROJECT TO INTERVIEW ALIENS AFTER SEPTEMBER 11, 2001 (April 2003) available at http://www.gao.gov/new.items/d03459.pdf.

The GAO found that as of March 2003, law enforcement officers had interviewed 3,216 aliens and that "the results are difficult to measure, and DOJ has not fully analyzed all the data obtained from the interviews or how effectively the project was implemented."

3. FREEDOM OF INFORMATION ACT: AGENCY VIEWS ON CHANGES RESULTING FROM NEW ADMINISTRATION POLICY (September 2003) available at http://www.gao.gov/new.items/d03981.pdf.

The GAO found that one third of all FOIA officers reported a decreased likelihood of their agency making a discretionary disclosure in the current Administration.

4. DATA MINING: FEDERAL EFFORTS COVER A WIDE RANGE OF USES (May 2004) available at http://www.gao.gov/new.items/d04548.pdf.

The GAO report highlights the types of and extent to which data mining occurs in the Federal Government, finding that "52 agencies are using or are planning to use data mining. These departments and agencies reported 199 data mining efforts, of which 68 are planned and 131 are operational . . . out all 199 data mining efforts identified, 122 used personal information."

5. REVIEW OF U.S. ATTORNEY GENERAL'S TRAVEL COSTS FOR USA PATRIOT ACT TOUR AND RELATED TRAVEL (October 12, 2004) available at http://www.gao.gov/new.items/d0595r.pdf.

The GAO examined and provided "information on the locations and costs of the U.S. Attorney General's travels known as the USA PATRIOT Act Tour, as well as the locations and costs of a series of trips in September 2003 referred to by DOJ as 'Life and Liberty' travel."

# D. Congressional Research Service

1. Elizabeth B. Bazan and Jennifer K. Elsea, Legislative Attorneys, Presidential Authority to Conduct Warrantless Electronic Surveillance to Gather Foreign Intelligence Information, Congressional Research Service Memorandum (CRS Memo) (January 5, 2006).

The CRS memo concludes that "it appears unlikely that a court would hold that Congress has expressly or impliedly authorized the NSA electronic surveillance operations here under discussion, and it would likewise appear that, to the extent that those surveillances fall within the definition of "electronic surveillance" within the meaning of FISA or any activity regulated under Title III, Congress intended to cover the entire field with these statutes."

2. Alfred Cumming, Statutory Procedures Under Which Congress Is To Be Informed of U.S. Intelligence Activities, Including Covert Actions, (Congressional Research Service Memorandum (CRS Memo) (January 18, 2006).

The CRS "memorandum examines certain existing statutory procedures that govern how the executive branch is to keep Congress informed of U.S. intelligence activities, reviews pertinent legislative history underpinning the development of those procedures, and looks at the notification process that reportedly was followed in informing certain Members of Congress of the President's decision to authorize the National Security Agency (NSA) to collect signals intelligence within the United States."

3. Elizabeth B. Bazan, Gina Marie Stevens, and Brian T. Yeh, Government Access to Phone Calling Activity and Related Records: Legal Authorities, Congressional Research Service (May 17, 2006).

This report "summarize[s] statutory authorities regarding access by the Government, for either foreign intelligence or law enforcement purposes, to information related to telephone calling patterns or practices. [It] also discuss[es] statutory prohibitions against accessing or disclosing such information, along with relevant exceptions to those prohibitions."

4. Gina Marie Stevens and Tara Alexandra Rainson, Data Security: Protecting the Privacy of Phone Records, Congressional Research Service (May 17, 2006).

"This report discusses recent legislative and regulatory efforts to protect the privacy of customer telephone records, and efforts to prevent the unauthorized use, disclosure, or sale of such records by data brokers." Gina Marie Stevens and Tara Alexandra Rainson, Data Security: Protecting the Privacy of Phone Records, Congressional Research Service (May 17, 2006).

# E. State Governments

1. District of Columbia, Maryland, and Virginia Advisory Committee to the U.S. Commission on Civil Rights, CIVIL RIGHTS CONCERNS IN THE METROPOLITAN WASHINGTON D.C., AREA IN THE

AFTERMATH OF THE September 11, 2001, TRAGEDIES (June 2003) available at http://www.usccr.gov/pubs/sac/dc0603/dc0603.pdf.

The Committee report found that "To the extent that government investigators target people based on their ethnic or religious background, these actions are at best ineffective protection against terrorism." The report describes the rise in hate crimes following September 11 and argues that current tactics to fight terrorism "pose a threat to civil liberties." It states that efforts should be made to "increase the U.S. public's understanding" of the Arab, South Bsian, Muslim, and Sikh communities.

2. Illinois Advisory Committee to the U.S. Commission on Civil Rights, ARAB AND MUSLIM CIVIL RIGHTS ISSUES IN THE CHICAGO METROPOLITAN AREA POST-SEPTEMBER 11 (May 2003) available at http://www.usccr.gov/pubs/sac/il0503/il0503.pdf.

The Report describes the increase in hate crimes against those perceived to be Arab or Muslim post-September 11 in the Chicago area. The report describes actions taken by local government, including the interviews of young male Arabs after September 11, which were perceived by the Arab and Muslim communities to be racial profiling. The report also found that the Arab and Muslim communities fear discrimination, and describes the consequences and concerns that arise as a result.

3. California State Senate Office of Research, THE PATRIOT ACT, OTHER POST 9-11 ENFORCEMENT POWERS AND THE IMPACT ON CALIFORNIA'S MUSLIM COMMUNITIES (March 2004), available at http://www.sen.ca.gov/sor/REPORTS/REPORTS_BY_SUBJ/GOVERNMENT/PATRIOT4-02.PDF.

The report reviews whether or not "the federal government, ostensibly to prevent further attacks, was targeting and harassing whole communities of largely Muslim immigrants living in the United States." The report investigates incidents of arrest, deportation, deportation, and interrogation, including immigration sweeps, secrecy provisions for courtroom immigration proceedings, and the 2/3/2003 FBI directive to "base terrorist investigations on demographic data of Muslim communities."

4. New York Advisory Committee to the U.S. Commission on Civil Rights, CIVIL RIGHTS IMPLICATIONS OF POST-SEPTEMBER 11 LAW ENFORCEMENT PRACTICES IN NEW YORK (March 2004) available at http://www.usccr.gov/pubs/sac/ny0304/ny0304.pdf.

The Committee found that law enforcement policies and practices have "pos[ed] a threat to civil rights and civil liberties, especially within New York's Muslim, Arab, and South Bsian communities." The report describes the negative consequences and potential implications of the Call-In Special Registration Program and the sharing of national databases on immigration status with state and local police.

WITHDRAWN

### About the Author

Sandra Lee Smith has taught grades from kindergarten through college in California and Arizona.

In response to the President's Report, *A Nation at Risk*, Ms. Smith participated in a project involving Arizona State University, Phoenix Elementary School District, and an inner-city community in Phoenix. Participants in the project developed a holistic approach to education.

### Photo Credits

Cover Photo: Chuck Peterson
Photos on pages 2, 9, 25, 29, 32, 37, 40, 45, 48, 59: Chris Volpe; page 13: Gamma-Liaison/Dr. Allan W. King; page 17: Gamma-Liaison/Roger M. Richards; page 20: Chuck Peterson/Blackbirch Graphics; page 26: Gamma-Liaison/James Metropole, page 39: Wide World.

Design/Production: Blackbirch Graphics, Inc.

IV-drug users are at high risk of contracting AIDS by sharing
needles.

HAZELDEN/ROSEN DRUG ABUSE PREVENTION LIBRARY

# HEROIN

Sandra Lee Smith

A HAZELDEN / ROSEN Book

To my brother-in-law, Richard,
whose expertise in the prevention of substance abuse
has been invaluable not only to the writing of this book
but to our community.

*The people pictured in this book are only models; they in no
way practice or endorse the activities illustrated. Captions serve
only to explain the subjects of the photographs and do not imply a
connection between the real-life models and the staged situations.*

Published in 1991, 1993, 1995 by The Rosen Publishing Group, Inc.
29 East 21st Street, New York, NY 10010

**Revised Edition, 1995**

This edition published in 1997 by Hazelden
PO Box 176, Center City MN 55012-0176

**Library of Congress Cataloging-in-Publication Data**

Smith, Sandra Lee
     Heroin / by Sandra Lee Smith
     (The Drug Abuse Prevention Library)
     Includes bibliographical references and index
     Summary: Discusses heroin, its unique qualities and
     dangers, and counsels against illegal involvement with
     the drug.
          ISBN 1-56838-166-2
          1. Heroin—Juvenile literature. 2. Heroin
     habit—Juvenile literature. [1. Heroin. 2. Drug
     abuse]
     I. Title. II. Series.
     HV5809.5S65 1991
     362.29'3—dc20                91-10676
                                            CIP
                                           AC

# Contents

# Introduction

*H*eroin, once known as the "heroic" drug, is one of the most addictive and destructive drugs available to teens today.

"I'm bored." Michael stretched out his long legs and shook back a lock of blond hair.

"Yeah," Jason agreed. "School sucks."

"Let's cut out of here."

"And go where?" Jason frowned, his dark brown skin crinkling around his eyes. "Ever since we quit smoking dope, life's been a drag."

Michael sighed. "What I wouldn't give for a joint right now!"

"I know. Where can we get one?"

Jason nodded toward a group of girls standing on the other side of the quad. "Maria has a stash in her locker."

"No kidding?" Michael straightened, paused for a minute, then sank back down. "We can't smoke now. If we get busted we'll be expelled for good."

Jason stood. "We can't get busted for asking."

"Cool it, Bro. I don't want to smoke, I just want to get high." Michael groaned as he watched his friend approach Maria. He half wanted him to come back; then again, if he scored...

Jason returned a few minutes later with Maria. Michael's interest perked up for the first time in days.

"I hear you wanna lift with no smoke." Maria smiled. "I've got just the thing."

Michael stood when he saw the foil in Maria's hand.

"A little Mexican tar, *hombre*."

Juan dropped the tray as the man brushed by. "Did you see him?" Juan barely noticed the tray Leo put back in his hand. "Wasn't that Shawn Clark?"

Leo cast Juan a wry glance. "You working with half a deck these days? Shawn Clark wouldn't be in a place like this." He

**8** gestured at the crowded room where he and Juan volunteered every Saturday afternoon to help feed the homeless drug addicts who drifted in.

"It was him, I swear," Juan insisted as he began to clear the next row of tables.

"Come off it. Clark was our star quarterback. He's got to be playing for some big-time college team by now."

"I heard U.C.L.A. recruited him," Juan agreed. "Still..."

Just then the man they'd been staring at turned around. Juan and Leo both froze. It was Shawn Clark, but it wasn't the Shawn Clark they had known. The once muscular body was now washed-out skin over bare bones. His eyes were sunken in his lined and haggard face. His hair stood on end, unkempt and dirty.

"He looks like a hundred miles of bad road," Juan gasped.

"That's heroin for you," Leo murmured. "It wastes you."

The baby screamed.

Saralyn shuddered as she glanced at her son's red, puckered face. "Shut up!"

The baby continued to wail.

"I can't stand it." Saralyn stomped out of the room and slammed the door. Tears

The athlete works hard to develop his body. He chooses not to harm it with drugs.

**10** rolled down her cheeks. If only she had some smack. It would calm her nerves.

Her fingers shook as she dialed the phone.

When Duane answered, she began to cry again.

"Saralyn, is that you?"

"Yes." She could barely speak.

"What's wrong?" Duane sounded worried. "You haven't taken anything, have you?"

"No," she managed to reply. "I need some stuff, D. I ache all over. My skin itches."

"Those are the symptoms of withdrawal. You'll get through."

"Can you bring me a candy bar or something?" She didn't want candy, she wanted the real thing. But she'd been craving sweets.

"Sure thing. Hang in there." Duane spoke firmly. "Remember your son. He needs to come off the drugs too."

Remorse coursed through Saralyn. Her son must feel as bad as she did. How was she to know he'd get high when she breast-fed him?

"It's okay, D. I'll make it." Saralyn hung up the phone and took a deep breath. Yes, she'd make it. She had to. She didn't

want her son to go through the hell she had experienced.

Each of these people has been exposed to the ups and downs of heroin. The thing about heroin is that it always ends in a down.

Humans are miracles of creation. Each one of us is unique and designed to get as much or as little out of life as we want. Free will and self-determination allow us to gain our achievements in our own ways. It is impossible to accomplish anything, however, if we destroy ourselves. Heroin is a chemical that destroys the body and the mind.

Our bodies have enough strength and resilience to temporarily resist what is poisonous. But repeated exposure gradually breaks the system down. Eventually the system just stops working. When that happens, you die.

You are a valuable human being. There is no other being created quite like you, no other person can accomplish what you can. You need your body and mind to be able to work at full strength and capacity. You have your own purpose in life to fulfill, your own goals to achieve. It is your responsibility to see that you keep yourself in good working order.

Poppies are beautiful flowers, but they yield a deadly substance.

# CHAPTER 1

# What Is Heroin?

*H*eroin is a chemical substance derived from the opium poppy. This beautiful flower grows in hot, dry climates. The pod left after the petals fall contains a white syrup that is collected by poppy growers. When the syrup dries, it hardens into a brown substance we call opium.

From opium, chemists extract many of our common drugs. Some of those drugs are used legally for medicinal purposes. Morphine and codeine are the most common ones. They are widely used by doctors as painkillers.

*14*     Heroin is also a common derivative, but it is illegal in most countries, including the United States. It is considered so harmful and dangerous that it is not even allowed to be used for medicinal purposes. Mainly that is because it is made from the garbage left over after making morphine.

That was not always the case. During the mid-nineteenth century a famous German chemist made heroin to help morphine addicts come off the drug. Morphine was widely used at the time as a painkiller.

The drug was considered a *heroic* substance. Soldiers from the Civil War up to World War I were given heroin to break them of their addiction to morphine. It was after the turn of the century that doctors began to realize that heroin addiction was far worse than morphine.

Now scientists have developed another chemical to assist the heroin addict. Methadone is used by some drug treatment centers throughout the United States to help heroin addicts withdraw. There is concern, however, that methadone is also addictive. In fact, some studies indicate that it is as addictive as heroin.

## *Manufacture of Heroin* 15

It is illegal to grow opium poppies in the United States. Even if we could grow them, a laboratory is needed to process the syrup into the powders sold on the street. Such labs are also illegal.

Most of the international supply of opium comes from poppy farms in two major areas: the Golden Crescent and the Golden Triangle. Poppy farms and factories are illegal in those areas also. But the people are so poor that they risk punishment to grow the flowers.

The Golden Crescent is in the Middle East and includes the countries of Iran, Afghanistan, and Pakistan. The Golden Triangle is in South Asia and includes Laos, Burma, and Thailand. All of these countries are very poor. A farmer can earn 97 percent more money from a crop of poppies than from the same amount of grain.

Most of these countries are engaged in wars. Because of that, police action is focused on warfare, leaving little time and money to fight drug trafficking. Also, these countries need expensive weapons. Drugs are often exchanged for arms.

**16**    In the western United States heroin is imported from Mexico. *Mexican Brown* is a poorly processed grade of heroin made from poppies grown south of the border. It is of very low quality, but the demand for it is so high that the makers see no need to spend money to process a better quality.

These social and economic conditions make it difficult to control the production of opium poppies. As long as people will buy their product, these poor countries will produce opium.

Transporting opium to the United States is illegal. However, opium slips through customs in many ways. Because of the increased attention of law-enforcement agencies, the drug scene on the streets is changing. Shipments of marijuana, which is strong smelling and bulky, are decreasing while opium and cocaine importation is increasing. The more compact substances are easier to smuggle into the country.

Unfortunately, the demand for all these drugs is high. Dealing them on the black market and on the street involves millions of dollars. The power of that much money makes it very hard to control the various

Drug-sniffing dogs help law-enforcement officers to check luggage at airports.

*18* sellers, dealers, and buyers. From the drug barons to the street dealers to the neighborhood pushers to the users themselves, greed and need rule supply and demand.

Because the market is illegal, it is not regulated. That leaves the business wide open to corruption, danger, and death. From the start of the chain in the Middle East and Southeast Asia, dirty laboratories begin the potential for death.

Buyers never know what purity or dosage they are getting in the packs of powder they buy. No laws control what is added to the substance. So a user faces not only addiction and the ill effects of the drug, but the possibility of overdose or poisoning or both.

Dealing the drugs is also dangerous. Heroin is illegal, so whatever level of the business you are involved in is criminal. Criminal activity not only is immoral but involves the dealer with immoral people. Those people are likely to cheat, steal, lie, and even kill. That happens at all levels, from the baron protecting his turf to the addicts who are so desperate for an injection that they kill for it.

You may think you are safe because friends or family supply your needs. But somewhere in your dealing you will come across a possibly life-threatening situation. It could be the quality of the heroin or the person you deal with.

## Other Names for Heroin

| | |
|---|---|
| The big H | Scag |
| H | Stuff |
| Smack | Elephant |
| Chi | Tiger |
| Dragon | Nanoo |
| No. 4 | Gear |
| No. 3 | China White |
| Harry | Black Tar |
| Junk | Chiva |
| Scat | Mexican Brown |
| Horse | Tar |
| Chinese | Mexican Tar |

A heroin addict shoots up—injects heroin to get one of many fixes in a day.

# CHAPTER 2

# How Does Heroin Affect You?

*H*eroin is a narcotic.  The word narcotic comes from the Greek word *narkosis,* which means benumbed.  Physically, heroin numbs the senses.

### Physical Effects

Our five senses enable us to survive in our environment.  Taste, smell, touch, hearing, and sight feed messages to our brain so that we can react to what is around us.  If we don't like what is around us, we have choices.  We can change the environment, move to a new location, or ignore what is there.  Most of us learn to function within the circumstances.

*21*

*22*     As teenagers it is not always possible to make changes. The choice to ignore is difficult, especially if the environment is depressing, lonely, or ugly. The addict's wish is to escape. Chemical substances deaden the senses and let one ignore the surroundings.

The problem with that form of escape is that whatever makes you want to escape doesn't change. Drugs wear off and there you are, still facing the same problems.

A first-time user of heroin often becomes violently ill, with vomiting and a severe headache. Peers or pushers say it will be better the second time. For some, it isn't. Occasional users often suffer from diarrhea, stomach and muscle cramps, and loss of appetite.

Heroin can be taken several ways. It can be smoked or swallowed, but neither way is very effective. The most common method of taking heroin is injecting it. *Skin-popping* is injecting the drug under the skin, not in a vein. A drug user's body builds up a resistance to almost anything it is given. Heroin is no exception. In order to get a high, a user needs more of it each time. Skin-popping soon becomes ineffective.

The user may then begin *mainlining*, injecting heroin directly into a vein. With frequent injections, veins may collapse. When new veins are used, *tracks* may appear on a *junkie's* body. Sometimes a user misses a vein. This can cause an abscess or develop into blood poisoning.

There are several grades of heroin. Many of them are poor. A user generally filters the heroin into the needle through a piece of cotton or a cigarette filter to get rid of any clumps. This leaves some residue on the cotton or filter. This residue is often diluted and given to a first-time user with the mistaken idea that it won't be a very strong dose. This procedure can be dangerous, especially if unsterilized cotton is used.

If you are allergic to heroin or any opiate, you can become violently ill and even die on the first fix. Heroin that has been made and handled poorly, is not measured, or is mixed with poison can cause overdose or death. There is no way of knowing when or if that will happen.

An overdose can cause heart failure, rapid heartbeat, shortness of breath, and ringing in the ears or head. Some heroin overdoses cause coma, or unconscious-

**24** ness. That is extremely dangerous, as victims can fall and smother or drown in their own vomit.

Daily use of heroin causes extreme constipation and a loss of appetite. Many addicts suffer from malnutrition for one of two reasons: First, they are not hungry. Second, and more commonly, the constipation becomes so painful that they don't want to eat more food.

### Emotional Effects

Most people get to heroin because they have been doing other drugs. As we have suggested, use of chemical substances is a form of escape. It is an emotional reaction to one's life situation. Instead of dealing with life, users choose to escape it.

Another emotional aspect of addiction to heroin and other substances is the *rip and run* thrill. Teenagers who do not see themselves as successful or do not see life as meaningful make a world for themselves that is filled with a series of daily purposes and successes.

The actual drug is not the purpose. It is the whole process of finding the stuff, getting the money for it, scoring the hit, and then riding the high. They are not

Counselors can help teens find a way out of the misery of drug addiction.

taking drugs, but *doing* drugs. Their day is a whole series of small, yet significant successes.

This false sense of purpose and accomplishment often replaces a teenager's view that life lacks real purpose and accomplishment.

Everyone can find some meaning and purpose in life. They can do so by searching deep within themselves and by setting and working toward goals. Choosing the escape of drugs leads only to a slow process of self- destruction. Repeated use of heroin or any chemical substance corrodes the brain, the organs, and the body. This path is a sure journey to death. Searching within and acting upon your values and goals is a road to life.

Running away from home makes many teenagers easy prey for drug pushers and pimps.

# CHAPTER 3

# The Start of an Addiction

*H*eroin is not very difficult to get. Most people, like Michael and Jason, get it from their friends. Others get it off the streets.

Major drug dealers often try to work through a network of high school students. This way they are in less danger of getting caught and also have better access to possible buyers. These outside dealers are usually the gangs and pushers who smuggle the drug into the country. The usual addict never meets these people. The addict gets his drugs from his friends who deal.

An addiction begins in experimentation. Someone hears a lot about a drug and decides to experience it for himself. However, heroin is so amazingly addictive that even experimenting with it just a few times can get you hooked.

28  Theo was already heavily into pot and acid when he first tried heroin. He'd tried cocaine before, but hadn't liked it. It made him too jumpy and paranoid. Heroin seemed just the thing. It chilled him out, made him feel good.

Soon Theo was using all the time. He never went to class; he just hung around school dealing to support his addiction. Before he'd started using, Theo had had lots of girls after him. But now he'd gone from looking like a healthy, attractive teenager to looking like a corpse. He'd lost his appetite, and when he did eat he became so badly constipated that it was hardly worth the effort. He rarely slept. Track marks ran all up his arms. His eyes were dull and always spaced out. He hardly ever showered. He was a mess.

Theo's parents finally got sick of their son's drug problem. He packed a bag and split.

Theo lived here and there—with friends for as long as they would put up with him, on the streets when he had nowhere else to go. Dealing no longer supported his habit, so he started stealing money, breaking into houses, and prostituting himself. He looked so bad that he barely made enough money selling himself to

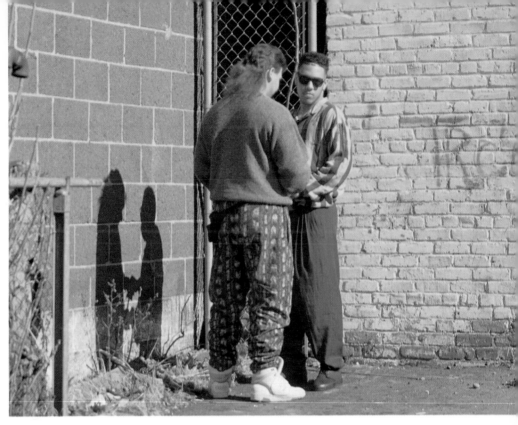

When you buy heroin on the street you could be buying anything.

support his habit, which now cost more than $50 a day.

Theo needed more and more heroin to get high. His normal dose would have killed a first-time user. His body had built up a tolerance to the drug. It was only a matter of time before Theo overdosed.

Friends who give or sell you drugs are just like any other dealer. They are not doing you a favor or trying to put excitement into your life. Most likely, they are dealing in order to support their own habit. They "do" the profit. For example, they buy an eighth of an ounce packet,

**30** called an *eight ball*. They take some of it for themselves, and then *step on it*, that is, add any white powder, such as baking soda or cornstarch, to bring the weight up. They then resell it as an eight ball. When you buy heroin, you can never know what else you're getting with it.

Sometimes users mix cocaine and heroin together and smoke the mixture. This is incredibly dangerous. A mixture such as this killed actor River Phoenix. He died of a heart attack. His system couldn't take that amount of drugs.

Heroin is a dangerous drug. It became a serious problem among young people in the late 1960s, so much so that it was the leading cause of death for young men in New York City.

Drug dealers know that most people begin using through friends. They offer free hits to students whom they consider possible runners until the targets are hooked. Then when they have to start buying their own stuff, the dealer tells them to sell some and take their share from the profits.

Some dealers offer female students free heroin until they get hooked. The girls are then forced to prostitute themselves for

their supply. The dealers usually use the girls themselves at first. When they tire of the girls they start them on a career in the streets.

Through this process, the dealers insure that they have a market and a network in which to move the market. Most gang members do not use drugs themselves. They see the results and don't want to destroy themselves. All they want is profit. They have no concern for you personally. All you are to them is supply and demand.

## *Family*

Unfortunately, many young people get drugs from family members. They often believe that they can trust such a supply. That is false security. The family member has to purchase the stuff from the same dealers the students at school do. It may not be the same person, but the heroin has traveled through the same unsavory channels.

The fact that heroin is illegal in this country and is not even allowed for medical purposes doubles its danger. Using even the cleanest heroin destroys your body, but unmeasured, unclean heroin can do so faster.

When parents drink and smoke, the stage is set for their teenagers to experiment with drugs.

# CHAPTER 4

# Why?

*T*here are many reasons people begin using drugs. No matter how reasonable
they sound, there is no excuse for doing
drugs.

### Family
The largest population of substance
abusers is the adult community. Therefore it should not surprise us to learn
that most teenagers are taught to do drugs
by their parents.

As children, we learn that the way to
resolve problems is a pill. We see our
parents smoke, drink, maybe even do
heroin themselves. Children naturally
copy their parents. The drugs may not be
the same, but the behavior of taking a
substance to cure, forget, or tolerate a
problem is.

*34*     Children who grow up in a substance-abusive home are much more likely to become addicts themselves. They learn that taking drugs is normal, is what adults do. When they become adults, they adopt the behavior they have been taught.

## Curiosity

Drugs are a great mystery to many teens. They are whispered about everywhere. Movies are made about them, songs are sung about them. Very few teenagers have ever actually been told everything they need to know about drugs.

For some reason, drugs are often regarded by young people, and actually by adults, as glamorous. All kinds of famous people are addicted to drugs or have died from drug use. Even though this should clearly point out the danger of drugs, it tends to have the opposite effect. People wonder what's so great about drugs that makes so many people use them.

There is something very attractive about the darkness and despair associated with heroin. It seems very real, very down to earth. The drug conjures up the image of a tortured artist, using drugs to find inspiration. However, the truth is that heroin will not bring inspiration. It

will take over your life until nothing is left but the need for the drug. The attraction of heroin is built on lies. If you want to be an artist, or a writer, or a musician, find your muse elsewhere. Doing heroin will only make you lazy and uninspired.

## *Peer Pressure*

Being a teenager is rough. Pressure comes from everywhere—your family, your school, yourself. Possibly the hardest thing to deal with is pressure from your friends.

If you are doing something that you know is wrong, but you want to keep on doing it, you have an inner conflict. That usually results in guilt. To get rid of that feeling of guilt, it is normal to try to justify your actions.

Students who do drugs often try to talk their friends into doing it because that makes their behavior seem more acceptable. If everyone else is shooting heroin, it must not be so bad a thing after all, right?

Peers who try to pressure you into doing drugs are not doing you a favor. They may be trying to justify their behavior to themselves. They may be trying to get you hooked so they can deal to you and support their own habit. One thing

**36** is certain. Any friend who is not willing to accept you for who you are and for the choices you make is no friend.

It can be hard to say no to a friend who is pressuring you. But you have to learn to make your own decisions. Your friend isn't living your life, you are. Do what feels right to you. Don't do drugs just because your friend tells you you're not cool if you don't. That friend is wrong.

### Pain and Hurt

Heroin resembles morphine, which is sometimes still used today as a painkiller. That is one of the biggest attractions of drugs in general and heroin in particular. They kill the pain of life.

Being a teenager is never easy. Life can be painful. Sometimes people with big problems turn to drugs as an escape.

If you can't cope with your life, if reality is simply too difficult for you, you may see drugs as a relief. Life can be very harsh. You may be suffering from abuse in your family. You may be living in poverty and see no chance of ever escaping. Someone you love dearly may have left you, through rejection or through death. Many things nowadays happen to teenagers that should never happen to anyone.

Living up to your responsibilities helps to create a positive self-image.

38  Heroin makes you feel numb. You forget about the problems that you can't face. You become lost in a kind of dream world. Drugs might seem like the perfect salvation from a life you can't handle.

However, this is one of the nastiest false promises heroin makes. Yes, the high will make you forget about your problems; but when you come down the problems are still there, waiting for you. And after a while you have a whole new problem to deal with: your new heroin addiction.

You can't resolve your problems while you're high. If anything, you're more likely to make them worse. The problems will not go away, and you cannot run from them forever. Getting into heroin just gives you a new set of problems.

Leaving problems unresolved is never a good idea. You have to learn to cope with whatever life throws at you. Using drugs is not a way of coping, it's a way of hiding. It doesn't make you strong enough to deal, it shows you to be too cowardly to stand up to whatever is so horrible.

Your life may be difficult. It may be unbearable. Every person at one time or another feels a sense of need. Every person at some point feels hurt and pain.

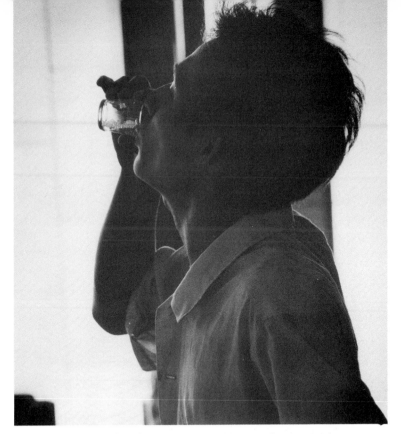

In an outpatient rehabilitation center, teenage heroin addicts receive daily doses of methadone as replacement therapy.

We always have freedom to choose how to handle the situation. We can choose to run and hide. We can choose to blame everyone else. We can choose drugs. The point is that it *is* our choice. We can always choose to face life as it is. We can also change it, but only through clear thinking.

There is no situation that we cannot change or survive. No matter how bad the circumstances, there is always somewhere to go, someone who'll help, and some way to climb out of it. Choosing drugs is one way. Choosing life is another.

Many teenagers lose friends to death from heroin overdose.

# CHAPTER 5

# A Life of Heroin

*H*eroin is not quite as swiftly dangerous as some people believe. It destroys
the body from the inside, slowly but
unstoppably. Yet many people do survive
for years despite daily use. However,
taking heroin regularly is incredibly
addictive.

People have remarkably short memo-
ries. Just a few years ago, heroin was
considered the drug of people who were
deeply suicidal. It was said that no one
who had any sense would put themselves
at the mercy of a drug that was so
certainly addictive and so certainly
deadly.

Recently, however, heroin has once
again come back in fashion. People have

*42* forgotten the devastation it can cause. Once again heroin is exerting its evil charm.

Users become addicted to heroin incredibly quickly. Heroin addiction is more severe than even cocaine addiction. It is impossible to stop using without getting professional help.

Recently, heroin has become much more pure than it was just ten years ago. Back then, a fix was usually 4 percent pure heroin—now the average is 65 percent pure. This higher grade of drug allows users to smoke heroin and get extremely high. Many people who were scared away from the drug by fear of needles became addicted by smoking.

What these smokers don't realize is that once you become addicted and your tolerance builds up, smoking will not be able to support your addiction. Almost all users who begin by smoking end up mainlining. Once again, this dark drug has tricked people into addiction.

Addiction to heroin rules your life. You don't think of anything but where to get your next fix. You don't do anything but get high. Nothing is important to you except the drug. Junkies almost never take care of themselves. They often get body

lice, they pay so little attention to hygiene.

In time you become a slave to the drug. You do not live your life; heroin lives your life. The drug becomes your master, your king, and your god. And eventually your life ends at the whim of that god.

## Health

When you choose to do heroin you choose to be sick. It is nearly impossible to stay healthy once you are hooked. The question is how quickly your body is destroyed.

Using heroin brings with it a whole family of health problems. You lose your appetite after a while. You become constipated so that even when you are hungry you don't want to eat. You lose so much weight that you look like a skeleton and usually suffer from severe malnutrition. You no longer take care of your physical appearance, and don't bother to be clean. You have needle tracks on your arms or on your legs, depending on where you shoot up. You have *abscesses*, where your skin caves in making an indentation where you missed a vein while shooting up. You may contract blood diseases from sharing needles, such as hepatitis,

**44** endocarditis, septicemia, and perhaps even AIDS. You won't be able to stay awake for any length of time. When you crash from a high, you will have horrible stomach cramps, sweats, and chills.

Then there is the danger of overdosing. Every time you get high there comes a point when you crave more heroin, you want to get even higher. That is one reason so many people overdose. When you reach this point, you are too high to realize that you are about to give yourself a fatal dose. Also, as your tolerance grows, you begin to need more heroin to feel anything. Your addiction gets to the point where every fix is enough heroin to kill you. And eventually, it does.

Have you ever seen someone overdosing? It is frightening. The user begins to have convulsions so strong that he or she travels across the room jerking and gyrating. He or she loses control of bodily functions—mucus pours out of the eyes and nose; the person drools or vomits, and may drown in the vomit; he or she may urinate or defecate all over himself. He or she may go into a coma for weeks, months, or years, or may never come out of it. The person may not die; he or she may only have permanent brain damage.

A heroin addict presents an attractive picture, don't you think?

45

## Emotions

If you start doing heroin to feel better, you are in for a big disappointment. Part

Loneliness and depression are frequent companions of drug addicts.

**46** of addiction is psychological dependency. It leads to depression and often to suicide. Addicts are sometimes forced into prostitution, dealing, and murder. They have no respect for themselves. Finally, they recognize their dependence on the drug and hate themselves for it. But still they won't stop. They are slaves to heroin, and there is no emotional pain worth that.

### Law

Heroin is an illegal narcotic. Trafficking, sale, even possession is a felony crime. Felony crimes mean time in prison.

First-time offenders caught using heroin for reasons not connected to any other crimes may be offered a diversion program. In such a program some states give teenagers the option of volunteering at their own expense to get counseling, drug prevention education, and periodic urinalysis. If they complete this program successfully, the charges can be dropped. Not all states have this option, nor do you have the choice on your second offense. In such cases you are charged as a criminal.

Another danger facing the user is that once you are arrested, or *popped*, you may no longer be trusted by your junkie

friends. They may think you are now working with the police. You may not be able to score a hit for a while after your arrest.

If someone is afraid you might *narc*, or inform to the police, he may give you a *hot shot*. This is an overdose of heroin laced with some kind of poison. It will kill you. Dealers sometimes give hot shots to people they don't trust, or even just to junkies who owe them money.

## Death

No matter which route you take when you do heroin, you always wind up at the same destination. If you don't get help, you will die. It's that simple.

Don't get yourself into that situation. Don't start doing heroin. You are too valuable a human being to let heroin control and end your life.

Positive activities with positive people are a good defense
against the temptation to do drugs.

# How to Get Help

*I*t is important to remember that no situation is ever hopeless. Many people who take drugs may find that hard to believe. You may think your condition is worse than it really is. Don't forget that heroin changes your brain.

Addiction is difficult, but *withdrawal is possible*. Habits are hard to break, but *behavior can be changed*. Sickness is hard to overcome, but *people are healed*.

## What to Do First

The first step toward help is admitting that you have a problem. The next step is to be willing to take action. The third step is to

**50** find help. The final step is to commit yourself to the path to recovery.

The first two steps involve you. You make your own choices about your quality of life. It may seem that you are trapped in your life, but that is simply not so. You decide how you react to your situation. No one can control your thoughts or your wishes.

No one can force you to take drugs. No one can force you not to. Maybe incidents of control do occur. For example, if you are in a hospital or in jail you may not be able to shoot up on heroin. If you are enslaved or captured by a gang, you may be forced to take drugs. But look back on your actions. Your own choice of behavior put you in those situations.

If you have allowed circumstances to open you to addiction to heroin, you can still choose to get out. Once you face the need and decide to withdraw, there are many places to go for help.

### Family, Friends, Religious Groups

The first place to go is to your family. Most drug addiction involves the whole family, either directly or indirectly. If other members of your family are involved

in substance abuse, including alcohol, they will need help as much as you do.

Maybe they don't take part in substance abuse. But if they create problems for you through physical or psychological abuse or neglect or misunderstandings, group therapy can help you solve your differences. If your family relationship is healthy, you will need the love and support of family members to pull you through the ordeal.

Sometimes teenagers do not want their family to know they are involved in drugs. There are other choices. Other relatives or close friends can help you. School counselors can suggest help. Family doctors will treat you or refer you to someone who specializes in substance abuse. Many communities offer social services that include teen centers.

One of the best sources of help is a religious organization. Most of the people in such organizations are trained in counseling and have access to community services. For example, Phoenix, Arizona, has an organization called Clergy Against Drugs. These inner-city pastors are trained in assisting young people who want to withdraw from heroin or other substances. Most large cities have Jewish

52 Family Services, listed in the telephone book as a resource for those of the Jewish faith.

Rapha is a national organization that offers in-hospital or outpatient care for substance abusers (1-800-227-2547).

Teen Challenge has offices in big cities.

Heroin is a powerful addiction. Finding professional help is the next step.

## Help Is a Phone Call Away

Whether your family is in on your decision or you are struggling alone, you will need trained assistance in withdrawing from heroin. Call a local hotline to find what is available in your area and which programs you can afford or qualify for.

Every major television network announces statewide hotline numbers to call for help. They usually follow a "Say No to Drugs" announcement.

The telephone book has listings in the Yellow Pages. Look in the "D" listings for *Drug Abuse Information and Treatment*. Call one of the clinics or centers and tell them what you need. If one is not the right place for you, they can refer you to other numbers.

If there are no drug listings in your area, try the "A" listings for *Alcoholism*.

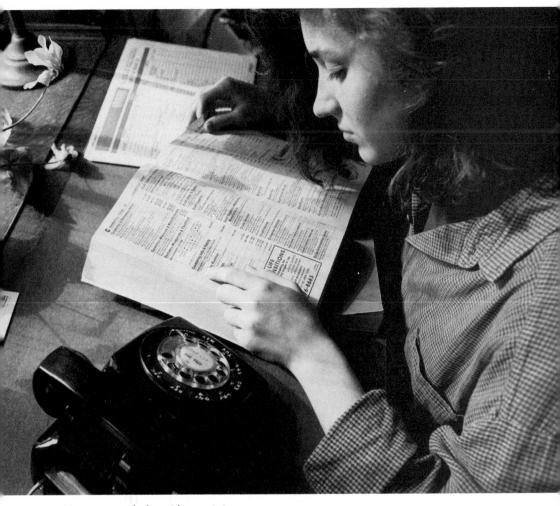

You can get help without giving your name on an emergency hotline.

These centers work with the drug abuse centers.

The advantage of phoning for information is that you can be helped to some degree without giving any personal information. The volunteer can tell you which

53

**54** clinics will treat you confidentially. Also, clinics range from free to over $2,000 per week in cost. Phoning can help you find the place you can afford. Always remember that help is just a phone call away.

## Hotline Emergency

The inside cover of the phone book lists emergency hotlines. They usually have the words *drug, emotional, help,* or *hope* in the number. For example, the number in New York is 1-800-622 HELP for the National Institute on Drug Abuse Treatment Referral. In Arizona the number 1-800-475 HOPE is advertised on television. These are important to know if you are with an overdose victim. Call 911 or one of the emergency numbers.

Some states have emergency teams that specialize in overdoses. Arizona has an organization called TERROS. These men and women rush to the scene in plain clothes and treat the victim without involving the police. That can be an important consideration. The sight of uniforms or the sound of sirens can frighten an overdose victim into a heart attack.

## Guidance

Every major metropolitan area and most counties have services for withdrawal from drugs. They range from government-funded projects to private hospitals. Religious organizations also provide counseling services.

Remember that substance abuse usually involves hidden causes. If you have been using heroin for any length of time, you will need to repair your thinking as well as heal your body. Good counseling and a relationship with a care group will help you to stay off the drug.

Kicking the habit will also mean changing some of your social habits. You might want to consider a new set of friends. Hanging around friends who are into drugs will be too great a temptation.

Treatment centers can introduce you to new friends who will understand what you are going through and can help you.

## Treatment and Rehab Centers

Since withdrawal from heroin "cold turkey" can be painful, many are afraid to quit. That does not have to be the case.

**56** Treatment centers offer controlled withdrawal with the help of other substances such as methadone and maltrexone. Some clinics employ acupuncture.

Such treatment enables a person to come off the drug slowly. It also allows him to function at work or school in a normal routine. Withdrawal does not have to be painful.

Unfortunately, many states do not offer methadone to teenagers unless they have failed one or two 21-day detoxification programs.

The programs for teenagers that have been most successful are the rehabilitation centers where they live with other teens coming off the drug.

Helping others is the best way to help yourself. The advantage of living with other addicts is that you can share experiences. There is someone who understands what you are going through.

Rehabilitation centers offer drug abusers a chance to take themselves away from their old environment in a setting that is drug-free. Through counseling and group therapy, they learn ways to rebuild their lives so that they can be free of dependence on heroin or other drugs.

Alcoholic Anonymous and Narcotics Anonymous achieve their success rates by helping their members renew their relationship with family and God. If you belong to a religious organization, or even if you go to a new one where your past is not known, you will be strengthened.

So much of the battle with substance abuse is an inner struggle. Much of the appeal of any drug is emotional and mental. You want peace, freedom from stress, and a sense of well-being.

These can be found on a permanent basis, but not through drugs. Get in touch with your inner self, and strength will come to help you battle the temptation offered by drugs. Find a true and spiritual relationship, and you will find peace, security, well-being, and love.

# Glossary
## Explaining New Words

**addiction** Inability to resist the urge for a drug.

**alternative** Choice between two or more courses of action.

**cold turkey** Quitting the use of a drug without any help.

**comatose** State of being unconscious, caused by disease, injury, or poison.

**constipation** Difficult passage of hard, dry feces.

**corrosive** Gradually eating away, like rust.

**cut** To mix heroin with a powder.

**derivative** Made from another material.

**eight ball** Eighth of an ounce packet.

**emulate** To try to be like someone.

**felony** Serious crime that results in severe punishment.

**hot shot** Overdose of heroin, or a dose laced with poison designed to kill the user.

**injection** Placing of a substance directly into the blood, usually with a needle.

**junkie** Person addicted to drugs.

**laboratory** Place where scientists work.

**mainline** To inject heroin directly into the blood through a vein.

**malnutrition** Poor health caused by not eating an adequate diet.

**popped** Arrested.

**prosecute** To charge in court with a crime.

**prostitute** Person who is paid for performing sexual acts.

**rehabilitation** Restoring to former health, or putting back into good condition.

**rig** The needle and tourniquet used to inject heroin.

**rip and run** Process of doing drugs in which you *rip* or get the drug and then *run* to find more.

**scoring a hit** Buying heroin.

**shooting gallery** Place where people gather to get shots of heroin.

**skin pop** To inject heroin under the skin, not directly into the vein.

**step on it** Slang term for taking some heroin out of a packet and adding back some kind of powder to make the packet look full again.

# Help List

- American Council for Drug Education
  204 Monroe Street
  Rockville, MD  20852
  (301) 294-0600

- National Clearinghouse for Alcohol and
      Drug Information
  P.O Box 2345
  Rockville, MD  20852
  (301) 468-2600

- Narcotics Anonymous
  World Service Office
  16155 Wyandotte Street
  Van Nuys, CA  91406

- National Federation of Parents for
      Drug-Free Youth
  8730 Georgia Avenue
  Silver Spring, MD  20910
  1-800-554-KIDS (5437)

- NIDA Clearinghouse for Drug
      Information
  P.O Box 416
  Kensington, MD  20795

# For Further Reading

Ball, Jacqueline. *Everything You Need to Know about Drug Abuse*, rev. ed. New York: Rosen Publishing Group, 1994.

Godfrey, Martin. *Heroin.* New York: Franklin Watts, 1987.

Kaplan, Leslie. *Coping with Peer Pressure*, rev.ed. New York: Rosen Publishing Group, 1994.

Lee, Essie E. *Breaking the Connection.* New York: Julian Messner, 1988.

**62** Morgan, H. Wayne. *Drugs in America*. New York: Syracuse University Press, 1981.

Smith, Sandra Lee. *Coping with Decision-Making*. New York: Rosen Publishing Group, 1989.

_____. *Coping through Self-Control*. New York: Rosen Publishing Group, 1991.

Sunshine, Linda; Wright, John. *The 100 Best Treatment Centers for Alcoholism and Drug Abuse*. New York: Avon Books, 1988.

Toma, David; Levey, Irv. *Toma Tells It Straight with Love*. New York: Bantam, Doubleday, Dell, 1981.

U.S. Department of Justice. *Drugs of Abuse*. Washington, D.C.: Drug Enforcement Agency, 1992.

# Index